INTRODUCTION TO BEHAVIORAL
SCIENCE FOR BUSINESS

Introduction to

Behavioral Science for Business

Blair J. Kolasa

Duquesne University

JOHN WILEY & SONS, INC.

New York · London · Sydney · Toronto

Library of Congress Catalog Card Number: 75-76056
SBN 471 49900 5

10 9 8 7 6 5 4 3 2 1

Printed in the United States of America

To Susan

Preface

The year 1969 marks the tenth anniversary of the publication of two reports that have had great influence on American education for business. *Higher Education for Business,* by Robert A. Gordon and James E. Howell, and *The Education of American Businessmen,* by Frank C. Pierson, and others, are so well known by this point that they can be easily identified simply by the use of the authors' names. While their scope extends to all phases of the curriculum, the reports are noteworthy for their recognition of the importance to prospective and active businessmen of exposure to the behavioral sciences. This book is one attempt to implement some of the recommendations of the two reports by providing a basic introduction to the breadth of the field, some concepts in behavioral science, and some of the results of research activity. Examples of applications in business settings or other areas of activity are included, but not in preference to discussions of basic concepts and findings. The reader will make the transfer, hopefully, to those areas where his interests or immediate activities lie. In addition, as is desirable in any work that purports to be an aid in education, this book should raise more questions than it answers; if it leads to any further inquiry, it will have done its job.

Authors have the good fortune, whether they recognize it or not, to receive the benefits of the influence of students and contemporaries. The latter, too, seldom realize how they may have contributed to the formation of frameworks for the conduct of later inquiry. This book, like the behavioral science thrusts generally in education for business, has been stimulated by earlier work by men like Herbert Simon, James March, Harold Leavitt, and Richard Cyert, all sometime faculty of GSIA at Carnegie-Mellon University, Harold D. Lasswell of Yale, Daniel Katz, Robert Kahn, and George Katona of the University of Michigan, Harold Guetzkow of Northwestern, Abraham Maslow of Brandeis, Frederick Herzberg of Case-Western Reserve, Mason Haire of M.I.T., Philip Selznick of California, and many others who have built meaningfully for business on the foundations provided by precursors of the present aggregate of activity in behavioral study. None of the above is aware of his influence in this case, but it is acknowledged gratefully, nevertheless.

Dean Joseph W. McGuire of Illinois belongs in the above category but has been more directly aware of the development of the present work and has been generous in his counsel. His help is most heartily appreciated. Others who viewed parts of the manuscript and offered valuable assistance are: Professors Eugene Laughlin and Eugene Friedman of Kansas State University, and Max Wortman, Jr. of the University of Massachusetts. At Duquesne, Dean James L. Hayes provided the kind of support that encourages effort. The usual disclaimer of their responsibility for the outcome accompanies the thanks of the author for their aid. Mr. John P. Young of John Wiley and Sons, Inc. has been very helpful in all work preparatory to publication while the superior editorial work of Mrs. Wendy Lemmert aided immensely in shaping the manuscript in its final form.

No work of this nature could emerge without the genuine interest of the individuals who typed and proofread the manuscript and generally aided in its preparation for publication. For their special role, thanks go to Mrs. Lee Ross and Mildred Lindbloom at Kansas State as well as to Goldie Caplan and Susan Haas at Duquesne.

Finally, I recognize that this effort has been stimulated by the positive sets of values for education held by my parents and extended family. My gratitude to them accompanies this realization.

Blair J. Kolasa

Pittsburgh, Pennsylvania, 1968

Contents

1

Introduction to
Behavioral Science

Behavioral science, most easily described as the scientific study of behavior, is a systematic inquiry into what *is* rather than what ought to be. It gathers facts about what people do rather than prescribes what they should do. In working toward that objective, most behavioral scientists focus upon human behavior. When research does extend to the study of animals, the primary interest is still in what these studies can tell about human behavior.

Any discussion of behavior usually finds many individuals who are willing to discourse on what people are like and what they do. It is not surprising to find this is the case. After all, why not? Have we not had the benefit of long experience in this world? Do we not know pretty much what to expect of others by this time? "Common sense" should give us the answer to most if not all of the problems! (It is entirely possible that some have a better understanding of human behavior than do others. To determine how you compare in this respect, try the short test in Table 1-1.)

Whether "common sense" is now or ever was adequate is a pertinent question at this point (common sense is, furthermore, probably not as common as many people believe). For any improvement on armchair speculation, "old wives' tales," or other unsystematic approaches, a more organized framework must be followed. The past can offer us many illustrations of attempts to organize facts surrounding the actions of people. Certainly, many artists and authors, along with others, have had perceptive views of human behavior. Shakespeare, Ibsen, Dostoevsky, and others have produced much insightful material. There are, without a doubt, many roads to a knowledge of man—the artistic, the poetic, and the philosophical. While it might be of value to recapitulate many of these thoughts and theories about human behavior, our interest should be strongest in the specific knowledge gained through scientific study. This is the province of the behavioral sciences.

1

Table 1-1.   Twenty Questions about Behavior (from Morgan, 1961)[a]

Indicate Whether the Statement Is True or False

1. Geniuses are usually queerer than people of average intelligence.
2. Only human beings, not animals, have the capacity to think.
3. Much of human behavior is instinctive.
4. Slow learners remember what they learn better than fast learners.
5. Intelligent people form most of their opinions by logical reasoning.
6. A psychologist is a person who is trained to psychoanalyze people.
7. You can size up a person quite well in an interview.
8. When one is working for several hours, it is better to take a few long rests than several short ones.
9. The study of mathematics exercises the mind so that a person can think more logically in other subjects.
10. Grades in college have little to do with success in business careers.
11. Alcohol, in small amounts, is a stimulant.
12. There is a clear distinction between the normal person and one who is mentally ill.
13. Prejudices are mainly due to lack of information.
14. Competition among people is characteristic of most human societies.
15. The feature of a job that is most important to employees is the pay they get for their work.
16. It is possible to classify people fairly well into introverts and extroverts.
17. Punishment is an effective way of eliminating undesirable behavior in children.
18. By watching closely a person's expression, you can tell the emotion he is experiencing.
19. The higher one sets his goals in life, the more he is likely to accomplish and the happier he will be.
20. If a person is honest with you, he can usually tell you what his motives are.

[a] Answers are to be found at the end of this chapter.

What Is Science

The behavioral sciences are sciences because of certain characteristics. Essentially, being scientific means following a particular method. The characteristics of this method will be outlined and then should be kept in mind when the behavioral sciences are defined later in this chapter. The presence of these characteristics is crucial for the often-asked question, "Is this science?"

What makes a science? Does it mean having equipment in a "laboratory" with a white smock for the "scientist" to wear? Chaplin and Krawiec (1960) reply:

Anyone can purchase a white robe and a laboratory full of scientific paraphernalia but the possession of such equipment does not qualify him as a scientist. Rather, both his scientific status and the value of the information he is collecting are evaluated according to the manner in which he *plans* his investigations, the *procedures* he employs in collecting data, and the way he *interprets* his findings.

Obviously something other than just a test tube and a lab coat is called for in order to make a scientist.

THE HALLMARKS OF A SCIENCE

The characteristics of a science do not necessarily include the possession of an array of gadgets; instead, they relate to a spirit of inquiry guiding an ordered intellectual approach to the gathering of data.

Characteristics

The features that are necessary conditions of scientific endeavor are implicit in the method. Using the scientific method means being

(1) systematic and (2) empirical

so that the information obtained in this way can be

(3) ordered and (4) analyzed

for the results to be

(5) communicable and (6) cumulative.

The scientist is, therefore, one who rigorously and with planned precision collects data which may be passed on to others to enrich the common fund of knowledge.

Being systematic means being orderly and proceeding according to plan in a manner that is not susceptible to bias. The attempt to gain knowledge must be without taint of personal or other prejudgment. Not only must the approach be objective, but the procedures and terminology must be precisely stated.

The empirical approach avoids armchair speculation or a priori systems with no actual basis. It concentrates on the collection of data. The behavioral science researcher wants to find out what is, much in the spirit of the famous television detective who wanted "the facts, Ma'm, just the facts."

The collection of data may occur in many different ways. Natural observation has been the oldest method used to gain information, and it is still one that behavioral research calls on. When it takes place in the original setting, it is called a field study. Something similar happens when a clinician gathers data about an individual or a group of individuals over a period of time. This "day book" approach has also seen much service in the history of behavioral science. Surveys where answers to questions are obtained and analyzed are of more recent vintage though the basis for the technique reaches back to the dawn of history. The ultimate data-gathering device of the behavioral scientist is considered by all to be the experiment; since the experimental method gives the researcher many opportunities to manipulate the variables, the ability to control conditions makes it a very appealing device for gathering data and accounts for its popularity.

The final step in the analysis of data through a logical or higher statistical treatment results in what Brown and Ghiselli (1955) call the rational phase of research in science. The methodology of both collection and treatment of data will be discussed in more detail in Chapter 3.

Science is also cumulative in that what is discovered is added to that which has been found before. Indeed, we ourselves, before we start, look around and find out first what has been done so that we need not start anew from a low base each time. We learn from past mistakes and obtain guides for the future. We build upon the base that has been left by others.

Scientific results must be communicable. For that matter, this may be considered a condition precedent for the cumulativeness of a science. In order for the area to be cumulative, the information in it must be able to be communicated to others. Full disclosure of specific procedures is called for, not only for communication of knowledge but also to allow for repetition of the study, if need be, by the original investigator or others. When a study is replicated and the second try provides results similar to the original, one can have much more confidence in those results.

Measurement

Among the factors frequently considered to be requisites for science, measurement is perhaps most often thought of as being one that is needed. This is not true, since many of the disciplines, even some of the physical sciences, do not call for measurement. Botany and geology involve taxonomy; demography or other descriptive disciplines do not, strictly speaking, depend on measurement. Valuable and desirable though it might be, measurement is not a prerequisite for a science.

Need for a Theoretical Basis

Theory, however, is a vital part of scientific endeavor. The term itself frequently arouses in the "hard-headed, practical man" a negative or pejorative connotation. Theoretical to him means "fuzzy minded" or impractical and therefore not worthy of consideration. Yet, as Kurt Lewin has said, "Nothing is as practical as a good theory." In any scientific endeavor theory is necessary.

A theory is a statement of relationships that are thought to exist between sets of facts. It is descriptive, and it is positive in that it describes what is as the describer knows it to be. Its value lies primarily in three facts.

1. It serves as a shorthand.
2. It is a predictor of things to come.
3. It serves as a guide on the basis of the prediction.

All of these serve as explanations of the facts, but a theory can be further recognized through three other characteristics.

1. There is empirical reference, that is, the facts are immediately available.
2. There is some connection or possible connection with other theories of a similar nature.
3. The statement of the theory admits of rejection or acceptance.

These three features represent the empirical, logical, and testing aspects of a theory, in that order.

Theories are often confused with other systematic approaches and it is well at this point to distinguish between them. A system of notation, while ingenious and self-contained logically, is not a theory. Few, if any, of the hallmarks of a theory can be recognized in a purely notational system. Measurement, while valuable in science by itself, is neither science nor a theory. Taxonomy, while very productive of information, is merely descriptive and falls short of being a full-fledged theory. The theory is a set of facts that the researcher believes is isomorphic with the real world. It must be in a state able to be tested.

Another concept often confused with a theory is that of a model. A model is an abstraction from the real world, that is, certain aspects of reality are picked up and placed within a theoretical framework. The model, like the theory, is representative of reality, but the model is not isomorphic with reality. A model is a small-scale representation with many important elements absent. It is not necessary that the model be true in every respect. What is necessary is that the model be helpful in letting us see what is possible in a situation (Braithwaite, 1953).

A hypothesis is often mentioned in the same breath as a theory. A hypothesis is merely a preliminary guess as to the validity of certain statements that are limited in scope and application. These statements are by no means as encompassing as a theory and are therefore more readily tested. McGuire (1964, p. 5) succinctly points out differences in meaning of the terms.

> A hypothesis may originate as an educated speculation. If it holds good in all circumstances it may be called a theory, and if it is sufficiently profound and universal it may be termed a "law." Because a generalization cannot be absolutely proven it is usually accepted after a number of tests, especially if it is compatible with existing scientific beliefs.

Hypotheses may be hunches and models may be crude representations, but a theory is a broader and more accurate picture of relationships between facts. Only with great trepidation and caution is one of these relationships labeled a law.

One final concept, that of a system, must be mentioned because it is becoming more salient in behavioral science (von Bertalanffy, 1956). This concept is one that incorporates the variables sketched immediately above into a cohesive, interacting whole. Not only are component elements of interest, but so also are the forces betweeen them. The entire "whole is more than the sum of its parts" and cannot be understood without simultaneously considering the interrelationships of all elements.

AIMS OF A SCIENCE

Without doubt, the true scientist wants above all to achieve understanding; he wants to know *why*. Mere knowing is not enough, however, as one must go on to that succeeding stage where the facts fit into a meaningful pattern. "Experiencing natural phenomena gives the scientist his facts, and his aim is to discover, accumulate, and interpret facts and relationships among facts" (Brown and Ghiselli, 1955, p. 36). This "search for truth" is best expressed by the word understanding, the general aim of science.

Other aims of a science include prediction. When one is aware of what is happening and why it is happening, prediction of events is possible. When predictions can be made, control can then be brought about. Control is often considered to be the ultimate application of scientific knowledge and endeavor.

UNIFORMITY IN SCIENCE

This matter is more frequently approached with the basic question—is science deterministic or probabilistic? In science we proceed on the basis of certain uniformities in nature. If we proceed in an experiment and manipulate the conditions, the outcome should be the same each time the identical conditions are manipulated in an identical way. We have come to expect this in science. In this situation the uniformity that we look for is one that is strongly deterministic; that is, the conditions that precede are inevitably followed by certain other conditions. In a chemical laboratory we mix certain chemicals and we assume that these elements, when properly mixed, will give us a particular compound. In social or behavioral science we are not prepared to attain such predetermined end results. It is this fact that leads many to think that the social or behavioral sciences are not really sciences. Here, however, there is uniformity, but it arises on a statistical or probabilistic basis. Wolfgang Köhler, is quoted by Rashefsky (1960) as pointing out that we can pick up hundreds of leaves and each leaf will be quite different from the one preceding it. We cannot state that the characteristics of one leaf will be present in exactly the same way in a second leaf. What we can say is that the average leaf will have certain characteristics and that the next hundred leaves will have certain characteristics within the limits we have set. The notion of probabilistic uniformity is perhaps even more important now in the physical sciences, as the Heisenberg principle has demonstrated. It may be that statistical uniformity is really all that can be expected in experimentation in physical sciences, too, rather than the deterministic uniformity most people have been led to expect.

Behavior

Faced with the difficulty or impossibility of studying the "mind" or other ephemeral concepts, behavioral scientists must concentrate on what can be studied, namely, behavior. Activity of humans (and animals) that qualifies under this term shows great variety. It includes everything from the decision making of the president of General Motors to the pressing of a button by a subject in response to a bell in a laboratory. Whatever is observable or measurable may be studied. There are extensions to something like the affective aspects of behavior or, more broadly, the experiential facets. Here, too, there must be something to study directly even though the indirect aspects are of most interest; some behavior does appear which represents those "other" aspects. Most behavioral scientists, however, prefer to stay within areas that may be more directly considered.

Certain fundamental assumptions underlying behavior should be emphasized from the beginning. Leavitt (1964, p. 12) has organized these assumptions about human behavior into a simplified structure showing behavior to be:

1. Caused.
2. Motivated.
3. Goal directed.

These assumptions rule out randomness or no-reason-at-all for behavior. There must be an external stimulus which causes the behavior which occurs. Motivation means some internal force that drives the organism; a secondary base that would not be activated without the initial stimulus. Finally, the behavior is again not random in that there is some end result toward which the organism points its activity.

There is a "logic" to behavior which contains all three of the features above. Even the "illogical" behavior of the insane shows causality, motivation, and goal direction. The behavior simply may not be our idea of "logic" or we may not understand how the behavior is "logical" (under Leavitt's framework) to the individual concerned.

The Science of Behavior

When an academic area is described, it is usually done in words. But verbal definitions are often difficult to frame or, when constructed, are frequently not very illuminating. This is especially true of behavioral science. Possibly the best way to define it beyond the preliminary attempt at the outset of this chapter is merely to point to what will follow in the book and say that this is what behavioral science is. This is in the nature of an *operational* definition whereby we indicate what is done at each step so that through the communication of these operations others know exactly what the situation is.

DEFINITION OF THE FIELD

There have been attempts to define this broad area within the scope of a few lines. Handy and Kurtz (1963, p. 6) provide what they believe is an all encompassing description of the approach of behavioral science by calling it "Transactionalism." By "Transaction" they mean "the name applied to the full ongoing process in a field where all pertinent aspects and phases including the connections among them and the inquirer himself are in common process." The same authors suggest that another term, "sign-behavior," differentiates the behavioral from the biological or physical sciences. Certainly, most of the study of man by behavioral scientists deals with symbolic activity or signaling while other sciences do not.

The behavioral sciences come to focus in three disciplines—anthropology, psychology, and sociology, though the scope of this broad area extends much farther, into other traditional academic disciplines such as economics, political science, psychiatry, jurisprudence, history, and into some of the applied areas of endeavor such as management, marketing, consumer behavior, and business administration as well as group dynamics, industrial morale, and related areas. These disciplines have been known as social sciences yet this older term does not fully express the tenor of the approach utilized in behavioral science. Behavioral science is more concerned with a direct collection of information about human behavior. Social science is more indirect and is based on broad and aggregative data. Just as the boundaries of behavioral science are somewhat unclear, so the differentiation between behavioral science and social science is not clearly delimited. The picture is further complicated by the fact that, as Berelson (1963, p. 2) states it, behavioral science is both *less and more* than the traditional areas of anthropology, psychology, sociology, and the more peripheral behavioral disciplines.

Behavioral science may be less than the specific discipline of psychology where a psychologist may study the biological aspects of vision or brain waves. Pure concern with the shape of pottery shards in archeology is not enough to include this subdivision of anthropology within the behavioral sciences. If the political scientist discourses on the structure of government without going into the political aspects of behavior, he too does not qualify for inclusion. In the same way, legal research may concentrate on case decisions and statutory interpretation without focusing on the behavioral basis of the actions.

Behavioral science may be more than the specific disciplines in that the bits of behavior to be studied cannot be viewed within the framework of one of the traditional disciplines alone. New interdisciplinary areas such as psycholinguistics, social psychiatry, forensic psychology, and communication have emerged recently. This last phenomenon points up one of the important features of this area, namely, that it is one unitary entity. The disciplines to which we traditionally refer represent artificial fractionations of this one broad body of knowledge. In some cases the barriers between academic areas have prevented communication across those walls. Recognition of common interest has come, however, and joint ventures in the nature of team research have increased in number in the recent past. Beyond this, the past few years have seen an increase in academic programs arranged along the interdisciplinary lines sketched above. Now, academic departments of organizational psychology, social relations, or communications have produced some individuals who, in their training, overlap many of the older areas.

Further evidence of the breaking down of the traditional academic disciplines comes in a perusal of designations given more and more to particular inquiries in the area of behavioral science. Game theory counts economists among its early supporters; these have been joined by many who call psychology their first academic home. So it is with decision-making theory, cybernetics, information theory, or organization theory.

It would be unrealistic, however, to state that workers in the traditional disciplines have ceded their identification with those familiar entities or even the newer groupings and now refer to themselves only as behavioral scientists rather than anthropologists or psychologists. Unification has not proceeded that far. The existent disciplines may be referred to by many of their members as the behavioral sciences, in the plural form which recognizes differences, while the term behavioral science, which emphasizes the unitary nature of the field, is used by fewer disciples. In the hopeful spirit of integration, this text will focus on the latter designation.

BEHAVIORAL SCIENCE APPLIED

Knowledge in and of itself can be valuable and interesting, but ultimately it should be put to some use. Research findings can be translated if need be and communicated to professional areas such as business, law, education, public health, medicine, industry, government, social work, and even agriculture. Many of the problems that face workers in each of these areas are those for which the professional man has no background or training. A religious body, for instance, has management problems for which theological seminaries have not or perhaps should not provide training. This may be duplicated in almost any organization one might mention. Broader areas such as mental health and rehabilitation call for a multiplicity of different skills and require, in addition, a knowledge of the administrative skills that may be necessary in coordinating the activity of the various professional groups involved in the handling of the problem. Similarly, other social problems present themselves at every hand—legislation, juvenile delinquency, urban renewal, and even something as prosaic as prison management are appropriate areas for the application of basic research in the behavioral sciences or action research in dealing with a specific problem. In all, it is possible to enlist the services and findings of the behavioral scientist.

THE EMERGENCE OF BEHAVIORAL SCIENCE

In this, as in almost any other area, it is difficult, if not impossible, to pick any date that meaningfully represents the start of activity within it.

It could be possible to start as far back as the fourth century B.C. in Greece and refer to Aristotle as the first behavioral scientist, a label he actually does merit in many respects. In the 1830's Comte coined the term sociology and began outlining the discipline which helps form the core of the behavioral sciences. Down through the years many others approached problems in a more-or-less systematic fashion. The area as we recognize it today, however, did not emerge clearly until the present century, although the groundwork was laid firmly in the latter part of the past century. Wilhelm Wundt at Leipzig and William James at Harvard were opening their laboratories and commencing the systematic attack on problems within the area of human behavior. This was less than ninety years ago, an insignificant span when measured against the spread of history, and a figure which, more than any other fact, calls attention to the youth of the field. Perhaps we can paraphrase Galileo, as did Merton (1963, p. 249), and say that the behavioral sciences comprise "a very new science of a very ancient subject."

Senn (1966) has noted that, while the term behavioral science was used sparingly before World War II, there were some researchers who considered the term a valid description of the work they were doing. In the early 1950's the designation was used with significantly greater frequency; the fact that the Ford Foundation began at this time to support a Behavioral Sciences Program with several million dollars does not seem to be an unrelated factor. At any rate, the label has become quite popular while the controversies as to who is and who is not doing behavioral research multiply. Stimulated by both World Wars, by the favorable attitudes toward science, and by the Ford Foundation and governmental agencies, behavioral science over the short span of time showed an increase geometrically not only in numbers of researchers, but in material produced. Merton (1963) notes that 90 to 95 percent of all behavioral scientists who have ever lived are still with us. The number of psychologists has doubled in less than 10 years. Similar increases have occurred within sociology, where the number of sociologists stands at roughly 10,000 (anthropology with approximately 1000 remains almost a primary group). Although the 20,000 psychologists make a small group compared to three times as many physicists and four times as many chemists (and 10 times as many physicians or lawyers), the large size amazes the older psychologists who easily remember when one knew almost everyone else in the organization.

At the same time that there has been an increase in numbers, there also has been a decided change in the emphasis of the activity. One active observer has labeled the changes "revolutionary" in pointing out that "in recent decades the field has become technical and quantitative, segmentalized and particularized, specialized and institutionalized, 'modernized' and 'groupized'—in short, Americanized" (Berelson, 1963, p. 8).

In twenty-five years the move has been from treatises in broad, theoretical terms to specific research projects by teams of technicians. Berelson goes on to say that some may consider this change as being from the broad and meaningful to the trivial and superficial. On the other hand, the trend may be viewed as an attempt to introduce precision into the study of a complex area, whereby we may obtain information upon which we can rely. Most researchers today prefer the latter, and it is this flavor that will probably prevail. Behavioral science is here to stay.

The Behavioral Disciplines

A closer look at the older, more traditional disciplines as well as some of the newer entities in this broad area should provide an even better appreciation of what goes on in the behavioral sciences.

The three disciplines comprising the core—anthropology, psychology, and sociology—must be included. Beyond this, the list is more or less arbitrary. Undoubtedly, mention must be made of economics, political science, and history. Education and jurisprudence should be included since, in many respects, they are often more behavioral than history, for instance, even though history perhaps receives mention in this area more often. The more applied areas such as management, marketing, and psychiatry are probably still better candidates for inclusion though they are all too often glossed over.

A final group that should be noted contains those recently formed and still somewhat ambiguous entities known as game theory, cybernetics, information theory, and organization theory.

BASIC DISCIPLINES

The basic areas comprising behavioral science are some of the long-familiar academic disciplines. Certain of them, however, may be placed closer to the core of the entire field than can others. Anthropology, psychology, and sociology are generally regarded as being in the center with economics, political science, and jurisprudence more at the periphery. While classification systems vary, a recent attempt to organize behavioral science literature (Bry and Afflerbach, 1968), for instance, encourages just such an orbital organization of disciplines around psychology as the core.

Anthropology

Anthropology is the study of man and his works. While this definition is certainly broad, the anthropologists have traditionally emphasized study of primitive (or, better, preliterate) societies in order to learn about man and his activities from early times to the present. The problems faced by the anthropologists are most frequently classified into four subgroupings (Kluckhohn, 1955, p. 319). Archeology analyzes the remains of past civilizations. Physical anthropology studies the biological features of man and traces evolutionary patterns. Social anthropology focuses on the forms of culture or technology and the impact they have on individuals and groups. Linguistics is the study of speech and relationships among languages. With the interest in culture and civilizations, or the concern with change in society, anthropologists may be called on to transfer information from basic studies to more applied areas. Much of this fundamental concern with man affects all phases of human activity at home and abroad. Strong cultural bases exist for war, peace, and mundane consumer behavior. Even designers of rapid transit systems must take into account anthropometric data as they decide on the measurements of seats and aisles.

Psychology

The term psychology comes from the Greek word *psyche,* the soul or spirit. This is a misleading description of the discipline today even though it fits the image generally held by people when they define the field as "study of the mind." The mind is obviously not amenable to study through the scientific approach; psychologists study behavior. The term behavior includes not only surface acts, which can be noted and measured, but extends also to those activities that constitute the "phenomenal" (experiential) aspects of the situation. Psychologists are concerned with concepts such as learning, sensation and perception, motivation, personality, attitudes, thinking, and problem solving—all within the framework of behavior. The areas of interest within psychology are so numerous that it is difficult to comprehend this array. In its development the field emerged eclectically from various "schools" or theoretical approaches (Boring, 1950). The differences, heatedly argued in the past, are no longer crucial though the flavor of psychology today shows some influences of the differentiations (Koch, 1959). John B. Watson's emphasis on behavior, and only behavior, remains as the core of psychology though the field has moved far from this extreme position. Psychoanalytic theory remains Freud's extensive contribution to the field. Still further kinds of dynamic theories are Gestalt psychology with its integrative organizational approach, and the newer views of man as a "self-actualizer" (Maslow, 1954) or as "standing out in the world" and experiencing it, according to the existential or phenomenological approach (May 1961).

While the focus of psychological research is on the basic core areas of learning and motivation, the immediate applications to the areas of business, government, and education are being made continuously. The fundamentals of human behavior are of practical interest in selection and training, communication in school and industry, and in most management and marketing situations. The applied psychologist may be testing applicants in the personnel department, but he probably will be even more interested in a topic like "motivation in the work group" to which he would apply concepts gained from basic research in physiological, social, and industrial psychology. In the same way, today's psychologist would be interested in the areas of individual and group decision making, patterns of influence and change in organizations, group processes, vocational choice and satisfaction, programmed instruction, attitudes and values in consumer and mass media situations, or (and this by no means exhausts the list) in conditions of human performance.

Sociology

Sociology is the study of the behavior of people in groups—"Sociology is the scientific study of patterned, shared human behavior . . . the ways in which people act toward one another" (Fichter, 1957, p. 1). From Comte to Durkheim, Cooley, Max Weber, and present-day sociologists, the emphasis has been on social groups, social behavior, society, customs, institutions, status, social class, social mobility, and prestige. Specific areas of study that constitute special subfields can be listed as follows. Urban and rural sociology, the sociology of race and ethnic relations, demography, communications, research, public opinion and attitude studies, collective behavior, the study of occupations, the sociology of medicine and social psychiatry, and social disorganization and deviant behavior are among the subfields in which considerable research and study are undertaken in the United States. Substantial attention is also given to such subdisciplines as political sociology, industrial sociology, the sociology of law, family sociology, the sociology of religion, educational sociology, the sociology of art, the sociology of knowledge, and sociology of science and invention (Alpert, 1963, pp. 58–59).

For the citizen at large as well as for the professional worker in many fields, the sociologist can provide a basis for action in everyday situations. Problems of segregation, law enforcement, labor-management unrest, mobility of labor, juvenile delinquency, urban or rural dynamics, and interaction in an industrial work group represent only a few areas of applications of the research techniques and conceptualizations available in this discipline.

Economics

The definitions of economics illustrate the current diversity of opinion as to what economics really is. The following broad definition by Von Mises

(1949, p. 880) may be contrasted with a more specific one given later. "Economics, as a branch of the more general theory of human action deals with all human action, i.e., with man's purposive aiming at the attainment of ends chosen, whatever these ends may be." A more specifically delineated definition has economics as "the study of how the goods and services we want get produced, and how they are distributed among us. This we call economic analysis. Equally economics is the study of how we can make the system of production and distribution work better. This we call economic policy" (Bach, 1960, p. 3).

The behavioral science features of economics cut across all the traditional categories used to subdivide the field, though the behavioral bases may be more evident in the areas of consumer economics or decision-making theory than in the more fundamental areas of price and economic theory or finance. The approach toward economic behavior, to qualify as a behavioral science, is described by Katona (1960, p. 8) as the study of the actions of people who play a role in economic trends. In economic psychology one must not only "analyze the results of human behavior [but] also . . . study the decision makers and the process of decision making, because motives, attitudes, and opinions influence actions and thereby what happens in and to the economy." Strict views of economics as the study of the "economic man" whose behavior is postulated as rational in striving for maximum utility under "perfect competition" is not, except in a complementary fashion, a part of the behavioral approach. Nor is a limitation to the behavior of commodities rather than of people included in this framework. Concern with actual decision-making processes and their results in the entire input-output system marks the behavioral approach in economics.

Political Science

Political science studies the behavior of individuals and groups within a political setting. The approaches may vary from studies of the structure of a government unit to the description and analysis of actual behavior of members of that political organization. The latter aspect is more behavioral than the former. Indeed, a classification system or a structuring of a situation can hardly qualify as behavioral. The earlier emphasis on political philosophy is less and less a significant part of today's scene, especially in the United States. Lasswell (1936, p. 13) illustrates the differences between the "science of politics which calls for the systematic statement of theory and the use of empirical methods of gathering and processing data and the philosophy of politics which justifies preferences."

The behaviorally oriented political scientist will eschew philosophy and will search for the empirical bases of behavior in politics and political parties, public opinion, pressure groups, public administration, voting, legislative activity, judicial decision making, organizations and institutions, culture and government, comparative systems, and international relations. The full scope of the field may be appreciated in a work like *Political behavior: a reader in theory and research,* edited by Eulau, Eldersveld, and Janowitz (1956). Theory in the behavioral approach is not ignored but emphasized. It is, furthermore, theory in the true sense and not a verbal substitute for the word "speculation."

History

Of the six main disciplines considered to be behavioral sciences, history probably qualifies least for inclusion in this area. Historians do study human behavior, but they study it with reference to a particular time perspective. The emphasis may be, and usually is, on the events themselves rather than on the behavioral actions that contribute to the outcomes. History then becomes a broad sketching of men, times, and places which, while it often may be social science, is not likely to be behavioral science. Recent contributions seem to be more in the direction of incorporation of concepts from other social or behavioral sciences to "contribute to the historian's understanding of why men, groups, and societies behave as they do" (Social Science Research Council, 1954, pp. 86–87). As things stand now, however, most activity in history shows an affinity for the humanities rather than for behavioral science.

Law as a Behavioral Science: Jurisprudence

The approach to law that is set upon a "theoretical" base rather than upon the practice of the profession has been known as jurisprudence. As in many of the areas above, the philosophical flavor of the discipline has been slowly giving way to the empirical. In the area of law the two tendencies have separated so much in the minds of most researchers that the term jurisprudence is less often being used to designate the newer, more empirical or behavioral approach and is becoming limited to the broader theoretical studies. The behavioral approaches to law are simply labeled in that way or are referred to as "law as a behavioral science." Recently the term "jurimetrics" has been proposed as the designation for the scientific investigation of legal problems (Loevinger, 1961) as a better description of the empirical thrust of this new discipline. This is the development in the law identified by Pound (1960, p. 32) as a move to a functional concern with problems and teamed with the social sciences in a study of values, expectations, and individual precepts. Behavioral researchers now are interested in problem areas such as the social dynamics in a jury, criminal responsibility, efficacy of legal methods, surveys of attitudes towards law, judicial decision making, and a host of other related areas. This differs from library research on statutes and cases which yield commentaries based only on the opinions of individuals or the written codes.

APPLIED AREAS

Certain action areas such as education, psychiatry, marketing, management, and administration represent more applied fields which must be included within the broad framework of the behavioral sciences. These professional areas do not really overlap the traditional disciplines mentioned above; instead, they draw upon them for the basic concepts with which they pursue their respective interests and activities. Mention of some areas by way of illustration must be made, although the reader is cautioned that the list is more extensive than can be covered here. Any profession or occupation dealing with people is involved in applications of behavioral science.

Education

The professional interests and activities in pedagogy are based on the basic findings of many of the fields of behavioral science, notably, psychology and sociology. Principles of learning and retention, growth and development, along with numerous other bits of information must be part of the reservoir of knowledge of the teacher in and the administrator of the educational endeavor. In addition, further understanding of social dynamics of the group and the community are proving to be an important requirement for anyone in today's educational structure.

Psychiatry

The diagnosis and treatment of nervous and mental disorders is the province of psychiatry. The psychiatrist is a medical doctor who has spent some time in learning the fundamental bases of human behavior in order that he may be able to treat the afflictions of his patients. He must gather and apply as much behavioral science knowledge as he can but, since he is a clinical practitioner, his direct involvement in basic behavioral research activities is minimal. This is more often the province of the psychologist, although clinical psychologists do engage in related activity—psychotherapy, the analysis of and therapy for problems of a psychological nature. A psychoanalyst (to help clear up another common point of confusion) is a psychiatrist who follows, more or less, the methods of treatment originally formulated by Sigmund Freud.

Marketing

The applications of behavioral science principles and results can be very useful in specific areas of business activity, among them, marketing. In the dynamic mechanisms of flow of goods and services from producer to consumer, the awareness of the nature of individual and social processes has immediate or long-range contribution to the success or failure of the enterprise. Consumer choice behavior often is a critical condition; the nature of influence and the channels involved represent leading topics for behavioral research in this area. Innovation and the diffusion of new products, creativity and the learning of responses are no less important social and individual phenomena that contribute to the total marketing process.

Management

The accomplishment of organizational tasks through coordination of the activities of others is the job of the manager. Since this role depends so heavily on the action of other people, it might be guessed readily that behavioral concepts and findings are crucial for the completion of managerial tasks. Motivation, learning, perception, and other basic facets of individual behavior form the foundations for effective performance in business organizations. The additional variables involved in such group and aggregate activity make it advisable for the would-be manager to acquaint himself with concepts of social behavior as well. Becoming even more crucial these days is the awareness of the broader environmental factors and dynamics that arise beyond the immediate organization and yet affect it in its functioning in the community and society.

Administration

The field of administration is considered by some to be synonymous with management. Where a distinction betweeen the two is made, administration is considered by most writers to be the activity of policy making or planning while management is the execution of such policy. Since the two functions are virtually inseparable, it would seem to be valid to consider management and administration as one and the same.

Administration has been used, however, to describe the functioning of coordinators or managers in the public sector or those executives in organizations such as hospitals or schools. Public administration has been an active professional area, and medical administration has been growing rapidly. Educational administration has developed almost exclusively under the aegis of schools of education and their pedagogical orientation.

Recent trends indicate growing recognition of the common base of specific areas of administrative activity. This reinforces some earlier positions reflecting the commonality of fundamental concepts underlying the variations found in specific locales. A pioneering effort by Litchfield (1956, p. 28) sketched the basic creed as being that "administration and the administrative process occur in substantially the same generalized form in industrial, commercial, civil, educational, military, and hospital organizations." Support for the whole area of administration as a significant entity is developing now not only in the form of research and writing, but in the reorganization of professional curricula or colleges as well.

NEWER FIELDS

The need for interdisciplinary attacks on new problems in the area of behavior has stimulated the growth of several new fields of science. These have arisen either through a "merger" of two areas or through an outright formulation of original concepts.

Game Theory

The theory of games and economic behavior by Von Neumann and Morganstern (1947) provided the impetus for the growth of game theory. The theory relates to the strategy employed in "games" (war or play) based on rational and statistical decision processes.

Decision Theory

This outgrowth of game theory incorporates more concepts to consider many of the difficult points that arose under game theory. Factors of subjective versus objective probability, choices under risk, and organizational decision processes must somehow be handled within a logical framework (Edwards, 1954; Cyert, Simon, and Trow, 1956) in the basic problem of selection of the best course of action in a given set of circumstances.

Organization Theory

A study of the functioning of the large, coherent social entities called organizations has proceeded slowly despite the recognition of its importance. Difficulties in definition of the field have slowed the development of an integrated theory of organizations. Some progress is being made, however, out of the diversity of views. Early work by Max Weber and Frederick Winslow Taylor has given way to the newer concepts of Barnard and Simon, among others (Rubenstein and Haberstroh, 1960). The functioning of individuals in organizations is now being studied from a systems standpoint as a move toward equilibrium and a pattern of roles and relationships, and from many other vantage points, but the underlying developments in these indicate an eventual convergence of views on what an organization is and how it functions.

Information Theory

This is a mathematical approach to questions of communication stemming primarily from the pioneering work of Shannon and Weaver (1949). Probabilities of selection of symbols in the communication process remain the crux of the area. From this point the applications move to the difficulties in securing accurate transmission and/or the information content of verbal material.

Communication Theory

This is a broadening of the concepts and applications of information theory to channels, systems, or psychodynamic variables that influence the basic communications.

Cybernetics

The science of communication and control has been called cybernetics (from the Greek for *steersman*), a term provided by Wiener (1948) who was the first to develop the concepts to any extent. The analogies between human and machine behavior, particularly in the concept of "feedback" as part of purposive or adaptive activity, have stimulated further conceptualization and application. Beer, in *Cybernetics and Management* (1959), feels that cybernetics may be applied to any and all fields because it represents a general theory of control.

Summary

Behavioral science is the systematic study of behavior. Use of the scientific method to gather facts in this area avoids speculation about what "is" and a normative discourse about what "ought to be."

The hallmarks of a science are present in the scientific method. Using the method means being systematic in gathering facts (empirical) to be ordered and analyzed so that the results may be reported and accumulated. Measurement is not necessary, though it is often helpful. Theory is needed, however, to serve as a shorthand way of showing relationships to serve as a guide for further meaningful activity. Theories are preceded by hypotheses, the preliminary statements of the validity of a set of facts. Theories also may be complemented by a model, an abstraction that represents reality.

Science aims to achieve understanding, to know why something happens, in order to predict events and thereby control conditions. Uniformity of events may be expected on a statistical basis rather than in a purely deterministic way.

Behavior (rather than "mind" or other concepts) is the subject of research because it can be studied. Behavior takes place in a logical framework because it is caused, motivated, and goal directed.

Behavioral science may be difficult to encompass in terms of one short, general definition. Characterizing the field as "sign-behavior" or "transactional-ism" is incomplete. Operational description of the composition of the traditional disciplines in the area is more enlightening. Not all of psychology, sociology, anthropology, or political science is included in behavioral science, however. Those aspects of the discipline that do not focus on the empirical and direct gathering of data on behavior are not behavioral. Some problems have been amenable to study only through combinations of methods or approaches from various disciplines. The knowledge and understanding gained from the disciplines and interdisciplinary activities often can be put to immediate use in applied areas such as business, education, or civic activity.

While attempts to study human behavior are age-old, scientific research and conceptualization on behavior began in the mid-nineteenth century within strict disciplinary lines. Regular use of the term behavioral science is even more recent; regular references to it seldom occurred before the 1950's. The field is new and growing rapidly; at least ninety percent of all behavioral scientists in history are still alive. The condition of the field represents a move from broadly theoretical studies to empirical and precise research.

Core disciplines in the behavioral sciences are anthropology, psychology, and sociology. Anthropology studies similarities and differences among the peoples of the world. The basic study of individual behavior is the province of psychology while sociology is concerned more with the actions of aggregates of people. More removed from the core of behavioral science are the disciplines of economics, political science, and history. Studies in these three areas, however, qualify for inclusion here only if they refer directly to empirical facts generated in behavioral frameworks. The study of law, too, can be behavioral as long as reference is made to actual behavior rather than being limited to the perusal of secondary opinions or conclusions.

Application of behavioral data in professional or occupational settings can be extensive. Basic findings of behavioral research serve to support action in the areas of education, psychiatry, or in areas of business such as marketing, management, or administration.

Newer fields in the behavioral sciences may represent interdisciplinary activities or novel attacks on problems. Game theory and decision theory represent strategy or choice behavior questions sometimes attacked in economics or psychology. Information theory, communications theory, and cybernetics represent the burgeoning interest in adapting mechanism and system approaches to the study of behavior. Organization theory recognizes the interrelationship of structure and function or regularized groupings with human behavior.

For Further Reading

The flavor of the behavioral science approach may perhaps best be gained by a look through some outstanding or representative works in the area or illustrative studies from a selection of journals.

Books

Simon, *Administrative behavior* (2nd ed. 1957).
Skinner, *Science and human behavior* (1953).
Allport, *The nature of prejudice* (1954).
Whyte, *Street corner society* (1943).
McClelland, *The achieving society* (1961).
Katona, *The powerful consumer* (1960).
Lasswell and Kaplan, *Power and society* (1950).
Cyert and March, *Organizations* (1958).

Journals

American Anthropologist
American Behavioral Scientist
American Journal of Economics and Sociology
American Journal of Psychology
American Journal of Sociology
American Political Science Review
American Sociological Review
Human Organization
Journal of Abnormal Psychology
Journal of Applied Psychology
Journal of Criminal Law, Criminology and Police Science
Journal of Marketing Research
Journal of Social Issues
Political Science Quarterly
Public Administration Review
Public Opinion Quarterly

The above represents a partial list of pertinent journals.

Bibliography

Alpert, H. (1963). Sociology: its present interests. In Berelson, B. (ed.). *The behavioral sciences today*. New York: Basic Books.

Bach, G. (1960). *Economics* (3rd ed.). Englewood Cliffs, Prentice-Hall.

Beer, S. (1959). *Cybernetics and management*. New York: Wiley.

Berelson, B., ed. (1963). *The behavioral sciences today*. New York: Basic Books.

Boring, E. (1950). *A history of experimental psychology* (2nd ed.). New York: Appleton-Century Crofts.

Braithwaite, R. (1953). *Scientific explanation*. Cambridge: The University Press.

Brown, C. and Ghiselli, E. (1955). *Scientific method in psychology*. New York: McGraw-Hill.

Bry, I. and Afflerbach, L. (1968). In search of an organizing principle for the behavioral science literature. *Community Mental Health Journal*, **4(1)**, 75–84.

Chaplin, J. and Krawiec, T. (1960). *Systems and theories of psychology*. New York: Holt, Rinehart and Winston.

Cyert, R., Simon, H., and Trow, D. (1956). Observation of a business decision. *Journal of Business*, **29**, 237–248.

Edwards, W. (1954). The theory of decision making. *Psychological Bulletin*, **51(4)**, 380–417.

Eulau, H., Eldersveld, S., and Janowitz, M., eds. (1956). *Political behavior: a reader in theory and research*. Glencoe, Ill.: Free Press.

Fichter, J. (1957). *Sociology*. Chicago: The University of Chicago Press.

Handy, R. and Kurtz, P. (1963). *A current appraisal of the behavioral sciences*. Great Barrington, Mass.: Behavioral Research Council.

Katona, G. (1960). *The powerful consumer*. New York: McGraw-Hill.

Kluckhohn, C. (1955). Anthropology. In Newman, J. (ed). *What is science?* New York: Simon and Schuster.

Koch, S. (1959). *Psychology: a study of a science*. New York: McGraw-Hill.

Lasswell, H. (1936). *Politics: who gets what, when and how*. New York: McGraw-Hill.

Leavitt, H. (1964). *Managerial psychology* (rev. ed.). Chicago: University of Chicago Press.

Litchfield, E. (1956). Notes on a general theory of administration. *Administrative Science Quarterly*, **1**, 1–29.

Loevinger, L. (1961). Jurimetrics: science and prediction in the field of law. *Minnesota Law Review,* **46,** 255.

Maslow, A. (1954). *Motivation and personality.* New York: Harper.

May, R., ed. (1961). *Existential psychology.* New York: Random House.

McGuire, J. (1964). *Theories of business behavior.* Englewood Cliffs, N.J.: Prentice-Hall.

Merton, R. The mosaic of the behavioral sciences. In Berelson, B. (ed.). *The behavioral sciences today.* New York: Basic Books.

Morgan, C. (1961). *Introduction to psychology* (2nd ed.). New York: McGraw-Hill.

Pound, R. (1960). *Law finding through experience and reason.* Athens: University of Georgia Press.

Rashefsky, N. (1951). From mathematical biology to mathematical sociology. *ETC., A Review of General Semantics,* **8,** 94–109.

Rubenstein, A. and Haberstroh, C. (1960). *Some theories of organization.* Homewood, Ill.: Irwin.

Senn, P. (1966). What is "behavioral science"—notes toward a history. *Journal of the History of the Behavioral Sciences,* **2,** 107–122.

Shannon, C. and Weaver, W. (1949). *The mathematical theory of communication.* Urbana: University of Illinois Press.

Social Science Research Council (1954). *The social sciences in historical study: a report of the committee on historiography.* Bulletin No. 64. New York: Social Science Research Council.

von Bertalanffy, L. (1956). General systems theory. *General Systems,* **1,** 4.

von Mises, L. (1949). *Human action: a treatise on economics.* New Haven: Yale University Press.

von Neumann, J. and Morganstern, O. (1947). *The theory of games and economic behavior.* Princeton: Princeton University Press.

Wiener, N. (1948). *Cybernetics.* New York: Wiley.

Answers to Table 1-1

All answers to the questions in this table are false.

2

History of
Behavioral Thought

The past serves to illuminate the present and, perhaps, even to predict the future if one takes seriously the motto emblazoned on the National Archives Building in the nation's capital. "What is past is prologue" is there for all, lawmakers and others, to see. Here, as in any field, what has gone on before can at least help us to understand better the present state of affairs. Here, too, the thinking of those of past ages can present some picture of human behavior; the statements of scientists or social and economic philosophers of the past serve as prologues to a detailed discussion of present concepts in the behavioral sciences.

As has been stated before, beginning dates in any complex historical study are not only hard to come by but often are impossible to establish. No sequence of human behavior and thinking ever has had one point where it clearly can be said to have started. Attempts to understand or explain the individual and social behavior of man undoubtedly have been made as long as man himself has been in existence on this planet. We can make many educated guesses about the relationships among individuals in groups or the results of contacts among people from the artifacts left behind; much can be inferred from plans of cities, pottery shards, or even paintings in caves. For a clear-cut view of social thought, however, we must leaf through the pages of history to a point in time where the daily activity of man began to be put down symbolically and on such material as can endure the ravages of centuries. The beginnings of writing represent a giant step forward in the course of human history. While early examples of written records do not amount to a full philosophical system encompassing most aspects of behavior, they nevertheless provide a sometimes extensive description of either actualities or normative guides. For science, the introduction of writing provided the most important basis, since without communicability there cannot be the cumulativeness necessary for science to emerge and continue.

Looking back at the history of thought generally, one can only be impressed by the "great leap forward" that took place in two widely separated periods. The Golden Age of Greece and the Renaissance marked a burst of intellectual energy that undoubtedly has no equal in the course of history. It is true that activity in these periods was high in almost all areas of endeavor, but learned discoveries played a significant part in generating further action or were stimulated by ongoing events. Cause and effect are, as always, hard to separate and indentify. Suffice it to say that an interrelationship exists.

Ancient and Classical Thought

The peoples of the Nile valley or those along the Tigris and Euphrates rivers provide us with our first clear organization of society where rules of social functioning can be studied readily. Few records of the legal codes of the Kingdom of Egypt have come down to us, though several writings containing political references exist. The most complete legal code, contained in the inscriptions of Horemheb at Karnak, is prefaced: "My majesty is legislating for Egypt to prosper the life of her inhabitants" (Maxey, 1948, p. 12). The famous *Precepts of Ptah-Hotep,* a series of sage sayings of an old vizier, are further references to various kinds of social activity that have been preserved in the ordinary everyday records of the Egyptians.

The outstanding example from the cuneiform records of the Babylonians is the Code of Hammurabi from the year 2100 B.C. These are laws said to have been organized by that king from a welter of prior customs and decrees, with an added measure of his own decrees which he felt had to be added. The notions of retribution and compensation, as with most early codes, predominate. Interesting differentials, such as in penalties for stealing, are contained in the code; the concepts embodied in it point to at least a rudimentary notion of normative approaches in this ancient society. For instance, theft of certain goods from a temple or palace called for a repayment thirtyfold, but only tenfold if stolen from a freeman (Kocourek and Wigmore, 1915, p. 391). More information comes from early Babylonian legal documents, which have been discovered and translated (*Ibid.,* pp. 680–695). These relate to transactions ranging from the purchase of a house or slave, agreements to repay a loan, and documents relating to family law—adoptions, wills, and marriage contracts.

Nor can the overwhelming contributions of the Jews be forgotten. The books of the Bible represent a coherent pattern of concern for regulation of society in order to promote a stable existence. Apart from the important move to monotheism, the dominant theme of Judiac thought lies in the concepts of justice and law; concerns for right and regulation are the prime social aspects in the legacy which we refer to as Judeo-Christian and may be traced most easily to this ancient people.

There is also a tendency for histories of thought to deal with western culture and ignore the many contributions to knowledge of human behavior that emanated from oriental sources. Confucius (551–479 B.C.) in China and Buddha in India were developing philosophical systems that had an impact on society at least as early as their learned counterparts in western lands were.

It was among the Greeks, however, that the flowering of philosophy brought out the greatest early stirrings of intellectual activity concerning the nature of man. Of all the Greek philosophers, Plato and Aristotle stand out in all respects, especially in their concepts of the relationships of man to society.

The highest intellectual activity in Greece was centered in Athens, almost to the exclusion of the other one hundred or more city-states. It also took place in a relatively short span of time, coinciding with the zenith of Athenian power and its destruction, as well as with the lifetimes of the three greatest philosophers of Hellas and, perhaps, the world. Socrates lived during the times of greatest influence and was put to death five years after the defeat by Sparta. Plato survived the Spartan domination while Aristotle taught and wrote under the rule of Macedon. No doubt the greatness of Athens helped each and others like them to emerge, but the three are even more responsible for the continuance of intellectual greatness in Athens after the decline of its political influence.

The turbulence of the period may have provided, as it so often has in history, a fertile ground for the aggressive and robust activity in commerce and economic development. While the conduct of trade did not bestow the highest prestige (Aristotle himself viewed the making of money as an evil), there were few effective arguments against those who developed power through economic means. Commerce thrived in Athens during the golden era, and its bustling businessmen found democratic ideas promising in their attempts to equal the old aristocracy or supplant it. It was this kind of ferment that provided a new base and the raw material for intellectual discourse on the nature of man and his relationships with others in a political entity.

In his "master plan" for a commonwealth, the *Republic,* Plato states that

---

Plato (427–347 B.C.), the pupil of Socrates and teacher of Aristotle, was an Athenian aristocrat gifted in physical and intellectual ways who lived during the height of the golden age of that city-state. While he discoursed extensively on many topics, his sociopolitical proposals in the form of a collectivistic utopian society have had the greatest recognition.

man cannot exist by himself and needs help. In getting this help, people align themselves under one of five forms of state; which one emerges depends upon the circumstances. He outlined five forms: timocracy, oligarchy, democracy, tyranny, and aristocracy.

Timocracy is characterized by military adventure and power, and oligarchy is a rule by the wealthy few. In democracy the masses control, often after a revolt, while tyranny represents the grabbing of power by parasites after an excess of democratic freedoms. In aristocracy philosophers are kings in a well-ordered society where love of wisdom and passion for justice is stratified with individuals at each level performing the tasks for which nature has best equipped them. Aristocracy illustrates many of the high points in Plato's ideal system of government. Plato believed that the highest form of rule was that of reason, with the intellect of the philosopher keeping the peace. He outlined his utopia based on the rule of the elite by reasoning deductively from that central position. The holding of things in common (including wives and children) on the part of guardians of the state was intended to help foster a concern with nothing else but governing. Such was the ideal of an aristocrat who put the rulers and the ruled into special separated niches with each group having its own role to play and all of this to be governed by the rule of reason (Taylor, 1960).

It may well be that Plato was genuinely concerned about the great social inequities of his day and offered his system as an answer to the turmoil. On the other hand, some observers see the system as the result of an attempt not only to maintain a status quo but even "improve" upon it by regressing. The past is often idealized by those who feel threatened in a period of rapid change, and "Plato's blend of reaction and Utopia" may reappear in the formulations of those who want to reestablish the past because they cannot understand what is happening to them and to their society (Roll, 1940, p. 32). Whatever the situation may be, no doubt remains that Plato left his ideal constructs as a legacy to later social philosophers and its impact is still being felt. The number of utopias stimulated by him increases almost daily; individuals distant in time and thinking, as Thomas More and Aldous Huxley, for example, clearly show the source of their concepts of social systems.

Aristotle outlined most of his sociopolitical ideas in his *Politics*. He considered man to be a political animal by nature, with the gregarious motive leading man to a collective form of existence. This positive force, however, was not as strong toward unity at the larger level as it was at the family level or, still more, at the individual level. Aristotle would have the state run by an expression of the interests of all the people; although individuals differed as to the ability they possessed, each could contribute whatever he had in order to maintain a stable whole. This concept of the state does not,

Aristotle (384–322 B.C.) was a physician in his native Thrace before coming to Athens to study with Plato. He lived there much of his life with intervals spent as a tutor, including a stint with Alexander the Great. Aristotle wrote authoritatively on so many subjects that it can be claimed that no other person has ever done so much in the intellectual sphere. For centuries he remained the resource for ultimate academic decisions and can still be called the first political scientist, psychologist, economist, physiologist, or almost any other designee.

as can be seen, put Aristotle too far removed from Plato. Aristotle maintained the division between the rulers and the ruled, much as his tutor did, and justified the need for slavery as the base of the structure. It was his ability and willingness to comprehend better the nature of the emerging patterns of society that puts Aristotle ahead of Plato in the area of analysis. When the great renewal of learning took place more than a thousand years later in Europe, it was Aristotle who provided the base for further specific activity; his system was based on a reality that was inductively ascertained and, therefore, stood the test of time better (not that everything Aristotle said was true, by any means). Plato was the more speculatively based thinker, spinning his system "off the top of his head." Aristotle discoursed on life as he found it, only occasionally elaborating further through speculation. When faced with the problem of formulating a model constitution, Aristotle was not content to sit at home and meditate. He collected, from the field, examples of 158 constitutions, then compared the features of all to formulate a basis for the new one. In *De Anima* we see this same relentless and monumental search for facts in nature. The reader may, at this point, guess why Aristotle is generally considered to be the father of behavioral science and the first political scientist, biologist, or psychologist.

It is, perhaps, an oversimplification to say that every thinker in western culture has been either a Platonist or an Aristotelian in his approach. It is certain, though, that much of what has been discussed in history with respect to man's functioning in society has been influenced by the statements of the two golden Greeks. It may well be that at the present we can subdivide the approaches taken by men of academic bent into the Platonic and the Aristotelian just as in the past we could identify the flavor of political theory in much the same way.

A then small city-state on the Tiber soon reached a level of power and influence that all but obliterated Greek functioning. The place of the Romans in history is due not at all to their original social and political concepts, since they had little if anything to say which was new. What they had they apparently took from others, notably, the Greeks. In the practical applications of political and legal constructs, however, they were unsurpassed; even to this day, the legacy of the Romans lives on in civil law and in other concepts of government. The energy and talent that they put into the administration of their commonwealth sets them apart in history.

Early Roman law, the *jus civile* (civil law), was the loosely knit body of laws regulating the life of the citizens of the city-state. As Rome grew, so did the diversity of peoples under the dominion of the Imperial City and a new kind of law (law of nations) had to be developed to cover all the foreigners. Little by little concepts from the *jus naturale* (natural law) came in to provide a still more rational and humane cast to the code. Codification of Roman law reached its highest point under the emperor Justinian, who, by 534, achieved a long-lasting, systematic organization of the legal system. The several volumes in the Justinian code passed the best of Roman law to posterity; it remains the basis for most of the codes of Europe and has influenced the common law of the Anglo-Saxon countries as well.

The Dark Interval

St. Augustine witnessed the fall of Rome to the barbarians and became convinced that the City of God was immutable just as the City of Man was

---

St. Augustine (354–430) is regarded as the greatest thinker of early Christian times. After what he considered to be dissolate youth, he came under the influence of St. Ambrose, bishop of Milan. His zeal from that time led him to carry on the administration of his Church as well as turn out a steady series of outstanding written works.

---

subject to decay, imperfect, and a necessary evil which had to be subject to the heavenly commonwealth. In the acts of human beings, said Augustine, there is an order which becomes for most individuals a rule to determine the outcome of their acts. This universal logic, the order of the cosmos, is a natural law governing the acts of members of mankind and regulating the relationships between them. This concept of natural law ruling the universe has been picked up, in one form or another, by other social thinkers and utilized as a part of the organization of a philosophical system. The notion of two autonomous commonwealths, one temporal and the other spiritual, has also been of great interest to scholars and practitioners of political and social bent and has reappeared frequently in later thought.

From Augustine to Acquinas is a long time, a period not completely void intellectually but so much so that this period was aptly titled the Dark Ages. Learning was undoubtedly kept alive by the monasteries and church schools but probably never before and certainly never since was the general functioning of a society so low. With Acquinas starts the rebirth of intellectualism.

> Thomas Acquinas (1227–1274), born in the Kingdom of Naples and student or teacher in Cologne and Paris, soon gained the reputation for being the most knowledgeable person since Aristotle. He took it upon himself to weld the works of antiquity with medieval developments in order to provide an all-encompassing system of thought as a proper accompaniment to the universal church. Such organization depends on central concepts of human behavior in society, and some of these have lasted long after the death of the saintly doctor.

At the time of Acquinas the heritage of the Greeks was slowly being reintroduced, often through Latin translation but more and more through the rediscovered works, in the original Greek, of Plato and Aristotle. It was natural for Acquinas, on discovering the wealth of thought in the social and political area by the Greeks, to grasp the basics in the organization of the philosophy and to graft on it the kinds of extensions that are necessary in a new age. Acquinas was a borrower, to be sure, but he did it in such a way and went so far with it as to create essentially a new system.

Not new is the concept of man as a social being, born to live in a dependent interrelationship with his fellows. It is man's nature, said the great Dominican, to be social, and the community emerges naturally from this social nature. Since man's nature comes from God, so his functioning is regulated, of necessity, by natural law. But this law of nature comes not from the random reasonings of individual men but originates from the thought and will of society acting as a whole, although at times one person may be acting for society as a whole. Then if society is natural, so therefore is government. Some kind of regulation of the conduct of individuals in a group must take place to further the common good.

The place of St. Thomas is secure in the sphere of theology and philosophy, certainly. In political and social thought he ranks as the great reviver of classic thought and the great innovator in the adaptation of the basic and great Greek ideas to the necessities of a changed world, a change that does not dilute the importance of the conceptualizations but even accentuates their value for those who came after.

The Renaissance
and Age of Reason

The second tremendous spurt in all spheres of activity, especially the intellectual, came in the period of interrelated events justly labeled the Renaissance. Whether the new spirit of learning influenced other activities such as discovery and expansion or was influenced by them is difficult, if not impossible, to answer. Again, it may be enough to state that all the factors are part of the same phenomenon and each is closely related to the others.

All of the factors in the new learning and the restless energy expended in the turbulent times of the Renaissance may not be identifiable, but there are some outstanding ones that can be mentioned. The use of gunpowder revolutionized warfare and altered social patterns because feudalism became outmoded. When Constantinople fell, Byzantine culture spread to the West and helped to encourage trade and the eventual discovery of America; in addition, the new learning that was stimulated was widely dispersed after the invention of the printing press. Most important, however, may have been the development of the Copernican theory with its removal of man from the center of the universe (Boring, 1950, pp. 8–9). Scientific theorizing and research spread quickly in the climate fostered by the discoveries in other lands and cultures, but more important was the liberating spirit that promoted fresh inquiry where before medievalists had relied on ancient pronouncements.

Nicholas Copernicus (1473–1543), a Polish astronomer-philosopher, changed the world by removing the earth, and man, from a central position in the universe. The impact of this on social thought was beyond measure, and the individual behavioral ramifications of the discoveries are present to this day.

The Copernican revolution brought out the scientist in Renaissance man. To one extent or another the thinkers wrestled with establishing an ordered system encompassing the facts they had obtained. While some dwelt more on physics or mathematics than on political or social facts, all represent the historical tradition for contemporary behavioral science.

This was the age of Galileo, Newton, Leibnitz, and of Harvey, the discoverer of the circulation of blood. Rene Descartes and Spinoza dealt with fundamentals of the intellectual process while Hugo Grotius and Jean Bodin developed concepts of jurisprudence which served to support thinking and research in later centuries. All played their individual and influential role in the development of science and social thought, though a closer look at some of the more proximate ancestors of behavioral science from this period provides not only a glimpse of the familial resemblances but further insight into the nature of those dynamic times as well.

It is perhaps typical of the turbulent times of the fifteenth and sixteenth centuries that this period should have produced two men who go down in

Sir Thomas More (1478–1535), well endowed in intellect and connections, rose rapidly in the tumultuous times of the England of Henry the Eighth to the exalted position of Lord Chancellor. When he could not in conscience side with the king in the break with Rome, More lost his office and then his head. Apart from his example, More's reputation rests upon his *Utopia,* a picture of an ideal commonwealth which indicates his social concern and the forces needed to meet the challenges of change.

history as complete opposites in thinking in the realm of social and political behavior. Niccolo Machiavelli, on the basis of *The prince* alone, stands out as one of the most castigated writers in history. Thomas More stands as one of the most respected personages in the chronicles of human events. In *Utopia* and in the lesson of his life, More demonstrates the high intellectual and ethical way.

Yet, in certain respects, one was as moral as the other. Certainly Machiavelli dealt with facts, or what he believed them to be, with respect to human behavior; at least two central concepts he developed have been used by others who would probably wince at being called Machiavellian. He argued that man

Niccolo Machiavelli (1469–1527), a well born public servant of Florence, is best known for his *The prince,* a frank and brutal blueprint for the governing of a state. As such, it may represent a philosophical system although it is as much an example of the empirical approach to political science. While Machiavelli wrote much more, some of it very light, his fame rests on the shocked response of the public to the honestly stated **prescriptions in *The prince.***

is motivated by self-interest; the state is the highest form of association and, therefore, the primary allegiance belongs to it. This is nothing more than the ancient Greek conception of the basic necessity in social living, which has been developed in this or related fashion by others down through the centuries. Perhaps historians have been too harsh with Machiavelli. He certainly abjured hypocrisy in "calling a spade a spade." He was a realist (although the line between realism and cynicism is a very fine one). As a researcher and reporter of "things as they were," Machiavelli is in the behavioral science tradition.

More's *Utopia* owes much to Plato, to be sure, yet departs from it significantly for adaptations of the basic ideas to sixteenth century England (or the twentieth century world?). More discourses on the need for social reform in the England of his time. Government, religious toleration, reform of the criminal law, health, education, and welfare—all of these and many others were topics discussed by More, with feeling and with a positive plan for implementation.

Sir Francis Bacon (1561–1626), son of an English chancellor, was himself Lord Chancellor to James I. His political career had many disappointments, but he kept active in the intellectual sphere. Bacon perceived the sciences to be organically connected, and his wide interests led him into various areas. His curiosity for factual data even led to his death when he caught a cold from packing a fowl with snow to determine the effect.

Francis Bacon represents a closer ancestor of the behavioral sciences even though his wide-ranging interests included much in the way of speculative philosophizing. His awareness of the need for empirical inquiry in the broad and integrated area of the sciences places him well ahead of most of his contemporaries in this respect.

In the midst of the turmoil in England from Elizabeth I to Cromwell, it is not surprising that Thomas Hobbes regarded mankind as in a state of "war of all against all." Although this statement hardly shows it, Hobbes

---

Thomas Hobbes (1588–1679), an English philosopher, related all social activity to the basic drive for power. Men were motivated, said he, by the pleasure that came from the attainment of power. In his major work, *Leviathan,* he pictured the state as one huge body keeping the individual elements together even though there was a struggle of each against the other.

---

really was a hedonist, but instead of relating all of man's behavior to pleasure seeking by itself, he believed that pleasure came only after power was obtained. Hobbes therefore considered man's most basic motive to be the desire for power. He states in his *Leviathan* that only the common power of the state to which men yield keeps this power struggle within bounds.

John Locke, a contemporary of Hobbes, better represents the Age of Enlightenment among the theorists of the social functioning of man. Man's rationality, Locke believed, enabled him to utilize all the fruits of his surroundings and to conduct himself with reasonableness, moderation, and full social control in a "Social Compact" with others. Locke saw the natural state of man as

John Locke (1632–1704) was an English philosopher whose *Essay concerning human understanding* (1690) established a base for later empiricists. Locke believed that concepts come from experience and that those ideas were associated or connected. His political beliefs of tolerance and liberty influenced many later political philosophers and activists.

a rational adaption to the situation and, indeed, went further to postulate this as a "natural law." The influence of Locke was felt not only by many of his contemporaries and successors, but it was also of great influence in the thinking of the founding fathers of the American Republic. Most believed in the ability of men to judge wisely and vote in the same way. Reservations which they may have had in differing degrees were expressed in the checks and balances of the Constitution, a system that was intended to provide the fullest expression of rationality while preserving the group from the consequences of the less-than-rational acts of its members.

On the continent a quiet yet significant contributor to the area we now know as the behavioral sciences spent his time in study and analysis. Charles Louis de Secondat (Baron Montesquieu) was born and bred a French aristocrat in a family full of notions of *noblesse oblige. The spirit of laws* in 1748

Montesquieu (1695–1755), a French nobleman, lived a comfortable life of early travel and later literary pursuits on his country estate. His *The spirit of laws* (1748) has influenced the political thinking of countless individuals and nations and represents the culmination of his painstaking study of the relationships between social facts and political or legal functioning. His reliance on empirical inquiry antedates the present behavioral thrusts in politics and law.

was the culmination of long activity, and his fame rests primarily on this one book, which probably has influenced more men in contemporary political life than any other, even though they may not have heard of the Baron.

Montesquieu anticipates the behavioral scientists in his painstaking collection of data concerning laws and social relationships. He states that his intent is to show that laws do not arise from whim or fancy but, instead, are social facts "arising from the nature of things." His attempt, further, is to rid man of his "prejudices," by which he meant those things that rendered men ignorant of themselves. Montesquieu's attempt to know society and its laws, to find out how they began, what function they perform, and what cause and effect relationships exist is the heart of his method. How much more can be asked of the prospective scholar in the behavioral sciences?

Many of Montesquieu's specific statements with respect to the proper procedures for establishing tranquility in a society were eagerly adopted by the founding fathers of the American Republic. A basic law and a system of checks and balances were introduced and further essentials of liberty such as freedom of speech were also quickly embraced. However greatly each of these specific points may contribute to social and legal functioning, the key point of Montesquieu's entire work is his awareness of and pointing to the fundamental purposes of laws and their relationship to the situational variables in the environment.

From Revolution to Revolution

Varied cross-currents followed in the wake of the many revolutions—industrial, American (1776), French (1789), The Revolution of 1848, and those engendered later by the ideas of Marx, Darwin, and others. From the French unrest to the attempts to stabilize Europe after Waterloo, much concern was voiced for the status of society.

England in 1776 was just on the threshold of the industrial revolution and all of its attendant social and economic changes. James Watt had invented the steam engine not many years before, and countless other devices were being turned out for widespread use in the new factories by inventors like Arkwright, Hargreaves, and many others. Perhaps one can understand the tremendous changes that took place then by noting some similar social changes in our immediate history which have been accompanied by labor strife, anxiety over automation, or frustration in unemployment. It is easy to see that a burgeoning economy with its attendant social changes would provide a setting for controversy in social and economic ideas. Politics, as usual, produced its debaters but it was in the area of economic thought that the most significant writings in this period emerged. Adam Smith, David Ricardo, and Thomas Malthus are considered together as the classical school, with Smith being known as the founder. Jeremy Bentham, James Mill, and John Stuart Mill later represent other lines of thought, sometimes close to the others, sometimes removed from them.

Adam Smith is best known for his contributions to economic theory, especially those in his *An inquiry into the nature and causes of the wealth of nations* (1776). More important, however, are the concepts like laissez-faire and hedonism that he believed underlie human behavior. Yet the systematization

Adam Smith (1723–1790) remains one of the most influential writers in the area of political economy by virtue of his treatise, *An inquiry into the nature and causes of the wealth of nations.* The ideas organized and propounded by this Scottish professor and lecturer have helped mould the intellectual foundations for free trade and a laissez-faire philosophy of management and government. This strong thrust toward a natural liberty of the marketplace has been challenged successfully by conceptions of control, but certain viable influences remain in contemporary thought.

included an emphasis on sympathy. Smith believed that our sense of justice is derived from the operation of sympathy.

Smith postulated an inherent natural law which he held to be superior to man-made law. The natural law meant a natural liberty for men which only artificial and unnecessary restrictions by a government could curb. It was quite easy for Smith to tie in the relationship between the natural law and laissez-faire with his view of economic liberalism.

His anticipation of the psychosocial concerns in modern mass production society is readily seen in his thoughts on the division of labor. Smith saw that through this division, man increased his production but also increased his dependency on others.

David Ricardo and Thomas Malthus followed Smith and polished the concepts which the founder first introduced. Ricardo furthered consideration

Thomas Malthus (1766–1834) is the father of population study. His *Essay on the principle of population* . . . (1798) outlined the problems of population growth which he saw as increasing faster than the food supply. Population would grow at a geometric ratio, said this English philosopher, were it not for the positive checks of famine, disease, or conflict. Even with these checks, the increases of population to the limit of food supply has a tendency to keep the standard of living low.

of a social reform movement in action and broad social foundations of economic history in his theoretical pursuits.

Jeremy Bentham was probably the most fervent exponent of hedonism as the basis for men's actions in society. In his opinion, men acted solely to secure pleasure and avoid pain. Bentham called this the "Principle of Utility" and built his system on it, even to the lengths where the degree of pleasure or pain could be measured if certain affective states were analyzed ("hedonistic calculus"). Nor was Bentham content to stay within the boundaries of psycho-

Jeremy Bentham (1748–1832), at times considered a somewhat eccentric Englishman, based most of his proposals for social action on "The Principle of Utility" which had its empirical basis in the measurement of pleasure and pain. All social action was to be evaluated on the basis of how much pleasure and how little pain was produced. The "greatest good for the greatest number" was the social ethic deriving from this simple hedonistic analysis of human behavior. This view influenced many during and after Bentham's lifetime, and the impact of "Benthamites" or "Utilitarians" was significant.

logical hedonism but extended it to ethical aspects. Men not only act to maximize their pleasure, but they ought to act so as to maximize the pleasure of others as well—"the greatest good to the greatest number." Bentham sounded the call for a down-to-earth empiricism which would be better able to pinpoint truths in human social and political existence. His interests in legislation and the reform of justice-dispensing agencies were based on that core of his philosophical system.

John Stuart Mill followed Bentham in time and thought. With his greater opportunities to reflect upon utilitarianism, Mill was able to refine and redefine the principles of utility enunciated earlier by Bentham and his disciples. *Laissez-*

John Stuart Mill (1806–1873) was the son of another English philosopher, James Mill, and like him was a Benthamite. The younger Mill refined the concepts of utilitarianism at the same time he was developing theory in the laissez-faire economic tradition of Adam Smith. Mill contributed significantly to most socioeconomic or political discussions on the salient issues of his day.

faire in economic and political matters remained the thesis of the Utilitarians, since Mill made few basic changes in the conceptual structure.

To the development of intellectual thought and action, George Wilhelm Fredrich Hegel provided his notion of the "dialectic" whereby every condition leads inevitably to its opposite just as, inevitably, that leads to a unity of

George Wilhelm Friedrich Hegel (1770–1831), a German philosopher, is best known for his formulation of the dialectic process of development of history and the concept of the "Great Absolute," an all-encompassing social entity. Hegel has been the godfather to authoritarian political movements of all shades ever since.

these opposites to form a better and more perfect whole. This concept of *thesis, antithesis,* and finally *synthesis* was picked up by Hegelians of Right and Left and we know it best today through its manipulation by Marx. Just as important an idea for the understanding of man's role vis-à-vis society, however, was Hegel's notion of something like a "Group Mind" above and beyond the minds of the individuals making up the group. This great Absolute is all-embracing, and the individuals within are but agents advancing it within the patterning of the dialectic, seeing it grow and develop through to a synthesis. Such absolutes can exist in the state to which men must give their allegiance. For Hegel the state was Prussia; in our day the legatees of Marx have their Absolute. Here, as then, morality lies in discipline; individual freedom lies in conformity to the functions of the Absolute. Yet, another picture seems to be painted by Hegel if one views his ideas overall. As Durant (1926, p. 297) says: "Such a philosophy of history seems to lead to revolutionary conclusions. The dialectical process makes change the cardinal principle of life"; with nothing permanent, politics should be an open avenue to change; "history is the growth of freedom, and the state is, or should be, freedom organized." The response to this, in history and in contemporary events, has ranged from a quiet and orderly progression to a violent and often nihilistic revolution.

At this same time, Auguste Comte provided a big breakthrough for social science (or the behavioral sciences) not only by formulating a structuring of the sciences and including the social ones, but also by starting to provide

> Auguste Comte (1798–1857), a Frenchman sometimes called the "father of sociology" because he coined the term, provided an early impetus for the social and behavioral sciences by insisting on an empirical base for social inquiry even though most of his own work was speculative in nature. While his concepts no longer have any force, Comte's greatest contribution remains the stimulation of further activity in sociology and social science.

the social sciences with an appropriate methodology and terminology. Comte coined the term sociology for the study of the social functioning of man but believed that it was not the final step up from the physical sciences. That last step was to be the culmination of activity in all the other areas and would fully account for the intellectual and affective aspects of man. Comte called this final science "la morale," but from his descriptions it could only have been psychology pretty much as we know it today. While much of Comte's structure is now archaic, he was well ahead of his time in anticipating the importance of an integration of the biological, social, and psychological approaches. This integration is seen today in the multidisciplinary team projects or the academic studies involving concepts from all or most disciplines involved in the study of man and his behavior.

   Other sociologists—LeBon, Tarde, and Durkheim—followed Comte. Durkheim felt that individual minds made up a collective mind and that religion

---

Emile Durkheim (1858–1917) was a French sociologist with research interests in the nature of social bonds between individuals and the group. He viewed integration of members in an organization as being fundamental in the stability of that entity. He introduced the concept of *anomie* to explain the lack of integration; suicide was viewed as an outcome of those basic processes. Durkheim, in his study of suicide, was one of the first to use statistical methods in research.

---

was the force through which the group mind made itself felt in the individual mind. Furthermore, through association of human beings, there arise behavior patterns and thoughts which are external to a single individual. Religion, of course, as well as suicide, *anomie* (normlessness), and the division of labor were to Durkheim facts of the social mind and extraneous to that of the individual.

   Karl Marx can be considered as outstanding an economist as, say, Adam Smith; his most important work, *Das kapital,* ranks with the *Wealth of nations*

Karl Marx (1818–1883) developed a conceptual system, dialectical materialism, to explain social functioning. His works, particularly *Das Kapital,* made extensive use of perceptive historical analysis but have been flawed by excessive adoptions as a political weapon. Marx, German born and educated, saw the close link between material circumstances and their social effects, with alienation being only one possible result of burgeoning technology.

---

as a substantial opus. It has the additional feature of having stimulated more controversy and more awareness of its philosophy than has Smith's staid thesis. The message of class consciousness and class conflict is by now so well propounded and documented that the revolutionary cast of this viewpoint need not be extensively pursued. It should be emphasized, however, that Marx's thesis is much more than a proclamation of revolution; it is an economic philosophy, a social document, and a view of history. The concept of the dialectic was taken from Hegel and put to work as an explanation of history.

   In 1859, a world already shaken by the publication of the Communist Manifesto in 1848 felt further tremors when a quiet English biologist published a book entitled *Origin of species*. At first glance, it is difficult to see how this work of Charles Darwin could cause such furor. True, the ideas expressed

> Charles Darwin (1809–1882) was an English biologist who, upon publication of his *Origin of species* in 1859, shook the world with the theory of evolution. Darwin's removal of man from the center of the universe stimulated the kind of emotional and intellectual controversy that contributes to the growth of science.

were revolutionary for their time, but these are usually slow in circulating through an *avant garde* and do not, even in our time, spread as quickly as fads. But spread they did until "Darwinism" became a militant idea. Darwin receives mention in the history of behavioral thought not so much for his basic ideas as for the fact that his action helped to advance the nineteenth century revolution in science and thought. Placid Victorian society was never to be the same again.

One of those who related Darwin's ideas to social functioning was Herbert Spencer who seized upon the doctrine of evolution and related it to the

> Herbert Spencer (1820–1903), an influential social philosopher of English Victorian society, developed a system of sociology founded on Darwin's biologically based theory of evolution. Spencer believed that social forms of organization and functioning were dependent on the natural process of evolution. Society, said he, moved toward greater complexity at the same time that individual characteristics became more important. A process of selection takes place that keeps the system in balance. This fundamental reliance on a "natural law" led Spencer to oppose social reforms through legal action as opposed to a natural process of adaptation.

hedonism of Bentham and the laissez-faire of Smith. Pain, said Spencer, constituted a threat to the existence of the organism; pleasurable activities were those related to survival, and it was thus natural to seek pleasure and avoid pain. The notion of survival of the fittest was introduced into psychological and social areas as well as the original Darwinian application to the physical and biological. It had Spencer opt for "rugged individualism" and oppose almost all the social legislation taking shape in the England of his day. Survival of the fittest was also a convenient rationalization for the activities of the "robber barons" of industry all over the world in the growing industrial development of the late nineteenth century.

> Wilhelm Wundt (1832–1920) was a German university professor who is most often designated as the first true psychologist. Originally trained as a physiologist, he later pursued his experimentation along psychological lines. The foundation of his first psychological research laboratory in Leipzig in 1879 is generally regarded as a starting point for the history of modern psychology. Wundt not only prepared many younger men for the field but also stimulated countless others through his prolific writing.

Against this backdrop, the infant science of psychology was developing, primarily as a consequence of the incomplete work of numerous physiologists. Wilhelm Wundt went to work in his laboratory at Leipzig in 1879, a date commonly accepted as the beginning of psychology, and in his precise fashion

> William James (1842–1910) pioneered psychology in America, and his laboratory at Harvard may have antedated others in the world. While he gradually drifted away into philosophy, his *Principles of psychology* (1890) greatly influenced the course of later events in the areas of studies of behavior.

produced an impressive array of basic findings. William James was active at Harvard just as early and, while his publication was not as extensive, he did show more breadth in his activities. In England, Francis Galton was busy

> Sir Francis Galton (1822–1911) pioneered present-day psychology in Britain, but his work has had more general influence. His extensive data gathering, especially on individual differences, has given substance and method for later empirical knowledge of attributes and abilities of individuals.

assembling anthropometric and psychometric facts to add to the growing store of data on behavior. In sociology the work of William Graham Sumner, George H. Cooley, and George Mead stood out at the turn of the century while in social psychology the first two books in that new field (E. A. Ross and W. McDougall) came along in 1908.

In France, Alfred Binet was proceeding in his own way along lines similar to those developed by Galton and eventually emerged with an appreciation of the facets of mental ability and a sequence of tests by which to measure them. This breakthrough stimulated the vast field of measurement which provides an immense body of information at present.

Alfred Binet (1857–1911) came to psychology after training in law, medicine, and biology. This background may have been responsible for the sound experimental approach he brought to research. He was not content, however, to keep his work in the laboratory. His extensive study of the intelligence of children enabled him to develop the standardized scales that have served as the basis for all the measurement of human abilities and aptitudes taking place today.

The field of economics received its impetus at the turn of the century in a variety of ways from the activity of Alfred Marshall, Thorstein Veblen, and John R. Commons. Of the three, Marshall was probably the most basic in conceptual thought, while both Veblen and Commons were more likely to put their arguments to the test in an action environment. To these should be added the name of Vilfredo Pareto who, though he can be identified as an economist, presented even broader and more dynamic sketches of social functioning, much as did his contemporary Max Weber (who also can be called an economist).

Max Weber was one of those prolific and insightful writers difficult to capture within the boundaries of a specific discipline. He was, certainly, a sociologist, an economist, and an historian; no doubt we may label him as

Max Weber (1864–1920) has been one of the most respected contributors to the social and behavioral sciences. His wide-ranging interests and prolific writing have stimulated further activity in sociology, political science, economic history, and business, to name only a few fields. Weber's writings and his participation in German political and intellectual affairs before and after World War I formed the basis for broader influence of academic activity. Even to this day scholars interested in power and bureaucracy, social stratification, and the sociology of religion and its relationship to economic activity owe a debt to Weber.

a social or behavioral scientist. Weber is well known for his relating of religion to economic development. In the *Protestant ethic and the spirit of capitalism,* he illustrates the ethic in Calvinistic Geneva and compares its growth to the growth of capitalism. The protestant ethic, said Weber, emphasizes the need for individual effort in a disciplined manner to accumulate evidence of predestination for the next world in the form of goods of this world. Hard work, thrift, and individual initiative marked the Puritans for salvation. This thesis has stimulated many students of society who have based much of their

> William Graham Sumner (1840–1910) was an early American sociologist whose major work, *Folkways*, established some fundamental concepts present in custom-related patterns of norms. His conservative background influenced his views on social and political issues and contributed to his emphasis on the force of custom in maintaining the social behavior patterns in a state of *status quo*.

work on Weber's ideas (Tawney, 1952; McClelland, 1961). McClelland has expanded Weber's thesis and has related the level of economic activity in whole nations to the extent of need for achievement found in individuals.

Current organization theorists have also been attracted to Weber, primarily through his concept of bureaucracy. Here he outlined in meticulous detail the characteristics and functioning of a bureaucrat (Gerth and Mills, 1946) and sketched the hallmarks of a bureaucracy. The term bureaucracy should not be considered as pejorative in this context, since it was Weber's name

> Charles H. Cooley (1864–1920) was an American sociologist widely regarded as one of the founders of sociology. He considered a central task of social inquiry to be the study of the socialization of the individual under influences from the primary group. One of the early pragmatists, Cooley followed this orientation in his work on the social nature of the self.

for what might be called administration. Today the bureaucrat would be known as a professional manager. Bureaucracy, stated Weber, is a hallmark of the modern state and is one of the foundations of capitalism. The regularity and order it brings to an organization or political entity is the reason for its existence.

> Alfred Marshall (1842–1924) was a British economist who might be considered a direct economic descendant of Adam Smith and J. S. Mill. Marshall emphasized that economic reasoning was not itself a body of laws or concrete truth but a method for the discovery of truth.

A potentate of old could rule by whim, collect taxes through extortion by underlings, administer everything personally, and still maintain some equilibrium in his domain; a complex present-day society needs a stable and continuing governing structure.

In somewhat the same way as Darwin and his followers, Sigmund Freud produced his own little revolution which spread from a small circle to notoriety on the outside and from widespread attacks on it to an almost grudging piece-

Sigmund Freud (1856–1939) undoubtedly has had a great impact on the world through his pioneering approach to understanding the behavior of man. In his medical practice in Vienna he developed the insights for which he became famous. The concepts of the unconscious mind and the libido not only provided a basis for knowledge but also a method of therapy, psychoanalysis. Freud's theory of motivation, then, has influenced psychologists and lay people alike so that the adjective Freudian is a common one.

meal acceptance. The name Freud is probably the best known name among all who have worked in the behavioral area. A further measure of fame is the acceptance of the validity of the label *Freudian* and the persistence of

Alfred Adler (1870–1937), an Austrian psychiatrist, broke with his teacher, Freud, and founded the school of Individual Psychology. Adler believed that much behavior was the result of compensation for inferiority and that each individual creates a unique life style.

circles of followers (who may not completely agree with what the old teacher had to say). Even those who disagree with the validity of many of the constructs have often incorporated the substance of several of those formulations.

The initial resistance to Freud may have concentrated on a central theme of his theory, the inclusion of a sexual basis for human behavior. Not only were staid Victorians shocked, but to this day certain aspects of the theory still stimulate emotional reactions one way or another. We can label Freud as a hedonist, somewhat in the manner of Bentham and other hedonists. For Freud, the principle of pleasure and pain had crucial meaning; what he did was construct a whole new world atop this basic concept, though he later modified this hedonism by superimposing a death instinct on the structure.

Freud's impact on the modern world, apart from behavioral science or just psychology, is unquestionably great. The influence on modern literature,

Carl Gustav Jung (1875–1961) was a Swiss psychiatrist who also, with many others, broke away from Freud's inner circle of disciples. The main drive, said Jung, was in the "will to live" rather than in sex. Patterns of behavior were also aided by a "collective unconscious" inherited by the individual from past generations.

drama, or even painting has been strong. The influence on day-to-day living in business, government, or religious institutions is no less.

Psychoanalysis, Freud's method of analyzing and treating personality problems, has become a movement, but even though others have adapted many

Vilfredo Pareto (1848–1923) was an Italian economist with broader sociological interests. He was originally trained as an engineer and practiced as such, but extensive writings in economics eventually won for him the chair of political economy at Lausanne. His view of social functioning focused on the systems of adaptation to maintain an equilibrium in society. He postulated a "circulation of elites" whereby stronger members of a society were allowed access to governing classes while weaker members were eliminated; conflict between elites were responsible for social change. In this analysis of individual and social functioning, Pareto emphasized the nonlogical basis for human behavior.

of the constructs for their use, a basic problem of validation of these concepts remains. While productive of a tremendous amount of insightful commentaries, the subjective framework or its elements cannot easily be put to a test; most present psychodynamic systems cannot be evaluated in the way we have set as an almost necessary prerequisite for behavioral science.

Frederick Winslow Taylor (1856–1915) was an American engineer who was determined to develop "the one best way" of accomplishing any task. His proposals and their outcomes have been grouped into what has been called the school of "Scientific Management" and have carried great weight with later attempts to introduce more efficiently engineered methods into industry.

Freud's work was paralleled by that of many one-time followers, among whom the most important two were Alfred Adler and C. G. Jung. Differences in emphasis accounted for the original break with the master, and these continued down through the years.

Frederick Winslow Taylor (1911) represents the application of the scientific method to specific industrial situations. In a way, what Wundt started in the basic discipline of psychology, Taylor continued in the factory. His meticulous, mechanistic, and mathematical approach developed into the "Scientific Management School," a movement that instantly appealed to the managers of factories and soon antagonized those who worked in them. Taylor's ideas spread rapidly and created many disciples who worked under various names—

Thorstein B. Veblen (1857–1929), an American economist, distinguished himself as a critical analyst of the social changes being wrought by the rapid development of business and industry at the turn of the century. He questioned the "conspicuous consumption" of the new and developing industrial society in his *The theory of the leisure class* and recognized other influences on social institutions of the new technology in various other works.

industrial engineers, efficiency experts, time and motion men, or system analysts. While Taylor's fame rests primarily on his contributions in a "practical" setting, it must be remembered that he and scientific management represent a view

John R. Commons (1862–1945) was an American economist with theoretical interests as well as an active participant in drafting model legislation in industry and government. His recognition of group controls in the orderly expansion of economic and political action places him well among the contributors to behavioral thought.

of man which must be taken into account. It rests not only on a mechanistic conception of man at work, but it incorporates the "rabble hypothesis" (Brown, 1954, p. 54) which considers that society is a mass of unorganized individuals, all alike and substitutable for one another. Taylor's approach was complemented by the work of Henri Fayol (1949) who, in 1916 in his *Administration industrielle et generale,* set the outlines for what has been the classical approach to organizations.

Elton Mayo (1880–1949) spent a considerable part of his productive life at the Harvard School of Business Administration. His earlier work at the Hawthorne Plant provided the basis for the Human Relations movement. Mayo believed that industrial harmony was critical to the continuation of a stable society and that an understanding of the needs of both management and workers was the road to social equilibrium.

Representing an entirely different view and undoubtedly one stemming from the reaction against the tenets of scientific management was the work of Elton Mayo (1945). Mayo qualified, more than anyone else, as the "founder" of the "human relations school." This movement arose, at least partially, from the now well-known studies in the Hawthorne plant of the Western Electric Company. As a result of the recognition of the importance of the social aspects of work performance, Mayo and others proceeded with the thesis that interpersonal relationships must be fostered for the fullest realization of the potential

---

John Dewey (1859–1952) was a philosopher-psychologist who strongly urged the intelligent attack on the status quo. Innovation, based on experimentation, was the hallmark of the kind of pragmatism that gave an American stamp to thinking and research on human behavior that continues to this day.

---

of individuals and groups. This is a recognition of man (call it a philosophy, if you wish) antithetical to Taylor's views but one viewed with more anxiety by managers who may be concerned with the effects on them when greater participation in decision making occurs.

A discussion of the precursors of present-day behavioral science could not be complete without at least a nod toward the contributions of John Dewey. This philosopher, psychologist, and educator played an important role in reinforcing the strong empirical approach to applied areas such as education.

Contemporary Outcomes

The patterns of behavioral thought in the past have influenced many other formulations through the years; this has continued to the present, of course. A look at contemporary positions, however, involves the related problems of identification and selection of those formulations that can be said to be significant. What one really needs is the test of time to winnow out the important theoretical or active positions. A selection of present theorists or researchers, then, is somewhat tenuous; a few may be mentioned but the reader must recognize that many more contributors to the behavioral science scene could be added.

In anthropology, Margaret Mead and George P. Murdock, among others, have been continuing in the tradition established a few years earlier by Franz Boas and Bronislaw Malinowski. In the area of law and the relationships with its social environment, Roscoe Pound and Jerome Frank have provided a set of constructs that many younger researchers and scholars have been able to use.

Floyd Allport in his *Social psychology* (1924) marks the transition to modern times in the discipline of psychology and, in many respects, in the behavioral sciences generally. Allport put the empirical stamp on social research, still based on theoretical formulations but moving further in that theory is put to the test.

In one significant step, Skinner (1938) solidified the basis in learning for present-day experimental psychology. His conceptual foundations and even later applications to areas such as programmed instruction have made Skinner a leading psychologist and representative of empiricists in the area of behavior. Carl Rogers (1951), on the other hand, represents a less physiologically oriented psychological tradition in his formulation of a clinical approach to an understanding of human functioning.

J. L. Moreno (1934) has provided many foundations for appreciating the interaction of individuals in groups. Beyond psychodrama, a technique for personal therapy, Moreno has developed techniques like sociometry. This latter approach, a simple sketching of the interpersonal attractions and repulsions, has been a fruitful basis for an understanding of intragroup dynamics.

Chester Barnard was an unusual businessman in that he stimulated further work in fundamental areas by providing academicians with conceptual formulations, pioneering particularly in organization theory. His *Functions of the executive* (1938) provided a discussion in depth of material on human relations, communications, authority, and many other concepts. He has influenced others like Simon (1957) in administrative or organizational areas. Simon, along with a few others (Cyert and March, 1963), is further affixing the empirical stamp on political, economic, or organizational studies or on newer interdisciplinary areas emerging from those traditional disciplines.

Mary Parker Follett (1941) also began to use social science concepts in formulating the relationship between individuals and the organization after the realization of the importance of social factors. Strother (1963) sees in Follett's work a renewal of the social contract theme for history and a predecessor of the ethical assumptions followed at this time by Argyris (1957), McGregor (1960), and Haire (1962). To this group we might add Maslow (1954) and Herzberg (1966). Maslow is best known for his concept of the *hierarchy of needs* and of *self-actualization* whereby man is motivated by an ordered set of needs. At the apex is the need for self-actualization, the need to be active in the most comprehensive and worthwhile spheres of human conduct or to fulfill one's potential to the greatest extent. It is on this point that Strother has commented that the proposition has an ethical base. It is a view of man that does indeed have a normative flavor.

In the area of political behavior the most prolific writer and researcher undoubtedly has been Harold D. Lasswell (1951). In a long series of works stretching back to the 1920's, Lasswell has developed the relationship between psychological factors and political behavior, particularly the ties between personality and politics. Much of this has been within a psychoanalytic framework. George Katona (1951) has forged the links between psychology and economics more than other economists and psychologists have been able to do. His activities follow the patterns of John R. Commons and Alfred Marshall but go far beyond into a more complete integration of economic and psychological material.

In sociology, Robert K. Merton (1949) and Talcott Parsons (1951) have stimulated further research. Parsons has developed a theory of social action which is intended to be a general theory of action rather than just a psychological or sociological one. It is an attempt to provide an integration of the behavioral sciences. The sociological base for Parsons' work shows some resemblance to Durkheim and Sumner in the emphasis on the normative aspects of society.

Philip Selznick (1957) has been a leading contributor to theory and research in sociology generally and, more specifically, in the social foundations of law as well as social behavior in organizational settings.

Basic Themes

A cursory review of some of the social, political, economic, or behavioral thought of the past or the present may provide the reviewer with glimpses of some recurrent themes or constellations of ideas. While it is difficult to collate these varied concepts to provide a semblance of a unitary picture, some attempt at organization may be made. In somewhat the same way, an attempt to outline an individual's ideas with a simple framework is at least misleading through generalization if not impossible to accomplish. There does seem to be, however, the flavor of the "Simple and Sovereign" idea in most historical or present-day formulations of the basis for human functioning (Lindzey, 1954). One may even wonder if this is not even a necessary precondition for the concept to be noted at all, if not accepted by a public larger than two or three students.

SPECIFIC CONCEPTS

Economists, particularly in the past, have concentrated on the rational basis of the "economic man." The two general notions fit together nicely. This approach states that man, faced with alternatives, chooses rationally between those alternatives in a way that will provide him with the best outcome. Man is presumed, under this concept, to maximize his gain.

The philosophers of the "Era of Enlightenment" often referred to themselves as the "Rationalists." Perhaps the idea that irrational aspects of human functioning were present did come to their attention, but it is probable that such notions were not permitted to intrude into the "higher order" formulations of rationality. Adam Smith, however, raised the possibility of the influence of the irrational and treated it at length. It was certainly given great impetus by the writings of Freud one hundred and more years later. At present, one cannot speak of a theoretical or applied system of human behavior without including both concepts, rationality and irrationality.

Hedonism, the doctrine relating all of behavior to the seeking of pleasure and the avoidance of pain, got its real start with Bentham's "hedonistic calculus." It is perpetuated in the economic theory of man in that it proposes that man will work to obtain money because money is pleasure. Its rational view is evident when it further states, in this context, that man will maximize by "buying low and selling high." That man does not always do this has slowly been recognized and economic theorists no longer hold to a purely rational hedonism.

Freud also represents an irrational type of hedonism, particularly in his earlier emphasis on the pleasure principle. The instincts, he said, seek pleasure, and any other factors we may see are simply overlays, supressions, repressions, or controls. A more behavioral use of the concept of hedonism, though it is infrequently viewed in this light, is in *reinforcement.* Either a reward (food or water, for example) or tension-reduction or shock becomes a matter of pleasure or pain which then reinforces the attendant behavior.

The notion of power or egoistic drive has come to the fore occasionally, more in nonprofessional circles, perhaps, though not limited to them. Hobbes declared that man's basic motive was the "desire of power after power that ceaseth only in death" (Lindzey, 1954, p. 13). This theme was later picked up by the German philosopher Nietzsche, who believed that the basis of all social functioning was the will to power. Both Hobbes and Nietzsche believed that pleasure came fundamentally from the exercise of power. Alfred Adler may be counted among this group. The basic reason for Adler's split with Freud was undoubtedly in his disagreement with the master's central concept of sex. To Adler, the basic theme in human existence was the striving for power. The inferiority complex and compensation represent for him the importance of the will to power.

Another frequently recurring theme has been the feeling for improvement of social conditions expressed in the form of ideal structures and circumstances. Plato's ideal, the *Republic,* gave rise in subsequent centuries to numerous plans or programs of social action, best expressed by More's *Utopia* (from which we derive the generic term for all such approaches). Interestingly enough, More's work was only one of many such books that emerged within a few years of each other in sixteenth century England. Variations on this theme have continued down to our own day.

A recurring analogy, from Plato to Hobbes to LeBon, is one that compares a group of individuals with the human body, or goes even further, in one variation of the basic theme, to postulate the existence of the "group mind." Certainly we talk these days about "the body politic" or the "head of the corporate body" much in the same fashion as Plato spoke of the philosopher-kings as the head of the social body.

Ideals or concepts often are antithetical to each other, or they represent polarities in attitudes. For instance, at present, a dichotomy in psychology (though a classification of a complex area into two or three categories leaves much to be desired) might be stated in terms of the behaviorists on one side and the more dynamic psychologists on the other; Skinner represents the more behavioristic of the psychologists while Rogers and Maslow represent various types of more dynamic theoretical positions. In somewhat the same way, Frederick Winslow Taylor and Elton Mayo represented polar positions. Taylor emphasized the mechanistic view of man at work; Mayo believed in a more open framework for greater individual need satisfaction.

DIFFICULTY WITH THE SIMPLE IDEA

As may be seen from the discussion above, the label "Simple and Sovereign" (taken from the idea of the single tax advocated by Henry George late in the nineteenth century) is one that may be applied to many of the conceptual frameworks built by authors, past and present. The least that may be said is that there is most often a central theme in the theoretical structure that is built. Perhaps this is a requirement for cohesiveness in organization or for greater ease in propagating the result. While the simple and sovereign idea may be convenient to view and use, the main difficulty is that it is too simple to represent reality adequately. Human behavior is too complex to portray adequately within a simplified framework. Overgeneralization often results in inadequate conclusions. Henry George, too, may have discovered that even in the limited area of taxation, his simple and sovereign tax on land was not viable in a complex economy.

We could err, however, by going to the opposite extreme and throwing up our hands in despair at the complexity of the problem. The difficulties involved are great, without a doubt, but there is no reason why we cannot approach the area systematically and gather data with precision to put together a clearer picture of human behavior. In this task, the philosophers and scientists of the past serve as guides; they do not represent either ultimate models for or limitations on activity in behavioral science.

Summary

The present state of an area or field cannot be understood fully without some awareness of the events that have preceded it. Study of the past can be helpful although we would not wish to rely on that alone as the basis for present decision making.

Some interest in human behavior undoubtedly has been generated from the days of man's first appearance on this planet. While there may be some educated guesses about earlier concepts of individual and social behavior from artifacts that remain, the advent of writing provides a better basis for knowing the extent and development of behavioral thought.

While various ancient peoples developed advanced social systems, the zenith of intellectual functioning in classical antiquity undoubtedly came in the Greece of the golden age. And of the illustrious complement of great men of that era, Plato and Aristotle stand out. Of the two, Plato was more the deductive thinker and developer of hypothetical systems. Aristotle deserves to be called the ancestor of behavioral science because of his bent for collection of facts as a prelude to organization of materials. The works of these two philosophers were at the core of Greek and Roman literature which helped stimulate the renewal of learning in Europe after the long, dark interval between Augustine and Acquinas. It was not, however, completely dark, as the feeble educational institutions maintained and developed the deductive approach that reached its high level under Acquinas and his peers.

It remained to others, however, under the press of uncommon events, to develop systematic inquiry into the nature of physical and social events. Copernicus altered man's concept of himself at a time when gunpowder hastened the decay of feudalism and travel widened not only trade but the world-view as well. Books and Byzantine culture did the rest; all this helped make a scientist of Renaissance Man. The tumultuous events produced individuals as disparate as More and Machiavelli, then Bacon and Locke, or Hobbes and Montesquieu. From Machiavelli's brutally honest empiricism to Montesquieu's hopeful reliance on social data, a wide range of philosophical thought helped to further early beginnings of the science of behavior just as it inspired political action.

The industrial revolution was but one of many revolutions; economic and political events were intertwined, as always. It is not surprising, then, that the economic writings of Adam Smith and Karl Marx have their political meaning and impact. Other intellectual concern for social welfare could be manifested in the utilitarianism of Bentham and Mill rather than the more militant rival philosophies. At the same time, a significant step was taken by Comte in the birth and christening of sociology in roughly the period when the physical sciences were beginning to stand on their own as areas of discipline. But the strong scientific imprint on behavioral areas did not come until later in the century as Wundt and other researchers pursued their interests in the tradition of the physiological laboratories in which they were trained.

Other revolutions shaped up in Victorian times as new views of man challenged cherished ideas. In somewhat the same way, Darwin and Freud shook their contemporaries and provided bases for fresh looks at the world and man's place in it. Both stimulated ideological movements in explanation of behavior that had wide social impact. Concurrently, other early behaviorists, in different ways, pursued their inquiries into the nature of individual and social functioning. Personalities as diverse as Galton, Binet, and Frederick Winslow Taylor observed, measured, and studied countless instances of behavior; Max Weber developed concepts of organizational functioning and traced the relationship between religion and the economy. These varied influences, and many more, have helped mould the present state of thinking in the behavioral sciences.

In the long unfolding of social and behavioral thought, certain patterns may be identified; particular themes occur, often in widely spaced periods of time. The concept of the rational man can be seen as well as the countervailing examples of irrationality, especially in Freud's contributions. Various views in history have focused on the pleasure principle (in both rational and irrational forms) or on the principle of utility—the greatest good for the greatest number. Egoism and power theories are represented as well, but by far the greatest recurrent themes are those framed in idealistic terms.

Most of the past and present concepts of behavioral bases have too much of the flavor of a "simple and sovereign" idea. Life is much too complex to resolve its important aspects to a neat and concise formulation. The unitary theme persists, however, and may even be necessary to provide a starting point for an approach toward a fuller understanding of human behavior.

Bibliography

Allport, F. (1924). *Social psychology.* New York: Houghton-Mifflin.

Argyris (1951). *Personality and organization; the conflict between system and the individual.* New York: Harper.

Barnard, C. (1938). *The functions of the executive.* Cambridge: Harvard University Press.

Boring, E. (1950). *A history of experimental psychology* (2nd ed.). New York: Appleton-Century-Crofts.

Brown, J. (1954). *Social psychology of industry*. Baltimore: Penguin.

Cyert, R. and March, J. (1963). *A behavioral theory of the firm*. Englewood Cliffs, N.J.: Prentice-Hall.

Durant, W. (1927). *The story of philosophy*. Garden City. N.Y.: Simon & Schuster.

Fayol, H. (1949). *General and industrial management* (Storrs, C., trans.). London: Pitman.

Follett, M. (1941). *Dynamic administration; the collected papers of Mary Parker Follett* (Metcalf, H., ed.). New York: Harper.

Gerth, H. and Mills, C. (1946). *From Max Weber: essays in sociology*. New York: Oxford University Press.

Haire, M. (1962). *Foundation for research on human behavior*. New York: Wiley.

Herzberg, F. (1966). *Work and the nature of man*. Cleveland: World.

Katona, G. (1951). *Psychological analysis of human behavior*. New York: McGraw-Hill.

Kocourek, A. and Wigmore, J. (1915). *Sources of ancient and primitive law*. Boston: Little, Brown.

Lasswell, H. (1951). *Political writings*. Glencoe, Ill.: Free Press.

Lindzey, G., ed. (1954). *Handbook of social psychology*. Reading, Mass.: Addison-Wesley.

Maslow, A. (1954). *Motivation and personality*. New York: Harper & Row.

Maxey, C. (1948). *Political philosophies* (rev. ed.). New York: Macmillan.

Mayo, E. (1946). *The human problems of an industrial civilization*. Cambridge: Harvard University Press.

McClelland, D. (1961). *The achieving society*. Princeton: Van Nostrand.

McGregor, D. (1960). *The human side of enterprise*. New York: McGraw-Hill.

Merton, R. (1949). *Social theory and social structure*. Glencoe, Ill.: Free Press.

Moreno, J. (1953). *Who shall survive?* Beacon, New York: Beacon House.

Parsons, T. (1951). *The social system*. Glencoe, Ill.: Free Press.

Rogers, C. (1951). *Client-centered therapy*. Boston: Houghton-Mifflin.

Roll, E. (1956). *A history of economic thought* (3rd ed.). Englewood Cliffs, N.J.: Prentice-Hall.

Selznick, P. (1957). *Leadership in administration*. Evanston, Ill.: Row, Peterson.

Simon, H. (1957). *Administrative behavior* (2nd ed.). New York: MacMillan.

Skinner, B. (1938). *The behavior of organisms.* New York: Appleton-Century-Crofts.

Smith, A. (1950). *An inquiry into the nature and causes of the wealth of nations* (Cannan, E., ed.). London: Methuen.

Strother, G. (1963). Problems in the development of a social science of organization. In Leavitt, H. (ed.). *The social science of organizations.* Englewood Cliffs, N.J.: Prentice-Hall, Chap. 1.

Tawney, R. (1952). *Religion and the rise of capitalism.* New York: Mentor.

Taylor, A. (1960). *The mind of Plato.* Ann Arbor: University of Michigan Press.

Taylor, F. (1911). *The principles of scientific management.* New York: Harper.

3

Data and Decision Making

This will be a chapter devoted to the methods by which behavioral scientists (1) gather information that they believe will be pertinent to the problem they are interested in, (2) organize the data gathered so that some conclusions may be drawn from them, and (3) draw those conclusions. It is a chapter devoted to method—the mechanics of research, including its important next-to-final stage, statistical treatment of data, and its ultimate point, the making of decisions.

There is one caveat that should be mentioned first (there are many more but these will, hopefully, be recognized in the delineation of this discussion). This is the danger inherent in the belief that technique is all that is of interest in this area. It should become evident to the thoughtful person who proceeds to uncover the elements of behavior that he cannot simply roll up his sleeves and go to work with the instruments. Not only does activity in this field require advance preparation but the data, once gathered, have to scrutinized to provide meaning from the bits; that is, they have to be viewed in the light of the relationships and associations with other material from the area. More important, the assumptions and premises underlying the gathering of evidence have much to do with the process of data collection and with the formulation of the results of that activity. Not only are the general assumptions underlying the scientific approach important (Chapter 1) but the various specific approaches to data collection each have their own peculiar underpinnings which could affect the results in one way or another.

Data Collection

Mention has been made in Chapter 1 of one of the hallmarks of behavioral science that is especially pertinent here, namely, that it is *empirical*. This field of discipline is not founded on speculation or "intuition" but is based on facts gathered in a systematic or scientific way. Nor is this approach normative, referring to the "ought" of behavior. Rather, it is descriptive of "what is." The "what is" can be determined, however, in many different ways. Just as "there are many ways to skin a cat," so there are many ways to collect data.

BEHAVIORAL RESEARCH

The important feature of the research of the behavioral scientist is that it concentrates on getting data at first hand. Secondary sources of data have been important for the historian who, by and large, digs into the writings of the past for his data. The student of law reviews judicial opinions, statutes enacted by the legislature, and commentaries by outstanding scholars. For those historians and law men, this activity is research. The behavioral scientist will not so designate it; for him this is only a review of the literature and the first step in the process. The gathering of primary data at the real source is usually the aim of the behavioral scientist. The methods to be outlined below have this characteristic in common.

There is one large area, however, where an apparent variation exists. Much information is available in records of various kinds—census statistics, newspapers, magazines, medical histories, business transcripts, and school records. The wealth of data has already been collected by someone other than the researcher. The behavioral scientist may then, even though this is a somewhat secondary approach, analyze the data available to him. He does do something with it, usually in a quantitative way and often in a creative fashion that provides information of a sort that could not be otherwise obtained (Webb, et al., 1966). The method of *content analysis,* which will be discussed later in this chapter, is another such technique.

OBSERVATION

The method of natural observation or the "field study" method is the oldest and probably still the most widely used method of gathering information. It was used by the ancients in their descriptions to others, and it is used at present by researchers in the field. Anthropologists studying the puberty rites of the Arapesh make use of it, but so do traffic observers who determine the nature and extent of vehicular activity at a particular urban location. In using this method the observer may go beyond being a nonparticipant in the behavior setting under study and may actually participate in the activity. A psychologist who is interested in the setting of group norms in an industrial work group may be hired, trained, and put to work in the midst of the very group whose activities he will observe. In either the participant or the nonparticipant approach, the role and actions of the observer may be hidden from the group or they may be aware of the real situation.

The method of natural observation may not, much of the time, provide very precise or intricate measures. It is all too often a haphazard note-taking venture with little else to supplement the casual or impressionistic results. There are, however, some structural situations with well-organized systems for observing and recording behavior. The method of Bales (1951) in assessing the interactions among individuals in groups on a twelve category system is illustrative (Table 3-1) of how much can be garnered by an observer behind a one-way vision screen. Mechanical adjuncts such as movie cameras, tape recorders, and stenographic systems may be used to overcome the observer's biological limitations.

The method of natural observation is limited in that control of the situation by the observer is not possible, although that disadvantage may in reality be an advantage—the method may have been chosen because the "natural" circumstances were considered desirable. What is more likely is that there was little opportunity to gain the information desired through any other approach. A further complication arises when the task of the observer, whether he be a participant or nonparticipant, is known to the subjects. It is certain that the activities of those who know they are under observation differ from their behavior when they have no idea that observations are being made.

Some of these difficulties are avoided in the use of a set of indirect approaches that should be mentioned at this point. With methods that can be called nonreactive (Webb et al., 1966), the researcher can garner information from past actions. In addition to data from records of various kinds, indirect data provide material for analysis. Erosion of floor tile is related to use, noseprints on museum cases are an indication of the level of childrens' interest in the exhibit, and the number of empty whiskey bottles in the household trash is evidence of consumption level. Other data bases are limited only by the ingenuity of the experiment.

THE LIFE HISTORY METHOD

This means of gathering data is based on the information gained in focusing on an individual and his emerging patterns of behavior. It may be referred to variously as the clinical method, the clinical history approach, or the case study. It is the method used by clinical psychologists when they try to determine the antecedents of a present pattern of behavior in order to understand better

Table 3-1. System of Categorization in the Observation of Group Relations (Bales, 1951, p. 59)

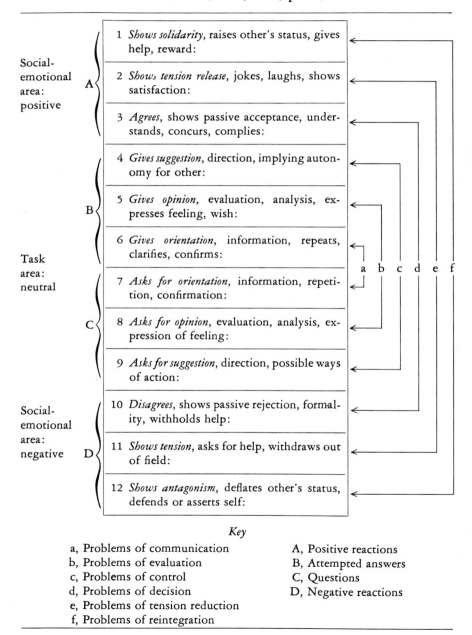

Social-emotional area: positive	A	1 *Shows solidarity*, raises other's status, gives help, reward:
		2 *Shows tension release*, jokes, laughs, shows satisfaction:
		3 *Agrees*, shows passive acceptance, understands, concurs, complies:
Task area: neutral	B	4 *Gives suggestion*, direction, implying autonomy for other:
		5 *Gives opinion*, evaluation, analysis, expresses feeling, wish:
		6 *Gives orientation*, information, repeats, clarifies, confirms:
	C	7 *Asks for orientation*, information, repetition, confirmation:
		8 *Asks for opinion*, evaluation, analysis, expression of feeling:
		9 *Asks for suggestion*, direction, possible ways of action:
Social-emotional area: negative	D	10 *Disagrees*, shows passive rejection, formality, withholds help:
		11 *Shows tension*, asks for help, withdraws out of field:
		12 *Shows antagonism*, deflates other's status, defends or asserts self:

a b c d e f

Key

a, Problems of communication
b, Problems of evaluation
c, Problems of control
d, Problems of decision
e, Problems of tension reduction
f, Problems of reintegration

A, Positive reactions
B, Attempted answers
C, Questions
D, Negative reactions

how a neurotic, for instance, "got that way." In this case, the analyst looks at the material uncovered in the individual's life history and, looking backward from his present position, identifies what he believes to be significant factors in the etiology of the client's or patient's behavior. A slightly different variation, from the standpoint of time, is the methodology used by a developmental psychologist who may follow an individual through time and keep a "daybook," as many fond parents do, which will be a record of the changes that take place over the period of study. Gesell's (1945) study of developing infants to establish norms for different ages and McGraw's (1935) study of the twins Johnny & Jimmy are examples of this longitudinal approach. An industrial sociologist would also be interested in the case history of a strike and in the background factors that seemed to be present in the genesis of the labor unrest. An anthropologist might utilize this same technique in tracing the adaptation of the individual in a primitive society to the rituals and traditions of the group.

The life history method has been criticized as being limited in its possibilities for generalization from the data. "After all," the critics often state, "the data are from one individual only and, therefore, are very limited in the amount of information they can provide us about other individuals or other situations." While this is a difficulty, it must be remembered that conclusions are often based not on the life histories of single individuals but on a conglomerate picture of life histories of many single individuals. After a period of time, a recurring pattern may cause the counselor to be suspicious of the significance of certain events in the past. Group case studies, too, are looked at not only in the light of the limited events emerging from the situation but are placed within the broader framework of knowledge of past and similar events before any conclusions are drawn. Perhaps the most significant statement to be made on the value of the life history method is the substantial accumulation of data from its use. It has been, particularly in clinical psychology, the basis for a wealth of insight for practitioners and the fruitful source of theory in the areas of self and personality.

The drawback in the method that does remain a serious one, however, is the difficulty the user may have in controlling the situation and remaining rigorously objective. The problem one has in maintaining scientific rigor is especially acute in a situation where collection of data occurs in a setting where selectivity by the collector of data can play a significant role. This difficulty occurs in the life history method as well as in the method of natural observation discussed above.

Another danger is that when we look at the results of the data gathering we might assume a relationship in a specific way between what now exists and what has happened in the past. The dangers inherent in thinking *post hoc, ergo propter hoc* are often very subtle.

SURVEY METHODS

When we wish to know the answers to certain questions such as "how do New Yorkers feel about the Mets?" or "what are drivers of Crudleigh V-8s like?" the approaches outlined above are unsuitable. It may seem at first glance that the observation method or the life history method could be used. Indeed they might, except that by the time enough information is gathered the basic situation has changed so that the limited answers are probably no longer meaningful. What has to be done is to establish a whole set of answers to the basic question at one and the same time; in other words, a survey must be made. The first and often only example of survey methodology that comes to most people's minds is the political poll, which they may then use to predict which of the candidates will win the coming election. While this may be a fascinating example of the opinion poll, it is by no means the most fruitful of the survey techniques. More information can be gained when the answers are arranged in categories that have been set up for other variables so that comparisons may be made. Do women show voting patterns different from men? What is the relationship between parents and children in opinions? Are there any personality pattern variations between those who buy convertibles and those who purchase the standard four-door sedans? The answers to questions such as these are much more meaningful than the answers "yes," "no," or "don't know" to the straight poll question such as, "In general, do you feel the president is conducting foreign affairs properly?"

The important technical problems in conducting a survey are those concerned with the following procedures.

(a) Formulating the questions.
(b) Setting up the sample.
(c) Interviewing.

In the first problem area, the matter of question formulation, the researcher has a choice, roughly, between the poll question or the open-end question. In the poll approach the investigator asks a question to which the respondent must answer with a simple "yes," "no," or "don't know." In the open-end question the investigator allows the answer to be given in the respondent's own framework and in his own words. There are advantages and disadvantages, of course, in either general approach. The poll question is easy to score and tabulate (for example, 40 percent yes, 50 percent no, and 10 percent don't know), although it does restrict the data because of its limited format—so limited, in fact, that often the answers may not represent the real feelings in the matter. The open-end question does not constrict the answer as much as does the poll question, and the reply given therefore may be more representative of the real state of the respondent's opinions than is the answer to the poll question. The chief problem with the open-end approach is that the answers are not simple and, before any conclusions may be drawn, they must somehow be grouped; out of a nearly infinite number of responses, some manageable categories must be constructed before the results can be reported.

A further difficulty in both types of questions lies in their phrasing. An obviously leading question is not too difficult to spot; those less leading may be passed by without recognition of their biasing propensities. The best of both techniques is possible with a combination of the two approaches, the "funnel" sequence, whereby the questions go from the very broad, open-end question at first to a more specific poll question at the end of the series. These and other interview problems are extensively treated by Maccoby and Maccoby (1954).

Let us assume now that the question is framed properly and that we are ready to proceed with the survey. Assuming also that we are interested in the opinions of the American people about the president's conduct of foreign policy, our question may be put to all 200 million of us (or should this be limited to adults, or to United States citizens and not aliens, or to all residents). If the question were directed to all the people in whom we were interested, the "population," we might be secure in knowing that we had a complete survey. No one, however, has the time, energy, and money it would take to do this complete a job on a national scale. In addition, by the time it could be completed, the basic situation undoubtedly would show great change. Suffice it to say that from a practical standpoint we must limit our respondents to a much smaller number in order to be able to have some reasonable time limit; in other words, we will have to take a sample of the population. The major concern at this point is to insure that the sample is representative of the population, that is, that the small group of respondents is a miniature of the larger group in every respect; this should be the population "in a nutshell." How a survey researcher goes about selecting the sample is the subject of many technical discussions, often very extensive. Here is a short, quick look at the problems.

How many should there be in the sample? Generally, the more closely we approach in number the population the greater confidence we may have in the value of our sample. Even more important than number, however, is representativeness; a sample of 300 carefully selected Americans can reflect American opinion better than a sample of improperly chosen individuals one hundred times that size.

How can the selection take place? One method would be to select a *random sample,* relying on the elimination of any bias through the laws of probability. If everyone in the population has an equal chance to be selected, any deviation from representativeness in our sample is only a result of the chance errors, which are predictable (see below). Often, however, supposedly "random" methods are far from that because of subtle and unrecognized biases operating in the selector. Pollsters who stand on the street corner to interview every tenth person must be careful indeed to do just that rather than interview those who appear to be good and pleasant prospects.

A *stratified sample* is one which is set up with the deliberate intent that it reflect the population in all variables under consideration. If we know the population has 50 percent men and 50 percent women, 4 percent farmers, 10 percent above age 50, etc., our sample will be selected to provide this kind of representation. The term *quota sampling* is often used for a less extensive variant of this technique. Often, an advertising agency will send out its interviewers with orders to get the quota of "ten men and ten women." With no other requirements evident, the "sample" is a very tenuous one indeed.

Area or block sampling selects respondents on a geographic basis. Larger areas are subdivided systematically until specific housing units are located. The residents of that unit are then the subjects of the survey and, if not at home, are the targets for "call-backs" until they are included.

In sampling from *lists*, the researchers may pick every tenth name, for instance, from a listing like a telephone directory, street lists of voters, etc. The source of error here is that often the surveyor may forget that while the sample may be randomly representative of the list, the generalization cannot be made to a population beyond the list itself. In 1936 the *Literary Digest* sampled from the telephone directory and then assumed that those who had telephones were representative of the general population of voters. On this basis they confidently predicted the election of Landon over F. D. Roosevelt (notoriety from this wide-of-the-mark prediction apparently proved too much for the magazine and it eventually disappeared from the scene).

With the sampling and the questions set, the last problem to handle before setting out in the field is whether to ask the question orally and receive a response orally from the subject or to do away with the interviewer and present a questionnaire. The interviewer may be face-to-face with the subject or may contact him by telephone; the questionnaire may be sent through the mail or be handed to the person and filled out at a convenient location. Questionnaires sent by mail and returned in the same way add an additional bias in that it seems certain that those who reply may differ in opinions on many issues from those who do not return their questionnaire.

Panel surveys are conducted with the same group over a period of time. Changes in response or the opportunity to survey more extensively are reasons why a panel approach may be used. What the process itself does to the individuals and their opinions over a period of time remains one of the more interesting questions a researcher might have to consider.

Depth surveys are attempts to probe more deeply in the psychological or psychoanalytic bases of the personality structure of the individuals being interviewed. Projective techniques of various kinds, interviews, or other armamentaria of the analyst are used. The technique does not receive wide use because of the cost in time and effort. It is necessarily limited to a very small number, a set of individuals further selected from the sample.

In addition to the difficulties associated with the form of the question and the sampling of the population, there are some fundamental problems of interpretation of survey results. These arise when relationships are traced between variables that are categorized and then surveyed along the divisions outlined. Causality cannot be easily determined—often all that can be said is that a relationship exists and influence may run in either direction. For instance, it may be difficult if not impossible to determine if one political party fosters "liberal" opinions or whether those with "liberal" attitudes join that particular party.

Despite the difficulties, the survey method remains as one of the more vigorous techniques. It is often the only one that can be used, as in a case where manipulation of variables is out of the question and we must take the situation as it comes. It is also the only way to accumulate a mass of data in a short period of time.

ATTITUDE SCALES

The measurement of attitudes is best done through the use of attitude scales. The attitude scale does not differ basically from the questionnaire in the survey method; it is a more refined variant of that approach. Because it is considered a basic technique by social psychologists and because it has some further important characteristics, it should be treated separately at this point.

An attitude is a basic predisposition or tendency to respond, positively or negatively, to a set of circumstances. As with many other variables an attitude can only be inferred from responses of the individual. In an attitude scale the individual responds to a set of carefully phrased questions. From these responses the individual may be placed at a point on an attitude continuum which numerically presents his position between the positive and negative poles.

There are two major types of attitude scales. Thurstone (1929) developed a scale that contains 11 points along a continuum of favorableness-unfavorableness. The 11 points are established by having judges place statements into eleven piles along the continuum. As a result, each of the many statements receives a scale value with, say, value 1 representing the strongly favorable attitude and 11 the strongest opposite. An illustrative scale is one that has been developed to measure attitudes toward war (Droba, 1930). Two items from the scale are given below, with the scale value in parentheses on the left.

> (1.3)   A country cannot amount to much without a national honor, and war is the only means of preserving it.
>
> (10.6)   All nations should disarm immediately.

Respondents are asked to check those statements with which they agree; a numerical score derived from the scale values of the items checked determines the placement of the person on the continuum.

The Likert (1932) scale asks for a response from among five that are in an ordered arrangement. A question on the Likert scale may be set up as follows.

World peace can come about only if nations are willing to arbitrate all controversies between them. (check)

☐	☐	☐	☐	☐
strongly approve (5)	approve (4)	undecided (3)	disapprove (2)	strongly disapprove (1)

The figures in parentheses represent the score for the particular responses. The final score can be either the cumulative one from all items or an average; either system places the person somewhere along the attitude continuum.

Other means of measuring attitudes are available from observations of behavior in specific situations to semiprojective techniques. Refinements of the Thurstone and Likert scales also have been made by other researchers. These will be discussed in more detail in Chapter 13.

SOCIOMETRY

While this term implies a broad category that includes all measures of social functioning, most behavioral scientists limit the use of the term to those methods specifically designed by J. L. Moreno (1953) to identify certain types of intragroup relationships. The sociometric test in this form determines and depicts the attractions and repulsions among individuals within a given group. Replies to a question like "with whom would you prefer to work" then can be arranged in tabular form or in histograms but are best translated to a visual form which highlights the individual responses and the patterns within the group. The simplicity of the technique and the graphic presentation of results have made the sociometric test a very popular and useful method. Figure

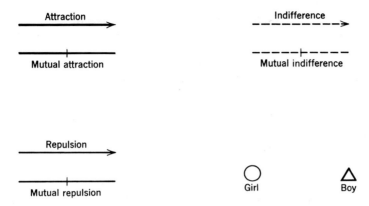

Figure 3-1. Key to sociograms (Moreno, 1953, p. 136).

3-1 contains a key to sociograms while Figure 3-2 includes several sketches which represent various situations in intragroup relations. While Moreno has sketched still other types of sociometric diagrams, such as comprehensive sketches of acts over a period of time, the sociogram have been the most useful in social research.

The sociometric method has been put to work in applied areas as well

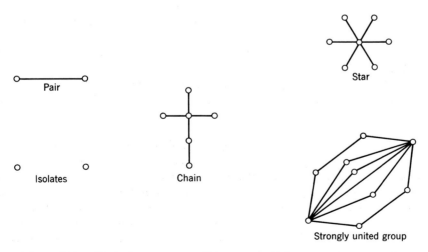

Figure 3-2. Typical structures within groups (Moreno, 1953, p. 137).

as in the development of basic social constructs. It has been used to study organizational effectiveness and morale in armed service units, to locate cliques in the classroom, to identify spontaneous leadership, and to determine interaction in many other practical settings. It has performed as a valuable tool in the detailing of concepts such as group integration, status, isolation, social distance, and informal social systems, among others. The technique, for all its simplicity, remains one of the most useful data collection and description systems.

CONTENT ANALYSIS

Much information worthy of study appears in static sources of information on human behavior or in more dynamic material such as appears in ongoing or recent communications. The method of *content analysis* is a scientific approach to the study of the "what" of communication of various kinds. Berelson (1954, p. 489) defines content analysis as "a research technique for the objective, systematic, and quantitative description of the manifest content of communication." The scientific description of the content is achieved through categorization of the material analyzed. The development of categories, then, is the crucial aspect of this systematic process.

Content analysis can be used to analyze material from many areas and to help answer interesting questions which cannot be answered easily through the use of other means. This method can approach questions like the following.

How do values in corporation communications differ from those in academic communications?

How are Negroes treated in short stories in the period from 1950 to 1955?

What is the "propaganda" content of certain communications?

Is there a difference between slogans used by the Russians and those used by the Red Chinese?

Categories in the content analysis technique are the crucial determinants of results. Berelson (1954, pp. 510–512) makes the distinction between "what is said" and "how it is said," that is, between substance and form. The "what" category includes subject matter, orientation or direction (pro or con), values, methods, traits, actor, source or authority, and origin and target. The "how" category includes form or type of communication, form of statement, devices (or "propaganda tricks"), and intensity. Once the categories are established, the problems of sampling and counting the verbal references remain.

PSYCHOMETRIC TECHNIQUES

Psychological tests have become one of the most used and useful measures of human characteristics. As such, they represent a very important method of gathering information about human behavior. Basically, tests are nothing more than samples of behavior obtained when individuals respond to a standard set of conditions. A comparison of the different modes and levels of response gives a picture of individual differences in addition to providing information about the single individual.

While schools are the setting for most of the information gathering by psychological testing, industry is also an extensive user of tests. There is, furthermore, no reason why tests cannot be used in many other settings as well; there is no inherent limitation to education and industry. The prediction of future performance in school, business, or other activity is probably the main reason for the use of tests in the initial selection procedures. We may be interested in identifying the intellectually gifted or those who are retarded, but the practical problems of picking a person to do a task, the diagnosis of academic difficulty, or the determination of training needs for a job most often take precedence.

Tests may be categorized in many ways. If the classification is based on the family of traits or characteristics measured by the test, the categories may be the following: aptitude, interest, personality, or psychomotor skills. On a time-reference basis, the tests in a particular area (scholastic measures, as an example) may be called ability, aptitude, or achievement tests.

Ability refers to a present state; aptitude refers to future performances and is, therefore, a predictive term. Achievement tests measure what has occurred, usually in uniform learning situations. The three concepts shade into each other, however, because a present state depends on the past and a present score can be used to predict future performance.

Measures may involve the use of language or they may be nonlanguage approaches. Tests may be so structured that they can be given to only one subject at a time, or they may be in a form that allows for administration to many at the same time. The measurement techniques may further be broken down as to whether a paper-and-pencil response is called for or whether a demonstration or other overt physical act is to be done. A single concept such as aptitude shows further variation by way of the particular aptitude areas that can be described. Mechanical, artistic, psychomotor, or scholastic aptitude measures are available in quantity. Scholastic aptitude measures may themselves be subdivided into levels of scholastic endeavor such as college or graduate work or into specific areas such as law, medicine, or engineering. Personality measures are often classified as to method of actual measurement;

personality inventories are paper-and-pencil questionnaires while projective techniques (the Rorschach or "Ink Blot" test, for example) require a response to an unstructured situation wherein the subject structures the stimulus according to the dynamics of his personality.

The responses from individuals on a test are scored according to some standard system which, in most instances, is an objective one. By itself, the obtained score does not possess much meaning unless it is related to the performances of others. Comparison with norms, the levels attained by a particular set of respondents, must be made before we can know where a certain score falls. The tests themselves must be carefully tested before use, and the test constructors or users must be concerned with the validity and reliability of the test. If the test measures what it is supposed to measure, it is valid; if the test gives consistent measurements, it is reliable.

Environmental and personal variables other than those being measured by the test can influence the result. The impact of motivation, cheating, malingering, or coaching on the test scores demonstrates the basic point that tests are merely samples of behavior and, as such, are subject to many influences extraneous to the technique. The widely known "I.Q." is not a magic number but a test score which can be derived in many ways. While well-established tests give remarkably consistent numerical results, variations can occur. Although they are not perfect in the task set out for them, psychometric techniques can and do provide valuable information which can seldom be obtained in any other way.

THE EXPERIMENTAL METHOD

This is the method which, ultimately, most behavioral scientists would like to follow in accumulating data in research. It has long been the keystone method in the disciplines included in the area, particularly in psychology. The attractiveness of the method to a behavioral scientist lies in the ability of the investigator to manipulate and control variables in which he is interested and to make precise measurements or, at least, systematic observation of the results of that manipulation. When we are able to do this, it is easier to disentangle cause and effect, probably the most basic relationship we might hope to uncover.

The classical single variable experiment keeps all variables under control and varies only one, called the *independent variable,* to determine what, if any, change takes place in the final factor, the *dependent variable.* This technique goes further and has two groups, the *experimental group* and the *control group.* The experimental group receives the treatment while the second group, the control group, does not. Any difference in the measured dependent variable is presumably the result of the action of the independent variable.

The method may be illustrated by the following example. Suppose we are interested in learning the effects of a particular drug on reaction time. The hypothesis may be that the drug in a minimal single dose inhibits reaction time or, more specifically, the pressing of a key to a light signal. The group of subjects would be divided at random into two equal groups, which are matched on every variable on which it is possible to match. One group is designated the experimental group and the other is the control group. The experimental group receives the drug dose (the independent variable) while the control group receives nothing (except a placebo or "sugar pill"). The reaction time of individuals in each group is measured (the dependent variable) and any significant difference in reaction time is therefore determined to be due to the drug (Figure 3-3). The control group is necessary primarily because the end result could conceivably have come about for some reason other than the variation in the independent variable.

The classic experimental method just described utilizes only the single variable change, but extension of this basic plan is possible to the point where several experimental variables may be present in the experiment or the action of the variable may be measured over time. For instance, two drugs may be introduced or other variables such as temperature, time, and size of dosage may be evaluated.

The prime attraction of the experimental method to researchers lies in its offering of a situation where the variables may be readily manipulated. It enables the scientist to advance further than might be possible were he limited to waiting while events occurred as he stood by. The precision with which the circumstances may be narrowed down and studied closely is a concomitant advantage making for greater acceptability of the results.

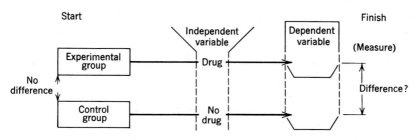

Figure 3-3. The classic single variable experiment.

There are, of course, disadvantages inherent in the method. Whereas there is an opportunity to reduce the number of variables to one or a few for more specific study, the difficulty arises of using the approach meaningfully in a complete context approaching that of real life. Reaction time, depth perception, and other skills are well studied in a laboratory setting. When we move to more complex activities, especially social situations involving many people, the experimental method is not as adaptable to many broad variables such as motivation, communication, or perception which are complex and interrelated in a social setting.

A further difficulty comes in attempting to generalize from the finding of the experiment to a more general population. Many of the experiments are conducted, for one reason or another, using animals for subjects. Many of the studies cannot use human beings because of the possibility of harm or suffering. In studies of deprivation, for example, it is possible to use rats to see whether food or water is the stronger drive. Animals also can be kept under control, bred where the genetic factors need to be well controlled and, generally, manipulated more easily than human subjects. The difficulty comes in the translation of the findings to the human area. While much of the physiological data is validly transferred, and some of the motivational findings may well be, other generalizations are to be made with caution (a few psychologists do not even care to make the transfer—they study animal behavior just for its own sake). Even when the subjects are human, a similar problem arises. Traditionally, the human subject has been the ubiquitous college sophomore. Why? Because he is readily available to researchers through his enrollment in beginning psychology or sociology courses. While college students are certainly human, it may well be that they differ in some significant ways from other classes of humans, particularly in mental ability, motivation, or attitudes, to name only a few areas.

Further criticisms of the experimental approach may include the point that the experiment is an artificial situation and that the behavior elicited is not representative of reality. This criticism may be valid for a poorly constructed experiment. Better designed ones can obviate much of the difficulty on this point, although it is probably true that people react differently when they know they are the object of study than when they are oblivious to scrutiny. With the two groups (experimental and control) present, this factor will presumably be the same for both, however. The knowledge of the actual purpose of the experiment is, moreover, withheld from the subjects until after the experiment is conducted.

With all its drawbacks, the experimental approach is by far the most rigorous weapon in the researcher's repertoire and, by virtue of this fact alone, it is the most desired of the approaches in the behavioral sciences. It will be the prime instrument in this area for a long time to come.

A REMINDER

The various methods of gathering data each have their own peculiar strong and weak points. Some situations call for study along lines approachable only through one method; other situations may require another method. Each approach may, furthermore, utilize various vehicles of data accumulation—the verbal report, a questionnaire, psychomotor responses, tests, interviews, or even records that have been made by others. However we approach the material and whichever way we assemble it, not much makes sense nor is it reportable until it can be organized. This is the subject of a later subdivision of this chapter.

Measurement

Measurement of behavior necessarily precedes arrangement of the data; treatment cannot take place until the data is gathered. Before any discussion of statistics, a few words must be said about measurement.

CONCEPTS

Measurement involves somewhat more than is ordinarily thought of when the term is used. Certainly we mean making quantitative determinations such as those of height and weight. The term extends to similar (but not the same) measures such as mental age or interest score. To go even further, we may consider categorization and placement within those categories as a measure. In a broad use of the term, dichotomies such as "yes" and "no" are measures and measurement is also what is accomplished with the concepts "more than" and "less than." While numerical statements are preferred (and even the dichotomies or categories can be converted into such), there is room under the concept of measurement for other than numerical results.

SCALES

If, on a particular variable, we can rank several individuals, we are establishing an *ordinal* scale whereby we know the order in which the individuals appear. For instance, test results might be reported as follows.

Individuals	Score	Rank
X	100	1
Y	50	2
Z	25	3

We can say that X is number 1, Y number 2, and Z number 3, and we have an ordinal scale. We *cannot* say anything more with certainty; we cannot say that X is twice as good as Y or four times as good as Z. In the same way, we cannot believe that a management trainee with a performance rating of 500 is twice as good as one with a rating of 250. The unwary may be deceived into thinking thus on the basis of our belief in the "magic of numbers." Certainly 100 apples are twice as many as 50 apples. To hold true in this fashion for all similar numerical statements, there must be a true zero point (as, for instance, no apples). This zero point is the requisite for a *ratio scale* where we not only start at a zero point but, in addition, know that the units of the scale are equal. Both these requisites are not possible to establish in most behavioral measures, especially in an area like intelligence, motivation, or achievement.

An *interval scale* lies somewhere in between. Each unit is equal to each other unit but, because of a lack of a zero anchor point, it cannot be said that any score is a percentage of another score. For instance, each degree on a thermometer means the same as any other degree but 20° F is *not* twice 10° F because 0° F is not really zero on the scale.

Organization of Data

With the mass of data accumulated as the result of even a simple experiment or survey, not much can be communicated until some sort of organization of the material takes place. With infinite or nearly infinite variation in behavior possible, without organization or categorization into more readily handled units the task of reporting results would be hopeless. We would have to report each bit of information and, when we did so, we would probably find it impossible to trace any relationships whatsoever. Mechanical and statistical procedures to make some order out of the lack of it must therefore be introduced at this juncture.

GRAPHIC DESCRIPTIVE METHODS

Data that have been collected can be cumbersome to handle and difficult to understand. A method that allows assembly of the information in meaningful form is to be desired. The simplest way of presenting material to a reader is undoubtedly the method of graphic representation whereby a visual pattern gives the global meaning of a complicated set of data at a single glance. If the ancient maxim attributed to the Chinese is correct, a picture here is worth a thousand words. Figure 3-4 provides some examples of simple graphic representation. The *pie chart* is effective in presenting a breakdown of sums. The total area of the pie represents 100 percent and each slice quickly shows the extent of the contribution to the whole by the various subdivisions; the area

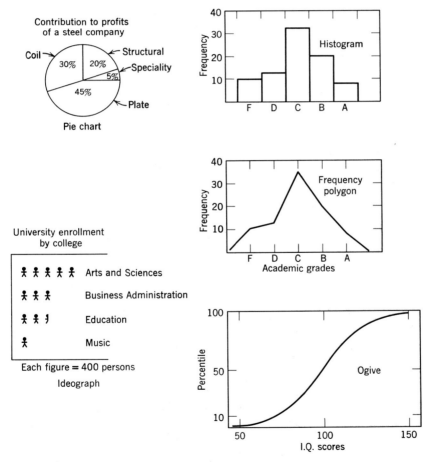

Figure 3-4.   Some methods of graphic representation of data.

of the slice shows the percentage in graphic form. The *ideograph* presents numbers of items in an array. In Figure 3-4 each school of a university contributes a particular number of "bodies," indicating the size of student enrollment in the school. The *histogram,* sometimes called a bar graph, shows the frequency of cases or number of items within a particular class; the *frequency polygon* does the same thing. The cumulative frequency curve, or *ogive,* shows number of cases or percentages and proportions between a zero figure and a total amount. The ogive in Figure 3-4, for instance, enables a viewer to determine how many persons fall within certain ranges of an I.Q. score and, of course, what percentage of individuals fall below or above a certain score (expressed in I.Q. units along the abcissa or horizontal axis).

There should be several words of caution interjected in this point. The unwary may easily be led astray under this dramatic yet simple presentation of data. Figure 3-5 presents an ideograph which purports to present the relative sizes of the armed forces of various countries. The difference is to be represented by the vertical measurement, yet the necessity to draw the bodies in true proportion emphasizes the areas involved. Even a long look at the relative magnitudes will impress the viewer with the apparent differences between the items.

Another source of confusion or error rests in the scaling, or lack of it, along either axis, the ordinate or abscissa. When a zero point is not indicated on the scale, the resulting figure is quite different in appearance from one drawn where the zero point is included (Figure 3-6). Stockholders of a corporation would undoubtedly react in different ways to the picture of growth of

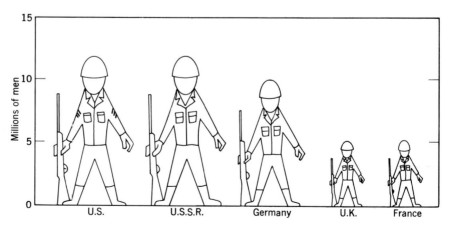

Figure 3-5.   An ideograph providing misleading comparisons of size.

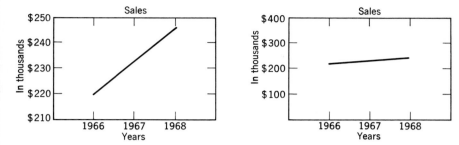

Figure 3-6. Presentation of the same information using two different scales along the vertical axis.

the corporation represented by the two line graphs shown in this figure.

A more subtle source of confusion arises from the use of an arithmetic scale when the changes taking place are more accurately reflected by a logarithmic scale. Figure 3-7 shows a straightforward representation of the population growth in the United States from 1790 to 1960. The population increased by the same number each year after 1850 but by a *decreasing ratio* or percentage each decade. Even more suspect are those graphic representations that go beyond the data available and purport to show a straight-line pattern of the present or try to predict the shape of things to come. Trend lines are sometimes drawn with present data to derive a simple pattern from a confusing array of data on a chart. Much variability in drawing this line is possible. Even more crystal ball gazing occurs when the "trend line" is continued by extrapolation. Investors in the stock market who buy or sell on the basis of such prediction are not the only ones affected by this type of guesswork.

DESCRIPTIVE STATISTICS

The average person associates the word statistics with mere counting of numbers of births, deaths, bathrooms, television sets, etc. Statistics goes beyond the simple totaling of specific events or aspects to the meaningful juncture of making some sense out of the myriad number of such instances. Statistical treatment enables us to summarize information to relate one set of facts to another, to determine the worth of data, and to translate the data we get to other sections, that is, to generalize. It is a tool without which behavioral science could not progress. Without statistics we would have little understanding

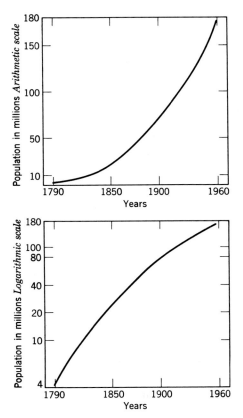

Figure 3-7. Population growth of the United States charted using arithmetic and logarithmic scales on the vertical axis.

of the data that have been accumulated through our use of the various methods of behavioral science.

With this framework, then, we find opportunities to attain some under-standing of behavior generally and the events surrounding it. To illustrate how meaning can be made out of material gathered, let us pursue the following example. First, suppose that in class you received a score of 350 on a test. Satisfied? You would, perhaps, wish to know "what does it mean?" before you answered. A better question at this point is "how have others done on this test?" Even with a true zero point (not present here), the score would have meaning only in relation to what others have done on the same test.

Is this better or is it worse than the performance of others; that is, what is the "average?"

Measures of Central Tendency

There is no single average as there are many ways of expressing the middle area of a spread of scores. What we ordinarily call the average is the *mean* or, more specifically, the *arithmetic mean,* since there are other types of means. The arithmetic mean is obtained by summing the values of the scores and dividing by the number of scores, an operation that can be expressed by the formula, $M = \Sigma X/N$. Another measure of "average" is the *median,* which is simply the *midpoint* of the distribution of scores. We count the ordered scores from the bottom to top (or vice versa) and stop with the score at the middle; that score is the median (a group of 25 scores, for instance, will have as its median the 13th score from the end). The third common measure of central tendency is the *mode,* the designation for the figure that occurs most frequently. In some reports it would be misleading or awkward to report the mean or median as, for example, we would hesitate to say that the average for families in a particular subdivision is 2.56 children and 1.75 bathrooms in their homes. The most often recurring figure (say, three children and two bathrooms) gives us a more appropriate picture. That, of course, is what each measure is supposed to do. The mean is more meaningful than the median in some situations, while in others the median may be. By way of illustration, let us consider the situation wherein a college senior is being recruited by the president of a small company who paints a glowing picture of the opportunities in that organization. "Come with us, boy," he says. "The average salary for our professional people is $15,400." Closer examination re-

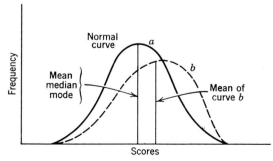

Figure 3-8.   Distributions of scores and measures of central tendency.

veals that the president makes $100,000 while nine other management people make $6000 apiece. The median or the mode is a more honest figure to us in this situation. Here lies the most important criterion of the use of measures. Our example (somewhat exaggerated, of course) shows the mean to be a measure that is influenced by extreme values, since each value has a weight in the determination of the average. The median is not so influenced since all we do is "count the heads" without ascribing any value to them. Each score is merely a point along a continuum. The mode is useful for reporting, especially with a large body of facts, a "typical" situation. All have their place in the statistical treatment of data. As a matter of fact, the more of them we report, the better picture the reader will get of our distribution. Figure 3-8 represents the discussion above in graphic form, including the interesting, but seldom seen, situation where all three measures—mean, median, and mode—coincide (curve *a*). Curve *b* shows the mean influenced by extreme high scores.

Measures of Dispersion

To return to the example with which we started this discussion, let us assume that your hypothetical test score of 350 occurs within a distribution where the mean and median both are 325. Compared to the "average," a score of 350 appears to be "above average." When we inspect the data more closely, however, we may find a distribution ranging from a score of 275 (curve *x* in Figure 3-9) or a spread of scores from 250 to 400 (curve *y* in Figure 3-9). These two distributions obviously do not mean the same thing. This illustration demonstrates the next body of information needed—the spread of the scores or, usually, the dispersion around the mean. The simplest measure

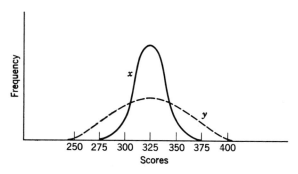

Figure 3-9.   Two hypothetical distributions of scores.

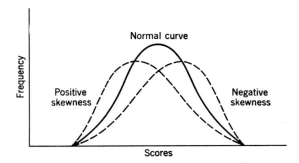

Figure 3-10. Normal and skewed distributions of scores.

of dispersion is the range, which is merely the difference between the highest and lowest scores. The range is not, however, a very good indicator of the shape of the curve and, in addition, is affected greatly by the inclusion of one or two extreme scores. A better measure of dispersion is one where a deviation score communicates not only something about the spread but also describes the curve formed by the distribution. The *average deviation* (*AD*) is the mean of the deviations of the scores from the mean (the formula for this measure is $AD = \Sigma d / N$). The *standard deviation* is a measure that is similar but more useful in further mathematical usage. For this measure of dispersion, the deviations from the mean must be squared, then summed, the mean taken, and the square root derived. The formula for the standard deviation is $\sigma = \sqrt{\Sigma d^2 / N}$ where σ (sigma), the lowercase Greek letter, stands for standard deviation (the upper case sigma, Σ, means, as above, summation). One sigma (σ) above and below the mean contains two-thirds of the scores in the distribution. A sigma representing a few numerical points, as in curve X in Figure 3-9, represents more clustering of scores than does curve Y in Figure 3-9, which has a sigma of large dimension. Obviously, a score of 350 means a relatively higher score in the distribution shown by curve X, since it represents a greater distance from the mean.

The *normal curve of distribution* is a curve that represents an ideal or "perfect" distribution for a variable, one toward which many curves describing human characteristics presumably tend. In reality, we often get curves short of this perfect symmetrical arrangement; curves often build up toward one side or the other. If scores pile up on the high side, this is known as negative *skewness* while the reverse tendency is seen in a *positively skewed curve* (Figure 3-10).

PROBABILITY

The concept of probability is an important one because it is fundamental to many of the uses of statistics and decision making. It is the basis for determining whether differences between groups are significant or not, and it helps one to guess at the validity of a sample by estimating the probability of the sample figure being a true figure. It is the basis for decision making in an actuarial area, such as insurance, where we know the number of persons likely to be alive at each birthday out of a total number. In other decision-making situations, the range between certainty and uncertainty of outcome contains the area of risky choices based on some awareness of the "laws of chance."

Probability deals with the occurrence of an event, and it may be defined as the expected proportion of times that event will happen with the expected proportion based on all the relevant information we can muster. The concept is best introduced by discussing the well-known tossing of a coin. When a coin is tossed, it is as likely that "heads" will appear as "tails" or that either side of the coin will appear one-half the time. If expressed in proportions, the relationship would look like this:

$$.5 \text{ (tosses)} = \text{heads}$$
$$.5 \text{ (tosses)} = \text{tails}$$

and the two proportions must add up to 1.00:

$$.5 \text{ tosses} + .5 \text{ tosses} = 1.00$$
$$\text{(heads)} \qquad \text{(tails)}$$
$$.5 \text{ heads} + .5 \text{ nonheads} = 1.00$$

The usual notation for the probability of the occurrence of an event is p and the nonoccurrence of the event is q; therefore: $p + q = 1.00$. The proportions cannot, of course, be less than zero or more than 1.00. If it is zero we are certain the event will not happen; if the probability is 1.00 we are certain that the event will occur every time.

The probability of the occurrence of an event may change as additional relevant information is obtained. In the coin-tossing problem above, the probabilities will remain the same unless some bias is present. The probability of an event such as survival of an individual until a particular age is obtained from a gathering of vital statistics representing the actual experience over a period of time. The overall probability of reaching a particular age can and does change with the change in actual numbers of survivors reported each year.

Heads and tails cannot appear at the same time—only one or the other can be present. This emphasizes the mutual exclusiveness of events in probability. The events are also said to be independent of each other. If the coin is unbiased the probability that heads will appear the fifth time is only $\frac{1}{2}$ even though heads may have appeared for four straight times before. Another aspect to probability is that as the number of trials increases, the actual results approach the theoretically expected frequencies (that is, "heads" has a probability of .50). This "law" of large numbers is the "law of averages" of which we spoke. It refers not to the probability of the occurrence of a particular event but to the overall distribution of examples of those events. For instance, it would be unwise to view the life insurance mortality tables as a prediction of a certain individual's reaching the age of 70. Instead, we would base a probability of this occurrence on the overall experienced mortality rate over the recent years.

RELATIONSHIPS

The knowledge of the relationship between variables is often of crucial importance to the behavioral scientist. While the ultimate use of the knowledge may be to predict on the basis of a relationship, the mere identification of a correspondence, if any exists, may provide valuable information.

Correlation

If height and weight increase with one another in a group of individuals, this might be of interest, but in practice an even more interesting relationship might be one where, in a group of individuals, scores on a particular test increase in a direct relationship with an index of performance obtained later. This is the typical situation where a selection device, a test, is used in industry and compared with a measure of performance, a criterion, so that a relationship, if any exists, may be used in the future to select others. An academic situation will be no different—the process of selection will unfold in exactly the same way; a test of scholastic aptitude will predict academic performance if the two variables "relate together" or are *correlated*. A graphic description of the initial placement according to scores and the basis for determining the correlation is in Figure 3-11. Each person is represented by a dot which indicates the coordinates of his placement on each measure, test and criterion. A high score on both measures is represented by point *A,* a set of low scores appears at point *B,* and the average is near point *C.* At this juncture a very neat and simple rectilinear relationship exists in a perfect positive relationship between test and criterion. But since things are seldom this perfect in real life, we find as we proceed that some scores deviate from the perfect line. Point *D* represents an individual who scored low on the test yet did well "on the

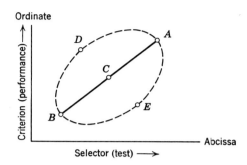

Figure 3-11.   A scatter of scores on two variables.

job" or criterion variable. The person represented by point E did well on the test and not so well in performance on the criterion. We expect a scattering of scores around the hypothetical straight line; but the closer the scores come to that line, the higher the relationship between the variables or the higher the correlation. The line represents a perfect positive correlation which is the coefficient of correlation represented by the small letter r and equaling $+1.00$ (usually the plus sign is understood and omitted). A line representing a perfect negative relationship, or an r of -1.00, should be drawn easily enough by the reader when he realizes that a negative relationship of this sort indicates a high score on one variable but a low one on the other. The widest possible dispersion of scores occurs when a circle encloses all scores; this phenomenon indicates an r of .00, or no relationship. The range of the coefficient of correlation, is, therefore, from -1.00 through .00 to $+1.00$. Moreover, an increase in the coefficient either way from zero is indicated graphically in the scatter of scores by a flattening of the circle to an ellipse (which gradually flattens to a straight line in the perfect relationship). The coefficient of correlation tells two things—the degree and the direction of a relationship between two variables. The plus or minus sign indicates the presence of a positive or negative relationship while the range from zero to 1.00 indicates the degree of the relationship. This latter figure may be difficult to interpret, however, without some experience. A correlation not far removed from zero is essentially a zero correlation (tests to measure if it is significantly large are available) and an r above .60 is very seldom seen. Measures are generally used in practice if correlations exist above .30 and if the number of the group from which it was derived is large.

The correlation coefficient, r, is more properly called the Pearson product moment correlation coefficient. There are many other ways of denoting a relationship between two variables, one of which will be described immediately below. The r is, perhaps, the most precise method and one which has been most often used. The r is obtained by using the formula $r = \Sigma xy / N\sigma_x\sigma_y$ where x and y are the deviations of scores from the means of the two variables and N is the number of cases.

Another method of calculation from ranks on the two measures is an approximation of the r. The rank difference correlation is known as *rho* and may be obtained through use of the formula $\rho = 1 - 6\Sigma d^2 / N(N^2 - 1)$ where d is the difference between ranks and N is number of cases. This is much easier to use, and a calculation of relationship between two variables may be accomplished in a fraction of the time usually taken to derive r.

Applications and Cautions

The correlation coefficient not only indicates the degree of correspondence between two sets of measurements but it can also be a means of predicting one from the other. As an illustration, we may consider the correlation between a selection test and performance. The important statistics are as follows.

	Selection Test T	Job Performance Measure P
Mean	50	300
Standard deviation	10	50

$r = .70$ between test and job performance

The two are, of course, positively related to a great extent. Without test T the best estimate of performance would be 300, the mean, and any error would be 50 points or less 68 percent of the time (the standard deviation). The best prediction of performance P through use of the test T could be made by using a prediction formula:

$P =$ correlation $\dfrac{\text{performance standard deviation}}{\text{test standard deviation}}$ (test score - test mean) $+$ mean on performance

Therefore, if the test score of the applicant is 60

$$P = .70 \frac{50}{10} (60 - 50) + 300$$

The predicted performance score is 335 while the error will be 35 or less 68 percent of the time. In this the error has been cut to 50 percent.

The practical applications of an aid to selection along these lines should be of interest to workers in many different areas—academic as well as business.

Lest this opportunity to decrease the error in predictions encourage one to make too optimistic statements of the value of prediction on this basis alone, it must be quickly pointed out that this is a valid approach over a period of time with a group. There is still not enough elimination of error to make prediction on an individual basis very accurate. With a number of opportunities, however, the odds will favor the statistician.

A more serious misappplication of information may come as the result of an assumption that a cause and effect relationship exists between the two variables. The number of cases of lung cancer has increased in the past five years; there are also more television sets now than there were five years ago. The positive correlation between the two factors does not seriously entice us into believing that one is the cause of the other. An even more subtle source of error can be in a relationship between each of the two variables and a third. The correlation of both with the third variable will make the correlation between the original two a higher one than would exist ordinarily, that is, it would be spuriously high. This might provide a basis for faulty decision making would we rely only on the correlation obtained.

Multiple Correlation

There are some situations where, when more than two variables are involved, it is valuable to know the relationships between those variables. Usually it is of interest to determine the correlation between a group or set of factors and one other variable. The correlation coefficient then represents the degree of relationship between the set and the single variable. The multiple correlation coefficient is labeled R, and the numerical index looks the same as an ordinary r with a range from -1.00 to $+1.00$. It should be noted here that not only is each of the variables related to each other variable, the multiple coefficient is the result of such relationships. A typical situation arises where a set of test scores obtained from a "battery" of tests may be used to predict performance on a job or in school work (the criterion). Each test will correlate to some extent with each other test and with the criterion. The correlation with the criterion will be expressed as the multiple coefficient, R. Table 3-2 illustrates a matrix of intercorrelations among the variables from which an R is obtained. This may lead to a regression equation whereby it is possible to make the best available prediction of performance on the criterion by substituting an individual's scores on each variable into the proper sections of the regression equation.

Table 3-2. Intercorrelation Matrix, Multiple Correlation and Regression Equations in a Comparison of College Quality Point Average and Four Selector Variables

	Intercorrelation Matrix				
	College QPA	Verbal Score	Math Score	High School Rank	English Achievement
QPA	1.00	.27	.25	.45	.16
Verbal	.27	1.00	.45	.23	.65
Math	.25	.45	1.00	.21	.35
High school rank	.45	.23	.21	1.00	.24
English achieve- ment	.16	.65	.35	.24	1.00

Multiple correlation between QPA (criterion) and four selector variables:
$$R = .50$$

Regression equation for prediction:
$$QPA = .14V + .08M + .37R - .06EA - 6.38$$

DETERMINATION OF DIFFERENCES

Frequently, the basic question in a behavioral research project will be whether there is a difference between two groups being compared. The comparison may be of an experimental and control group on a variable or it may be concerned with a difference in a particular score of two groups, say, men and women. The behavioral researcher, in trying to answer the question of possible differences between groups, begins with the *null hypothesis.* The null hypothesis is merely a supposition that no difference really exists between the groups; if a difference does occur, the null hypothesis is rejected. The difference, however, may be small and/or due entirely to chance factors rather than to real differences between the groups. The tests of significance of difference are based, therefore, on the concepts of probability and distribution of data. If the obtained difference is larger than what might be expected on a basis of random distribution of measures around a mean, the null hypothesis may be rejected. There are, however, many degrees of uncertainty to consider. Expressed in percentages, we may be secure in feeling that 95 or 99 percent of the time a true difference exists. This is the *level of confidence* and is usually stated as the 5 or 1 percent level of confidence, respectively.

The Critical Ratio

This index compares the difference between the means of the two groups with the standard deviation of that difference:

$$CR = \frac{D}{\sigma D}$$

A critical ratio higher than 3 gives a high probability of a real difference between the means, since the probability is slight that a chance score would be found more than three sigmas above or below the mean. The null hypothesis stating no difference between the means of the groups may therefore be rejected. If the 5 percent level of confidence were chosen, a CR of 2 or higher would permit a rejection of the null hypothesis. The CR is based on the assumption that the data is distributed normally. A similar test, the t test, is used for nonnormal distributions. In a business setting we might be interested in whether there is a difference in performance scores between a group of managers who participated in a training program and another group who did not. Mean scores were as follows.

> Managers with training   125
> Managers without training   121
> Difference between means = 4
> Standard deviation of differences = 3

On the basis of this comparison, it is evident that the critical ratio of 1.33 is well below either the 5 or 1 percent level of confidence. We would have to conclude that the difference between the means is not a significant one.

Chi Square

Where there are many different outcomes possible and it is important to determine whether differences arise by chance, the Chi Square (χ^2) test may be used. The technique is based on the determination of whether the obtained figures deviate from results expected on the basis of an a priori or expected distribution. For instance, in 100 tosses of a coin we might expect 50 heads and 50 tails, but we get 35 heads and 65 tails instead. Is there something at work here that should put us on our guard? The chi-square tests may give us a lead:

$$\chi^2 = \frac{(O - E)^2}{E}$$

(O is the observed figure; E is the expected one.) For this situation,

$$\chi^2 = \frac{(35 - 50)^2}{50} + \frac{(65 - 50)^2}{50} = 9$$

This is a figure which, when appropriately entered into a chi-square table, shows that the difference is significant at the 1 percent level; this means that a deviation of this size would occur by chance only one out of one hundred times. This is an opportunity to place a reasonable amount of confidence in the statement that something other than chance is at work.

In another setting a tie salesman might wish to determine whether any tie style is selected significantly more often than any other. On the first day of a sale, he observes that 180 ties are sold. On the basis of chance, the total could be broken down into 60 ties of each pattern, when, in fact, 75 stripes, 50 foulards, and 55 plain designs were sold. Is this a significant finding? Our χ^2 formula will again provide some basis for a decision.

$$\chi^2 = \frac{(75 - 60)^2}{60} + \frac{(50 - 60)^2}{60} + \frac{(55 - 60)^2}{60} = 5.83$$

This result, when compared with a χ^2 table (with two degrees of freedom), indicates that we can be more than 90 but less than 95 percent confident that the differences did not arise by chance and the results represent real differences in buying patterns. Most experimenters prefer a higher level of probability—at least the 1 percent level, or 99 percent confident—but our tie salesman may be willing to settle for less. Remember that statistical tests do not relieve us of the necessity for making decisions, they provide only the bases.

The Sign Test

A good measure of difference in many situations which are met in business applications is the Sign Test because no assumptions such as normality of the distribution or independence of scores have to be made. Suppose we are working with a group of people and, in a fairly typical "before and after" situation, we are interested in whether our advertising campaign has changed their attitudes toward "Crunchies," a well-known breakfast cereal. We can array the data as in Table 3-3.

The probability of obtaining the two minus signs in a random sample of 6 plus and minus signs is fairly large and if we use the .01 level of significance, means that the probability of a real difference is not very great.

Another application of the test may be where we are interested in finding out whether a management development program improves the functioning of middle management people or whether a supervisor training program cuts

Table 3-3.   Data for a Sign Test from a Hypothetical Survey on Attitudes toward "Crunchies," a Breakfast Cereal

Person	Before	After	Sign	
1	For	Against	−	The sign marks the
2	For	For		change from the before
3	Against	For	+	condition to the after
4	For	Against	−	condition
5	Against	For	+	
6	Against	For	+	
7	For	For		
8	Against	For	+	

down on the number of grievances filed. In both cases the "before and after" comparison may be handled as in the illustration above.

Analysis of Variance

This has often been called one of the most refined and powerful tools in behavioral research (Senders, 1958). It is a method for testing the null hypothesis that several samples were drawn at random from the same population. The index of difference obtained through the analysis of variance is the F ratio, the ratio of two estimates of variances being compared (the variance is the square of the sigma or standard deviation):

$$F = \frac{V_1}{V_2}$$

The analysis of variance technique is not only similar to the t test or the critical ratio, it is really a more general test of significance of which t or CR are special cases (McNemar, 1955, p. 261). The same kinds of business or educational research problems can be handled with the F test as with CR or t. We may wish to know whether two kinds of training programs are significantly different, but the analysis of variance can be extended to compare groups under several treatments. We might be interested in productivity under different incentive conditions. Workers might be divided up and each group paid differently—straight salary, straight piecework, or salary plus incentive, for example. The resulting F ratio would allow a conclusion as to whether the differences between treatments are significant or not.

Data Subdivision

This simple means of analysis of information calls for a progressive subdivision of data according to the variables of interest to the researcher. Table 3-4 illustrates how the subdividing of the collected data is made according to categories based on the variables deemed important. From this splitting the researcher may trace relationships and differences between groupings and in this way note the significance of each variable. In the simple hypothetical situation made up for illustration in Table 3-4, it is possible to compare attitudes along the variables of sex and residence. Political, economic, and other social behavior is often under scrutiny by the use of this tabular approach.

Table 3-4. Data from a Hypothetical Survey of Attitudes toward a "Fluffo" Soap Commercial (in Percentages)

	Men			Women			Total	
	Rural	Urban	All Men	Rural	Urban	All Women	Rural	Urban
Positive	10	15	12	20	30	25	15	22
Neutral	20	70	50	30	40	35	15	55
Negative	70	15	38	50	30	40	60	23
Total	100	100	100	100	100	100	100	100

Models

A further way of organizing the material obtained through empirical data gathering is to order it in a fashion that provides meaning through graphic or mathematical translation. We can abstract from reality and place these elements in a model that, hopefully, indicates important aspects of the situation and relationships between them.

GRAPHIC MODELS

The representation of reality through graphic means is an old technique, as we have already mentioned. Various aspects of human functioning may be described graphically; these may represent certain phases of individual and group dynamics, or they may represent bases for future activity such as decision making.

A Model of Motivation

March and Simon (1958, p. 49) sketch a general model of motivated behavior which includes the notion of adaptation (Figure 3-12). The model illustrates the following statements of the motivational bases of behavior.

The lower the satisfaction of the organism, the more it will search for alternative programs. With greater search there is a higher expected value of reward. The higher this expected value of the reward, the greater the satisfaction and the higher the level of aspiration. With higher level of aspiration, satisfaction is lower.

Decision Diagram

An approach toward decision making in an applied setting is illustrated by Haynes and Massie (1961, p. 376) in their graphic description of the alternatives faced in opening branch department stores and the probable consequences thereof. The diagramming is often called a *tree diagram,* with the branches representing the alternatives with the degrees of uncertainty involved in each path from the original decision to each of the consequences (Figure 3-13). As with other models, this graphic approach aids in systematizing the decision making of individuals by requiring the "spelling out" of the important factors to be considered.

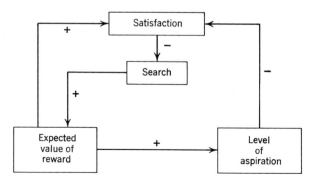

Figure 3-12.   A graphic model of motivation (adapted from March and Simon, 1958).

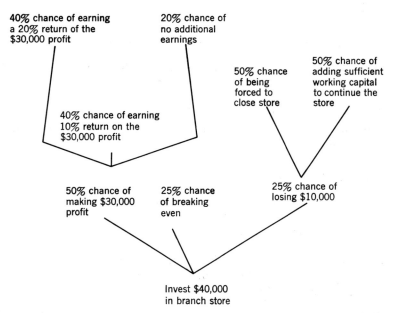

40% chance of earning a 20% return of the $30,000 profit

20% chance of no additional earnings

50% chance of being forced to close store

50% chance of adding sufficient working capital to continue the store

40% chance of earning 10% return on the $30,000 profit

50% chance of making $30,000 profit

25% chance of breaking even

25% chance of losing $10,000

Invest $40,000 in branch store

Figure 3-13. A tree diagram outlining alternatives in a business decision (Haynes and Massie, 1961, p. 376).

An Organizational Model

A simplified graphic model of some aspects of organizational functioning has been sketched by Gouldner (1954) to show the relationships between the factors (Figure 3-14). In it Gouldner postulates that low motivation and performance bring on closer supervision which, in turn, increases tensions. Rules that emerge have a tendency to mitigate tensions but also to reinforce the low performance and the lowered motivational level. March and Simon (1958) have developed Gouldner's concepts further by describing in graphic form the relationship between the emergence of rules as a demand for control and the maintenance of structure in an organization. Both intended and unintended results are noted in the model.

MATHEMATICAL MODELS

Closer to the verbal models of a natural language are those employing mathematical notation as an expression of structure and function in human

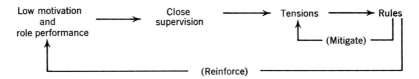

Figure 3-14.   A model of organizational behavior (Gouldner, 1954, p. 178).

behavior. These, too, may describe individual dynamics and interaction in a group, or they can describe the parameters of a problem in preparation for decision making.

A Psychosocial Model

Simon (1957, p. 99) has reduced to mathematical terms a social system outlined earlier verbally by Homans (1950). In utilizing variables that are functions of time, Simon combines the following:

$I(t)$ the intensity of interaction among the members
$F(t)$ the level of friendliness among the members
$A(t)$ the amount of activity carried on by members within the group

The designation (t) refers to time, since the model is concerned with interaction over time. The variables can then be combined into a relationship, $I(t) = a_1 F(t) + a_2 A(t)$, which is the mathematical expression of what Homans expressed verbally, namely, that the intensity of interaction increases with the level of friendliness and the amount of activity in the group. Still other equations by Simon have developed related concepts along more complex lines. The resulting mathematical statements represent the circumstances in the group with much more precision than may be possible with purely verbal descriptions. This is the primary value of the use of mathematical models.

An Industrial Model

Linear programming is a method of presenting variables quantitatively for decision making. It involves the following considerations: (1) seeking an objective, usually the attainment of an optimum such as maximizing or minimizing a position by (2) selecting from among alternatives within (3) certain constraints or limits.

An additional technical requirement is that the relationships between variables are linear. Using mathematical descriptions of linear relationships, a decision maker may be active in many practical situations. A production scheduling problem involving the optimum use of various pieces of equipment and the arrangement of optimum conbinations of products to be produced, the "product mix," is an extensive use of the method. The concept of mix may be extended to production of the product itself, as in "blending" in the oil industry to produce different types of gasoline. Finally, decisions as to transportation of supplies or finished products from suppliers to plants to markets also can be made more meaningfully through the models of linear programming.

A simple illustration of the use of linear programming in scheduling production of products is given in the following problem. Assume that a manufacturer of a line of stereo sound systems produces one such system. There are two models in the line, one standard and the other deluxe, with the following time schedule for assembly and finishing.

Model	Assembly Time	Finishing Time
Standard (s)	10 min.	9 min.
Deluxe (d)	10 min.	15 min.
Total	300 min/day	360 min/day

In actual production the relationship between products would be:

$$s \geq 0$$

$$d \geq 0$$

$$10s + 10d \leq 300 \text{ (assembly)}$$

$$9s + 15d \leq 360 \text{ (finishing)}$$

If the profit from the products is five dollars for the standard model and seven dollars for the deluxe, then total profit, P, would be:

$$P = \$5.00s + \$7.00d$$

A graphical representation of the limits appears in Figure 3-15 where the lines mark off the production constraints. The shaded area represents the polygon within which the company must work in making a decision. A numerical solution to the problem exists though it is cumbersome. Fortunately, we already know (from other evidence) that the optimum solution lies at one of the corners of the polygon *ABCD*. We can therefore substitute the corner figures into the profit formula:

A (nothing) $\$5 (0) + \$7 (0) = \$0$
B (all deluxe) $\$5 (0) + \$7 (24) = \$168$
C (intercept) $\$5 (15) + \$7 (15) = \$180$
D (all standard) $\$5 (30) + \$7 (0) = \$150$

This solution can then aid in the decisions involved in production scheduling.

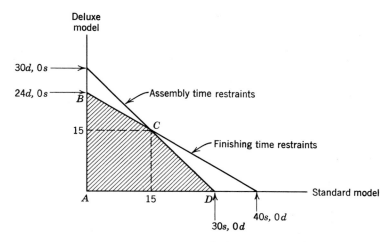

Figure 3-15. Graphic representation of factors in a linear programming problem.

Other practical problems are more complex, of course; seldom are only two variables involved. With other aspects of concern, the problems and data get more complex and involve much more computation or processing. The basic approach sketched above remains the same, however.

COMPUTER SIMULATION MODELS

The analogy of electronic computer processes to the operations of human thinking has been noted from the very beginning of experimentation with these data devices. The computer has even been called a "giant brain." This is a misnomer because the computer, despite its size, is not greater in functioning than the human brain, nor is it like the brain in form. It can, however, be used to duplicate or simulate the processes of thought and thereby provide many important guidelines to the study of decision making.

Simulation of thinking proceeds by developing programs of instructions to the computer; the programs are based on precise delineations of steps which are presumably those a human follows in making a decision. An added value of this procedure comes from performing the activity, since if one states steps in a process such as this, one thereby learns quite a bit about that process. Gelernter and Rochester (1958), for instance, have developed a program for the solution of geometry problems where the solutions occur on the basis of static stored basic information. No change occurs in the stored material except that it can be combined in different additive ways. On the other hand, simulation of complex concepts involves changes in the material (a duplication of learning in the human) as Hovland (1963) has discovered in attempts to simulate the acquisition of complex concepts through experience. Various approaches also may be added to a basic process; strategies and shortcuts which resemble human "hunches" and moves are possible in a computer program. Checker-playing machines have been surpassed by chess-playing machines with moves considered two or three steps ahead.

Simulation of social behavior is also possible even though it is more complicated. The patterning of interaction calls for too many combinations if all are considered, but the broad descriptive outlines may be sketched in a computer program. Roles of individuals and their patterns of proceding can be sharpened in a quantitative analysis aided by the high-speed computer.

Electronic Computer Applications

There is hardly any doubt that recent rapid advances in technology have provided expanding opportunities for the researcher or worker in all professional fields. Each of the areas of data collection and treatment mentioned in this chapter are affected by these technical facilities which were virtually unavailable a decade ago. Efficiency and scope of research or day-to-day work have been improved or enlarged by the electronic digital computing devices because they provide the following advantages.

1. Great speed of operation (in milliseconds).
2. Storage of data ("memory").
3. Rapid access to the stored material.

The computer does not do anything that has not been done before; it just does it faster and cheaper. The computer also will not, at this time anyway, turn out anything that has not been put into a form that it can accept and process.

COMPUTER SYSTEMS

Computer systems may be divided into four functional units: input, storage, central processing, and output devices.

Input

. Data are fed into the system by means of input devices. Before this can be done, however, the data must be converted into a set of symbols which can be assimilated by the computer system. Moreover, the symbols must be recorded on media compatible with the requirements of the system. Information may be placed on the following media.

(a)   Punched cards.
(b)   Paper tape (may be punched as cards).
(c)   Magnetic tape.
(d)   Magnetic ink characters (bank checks now carry these).

The symbols carried on the above devices must be in a form that can be represented within the machine. The form in which computers function is called the binary mode, an arrangement that indicates only two possible states. A switch is either on or off, a light is on or off—these are binary modes. A binary system of notation uses only two symbols, zero (0) and one (1). The binary digits are commonly referred to as *bits* (a contraction of binary digits) and, though simple, they can symbolize more complex numeric and alphabetic characters. Numerals, for instance, may be represented as in Table 3-5.

In some computers the binary notation used is directly related to the binary system; in other computers the relationship is more remote even though based on the above system. The data are placed on the mediacards, on tape, or in magnetic ink, according to the binary system. Input devices read or "sense" the data before they are sent to storage.

Input of information proceeds after translation into a code through programming. The writing of a program in actual machine code is seldom warranted. Instead, a program may be written in a language closer to the

Table 3-5.   Representation of Numerals in the Binary System

Our Numerals	(16)	Place Value (As Indication) (8)	(4)	(2)	(1)	
1	0	0	0	0	1	1—00001
2	0	0	0	1	0	2—00010
3	0	0	0	1	1	3—00011 (2 + 1)
4	0	0	1	0	0	

programmer's own familiar language, which is then converted into machine language by the processor in the computer system. Various approaches are possible involving compromises between ease of writing or facility of input into the system. Program languages such as FORTRAN and COBOL are available for use in wide areas of operation.

Storage

Information must be placed in storage before it can be passed on to central processing. This information can be either a set of instructions, data, or reference data such as tables or constants. The actual "hardware" for storage, the storage devices, may be magnetic core assemblies, magnetic drums, or magnetic disks. Storage has often been compared to a set of numbered mailboxes in a post office wall. Each box is a location; to use it, the address must be known. The information at that address can be used over and over but if replaced by new information, that new data then occupies the address.

Central Processing

The supervision and control of the entire computer system is the function of the central processing unit (CPU); it performs the arithmetic and logical operations on the data input. In addition to doing addition, subtraction, multiplication, and division, the CPU also performs under instructions like "stop on error," "branch if equal," "add if plus," and many other logical operations.

Output

Information emanating from the computer system may be in the form of punched cards with the punches designating the information in the same way it is represented in the input stage. More direct is a printing of the information, the printout," which can be done by either a special typewriter or by a high-speed printer. The speed of the printout can vary from 10 to 2000 characters per second.

USES OF COMPUTERS

Computers perform in various areas, some mundane or routine and some rather complex. Some of the uses are of greater interest to the researcher in the behavioral sciences even though each application can be and is used for basic and applied research in the behavioral and social areas.

Calculations and Record Keeping

Straightforward calculations of number of hours worked, number of items in an inventory, or elements of the accounts of customers are of direct and important interest to business organizations. Thousands of calculations are necessary to keep abreast of the information input in making up a payroll, keeping track of tax payment, analysis of turnover of items in stock, and many more. Similar input of information is required by the researcher as data is collected and assembled.

The arrangement of data in the meaningful ways described earlier in this chapter is advanced by computer technology. With a minimum of effort and time, means and standard deviations, correlations, and other statistical operations provide the researcher with a clearer idea of the meaning of the study.

Comparisons in Recurring Operations

Once a particular program has been arranged, the computer will be able to provide an output which quickly responds to variations in the input. In linear programming, for example, the optimum solution may be obtained by finding the best combination of variables through thousands of simple repetitive calculations. Prediction of election results from little data on the basis of comparisons with the expected is another example of this use of the computer.

Information Retrieval

Increasingly rapid expansion of information in all areas of activity has severely burdened the workers in most fields. It is becoming more and more difficult to keep up with material in one's own field, much less worthwhile material in related fields. Ordinary methods of retrieval are no longer adequate for the task at hand, and an increasing amount of information is being transferred to computer storage for swift recall on demand. Access to this bank of information may be by the use of "key words" where the researcher determines the identifying words or phrases that will call forth from computer storage either an abstract or a complete text which contains that particular key set of words. While complete information centers are no further than the planning stage, some areas of specialization have retrieval capabilities. The "Pittsburgh program" (Aspen Systems Corporation, 1969) has been able to place some statutory and case material on tape and can conduct searches in response to requests. In the medical area there are possibilities for the use of electronic computer systems in medical diagnosis. After a physician puts into the computer a set of observed symptoms, these are compared with an extensive variety of characteristics of disorders and the result of such comparisons are printed out. The completed diagnosis is not made, of course, but the physician should be aided in his decision by virtue of the additional information or rearrangement and comparison of existing information. Access to data banks is possible also in business where the information gained can be used to provide a better basis for decisions of all types.

Control

Guidance and control systems have existed since man began (man is the oldest servomechanism around), but now the increasing efficiency resulting from speedy calculation makes certain guidance and control systems available where they have not been possible before. Guidance of missiles, space ships, airplanes, or submarines is fostered through the rapid processing of information fed back to the system. In industry, manufacturing processes are increasingly coming under the control of computer programs. Oil refining, chemical processing, and now steel making are being regulated by electronic control methods. Production of machinery is also directed by automated devices controlled by programmed instructions.

Simulation

One of the more complex means of computer use is the duplication of mathematical or symbolic models of a system to permit manipulation of it for continuing study. Simulation of behavior of individuals or groups and the activity of business or other organizations may be conducted. Time is compressed so that greater variation in activity is possible. Future performance may be predicted, based on the end result of the many manipulations of the model. Often, simulation has an additional purpose—that of educating prospective students of business when management of an enterprise can be duplicated in many respects by a business game.

Programmed Learning

Autoinstructional devices permit the student to proceed at his own pace and, ideally, along a path determined by his response. Simple programmed texts or related techniques do not do this to any great extent. A computer program that would present the information step by step and then branch to appropriate next steps for each student is now technically feasible. In an advanced system not only does the student respond to a visual display on his own keyboard but the response is possible in auditory and visual means to reinforce the correct response even more.

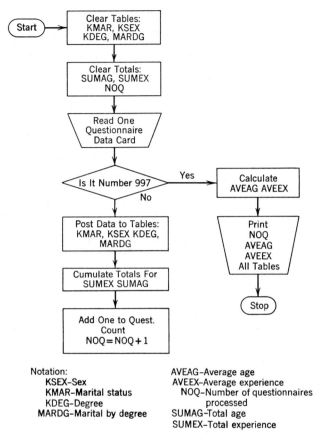

Figure 3-16. Flow chart for operations treating data in questionnaire from professors of business administration (IBM, 1964).

AN ILLUSTRATIVE PROGRAM

A rudimentary illustration of steps in the development and use of a program that processes behavioral information is presented in Figure 3-16 and Table 3-6. They describe the treatment of data received on the basis of a simple questionnaire eliciting information on sex, age, marital status, years of teaching experience, and degree from a hypothetical group of professors of business administration. It can readily be seen how data gathering and analysis, the core of the job of the behavioral scientist, has been greatly aided by the computer, and how the lot of a researcher is a somewhat happier one.

Table 3-6. Questionnaire for Survey of Professors of Business Administration and Eventual Printout of Information (Adapted from IBM, 1964)

QUESTIONNAIRE
SEMINAR FOR PROFESSORS OF BUSINESS ADMINISTRATION

Directions: Please record your answers to the following questions in the boxes to the right of the question. Enter leading zeros; that is, if there are two boxes and your answer is say, 5, please enter 05.

Answers to this questionnaire will remain anonymous.

1. Sex: 1 = male; 2 = female
2. Age: record to the *last* birthday
3. Marital status: 1 = single; 2 = married; 3 = other
4. Number years teaching experience
5. Highest degree: 1 = bachelor's; 2 = master's;
                                       3 = doctor's

COMPUTER OUTPUT

QUESTIONNAIRE ANALYSIS

NUMBER QUEST.	AVERAGE AGE	AVERAGE EXPERIENCE		
21	39.7	10.1		

	MALE	FEMALE		
SEX	19	2		

	SINGLE	MARRIED	OTHER
MARITAL STATUS	2	18	1

	BACHELOR	MASTER	DOCTOR
DEGREE	0	5	16

MARITAL STATUS	BACHELOR	DEGREE MASTER	DOCTOR
SINGLE	0	0	2
MARRIED	0	5	13
OTHER	0	0	1

STOP

Summary

Decisions in the behavioral sciences must be based on the results of empirical data gathering, organizing, and testing. All this is done by systematic means that have been programmed beforehand.

Observation of events in a natural setting, with the observer participating or not, is usually a less precise method. It is sometimes the only one appropriate or the only one possible at the time. The approach can be improved by structuring specific categories for more orderly observation and recording of behavior.

The life history or the clinical method involves the gathering of information from the report of an individual in a face-to-face situation. Material from a client or patient can be helpful in understanding present behavior. A variation of this approach is the sketching of progress of an individual over a period of time.

Survey methods collect responses to a structured situation from many individuals over the same limited period of time. The technical problems in survey methodology lie in formulating the questions, setting the sample of individuals, and interviewing. Open-end questions allow for a variety of responses but are difficult to score; poll questions restrict the replies to the categories used, but the scoring and reporting of responses is easier. A sample, a small part of the target group, is obtained because it is unlikely that everyone could be contacted. It is crucial that the sample be representative of the population, the group under study.

Attitude scales are variants of the questionnaire. Subjects reveal their attitudes through responses to questions that are first scaled and then scored after the replies are obtained. Predispositions to react positively or negatively on an issue are thus summarized in objective form.

Sociometry is a technique that obtains preferences for interaction and sketches the responses in diagrammatic form. The results present a picture of the dynamics within the group studied.

Content analysis surveys the substance of communications. What is said and how it is said may be of significance in pointing out the underlying bases of behavior.

Psychometric techniques are the structured situations eliciting respones that can be scored in a standardized way. These are most often tests of factors such as ability, aptitude, interest, achievement, or personality.

The experimental method is preferred by many behavioral researchers because conditions may be kept under more control in this approach than is possible in other methods. The classic example involves a comparison on an end result (the dependent variable) of an experimental and control group where the experimental group gets a different treatment (the independent variable). The method cannot be used in all circumstances; even when it can be employed there are questions about the artificiality of the controlled conditions.

Measurement may be quantitative and numerical in form, though it need not be. Scales can provide for a ranking of data with no other information implied, or they can, at the other extreme, be organized with a true zero point and equal intervals.

In any meaningful study, data are so extensive that some organization of them must be made before any meaning can be extracted.

Graphic methods provide visual patterns to give a quick and easy summary of information. Because the material is necessarily oversimplified, the diagrams may be misleading. Particular attention must be paid to the way in which the scales and graphs are drawn.

Descriptive statistics give a picture of the placement and the distribution of the data. Measures of central tendency give the "average" of scores, while the dispersal is shown by measures of deviation.

Probability refers to an expectation of an occurrence of an event. Prediction of conditions or the testing of hypotheses are based on the concepts of probability.

Relationships in the data can be determined, if they exist, through the use of correlation. If two or more variables are related, that is, an increase or decrease in one is accompanied by a corresponding change in the other, a correlation exists. The extent and direction of the relationship is of importance in this approach to getting meaning from the data. Knowing the correspondence between two variables also enables a researcher to predict one from a knowledge of the other. Where more than two variables are involved, a multiple correlation can be calculated.

Differences between individuals, groups, conditions, or sets of factors can be scrutinized to determine if these are significant differences or ones arising on a chance basis. The differences may be tested with techniques that vary with what is being compared. Differences between group performances, deviation from a hypothetical condition, or changes as the result of time or treatment represent uses of different techniques.

Graphic models represent a sketching of patterns of behavior in order to understand that behavior better. A model can represent varying sets of conditions, from behavior in an organization to the sketching of phases of decision making.

Mathematical models present behavior patterns in the form of mathematical notation and relations. Scheduling of work for maximum effectiveness is an industrial example; linear programming is one such technique.

Computer simulation models utilize data processing technology to simulate various aspects of behavior, from human problem solving to organizational functioning.

Electronic data processing technology provides an ever-expanding aid for the conduct of virtually every area of human endeavor. Data devices are unexcelled in providing great speed in operations, including access to extensive storage of data. Operations must be programmed so that the machine can treat inputs properly to provide the outputs that are meaningful for the user.

Bibliography

Aspen Systems Corporation (1969). *Searching law by computer.* Pittsburgh, Pa.: ASC.

Bales, R. (1951). *Interaction process analysis.* Cambridge, Mass.: Addison-Wesley.

Berelson, B. (1954). Content analysis. In Gardner, L. (ed.). *Handbook of social psychology.* Reading, Mass.: Addison-Wesley.

Droba, D. (1930). *A scale for measuring attitude toward war.* Chicago: University of Chicago Press.

Gelernter, H. and Rochester, N. (1958). Intelligent behavior in problem-solving machines. *IBM Journal of Research Development,* **2,** 336–345.

Gesell, A. (1945). *The embryology of behavior.* New York: Harper.

Gouldner, A. (1954). *Patterns of industrial bureaucracy.* Glencoe, Ill.: Free Press.

Haynes, W. and Massie, J. (1961). *Management: analysis, concepts and cases.* Englewood Cliffs, N.J.: Prentice-Hall.

Homans, G. (1950). *The human group.* New York: Harper.

Hovland, C. (1963). Computer simulation in the behavioral sciences. In Berelson, B. (ed.). *The behavioral sciences today.* New York: Basic Books.

International Business Machines Corporation (1964). *A FORTRAN primer with business administration exercises.* White Plains, N.Y.: I.B.M.

Likert, R. (1932). A technique for the measurement of attitudes. *Archives of Psychology,* No. 140.

Maccoby, E. and Maccoby, N. (1954). The interview: a tool of social science. In Lindzey, G. (ed.). *Handbook of social psychology.* Reading, Mass.: Addison-Wesley.

March, J. and Simon, H. (1958). *Organizations.* New York: Wiley.

McGraw, M. (1935). *Growth: a study of Johnny and Jimmy.* New York: Appleton-Century.

McNemar, Q. (1955). *Psychological statistics* (2nd ed.). New York: Wiley.

Moreno, J. (1953). *Who shall survive?* (2nd ed.). Beacon, New York: Beacon House.

Senders, V. (1958). *Measurement and statistics.* New York: Oxford University Press.

Simon, H. (1957). *Models of man: social and rational.* New York: Wiley.

Thurstone, L. (1929). Theory of attitude measurement. *Psychological Bulletin,* **36,** 222–241.

Webb, E., Campbell, D., Schwartz, R. and Sechrist, L. (1966). *Unobtrusive measures: nonreactive research in the social sciences.* Chicago: Rand McNally.

4

The Development
of Individual Differences

Although it may have its troublesome aspects, one of the most fascinating opportunities for one who is a parent is to be able to watch the emergence of an individual right before his eyes. This interest and the recognition that adult patterns are formed very early in the individual's life may be reason enough for the student of behavior to be interested in the developing of a person. Wordsworth expressed this by stating that "the child is father to the man."

This concern with the early years of development has been seen in the behavioral sciences primarily in the activity of child psychologists with their mapping and interpretation of various aspects of the child's functioning. The information gained has not only provided basic knowledge in the area of human behavior, but it has also provided practical guidelines for those who have some need for it in their daily living, whether they be parents, teachers, social workers, court attachés, or members of many other professions. But why should individuals in business be interested in developmental patterns? The reason is that business depends on people and decisions that must be made depend on a knowledge of people and what they can do at particular times during their lifetime. Furthermore, a better understanding of present behavior and how to cope with its problems comes only after an awareness of how people "got that way." These basic interests should be more important to the decision maker in business than should any limited approaches to information such as that needed to conform to the Federal statute restricting job descrimination on the basis of age.

The history of a person moves from childhood, through adolescence, to adulthood (though we may not be sure when these labels apply). In the past, the stages have been artificially delimited for study—the child from the adolescent, the adolescent from the adult. The subdisciplines of psychology reflected this in that the child psychologist and the adolescent psychologist were frequently differentiated. The artificial boundaries between them disturbed most of those interested in these areas, so that gradually the lines between them disappeared and many began to call themselves developmental psychologists or researchers in growth and development. The newer approaches and designations point out much more realistically that study of the individual in his growing cannot be cut into precise pieces, for if we do we lose that picture of the continuity of process which is important to keep in mind.

Interest in continuing even further along the developmental span has increased in recent years. There is the realization also that we know little about a group that is increasing in number each year—those in their advanced years. The problems of adjustment and activity and their application to the "senior citizens" has stimulated the growth of gerontology, the study of the aged (we should not forget, however, that while the absolute number of older people is on the increase, percentages may be more static—about half of all the citizens of the United States are below the age of 26).

The researcher interested in the abilities and aptitudes of the human person may focus on fundamentals or be interested in applications of knowledge. Those interested in specific areas such as business and industry, education, and government may find that much work has been done which will help them to understand human behavior in their setting. Frequently, they find that the emphasis on traditional categories or the lack of interest in the older and younger person have limited or scattered the knowledge that they need.

Nature and Nurture—Heredity and Environment

Where does one begin in the description of this process of development? Certainly from the very moment of conception. To fully explain many of the aspects of the process of development, however, we must really go back even earlier in point of time. What an individual is now is shaped by many forces present before his birth. These are primarily biological, but social forces in a historical background also play a role. While certain genetic arrangements determine the physical and functional basis of an individual's behavior, what is not to be ignored is the contribution to development that comes from the culture into which the individual is born. There is a social heritage which is transmitted by many media, the most immediate of which is the family. Not only must both heritages be considered, but their interaction in the lifetime of the individual must also be taken into account.

This is the basis for what is probably the most intriguing question in this area, namely, how much of what we are is due to heredity and how much to environment. This question, "nature or nurture," has been posed and probed by many researchers right up to the present. While the picture is a complex one and the problems even more so, there are some conclusions that may be drawn. Keep this fundamental problem in mind. It will help you to assemble the material more meaningfully, but more important, it will help you to handle the statements of those who proceed upon certain assumptions about human behavior. Such fundamental positions are recognizable in statements like "you can't make a silk purse out of a sow's ear" or, the opposite, "clothes make the man." These attitudes persist in broader social circumstances and may play a significant role in individuals for or against social welfare projects, foreign aid, juvenile courts, or almost any activity in society. In business a decision avoiding the hiring or training of ethnic minorities may be generated basically from an assumption about the "impossibility" of altering "natural" conditions.

The Span of Development

Until fairly recently, the interest in the life history of a person has been casual rather than scientific, and there has been more concern with subdividing the span into rough time periods rather than viewing it as a continuous process.

We are familiar with traditional designations such as infancy, childhood, adolescence, adulthood, and old age. These often have been reinforced with arbitrary age limits imposed by legal institutions to point out permissible or appropriate participation in the functioning of political or social groups. Setting the voting age at 21, for instance, represents a feeling that adulthood and full participation in society comes at that age level and not before.

Other differentiations of the age span vary with the awareness of the author or with his specific orientation to behavior. Shakespeare outlined his ages of man; Erikson (1963) has expanded that basic concept to a view of man explained along psychoanalytic lines. In this "Eight Ages of Man" Erikson not only characterizes states of behavior in a novel fashion but identifies those levels of development in polar terms, from the earliest period of *basic trust* versus *basic mistrust* through other stages, including *identity* versus *role confusion,* to the final experiences of *ego integrity* versus *despair.* Infantile trust leads to the ego integrity of the mature adult, says Erikson, with the other aspects included in their turn in the developmental process. In this sequence the problems of identity occur in the beginning stage of youth, well after the striving for individual autonomy that takes place in childhood.

INFANCY AND CHILDHOOD

In the more traditional identifications and discussions of this early period of the life history, most observers of behavior have emphasized the importance of the first years of life. In his work, Freud pointed to the possibility of identifying the basis for adult personality patterns in the problems of early childhood. Freud, however, did not work with children; his contributions came in stimulating later psychoanalytically inclined observers to do research on the early stages of development. This influence and the main impact of his ideas fostered a general acceptance of many of Freud's developmental concepts, even by those who do not consider themselves Freudian in orientation.

Other researchers of widely varying viewpoints have provided a more specific view of the behavior of individuals in the early stages of the life span. Alfred Binet, in developing his measure of mental ability at the beginning of this century, established some clear norms of test performance at each age. More recent is the line of experimentation and observation by Piaget and his associates in Geneva (Mussen, 1963). Piaget views the development of the child as being a process of adaptation to the world where the means of handling the environment proceeds in stages. Up to age two the child is immersed in problems of his sensorimotor operations. Preconceptual thought, where concrete things are recognized as standing for real ones, develops before age four though classification of these concepts takes place up until age seven. Even at this age, however, the child is tied to concrete states (though in greater number) and not until approximately age 11 is there a move to abstract thought and use of logic and hypotheses. While the stages may be too rigidly defined, Piaget's research does show the changing nature of the individual and his ability to proceed in the world. As an illustration of specific aspects of development in this part of the life span, it has few equals.

ADOLESCENCE

The transition from the early developmental period to the one we call adolescence is not clear cut. A convenient dividing line is the attainment of puberty, but since this comes at different times for different individuals and since even the physical manifestations are probably the less crucial features, the line between the child and the teenager is hard to draw.

The period when the person is no longer a child though not yet an adult is often pictured as a stressful one, at least in our culture. That this need not be so was pointed out long ago by Margaret Mead (1928) in her reports on primitive societies. In certain primitive cultures, but not all, the passage from childhood to adulthood is achieved without stress and strain. The transition to maturity is accomplished most effortlessly by those groups that deliberately make the process a clear and easy one. There, the passage to adulthood is significant and marked by *rites de passage,* the ceremonies indicating a new status. It may be regretted that, all too often, no clear guides or ceremonies exist in modern society. The "magic age" of 21 is a rather late and weak counterpart marked only by the right to vote and imbibe. At any rate, the period is one of great energy and idealism; it is not clearly different from adulthood in many respects, especially in late adolescence, and not enough different to support either the legal protection of the "infant" or denial of civic activity until the traditional landmark of 21 is reached.

MATURITY AND OLD AGE

The discussion of adolescence was curtailed, deliberately, because it can be a short phase or an unclearly defined period in the life span. In many cultures, youth are admitted to full membership in the group much sooner than they are in Western cultures generally. There is some basis for this early acceptance into adulthood. Performance on tests of mental ability reaches a peak at about age 16, although this high level must be viewed with a recognition that general intellectual performance also depends on the ability to evaluate, which is aided by experience. While the physical development of an individual may proceed at a slackening pace to about age 25, many sensorimotor abilities are at their highest level at about age 19. Reaction time, speed, and adaptability to new situations are best at this age. That accident statistics do not reflect this is, again, a function of experience as well as attitudes, and more particularly of attitudes.

In the period of maturity we may be faced again with dogmatic positions on behavior of individuals at certain ages. The statement that "a man is over the hill at 35" may be offset by one that states "life begins at 40," but industry has all too often preferred the former to the latter. Notions of the proper age for retirement focus on age 65 as the criterion. Pointing to examples of cases where people have, indeed, deteriorated after retirement at age 65 is a good example of the self-fulfilling prophecy.

The accuracy of common notions regarding development or aging and the behavior to be expected at each age will be determined in specific sections to follow in this chapter. In prior or present discussions of this area of behavior, a distinction between development and aging often has been made. In a continuous phenomenon like life through its entire span, however, such differentiation is not easy or meaningful and leads to a certain amount of discussion or disagreement. A casual way of referring to the two has been to split the life span in half and call the first part development and the second half aging. This is unsatisfactory because it implies that different principles are involved (growth versus negative growth or development versus deterioration). A more satisfactory way of looking at the problem would be to consider aging as the point in time when the forces of growth have arrived at a relatively steady state (Birren, 1959, p. 13). While it may not provide a comprehensive answer, this delineation at least leaves the door open for research that is not based on too many fixed assumptions. It is well to remember also that the research results below on specific characteristics or abilities reflect the variety of concepts and scales of age—biological age, psychological age, mental age, and social age.

Individual Differences

What can be known about individual differences must come from measurement of some kind. The measure may be of a very objective and precise nature or it may be a very casual one. It may be obtained through observation, in an interview, or by means of a "test." In short, all techniques in the previous chapter can be used to gain this information, and more than a single limited appraisal is available, hopefully, in most situations involving understanding of individual and group differences. Such knowledge serves as the basis for applications not only in education and industry but also in broader functioning on the community scene. An understanding of the nature of differences, if such do indeed exist, makes for more effective citizenship in present-day society.

THE DISTRIBUTION OF TRAITS

Most human traits are distributed along a continuum, with most people in the middle and few at either extreme. The resulting curve is called the normal curve of distribution, a concept already noted in Chapter 3. Here it is important to note additional features about the normal curve which any student of individual differences should know. Figure 4-1 shows the proportion of individuals at different points of the continuum. The curve contains about two-thirds of the individuals within the range from one sigma, or standard deviation, above the mean to one sigma below. The curve may represent the distribution of many traits such as adult height, weight, or I.Q. scores. In the latter case, the mean would be 100 and the standard deviation 15.

As we get further away from the middle of the spread of scores, we find fewer individuals. With I.Q. scores, for instance, an I.Q. of 110 is not

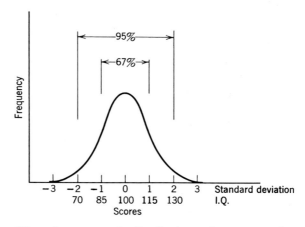

Figure 4-1. Normal curve and distribution of scores (I.Q. scores as an illustration).

unusual while one of 150 certainly is; a man 5 feet, 10 inches high does not stand out in a crowd but one 7 feet tall does.

The normal curve is a hypothetical result which, in practice, is approached but not reached though a large sample of the general population should provide a curve close to it. A selected sample will probably show a curve skewed toward one end of the continuum or the other. Personnel administrators in industry are not too surprised to find that management trainees for their company may tend to cluster on the higher side of a continuum of mental ability. They have already been preselected in school; many, but not all, of the earlier "dropouts" are from the middle to lower range of ability.

INDIVIDUAL TRAITS

There are many different aspects of individual functioning in which we may be interested. The trait areas that can be considered may be organized in various ways but continued usage over the years has set categories that are by now familiar and useful. Most workers in personnel or related activities consider the following trait areas to be the important ones: (a) mental ability, (b) mechanical aptitudes, (c) psychomotor skills, (d) interests, (e) personality, (f) scholastic aptitude, (g) achievement, (h) clerical abilities, and (i) language ability. These areas may be subdivided further, or there may be a larger grouping made for a particular purpose.

Any confusion in this area is compounded further by some difficulty in distinguishing between the instruments that are used to measure the traits or characteristics, since similar tests may be used to determine ability and aptitude or achievement and aptitude. These terms may be separable on a conceptual basis but in practice may be a bit confusing. *Ability* refers to a present state or condition of the individual. It relates to what he is able to do at the time of the test. *Aptitude* refers to capacity of the individual for a particular kind of activity and is future oriented in that it attempts to assess his level of performance at some later time. *Achievement* is what a person has accomplished in a specific area.

The distinctions in action are not as easy to make, however. A test of mental ability, for instance, may be a measure of scholastic aptitude because later performance in school is undoubtedly based on mental ability to a high degree. The capacity for learning in that specific setting depends heavily on this particular ability. It may also be true that aptitude for most managerial tasks may be shown by present mental ability measures. An achievement test can also serve as a predictor of future performance. A test of typing, for example, not only measures the level of attainment of that skill but may also be used as a measure of aptitude for a task such as key-punch operation. The person has had typing instruction and experience but no key-punch experience. Because of the nature of the future task, however, the typing level may be used as a predictor.

Personality tests measure those dimensions of an individual that play a role in his reactions to life situations. "Personality" includes motives, tendencies, and even the abilities listed above. Very broadly, it refers to the social self of the individual but includes those deeper traits that influence interaction. The list of trait names included in the area of personality could start with those such as "sociability," "excitability," and so on for an almost endless series. Personality tests usually consist of items that sample behavior by asking what the subject would do in hypothetical situations.

Interest patterns may be considered as part of personality but are thought to be important enough to be measured separately. The activities an individual would prefer to pursue can bear some relationship to his later effectiveness on a job. Other things being equal, interest in the activities required in the task should lead to greater effectiveness in it.

CAVEATS IN APPRAISAL

In obtaining and using information about individual differences, the decision maker must be aware of many factors that should make him cautious about applying the results obtained. This is especially true in selection situations where persons are chosen for specific tasks. This area probably provides the most common use of information about individual differences in industrial, academic, or other organizational settings.

Concern with the Use of Tests

Criticism of testing, particularly in industry and in the schools, waxes and wanes but seems to be more extensive and emotional in recent years. Two types of concern usually emerge; one questions the adequacy of the technique while the second centers on the feeling that testing constitutes an invasion of privacy. Since psychologists have been more involved, on the whole, in the structuring of tests than has any other professional group, significant responses to sensational authors and concerned citizens have come more often from them (Amrine, 1965). These reflect the concern of the profession for proper standards.

The most obvious rejoinder to critics is that tests are not infallible. Perfection is to be sought, perhaps, but to reach it is outside the realm of possibility. No one knows this better than the trained professionals who are aware of the limitations of the technique. The hazards come in situations where, as Alexander Pope remarked, "a little learning is a dangerous thing," and users of tests remain insensitive to the difficulties present in interpreting results.

Of all the tests, the mental ability or scholastic aptitude measures are the best established but, even here, there are variations. The Stanford-Binet is an old reliable measure of mental ability but is one that is appropriate for subjects between the ages of six and sixteen. For adults, other (better designed) measures are available. Recent concern in the area of civil rights has included the protest that most minority group members, primarily Negroes, have been discriminated against in the use of tests for job selection based on a particular cultural experience. Ideally, a "culture free" test might prove to be more acceptable and desirable but, even if one were available, the selection program would require that the test help to predict performance on the job. If that job performance requires preparation of a particular kind or a basic fund of knowledge, a test must measure these aspects in order to be valid. The personnel administrator must, at the same time, be objective in determining whether certain abilities really are critical on the job. The personnel man in industry who selects on the basis of the color of the applicant's tie is not likely to be doing his task well.

The possible violation of the legal right to privacy when tests are used is another concern which is being voiced with greater frequency. Recently, in the *American Psychologist,* a professional journal, Ruebhausen and Brim

(1966) outlined legal aspects of the problem and pointed out what seem to be the prevalent attitudes of the profession. The authors maintain that in all research the lead should be taken by the scientific community through its own codes, attitudes, and behaviors; absolute rules allowing a probe beyond decent inquiry are intolerable to free men in a free society. A code of ethics is suggested for all researchers, including users of tests, which recognizes and affirms the claim to a private personality and a positive commitment to respect this in research. To the fullest extent possible, consent of individuals should be obtained; where this is not possible, the officials should be satisfied the social good of the project outweighs the social value of claims to privacy. Identities of individuals should be protected from disclosure, and the data are not to be used for other research without additional consent or overriding considerations of public interest.

Personality measures have borne the brunt of the criticism on both counts. These tests are more open to censure, and such action often has much support from professionals in the test and measurement field. Personality tests have long been difficult to construct and use with a secure frame of mind. On the whole, however, these techniques do provide some information; frequently, it is much more complete than can be obtained in any other way, if it can be gained at all. As an easy criticism suggests, personality tests are subject to "faking" or alteration of results but any good tester knows this when he uses them for selection purposes. In this he has help from an increasing number of techniques that can help spot the alteration of responses.

Much of the concern really stems from the anxiety that is felt when probes are made into a sensitive area. The situation is aggravated by the reaction to the terminology often used. Negative connotations in test scores termed "paranoia" or "psychopathic deviation" provide a basis for apprehension. One must have experience to know that these are only labels for certain scores and to understand what these labels do and do not mean.

Test Factors

Close attention to certain attributes of measurement devices may avoid many of the problems that sometimes arise in the use of the tests. The difficulties are usually in connection with interpretation of the results of measures.

Scores. A simple but potentially misleading aspect of a test is the manner in which the results are reported. The performance on most measures is described in terms of a single overall quantitative index. That numerical score may give many people the impression of more precision than really exists. Since we have learned very early that the numeral 100 refers to a number greater than 99, it is quite easy to assume a similar situation exists when test scores are reported in this way. In reality there may be no significant difference between two such test scores.

Profiles. The one general score may also fail to provide enough information for the appraiser. A "catchall" measure of mental ability, for instance, includes many specific abilities which go to make up the overall picture. These factors often can be scored and reported separately; the resulting profile of subtest scores provides more meaningful information about the individual through the patterning of scores than does a single numerical total score. Some results, furthermore, can be reported in no other way; the profile pictured in Figure 4-2 reports results of scoring on a well-known inventory where a total score would be meaningless. A total score on a test of mental ability does indicate an overall placement for the person along a continuum, but the profile of subscores shows the weak and strong points in a realistic way.

Norms. Numerical scores by themselves mean very little or nothing unless we have some idea of where they fit in a overall scheme. A score of 292 on a test, for instance, does not tell us much unless we know how others have done in the past or how they perform ordinarily. This necessity for comparison with others may already have been inferred by the careful reader. Test manuals should report not only the means and standard deviations but also should identify the individuals to whom the tests were administered in the process of standardization. An "average score" could mean that obtained by eighth-graders, college students, steel mill janitors, or insurance company file clerks; it would be of significance to know where the group was obtained as well.

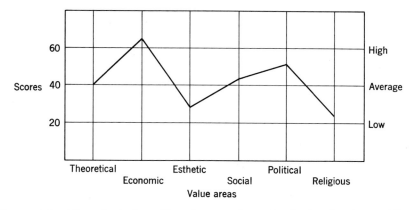

Figure 4-2. Hypothetical profile of scores from the *Scale of values* (Allport, Vernon, and Lindzey, 1960).

Reliability. A measure can have no real use unless it is steady and consistent in the results it gives. Just as a rubber ruler would not give consistent measures, a test could not provide meaningful information if it were not capable of giving a stable set of scores. This concept of consistency is what is meant by reliability of a test.

Validity. If a test measures what it is supposed to measure, then it can be said that it is valid. This aspect may be determined from an inspection of the nature and content of the items of the test; in this instance, the validity that we determine is *face validity* or that obtained from the surface appraisal of the test. More than this is desirable, however.

The Criterion. This is the concept that must be considered in connection with validity. A criterion is a standard; we compare any tool or artifact with it to see how our recent product "measures up" to it. In much the same way, test results are compared to some other indicator to see how closely they approach that measure. In an industrial situation we may be interested in performance on a particular job. A measure of job performance would be a criterion to which we could compare performance on a test. Hopefully, such a criterion of job performance would be objective, that is, be a specific measure such as "number of widgets produced per hour" or "number of rejects." Performance figures such as these may be affected by circumstances beyond the ability of the individual to control, or the activity may be such that no objective measure is possible. In that event, a subjective evaluation, such as a foreman's rating, must be substituted. In either case, the true job performance levels may not be reflected by the obtained results. This is known as *contamination of the criterion.* The supervisor who rates management trainees on the basis of whether or not they wear Brooks Brothers suits contaminates the criterion by doing so if that factor does not play a role in successful performance of the job. Unfortunately, such criteria are often present without our awareness of them.

Use in Selection. Comparison of the test and criterion is valuable when the use of test results to predict performance on the criterion enables one to select on that basis. If the relationship between test and criterion exists to any appreciable degree, we say the test has predictive validity and put it to work. This relationship is demonstrated by correlating the two scores, test and criterion, for each individual in the group (see "Correlation" in Chapter 3). In an industrial situation the test could be one of mechanical ability while the criterion would be a job performance rating. A sketch of the scores in a typical case of this kind is presented in Figure 4-3. Each dot represents a person, and the location of each dot indicates his performance on both measures. Notice the tendency of the dots to move to the upper right-hand

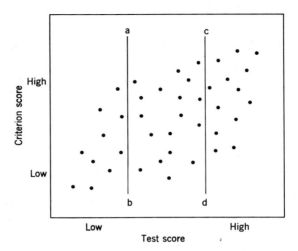

Figure 4-3.   Scatter of scores on test and criterion.

corner even though the scatter of scores shows less than a perfect relationship. Some who score high on the test score low on the job, and vice versa. If a perfect relationship existed, a straight line would result.

The Selection Ratio. Even though the relationship between test and criterion is less than perfect, the personnel administrator will find it useful for selection of workers. Flexibility in its use, however, provides different results under different circumstances. If, as would happen in a "tight" labor market, we would need to select a large percentage of the applicants, the cutoff line could be made about where line *ab* appears in Figure 4-3. With many more applicants than needed, a lower selection ratio would result if line *cd* were used. Here, only one of four would be chosen, with the percentage of successful workers on the job increasing as a result. A number of less successful workers would still be included, of course, since the correlation between test and job is not a perfect one.

Diagnostic Use. The preceding discussions of uses of measurement focused primarily on selection of individuals. Such choices carry with them the concomitant rejection of others. When this result may not be possible, under conditions of full employment or a policy of acceptance of virtually all applicants, emphasis can be placed on the use of measures to identify the areas of strength in the pattern of abilities shown by the individual and to use the results in placing him in a job. This wider approach often has more to recommend it than does the narrower use of testing to fill specific job situations.

The Biological Basis for Behavior

Most human traits or characteristics have a firm biological basis. The fundamental mechanisms are in the genetic pattern as it emerges anew in the pairing up of the chromosomes from the germ cells of each parent. Each mate has a peculiar genetic alignment as the result of the very same process, one which has been repeated each generation in turn. Though each individual alignment is different, there are enough combinations similar to those of the parents and other relatives so that we are able to see the evidence of those similarities in the surface features of individuals in the same family.

THE BASIS FOR INDIVIDUALITY

Each person has billions of cells in his body, and each cell is much like another in fundamental structure. The nucleus, or center, of the cell contains 23 pairs, or 46 in all, of the tiny, rod-like bodies called chromosomes; these are really intertwined to give the appearance of a ball of string. Each chromosome contains countless tiny bodies called *genes.* Each chromosome and each gene in the chromosome are paired to provide the characteristics of the person. Only one qualification to the above information need be made here, but it is an important one. The germ cells, sperm and ovum, are split so that they contain only one side of the pairing, or 23 chromosomes in all, rather than 23 pairs. It is thus easy to see how each partner then can contribute one side of the pair which the new individual will possess.

The pairing is even more complicated, however, in that each side of the pair of genes is not equal in its contribution to the characteristic that results. One of the pair of genes is *dominant* while the other may be *recessive.* The characteristic that appears is that which is represented by the dominant gene. Brown eyes are a dominant trait while blue eyes are recessive, so that when a brown gene is paired with a blue gene, the individual has brown eyes. Blue eyes come about only when two blue genes are paired. Other characteristics appear in the same fashion—hair color and texture, color blindness, hearing, and limb proportions, to mention only a few (women may find it difficult to believe that curly hair is a dominant trait since there is apparently so little evidence of it in their world).

The genes are not affected by life experiences; no acquired traits can be passed on to progeny. Changes called mutations do occur, however, apparently as the result of "accidents" such as X-ray, cosmic ray activity, or other little understood forces.

Chromosomes may also be pinpointed as the vehicle by which another determinant of behavior is itself determined. Sex is a variable that is of interest not only biologically but also socially or culturally. The mechanism by which sex is determined is basically simple; one chromosome pair is responsible. Remembering that one side of the pair comes from one parent and the other side from the other parent, we can guess that the split of the pair somehow determines the sex of the offspring. Each cell (except the germ cell) of an individual has a pair of sex determining chromosomes. In the female this is a nicely matched pair of usual size. The male, however, has a regular sized one along with a somewhat smaller one. The regular sized one is called an X chromosome while the shriveled-up one is called the y chromosome. Each female, then, has two X chromosomes, while the male has an X and a y. (To say that the only difference between boys and girls is the y chromosome is to pass on a facetious oversimplification.)

An even closer look at the mechanisms of heredity shows that genes may be seen more specifically as being very complex packets of *deoxyribonucleic acid* (DNA). The chain of DNA molecules carries a code for its own reproduction and the production of enzymes. It can produce various types of *ribonucleic acids* (RNA). One of these is a "messenger RNA" which is assembled according to the code of the DNA molecular structure and is then sent with the genetic information to the synthesizing areas of the cell to continue the process of building the individual.

THE NEW AND DIFFERENT INDIVIDUAL

As has been stated above, the germ cells of the individual contain one side of a pair of chromosomes. When the germ cells meet, that is, when the sperm cell fertilizes the ovum or egg, a new single cell, which is the new individual, is formed. Within one day the single celled organism divides into two and, in another day each of these divides into two; in a very short time this multiplication produces an organism composed of billions of cells. (To fully appreciate how rapid and extensive the buildup is, take a penny and double it the first day, take the result and double that, and so on for each day for one month; the total may surprise you.) Along with growth there comes a differentiation of cells as they begin to specialize in many different tasks; not all cells do the same thing.

PATTERNS OF DEVELOPMENT

There are certain patterns in the development of the organism, both *in utero* and after birth, which are the same for all. The time of onset of physical growth or behavior may vary among individuals, but the sequence does not. Attainment of certain abilities or skills may occur at different times, but the order remains the same for all.

The new organism unfolds according to two set plans; it grows and develops as follows.

1. Cephalocaudally.   2. Proximodistally.

The first pattern means that the development proceeds from head to tail (the word comes from the Greek words for head and tail). The second term refers to the fact that the individual structures show growth and development from the midpoint to the extremities, or from the proximate parts to those that are more distant.

Before birth, the embryo and foetus are seen to be almost "all head"; that is, the early brain and central nervous system structures predominate. The embryo resembles a tadpole with its large head and small tail, the tail eventually becoming the rest of the body of the person. Development along the midline of the individual also proceeds ahead of the development of the extremities. The brain and spinal cord are formed first. Arms and legs appear first as tiny buds; not until much later do the fine features of the hands and feet develop.

The two predominant patterns of development continue after the individual leaves his sheltered existence and has to face the more variable environment of the outside world. The average infant of one month can begin to raise his head when placed on his stomach but cannot raise his chest until about a month later. Lower parts of his body do not come under control until several months after this (we see that the child can crawl before he can walk). The proximodistal patterns are not as evident as the cephalocaudal patterns just mentioned but they are important in the scheme of things. The infant is able to make broad or gross movements of the arm before fine manual dexterity is achieved. The average six-month-old swings his whole arm to get a toy block and, when contact is made, palms it very clumsily. By his first birthday, however, he can grasp the block in the prehensile manner of the adult. This latter ability, incidently, is much more important than most people realize. The ability of the human to use the thumb in opposition to the fingers makes man a "skilled toolmaker" and has helped to set him apart from infrahumans.

It is important to repeat, finally, that while the sequence of behavior is the same for all, the timing may be different. Some infants get to walk or talk earlier than others. Those who turn out to be retarded usually have been late in achieving the simple skills. On the other hand, it is reassuring to know that not all children who are late walkers or talkers turn out to be less gifted than average.

INPUT PROCESSES

Information receiving, or sensation, serves as a basis for behavior. While not as crucial, perhaps, in overall functioning, the senses do play a role in the formation of patterns of behavior. The part that age factors play in the reception of stimuli concerns us here.

The structures that serve as information receptors for the organism are complete and ready to function even before they are necessary. Well before birth, the receiving structures are ready to be used even though pathways to the brain, such as the optic nerves, are not completed until late in the period of pregnancy. The cortex of the brain may not be functioning at birth, but all the preliminary stages of the system are ready and working. The fetus at six months *in utero* is apparently sensitive to noise. A conditioned reflex may be elicited in the growing organism at about the same time.

There is some question as to the sensitivity of the organism in the early period of life, but it is well known that in the first grade children still need large-sized letters in their reading books. From this point in life, visual acuity seems to improve, then level off and remain at a high level until fairly late. Chapanis (1950) tested the visual acuity of a group of subjects from ages 5 to 79. The results showed a rise in visual acuity to age 15, a leveling-off

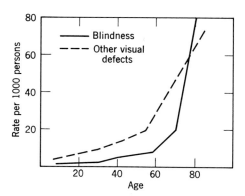

Figure 4-4.   Age and blindness or visual defects (from U.S. Department of Health, Education and Welfare, 1959).

until age 50, and a decline from that point on. Visual defects and blindness do increase considerably after age 40, though the number is still only 80 per thousand even as late as age 80 (Figure 4-4). With respect to audition, it has been noted frequently in the past that older persons are not as sensitive to higher frequency tones as younger people. The loss occurs in the range of 10,000 cycles per second of above. Frequently, a pattern of "tonal islands" may be seen where the loss of acuity occurs in a few scattered parts of the range of sensitivity. Men suffer more of a loss than women, a finding that may be at least partially accounted for by the greater exposure of men to high intensity industrial noise. That age factors are also responsible is shown by further studies which found reduced acuity after age 64 (Birren, 1964, p. 98).

Structures for taste and smell seem to show some anatomical changes with age, but the exact nature of the changes have not been pinpointed. Cooper et al. (1959) found little, if any, change in taste sensitivity up to age 50. The substantial decline in ability to taste apparently comes considerably later. Very old people may be seen to season their food with great abandon and complain that "things don't taste like they used to."

The skin senses show some decline in sensitivity with age. Sherman and Robilland (1960) noted a 20 percent difference in pain sensitivity between those in their 20's and those above age 65, with the striking decline after 70. This study also found that women were more sensitive to pain than were men.

CENTRAL PROCESSES

The cognitive processes are probably the most critical functions in behavior. Any differences in this area with respect to age are important to note, therefore, for a better understanding of human activity.

Perception

Few studies of age differences in perception have appeared. Landahl and Birren (1959) had subjects judge weights with both hands and noted the speed and accuracy in perception of differences. Generally, the older subjects (ages 58–85) performed at about 65 percent of the level demonstrated by the younger subjects (ages 18–32). Interestingly, there were no differences when the judgments were made using the same hand. There was also no difference in time taken when difficult judgments were to be made. Crook et al. (1958) found no differences in visual perception between the ages of 20 and 50 when conditions were optimum. When illumination or time was reduced, the differences between young and old were significant.

Learning

Conditioning, the most basic kind of learning process, comes about more slowly in older subjects than in young adults or children. Braun and Geiselhart (1959), along with others, state that part of the problem in achieving the new response may be because the old patterns are firmly established. Maintaining the predisposition to respond or keeping the stimulus at a high enough level of intensity may be a further problem.

In a more complex and realistic setting, the results in learning tasks may not show any differences resulting from age. In an industrial setting involving workers in many different occupations, the U.S. Department of Labor (1963) found very few areas of difference between old and young workers in learning new procedures. The information upon which the conclusions were based came from retraining sessions organized to meet technological changes. Older workers were not consistently or significantly poorer in training than the younger workers and, in some ways, were better.

Transfer of training may be a crucial point for the trainer to consider. What has been learned earlier may interfere in learning a new and different task. On the other hand, the experience accumulated over the past may help in the learning of the new task if that new situation has many of the elements of the old and familiar activity.

Other factors in the actual on-the-job situation may be more important contributors to performance. Bowers (1952) found that, while older workers learned less readily, there was no difference between young and old in job knowledge, accuracy, or dependability.

Mental Ability

Most of our information in this area comes from the use of tests labeled mental ability, scholastic aptitude, or intelligence, where the performance of individuals of various chronological ages may be determined fairly easily. While factors extraneous to those measured by the test may influence performance at any age, it is not true that adults are more defensive about their performance on a test than are adolescents. Older subjects are usually interested in the task at hand, although they may not be as involved in the process or believe that these are really problem-solving tasks. This makes comparison of adult and adolescent scores a bit more difficult.

Since tests of mental ability are ordinarily composed of different kinds of items measuring different aspects of intellectual functioning, we may expect that a breakdown can be made into specific subtests with a subsequent variation between subtest scores. A total score on the test would reflect the position that mental ability is a general grouping of specific kinds of abilities. In this framework it is possible to develop individual profiles as well as plot differentials in test performance at various ages. In an early project Jones and Conrad (1933) tested all those between 10 and 60 in a New England village. Mental ability was found to increase to a peak at age 16 and decline somewhat to 60. In subtests which require rapid adaptation to new situations the young were superior to the old, but where past experience is valuable, as in vocabulary and general information, the older subjects maintained the level they reached at approximately age 16 and sometimes even improved on their earliest performance (Figure 4-5). While there are different results even with verbal tests, performance on linguistic measures generally remains the same or increases with age. Nonverbal tests, however, often show a decrease in performance

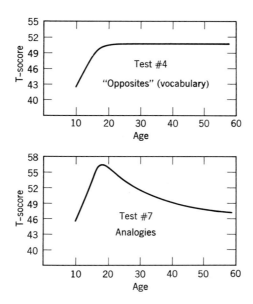

Figure 4-5. Age and performance on two subtests of the Army Alpha (Jones and Conrad, 1933).

with age (Foulds and Raven, 1948), but verbal ability is usually more critical than nonverbal ability in many settings. In either scholastic activity or professional work situations, language level remains the best indicator of ability and predictor of performance.

Concept Formation

The process of forming concepts involves representing, through reasoning based on experience, the common aspects of objects or situations that are otherwise unlike. Time, life, apple, or red are concepts that are formed in certain stages in the development of the cognitive functioning of individuals. Concepts may be formed through observation, but these may be inadequately based. To an average eight-year-old the concept *life* means ability to move; to him a bicycle would have life for this reason. In later life more complex concepts may be based on inadequate knowledge. The concept of intelligence, for instance, is an important one for the personnel man, but his activity may be fraught with danger if he pursues his job with an imperfect knowledge of testing.

Much of the information about concept formation in the young comes from the studies of Piaget and his co-workers (Inhelder and Piaget, 1958) who have noted the development of concepts such as those of number, magnitude, order, and conservation of matter. Piaget found that young children will say there are more pennies in front of them when the experimenter spreads the coins out so that the boundaries are greater. In the same way children do not have the concept of constancy, that is, knowing that size and weight remained the same when a ball of clay is flattened; at age two to four the child thinks there is more clay when the ball is flattened, and even at age nine the concept of constancy of mass is not present in many respects.

At the other end of the age continuum there may be a tendency for the older person to adhere strongly to concepts that have been formed on a simple basis. When one forms a concept by paying attention to only one obvious facet such as color or size, the approach may be labeled a *concrete* one as opposed to an *abstract* conceptual process which tries to pull out all appropriate aspects of the situation. Thaler (1956) found that older persons had a tendency to sort figures on the basis of one attribute alone rather than to make the additional classifications which were available.

In other words, with respect to concepts the development comes in a certain sequence or pattern with increasing age and experience. In old age inflexibility of function limits the full utilization of the available elements.

Problem Solving

While there has been a scarcity of information on the relationships between age and problem solving, what little there is seems to point to some differences in approach toward problems and their solution as individuals get older. Chown (1961) states that the basis for the superiority of the young lies in their willingness to analyze the problems rather than rely on associations as do older subjects. The older individuals do not have the strong problem-solving orientation that generates hypotheses and tests them. Friend and Zubek (1958) interpreted the poorer scores of older workers on a test of critical thinking as stemming from a lower objectivity and a greater inflexibility in answering the question. Inspection of a graph (Figure 4-6) charting performance, however, shows no appreciable difference between subjects of age 20 and age 60. This minimal difference may be more significant than any drop after age 65, a result that may stem from other factors.

Language

Speech is characteristic of the human species—no known group of people is without some language. It, too, shows a distinct pattern of development which is the same for all, though age in reaching particular points in the sequence may vary. Generally, all the speech sounds that are necessary come into use by about six months of age in the form of random babbling. By nine months the child can imitate sounds and, when he is one year old, he

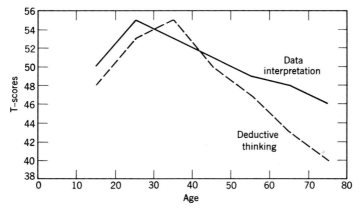

Figure 4-6. Age and performance on a test of critical thinking (Friend and Zubek, 1958).

can say the exciting first word. The size of vocabulary increases rapidly; at 18 months the usual number of words in the repertoire is only five or six but at two years it is 250. On the average, speech develops earlier in girls than in boys and is maintained at a higher level. Usually, the more intelligent the child the better the speech; a similar positive relationship exists between language ability and skills of other kinds, including psychomotor skills, to a slight degree. Higher social position, better homes and opportunities to learn, along with fewer siblings are some of the environmental factors that are directly related to language ability.

OUTPUT: PSYCHOMOTOR ACTIVITIES

Psychomotor activities are those actions involving some voluntary movement of the body ranging from fine manual dexterity to more complex coordination of limb and trunk movements. Psychomotor refers to simple movements such as grasping as well as to complex acts involved in the assembly of a complicated piece of machinery.

It may be casually noted that older people are slower generally than are younger persons. If psychomotor skills show a change over life span of the individual, such changes show up primarily in terms of speed and/or timing. The entire behavioral output in a person's activity, however, is not the result of psychomotor processes alone. Since reaction time refers to the total span between sensation and response, more than something purely physical is involved. While at this point we may concentrate on the latter phases of the action process, the earlier elements of behavior cannot be forgotten. Nor can we forget that here, as well as with other matters, there are other variables which influence the end result; personality, mental ability, and social and cultural factors play a role in even the simplest motor responses people make.

All this activity is possible as the result of maturational processes. When structures are developed, activity can then take place; pushing a child into a certain activity before he is ready not only is not effective but may have undesirable concomitants as well. Practice does not hasten the skill (Gesell and Thompson, 1943, p. 216). Dennis and Dennis (1940) found, furthermore, that those children whose movements were restricted walked no later than those who had freedom of movement.

The control that an individual achieves over the early developmental years is the result of learning superimposed on the maturation of the structures involved. The younger adult at maturity has reached a point where presumably all physical excitation and activity is at its peak of efficiency. Increasing experience may, however, compensate later for a slackening of the physical bases for activity. Work may be performed with ease by the knowledgeable employee while the newcomer may be severely taxed by it.

This may be a reason why studies in industry often show insignificant changes in psychomotor performance of workers through the life span, at least to age 65. Experimental studies do indicate some changes, however, in certain specific kinds of skills though the pattern is not uniform for all. Welford (1958), in a summary of the changes over time in particular skills, identified these as arising in the central control and guidance of actions coupled with changes in attitudes. While there was great variation among individuals at any age, in many tasks the subjects worked well within their capacities. In other tasks minor changes in layout brought about satisfactory or superior performance.

Personality

Personality is a broad, amorphous designation relating to fundamental approaches of persons to others and themselves. To most psychologists and students of behavior, this wide term refers to the study of the characteristic traits of an individual, relationships between these traits, and the ways in which a person adjusts to other people and situations. The characteristic ways of responding to life's situations is at the core of human behavior. The development of individual differences in this area should be, therefore, of prime interest.

PERSONALITY DEVELOPMENT

In the early formative years the shaping of the personality of the individual is done by many forces, the primary ones originating within the family. Since the family is the greatest source of socialization (the social process whereby individuals learn to interact with others), the direct contacts within the family are significant, perhaps for more than one generation. Bowlby (1952, pp. 82–83) maintains that the lack of a normal home life in a child makes for a bad parent, a bad parent makes for deprivation, and on and on for generations in "lock step." Harlow's (1962) monkeys made poor mothers when they themselves were poorly mothered. Apparently, an important feature in the development of personality is a stimulation from the contact with and warmth from loved ones. With less affection, less strength of character develops. Stronger super-ego control comes with growth under supervision that is love based;

the development of conscience proceeds more strongly when the control exercised by parents is firm but fair, permissive not punitive, and one that offers guidance with an affectionate base. On the other hand, punishment may show effects that are undesirable. Severe punishment for aggression not only makes for anxiety in the person punished but, even more important, the later expression of aggression is made more likely and delinquency more common.

Rigidity and rejection in discipline can lead also to an overdependency in the child; anxiety is easily aroused when the child perceives the forcing of independence as a rejection by parents at a time when his main concern is for support from an ordered and secure world. Too much and too long continued nurturance, however, can lead to dependency as well.

McClelland (1953) has related the drive for achievement to certain experiential factors early in the life history. He found a high relationship between an achievement need and an accenting of independence training in the culture. The earlier the demands on the child or the stronger the parental pressure to achieve, the stronger were the manifestations of the need-achievement pattern. The stressing of achievement was not without parental love, however; clear expression of affection, even physical, was more often the experience of the striver for achievement.

Other studies of personality carried out over at least part of the life span show both consistency and change in traits. A longitudinal study of married couples carried on up to 18 years of married life indicates a stability of personality traits in each partner (Kelly, 1955). In that period of time there was no increase or decrease in correlation of personality scores of the married partners. Living together does not increase the resemblance between mates; apparently, there is little reason for prospective brides to hope to "marry the man today and change his ways tomorrow," at least toward similarity with her. While the study did find changes taking place with respect to attitudes, it is established that enough stability in personality exists in the development from childhood to early adulthood to lend emphasis to an earlier statement in this chapter, namely, "the child is father to the man." Enough changes can be superimposed on this core structure, however, to make one careful of assuming that no change can or does take place.

Personality functioning in later life seems to be a matter primarily of the extent to which social interaction takes place. A series of studies at the University of Chicago (Tobin and Neugarten, 1961) has emphasized that a prime personality trait is the move toward personal relations with others. While it may be characteristic of the aged to be less involved in their environment, those happiest were those who maintained contact with their surroundings. The importance of this factor is stressed by further findings of extreme behavioral, even physical, reactions to environmental changes. It has been observed that the death rate increases for elderly patients being moved or widows who are recently bereaved (Aldrich and Mendkoff, 1963).

MENTAL HEALTH

More serious emotional or affective responses are part of the problem of psychopathology, the study of mental diseases. In an extensive survey in the New Haven community, Hollingshead (1958) determined the prevalence of diagnosed neurotics and psychotics by age and sex. Figure 4-7 shows a high peak at about age 35 for the neuroses, while it also demonstrates the steep increase with age in psychotic involvement. Neurotic disabilities are not as severe as psychotic ones in that an individual with neuroses is in touch with reality while a psychotic is not. Neurotic problems are not frequent in old age; at that time the psychoses are more of concern. Even within the general category of psychosis there are some further differentiations according to age.

About 25 percent of the first admissions to mental hospitals consist of schizophrenics, and the same percentage is diagnosed as suffering from the old-age disorders such as arteriosclerosis or senile brain disability. The other half of the new patients are distributed through many miscellaneous categories.

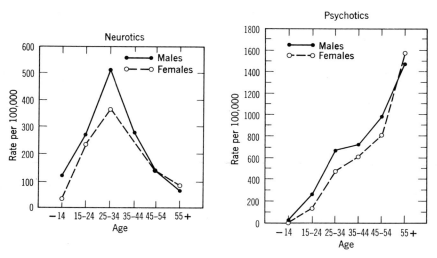

Figure 4-7. Prevalence of neurotic and psychotic patients in the New Haven community by age and sex (Hollingshead, 1958, pp. 430, 431).

The senile disorders are all based on organic changes in later life; schizophrenia, on the other hand, is a *functional,* or nonorganic, disorder which appears more often in the young. Since the schizophrenic is younger at admission, he stays hospitalized longer than the senile patient who may stay only a year or two prior to death. A more extensive discussion of the details of psychopathology and therapy is in Chapter 8.

It is well to remember, however, that it is easy to overexaggerate the impact of senile diseases. No more than 2 percent of the older age group can expect to be hospitalized for mental illness (Birren, 1964), a figure not significantly different from other age groups. It is important to note, too, that the physiological changes associated with old age, such as arteriosclerosis, do not necessarily bring the behavioral changes commonly assumed in senility.

RETIREMENT

The effects of retirement on personality can be significant; this is a critical point in the life of someone, particularly the male, who has kept busy and happy in an occupation of his choosing. For some, the period of retirement may be eagerly awaited, however; many government employees opt for early retirement when this is available to them.

As has been the case with other aspects of the aging process, the effects of retirement on personality show a range of individual differences. Physical changes do not occur at the same rate or in the same way for everyone nor is there a typical pattern of adjustment in retirement. Some workers may be vigorous and alert until forced to retire. Then illness or senility may set in as a result of their being unable to cope with the enforced boredom. Others keep busy with activities they had always wanted to pursue but never could. Cavan et al. (1949) present "word portraits" assembled in a study of old age and retirement. The extensive variation in behavior seen in only a small number of individuals impresses the reader with the variety of response; the range of behavior may be greater here than at any other stage or condition of life.

A further picture of personality differences emerges from research known as the "Berkeley Studies" (Reichard et. al., 1962). Compared with preretirement men, the retired were characterized by less defensiveness and insecurity. The older were generally (though not all) more satisfied with their lives or more accepting of the course of events in their pasts. The investigation found a positive relationship between earlier success, higher education, and good health, on the one hand, and successful aging patterns on the other. Those who adapted

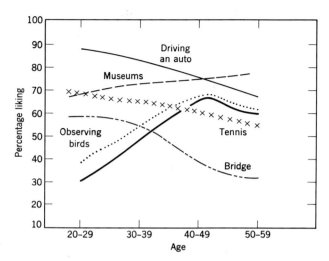

Figure 4-8. Changes in interests with age (Pressey and Kuhlen, 1957).

well continued to seek out healthy social relationships as they had in the past. Life for them produced even less stress than earlier.

INTERESTS AND ATTITUDES

Some changes in interests over the age span have been concisely sketched by Pressey and Kuhlen (1957) and reproduced here as Figure 4-8. The authors used results of the Strong Vocational Interest Blank to determine the interests of a sample of individuals in each age bracket. The resulting patterns show a trend toward less competitive activities and less excitement but no lessening of intellectual activities. Meyersohn (1961) indicates that while television viewing remains unchanged over the life span in terms of hours spent, preferences indicate a shift to variety or game programs in later life. The interests of the young are differentiated more on the basis of sex. Boys find more appeal in football, fishing, marbles, bicycles, and machinery, while girls play house, hopscotch, sew, and play at cooking. Adolescents keep somewhat the same patterns of "masculine" and "feminine" interests but with some close parallels at certain points. Table 4-1, for instance, shows reading to be the most favored activity for girls while it is in second place for boys. Not only is the percentage for girls much higher than for boys, but the content of the material read differs significantly.

Table 4-1.   Percentage of Adolescents Engaging in
Certain Leisure Time Activities (Bell, 1938)

Activity	Boys		Girls	
	Percent	Rank	Percent	Rank
Individual sports	22	1	11	5
Reading	17	2	35	1
Team games	16	3	1	8
Loafing	13	4	5	6
Dating and dancing	11	5	14	2
Movies	9	6	12	4
Hobbies	6	7	13	3
Radio	2	8	2	7

Social and Cultural Factors

While most people recognize at least the surface aspects of the physical changes which occur in development throughout the life span, their attention may not be focused on the important effects of the immediate environment on the growing person. Socioeconomic forces in society at large shape the individual in his move toward maturity and affect his outlook and that of others toward him in his old age.

ATTITUDES OF SOCIETY

Prevalent views of individuals and groups in society usually appear with particular "themes" for each age grouping. These outlooks are usually oversimplified in presenting a picture of "typical" behavior. They may be termed *stereotypes* or a sort of shorthand method of describing behavior. We often associate sagacity and achievement with age, assign speed and excitability to youth, and generally attribute to either sex a set of characteristics that individuals may or may not possess. In our society the elder male has been the one who occupies a position of responsibility, and legal restrictions, for instance, follow suit. No one is regarded as responsible for his commercial transaction (with exceptions, of course) until the "magic age" of 21. Until then, contracts by infants (anyone under 21) may be repudiated by them. Political participation is also a privilege accorded only to those who have passed that magic milestone. All these decisions represent the attitudes of society, no matter how they may be expressed.

In much the same way, 65 is looked on as a significant milestone. In practice it may do more in shaping people's behavior than any other age although 35 as a cut-off point consideration for employment by industry runs a close second. We should ask whether these points in the age span represent a significant boundary and, if so, how much it affects the situation. The extensive variation in behavior encountered in answering the questions leads us to some conclusions. Certainly all of us have encountered "old maids" at 22 and "youngsters" of 70. Individuals show enough variability to dispel most stereotypes as to behavior.

How then have we arrived at certain cut-off points? The age of 65 as a criterion age for retirement is used undoubtedly because a group of Federal civil servants somewhat arbitrarily picked that figure as the start for OASI or Social Security. The setting of adulthood at 21 is somewhat more obscure. At any rate, it seems to be part of the age-old use of multiples of seven for age boundaries—seven as the "age of reason" and 14 as the "age of consent." Stereotypes may be false, or partially so, in concepts of age and behavior. More important than their validity, however, is the fact that their existence sometimes causes reactions to them as if they were true. If company personnel have generally believed a man is "over the hill at 40," this feeling remains in their office behavior despite the federal statute regulating the discrimination in hiring on the basis of age.

Variations occur, of course, not only between societies but also within them from level to level; changes over time also take place. Attitudes toward the aged have changed from an earlier era when elderly parents were the responsibility of the children. Changes in patterns of living along with the greater inclination to have community agencies play a role are immediate factors in present attitudes toward the aged. The laws covering age discrimination also reflect changing attitudes, at least on the part of some members of society.

Companies, too, have differed in their general frame of reference with respect to aging and employment. Some companies maintain a great deal of pride in being able to employ an individual over most of his life span and prestige accrues to the older employee in all positions, especially at the skilled and managerial levels. Other companies have a strict policy of retirement at 65 or even before. While this is not unusual, in some organizations the pressure on the older workers to leave and make room for the younger ones on the treadmill behind them makes the company policy more emphatic.

SOCIOECONOMIC INFLUENCES

The development of the individual proceeds under the influences of many socializing forces and agencies, from the nuclear family to more distant or global groupings. The attitudes in different strata of society, if they are different, help shape the person in that level or grouping accordingly. Parents are apt to raise their children in the same way they were raised, whether or not they recognize this in their behavior. When the broader social influences arising from class placement do play a role, their effects are perpetuated through future generations.

Child-Rearing Practices

Parents in higher socioeconomic levels have traditionally been among the first to adopt those practices of rearing children which have been promoted by "experts" and have done so with greater enthusiasm. This has had its effect on the behavior of the developing individual. There is some later evidence, however, that indicates that these class differences may be narrowing (Bronfenbrenner, 1958). Perhaps this is because more information is being communicated these days to reduce the transmission lag between the classes, although Bronfenbrenner hypothesizes that it results from the increasing income and education of the working classes. Differences in attitudes and other aspects of behavior seem to persist in the parent-child relationships, however, as the result of differences between classes. Bronfenbrenner has reviewed studies from widely separated locales and has summarized the differences which have emerged. Lower-class families, in general, seem to exercise less control over aggression and sexual expression. Discipline is more physical as opposed to the greater use of reasoning in higher socioeconomic levels. Middle-class parents are more prone to stress achievement and encourage education. A more equalitarian atmosphere is fostered in middle- and upper-class homes as opposed to the more rigid authoritarianism enforced by physical punishment in groups lower on the scale.

Lest anyone doubt that attitudes of parents have any influence on their children, results from several research studies have indicated close correspondence between family members in attitudes and values. The classic study by Newcomb and Svehla (1937) showed the high correlation between attitudes of parents and children with a further consistency in patterns. The relationship between parents and children was higher than that between the children and their peers. The correlation in attitudes between the children and their teachers was even lower than in the first two comparisons.

Beyond the Family

There are other influences beyond those arising from the social placement of the family as individuals are exposed to agencies outside the home, particularly the school. The difference in values, however, may give rise to conflicts of roles, attitudes, and values in the person. Too great a gulf to bridge may foster delinquency, school "dropout," or further dysfunctional behavior. On the other hand, sometimes the outside agency helps to alleviate emotional problems arising in the immediate home environment. Children from broken homes or disrupted families may find release in school or play activity. Membership in social groups may provide a base for a better personality integration in the developing individuals. Riley et al. (1961), for instance, found a strong relief from intrafamily tensions through membership in a peer group.

Class membership may be related to basic factors such as health, morale, and attainment. Generally, the higher the social-class level, the more the person expects and the greater are his attainments. Higher educational level, better dietary habits, better housing facilities provide not only a higher level of physical hygiene but of mental hygiene as well. All the positive factors have a tendency to be interrelated so that the picture is one of greater accomplishment and greater "happiness." Kutner et al. (1956), in a study of a sample of persons over 60 in New York, found that high morale is associated with high economic status. Lower levels of satisfaction at the lower socioeconomic levels were associated with the drudgery that comes with less respected occupational placement. The authors effectively dispelled the old stereotype "poor but happy."

Mental Illness

The classic study of a community and its population by Hollingshead and Redlich (1958) found a relationship between class placement and types of mental illness. Psychoses were most often diagnosed in the lower classes; by age 55 a ratio of 7 to 1 was found between the upper and lower class levels in the community. There was a slight increase in neurotic disorders in going from the lowest class to the top. The importance of the social factors throughout the life span of the individual is emphasized by a similar study which concluded that lower parental socioeconomic status tends to provide the child with smaller chances of achieving a well state during adulthood (Srole et al., 1962).

Physical Disability

In the physical area the same relationships between socioeconomic status and health are present. The lower income groups, when this is taken as an indication of socioeconomic level, show a higher disability rate (Birren, 1964). Older persons, on the basis of lower income, may represent a proportionately greater part of the group but, even when it is held constant, the relationship still holds. In studying rejections for Selective Service, mortality rates, and socioeconomic status, Birren (1964) found that differences in health statistics between whites and Negroes disappeared when both groups were equated on the basis of income, occupation, and place of residence. This points out a clear basis in socioeconomic factors rather than ethnic or racial ones.

Achievement

Questions of occupational achievement or productivity do not occur in a society until adulthood; in this respect dependency on others is more prolonged in western culture, and full participation in the society comes later than in preliterate or simple cultures. The entry into meaningful employment is even more delayed at higher professional levels where preparation for work takes more time. The age span considered meaningful for us in this section of the chapter is, therefore, from the late teens to the 70's and beyond.

EMPLOYMENT PATTERNS WITH AGE

The percentage of active workers past age 65 has showed a steady decline in the United States since the turn of the century. In 1900 about two-thirds of males over age 65 were still in the labor force, while by 1962 this figure was about one-third (Birren, 1964). Although this trend brings with it mixed results in a social context, the question paramount at this point is whether there are any relationships between age and productivity.

Data on age and productivity are usually very difficult to interpret. Physical or physiological factors may play a heavier role in performance on unskilled and semiskilled jobs than they do for professional and managerial positions. Even at lower levels, however, jobs are often "age-graded" in the sense that workers gradually shift into different positions as they get older, whether or not there is any specific policy of the company to this effect. An additional factor to consider is that evaluation of workers may be based more on their external characteristics. Age is often enough to place the worker into a higher category, since we usually regard greater experience and age as being closely related and, therefore, efficiency often correlates with age. Often, however, this view is altered when it is the opinion of supervisors that their older workers are slower to learn than the younger ones. Without any better objective evidence, either view may be a misleading myth or stereotype. Further complications of data come from the conditions of work; if production seldom exceeds

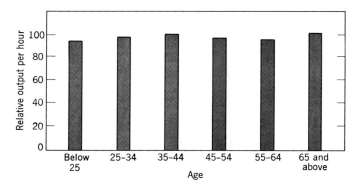

Figure 4-9. Relative output per hour of women office workers by age (U.S. Department of Labor, 1956).

a modest level of output, the measures of performance may not show any significant differences between individuals.

Job Productivity

A study of women office workers by the U.S. Department of Labor (1956) showed no essential difference in output over the age range from under 25 to 65 and over (Figure 4-9). The younger women were even slightly below the levels achieved by the older women. In a study of sales activity, Maher (1955) obtained relationships between age and performance on a large sample of salesmen. Older salesmen turned out to be better than the younger ones; some correlations between age and other variables were as indicated below.

Age and knowledge of products	.59
Age and customer relations	.30
Age and sales	.28
Age and overall sales ability	.28

It was also found that the salesmen over age 60 were selling, on a per man basis, over 50 percent more than those of age 30.

Further evidence of the absence of significant differences in work performance at various ages comes from a study by Bowers (1952) where for traits such as accuracy, initiative, job knowledge, tactfulness, and cooperativeness there was no difference between age groupings from ages 18 to over 60. Older workers were considered slower but not much so. They were rated higher on steadiness and conscientiousness.

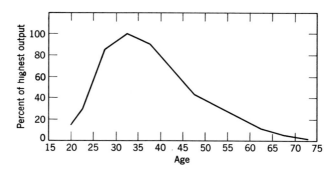

Figure 4-10.   Age and significant contributions by chemists (Lehman, 1953, p. 15).

Professional Achievement

Achievement of individuals at a higher occupational level has been extensively studied by Lehman (1953) who compiled biographical as well as achievement data from a wide variety of sources. He was then able to sketch some relationships between age and scientific or literary accomplishment. In the scientific area, Lehman found that his sample of chemists made their greatest contributions during the period between ages 35 and 40. Using this peak period as 100 percent, the curve sketched in Figure 4-10 indicates the percentage of the peak period, which is represented by the contributions of chemists at different ages. At age 50, for instance, these same chemists make about 40 percent of the contributions they made ten to 15 years earlier. It seems that

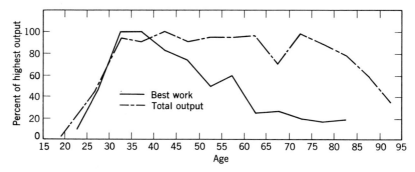

Figure 4-11.   Quantity (total output) and quality (one best treatise) of 182 deceased philosophers (Lehman, 1953, p. 47).

in the physical sciences and mathematics an individual may do significant work early as the result of the mastery of a highly specific set of facts. In an area such as philosophy, outstanding work also may come fairly early as well but, perhaps more important, total output is maintained at the same level over decades (Figure 4-11).

In industry, figures on placement show a somewhat different pattern. The relationship between age and industrial leadership is shown in Figure 4-12 where the solid curve shows a normal distribution of a sample of almost 3000 business leaders around a mean age of 57. The dotted curve in the figure corrects for the disproportionate numbers of young people in our population and puts a theoretical peak at a more advanced age.

Income may be one further measurement of achievement; in some areas it may be the only measure available. Gordon (1960) collected income data of various groups and individuals in the United States for two separate years, 1948 and 1957. The subsequent distributions show, first of all, the disparity between men and women. More important, it indicates that rise in personal income is greatest over the years mentioned in the middle age brackets; not much change takes place in the teens or beyond 65. Income is at a steady high level from age 35 to 55 with the highest earning power overall at age 45 (Figure 4-13).

OTHER FACTORS IN ACHIEVEMENT

Some aspects of the job situation affect performance only indirectly and yet may be so influential that they cannot be ignored in a survey of this

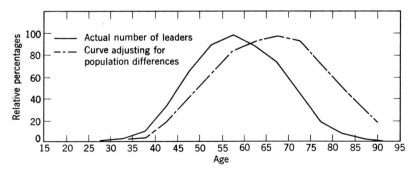

Figure 4-12. Age versus outstanding commercial and industrial leadership (Lehman, 1953, p. 157).

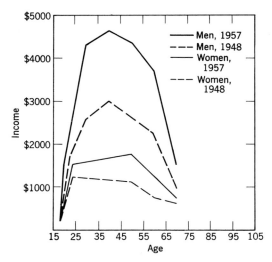

Figure 4-13.   Median income by age for men and women in the United States in 1948 and 1957 (Gordon, 1960).

nature. Total output could vary as the result of these more than through many direct influences.

Absenteeism

While many of the direct indications of achievement already presented above may be difficult to interpret at times, in the matter of absenteeism we have clear-cut and continuing evidence. From many reports it is clear that conscientiousness of attendance at the job increases with age. There is less absenteeism among the older workers than among the young. Kahne et al. (1957) demonstrated that the absence rate of workers over 45 was far less than that of workers below 45, with the 45–55 age bracket slightly superior to the still older ones. This difference resulted from somewhat longer absences among the over 55 group. When the older workers are absent (not often), the period of absence is longer, but the younger workers are absent more often. Van Zelst (1954) confirmed these findings in his studies of age and accidents.

Reassignment

It has been noted that the older worker may drift off into easier employment or do the job at a level of activity where inadequacies do not manifest themselves. This same approach may be used more positively by companies to utilize their older workers more effectively. Gilmer (1966) points out an extensive survey for a New York State legislative committee which noted widespread attempts by industrial organizations to redesign the job or reassign workers to jobs in which they might function better. As a result, most concerns have found benefits accruing from better performance on the job along with the superior attendance at work by older workers.

ACCIDENTS

The frequency of accidents and their severity may differ at various points in the developmental continuum, but the findings are not always clear. Gordon (1949) points out that deaths from home accidents in 1945 were highest in those below age five or past 65; those in between suffered fewer deaths even though they were most active. This finding underestimates the importance, however, of accidents for children and young adults which are the principal causes of death for this group. Sex plays a role as well; young males experience more accidents than young females, though this relationship is reversed beyond age 65.

The finding that young males have more accidents than young females, particularly in motor vehicles, is not a novel statistic; insurance companies, driver education programs, state police, and almost everyone else accepts this as a fact. The raw data indicate female superiority in driving yet, when analyzed further, several points may be raised. No doubt the male role in our society calls for men and boys to be dominant and aggressive. Males "must" assert their masculinity, and they are more apt to do the driving on dates. At a younger age men spend three times as much time behind the wheel as do the women, drive more at night, and are less supervised by parents than are girl drivers. When these social and psychological factors are added to the situation, the driving superiority of women tends to disappear. When women begin to drive more, to schools and supermarkets, their accidents increase (McFarland and Moore, 1960). While an understanding of these social foundations may not necessarily change the insurance rates for young drivers, the analysis does point out a few of the difficult problems of interpretation of accident statistics.

Accidents on the job vary by age with results and interpretation similarly difficult. King (1955) found that a simple positive relationship between age and accidents was misleading in that different types of accidents affected younger and older agricultural workers. Younger workers had injuries to parts of the body used in their work while older workers had injuries not directly related to their job. King identified the difference as being due to different exposure to risk, particularly in the greater skill with tools as the result of experience. Van Zelst (1954) found that the younger workers had more accidents than did the older workers. It was suggested that younger employees are not as familiar with industrial plant hazards and also have a tendency to be placed in the more hazardous job positions. That the younger employee may be more impulsive and less cautious is a strong possibility as well. At least one earlier study (Stevens, 1929) has shown, however, that older employees had more than their share of accidents. This may be simply an indication that variation from one industry to another could exist or that other circumstances may vary to produce different results.

Age—Recapitulation

One last comprehensive look at the life span of the human being underscores the importance of individual differences. While there may be some characteristics of different age groups or some age-related aspects of behavior may emerge, one must always be careful in making general statements about the abilities of individuals of different ages. Subjects may or may not have certain capabilities; rather, we may, because of myths or stereotypes based on age, endow them with certain qualities. Our perception of their actions will be moulded accordingly.

Differences between people of the same age may be great as the result of social and personality factors; there may be wide variations in basic physical factors as well. Selye (1956) has noted that the amount of "wear and tear" to which the person has been exposed, not time elapsed since birth, is a true measure of physiological aging. While physiological age may be more important for performance in unskilled or manual tasks, it does play a role in all types of activities. More important is a reminder that one objective fact, such as chronological age, may not be an accurate indicator of ability or capacity. Other factors may be equally responsible for the wide range of differences in the behavior of individuals.

Summary

The development of an individual unfolds through a steady sequence past maturity and into the stages of nongrowth to a terminal point. What people at all ages are like, what they can do, and how they are affected are some of the most important questions a behavioral scientist can ask as he views the long span of an individual's existence. Knowledge of the accumulating experience of people is valuable in itself and in serving as a basis for present understanding of their behavior and prediction of future activity.

The process of development begins before birth and has antecedents prior to that. How much of our functioning is due to heredity and how much to environment is more than a scientific question, since it represents some fundamental assumptions of most people about human behavior.

Stages of development have been identified in various ways by investigators, both in a broad framework over the entire span or in specific ages and areas such as cognition.

Individual differences are basic facts in the study of behavior, as even the uninitiated are aware. What is not as obvious is the exact distribution of traits or characteristics such as mental ability, aptitude, interests, and personality. Most traits are distributed in the population in a fashion that finds a majority of individuals clustered in the center of the range with fewer and fewer to be found toward the extreme positions along the continuum.

Some hidden dangers lie in the appraisal of abilities or other traits in an applied situation. Testing has long been a source of anxiety to many people as, first, an invasion of privacy and, second, a technique that has not been valid in many situations. Concern with ethical problems increasingly occupies the attention of researchers; the matter of qualifications is less difficult in the hands of qualified personnel with the knowledge built up over a longer time of the attributes and drawbacks of the various measures. The knowledgeable user is familiar with the meaning of scores and the fundamental characteristics of tests in addition to the uses of measures to diagnose for placement of individuals as well as to predict performance in any organizational setting.

Individuality is based on the biological mechanisms steered by heredity, with adaptations as the result of environmental influences. The individual, even though he bears some resemblance to others in form and developmental patterns, is a unique person. This should be kept in mind even though discussions of development must, of necessity, refer to a summary picture of activity with respect to age.

Input areas show some decline at about age 70 from the peaks of sensitivity in the teens, but the difference usually amounts to 20 percent or less and the relative number of individuals with serious defects remains under 10 percent.

Cognitive processes also show only a small decline in overall level between the teens and the 70's, though there may be variations with respect to different subareas. Learning new things and solving problems shows some decline which is compensated for by an increase in reasoning and general information. Language, once built on favorable aptitude and environmental bases, continues at a steady level through the years.

Adult personality shows the impact of early experiences. Not only is there a consistency in personality patterns through the years, but there is a continuation of child-rearing patterns through generations.

Mental health has many implications for the community beyond individual involvement. Psychotic disorders rise with age, though neurotic disorders show a peak at about 35.

Retirement may be stressful for many workers. Those who have successfully coped with stress in their lifetime are able to adjust better to the problems of enforced retirement.

Interests change through the life span from active and competitive to sedentary and integrative.

Attitudes of society have formed in stereotypes, some widely held, about age and its concommitants. The attitudes of a group toward the youthful or aged can shape the behavior of the age groups as much as any other factor can. More attention should be paid to actual abilities and performance of persons than to notions that may not be accurate.

Socioeconomic factors play a vital role in shaping behavior. The influences arise from child-rearing practices or from the broader influences of the class or geographic membership group. Mental and physical health is apt to be poorer in the lower socioeconomic levels.

Performance on the job seems to vary little with age; older workers perform as well as younger workers and, in addition, are less likely to be absent or have accidents. Knowledge of the job is apt to be higher at older age levels. Contributions in arts and science can vary with age. While the integrative areas such as philosophy may show output from men of all ages, a definite peak for contributions by scientists and mathematicians comes in the 30's. Industrial leadership is concentrated in the age group from 50 to 60.

A look back at research findings on the abilities, aptitudes, and achievement of individuals of all ages highlights the individual variability to be found at all levels. Social and personality factors as well as physical ones play an important role in shaping performance throughout the life span. Attention should be paid to these rather than to routine evaluations or stereotypes about what people are like or can do.

Bibliography

Aldrich, C. and Mendkoff, E. (1963). Relocation of the aged and disabled: a mortality study. *Journal of the American Geriatric Society,* **11**, 185–194.

Allport, G., Vernon, P., and Lindzey, G. (1960). *A study of values* (3rd ed.). Boston: Houghton-Mifflin.

Amrine, M. (1965). The 1965 Congressional inquiry into testing: a commentary. *American Psychologist,* **20**, 859–870.

Bell, H. (1938). *Youth tell their story.* Washington, D.C.: American Council on Education.

Birren, J., ed. (1959). *Handbook of aging and the individual.* Chicago: University of Chicago Press.

Birren, J. (1964). *The psychology of aging.* Englewood Cliffs, N.J.: Prentice-Hall.

Bowers, W. (1952). An appraisal of worker characteristics as related to age. *Journal of Applied Psychology,* **36,** 296–300.

Bowlby, J. (1952). *Maternal care and mental health.* World Health Organization, Monograph Series No. 2.

Braun, H. and Geiselhart, R. (1959). Age differences in the acquisition and extinction of the conditioned eyelid response. *Journal of Experimental Psychology,* **57,** 386–388.

Bronfenbrenner, U. (1958). Socialization and social class through time and space. In Maccoby, E. et al. (eds.). *Readings in social psychology* (3rd ed.). New York: Holt, Rinehart and Winston.

Cavan, R., Burgess, E., Havighurst, R., and Goldhammer, H. (1949). *Personal adjustment in old age.* Chicago: Science Research Associates.

Chapanis, A. (1950). Relationships between age, visual acuity and color vision. *Human Biology,* **22,** 1–31.

Chown, S. (1961). Age and the rigidities. *Journal of Gerontology,* **16,** 353–362.

Cooper, R., Bilash, I., and Zubek, J. (1959). The effect of age on taste sensitivity. *Journal of Gerontology,* **14,** 56–58.

Crook, M., Alexander, E., Anderson, E., Coules, J., Hanson, J., and Jeffries, N. *Age and form perception,* USAF School of Aviation Medicine, Randolph AFB, Texas, Report No. 57–124.

Dennis, W. and Dennis, M., (1940). The effect of cradling practices upon the onset of walking in Hopi children. *Journal of Genetic Psychology,* **56,** 77–86.

Erikson, E. (1963). *Childhood and society* (2nd ed.). New York: Norton.

Foulds, G. and Raven, J. (1948). Normal changes in the mental abilities of adults as age advances. *Journal of Mental Science,* **94,** 133–142.

Friend, C. and Zubek, J. (1958). The effects of age on critical thinking ability. *Journal of Gerontology,* **13,** 407–413.

Gesell, A. and Thompson, H. (1943). Learning and maturation in identical twins: An experimental analysis by the method of co-twin control. In Barker, R., Kounin, J., and Wright, H. (eds.). *Child behavior and development.* New York: McGraw-Hill.

Gilmer, B. (1966). *Industrial psychology* (2nd ed.). New York: McGraw-Hill.

Gordon, J. (1949). The epidemiology of accidents. *American Journal of Public Health,* **39**, 504–515.

Gordon, M. (1960). Aging and income security. In Tibbitts, C. (ed.). *Handbook of social gerontology.* Chicago: University of Chicago Press, 208–260.

Harlow, H. and Harlow, M. (1962). The effect of rearing conditions on behavior. *Bulletin of the Menninger Clinic,* **26**, 213–224.

Hollingshead, A. (1958). Factors associated with prevalence of mental illness. In Maccoby, E. et al. (eds.). *Readings in social psychology.* New York: Holt, 425–436.

Hollingshead, A. and Redlich, F. (1958). *Social class and mental illness.* New York: Wiley.

Inhelder, B. and Piaget, J. (1958). *The growth of logical thinking from childhood to adolescence.* New York: Basic Books.

Jones, H. and Conrad, H. (1933). The growth and decline of intelligence: A study of a homogeneous group between ages of 10 and 60. *Genetic Psychology Monographs,* **13**, 223–298.

Kahne, H., Ryder, C., Shegireff, L., and Wyshak, G. (1957). Don't take the older workers for granted. *Harvard Business Review,* **35**, 90–94.

Kelly, E. (1955). Consistency of adult personality. *American Psychologist,* **10**, 659–681.

King, H. (1955). An age-analysis of some agricultural accidents. *Occupational Psychology,* **29**(4), 245–253.

Kutner, B., Fanshel, D., Togo, A., and Langner, T. (1956). *Five hundred over sixty.* New York: Russell Sage Foundation.

Landahl, H. and Birren, J. (1959). Effects of age on the discrimination of lifted weights. *Journal of Gerontology,* **14**, 48–55.

Lehman, H. (1953). *Age and achievement.* Princeton: Princeton University Press.

McClelland, D., Atkinson, J., Clark, R., and Lowell, E. (1953). *The achievement motive.* New York: Appleton-Century-Crofts.

McFarland, R. and Moore, R. (1960). *Youth and the automobile.* Washington, D.C.: Golden Anniversary White House Conference on Children and Youth, Inc.

Maher, H. (1955). Age and performance of two work groups. *Journal of Gerontology,* **10**, 448–451.

Mead, M. (1928). *Coming of age in Samoa.* New York: Morrow.

Meyersohn, R. (1961). A critical examination of commercial entertainment. In Kleemeier, R. (ed.). *Aging and leisure.* London: Oxford University Press, 243–272.

Morgan, C. and King, R. (1966). *Introduction to psychology* (3rd ed.). New York: McGraw-Hill.

Mussen, P. (1963). *The psychological development of the child.* Englewood Cliffs, N.J.: Prentice-Hall.

Newcomb, T. and Svehla, G. (1937). Intra-family relationship in attitude. *Sociometry,* **1,** 180–205.

Pressey, S. and Kuhlen, R. (1957). *Psychological development through the life span.* New York: Harper and Row.

Reichard, S., Livson, F., and Petersen, P. (1962). *Aging and personality.* New York: Wiley.

Riley, M., Riley, J., and Moore, M. (1961). Adolescent values and the Riesman typology. In Lipset, S. and Lowenthal, L. (eds.). *Culture and social character.* New York: Free Press.

Ruebhausen, O. and Brim, O. (1966). Privacy and behavioral research. *American Psychologist,* **21,** 423–437.

Selye, H. (1956). *The stress of life.* New York: McGraw-Hill.

Sherman, E. and Robilland, E. (1960). Sensitivity to pain in the aged. *Canadian Medical Association Journal,* **83,** 944–947.

Srole, L., Langner, T., Michael, S., Opler, M., and Rennie, T. (1962). *Mental health in the metropolis.* New York: McGraw-Hill.

Stevens, A. (1929). Accidents of older workers: relation of age to extent of disability. *Personnel Journal,* **8,** 138–145.

Thaler, M. (1956). Relationships among Wechsler, Weigl, Rorschach, EEG findings, and abstract—concrete behavior in a group of normal aged subjects. *Journal of Gerontology,* **11,** 404–409.

Tobin, S. and Neugarten, B. (1961). Life satisfaction and social interaction in the aging. *Journal of Gerontology,* **16,** 344–346.

U.S. Department of Health, Education and Welfare (1959). *Impairments by type, sex, and age.* Washington, D.C.: Government Printing Office, Series B-9.

U.S. Department of Labor (1956). *Job performance and age: a study of measurement.* Washington, D.C.: Government Printing Office, Bureau of Labor Statistics, Bulletin No. 1203.

U.S. Department of Labor (1963). *Industrial retraining programs for technological change.* Washington, D.C.: Government Printing Office, Bureau of Labor Statistics, Bulletin No. 1368.

Van Zelst, R. (1954). The effect of age and experience upon accident rate. *Journal of Applied Psychology,* **38,** 313–317.

Welford, A. (1958). *Aging and human skill.* London: Oxford University Press.

5

Behavior: An
Input-Output
System

The behavior of an individual is based, first of all, on the information that comes in from the outside. Without a stimulus (the physical energy that excites receptors) there is no input, that is, no information that can be handled by the internal processes prior to action by the organism. The entire situation has traditionally been described as a stimulus-response process, especially by psychologists who consider the S-R bond to be basic in behavior. To those concerned with the organism a little more, the formulation would appear as S-O-R, the O standing for the organism.

Model of a System

It may be more advantageous in many respects to view this process from a standpoint that emphasizes the systematic interrelationships within and without the functioning entity. To conceive of the organism and the contiguous variables as a system may seem strange at first, but a description of behavior in terms of a systems model can foster a better appraisal of the processes involved. We know from Chapter 1 that the value of a model lies in the opportunity to approach some visualization of reality; the model system sketched in Figure 5-1 attempts to do this. The model accounts for inputs and outputs, or stimuli and responses, through a central processing function. This central area is the important area of cognition composed, for our purposes here, of perception, core processes, and decision making. Central information processing includes the function of information storage or, as it is more commonly known, memory. The separation in the model into discrete functions makes it easier

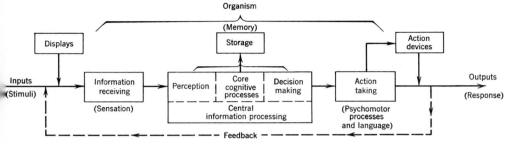

Figure 5-1. A systems model of behavior.

to visualize the difference between information receiving, for instance, and the central process of perception. Also, stimuli (inputs) are clearly separable from sensation (information receiving).

Feedback is an important aspect of behavior. This concept refers to the return of information from the outputs to serve as further inputs. The process changes the later outputs as the system corrects or alters its functioning. The notion of feedback is a central one in the area of cybernetics (Wiener, 1948) or the description of behavior as a control or steering process. The presence of feedback information is the basis for a *closed-loop system*. The process in this type of system is a continuous one under control as the result of the information being fed back through the system. A *line system* is one that has no control once it is activated; it continues functioning without the altering of its activity through feedback. Man functions as a closed-loop system, since the feedback alters performance to keep the activity under control. A guided missile operates in basically the same fashion.

When systems theorists speak of a man-machine system, they are introducing no new views. The extension of the organism into a broader system involves the same concepts as are useful in describing the controlled functioning of the person. The model in Figure 5-1 covers both the human organism and the "hardware" with which he is surrounded.

Inputs and Information Receiving

The functioning of a system first depends on the inputs that are introduced. In considering behavior as a system, the inputs are presented through displays and are received by the sense receptors. These, in turn, send the information along in a different form to the central processing units of the system, the cognitive functions.

DISPLAYS

The term display is used in systems to refer to a presentation of information by means of symbols. Information in the environment is very often in a form that cannot be introduced into the system; conversion of that information to a form that can be presented to the senses and the presentation of that information is the task of the display. Information such as speed, air pressure, or temperature can be sensed by an individual only imperfectly; more accurate information is given in visual form from a dial, measuring device, or other mechanism.

Displays are possible in many forms with as many variations as there are senses. Visual displays are most often met, although auditory displays are also common. Information, too, can be converted to signals which are capable of being picked up by the skin senses or the olfactory and taste sense receptors. In any of the sense areas the fundamental concern of the systems analyst is the presentation of the maximum amount of information in the quickest and most effective way possible. The proper reading of an altimeter becomes crucial for the airline pilot and his passengers. Other readings may not be as immediately critical but can, in the long run, be the basis for success or failure in industrial or other tasks.

The purpose of displays is to provide readings which may be processed. These readings are usually of a quantitative nature, but they may be qualitative as well. Even simpler is a reading that is only a check of the system or its functioning.

The accuracy and speed of such readings are crucial questions; the efficiency with which the displays can function are questions of design.

A few general principles of display design may be stated as follows.

(a)   Single positions for fixation of attention are superior to those arrangements where many refixations are possible. The "open window" or counter is superior to the moving dial (Figure 5-2).

(b)   Where movement is called for, the entire range should be identified.

(c)   Markings should be scaled to the smallest unit to be read; if time is limited, fewer markings should then be used.

(d)   Numerals should be horizontal to the line of sight, not obscured by the pointers, and the direction of increase in the scale values indicated (Fitts, 1951; McCormick, 1957).

Many other specific aspects may be of importance. The height and width of letters, their shape, the color of figure and ground—all should be considered, whether it be as prosaic as a highway sign or as complex as a pilot's cabin in an aircraft.

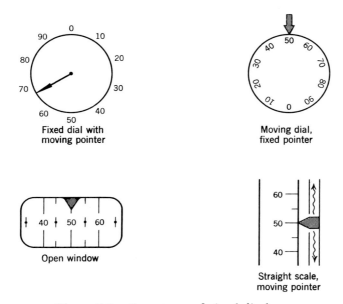

Figure 5-2.   Some types of visual displays.

SENSE RECEPTORS

All of the foregoing physical factors are of little consequence in behavior unless they are introduced into the human part of the system. Sensory equipment has the task of receiving and relaying the physical changes taking place on the outside.

Vision

Most of the information we receive from the world comes via this sense-receptor area. The eye is an instrument capable of extraordinary feats. Under proper conditions it can see the flare of a match 50 miles away, or view a wire $\frac{1}{16}$ inch in diameter at a distance of $\frac{1}{2}$ mile. The stimuli that we eventually experience as light are really emissions or reflections of electromagnetic energy. Not all of this radiant energy can be received by the human eye; it can pick up only a small part of the electromagnetic energy continuum. This energy may be considered to be transmitted in wave lengths from a frequency as short as 10–14 meters to a length of 10^{-8} meter. Only a small part of that frequency range is visible to the human eye—a narrow band near 10^{-6} meter or from about 400 to almost 800 millimicrons (a millimicron is one thousandth of a millionth of a meter).

The eye often has been compared to a camera, and this analogy is somewhat valid. Light comes through a lens with a mechanism for altering the opening through which the light must travel. The *iris,* the colored part of the eye, changes the size of the *pupil,* the opening, to admit the required amount of light. This change occurs without control on our part; it is a reflex action. The image is projected on the rear wall of the eyeball, just as the image in a camera is focused on the photographic film at the back. The sensitive wall is known as the *retina* and is composed of very small cells shaped like rods and cones. The cones are concentrated in the center, especially in a very sensitive spot called the fovea; the rods are more common at the periphery of the retina. The cones are believed to be more important than rods for color vision or may even be the sole receptors for color.

The lens of the eye changes shape to focus an image on the retina. When the lens bulges, the focal point is closer to the lens; when the lens flattens, the focus is farther back. An inability of the lens to focus the image on the retina causes the visual difficulties of near and farsightedness. Further problems arise when, because of imperfections in the lens, the image is distorted (astigmatism).

Sensitivity of the eyes may be of importance in many ways. The smallest amount of light that may be seen (absolute threshold) and the barest difference that may be seen between two lights (contrast threshold) are two aspects of interest. Another type of sensitivity is that of dark adaptation or ability to adjust to lowered illumination.

In the matter of color sensitivity, it is often said that "all cats are gray at night" or that colors are difficult if not impossible to perceive under reduced illumination. Not only is everything gray at the extreme but the colors are relatively brighter or duller as the amount of light decreases. At twilight, greens and blues seem brighter than reds while the opposite is true in intense sunlight. This phenomenon, known as the *Purkinje effect,* adds to the problems of sensitivity. For instance, courtroom testimony based on observations at dusk or night may be quite inadequate or misleading. Additional difficulty comes with the use of lights with properties that alter the color characteristics of the product.

Color has been used effectively in many situations. In advertising, the ads in color attract more attention from the readers than do those in black and white (Lucas and Britt, 1950). While certain colors seem to be associated with specific moods or environments, there is little evidence that people's behavior is seriously affected by the color alone. A more important impact of color lies in its use in information receiving. Color coding has been employed for a significant period of time, so that red and green signify much to most people. Use of contrast, such as in diagonal yellow and black stripes, not only increases visibility but signals greater attentiveness when this type of coding is learned. Contrast and color coding may be of importance in uses ranging from highway signs to the increase in legibility of books and periodicals.

Acuity, or the ability to see fine differences in stimuli, is the final factor to be considered. The most familiar test of visual acuity is the eye chart with letters of varying size. The designation 20/20 means that a person is able to see at 20 feet what an average person sees at that distance. Acuity of 20/200 means subnormal vision because the subject can see only those letters at 20 feet that an average person can see at 200 feet. Acuity is best in the center of the visual field; at the periphery, it is not as good. Acuity also depends on the level of illumination and how the lighting is placed. Contrast and glare also affect the way in which people see in their environment.

Audition

While vision is the most used and valued of the senses, it may be that hearing is even more important in many situations. In audition, the physical changes in air pressure are caused by the vibration of some object. These pressure waves stimulate the ear and cause us to experience sound.

Auditory stimuli have three characteristics: frequency, intensity, and complexity. Frequency is a measure of the variation in a wave and is expressed in terms of cycles per second. Intensity is the extent of the sound pressure, expressed in decibels. There is, further, complexity in the tones we actually hear since, in reality, we seldom hear pure tones of one frequency except in the laboratory. It is important to remember that these three aspects are characteristics of the physical stimuli; what we experience is not exactly the same thing. The psychological counterparts of the physical aspects may be listed as follows.

Physical	*Psychological*
Frequency (cycles per second)	Pitch
Intensity (decibels)	Loudness
Complexity	Timbre or tonal quality

None of the above attributes stands alone; in actual situations each factor alters the others. Pitch, for instance, depends not only on frequency but also on intensity. Changing pitch may be experienced without changing frequency, just by altering intensity.

The ear is the mechanism that transforms the physical pressures of the sound waves into the psychological experience. The outside fleshy part we commonly refer to as the ear has very little work to do. It only cups the sound waves to transmit them better to the internal structures. The sound waves enter the canal of the ear and strike the eardrum, causing it to vibrate. These vibrations are transmitted to the bones of the middle ear and are passed on by them to the inner ear. At this point, the actual process becomes a matter of dispute. There is no doubt, however, that electrical potentials can be recorded in the inner ear (Davis, 1959). These are nerve impulses believed to be produced by the movement of hair cells in the tiny *organ of Corti* brushing against a nearby membrane. All of this takes place within the larger structure, the fluid-filled cochlea.

The range of frequencies to which a human is sensitive runs from about 20 cycles per second (c.p.s.) to 20,000 c.p.s., although the range in which a person hears best is between 1000 and 4000 c.p.s. Other species have a higher upper limit—dogs hear sounds above 20,000 c.p.s. while bats presumably are sensitive to considerably higher frequencies.

Loss of sensitivity as well as deafness from early age causes not only problems of communication but adds emotional problems as well. We rely so much on the spoken word and receive so many of our cues from the social situation through audition that any impairment has serious consequences. Not only do we need to know what others are saying but we also need to hear ourselves speak in order to learn to speak and to continue to speak properly. The suspiciousness of the deaf, along with frequent shyness and seclusion at work and in other social situations, is not difficult to understand.

While there may be some nerve loss leading to hearing loss with older age, a more important source of loss may come as the result of exposure to high intensity noises. Glorig and Wheeler (1955) found that, with sounds of about 100 decibels intensity, greater hearing loss came with greater exposure. The hearing loss was greatest between 4000 and 8000 c.p.s. That intensity level may be found in a large weaving room or woodworking shop, although the noise inside most subway cars closely approaches it.

OTHER SENSE AREAS

The lower senses may be grouped into the *chemical senses,* which include smell and taste, the specific skin senses, and the *proprioceptive senses,* which receive information about posture and balance through receptors in the inner ear and muscles.

The Chemical Senses

This area includes the senses of smell and taste. Of the two, the most sensitive mechanisms are those involved in smell. We receive this experience when the chemical particles in the air stimulate olfactory receptors high up in the nasal passages. To get a better smell we may "sniff" to get more air up into the passages. In the same way, warm food is usually more appealing than its cold counterpart because the fragrant particles move more when hot. The sensitivity of our olfactory receptors can be very acute. Artificial musk, for instance, can be smelled when only .00004 milligram of it is present in a liter of air. Ether needs a much heavier concentration—something like 40 millionths of an ounce to a quart of air—before we can detect it (Morgan and King, 1966).

The sense of taste could justifiably be broken down into four senses because there are four separate kinds of receptors, those for sweet, salt, sour, and bitter. Each of these aspects of taste has its own kind of receptor or *taste buds* with each type of bud concentrated in specific areas of the tongue and throat.

Most of the sensations we get from eating come through the receptors of smell rather than taste. We have noticed that when we have a nose cold we just can't "taste" the food. Actually, taste is relatively unaffected; the olfactory bulb receptors are made insensitive, and it is difficult if not impossible to identify the food by taste sensations alone. When we compliment our hostess at dinner, it would be more accurate, then, to say "this food smelled good" rather than refer to taste.

While separate receptors have been identified for taste, no such simple physical categorization can be made for smell. Without a clear-cut idea of what the primary odors are, or even if they do exist, arbitrary systems must be used. There are several in use but more common among industrial chemists is the four-category system of basic odors (Crocker, 1945) which calls for acid (vinegar), burnt (roast coffee), fragrant (musk), and caprylic (goaty).

The answers to the question of what actually happens when we taste or smell remain unanswered. There must be some kind of coding of the inputs in both areas. Erickson (1963) measured the electrical responses of single fibers of a taste nerve and found that many of them responded to different taste stimuli, but to different extents. Apparently, the patterns of firing of the nerves were decoded by the cortex of the brain. With respect to olfaction, a current concept (the "lock and key" theory) considers that differently shaped molecules fit into different olfactory receptors and fire just those where the fit occurs (Amoore et al., 1964). This is a good possibility because we do know that minute traces of substances can be picked up by our receptors of smell.

The Skin Senses

Here, too, there is more than just one sense; four distinct skin senses can be identified. There are separate receptors for *hot, cold, pressure,* and *pain* with each of these kinds of receptors clustered in various broad areas of the body covering. While some cold or hot receptors, for instance, react also to pressure or pain, the receptors are specialized and may be easily located and charted on the skin.

While stimuli of the skin senses may not be a leading source of inputs in human behavior, they are nevertheless important in a vital matter such as feedback and preservation of the organism. Pain receptors, in particular, provide us with a means of avoiding potentially destructive situations. In those rare cases where individuals do not sense pain, severe damage has been caused by burns or bruises of which the individual was unaware.

On a more limited basis, there has been a growth of interest recently in the use of the skin senses as communication channels. Human factors research is interested in how effectively workers can receive information by size and shape of devices they use. The airline pilot at the controls or a machinist turning a wheel can receive much more than the ordinary basic tactile information people generally use.

The Proprioceptive Senses

While all of the senses already mentioned provide a wide variety of inputs, a big gap in information crucial for human functioning would exist were it not for this class of senses. We need information about our position in space and the relative positions of the parts of our body. This is obtained through the *vestibular* and the *kinesthetic sense* receptors.

The vestibular sense receptors are located in the semicircular canals and the otolith organs of the inner ear. These have nothing to do with hearing, but they do provide information about balance. An inner ear disorder will often disrupt this sense of balance. Stimulation of these receptors can also cause motion sickness at times in many persons. While the exact mechanisms involved are not clear, particularly the link with the alimentary tract or the drugs that affect it, the importance of this sense is well established.

The kinesthetic sense receptors are in the muscles, tendons, and joints of the body. Information about and coordination of all of our skilled movements comes primarily from these receptors. Visual inputs may give us some idea of the location of our body members and how to coordinate their activities, but the kinesthetic inputs are more crucial in the process. We see how important the sense area is by observing those whose afferent nerve pathways are cut or damaged. Speech, walking, or other skilled psychomotor activities are severely affected.

INTEGRATION OF INPUTS

The end responses to sensory stimuli come as the result of not one but many types of sensory inputs. The cues we receive from the outside situation are many and varied; when we evaluate and take action it is because of an integration of the sensations. We hear the report of the gun soon after and in connection with the sighting of the smoke of the gun powder; we may even smell that powder as well. Thus, each sense area acts in concordance with another so smoothly that often we do not realize that more than one type of cue is needed. Judging a person's emotion from a facial expression alone becomes difficult or impossible without other cues. We usually have other information, mainly a knowledge of the context in which this took place.

More interesting are those circumstances where inputs from different sense areas do not agree. The straight stick looks bent when plunged into water, and a sound may seem to appear from the wrong direction if it bounces off nearby buildings. This faulty organization of input is called an *illusion;* it represents the more complex organization which occurs deeper in the system and should be discussed under the heading of perception in the central information processing area.

Central Information Processing

The critical central area in the system sketched in this chapter is that which has long been labeled *cognitive processes.* Simon and Newell (1964, p. 281), among others, reflect the systems approach to this area by emphasizing that "the thinking human being is also an information processor and the output of the processes, the behavior of *homo coqitans,* should reveal how the information processing is organized." This general topic deserves closer and more extensive study and, for this reason, will be treated in greater length in a later chapter (Chapter 7). At this point, a short delineation in systems terminology and concepts is in order.

PERCEPTION

Perception is the phase of operations that takes place after information receiving but one that is well-nigh indistinguishable from it. It has been defined in various ways, but it refers basically to the manner in which a person experiences the world. Information receiving is only the beginning of the functioning of the part of the subsystem we refer to as the organism. Something must happen to the inputs as they are received, altered, and then sent along to other central information processing phases. The organization of inputs into an arrangement that has meaning for the person is the experience called perception.

Set

The predisposition to respond in a particular way is another part of the way in which input is translated into meaningful terms. A predisposition of a specific kind will determine what parts of the input are selected and are available for organization. An accountant is more likely to be predisposed to pick up discrepancies in accounts being reviewed than is an engineer viewing them, while the latter undoubtedly would be more alert to malfunctions in equipment during a plant tour.

Scanning

The organism part of the system must be in a state in which the input will be transmitted through to the central informational processing area. This is not fundamentally a question of capacity, since that is a matter of sensory input and information receiving. Here, a more informative term might be *attention*. To derive meaning from the sensory input, the person must be alert or attend to the varieties of input. The line of research which is often called *vigilance research* is an example of attempts to address this problem.

Scanning is fundamentally a search process. Here, the individual attends to input in a regular and successive way. He pays attention in a selective way to the elements which are presented as inputs when he scans the range of information received.

The selection of successive inputs provides observations which are compared with stored impressions. This comparison with the stored material results in a recognition or identification that has meaning. This placing of information into classes is the essence of perception.

In complex information processing tasks, the perceptual problems may be critical. Not only does there have to be as unambiguous a stimulus as possible but the personality dynamics of the human operator in the system must be recognized. As Campbell (1958) and others have emphasized, there is a tendency for the individual to distort the meaning of the input or to ascribe meaning that was not intended. The operator in a system, to a great degree, perceives what he needs or wants to perceive. Since the situation often calls for an unequivocal response, the scanning can be cut down by providing input which is unambiguous. Input which can symbolically related to the task will help in perceptual identifications. A coding of inputs will speed perceptions as well. Schipper et al. (1957) found improvement in the effectiveness of aircraft controllers when they coded positions of aircraft they were guiding by using clock positions rather than simple recognition of blips on a radar screen.

CORE COGNITIVE PROCESSES

A further step into the cognitive area involves more than the organization or classification found in perception. The next phase of the behavioral sequence in the central processing area may be referred to by many names. *Thinking, reasoning,* or *problem solving* are some of the labels used to identify the processes involved in the center of the behavioral system. In Chapter 7 a further look at this critical process in behavior will emphasize the research and conceptualization occurring, and a more detailed discussion of these concepts and their refinements is due there.

Information processing theories generally deal with the constructs associated with the processing of symbols. Various operations utilizing a list of symbols (changing, deleting, inserting, or copying) form the basis for a sequence, according to rules of operations or a program. Memories, providing information for simple information processes, may be interconnected in some order or combined by a definitive set of rules into whole programs (Newell, Shaw, and Simon, 1958). The behavior generated by the operations of this kind of information processing program is the kind that promises to give more objective information about these central processes.

DECISION MAKING

Further processing in the central cognitive area comes before the final responses of action taking. After evaluation or judgment some step must be taken; a choice among alternatives available has to be made. This selection among alternative courses of action is decision making.

The greater the number of alternatives, the greater is the complexity of the decision-making process and, not surprisingly, the time required for the decision increases with the number of decisions possible. Simple reaction time data reported by Fitts (1953) shows the increase in reaction time with the increase in number of fingers to be used in responding to a signal (Figure 5-3).

Decision making proceeds according to rules. The purpose of the rule is to identify the way the system must operate to achieve the continuation

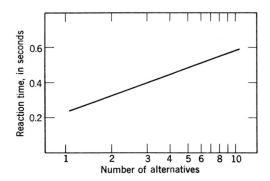

Figure 5-3. Relationship between complexity of problem and reaction time (Fitts, 1953).

of activity to the output. A rule may be seen in the simple relationship of "if this is so, then that must be done." The course of action to be followed becomes the last link in the central information processing function and the action-response takes place.

Decision rules are, unfortunately, not easy to identify. The same difficulties in understanding of the process exist here as in all the cognitive areas. We may be able to reach decisions without difficulty but be completely unable to know how it was done much less report to others on the exact steps. Nevertheless, models for decisions by people generally have been made and have served to encourage further research. In applied settings one should try to specify as much as possible the decision rules as they appear to be pertinent in that situation. The clearer the decision rules, the more effective the action.

Action Taking and Outputs

Outputs of the system are the end results of the operations that have been described above. The traditional concept of response is one which covers the area under consideration. The terminology from engineering psychology perhaps is more descriptive in that it outlines the several aspects of the functioning of the system or organism. It is clear that the responses or outputs are the final results of the actions of the effector processes or the action-taking subsystem. While the model of the entire system may conceptually separate the action taking from the output part of the system, the two must be considered together under one heading, much as the inputs and information receiving processes were considered together earlier in this chapter.

PSYCHOMOTOR RESPONSES

Signals from the central information processing centers are transmitted through motor nerve pathways to various parts of the body, primarily the muscles. The resulting physical movements are the above-mentioned psychomotor responses. While verbal outputs are important, most studies concerned with output in a system will be in the area of psychomotor activities.

There are many kinds of movements possible in the completion of a task in the flight compartment, in the office, at home, or on the production line. While it is possible to classify the movements in several different ways, the following categories are the most commonly used and lend themselves to more extensive treatment.

Simple Positioning

A simple positioning movement involves an action where a part of the body moves from one location to another. It is a move that can be clearly differentiated from any other; it has a definite start and a clear end. Examples of a positioning movement would be throwing a light switch, twisting a knob from one position to another, or any simple reaching for an object, which is one of the most common of the motor activities.

Static Reactions

Where the extent of the positioning movements could be quite large, a static action shows minimal movement although, in the small activity that it requires, it does resemble a positioning move. A static response requires some exertion, but the mobility of the members is limited. Here, some sort of force is called for either to grasp an object or to hold it or to maintain pressures on a brake pedal.

Sequential Movements

In this class of movements some activity is taking place over a period of time within a well-defined pattern. Sequential movements may be further broken down into *continuous, repetitive,* and *serial movements.* Continuous movements require continuing adjustments to the nature of the stimuli within the task itself in order to maintain control over the task elements. Controlling the steering wheel of an automobile or following the guidelines of a pattern with a machine are examples of a continuous movement. A repetitive movement is one where the same discrete activity takes place over and over again. Tapping, hammering, or turning a wheel are examples of this. Serial movements involve a long series of independent movements which are arranged in a sequence. They may vary in complexity from a task such as typing to the elaborate checklist procedure in getting ready for takeoff in an aircraft.

Tense and Ballistic Movements

Another means of classification would be to use a parallel set of categories such as *tense* and *ballistic* movements. The tense movements involve the reaction of the body members on the forces applied against them. Trying to keep an object in a track where there is pressure to leave it would be an example of a tense movement. A ballistic movement, on the other hand, does not require the tension in the muscles; once the force is applied, the object reacts under its own momentum. Swinging a golf club or hammering a nail would be an example of a ballistic movement.

Movements in Combination

Not only can movements be classified in different ways, as indicated immediately above, but most practical activities call for rather involved combinations of different types of movements in a sequence. Not only is hammering a repetitive ballistic movement but, in most situations, it calls for a certain amount of positioning or other types of movements as well. Any extensive operations will call for many different motor activities. The nature and extent of the feedback from the motor outputs also enter into a description of motor activities. A positioning movement may be made with the help of visual feedback, or it may take place without any visual control. In that case, it is known as a *blind positioning movement*. There may, of course, be other cues (kinesthetic, for example) to provide information. A worker who throws a switch without looking is making a blind positioning movement.

Action Taking or Control Devices

The mechanical devices contributing to outputs of human systems are many and varied. Strictly speaking, a pencil is a device which aids in producing a specific kind of output. A complex piece of machinery activated by an operator represents the other extreme. The more common and significant elements of control systems may be outlined very simply.

1. Activation devices (with discrete settings)

    (a)   Hand-push button   (c)   Toggle switch
    (b)   Foot-push button   (d)   Rotary selector switch

2. Continuous controls (with quantitative setting)

    (a)   Knob   (c)   Wheel   (e)   Pedal
    (b)   Crank   (d)   Lever

Each type of action-taking device may leave further important properties for a systems study. Generally, more feedback from the activation will be sought in the coding of controls. This may be accomplished through the use of size, shape, color, location, or surface variations. Coding should be arranged to provide the maximum of cues. When coding according to shape, for instance, the shapes should be geometric ones which are not easily confused and which have some symbolic relationship to the task being performed. A symbolic arrowhead on a lever can point to the direction of greater power, for example.

The cues from coding are primarily for feedback. The functioning of the output devices themselves are of more immediate interest in the study of the output area itself.

PERFORMANCE

In a study of motor activities, the elements of performance in which the human factors scientist is interested are those related to efficiency or performance on the job. These relate primarily to speed and accuracy, although amount of effort needed to control, or strength of response, are also factors of concern.

Reaction time is usually of first interest. Simple reaction time is the time needed to make a simple response to a single stimulus. Complex reaction time is that which is needed to make an involved and comprehensive discrimination with a complex set of stimuli. These are characteristics that are common to all of the various types of movements, and reaction time will vary with the type of task. Overall, however, it may easily be guessed that reaction time increases with an increase in the number of stimuli. Baxter (1942) found this to be the case but noted, in addition, that reactions to sound were faster than reactions to visual stimuli. Reactions to touch also seem to be faster than those to visual stimuli.

In positioning with visual cues, concern will be whether speed or accuracy of performance is of greater interest. There will be a difference, too, whether this positioning will be one handed or with two hands. One-handed positioning is best when short distances are involved; in any case, both speed and accuracy are superior when positioning is at about a 60° angle from direct center (Briggs, 1955). Two-handed positioning is most accurate directly ahead, although the movements are made slightly faster at a 30° angle from a straight-ahead position. Blind positioning or those positioning movements made without visual cues are most accurate when straight ahead and somewhat below the shoulder height (Brown et al., 1948).

In action taking generally, the smaller the control mechanism, the faster the carrying through of the activity. This assumes that there is no friction or torque; in that case the device must be a little larger to overcome the inertia. If some pressure has to be used to overcome inertia or resistance, the position of a handwheel or crank should be at an angle and somewhere near the midline of the operator (Davis, 1949). When positioning knobs, the most accurate settings can be made at the 12, 3, and 9 o'clock positions (Chapanis, 1951).

With respect to force exerted by the human in the system, several conclusions may be reached. When pushing in a horizontal plane, greater force comes in a movement straight ahead rather than at an angle. If force is to be exerted below the shoulder, a positioning of the device about 3 feet below the shoulder level is better than any other level higher up nearer the shoulder. For above-the-shoulder work, the maximum force comes with pulling downward (Provins, 1955). From a seated position, greater strength can be exerted if the legs are pulled up at an angle rather than being parallel with the horizontal. Pushing or pulling in a horizontal plane can exert more force than any other movement of the arms, up or down, in or out (Hunsicker, 1955).

Optimum Conditions

A common characteristic of human motor performance lies in the fact that there are certain conditions under which optimum performance takes place. Greater departure from these optimum points in the center results in a lowered performance. The drop in effectiveness occurs on both sides of the optimum range. This has been identified by Helson (1949) as the "U hypothesis" because a charting of performance under a range of a particular variable being studied turns out to be a curve which looks like the letter "U" (Figure 5-4).

ENVIRONMENTAL FACTORS

The conditions under which outputs take place affect the functioning of the system as a whole. Variables such as temperature, humidity, sound,

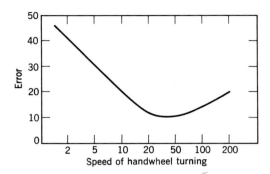

Figure 5-4. Curvilinear performance along a range of a variable (Helson, 1949).

or noise affect the functioning of the system. Actually, all these are really inputs into the system; here, however, we focus on how these general environmental inputs affect the psychomotor processes.

Heat Exchange Processes

The role of both temperature and humidity as environmental variables can be better understood in a discussion of the basic process involved, the heat exchange process. Air temperature and humidity as well as its circulation do affect the performance of individuals and their feelings of comfort. All this takes place, however, as a concomitant of the heat exchange process. There are four methods of heat exchange, namely, *convection, conduction, evaporation,* and *radiation.* In convection the heat is transferred by the air, while in conduction the heat transfer occurs as a result of the direct contact with heat-giving or heat-taking objects. In evaportion the heat loss or gain is the result of evaporation through perspiration or the loss of moisture from the lungs. Radiation is the direct exchange of thermal energy between objects.

Performance

There is a significant decline in performance on most tasks when the effective temperature goes above 90°. Not only is output affected quantitatively, but it is qualitatively affected as well (Mackworth, 1946). Errors rise steeply at about this point in the temperature scale. Accidents also occur with greater frequency when this temperature level is reached and surpassed. At the other end of the scale, cold temperatures seriously affect activities that are primarily manual in nature. Intellectual activities are not as seriously affected by cold temperatures as they are by high.

Comfort

Most people report feeling comfortable somewhere in the range between 65° and 75° fahrenheit. This range may vary depending on age, the time of the year, and other factors. They usually feel more comfortable in the upper part of the range in summer, while in winter there is a preference for the lower part of that range, between 65° and 70° fahrenheit. Outside temperature is not the fundamental factor in feelings of comfort, however; the skin temperature is the critical factor. When their skin temperature is somewhere close to 92° fahrenheit, people are comfortable (McCormick, 1964).

Auditory Inputs

Studies of effects of sound on human performance usually focus on that kind of nonharmonic sound which is casually called noise. The relationship between excessive noise and loss of sensitivity in the auditory area has already been noted. With respect to the effect of noise on human performance, however, the results are not as clear cut. There is some indication that noise may have an impact on performance on the job, but there are just as many studies that show no effect. It may well be that performance does maintain itself at a high level under noise but only as a result of adaptation to this set of circumstances in the people involved. Performance then comes at a higher cost to the individuals having to operate under the slightly more adverse conditions.

Illumination

Studies of the effect of illumination on performance have generally shown an expected positive relationship between the two factors. Both in the laboratory (McCormick and Niven, 1952) and in the plant (Luckiesh, 1944), increased output accompanied a rise in the level of illumination. The only qualification that must be made is that, as in so many other situations, the influence of other psychological factors is no doubt partly responsible for the results. In practical applications other factors such as glare and distribution of light must be considered in addition to the level of illumination.

Space and Equipment

The performance of the individual in the "envelope" within which he operates requires a study not only of the psychomotor functions outlined above but also a scrutiny of the more immediate environmental factors. Questions of extent of work space and placement of equipment require anthropometric as well as psychometric data. Since people are not alike physically, those variations

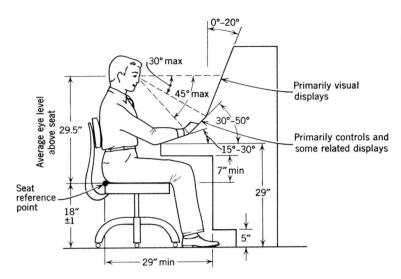

Figure 5-5. One possible arrangement of a display and control console (McCormick, 1964, p. 376).

in body size and type must be considered. The human factors specialist will concern himself with the "average" or the "extreme individual" and may design the quarters for the range of sizes involved. Whether standing or sitting is involved, the optimum placement of work surfaces is of further interest. While exact placements will differ with the type of task and other factors, an illustrative point from Schroeder (1951) suggests a 36 inch height for ironing while standing and 28 inches while sitting.

Placement of visual displays and location of the control devices represent an integrative extension of the principles of space design. Figure 5-5 is suggestive of seating with respect to placement of visual displays and controls. Visual display should be placed at a perpendicular angle to the eye. Control devices must obviously be within the limits of optimum reach (this is not, however, a circular area around the individual). The reach may be further affected by the angle of the backrest as well.

Summary

Behavior may be described in general systems terminology within the broad concept of an input-output system.

Stimuli are the inputs for the system and may be introduced by visual displays in addition to their direct entry into the system from the environment. The information receiving processor function has been known as sensation. Here, the material from the outside is received and converted by the various sense organs of vision, audition, smell, taste, those on the skin, in the inner ear, and muscles.

The organization of the information inside the system for a meaningful outcome takes place as the central information processing function. The first step in this process is perception, the organization of stimuli in an orderly way. This happens in routine or very dynamic ways; individual personality factors, shaped by experience in a society, play an important role in organizing the new sensations that come in. The central processing continues to provide the basis for decision making and action taking. This core activity has been very broadly labeled as thinking or cognition. Memory or information storage serves as a concomitant function of central processing.

Action taking, with or without action or control devices, is the output phase of the system. What has been known as the response part of the stimulus-response link is the result of verbal and psychomotor processes. Here, the emphasis has been on the basic movements or motor activities taking place within an environmental setting. Environment factors such as temperature, sound, and space are, in reality, inputs but are of direct concern in assessing their influence on psychomotor functioning.

Bibliography

Amoore, J. et al. (1964). The stereochemical theory of odor. *Scientific American,* **210(2)**, 42–49.

Baxter, B. (1942). A study of reaction time using factorial design. *Journal of Experimental Psychology,* **31**, 430–437.

Briggs, S. (1955). *A study in the design of work areas.* Lafayette, Indiana: Purdue University. Unpublished dissertation.

Brown, J. et al. (1948). The accuracy of positioning reactions as a function of their direction and extent. *American Journal of Psychology,* **61**, 167–182.

Campbell, D. (1958). Systematic error on the part of human links in communication systems. *Information and Control,* **1**, 334–369.

Chapanis, A. (1951). Studies of manual rotary positioning movements: I. The precision of setting an indicator knob to various angular positions. *Journal of Psychology,* **31**, 51–64.

Crocker, E. (1945). *Flavor*. New York: McGraw-Hill.

Davis, H. (1959). Excitation of auditory receptors. In Field et al. (eds.). *Handbook of Physiology*, Vol. I. Washington, D.C.: American Physiological Society, 565–584.

Davis, L. (1949). Human factors in design of manual machine controls. *Mechanical Engineering*, **71**, 811–816.

Erickson, R. (1963). Sensory neural patterns and gustation. In Zotterman, Y. (ed.). *Olfaction and Taste*. Oxford: Pergamon Press, 205–213.

Fitts, P. (1951). Engineering psychology and equipment design. In Stevens, S. (ed.). *Handbook of experimental psychology*. New York: Wiley.

Fitts, P. (1953). The influence of response coding on performance in motor tasks. In *Current trends in information theory*. Pittsburgh: University of Pittsburgh Press.

Glorig, A. and Wheeler, D. (1955). An introduction to the industrial noise problem. *Illinois Medical Journal*, **107**(1).

Helson, H. (1949). Design of equipment and optimal human operation. *American Journal of Psychology*, **62**, 473–479.

Hunsicker, P. (1955). *Arm strength at selected degrees of elbow flexion*. Wright-Patterson Air Force Base, Ohio: Wright Air Development Center. Technical Report 54–548.

Lucas, D. and Britt, S. (1950). *Advertising psychology and research*. New York: McGraw-Hill.

Luckiesh, M. (1944). *Light, vision, and seeing*. Princeton, N.J.: Van Nostrand.

Mackworth, N. (1946). Effects of heat on wireless telegraphy operators hearing and recording morse messages. *British Journal of Industrial Medicine*, **3**, 143–158.

McCormick, E. (1957). *Human engineering*. New York: McGraw-Hill.

McCormick, E. (1964). *Human factors engineering*. New York: McGraw-Hill.

McCormick, E. and Niven, J. (1952). The effect of varying intensities of illumination upon performance on a motor task. *Journal of Applied Psychology*, **36**, 193–195.

Morgan, C. and King, R. (1966). *Introduction to psychology* (3rd ed.). New York: McGraw-Hill.

Newell, A., Shaw, J., and Simon, H. (1958). Elements of a theory of human problem solving. *Psychological Review*, **65**, 151–166.

Provins, K. (1955). Effect of limb position on the forces exerted about the elbow and shoulder joints on the two sides simultaneously. *Journal of Applied Physiology,* **7,** 387–389.

Schipper et al. (1957). *Terminal system effectiveness as a function of the method used by controllers to obtain altitude information.* Wright-Patterson Air Force Base, Ohio: Wright Air Development Center. Technical Report No. 57.

Schroeder, F. (1951). *Anatomy for interior designers* (2nd ed.). New York: Whitney.

Simon, H. and Newell, A. (1964). Information processing in computer and man. *American Scientist,* **52,** 281–300.

Wiener, N. (1948). *Cybernetics.* New York: Wiley.

6

Modification Mechanisms: Learning and the Acquisition of Skills

Learning is generally considered to be one of the fundamental bases of human behavior, if not, as many psychologists believe, the most important source of information for those who wish to understand the underlying mechanisms. This emphasis on learning may come as a surprise to the casual observer who, up to this time, may have considered learning to be an activity that takes place in a limited academic situation. It is to be hoped that learning does indeed occur in the classroom, but far more of it undoubtedly takes place on the outside. Humans and infrahumans learn, in either simple or complex fashion, from the very first opportunity to react to sensory stimuli. Learning takes place everywhere and throughout the entire existence of an individual.

Learning is the modification of behavior as the result of some experience. The definition is a broad one which includes much more than a casual dictionary definition might indicate. Learning to avoid fire, to walk, to drive a car, to memorize a poem, to get to know the implications of alternative courses of action—all these activities varying in type and complexity are based on the occurrence of mechanisms that produce a change or, as the title to this chapter indicates, act to modify behavior.

Finer distinctions may be made between the learning of psychomotor tasks and the development of concepts or between the acquisition of skills and the more discriminative kinds of learning. The distinctions are important even though these are often obscured by the emotional approaches which sometimes emerge, for example, in arguments over what is training and what is education. It is important to note here mainly that learning represents a broad behavioral area that encompasses training, the acquisition of skills, education, "management development," or any other similar change or modification process.

Learning cannot be considered apart from other basic aspects of behavior such as sensation, perception, and motivation. Modification of behavior output requires the functioning of input processes; sensation and perception are crucial determiners of the change process. Just as important, if not more so, is motivation for without motivation no learning or change in behavior is discernable.

It is necessary for professional people to understand the ways in which learning takes place in order for them to be effective in their work. Certainly the teacher in the classroom ought to know what really happens in this process of learning. No less should the manager of people know these basics of behavior, particularly when we view the manager as a "change agent" in his role of getting things done through the activities of others, a job which often requires the modification of much behavior.

Basic Processes

Fundamental processes in the modification of behavior can be so simple as to cause some observers to doubt that what is taking place is commensurate with their idea of learning. It must be remembered again that the classroom is not the only place where learning takes place and, also, that the most extensive ramifications of finite mathematics are based on original elementary associations such as "one and one equals two."

CONDITIONING

The simplest kind of learning may be seen in the processses of conditioning. The term conditioning refers to the modification of behavior under the two related sets of circumstances described below.

Classical Conditioning

The first experimental delineation of conditioning occurred as an outgrowth of some physiological studies early in this century by the Russian scientist Ivan Pavlov. Pavlov was interested in the secretion of glands and, in the course of his experiments, noted that the dogs he worked with could be made to salivate as the result of presenting stimuli other than the food which, in the past, had caused the dogs to salivate. Dogs do not ordinarily salivate at the sound of a bell, for instance, but Pavlov was able to get them to do so after a sequence of presenting the food and the bell together. After this pairing, the bell alone would produce the effect. Pavlov labeled the process conditioning and called the food the *unconditioned stimulus* (US) while the other stimulus,

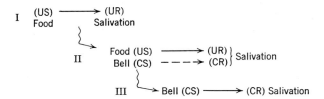

Figure 6-1.   The classical conditioning process.

the bell, he termed the *conditioned stimulus* (CS). The salivation is the *uncon-ditioned response* (UR) and, when produced under the new circumstances, is the *conditioned response* (CR). A schematic version of the procedure and outcomes is sketched in Figure 6-1. Pavlov found further that sounds similar to the original bell would have the same effect; that is, a generalization occurred whereby the phenomenon spread (generalized) to other stimulus situations. The greater the difference in tones, however, the weaker the effect. Pavlov also found that the response would not be maintained indefinitely but would be lost, that is, *extinction* would result. To revive the response or to maintain it, *reinforcement* of the response was necessary. In this situation the reinforce-ment was the pairing of the bell with the food.

There are many other aspects of interest in the process of conditioning. Further details are readily available in most introductory textbooks in psychology (Morgan and King, 1966; Krech and Crutchfield, 1962). Here, it is important to note the significance of the development of the concepts of conditioning by Pavlov and others. The illustration in experimentation of these basic proc-esses of learning represents an important contribution to an understanding of the elements of human behavior. Some theorists view all learning as arising from conditioning; even if this viewpoint is not shared by others, there is still recognition of conditioning as an important basic process.

Operant Conditioning or Instrumental Learning

Another experimental situation years after Pavlov's work gave rise to an-other type of conditioning. In the mid-thirties B. F. Skinner (1938) constructed a box in which a rat could be placed. A bar or lever on one wall of the box produced a food pellet when pressed by the animal. The distribution of pellets could be regulated from one at each pressing to one at variously spaced intervals. Obviously, naïve rats do not have bar pressing in their repertoire of skills. They do, however, adapt their activity toward bar pressing after a series of deliveries of food pellets when they happen to press the bar while

motivated by the need for food. Getting the food pellet is clearly the reinforcement for the rat, and he rapidly modifies his behavior accordingly. The difference between this type of conditioning and the Pavlovian or classical conditioning lies in the fact that the organism is reinforced as a result of something
it does. Out of an infinite number of acts, some bit of behavior is reinforced;
other behavior is not. The reinforcement of that bit of behavior makes it
more likely that the organism will engage in that act in the future. Skinner
also found a very interesting result which would probably not be guessed
by the use of "common sense." He noticed that when the rat was reinforced
only part of the time and did not receive a pellet at every bar pressing, the
activity was more resistant to extinction than when the rat received a pellet
at each press. The obvious lesson is that when there is some action we wish
to perpetuate, it should not be rewarded each time it happens. On the other
hand, an undesirable act may be hard to eliminate because even if it is seldom
reinforced, that partial reinforcement makes it highly resistant to extinction.

Applications

Illustrations of conditioning so far have emphasized the simplicity of
the processes. Something so basic may indeed show many simple instances
yet the phenomenon of conditioning may be found in more complex and applied
situations upon closer inspection. Conditioning takes place early in life when
a loud, frightening noise accompanies the arrival of a white furry animal.
The fear-response to a sudden sound becomes the conditioned response to
the animal; no wonder some adult individuals are uncomfortable in the presence
of white furry things.

People become important and, therefore, their presence is reinforcing
because from the very beginning they have been around to satisfy the basic
physiological and physical needs. A smile itself becomes a reinforcer on this
basis. The phenomenon is known as *higher-order conditioning* and is the result
of a buildup of conditioned responses. Even the simple Pavlovian response may
be seen in the classroom when the bell sounding the end of the class triggers
the usual slamming of books and the putting away of pens and pencils or the
throwing down of tools when the factory whistle blows at quitting time. More
complex variations on this theme ought to suggest themselves to the reader.

Conditioning takes place in the verbal area as well. The strange jottings
below do not, for most of the readers of this book, cause any meaningful
activity to emerge:

КОММЕРЧеский   ДИРеКТОР

The reason these markings cause a response to be elicited or to develop within an individual clearly lies in the pairing of the ordered letters with the original unconditioned stimulus, the object itself. The response to the letters by someone without the previous conditioning would be completely different.

PERCEPTUAL AND DISCRIMINATIVE LEARNING

In some novel experiments with rats, K. S. Lashley (1930) and others have been able to demonstrate another kind of basic learning process. Lashley placed a rat on a platform facing two windows. Each had a door which could be marked any way the experimenter wished. One of the doors would open when the rat jumped against it and would permit the rat access to food. The other would remain closed and give the animal nothing more than a bump on the head. In time the rat would learn to perceive the elements of the right choice. (Note that a design or color on the correct door is only one possibility—the correct choice could be indicated by placement, left or right, or could be alternated.) There are various aspects of the situation to which the rat can respond, and it learns that a particular one is correct.

Some learning theorists prefer to consider this type of learning and the situation described under operant conditioning above as more understandable when considered as *trial-and-error learning.* Most of the researchers draw on the early experiments of E. L. Thorndike (1898) with animals escaping from a puzzle box. The "laws" of learning which emerged from the experiments became the basis for many applications in education to this day. It is true that much of our learning activity does resemble the many movements of a trial and error approach; that label does not do more, however, than describe what some kinds of learning activities look like. It does little to explain them.

CONCEPTUAL AND INSIGHTFUL LEARNING

More complex processes of learning may be seen in other types of experiments. Observations of tasks given chimpanzees or other primates have provided much data in this area; the work of Köhler (1925) is particularly interesting. Köhler described the behavior of several chimpanzees when faced with a problem of obtaining food placed beyond their reach. A sudden grasp of a stick, previously unused, and the scooping in of the food with the stick is strong evidence of learning that can be called insightful. A sudden awareness of how a problem can be solved without any trial and error preceding it describes insight learning.

At this stage the complexity of the processes of acquisition of knowledge or modification of behavior has reached a point where it can be discussed more readily under headings such as problem solving, reasoning, or cognitive processes. This is an arbitrary dividing line, of course, and it puts these higher order processes into the next chapter (Chapter 7).

Principles of Learning

Certain fundamental aspects of the learning situation either must be present for us to be able to say that learning takes place or they affect the process to such a degree that no discussion of learning can be conducted without a mention of them.

MOTIVATION

The concept of motivation is basic because it must precede consideration of other factors in learning. Without motivation, learning does not take place or, at least, is not discernable. Motivation may be seen at different levels of complexity of a situation. A thirsty rat will learn the path through a maze to a dish of water; it is not likely to do as well, or even move purposefully at all, if it is satiated. On a broader level, a college student must have the need and drive to accomplish a task and reach a specific goal. None of this is particularly difficult to understand except that in practice the subtleties that surround the learning situation make it more difficult to recognize the basic problems. Often the individual may be unaware of the deep resistance he has to playing a particular role or participating in a project for which he is undergoing training. The perception by the person may be altered by the deeper emotional response and adversely effect the course of the training. All this at a time when the trainee (very sincerely) may voice his eagerness to learn. Torrance (1950) provides some examples of the subtle interference of learning by unconscious resistance to it, including an interesting self-analysis of the difficulty in learning to keep in step as an army private. "Fighting the problem" is sometimes the reason for the resistance to the introduction of new techniques in business.

SET OR LEARNING TO LEARN

The term *set* is used here the way it most often is in psychology, that is, as a predisposition or a tendency to respond. In connection with learning, the concept of set goes beyond mere discussion of motivation; it has mechanical aspects which influence the course of learning. Harlow (1949, p. 51) calls it "learning to learn" and says that this changes the organism from one that adapts by trial and error to one that seems to develop hypotheses and insight. In an actual training situation, learning how to do similar but easier tasks in prior practice will make learning less difficult in the learning session. What the instructor does before training begins, even though it may appear to be innocuous, can influence results. When Ray (1957) asked trainees to describe their plan of learning ahead of time, the trainees learned faster and made fewer errors in the learning session.

REINFORCEMENT

It has already been noted that reinforcement is a fundamental condition of learning. We can say that without reinforcement no measurable modification of behavior takes place. In the basic experiments on learning, the reward which accompanied or followed the behavior was the reinforcer of that behavior. In broader applied settings there are many ways in which reinforcement takes place. Seldom is the satisfaction of a basic physical need an important reinforcer in practice; social reinforcers are more crucial in everyday events. The approval of others when we do the right thing, recognition, a personal feeling of accomplishment, self-satisfaction in getting the correct answer, information about progress and achievement, or a monetary reward are all possible reinforcers. A training program must recognize which reinforcers are operative and most effective in that particular situation. Too often, managers in industry rely on money as a reinforcer when other, less tangible, factors are more important.

LEARNING CURVES

When learning takes place, the acquisition of knowledge or skill is measurable and may be charted. A visual display of the progress gives a clearer picture of the development than might otherwise be obtained. No such phenomenon as *the* learning curve exists nor can it be stated as an entirely hypothetical construct. A learning curve merely represents performance on the part of an individual or group over time or a series of trials. Certain patterns may be frequently met, however; some of these are sketched in Figure 6-2 (a caution about the regularity of the lines—these have been smoothed to show the apparent shapes of learning curves; in reality, the progress is less regular). Curve *a* is called a *negatively accelerated* learning curve while the

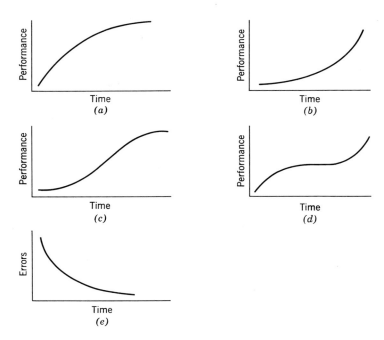

Figure 6-2.   Some curves of learning.

curve for *b* is a *positively accelerated* one. Curve *c* is an "S" curve which may be a combination of the preceding two; curve *d* may also be a similar combination. Curve *e*, though it is quite different from the other four, is still a learning curve. Since the ordinate (the vertical axis) is in terms of errors, the declining curve is in reality a sketch of progress in learning.

Some educated guesses as to the basis of the differences between the curves have focused on individual differences or type of material. Simple tasks may result in high early performance that soon approaches or reaches a ceiling. Difficult tasks can deter individuals; a gaining of insight into the problem can trigger a sudden rise in performance. It should be clear that one cannot expect the same patterns in the learning of a simple assembly task as in the attainment of a more complex set of concepts in managerial action.

THE PLATEAU

Curve *d* in Figure 6-2 shows a leveling off in performance after a rise. This level is maintained until, ordinarily, there is a further rise in performance to a higher level. This result is known as a plateau. While only guesses may be made as to cause (for instance, it may be the result of a need to reorganize or to "catch one's breath"), none of the explanations are entirely satisfactory; what is important to note is that it does exist and should be taken into account by anyone responsible for the administration of specific programs. In training programs in industry or elsewhere, the period of the plateau can be an extremely discouraging one for the trainee. No improvement has taken place for awhile and none seems in the offing; yet experienced workers are seen as performing at a far higher level. A realization by trainer and trainee both that this is part of the usual course of events alleviates much of the difficulty.

DISTRIBUTION OF PRACTICE

How the practice trials or sessions are arranged greatly influences the shape of the learning curve. Many investigators have found that, given the same amount of practice time, more efficiency is gained in the learning process by spacing the sessions rather than having the practice massed. As early as 1885, Ebbinghaus, a pioneer in learning studies, noted that when he memorized the material, he did better when he spaced the trials over three days than when he tried to mass the practice in one day. Further research indicates that spaced practice is particularly effective where rote material is fatiguing or where the problem solution would be delayed because of a wrong mental set (Kendler et al., 1952). Spacing alone may not always be effective; Ericksen (1942) found that conceptual or insightful learning was best with massed practice followed by shorter periods spaced over time.

The lesson for college students should be obvious; don't cram! Subject matter studied over the course of a semester is learned better than when attempted all at once the night before an examination. Trainers in industry will often find the same factor influencing results; scheduling the practice sessions over a period of time with intervals in between aids learning. In much the same way a college course taught three times a week over a semester probably yields better results than if massed into a few consecutive days in the summer session.

ACTIVE VERSUS PASSIVE LEARNING

A subject who does something more than act as a passive blotter learns more efficiently; participation in a program of learning leads the learner along more rapidly. While some may feel that the easiest way to assimilate knowledge is to try to get it by "osmosis," the experimental evidence contradicts this. Hovland, Lumsdaine, and Sheffield (1949), for instance, found that soldiers acquired the use of the phonetic alphabet by rote more easily when they actively engaged in the learning procedures. The principle of active learning has become one of the important reasons for the development of programmed instruction, since the programmed approach relies on the active participation of the individual throughout the entire process. The learner does something and that activity aids in the attainment. The old recommendations for "learning by doing" have further meaning in techniques that rely on simulating a job problem and requiring the trainee to act as if he really were the person called on to accomplish the task.

KNOWLEDGE OF RESULTS

Since man is a purposeful being, that is, goal directed, he needs to have some idea of not only where the goal is but what his placement is with respect to that goal. No meaningful progress can be made and, therefore, no learning can take place unless there is some knowledge of how one's actions approach the desired norm. Knowing where the missile falls with respect to the target and how much to correct for the deviation is crucial. The more information we have and the sooner we have it the better. A trainee who has no idea of what is expected of him or whether what he is doing is right or not has little more chance of improving his performance than does a blindfolded dart thrower who has no idea where the target is or how close he is coming to it on each throw. In practice a trainee without information will usually try to generate his own knowledge of results, that is, select a goal he thinks is correct and adjust his performance accordingly (Ammons, 1956). Without a proper criterion set by the trainer, however, the subject will operate with respect to an unsatisfactory goal.

Lindahl (1945) illustrates the importance of knowledge of results in industrial training. Workers had to learn to cut discs from a tungsten rod, a task which required complex hand and foot coordination. Trainees were able to see their action patterns traced on paper as they attempted to duplicate the patterns of experienced operators. Figure 6-3 shows tracings indicating progress made over the period.

One of the advantages of programmed instruction, which will be discussed below, is just this opportunity to provide the learner with "instant feedback." The subject has immediate knowledge of whether his answer is right or wrong.

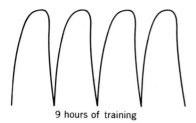

9 hours of training

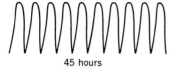

45 hours

Experienced operator

141 hours

239 hours

Figure 6-3. Recorded movement in training (Lindahl, 1945).

In industry an annual review of a man's performance provides some knowledge of results but "too little and too late" might be applied to this procedure; once a year is not enough and too often supervisors, through distaste for the process or for other reasons, seldom provide the amount or kind of information needed for progress.

Repetition has often been cited as one of the fundamentals of learning. By itself, repetition means nothing; the critical factor is the knowledge of the results of one's activity. One could repeat an action all day with no improvement in performance if there were a lack of knowledge of the results of the activity.

MEANINGFULNESS OF MATERIAL

Much research has been done on the relationship between meaningfulness of material and learning. That of Noble (1952) is one of the latest in the series. All indicate that the more meaningful the material, the better learning proceeds. As a matter of fact, if there is no meaning in the task, the learner will often attempt to impose one. Acquisition of nonsense syllables proceeds more slowly than that of prose or poetry. On a broader scale, a program of learning where each task is depicted in terms of its relationship to other tasks makes for meaningfulness. Knowing the "big picture" and understanding how each element fits into it speeds the acquisition of those elements themselves and the series as a whole. Trainers may have available to them certain techniques that increase meaningfulness for trainees. Organizing meaningful units, creating association with already familiar terms, and providing a conceptual basis or logical reason for the material are some of the practical possibilities.

WHOLE VERSUS PART LEARNING

This question is related to the matter of meaningfulness of material and the problem of massed or spaced practice. How to group the material to be learned is the crucial point here. Whether to split the task into segments (and, if so, what size?) or to undertake the task to be learned as a whole seems to depend on many interrelated variables. Hovland (1951), in a survey of experiments, found that variables such as interest and fatigue in the individual or size and structure of the material played an important role. He summed up the findings by noting that, other things being constant, the best procedure is to use the largest units that are meaningful to the individual and that are within his intellectual capacity.

TRANSFER OF TRAINING

When what has been learned in the past influences what is being learned, transfer is taking place. Note that the influence may be such as to be helpful in learning the new task or it may be detrimental. Where the old material aids in the acquisition of the new, there is *positive transfer;* where the old interferes with the new learning process, there is *negative transfer*. When I drive my foreign sports car with a four-speed gearshift and then switch to an American car, I take a strong chance of stripping the gears by engaging in the movements called for by the four-speed system. A more serious problem arises where an airline pilot who has been trained to a high degree on one particular airplane is transferred to a new cockpit with control and information devices differing from the older arrangement. In a new situation it is too easy to respond with an old pattern of behavior; negative transfer at times like these has serious consequences.

More common situations involving transfer arise when a trainee responds to stimuli in a training program in a manner learned prior to the program. These responses not only may be of no help, they may be detrimental to the new learning. Students learning to type, for instance, are probably better off if they have never been at the typewriter keyboard. Those who have used the "hunt and peck" system with two fingers are usually handicapped by the negative transfer.

A final note—pure positive or negative transfer does not exist in practice. The actual situation has in it elements of both. In the change of cars discussed above, there is positive transfer in that the movements have much similarity and knowing how to shift gears in one car transfers to aid in shifting gears it the second. We would be more painfully aware of the negative transfer in that same circumstance. The situation is a mixture of both, and we ordinarily label it according to which type is preeminent.

Measures of Performance

Implied in all the discussions of learning is the factor of measurement. While modification of behavior may indeed be taking place, unless there is some way to note those changes no one can really say that learning has occurred. What we can know about learning comes as the result of measurement of performance in specific situations. Tests made during a period of trials determine levels, and the change which is recorded is called learning. Later tests after the trial period are measures of *retention;* these scores indicate how much has been retained over a period of time after the trials have ended. What is called *remembering* is really the result of measures of retention of learned material. The important thing to note is that learning and remembering are really part of the same phenomenon. Where we stop the trials determines the dividing line between the two; the basis of information for both areas, however, lies in measurement.

MEASURES OF LEARNING

As we have seen in the curves of learning, measures of level of attainment during trial periods form the basis for comparisons of levels to determine if modification of behavior has taken place as the result of those trials. If levels of performance increase we say learning has taken place or a skill is being attained. The level of performance ordinarily is charted with relation to the lapse of time under consideration or to the number of specific trials.

Learning to a Criterion

In experiments a criterion of performance is usually set. It may be, for instance, the first correct recitation of a list of words to be learned. The raw material of learning experiments more often consists of nonsense syllables, that is, three-letter words that are meaningless. These are chosen to provide relatively "pure" verbal material free of any emotional or intellectual associations which could contaminate the findings of a learning experiment. Obviously, if meaningfulness is a factor to be studied, other material must also be used.

Overlearning

A continuation of trials beyond the usual criterion of a correct recitation once or twice represents a higher level of learning than in the method of learning to a criterion.

MEASURES OF RETENTION

While there are many possible ways of measuring retention, three methods are most often used.

1. Recall.
2. Recognition.
3. Relearning.

Each has some distinctive features and advantages in information gathering. Performance tests made over a period of time after learning trials are ended provide the basic information for what we speak of as remembering. The phenomenon refers to the availability of information that has been learned. A more appropriate term for this is *retention,* and the measures that are made have been the subject of many experiments.

Recall

In recall the subject is required to call forth or reproduce the elements of the material learned. The typical essay examination in school is an example of the approach; in experimentation the technique of measurement is apt to be more refined, however, than the casual scoring often encountered.

Recognition

These measures are based on the subject's picking out, from material presented to him, the elements that he acquired in the prior learning process. This method is the basis for multiple choice or matching examinations. Since this requires mere recognition of familiar material, it usually gives a higher retention score than recall. At the same time, since chance guessing introduces an extraneous factor, correction for guessing is often made.

Relearning

The method of relearning is one pioneered by Ebbinghaus in his studies of learning and retention. Ebbinghaus determined the time it took him to memorize a list of nonsense syllables and then, after a lapse of time, he noted how long it took to relearn that same list. The difference in time taken was expressed as a percentage. If the relearning time was 60 percent of the original time, the retention was 40 percent. With other lists and additional intervals of time, Ebbinghaus was able to chart a "curve of forgetting" or retention, as in Figure 6-4. The relearning method of measuring retention is also known as the *savings* method, since the results indicate the amount of material saved.

It may be discouraging for the student to see the small amount of material

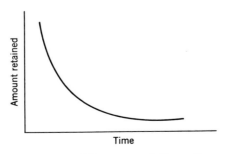

Figure 6-4. The curve of forgetting.

retained after a period of time. On the other hand, it will not be as difficult to relearn the material, since a percentage of it is saved.

INDIVIDUAL DIFFERENCES

Characteristics of the individual in the learning situation are important variables to be considered. Mental ability, age and intelligence, motivation and interest, prior experience—all are factors that determine the shape of the learning curve (McGeoch and Irion, 1952).

Ability

For the most part, those with more ability in the intellectual area learn more rapidly; aptitude for the task shows an even closer relationship with performance. It may be somewhat frustrating for trainers to find that at the end of a training program, the gap between the best workers and the poorest ones is even greater than before. It had been hoped, perhaps, that all would reach the same level of competence. An encouraging note in this situation, however, is that all trainees probably improve their performance as the result of the training.

There is some further encouragement to the "slow learner" in that Underwood (1954) has shown that speed of learning is not the crucial factor in retention; the level of learning reached determines how much is remembered. It is true, however, that the slower one proceeds, the less material one can cover. One may overlearn a small amount of material and retain that little bit well. A slower student will take longer to study or, with the same amount of time available, learn less than someone speedier.

Age

The relationship between age and learning ability has been sketched for the verbal area by Thorndike et al. (1928). A sharp increase in verbal learning performance is seen up to the ages of 17 to 20 with a leveling off until about 50 or 60 years of age. This is consonant with evidence presented in Chapter 4.

Other Variables

The reader is also reminded that motivation, including attitudes and intent to learn, is another important variable in the learning and retention process. This area has already been discussed above under "Principles of Learning."

RETROACTIVE INHIBITION

Experimental evidence is clear that the processes of retention are affected by what occurs after the material is learned. Mere lapse of time is not a crucial variable, that is, forgetting is not a matter of "decay" of information but comes about because other, newer material pushes the older material further into the background of our "memory storage" and makes access to that earlier material more difficult. Theoretically, then, we really forget nothing; what we keep learning interferes retroactively with what has been learned. There is some clinical evidence for this in experiments on reconstruction of earlier life experiences under hypnosis.

Retroactive inhibition or interference effects are studied under an experimental design as follows:

Experimental Group
    Learn Task A   Learn Task B   Test on Task A
Control Group
    Learn Task A   Test on Task A

Superiority of the control group on Task A when tested would show the inhibitory effects of learning Task B. This is generally what experimenters have found. It is clear that retention of learned material would be greater if there were no interpolated activity between learning and later testing. Unfortunately for the student, there is no way to provide some kind of "suspended animation" before an important examination. Experiments have, however, used sleep as a condition quite close to total immobility. Van Ormer (1932) compared retention after intervals of sleep and after activities while subjects were awake. Retention was significantly higher when sleep intervened than when wakeful activity took place.

QUALITATIVE CHANGE

The methods of measuring retention which have been outlined above are all quantitative. The results show amounts of material retained but provide little information as to the kind of changes that occur over time.

Bartlett (1932) noted changes in verbal material over a time period. He presented an American Indian folk tale to a group of British university students and tested their recall after various intervals. In addition to the expected quantitative decline, Bartlett found interesting qualitative changes. In general, there was a tendency to simplify or to put the tale in one's own terms. Certain features stood out, however, because of unusual aspects or associations. Bartlett also noted changes in the reproduction of figures. Over an interval of time, subjects would draw a figure from memory; each successive reproduction showed distortions until a more symmetrical and complete figure or one more familiar to the subject emerged.

Levine and Murphy (1943) noted that individuals learn and remember material that is congruent with their social attitudes better than material that is not. Anticommunist students learned and remembered anticommunist prose passages better than the procommunist passages. Procommunist students did better with the procommunist material.

REPRESSION

Repression is a kind of "forgetting" that is based on a defense mechanism of which we are unaware. As a result of this dynamic feature, one is able to lose awareness of a fact that would otherwise cause fear or anxiety. This is not the same kind of mechanism operative in ordinary forgetting nor are we conscious of its existence; it is a phenomenon that comes into play to prevent anxiety without our willing it. When a social event passes without my attending it, I might wonder whether I really wanted to attend and therefore conveniently "forgot." Dentist appointments, people's names, and events in one's past are all subject to the occurrence of repression.

PHYSIOLOGICAL FACTORS

Some evidence has been accumulated from basic research on memory that indicates that the underlying factors in this process are physiological in nature (Deutsch, 1962). It is thought that different processes or different degrees of development of a common process are involved, so that we might speak of "short-term" and "long-term" memory. It has also been hypothesized that a change in structure of ribonucleic acid (RNA) is the molecular basis of memory (Dingman and Sporn, 1964).

Training Programs

Applications of learning principles to training programs are made in many and varied ways. Training programs differ in length, complexity, extent of use of principles, and in objectives. Many of them have certain characteristics in common, a factor that makes for overlapping classifications.

OBJECTIVES OF TRAINING

The major question which must be asked even before the training begins is "training for what?" The matter of identification and selection of objectives determines the entire course of the instructional program and cannot be overlooked or minimized. Some programs operate to provide a mere acquaintance with the ramifications of a problem or an organization. Such approaches are often plainly labeled as orientation programs. Other situations are set up to provide an extensive grounding in specific skills, be they mechanical or managerial.

General rules may be stated in setting objectives for training programs. The objectives should be derived from what is actually required for the job performance. They should also be communicated to the students after being arranged in hierarchical order. Each unit of instruction must be based on the knowledges and skills already within the repertoire of students before the training begins, so that new material is reasonably within the achievement level of the students (Crawford, 1962, p. 326). These rules allow curricular decisions to be made on sound principles of learning applied to those areas where skills and knowledge are important to the completion of the task.

TYPES OF PROGRAMS

Actual training programs encountered may vary from casual and general approaches to highly organized efforts to inculcate specific skills. "Orientation" programs, for instance, are frequently met but may consist of nothing more than a tour of the plant. Other techniques usually show more structuring.

"On-the-Job" Training

This, too, is a term that is widely used and may cover rather diverse circumstances. It is very often seen in the casual introduction of a new worker to the work situation itself. An experienced worker is then asked to show the trainee "the ropes," a course of action hardly to be recommended. The approach assumes that the experienced worker not only can communicate the elements of the skill involved but that he will put into practice the principles of learning, an assumption that is usually unwarranted.

Apprentice Training

In newer versions of the medieval relationship between a master craftsman and his pupil, this is still considered an important type of training approach.

Apprenticeship could, however, be considered as a schooling approach, though it also has hallmarks of on-the-job training. An *internship* in medicine or a *clerkship* in the law is a form of apprenticeship or even on-the-job training. These are only as good as the trainer and the training program; those who believe that experience is a good teacher should recognize that indeed it is but it may be teaching the wrong things. The "school of hard knocks" is usually a much too traumatic and expensive way of learning something.

At higher levels in industry, management trainees are often given real company problems for discussion and recommendation of alternatives for solution. The device of naming them to "Junior Executive Boards" adds a touch of realism to the task even though in their conclusions they perform a staff function with no final executive powers.

Supervisory and Managerial Training

The training of individuals who supervise the activity of others has assumed greater proportions in the past few years as almost all industrial organizations of any size have or hope to have a training program for management personnel. Whether the label used refers to supervisors or managers makes little difference in the actual content; the training differs in degree or extent, not in kind. Managerial is the adjective more often used for training of those at higher levels of the organization where more time in training and a more extensive program is ordinarily available. Supervisory training is offered at the first-line supervisory level and is usually less extensive. There is actually no difference between the two in terms of basic learning principles.

Though the jobs of foremen have shrunk over the years in terms of extent or responsibility, there still remains a large core of job duties for which training is desirable. While there is a need for knowledge of the skills possessed by subordinates, a more critical area is that of social or human relations skills. Many of the types of training programs already mentioned above are put to use in managerial and supervisory training; the most appropriate ones, however, are those which are particularly suitable for the development of interactional skills. Role playing, T-Group sessions, and the management game are some of the approaches that are valuable for the purpose.

School Training

This type of training approach undoubtedly needs little introduction. There are about as many variations, however, as there are opportunities to open up classrooms. These range from the specialized training institutes organized by a particular company in order to fill the need for workers with specific skills to very broad educational institutions. The classroom in the company is often virtually indistinguishable from the high school or college classroom.

Secondary or college education and training is often considered as a pre-training situation in that the course programs are seldom specifically geared to later employment but do serve as preliminary preparation.

Vestibular Training

This approach to task learning concentrates on the acquisition of skills in a setting removed from the work scene but with all the attributes of the real situation. In industry the training would take place on a typical machine in a room off the plant floor, hence the name vestibule.

Simulation

Simulation programs vary widely, with many of them having elements seen also in other approaches. The gamut runs from business games in college or other training programs to the use of various mechanical devices such as the Link trainer for pilot training. In the business game a simulated marketing, production, and financial situation is arranged while the students respond as if they really had to make decision affecting the enterprise. One of the earliest extensive business simulation programs was the *Carnegie Tech Management Game* (Cohen et al., 1964), whose authors set out to provide a challenging environment for students wherein they would be able to develop the skills that managers need. They believed that the complex structuring of data and circumstances in the game allows for the acquisition of several abilities, among them the ability to set goals and to forecast and plan. Along with this, the game gives the opportunity to play the role of generalist and specialist and to organize and use information from a complex environment. Not the least is the additional chance to learn to work effectively with other people. The game provides players, arranged in groups of five to ten, with 1000 to 2000 pieces of information for each "month" of play. The players are able, from this information, to make over 300 decisions each simulated month.

Team Training

Most learning or training programs concentrate on the individual. In an increasing number of situations, however, the individual is called on to function as a part of an operating group. The training of aircrews recognizes that three or more individuals must work as a team. Here, as in individual training situations, a simulation device or program may be used.

Team training on a larger scale is often called *system training*. Biel (1962) describes such a program used by the Air Defense Command to train individuals and teams in the overall system represented by the Aircraft Control and Warning System. Simulated conditions are set up for communication and coordination among units of the system. Each individual and each team must function as they would in a real situation. Radar information is introduced; crews process the information from the radar scopes and send simulated aircraft to intercept unidentified aircraft. Simulated systems training is valued because it provides training that system members could not get otherwise.

Group Dynamics Techniques

Many tasks require a high level of skill in interpersonal relationships. Skills in the social area are seldom, if ever, acquired with the training programs sketched so far; the nature of these abilities calls for approaches of a different sort. Variations of group techniques have been used in many training programs pointed toward managerial or other influence-transmitting activities.

Role playing requires participants to adopt specific roles or to develop them extemporaneously in a hypothetical social situation. Considerable insight is possible into one's behavior and that of others as the result of a properly structured dramatic experience. A supervisor playing the role of an indignant female employee he usually supervises on the job can learn as much as or more than the other supervisors in the audience. Not only is there learning of facts or skills on an intellectual basis but, even more important, the emotional or feelings content of situations emerges from the play. *Psychodrama* is the name applied to this technique when it is used in clinical or therapeutic settings. The same prophylactic results are often by-products of the role-playing sessions in industry.

The *T-Group or Training Group Method* has been identified also as "the laboratory method of training" or "sensitivity training." The multiplicity of labels indicates the amorphous concept of the methodology involved.

This general approach probably stems from the ideas and activities of the Research Center for Group Dynamics under the leadership of the late Kurt Lewin. The basic concepts were carried out in sessions at the National Training Laboratory at Bethel, Maine, beginning in 1947 and continuing to this day, but there has been no single outstanding and definitive delineation of the method. Perhaps each individual and each trainer perceives the program differently and contributes to the proliferation of variations on the main themes. A near consensus does exist, however, with respect to central concepts, and most practitioners will agree that the laboratory method provides a setting in which group processes can be observed and studied. The objectives are to train group members to recognize when processes are appropriate to the task, what the consequences are, and how members contribute. How leaders aid these processes or how a group with inappropriate processes may be helped to improve are additional facets (Thelen, 1963, p. 130). The trainer assigned to each small group has the task of providing significant experiences from which people in the group of 15 to 20 can learn. The trainer's job is to facilitate the airing of feelings in the problem-oriented group situation. Many of those who use the label "sensitivity training" are apt to emphasize the cathartic nature of the expression of feelings and pay less attention to the other aspects of the learning situation. In practice the interpretations or comments of members could be traumatic for a person and detrimental to learning. Supporters of sensitivity training believe it to be a good way of finding out how others perceive you; this is a bit of knowledge that is important in interpersonal activities and yet is often very difficult to obtain.

The Case Method

Some academic and business programs have used the case method approach to develop awareness and skills in many functional areas. Programs in training for business have adapted a form of this method which has become traditional in law schools, namely, the study and analysis of cases, the reports of and rationale for judicial decisions on points in controversy in court. The case method in business is, instead, a study of descriptions of actual situations. Analysis of the problems with an attempt to provide possible solutions is the basis for the educational value to be gained in this approach. The *problem method* is a less extensive variant of the case method where a short anecdote serves as the basis for analysis and hypothetical response.

MEASUREMENT OF TRAINING

Evaluation of learning in an applied setting should be carried out on a systematic basis. The progress toward meeting the training needs outlined must be determined by something more than a simple impression or opinion of performance. In academic course work or in industrial training, specific and objective measures of progress toward a specified goal are highly desirable.

The fundamental measures of retention of material sketched above serve as the basis for measurement in applied areas. In the area of education, measures of performance are tests of achievement consisting of items constructed from material which has been learned. Recall and recognition items in achievement tests are familiar to all who have been through school.

In industry measures of achievement may take different forms. Often, since the objective may be to train people for production, some indication from production figures serves as a measurement of skill. These production figures may be direct measures of output (number of "widgets" produced per hour or day) or they may be based on percentage of workers meeting a standard or on the time required to do a job. More indirect measures of performance may relate to the number of rejects or the decrease in costs and breakage. Even more indirect are measures that point out changes in absenteeism or turnover. Where the objective is the presentation of information, as in orientation training, achievement measures similar to those found in the classroom are appropriately used.

The most difficult problems of evaluation lie in the area of human relations skills training. Supervisory and managerial training programs are, for this reason, less amenable to objective review procedures.

Aids to Learning

Learning can be affected by physical or material factors in the situation as well as through the operation of the intrinsic features heretofore mentioned. "Hardware" is becoming more important as trainers in all areas of society begin to recognize the extent of assistance that is available to make their role more effective.

AUDIO-VISUAL AIDS

Almost any method of presenting material to be learned could be called an audio-visual aid. These might be subdivided into those utilizing visual stimuli, those using the auditory sense areas, and those using both. Needless to say, any of the other sense receptor areas could be brought into play as well, but not many examples of other sensory inputs exist apart from some novel uses of odor in advertising or limited kinesthetic stimuli in Link Trainers or other skills-learning apparatus.

A quick enumeration of some of the better known aids to learning will serve as a reminder of their existence. Textbooks, programmed instruction, periodicals, theatricals, and graphic displays of all kinds may be considered audio-visual aids to learning. Another obvious device is the blackboard, scarcely newer than the clay tablet or marble slab of the ancients yet one that remains one of the most useful of all present aids. Flipboards present a series of messages on cards, large and small, which are flipped in sequence. Opaque and transparent projectors throw static pictures on walls or ceilings. These may even include an audio message, although the movie film projectors are more likely to add sound. Radio still remains a largely untapped resource, although many school systems receive radio programs from educational networks along with television productions. Tape recorders or disc recordings either provide feedback on an individual performance or serve as a means of preserving lectures permanently. Some systems are so complexly structured that a central bank of tapes provides a "dial-a-lecture" service on call from remote stations. Further descriptions of aids and training devices may be found in works by Biel (1962) and Brown (1964).

Of greater concern, more likely, to the student of learning in an applied setting is an appraisal of the limitations or the value of the various aids to learning. Evaluations of the instructional impact of television indicate the important contributions of applied learning studies which this research has made. Perhaps the most extensive review of the literature is that of Schramm (1962) who presented a summary of the results of almost 400 comparisons of television and conventional instruction. In 65 percent of the cases there was no difference between the techniques in results obtained, and in 20 percent of the cases the difference was in favor of the television presentation. Attitudes and results obtained favored television more in the lower grades than at the college level. Further indication of the importance of attitudes lies in the variation in acceptance of television in different subjects. Science and mathematics courses or those using demonstrations were considered more valuable. Just as significant an indication of the role of attitudes is that instructors who used television favored it while those who avoided it were suspicious and reluctant. This is not surprising, since it reflects similar findings in other attitude studies.

The experimental findings in the area of television instruction are much the same as those reported earlier in studies of the use of films in the classroom—the two media are basically the same technique. Wendt and Butts (1962) present an extensive survey of recent experimentation with films which helps to point out possible pitfalls for the trainer or teacher. Films can be an effective medium if the principles of learning outlined above are followed in the classroom use of films; learning proceeds to the extent that the basic principles are recognized and used. The set is particularly important—students will learn if they are prepared for the material and told that they will be tested on it. Abilities and interests play a vital role as well. Finally, attitudes are important here, too; one specific recurring finding is that unfavorable attitudes develop when a series of daily films extends for a month or more. These unfavorable attitudes most assuredly affect performance in the learning situation.

Despite some drawbacks, the advantages of film, television, and other aids to learning remain. By use of these media, material can be presented that could not be available otherwise. Through films or recordings we "take journeys to other times or other places." The same format can present material over and over again in exactly the same way each time and be available at all hours. No live lecturer could or would be able to do the same.

SIMULATORS

Various devices are available which can reproduce actual job situations for the trainee with a high degree of realism. The subject is able to experience stimuli and respond in much the same way he would be called on to do later on the job. The Link Trainer, a device for training airplane pilots, is the best known example of a mechanical simulator. Figure 6-5 shows a flight simulator for a U.S. Phantom II jet aircraft where all visual displays and control devices operate realistically to give the pilot-trainee feedback at all times. The technique is good not only for training to a level of proficiency but can be valuable for continuing training to maintain that level. Emergency situations seldom met in actuality, yet critical if they do occur, can be presented often in the simulator.

Figure 6-5. Weapons system simulator for the Phantom II, a two-seat, all-weather jet (Link Group, General Precision Systems Inc.).

PROGRAMMED INSTRUCTION

The greatest amount of interest in education and training circles in recent years has been stirred by the development of a systematic approach toward presentation of material to the learner. Because of this, but more because it illustrates many of the principles of learning outlined above, programmed instruction will be treated more extensively here.

The label "teaching machines" has stirred the interest of many, although that term is a misnomer because the concept of programmed instruction is broader than the mere use of "hardware." While machines represent a significant part of this approach to training and education, the presentation of material may be made in other, often less expensive ways. A book, for instance, may consist of pages of material that are arranged in the same way as is the machine-presented material.

The main characteristics of programmed instruction techniques are:

1. Presentation of material in small units called "frames" in a specific sequence.

2. The student considers these at his own pace.

3. Each frame calls for a response.

4. The response receives immediate feedback, and a correct answer is reinforcing while incorrect answers may be corrected.

5. The entire approach is built on an empirical and student-oriented basis. Goals and arrangement of steps are determined by actual results.

6. The procedure makes for better student motivation.

Most of these principles are fundamental in learning and have been in use for some time (perhaps since Socrates). Recent research and development has, however, sharpened the thinking which now goes into the use of this approach to training and education.

Development of Programmed Instruction

Sustained interest and research in programming is a matter of little more than ten years, yet in that time the field has unfolded rapidly. The flurry of activity followed B. F. Skinner's reports (1958) of his research in the mid-1950's. Skinner's work stemmed logically from his basic experimentation in learning and focused on the concept of reinforcement. Even before this time there had been activity in research and development, particularly in the armed forces during and after World War II. Earlier than this, however, Sidney L. Pressey of Ohio State was active in the construction and use of machine techniques for instruction and scoring of responses (1926). While

Table 6-1.   A Completion Frame (Holland and Skinner, 1961)

Performing animals are sometimes trained with "rewards." The behavior of a hungry animal can be "rewarded" with _____.

Pressey did publish results of his work, interest in the technique remained dormant until revived again after 1945.

Basic Approaches to Programming

While there are many examples of variation in the construction of programs, two basic approaches may be identified. Skinner (1958) and his co-workers have favored programs that call for an actual response, or a constructed response. The items require either the actual writing in of the response on a blank line or other constructive effort on the part of the respondent. One such frame is given in Table 6-1. The Skinner approach is often termed a *linear* system because the items are considered in an unvarying sequence. Each of the frames is "lined up" in a certain order to be followed by each respondent.

The other basic approach to program construction may be labeled multiple-choice programming. This was the system Pressey used when he had students punch keys on his early machine to indicate their choice of the correct response. A later illustration of a multiple-choice item appears in Table 6-2.

The multiple-choice programming approach is sometimes called the "branching" method because of an important variation which is often added to the technique. Each response in the frame may be programmed to lead to a different point in the sequence of frames. If a respondent shows understanding of

Table 6-2.   A Multiple-Choice Item (Keislar, 1959)

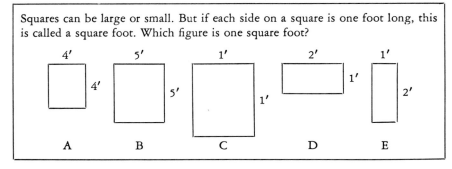

Squares can be large or small. But if each side on a square is one foot long, this is called a square foot. Which figure is one square foot?

Table 6-3.   An illustration of a "Scrambled Item" (Crowder, 1960)

In the multiplication $3 \times 4 = 12$, the number 12 is called the product and the numbers 3 and 4 are called the
      page 15 quotients
      page 29 factors
      page 43 powers

(if the student chooses page 43)

---

    page 43
Your answer was: "powers"; we'll get to powers of numbers pretty soon, but we're not there yet. The numbers that are multiplied together to form a product are called "factors" not "powers." Now return to page 1 and choose the right answer.

---

the frame by choosing the correct response, he is sent on to the next phase. If the choice is an incorrect one, the student is sent back for further study to a point which is indicated by his incorrect response. An extensive use of this method appears in the "scrambled book" developed by Crowder (1959). Table 6-3 contains a sample item. Crowder also refers to his system as *intrinsic programming* because the student himself determines the next material he will be exposed to rather than have the set program of the program writer determine it for him.

Teaching Machines

The basic approaches toward programming may be presented in many mechanical ways. The best of such devices already developed and available is quite extensive. Only a quick glance at the varieties on the market is possible here.

Pressey's early machine was a box with a revolving drum with an item in an open window; pressing the correct button permitted the drum to be moved on to the next frame. Skinner first used a similar "slider machine" which allowed the student to write the correct response in the frame exposed by a window and then slide it on to the next frame to check his response and start the new frame.

In World War II the armed forces had already begun to develop more complex mechanical devices which received extensive use by the mid-1950's.

The most significant steps being taken at the present time, however, are those which utilize the capacity of the computer to provide extensive and immediate aid to the student. In 1958 the International Business Machines Company combined the IBM 650 computer and an electric typewriter input to provide the student a linear sequence with quick feedback for responses. Needless to say, such elaborate arrangements are infrequent because of expense, although increasing mass use may facilitate their introduction.

Considerations in Programming

Virtually all of the principles and problems outlined in this chapter are applicable in setting up and using a programmed approach in instruction. The technique further offers its own unique variations of the fundamentals of learning. Some of these factors should be pointed out to give an idea of the problems to be met. The type of item, its length and position, the size of the steps, the conceptual approach, and the material used need to be studied carefully. Individual factors and the learning environment are important here as well.

Are Teachers Unnecessary?

With the increasing introduction of programmed instruction, the notion of replacing teachers in a training program occurs to many, even to the teachers themselves. The thought is a source of anxiety to some and a hope to others. The elimination of a human instructor is not only unlikely, it is undesirable. First of all, we cannot duplicate, in a program, the complex treatment which is necessary in any advanced area. Programmed instruction can provide, however, the basic information which is necessary for proceeding further in understanding and problem solving in most academic disciplines. The lesson should be obvious. Those instructors who "read the book" to their classes perform a function that programmed instruction can do better, and they can be replaced. The need for superior discussion leaders, however, will be greatly increased. The mentor who can carry the students into advanced work once they have had the basic material has always been in short supply. This demand will become even greater in the future.

Summary

Learning is an important base for behavior; what we are is largely the result of what has happened to us, that is, what we have learned.

Learning can take place at many levels of difficulty and in various ways. Conditioning is a simple kind of learning where a new behavior is added because it either accompanies the old and is thus reinforced (classical conditioning) or because some new behavior is reinforced (instrumental conditioning). Perceptual discrimination is another form of learning wherein a correct response is picked out and reinforced. Even more complex is the insightful kind of response consisting of many elements that are finally put together properly.

Basic principles of learning are those fundamental and common to all learning situations. No learning takes place without motivation: the process of goal-directed need satisfaction. Set is the predisposition to respond that helps mold the behavior in the learning situation, while reinforcement is the reward condition that makes it more likely that the reinforced behavior will take place. The learning can take place in various patterns that can be sketched graphically as curves of learning. A curve may have a leveling off somewhere in the midst of a period (plateau).

How the practice is distributed, that is, whether massed or spaced, makes a difference in the rate of learning; under most conditions spaced is superior to massed practice. When the learner is involved in the process, learning is more effective than when he is passive. If the material is meaningful, learning proceeds faster than when there is little or no meaning inherent in it. Knowledge of results is not only important but necessary for learning to take place. When what has been learned before aids in the learning of a new task, there is positive transfer of training; negative transfer is where the old hinders the new. Finally, learning by whole as opposed to part by part may make a difference in the rate at which it may be accomplished.

Measures of learning are those made during the learning trials. Measures of retention are those tests of level after the trials have taken place. Three common methods of measuring retention are recall, recognition, and relearning.

Individual differences affect learning. In general, the most important variable is intelligence; those with greater ability learn more, faster. Learning new material is at a peak at the mid-teens, and the aptitude declines very gradually thereafter. Motivation plays a most important role, as always.

What happens to learned material over a period of time? None is truly forgotten but may not be remembered because new material is learned that takes the place of the old (retroactive inhibition). Qualitative changes take place over time with repression being the most dynamic mechanism. Repression is not a conscious forgetting—the blotting out of the set of circumstances is taken care of at an unconscious level.

Training programs must, first of all, be well planned. The objectives of training should be clearly determined in advance of the training program.

Different approaches to training are possible, and the variations allow many classifications. The program may be called orientation, on-the-job, apprentice, vestibular, school, or supervisory and managerial training.

Simulation programs represent a newer approach in that an entire real-life problem in miniature is used as a learning situation. Group dynamics techniques use the findings of small group studies to foster awareness of interpersonal problems in organizations.

Measurement of training uses those measures of achievement that reflect performance. Different measures must be used in verbal and in industrial situations.

Aids to learning consist of a large number of audio-visual aids from blackboards to movies or television. Use of educational television in the classroom indicates at least as good results as traditional classroom techniques and frequently even better.

Simulators are devices that duplicate, in so far as is possible, the circumstances of the job without its dangers and drawbacks. The earth-bound Link Trainer to prepare pilots is one such device.

Programmed instruction, whether in machine or book form, represents a new and dynamic development in education and training at all levels. Material is presented in small units that students consider at their own pace. Each item calls for a response, and the learner knows immediately whether the response is correct or not. The system is based mainly on the learning principles of motivation, knowledge of results, and reinforcement.

Bibliography

Ammons, R. (1956). Effects of knowledge of performance: a survey and tentative theoretical formulation. *Journal of Genetic Psychology,* **54,** 279–299.

Bartlett, F. (1932). *Remembering.* London: Cambridge University Press.

Biel, W. (1962). Training programs and devices. In Gagne, R. (ed.). *Psychological principles in system development.* New York: Holt, Rinehart and Winston.

Brown, J., Lewis, R., and Harcleroad, F. (1964). *A-V instruction: materials and methods* (2nd ed.). New York: McGraw-Hill.

Cohen, K., Dill, W., Kuehn A., and Winters, P. (1964). *The Carnegie Tech Management Game.* Homewood, Ill.: Irwin.

Crawford, M. (1962). Concepts of training. In Gagne, R. (ed.). *Psychological principles in system development.* New York: Holt, Rinehart and Winston.

Crowder, N. (1959). Automatic tutoring by means of intrinsic programming. In Galanter, E. (ed.). *Automatic teaching: the state of the art.* New York: Wiley.

Deutsch, J. (1962). Higher nervous function: the physiological bases of memory. *Annual Review of Physiology,* **24,** 259–286.

Dingman, W. and Sporn, M. (1964). Molecular theories of memory. *Science*, **144**, 26–29.

Ericksen, S. (1942). Variability of attack in massed and distributed practice. *Journal of Experimental Psychology*, **31**, 339–345.

Harlow, H. (1949). The formation of learning sets. *Psychological Review*, **56**, 51–65.

Holland, J. and Skinner, B. (1961). *The analysis of behavior: a program for self instruction*. New York: McGraw-Hill.

Hovland, C. (1951). Human learning and retention. In Stevens, S. (ed.). *Handbook of experimental psychology*. New York: Wiley.

Hovland, C., Lumsdaine, A., and Sheffield, F. (1949). *Experiments on mass communication*. Princeton: Princeton University Press.

Keislar, E. (1959). The development of understanding in arithmetic by a teaching machine. *Journal of Educational Psychology*, **50**, 247–253.

Kendler, H., Greenberg, A., and Richman, H. (1952). The influence of massed and spaced practice on the development of mental set. *Journal of Experimental Psychology*, **43**, 21–25.

Kohler, W. (1925). *The mentality of apes* (Winter, E., trans.). New York: Harcourt, Brace & World.

Krech, D. and Crutchfield, R. (1962). *Elements of psychology*. New York: Knopf.

Lashley, K. (1930). The mechanism of vision. *Journal of Genetic Psychology*, **37**, 453–460.

Levine, J. and Murphy, G. (1943). The learning and forgetting of controversial material. *Journal of Abnormal and Social Psychology*, **38**, 507–517.

Lindahl, L. (1945). Movement analysis as an industrial training method. *Journal of Applied Psychology*, **29**, 420–436.

McGeoch, J. and Irion, A. (1952). *The psychology of human learning* (2nd ed.). New York: Longmans Green.

Morgan, C. and King, R. (1966). *Introduction to psychology* (3rd ed.). New York: McGraw-Hill.

Noble, C. (1952). The role of stimulus meaning (m) in serial verbal learning. *Journal of Experimental Psychology*, **43**, 437–466.

Pressey, S. (1926). A simple apparatus which gives tests and scores—and teaches. *School and Society*, **23**, 373–376.

Ray, W. (1957). Verbal compared with manipulative solution of an apparatus problem. *American Journal of Psychology*, **70**, 289–290.

Schramm, W. (1962). Learning from instructional television. *Review of Educational Research, 32,* 156–167.

Skinner, B. (1938). *The behavior of organisms.* New York: Appleton-Century-Crofts.

Skinner, B. (1958). Teaching machines. *Science,* **128,** 969–977.

Thelen, H. (1963). *Dynamics of groups at work* (Phoenix ed.). Chicago: University of Chicago Press.

Thorndike, E. (1898). Animal intelligence. *Psychological Monographs,* **1(8).**

Thorndike, E., Bregman, E., Tilton, J., and Woodyard, E. (1928). *Adult learning.* New York: Macmillan.

Torrance, E. (1950). The phenomenon of resistance in learning. *Journal of Abnormal and Social Psychology,* **45,** 592–597.

Underwood, B. (1954). Speed of learning and amount retained: a consideration of methodology. *Psychological Bulletin,* **51,** 276–282.

Van Ormer, E. (1932). Retention after intervals of sleep and waking. *Archives of Psychology,* **21(137).**

Wendt, P. and Butts, B. (1962). Audio-visual materials. *Review of Educational Research,* **32,** 141–155.

7

Cognitive Processes

It is not unusual to see, in the offices of many of the country's leading corporations, a sign which exhorts the employees to . . . THINK. This ubiquitous reminder is merely a small example of how much this activity is prized. We recognize the centrality of this process and place a high premium on it.

What this quality is may be a bit more difficult matter on which to reach an agreement. The word "think" may mean many things at different times; it often is used to denote different aspects of the cognitive processes or even other psychological activities. For instance, we may be urged by parents or teachers to "think about what we are doing." In this case, the command is to pay attention or be aware of what is happening and, therefore, refers to the preliminary perceptual process. A simple associational process of calling forth an image can result from the request to "think of an apple." Closely related is the activity that psychologists call *autistic,* the fantasy or daydreaming sort of thinking which is a response to deeper wish-fulfillment drives. Imagination is a more complex or problem-solving version of this autistic kind of thinking. Another kind of request—"think where you left your umbrella"— means a demand for recall and is better labeled as *remembering.* More complex activity is the kind of thinking that involves an extensive effort, as in solving a problem or in reasoning through to a logical conclusion on the basis of consideration of evidence. Still another frequent use of the term thinking is in connection with a question such as, "What do you think of the President's policies in foreign affairs?" This last meaning of the term refers to opinions or beliefs rather than to cognitive processes per se. While some basis of beliefs lies in the central processes, these phenomena are shaped even more by affective experience and social influences. These are important enough to be viewed separately later (Chapter 13). Here, all mentioned variations except the very last usage of the term "thinking" will be recognizable in the present discussion of the cognitive processes.

The model of behavior sketched earlier (Chapter 5) on the basis of an

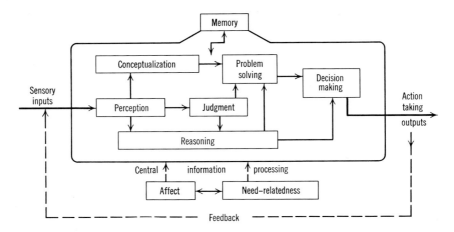

Figure 7-1.   A systems model of central information processing.

input-output approach discussed the critical central processes primarily in terms of information processing technology. This is a new and, to many researchers, an appropriate way of structuring a study of this area. There have been, however, more traditional and more extensive ways of considering the functioning of the higher level cortical activities. The designation of *cognitive processes* has been the usual general label; beyond this, there has been greater variation in the views of the more specific processes. These variations from the information processing model provide a more complete picture of research activity and results. In doing so, they do not cause rejection of the information processing model either in its entirety or in part; they extend or complement it. At this time, it is possible to reintroduce the schematic model of behavior and add to the description of the central information processing functions (Figure 7-1).

Definition of the Field

With little doubt this important area of human behavior remains a most complex and difficult field of study. As might well be guessed, the problems inherent in studying the processes within this category are great. The difficulties in systematically observing overt behavior are troublesome enough; when we move to the outer edges of behavior and attempt to study its phenomenal aspects, we are treading on shakier ground. It is no wonder, then, that there are many disagreements in this area, beginning with definitions of terms, even though these processes have been studied with scientific rigor since the earliest days of a systematic approach to behavioral problems. The difficulties are magnified further by the fact that a sample of behavior in the cognitive area will contain an intertwining of many of these processes all at the same time.

Definition may serve as a basis for the discussion of the cognitive processes even though a reviewer must be cautioned to expect some variation in the uses of terminology. What follows here, however, has a great deal of acceptance from those who are working in this field.

Thinking is the representation of "reality" or the world outside, whether present or not, through the use of symbols or images. The process is a common one, and the actual representation may vary from the simple processes to the very complex—from reminiscences and remembering, at one end, to the judgments involved in deciding on a course of action, a decision that is based on a recombination of past associations.

Reasoning is just such a recombination of past experience to provide a meaningful response to a situation. Reasoning is a term sometimes used in place of problem solving or even decision making but is viewed, more correctly, as a process basic to those activities.

Problem solving is goal-directed activity which must surmount some kind of obstacle on the way to that goal. True problem solving is much more, however, than an habitual reaction to a problem; it calls for more thought in the accomplishment of a result than does a mere conditioned response.

Decision making means choosing between alternatives and deciding on a course of action. Alternatives may vary from a simple binary situation (go, no go) to one where the number of alternatives is infinite. Decisions usually must be made under conditions of imperfect information. While often there is the implication that the decisions are such as to reach some optimal result, this may not be justified on the basis of empirical evidence.

Perception is the experience people have as the proximate result of the sensory inputs. The process is one of selection and organization of sensations to provide the meaningful entity we experience.

Conceptualization is the cognitive process from which evolves a common property of or a relationship between objects or conditions which then can be represented by a term or name.

Judgment is the evaluation and estimation of the characteristics of a situation. We may perceive a person far away, but judging how tall he is involves more activity than is present in perception. Some standard for comparison, present or past, is called into play to make the determination.

Creativity involves innovative thinking which provides either better, more ingenious, or more esthetic results than usual. It differs from *originality*, with which it could be confused, in that original thought merely means something new or different without the value or utility implied in creativity.

Discussions of thinking should further keep in mind other aspects of this area, namely, those which touch on the *content* and *scope* of the thinking process. Questions of content, efficiency, and level of thought come into the picture. Other variables which play a role in the thinking process range from personal background and experiential factors such as attitudes, beliefs, or group membership to factors such as intelligence, language (and its structure), and physical condition. Basic psychological concepts like motivation, perception, and learning also play their ever-important role in the unfolding of thinking, as they do in other areas of behavior.

Perception

Perception is a basic cognitive process with many variable aspects to affect behavior. It may be defined as the organization of material which comes in from the outside at one time or another. Perception may also be considered as the interpretation of the data that is received from inputs. The system, or organism, recognizes the information, assembles it, and makes comparisons with material previously stored in the "central information processing storage." This involves a whole history of what has happened to the individual over his lifetime, since it is the organization of inputs through an inner process that is dynamic, that is, a constantly changing one. It is a process that shapes whatever comes in from the outside; in turn, what is there is changed by what comes in.

We find eventually that the television and radio commercial "it's what's up front that counts" is not really so. What's up front is not as important as what's inside. Objective reality often means less than what is inside because what is inside shapes what comes in from the outside. By way of illustration, we might take a very prosaic example. A boy and a girl walking down the street, both with 20/20 vision and no color anomalies, see at the same time a shapely young female walking 10 yards in front of them. Both *see* the same thing, but is the impact of this vision of loveliness the same for both? Obviously not. In much the same way, when a couple goes to a baseball or a football game, the man, probably better versed in the sport, picks up much more information on the game than does his woman companion who may be more interested in the muscles of one of the players or the costume worn by the woman several rows in front. An experienced engineer scanning a panel of dials in front of him gets more out of this information than does the manager visiting from the central office.

BASIC FACTORS IN PERCEPTION

While social and other environmental factors are seen to be influential in helping to determine perceptions, before those myriad ways of influencing may be considered, more fundamental factors must be pointed out. These are pretty much the same for all individuals.

Perception is, first of all, a selective process. We select a certain amount of information from the outside simply because we cannot assimilate all of the information coming in. All of these physical changes may be impinging upon us, but only certain stimuli are taken in and responded to. The stimuli may be of two kinds: those of which we are aware and, therefore, can recognize fairly readily after selection or they may be below the threshold of our awareness, that is, those of which we may not be cognizant yet which do influence us. It is a little more difficult for people to believe that some of our behavior is determined by stimuli that are below the level of consciousness.

The basic factor in those perceptual situations within the limits of awareness is attention. When we attend to a situation, we focus on that set of circumstances. These elements of the experience stand out from others on the periphery. Many stimuli may have been attended to for a long period of time yet, suddenly, we shift to another set of stimuli and perceive something that was going on all the time. For instance, the baseball game comes through to us on the radio very clearly after the study period is over. It had been on all along, but only now did it intrude. Had the radio been blasting, we probably would have perceived at least part of the program, since *intensity* is a factor that plays a vital role. This lesson has been learned by advertising on radio and television (although the fanfare of trumpets to announce an important message is really an old device). In the visual area, *size* is the condition comparable to intensity. Closely related is *contrast.* Here, too, the television advertisers have learned to give the commercial several decibels above the level maintained in the program. They have also found *repetition* to be valuable in "getting the message over."

All of the factors immediately above are characteristics of the external situation. More internal in operation are the dynamic organizing features of perception. In a situation presenting a set of figures, an individual is not content with a mass of unorganized figures, he devises and perceives what can be called a good *gestalt* or fine form. A set of four dots equidistant from each other at ninety degree angles are perceived as a square. We have

Figure 7-2.   Reversible figure and ground.

a tendency to organize in a way which makes for a "proper" or "right" result, or at least we perceive a figure with boundaries as a unitary whole. *Symmetry* is imposed on a figure that may not really possess it. *Continuation* is the phenomenon that finishes a line, a piece of music, or other sensations. An incomplete circle will be perceived, more than likely, as a complete circle. Figures which are alike or close together are grouped on the basis of similarity or proximity. In the following arrangement, we impose upon the raw data more than is really there. A row such as XXOOXXOOXX is a grouping of Xs and Os by twos rather than a line of Xs and Os. Another tendency in perception is to perceive *figure and ground;* that is, we distinguish a central object from the surroundings. Often this is reversible, as the famous "cup-faces" in Figure 7-2 illustrates. A picture on a wall is a figure, the wall is a ground. In the auditory area we hear a melody; the chords represent the ground.

Adaptation level is a concept developed by Helson (1964) to explain the changes in perception as the result of the context in which the figures or events are perceived. Helson's experiments use different extreme stimuli (anchors) for subjects to use as comparison for a judgment in simple experiments, but the concept has been extended to more complex social activity as well. On the job, for instance, an average worker may be perceived as a poor one when he is with a group of good workers but may seem quite good when the rest of the team are poor.

In the terminology of engineering psychology or human factors systems, we might consider perception as being based on *scanning* and *coding*. Scanning is a search process whereby we attend selectively to various characteristics or properties and then put them into particular categories. This categorization, or putting the stimuli into a meaningful system, is often called "coding." This part of the process is a representational one in that a category takes the place of and stands for the "reality" which has been searched and coded.

Illusions are also interesting examples of the power of perception. The final perception which does not agree with other perceptions or reality is called an illusion. Figure 7-3 contains a few examples of well-known illusions. Another example is often referred to as the *phi phenomenon* or *apparent movement*. Some electrical advertising signs flash on and off in synchronized patterns which give us the illusion of movement. We are also "fooled" at the movies; the pictures do not move but are static photographs projected so rapidly that we perceive movement by the actors.

Another type of internal factor influencing perception is even more variable and powerful in producing variation in perceptions by individuals than the

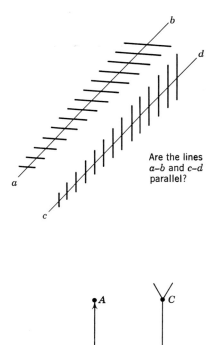

Are the lines
a–b and *c–d*
parallel?

Which vertical line is
longer—*A–B* or *C–D?*

Figure 7-3.　Some common illusions.

factors discussed immediately above. *Expectancy, interests,* or *motives* provide possibilities for widely differing organizations of inputs. Expectancy is more often referred to as a *set* or tendency to respond. When we are told that we will be tested on perception, we pick up more information in this area than if we are not told. The interests of a metallurgical engineer are such that a trip to a steel mill will cause him to organize more of the visual material than an ordinary visitor would. The dynamic variable of motives or drives can play an important role as well. Advertisers have noticed that attractive females on ads sell products. Sex has an appeal in our culture while, in another cultural setting, some other drive which has been limited will probably have more appeal. All these dynamic variables are the basis for the broader cultural and social factors which operate in more complex fashion.

SOCIAL AND CULTURAL FACTORS

Other variables play a very important role in the process of perception. Such factors as attitudes, values, motives, stress, a person's background, whether or not other people are present, or whether the others have a great deal of prestige are all factors that go into shaping perception. Many cues are present even though rationally some may seem to be irrelevant. Very frequently, the "irrelevant" cues are those which prove to be of most importance.

One of the earliest studies demonstrating the importance of attitudes or values was the work of Postman, Bruner, and McGinnies (1948) where words were presented tachistoscopically, that is, by an apparatus that gave very brief exposure to each word. These words were taken from value areas as measured by the Alport-Vernon Study of Values, value areas that showed political, aesthetic, theoretical, economic, religious, and social biases. The greater the interest of a person in a particular area, the more rapidly he would recognize or perceive words when they were briefly presented. This was done so quickly that individuals were not aware of them and could not definitely state them exactly, but subjects were able to predict or guess or recognize the words when these had high value for them. A word like "bank" or "money" was more readily perceived, even when presented below the threshold of recognition, by individuals who had high values in the economic area. Another study by Bruner and Goodman (1947) took children from prosperous homes and compared them with children from poor homes on a task of adjusting a patch of light to the sizes of various coins, either with the coins readily available or from memory. They found that the boys overestimated the size of the more valuable coins and underestimated the size of the less valuable coins. This did not happen in the situation where the same boys were to compare the patch of light with paper disks. In addition to this, it was significant that the distortion of size of coins was greater for the boys from poorer homes.

Other experiments further demonstrate the close relationship between the basic underlying motivational processes and the process of perception. Levine, Chein, and Murphy (1942) presented a group of subjects with food pictures placed behind a screen through which the food could not be clearly perceived. With increase in the time and food deprivation, subjects showed more associations connected with food.

Bruner (1958) emphasizes that there are two significant factors emerging from this series of studies. Perceptional readiness, that is, the set or the tendency to respond to items that are represented, reflects not only the needs and the goal striving of the individual but also the presence of an element of familiarity or predictableness of perception. We have a tendency to perceive what we expect to perceive. If an incongruity occurs, it is readily perceived as the usual event. Bruner and Postman (1949) presented playing cards with color and symbol reversed. Subjects perceived the briefly presented cards as being congruous; that is, hearts and diamonds were red and spades and clubs were black even though the actual cards had the reverse combinations. We usually perceive on the basis of what we have learned over a long period of time, either in physical or social events. If we hear behind us the sound of walking feet we turn around and perceive the person on the sidewalk walking behind us. This is a very straightforward and not very dynamic example of perception and then action. When we do not have a clear-cut situation, however, there is more opportunity for a variety of responses. In a social situation we may perceive hostility in another person if this is what we expect and our perception of hostility, even though there may be no foundation for it, "confirms" our prior expectation.

The conclusion that we can come to from the experiments is that what we perceive depends a great deal on not what is out there but what we ourselves bring to the situation—our own needs, drives, or predispositions. The process of selection is present, but this is very much a changing one; it is very creative and dynamic. In our relationships with others we are interdependent with other people. Since most of our satisfactions come in the social area from interactions with others, it is obvious that much of what occurs is a result of what we bring to the situation. The perceptions formed in our interactions with other people are affected not only by those same basic factors or variables that determine our perceptions of simple objects or pictures; when we are in a social relationship interacting with others, there are many more combinations of factors influencing our perception.

It is true, as stated above, that our perception proceeds along established lines, along a rut that has been pretty well fixed in our past. In this sense, a biased perception of people and events has been called a *stereotype*. Stereotype is a term first used by Walter Lippmann, who wrote about them as being "pictures in people's heads." These pictures determine the perception of others in ways that may vary widely. The prejudgment of others based on their membership in certain groups is a common example—"Lusatians are lazy, Transylvanians are industrious, and bankers reserved." It may extend to other people whom we meet in our daily activity—people in management, people in the union, people in college, or people in the club.

It may be that perceiving others with whom we deal in a stereotyped way limits our efficiency. Mason Haire (1955), in an experimental approach to labor and management relations, discusses perception by one side in a power conflict with the other and the roles that emerge. Haire concludes from his study of words used by subjects to describe others and themselves that there are differences in the impression of a person when he is viewed as a member of management and when he is viewed as a labor man. Management and labor perceive the other as less dependable; each person in the group "sees" persons in their group as appreciative of their own position and views the other as deficient in emotional characteristics, interpersonal relationships, and in reasoning. Labor sees itself and management differently, and management sees itself and labor differently. It seems clear from this and similar findings that a proper basis for decision making often may not exist in crucial social and industrial situations.

Core Cognitive Processes

Further inquiry into the central information processing functions leads to a consideration of those various processes that have usually been called *thinking*. Since they are more complex than the preliminary organizing processes of perception, there is also likely to be more agreement on the adjective *cognitive* for these deeper aspects of functioning.

CONCEPTUALIZATION

Concepts refer to the general classes of concrete things or mere ideas which are arranged on the basis of common elements or relationships. These commonalities are a significant part of the symbolic processes that take place in cognitive functioning. Symbols seldom refer to one specific event or object by itself; instead, they stand for the general class. "Apple" has meaning for us primarily because that object is part of the general run of apples with which it shares certain characteristics. Our language serves as the means of "carrying these classes in our heads," referring to them, and transmitting them to others. Without such classification we would be completely bogged down in everyday activities if each specific object or event were handled as a new and completely different thing. Classes are necessary for any effective functioning in the world.

Types of Concepts

We may identify three types of concepts (Bruner et al., 1956). The classification may be on the basis of the common elements that may be abstracted or "taken out" of the situation. The concept of redness refers to the aspect that rubies, apples, and red wagons have in common. This is termed a *conjunctive concept.* The second may be a class that contains members arrived at through different means; a strike in baseball is either where the hitter swings and misses, or is when the ball is thrown over the plate and between the shoulders and knees of the batter, or is a ball that is hit by the batter outside the boundaries of the playing field. This is a *disjunctive concept.* The third type is a *relational concept* covering the relationships between items as in "bigness," "clarity," and "fairness."

Concept Formation

In general, the process of learning concepts begins with the discrimination of common properties or relationships. This kind of awareness of the requisite features is called *abstraction.* The abstracted property is then labeled with a word to identify it in everyday use. The word is not the same thing as the concept nor do we even need the word; the concept stands by itself. In practice, however, the two are so closely intertwined that we usually consider them as one.

Concepts may be learned in several different ways. A child may have his discriminations reinforced when he attaches the label "apple" to some objects but not to others and is praised for doing so. Later, many other words may be used for developing a concept through definition. Young children may never have seen a buffalo, but it may be described for them. Later in life, definitions of concepts come in the even more complex form you are getting in this and other books. A similar approach may focus on the classification involved in the study of a field. The broad conjunctive concept "toolmaker" on the industrial scene is built up much as a botanist will classify and group a series of plants or a zoologist will group certain animals as "mammals." A final way of building a concept is to have it emerge as the result of its use over a period of time. The context may provide enough cues so that eventually we get an idea of what is meant.

One of the earliest investigators of the development of concepts, and still one of the most active, is Jean Piaget of Paris and Geneva. Piaget has worked with children on the assumption that the development of concepts can best be studied in the young and has concentrated on the unfolding of logical and mathematical concepts from an early age to maturity. The various stages in the development of concepts have been discussed earlier (Chapter 4). The several phases, from the sensorimotor period to the age of formal operations, represent the fundamental aspect of *adaptation,* the equilibrium toward which the organism moves as the result of the interaction between it and the environment. Piaget considers two aspects as the key ones in the process. The first is the movement away from a solely egocentric orientation while the second key factor is the development of *operations,* or those actions which have been internalized. A child learns to manipulate beads and soon is able to do so without the actions—in psychological manipulations, even if it takes awhile before words are used to describe the basis of and predict the actions. This interiorization of actions is considered to be the origin of thought.

Piaget's work does have its critics. A recurring complaint centers on the absences, at times, of strict controls in the experimental procedure and the looseness of reporting. Despite these concerns, the output from the series of studies over the years has been impressive.

More recently, Bruner and associates (1956, 1966) have been conducting their own series of experiments in cognition. While acknowledging a debt to Piaget, they have picked up where Piaget left off and have considered concept formation in adults. The experimentation is also a bit more specific and precise.

The Bruner experiments to identify the characteristics of concept formation focused on *strategies* in the solution of problems or the accomplishment of tasks. In general, the experimenters tried to determine how people attained concepts and how their approaches differed from "ideal" strategies developed beforehand by the experimenters on the basis of their logic and simplicity.

JUDGMENT

A judgment involves an estimate of the characteristics of the situation. An observer may perceive an object at a distance as an automobile. It falls into a classification we have already established. How large or how far away it is, however, requires more than a mere categorization. An active process of judgment or evaluation is called for. We dip into our memory storage to compare the new information perceived with what has been stored. Judgments of size, distance, weight, true brightness, and extent are all possible.

There are two types of judgments that may be made. An *absolute judgment* assigns a value set on a continuum that has been established through experience. To say a man is 6 feet tall represents an absolute judgment. A *comparative judgment* involves the evaluation of two or more objects presented. We are concerned with determinations of a relative nature when we judge one person to be taller than another or the speed of a car greater than that of another vehicle.

REASONING

Reasoning is another important part of the cognitive area of thinking, if the term thinking is used in the broad sense. Certainly, reasoning refers to much more than the simple associational processes that occur without much effort. Reasoning is the more involved handling of problems and their solution according to some systematic approach or the following of rules. If a person pays attention to the rules and reaches certain conclusions as a result, we may say that he is logical in his thinking and reasonable. If the rules are not followed, the person's thinking is labeled "unreasonable" or "foolish."

Rules for reasoning have been systematized over the years, and the result has been known as *logic*. When people follow the rules, we say they are thinking logically. One may learn a syllogism such as the following example.

1. All businessmen are men.
2. All men are mortal.
3. Therefore, all businessmen are mortal.

Logic may not be present, however, in many such ordered statements. A fallacious syllogism is not always easy to spot. Take the following syllogism, for instance, for industry.

1. More output means more pay.
2. More pay means more inflation.
3. Therefore, we should cut output.

The reader can, hopefully, point out the source of the difficulty in logic.

Logical approaches are affected even more by factors that commonly accompany the reasoning attempts. Logic may be turned aside by the sheer complexity of material or emotional concomitants of problems. The format of the propositions may induce responses not based on logic; when statements are made positively, for instance, the tendency is to reject negatively stated conclusions. Even more distortions can come when attitudes and beliefs affect the deductions. An experiment by Morgan and Morton (1944) vividly illustrates the influence of prejudices on reasoning. A syllogistic test was given in two forms, one using neutral designations X, Y, and Z. The second form was cast in a way that evoked strong opinions about the strength of air power versus battleships. In reality, none of the conclusions could follow logically, and the neutral form and the emotionally tinged one evoked quite different responses.

While people do have the capacity to use logic, other forces contend with it to take the upper hand at times. Emotion may overcome reason without our being conscious of it.

PROBLEM SOLVING

The kinds of processes that occur in the attempts to solve problems may be isolated in broad form. Very simple approaches to problems may consist of following a sequence that has been learned by rote and that by now may be mechanical or habitual. The arithmetic student will add a column of numbers or the mechanic will service a business machine in a routine order without puzzling over it to any great extent. Sequences learned earlier are followed with no difficulty. Sometimes those earlier solutions came accidentally as the aftermath of trial and error attempts, seemingly not very high-level thinking, but perhaps some basic hypothesis guiding the action may be present without our knowing it. In general, however, such attempts are not overly efficient.

The rote or mechanical processes may lead to a sudden and new solution, one often called the "aha" response, or *insight*. Insightful solutions may be so long in coming when the thinker is baffled by a complex problem that the sudden experiencing of a solution is overwhelming. Archimedes lost touch with his surroundings when he jumped out of the bathtub at the moment of his insight into the solution of the king's problem and ran naked through the streets shouting, "Eureka!" Even though these solutions may appear suddenly and the creator may be unaware of the exact steps in the process, these do not materialize out of nothing. There has been a long period of preparation and trial preceding the sudden burst of a conscious solution.

Steps in Problem Solving

The most information about the procedures in problem solving may come when the solution appears as a result of an understanding of the steps involved and the relationships between them. An awareness of general principles and the putting of them to work in specific problems often can be verbalized by the individual problem solver. The emergence of *functional solutions* from general solutions is a step before those by which particular problems may be solved. This focus on the functional is the important aspect of the problem-solving approach through understanding.

An extensive inquiry into functional solutions has been made by Duncker (1945) in the belief that one of the most important aspects of problem solving is the goal-determined search for functional solutions. A well-known problem he propounded to his subjects concerned the case of a patient with a stomach tumor. Rays which can destroy human tissue can free him of the tumor; the big difficulty is that the rays also destroy healthy tissue. The problem is one of destroying the tumor without destroying the other tissue. Figure 7-4 is a tree diagram which illustrates steps in a problem-solving approach. Level 2 contains general solutions; level 3 has the functional ones with specific solutions coming at level 4. The best solution is to let weak rays which do not hurt tissue focus at the site of the tumor. The combination of rays is powerful enough to destroy the tumor.

Computer Simulation of Problem Solving

The analogy of thinking to electronic data processing has been made often. Many people refer to electronic computers as "giant brains" and call their behavior "thinking." A great deal of anxiety often accompanies such statements; some individuals reflect concern, in their comments, about being replaced in their jobs. Others scoff at the possibility of "intelligent behavior" on the part of machines, while still others, the avant-garde in this area, maintain that the answers to whether this is comparable to thinking will come from future research and not from cherished opinion held firmly in ages past.

Whatever the outcome, the present state of the science of simulation is such that we can make some initial steps toward understanding the cognitive processes. We can develop a program, based on protocols of problem solving, that may identify the sequence of "instructions" that a human central processing system probably follows in an approach toward the solution of a problem. This can then be used to program instructions for a machine to follow through the process in much the same way. The central value in doing this is in the specifying of the steps in the process. If we can be specific enough about a cognitive process to be able to formulate a program to be followed by the computer, we already must have learned something about the process. Human strengths and weaknesses emerge from the comparisons; machine memory is not as fallible as the human counterpart, and access to detail is ordinarily much faster. On the other hand, the human information processor is able to consider a considerably greater number of alternatives to decide on an efficient solution.

This comparison underscores two general types of programs followed in problem solving. A program that would force a consideration of all elements

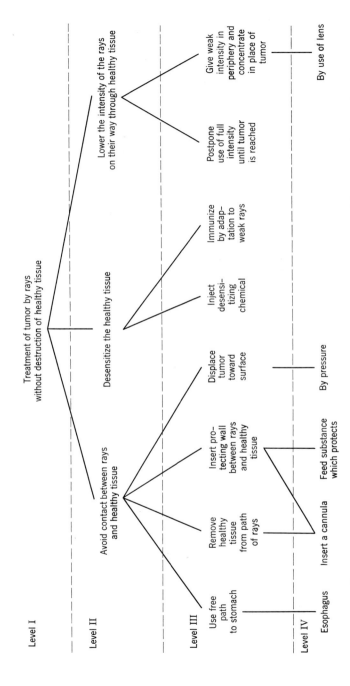

Figure 7-4. A tree diagram showing solution to the "tumor" problem (Duncker, 1945).

available and come up with a solution could be possible given enough time and effort. We might consider comparing all aspects of all investment possibilities in the securities market, for instance, and eventually reach some conclusions. Such "brute force" procedures are known as *algorithms*. Needless to say, human problem solving does not entail such fantastically extensive consideration of alternatives. We are used to being selective in our proceeding to a solution. We use "hunches," strategies, or simplifications to limit our search. These approaches are called *heuristic* methods and, because they are shorter and more practical, they are used most often. Even though they may not be as good in the long run because they may overlook the best solution, these are the methods that get greater use and for this reason are of greater interest to students of problem solving.

Heuristic methods may be identified as *special-purpose* or *general-purpose*. An approach useful in the past or working backward from a previously known solution represents the special-purpose type of heuristics. One general-purpose approach which is frequently used involves *means-end analysis* whereby problems are converted into targets that are closer and the gap between what is done and what is to be done is gradually reduced.

One theoretical formulation of problem solving that highlights means-end analysis has been developed by Newell and Simon (1963). Their General Problem Solver (GPS) attempts to set up a system that attains a goal by setting up subgoals, if such are needed, and reducing, through operations, the differences between goal states and subgoal states.

Problem Solving in Practice

Problems faced in putting research findings to work may be many and varied. Costello and Zalkind (1963, p. 373) list some of the barriers to problem solving such as an inappropriate set or predisposition, unavailability or ineffective use of information in a new situation, a faulty analysis of the problem, or other handicapping characteristic of the problem solver.

They go on to outline some effective problem-solving procedures in the two areas of set and utilization of information (pp. 374–385). Set may have developed strongly from the problem itself or from the background and experience of the person. Shifting the set by rearranging the problem, seeking other positions, or "moving about" in many ways often can provide new viewpoints. In the area of information utilization, having more associations available may produce more and better solutions to problems; sometimes, however, there may be too much information available, and the excess can hinder problem solving. Often, the solutions come by simply making more effective use of what information we have.

Decision Making

Decision making means making a choice among alternatives. The alternatives may be many and varied or there may simply be two states from which to choose. There may be much information available about the different states and the outcomes attending their choice or there may be very little. Generally, decisions must be made under conditions of imperfect information. Decision makers may like to think that their decisions aim for optimal results, and often this is implied in discussions of decision making. In this light some writers look to the process as being a rational one with clear-cut logical or statistical bases. Others can cite good empirical evidence for decisions influenced by personality and social factors and leading to outcomes with other than logically optimal bases.

Decision making is used by some writers to mean the same as problem solving. The two are, certainly, close, and there is little doubt that problem solving is a basic cognitive process which underlies or precedes decision making. Let us merely follow the model which indicates decision making to be a "mature" aspect of the central processes and consider the present state of this cognitive factor, a concept that is important enough to be treated separately.

DECISION THEORY

The basis of decisions, particularly in the area of business or related activity, has been of interest for many generations, at least, but more precise theorizing and applications of mathematicians and behavioral scientists became significant only since the early 1950's.

Decision theory is concerned with the statistical concepts of probability underlying choice in addition to other behavior factors which vary the purely mathematical foundations of a decision. Attention may be focused on the relationships between the information a decision maker has about possible events and the subsequent decisions he makes. Information available can vary widely along a continuum to provide a state of certainty or uncertainty for the decision maker. The continuum is often cut, somewhat arbitrarily, into areas of *certainty* and *uncertainty,* with *risk* occupying the middle position.

Certainty

Certainty has long been the fundamental prop for the traditional economic theory of business firm activity. This theory simply assumes that alternatives are known to the decision maker and that one choice among factors such as costs and production will lead to a maximization of profits.

Determination of a maximum may be made in the industrial situation through the use of techniques such as mathematical programming. An example of simple linear programming has already been given in Chapter 3 where, with certain constraints and assumptions, the maximum profit could be obtained by proper scheduling.

The limitations of mathematical programming, or other similar techniques, in the complex situations in which organizations find themselves have prevented any full development of a theory of behavior based on certainty. Not only are there many variables to determine with certainty, there are strong doubts whether firms really do maximize profits, considering all the behavioral constraints to which firms are subject (McGuire, 1964, p. 118). In combination with other approaches, some progress may be made toward a more accurate description of decision making in organizations.

Uncertainty

When there is no way in which the decision maker can assess the probabilities associated with outcomes, uncertainty is the condition present. The decision maker may not be aware of the absence of any basis for a clear appraisal of alternatives and may justify his choice one way or another. The researcher in the area of decision making will not be satisfied with rationalizations, however, and will attempt to reconstruct the criteria that are likely to be used.

An illustration of a practical situation of decision making under uncertainty could be that of a businessman who may be faced with the problem of whether or not to open a branch store. With no awareness of the probabilities surrounding the decision, the executive may focus on aspects that he believes contributed to his decision. In this he is motivated by the belief that all his decisions must be rational, and he searches for "rationality" in the explanation.

With uncertainty, however, the probabilities for each alternative are unknown. The actual decisions are, therefore, based on specific criteria or strategies. These criteria represent assumptions about the circumstances from which the decision maker will proceed in his choice behavior. The criteria may have conservative or optimistic bases, even though they all represent attempts to optimize in some way. To one extent or another, they also point out the individual nature of the criteria for decision making and the behavioral bases for the selections made.

The simplest assumption about the probabilities of alternatives is that, since these future states are unknown, they should be considered equal (the *Laplace criterion*). The *maximin criterion* is a conservative one pointing to the alternative that produces the maximum of the minimum returns. This strategy is a pessimistic one concentrating on safe minimal payoffs. A strategy that selects (as in costs) the minimum of maxima (minimax) is the same approach. Other criteria have been suggested to expand these basic treatments and account for further influence of individual personality factors (Savage, 1951; Shackle, 1955).

Risk

Risk occupies the middle ground between certainty and uncertainty. Here, the decision maker knows the probabilities of each state with which he must concern himself. This means he has less information than under certainty but more than he would have with uncertainty.

While the decision maker knows the probabilities of the alternatives, these have been established on the basis of a large number of past occurrences. The risk comes in not being able to predict the happening of a specific outcome, even though the distribution of a large number of outcomes is known on the basis of the "law" of large numbers. This a priori evidence serves as the basis for selection by the decision maker, a process that tends, presumably, toward a maximization of gains. Actual decision making, however, does not proceed as clearly and as easily as might be indicated. As with uncertainty, the many statistical and behavioral concomitants make the choices in risky situations extremely variable. There may have been few instances in the past to provide the basis for decisions. Of even more importance in the process is the matter of influence. Money is an objective measure of a goal such as maximization, except that in most situations amount of money is not the central issue. A better basis for the decisions of individuals lies in the concept of *utility* rather than monetary maximization.

UTILITY AND PROBABILITY

Utility and probability are considered by many theorists to be more important bases for decision making. The objective probability of an event occurring may not be as important, however, as the subjective probability that the decision maker has in mind. Combining subjective probability and utility gives us the concept of subjectively expected utility (SEU). Success or failure becomes, not an objective state, but a subjective one tied to attitudes toward achievement. Siegel (1957) concentrates on the level of aspiration of the individual to shed some more light on utility and decisions. Table 7-1 represents a situation where there is a different payoff for outcomes under two alternatives. If a person has an aspiration level of 4, then anything less is failure for him. He expects greater utility from A and will choose it over B, which has greater value.

Atkinson (1957) goes somewhat further with the concept of level of aspiration and concentrates on the value to the individual of goal achievement

Table 7-1. A Payoff Matrix Table (Siegel, 1957)

	Alternative A	Alternative B
If heads	4	3
If tails	0	3

rather than the utility placed in the goal. This general concept is developed to the point where several aspects of behavior underlying decision making can be related. Atkinson considers that a person is influenced in risk-taking decisions by the interaction of six factors:

Motive	to achieve to avoid failure
Incentive	the positive value in success the negative value of failure
Subjective probability	of success of failure

He maintains that incentive and subjective probability are tied to the difficulty of the task. In a decision-making situation a person with strong motivation to avoid failure will choose alternatives that would keep his anxiety about failure low; he would set a level of aspiration very low, where he is not likely to fail, or very high, where failure is not embarrassing. An individual with a strong achievement motive will choose tasks of moderate difficulty where uncertainty is greatest because he acts to maximize his anxiety about failure to aid his strong drive for achievement.

SATISFICING

Most decision-making theories up to now have been based on clearly economic views of man's behavior. The notion that the decision maker considers all alternatives and rationally chooses the one which will provide him with the optimum result is the characteristic feature of such views. Simon (1957) takes issues with this notion of "economic man" and postulates a decision maker of limited rationality whom he labels "administrative man." Under this view, man does not maximize or select the best alternative available; he *satisfices* in that he selects alternatives that are good enough. He does so because he cannot or will not be aware of all alternatives due to time or ability limitations. In the area of business, such satisficing criteria are illustrated in the phrases "share of market," "adequate profit," and "fair price" (Simon, 1957, p. xxv).

Motivation and Affect in Cognition

No psychological variable can be considered in isolation, of course, since in even the simplest of situations several factors interact and influence each other. In cognition, as in other areas, motivation is an important variable.

Even a casual observer can notice variations in performance of a task. A subject in an experiment shows activity above and below a mean level. A worker turning out a product will sometimes fall far below his average hourly production and sometimes will exceed it. Undoubtedly, fatigue or other physical conditions play a role, but more often the factor of motivation is responsible. The level of motivation may be low with underachievement as a result. A high level of motivation can produce a high level of achievement, although at times this same high level of motivation can bring with it a lower achievement level because the person may be so anxious to succeed that the tension is handicapping.

Motivation implies a goal toward which the movement occurs as well as the "reason behind" the action. The inner needs give rise to the observable behavior. On this much there is agreement even though the specific mechanisms are the subject of discussion. Specific theories lead off the treatment of motivation in Chapter 8; here, a basic description of the process may shed light on its influences on the cognitive processes.

BASIC FACTORS

Motivation begins with a need, a lack or deficit in the organism. This disequilibrium causes the organism to act in a specific fashion, not at random but with some purpose. This means the behavior is directed toward a particular goal. The reaching of the goal satisfies the need and restores equilibrium. Such is the motivation cycle.

This concept of motivation is easily seen in the basic physiological needs. A deficit of water in the tissues gives rise to water-seeking behavior. Drinking water and having it get to the tissues is reaching the goal that satisfies the need. Most real-life situations are more complex, however, and relate to the extensive needs beyond the basic ones. The social needs are deeper and more dynamic; they are harder to work with conceptually but are undoubtedly more important in most of the situations with which we have to deal every day. Needs such as affiliation or prestige cannot be measured accurately, but their role in human events is beyond question.

COGNITIVE RELATIONSHIPS

In the cognitive processes, what moves us to forge ahead to a solution? A sign of approval, a smile, or a pat on the back is a satisfaction of a social need and one that is potent from the days of early childhood to adulthood. The businessman who solves a knotty industrial problem makes money in the process, but the money signifies social approval in addition to other visible aspects of approval, as in the acclaim he gets from others. Security also is gained when one is rewarded for the valuable results that emerge from the higher-order reasoning and problem-solving approaches.

A more important basis for much cognition may be, however, in the needs that have been postulated as being general—needs such as activity, curiosity, and manipulation. Rats and monkeys pay attention to aspects of their environment, and monkeys will play with puzzles. People of all ages seem to be fascinated by puzzles and problems of all kinds, and this may be a general basis for behavior. The need to organize meaningfully may be a strong aspect of motivation and the most important prop for thinking and problem solving. The rewards from doing the job or solving the problem may be enough reinforcement for many people. The self-satisfaction coming from the intrinsic aspects of the job may, however, be extended by the self-respect and esteem which come because society values thinking highly and places a high premium on the end products of problem solving.

INFORMATION PROCESSING CONCEPTS

In the past, information processing theories of cognition have been criticized for their ignoring of, for the most part, motivation and the affective states of man (Neisser, 1963). Some responses have been made (Tomkins and Messick, 1963) and, more recently, Simon (1967) has charted a theoretical relationship, couched in processing terms, between motivation and emotion on the one hand and cognitive processes on the other. The central concept is that of a serial information processor with multiple needs adapting to and surviving in an environment that presents unpredictable threats and opportunities. There are two central mechanisms involved; one is a goal-terminating mechanism which permits the processor to satisfice with action terminating when a satisfactory situation has been achieved. The second is emotion (an interruption mechanism) which allows the processor to respond to urgent needs. The model thus permits recognition of the many motivating factors operating simultaneously in an adaptation to an environment. In this way Simon endows information processing theories with those qualities that Neisser (1963) pointed out, in his criticism of processing theory, as being motivational characteristics of human thought and, therefore, necessary in any model. These include the concept of multiple motives operating simultaneously and the presence of emotions and feelings in the cognitive processes. This sketching, however, can go beyond information processing ideas to show generally the close and complex interweaving of thinking and motivation. These variables, along with many others, play a vital role in the more global constructs of personality to be discussed in the next chapter.

Creativity

Creativity has long been one of the more highly prized attributes of human functioning even though at times one may wonder about the value placed on it in specific situations. There is a certain amount of ambivalence evident in views of creative individuals in organizations. On the one hand, we may recognize that creativity is crucial for the growth of the company and yet still be disturbed by some of the deviance from group norms on the part of some individuals. Costello and Zalkind (1963, pp. 414–415) try to resolve the dilemma by postulating that high creativity is tolerated only in exceptional members of an organization but the basic emotional reactions generally remain.

It should be recalled that originality and creativity are not the same. Any novel or different idea is original while creativity is the introduction of an idea or product that has social value. The contribution that is made must be "good" for the group.

CHARACTERISTICS OF CREATIVITY

In his introduction to *The creative process,* Brewster Ghiselin (1952, p. 4) reiterates the difficulties involved in detecting and recognizing creative talent. In the first place, "Every creative act overpasses the established order in some way and in some degree, it is likely at first to appear eccentric to most men." It may be perceived as nothing more than dissatisfaction, but to the creator it may involve a disordered excitement and then a state of suspense yet certainty as he is drawn toward clarification in the conscious sphere.

Spontaneity is a hallmark of the process; conscious determination to be creative does not seem ever to take place; affect is the guide to the unfolding of the creative surge, and intellect plays no role visible on the surface. The end of the development, it is to be remembered, is not mere novelty but use—the concept of value stressed in the definition of creativity.

In the scientific area some more objective guidelines to creativity may be gained from discussions of patentability of discoveries or inventions (McPherson, 1963). When the novelty extends to the "inventive level," the protection from the legal process may be obtained. The characteristics of the innovation must include the solution of a problem in a novel way, representing a great stride forward after much experimentation before achieving success. The invention must also meet an unfulfilled desire, with a rise in business following its introduction. While these practical guides to patenting may not provide direct insights into the creative process, they do represent evaluations of its products.

In an empirical attempt to identify some characteristics of creativity, Getzels and Jackson (1962) gathered data on highly creative and highly intelligent high school students. They chose the top 20 percent who were in one category but not the other and then compared the two groups in several ways. In scholastic performance the two groups, the high I.Q. and the high creative, achieved at the same level despite a 23 point difference in mean I.Q. Teachers' ratings on the degree to which they enjoyed having particular students in class showed that the high I.Q. individuals were preferred to others in the group; no such preference for the high creatives emerged. Both groups ranked "social skills" as the quality they would most like to possess (virtually the entire school did the same, however); the main difference came in the high ranking for "sense of humor" by the creative students when the high I.Q.s ranked it last. The high intelligence group demonstrated a close relationship between qualities desired in themselves and those they believed were needed for success later on, as well as those they believed their teachers thought were desirable. The high-creative adolescent, however, valued qualities different from those he perceived as leading to success or as being desirable to his teachers. It is, therefore, not too surprising to find that career aspirations differed radically as well. Almost two-thirds of the creatives gave unconventional career aspirations while only 20 percent of the high I.Q. students did so. The authors summarize by picturing the creative individuals as having the ability and drive to "diverge" from the usual and ordinary while the high I.Q. student has the need to control and focus his activity within the customary channels, come up with the "school solution," and all the while stay away from risk and uncertainty.

The apparent distinction between creativity and intelligence is misleading, however. The two factors are different but can be present in the same individual. Mednick and Andrews (1967), as a matter of fact, have noted no decline in creative ability as intelligence increased in their sample of students. Low correlations between intelligence and creativity are found often in studies using samples of individuals within a restricted range of mental ability, and the range of creativity may be very great at high I.Q. levels (McNemar, 1964). The analogy was made to the weight of individuals on a football team; it takes a lot to be on the team but once on it, the range of performance is unrelated to differences in weight (Steiner, 1965). It can be said, in summary, that it would be nice to have a team of individuals high on both factors, intelligence and creativity, in many situations in industry or education.

The relationship of creativity to personality cannot be slighted either. The patterns in the high school students studied by Getzels and Jackson (1962) have been found in other settings. Highly creative individuals have a richer fantasy life and are more apt to pay heed to "inner voices" when making a judgment and to stick to that stand despite social pressure (Barron, 1965). The resulting pattern of behavior indicates that creatives express whims and impulses yet have an ability to control and manipulate in a realistic way. Creative individuals may not be hampered by anxiety in their activity; persons with low levels of anxiety have performed significantly better on tests of divergent thinking than do individuals with high levels of anxiety (White, 1968).

CREATIVITY IN PRACTICE

Some of the attempts to put the concept of creativity to work have proved disappointing. For instance, tests for creativity have been compared with ratings of creativity on the job and have been found to be unrelated or, even more discouraging, to be negatively correlated with performance (Jex, 1963). As teachers constituted one group studied, the author suggested that perhaps ingenuity in teachers is not rewarded but penalized in most school systems. An identical question seems to be of concern to many other researchers who are represented in the same compendium of research on creativity (Taylor and Barron, 1963).

The concern has been voiced before in many settings, particularly business and industry. Do organizations reward the kind of deviance that often accompanies creativity or is a higher premium placed on docility and absence of stimulation? It has been stated frequently that Benjamin Franklin or Thomas Edison could not find a job today. Perhaps so, but empirical evidence from more precisely phrased experimental inquiries has not yet appeared in quantity. The matter does remain, however, a very provocative one in many professional areas as well as in business. A more penetrating question might be raised as to whether there are any aspects of organizational functioning that are associated with creativity of individuals within them or of the entity as a whole. Many of the characteristics of organizations that can be called creative are those traits identified in individuals. Creative organizations have open communication systems that encourage ideas and contacts with others (Guetzkow, 1965). This type of organization encourages marginal, unusual types who can operate under conditions for freedom of inquiry and discussion. The organization itself is more decentralized, less authoritarian, and more risk taking in producing an atmosphere that permits less conformity and more "fun."

In practice there may be less opportunity to implement these guidelines. In an intermediate position March and Simon (1958) believe the answer lies in setting creative individuals apart from the rest of the organization and eliminating routine tasks as well as reinforcing creative behavior.

The possibility also exists that steps can be taken to develop the potential for creativity that exists within the organization. Apart from direct efforts to introduce many of the characteristics outlined above, other approaches are deemed possible in providing a base for innovative activity. Sensitivity training, for instance, can be used in a Business Administration program to allow students to interact and contribute to the curriculum as "a means of mobilizing potential" (Culbert and Culbert, 1968). Advocates of "brainstorming" (Osborn, 1957) believe that the number of ideas and their value will increase under the social facilitation of group activity. The brainstorming group is instructed to produce as many ideas as possible without criticism of any part of the output. While solitary thinkers may well produce more ideas, as some researchers believe, the social stimulation in the brainstorming process can be effective.

The Physiochemistry of Cognition

Many researchers have long felt that the ultimate basis for cognitive activity lies in chemical factors in the functioning of the organism. Experiments with learning and memory have postulated that changes in structure of RNA molecules within the cell are responsible for behavioral outcomes (Dingman and Sporn, 1964). This has led to suggestions that it is possible to transfer patterns of learned behavior by injecting RNA from a trained animal into another untrained one. A complementary line of attack is that which seeks to determine the effects of drugs that block protein synthesis. While not enough information is at hand, there is some indication that protein synthesis is required for the consolidation of memory (Agranoff, 1967). More recent research with humans has focused on substances such as pemoline to stimulate the enzyme that apparently controls RNA production. While definite conclusions cannot be reached, there is some evidence that pemoline, at least, acts only as a stimulant without lasting effects on cognitive performance. While results such as these might be disappointing in the lack of clear evidence of activity, the future holds some exciting, and frightening, possibilities for understanding and control of cognition.

Similar extensive interest in various quarters also exists in connection with the use of psychedelic drugs or psychotogens such as marijuana or LSD. Numerous claims have been made for the "mind-expanding" qualities of the substances (Leary, 1966). There may be some output of unusual works of art or music (Berlin et al., 1955), but the use of LSD more typically causes confusion, inappropriate action, difficulty in thinking, and quite generally impairs intellectual processes (Jarvik, 1967). Findings such as these have helped to stimulate legislation with strong sanctions to curb the problems of drug abuse. With respect to marijuana, little information exists as to its effect on cognition; at this time, support for sanctions is apt to focus more on its dangers such as the potential for psychological dependence (American Medical Association Committee on Alcoholism and Drug Dependence, 1967) rather than a discussion of its cognitive aspects.

Summary

Thinking is a highly prized activity when the term refers to more complex cognitive processes. It is often used, however, to indicate other psychological activities such as attention, remembering, or even attitudes or opinions.

"Thinking" can cover a wide range of specific processes even when it is limited to the cognitive area. It may be considered in the framework of a systems model as central information processing in addition to being designated in more traditional terms.

More specifically, thinking may be considered as the representation of reality through the use of symbols or images. Reasoning is at the more complex end of a continuum where there is a recombination of past experience to provide a meaningful response to a situation. It is basic to problem solving, the surmounting of obstacles to a goal, and to decision making, the choosing between alternative courses of action. Judgment enters into the general process when the evaluation of events occurs as does conceptualization, the identification and representation of properties and relationships.

Preceding the complex cognitive activity is the process that organizes incoming information. This first experiential aspect of cognition is perception. At the other end of the cognitive continuum is creativity—the novel, innovative, and ingenious thinking that provides something superior to ordinary solutions.

In its function of organizing material coming in from the outside, perception is molded by previous simple and complex physical or social factors.

Size, intensity, repetition, and other aspects affect the organization of material. More important, individuals respond to stimuli in basic ways, most often in an attempt to impose regularity or "wholeness" upon the information. The dynamic factors of interests or motives further shape the material coming in from the outside while social experience plays an additional role in the same way.

Perception is also a selective process. Because so many stimuli impinge upon the individual, not all can be assimilated; those that are picked out are selected on the basis of established patterns. When responses are made according to these oversimplified stereotypes, meaningful everyday activity is apt to be limited.

More central cognitive processes can be treated by starting with conceptualization. Concepts are the classes that are developed on the basis of common elements or relationships; without some classification of data, no meaningful activity could take place. Various categories can emerge in many different ways, and research on how concepts develop is basic to further understanding of cognition.

Judgment is the making of absolute or comparative estimates of a situation. Reasoning is an even more complex activity calling for a cognitive conclusion as the result of systematic following of rules or logic. Many impediments to reasoning exist, including emotional ones.

Problem solving, a further extension of the cognitive processes, is an attempt to surmount barriers to reach a specific goal. Routine or rote approaches may solve a problem through trial and error or by leading to an insightful solution. Steps in problem solving have been postulated from research studies but are now being made more explicit by attempts to simulate human problem solving with electronic computing devices.

Decision making has received more attention in recent years. In the choosing between alternatives, other cognitive factors are basic to the decision, the final choice point. Decisions must be made under conditions of imperfect information, since all aspects of all alternatives usually cannot be known. Decisions are made under conditions of certainty (rarely), uncertainty, and risk; the more probable is the middle circumstance where some but not all information is available. Various criteria or assumptions can be followed in selecting alternatives under each if the three conditions. Utility and probability are important factors in the making of decisions. The proposition that decisions are made to maximize some aspect of the outcome is open to question; decision makers are more likely to "satisfice," or select the best alternative available after less than a maximum search.

Motivation and affect play an important role in cognition, as they do in other areas of behavior. The drives underlying actions have an impact on problem solving through reinforcement from the solution. Cognitive achievement and underachievement reflect the needs and values of an individual and his society. Information processing concepts can provide a better understanding of this phase of the process as they have in systems models of cognition generally.

Creativity is more than novelty. Something new or different is creative, and therefore prized, only when it makes a valuable contribution. Ambivalence may exist toward creativity and creative individuals. Creativity may result from activity that is unconventional or divergent from a mainstream. The tensions built up in an organization as a result may not be manageable.

Some recent experiments to determine the biochemical bases of cognitive behavior have provided inconclusive but provocative results. Other research on drugs to stimulate cognition or creativity also has not provided, as yet, any intellectual rationale for their use.

Bibliography

Agranoff, B. (1967). Memory and protein synthesis. *Scientific American,* **216(6),** 115–122.

American Medical Association Committee on Alcoholism and Drug Dependence (1967). Dependence on Cannabis (Marijuana). *Journal of the American Medical Association,* **201,** 368–371.

Atkinson, J. (1957). Motivational determinants of risk taking behavior. *Psychological Review,* **64(6),** 359–372.

Barron, F. (1965). Some studies of creativity at the Institute of Personality Assessment and Research. In Steiner, G. (ed.). *The creative organization.* Chicago: University of Chicago Press, 118–129.

Berlin, L., Guthrie, T., Weider, A., Goodell, A., and Wolff, H. (1955). Studies in human cerebral function: the effects of mescaline and lysergic acid on cerebral processes pertinent to creative activity. *Journal of Nervous and Mental Disease,* **122,** 487–491.

Bruner, J. (1958). Social psychology and perception. In Maccoby, E., Newcomb, T., and Hartley, E. (eds.). *Readings in social psychology* (3rd ed.). New York: Holt, Rinehart and Winston.

Bruner, J. and Goodman, C. (1947). Value and need as organizing factors in perception. *Journal of Abnormal and Social Psychology,* **42,** 33–44.

Bruner, J., Goodnow, J., and Austin, G. (1956). *A study of thinking.* New York: Wiley.

Bruner, J., Olver, R., Greenfield, P., et al. (1966). *Studies in cognitive growth.* New York: Wiley.

Bruner, J. and Postman, L. (1949). On the perception of incongruity: a paradigm. *Journal of Personality,* **18,** 206–223.

Costello, T. and Zalkind, S. (1963). *Psychology in administration: a research orientation.* Englewood Cliffs, N.J.: Prentice-Hall.

Culbert, S. and Culbert, J. (1968). Sensitivity training within the educational framework: a means of mobilizing potential. *Journal of Creative Behavior,* **2**(1), 14–30.

Dingman, W. and Sporn, M. (1964). Molecular theories of memory. *Science,* **144,** 26–29.

Duncker, K. (1945). On problem solving. *Psychological Monographs,* **58(5)** (whole No. 270).

Getzels, J. and Jackson, P. (1962). *Creativity and intelligence: explorations with gifted students.* New York: Wiley.

Ghiselin, B. (1952). *The creative process.* Berkeley and Los Angeles: University of California Press.

Guetzkow, H. (1965). The creative person in organizations. In Steiner, G. (ed.). *The creative organization.* Chicago: University of Chicago Press. 35–49.

Haire, M. (1955). Role perception in labor-management relations; an experimental approach. *Industrial and Labor Relations Review,* **8(2),** 204–216.

Helson, H. (1964). *Adaptation-level theory.* New York: Harper and Row.

Jarvik, M. (1967). The behavioral effects of psychotogens. In DeBold, R. and Leaf, R. (eds.). *LSD, Man and society.* Middletown, Conn.: Wesleyan University Press. 186–206.

Jex, F. (1963). Negative validities for two different ingenuity tests. In Taylor, C. and Barron, F. (eds.). *Scientific creativity: its recognition and development.* New York: Wiley.

Leary, T. (1966). Interview. *Playboy,* September 1966.

Levine, R., Chein, I., and Murphy, G. (1942). The relation of the intensity of a need to the amount of perceptual distortion; a preliminary report. *Journal of Psychology,* **13,** 283–293.

McGuire, J. (1964). *Theories of business behavior.* Englewood Cliffs, N.J.: Prentice-Hall.

McNemar, Q. (1964). Lost: our intelligence. Why? *American Psychologist,* **19,** 871–882.

McPherson, J. (1963). A proposal for establishing ultimate criteria for measuring creative output. In Taylor, C. and Barron, F. (eds.) *Scientific creativity: its recognition and development.* New York: Wiley.

March, J. and Simon, H. (1958). *Organizations.* New York: Wiley.

Mednick, M. and Andrews, F. (1967). Creative thinking and level of intelligence. *Journal of Creative Behavior,* 1(4), 428–431.

Morgan, J. and Morton, J. (1944). The distortion of syllogistic reasoning produced by personal convictions. *Journal of Social Psychology,* 20, 39–59.

Neisser, U. (1963). The imitation of man by machine. *Science,* 139, 193–197.

Newell, A. and Simon, H. (1963). GPS, a program that simulates human thought. In Feigenbaum, E. and Feldman, J. (eds.). *Computers and thought.* New York: McGraw-Hill, 279–293.

Osborn, A. (1957). *Applied imagination* (rev. ed.). New York: Scribner's.

Piaget, J. (1954). *The construction of reality in the child.* New York: Basic Books.

Postman, L., Bruner, J., and McGinnies, E. (1948). Personal values as selective factors in perception. *Journal of Abnormal and Social Psychology,* 83, 148–153.

Savage, L. (1951). The theory of statistical decision. *Journal of the American Statistical Association,* 46, 55–67.

Shackle, G. (1955). *Uncertainty in economics and other reflections.* Cambridge: Cambridge University Press.

Siegel, S. (1957). Level of aspiration and decision making. *Psychological Review,* 64(4), 253–261.

Simon, H. (1957). *Administrative behavior* (2nd ed.). New York: The Free Press.

Simon, H. (1967). Motivational and emotional controls of cognition. *Psychological Review,* 74(1), 29–39.

Steiner, G. (1965). Introduction. In Steiner, G. (ed.). *The creative organization.* Chicago: University of Chicago Press, 1–24.

Taylor, C. and Barron, F. (1963). *Scientific creativity: its recognition and development.* New York: Wiley.

Tomkins, S. and Messick, S., eds. (1963). *Computer simulation of personality.* New York: Wiley.

Wertheimer, M. (1959). *Productive thinking* (enl. ed.). New York: Harper and Row.

White, K. (1968). Anxiety, extraversion-introversion, and divergent thinking ability. *Journal of Creative Behavior,* 2(2), 119–127.

8

Needs and
Need-Satisfaction

The crucial question in human behavior must undoubtedly be the simple one—WHY? This search for understanding of the basis for reactions of individuals has occupied mankind since the dawn of humanity.

The continuing quest for answers to the question of "what makes people tick" comes to focus primarily in a discussion of the material that forms the basis for this chapter. While we must understand the biological bases for individual functioning and the adaptation to the environment which comes in the learning process, more of a crystallization occurs in an inquiry into the variety, mode, and style of the responses people make in everyday situations as the result of the personality determinants which go into the shaping of the individual and his interactions with others.

The concept of needs and their satisfaction forms the core of this closer look at the dynamics of behavior. From needs at the center, consideration of related concepts continues to other aspects of behavior; motivation, personality, conflict, stress, frustration, mechanisms of defense, adaptation syndromes, mental health, job satisfaction, and morale are all of concern in many and varied situations. One should recognize the centrality of needs in human functioning in all settings—industrial, academic, social, or other institutional framework. Not only are needs and related concepts important variables in the world of work, they are crucial determinants in all areas of human functioning.

Personality

Personality is like the weather—everybody talks about it, but (and here we change the simile!) all too often they mean different things. To some students of behavior it means a general sum of traits or characteristics of the person; to others it refers to a unitary mode of response to life situations.

241

It could mean all of this and more to still other researchers, or it could be seen as a concise yet complex concept. "Personality is what man really is," says Allport (1937). Hall and Lindzey (1957) give up the troublesome task and state merely that personality is defined by the empirical concepts of the theory propounded by a particular personality theorist and invite the reader to determine these from the text of their book.

Despite the wide range of meanings, there is a consensus that the concept is important. There is also agreement that it does *not* mean what people casually refer to as personality when they describe an effective set of social skills or evaluate an outstanding aspect of the impression created in others. Realizing that no definition can really do justice to the wide range of concepts of personality, a tentative one still should be made at this point. Personality may be said to encompass the characteristic traits and patterns of adjustment of the person in his interrelationships with others and his environment. This definition points out not only the structuring of personality but its dynamic qualities as well.

PERSONALITY THEORY

While questions of human behavior have been asked by philosophers, artists, and plain, ordinary people for a long time, with increasing knowledge about ourselves the replies become more sophisticated. Most of the present-day formulations represent an integrated system of explanations based on insights gained from clinical experience with a series of individuals met in clinical practice. Tests of personality, experimental findings, and survey evidence may add to that base in the formation of theories of personality, but the single observer has remained the most prolific contributor to this body of thought.

Theories of personality may sometimes fall short of the tests for scientific theories outlined in Chapter 1, but they have served a purpose. They do organize and channel thinking toward important problem areas and thus may stimulate more research even if they remain in a form that defies complete verification. No one doubts that the outstanding personality theorists of past and present have generated ideas that often provoke controversy and have presented patterns of behavior despite the inability of researchers to verify most of the conclusions scientifically. Certainly Freud's formulations, for instance, are weak from the standpoint of empirical validation but stand as powerful contributors to the self-awareness of individuals of the present century.

THEORIES OF PERSONALITY

Grouping personality theories and labeling the resulting categories becomes a task even more difficult than that of defining personality; the reasons for this are the same as those for definition. Each theorist cannot really be grouped with another, even though they may have operated from similiar positions. Since the theories are products of individuals, a discussion of each contributor to the general body of theories will provide continuity. Throughout, the reader may be able to trace threads of similarity that tie individuals together in certain ways, but a discussion of this nature here must, however, be very limited and sketchy. In some instances the theorist is well known to the literate, and the summary will serve as a refresher of memory; in other instances the discussion may be an exposure to other personality theorists previously unmet. For further reading, a full textbook in personality theory (Hall and Lindzey, 1957; Stagner, 1961) is highly recommended.

Freud

Sigmund Freud's greatest contribution to the knowledge of human behavior is his development of the concept of the unconscious. The notion that man is motivated by unseen forces more than he is controlled by conscious and "rational" thought was enough to shake his contemporaneous society, even without his adding other constructs of psychoanalytic theory—the *id*, the *ego,* and the *super-ego*—a structure of personality based on the hedonistic pleasure principle of satisfaction of instincts.

The id is the reservoir of the basic drives called the *libido*. The id would proceed unchecked to satisfy motives were it not for the channelling of the activity into acceptable ways by the ego. Even higher order restraints are imposed by the super-ego, a concept roughly corresponding to the notion of conscience. Freud believed that instincts could be classified under *life instincts* and *death instincts.* Life instincts are, among others, hunger, thirst, and sex; the energy involved in their activity is the libido. In the formulation of his theories Freud paid most attention to the life instinct of sex, and in his preoccupation with this instinct he treated almost all behavior as originating on the basis of the sex drive. Perhaps this notion, more than the concept of the unconscious or the lack of verifiable hypotheses, was responsible for the impact of Freud's ideas on society and for the concentrated and intense attacks by individuals and groups on him and his statements. Some of the criticism of Freud and psychoanalysis is based on misconceptions of the theory, but more is undoubtedly the emotional result of the bringing of "sensitive" material to people's attention. The concern over the difficulty of validating the conclusions takes second place to the acknowledged stimulus to thought and treatment which psychoanalytic theory provided. Then, too, one wonders how rigidly a reader must adhere to constructs like the id, since if it is considered only as a model of the structure of personality, it can serve to increase understanding. That Freud was provocative in his statements there is no doubt. There is even less doubt of his impact on art, drama, literature, or our everyday world in general.

Alfred Adler and Carl Jung

Both these personality theorists began as members of Freud's inner circle in Vienna but soon rebelled against the master and left psychoanalysis and its organizer behind. Both found the emphasis on sex as the explanation for most behavior untenable. Jung developed an approach to therapy that is called *analytical psychology,* a system that includes some concepts similar to those of psychoanalysis. The ego and the unconscious are part of Jung's theory, but he took the unconscious further and postulated a *collective unconscious* reaching back through previous generations to the dawn of history. Personality, said Jung, is based on predisposing patterns from the past which are inherited by every individual. An *archetype* is such an image or thought form which is passed on through the ages in the collective unconscious.

This notion of the hereditary transmission of acquired characteristics is one of the concepts least acceptable to present-day scientists. From the behavioral standpoint, even more interest can be focused on the logical outcomes of this kind of thinking. It places a strong emphasis on the past as a basis for the present activity of an individual. Yet Jung did not stop here. He stated that the functioning of a person is as much future-oriented as rooted in the past. Man can act in the light of knowledge to come and "the psyche creates its own future" (Jung, 1916). In his belief that man is not wedded to the past but can effectively create his future, Jung was a dynamic optimist.

Adler (1927) was considered by many to have been the crown prince of psychoanalysis before he broke with Freud. Like Jung he found the explanations based on sex unacceptable. Instead, Adler considered the main drive motivating man to be the thrust for superiority; the concepts of *compensation* and the *inferiority complex* follow easily in the unfolding of a system based on a drive for power. This striving to overcome a weakness and become superior in another area—the poor student who then tries to excel as an athlete—is given as a prime example of the basic drive. Adler differs basically from Freud and Jung in that the other two base their theories on innate or biological factors and functions while the basis for Adlerian thinking lies in social inter-relationships. This, along with the emphasis on individual uniqueness, style of life, and the creative self, place Adler close to many present theorists, including some who consider themselves psychoanalytic in orientation.

Neo-Freudians

A few contemporary theorists might be grouped very loosely under this label. Even though their departure from Freudian constructs may be extensive, most acknowledge at least some influence of psychoanalysis.

Karen Horney (1937, 1945) focuses on anxiety as a basic factor in understanding personality dynamics. The anxious person develops tactics to cope with anxiety-producing situations; these are inappropriate methods of solving problems that Horney labels *neurotic needs*. The ten neurotic needs are separable into those:

(a)   Moving toward people (affilation, love).
(b)   Moving away from people (independence).
(c)   Moving against people (power need).

When problems cannot be solved through conflict of needs or otherwise, certain needs tend to dominate the lives of the persons.

Erich Fromm points to the condition of man as he becomes isolated from others as, in growing up, his primary ties are cut. This individual chronological process mirrors the increasing isolation of individuals in Western society which came with the freedom engendered by the Industrial Revolution or the Reformation. Fromm believes that personality can be understood best by viewing the behavior that arises through the satisfaction of the needs expressed in the process of isolation. A need to affiliate with others may be the motivation to "escape from freedom," as the author entitled one of his works (1941). Combining all aspects of his theoretical stand, Fromm ends by outlining the perfect society, one "in which man relates to man lovingly, in which he is rooted in bonds of brotherliness and solidarity" (1955, p. 362).

Erik Erikson (1951) emphasizes the developmental aspects of psychoanalysis and postulates the search for *ego integrity* as the fundamental aspect of personality. This search involves identification with models, and where these are difficult to come by because of vague and shifting goals, problems ensue. The eight stages of problem areas already have been mentioned in the discussion of development in Chapter 4.

Harry Stack Sullivan demonstrated, in his *Interpersonal theory of psychiatry* (1953), the importance of the crucial social mechanisms in the development of individuals. His emphasis on learning in social situations probably makes him further removed from Freud and the other theorists, and the novelty of the approach may well put him into a separate conceptual category. Sullivan has stimulated a considerable amount of interest, and his work has attracted a wide following.

Trait Theorists

That personality may be seen primarily from the standpoint of understanding the patterning of traits or the needs that arise from them is a central position taken by a few theorists. Gordon Allport not only accepts this basis but states further that each individual has a set of traits shared by no one else. This uniqueness emphasizes the psychology of the individual that Allport has developed.

Raymond Cattell (1950) has developed a similar set of traits primarily through the construction of tests and the determination of factors or trait families which may emerge from these psychological measures. The quantitative results are representative of the extensive activity in assessment of personality in many settings—school, business and industry, government, and therapy—as the result of inquiry through paper-and-pencil questionnaires (see Chapter 4). A theoretical formulation, based on factor concepts, emerges with terms like tender-mindedness, somatic anxiety, energetic conformity, dominance, and many other similar descriptive terms.

William Sheldon's (1940) *Constitutional psychology* has some of the features of the trait theory except that his organization is based on physical characteristics. For this reason the theory may actually be considered as standing off on its own. The tracing of relationships between physical structure and personality is nothing new, since the ancient Greeks developed a classification scheme on a physical basis which has been perpetuated largely through widespread stereotypes such as "jolly fat man" and "humorless thin man." Kretschmer (1925) and others have preceded Sheldon in a systematic approach, but Sheldon carries the structuring further by stating that physique is composed of three components.

> Endomorphy—soft and spherical structure.
> Mesomorphy—tough and muscular body.
> Ectomorphy—linear and fragile.

On a seven-point scale for each component, a rating of 7–1–1 indicates a person high in endomorphy and low in the other two factors.

The relative presence of these three physical aspects points to specific patterns of personality. Three dimensions of temperament are believed by Sheldon (1942) to be related to body types.

> Viscerotonia—love of comfort and affection.
> Somatotonia—physical adventure and risk taking.
> Cerebrotonia—restraint and inhibition.

While Sheldon believes that a close relationship exists between his dimensions of structure and personality, most other investigators find only slight correspondence, if at all. There is still not enough information to support the popular stereotypes, although the interest in this may continue.

Learning Theory

The crucial position that learning plays in the development of behavior has already been emphasized (Chapter 6), so that it is not surprising that many psychologists have started with this fundamental concept and have elaborated on it to explain personality. Some have drawn on psychoanalytic or other ideas to expand their theoretical systems. John Dollard and Neal Miller (1950) are probably the two theorists out of a large group who have most pursued this problem to develop a framework for understanding personality. Central notions are those familiar in general learning theory; reinforcement of certain mechanisms used by the individual to reduce anxiety leads to learning of those modes of adjustment (defense mechanisms). The analysis of the process continues in S-R terms and, for this reason, is known also as Stimulus-Response Theory. Some further and more specific indications of this approach will become evident in the discussion later in this chapter of applications of theory to common situations.

Need Theory

Sufficiently different from the formulations above, yet with many similarities to them, is the theoretical structure developed by Henry A. Murray (1938). A long list of needs in this system accounts for the dynamics of personality. Murray was influenced greatly by Freud in his use of a projective test, the Thematic Apperception Test (TAT). Analysis of responses to ambiguous pictures enabled Murray to postulate needs such as $_n$Abasement, $_n$Achievement, $_n$Affiliation, $_n$Aggression, etc. Behavior is explained further in dynamic ways in terms of Press on properties of the situation such as $_p$Family Insupport, $_p$Affiliation, $_p$Friendships, $_p$Inferiority, and $_p$Lack or Loss.

Murray's work has stimulated further interest and activity among students of personality. Even more important, perhaps, is the influence he has had on researchers such as McClelland (1961), who has taken the concept of $_n$Achievement and has related it to ecomonic behavior on a large or small scale.

Holistic Theories

Holistic, organismic, or field theories have in common an emphasis on the totality and interrelatedness of all behavior. This approach treats the organism as a whole to a greater degree than do any of the other theoretical formulations. Beyond that common thread there are, as with all the theorists, enough differences to make each stand out somewhat.

Abraham Maslow has concentrated on the concept of needs developed from the study of positive and optimistic aspects of man's total functioning, not from a "pessimistic, negative and limited conception" of him. In *Motivation and personality* (1954) he structures various levels of needs, the *hierarchy of needs,* with the most important one being the need for self-actualization. Maslow says man has a basic striving to satisfy a need for fulfillment of all his potential.

Maslow has generated interest in circles far beyond the academic. He has influenced contemporary students of business who, like McGregor (1960), have used his formulations to illuminate specific problems in administration or labor relations. Maslow's concept of a hierarchy of needs is, further, a stimulating one for discussion of needs and is useful for a model to explain many specific aspects of behavior. It will be used in this way in discussions below.

Carl Rogers (1951) organizes the concept of what man is in terms of the *organism,* or total individual, operating in a *phenomenal field,* the entire experience of the person. The patterns of perceptions in this field are the basis for the self which learns to be consistent with itself and the environment; instances where this is not the case are perceived as threats to the organism. Rogers is best known for a system of psychotherapy which is called *nondirective therapy* because the clinician does not force or direct the experience into channels already established by him. The emphasis is on mirroring the feelings of the client, as the title of Rogers' best known book indicates (*Client-centered therapy*).

The subjective and experiential approach, which Rogers drew on for his system, is developed further by a school of thought sometimes labeled *phenomenology.* The basic position in this formulation is that "reality" for the individual consists of what he perceives in his field or experiences. The subjective reality is more important in understanding his behavior than is the physical situation. This body of thought has not been well developed up to this time in psychology, but interest in it is likely to grow. Combs and Syngg (1959) have been the earliest exponents of this general approach although they have preferred to label their system a perceptual view of behavior.

A newer approach toward personality which includes many of the concepts of the holistic theorists is sketched by Herzberg in *Work and the nature of man* (1966). In it the author has gone to great lengths to make applications of his basic concepts to the world of work. Herzberg considers that man has two dimensions. One aspect of man is the *Adam,* or the animal nature, where the goal of the organism is to avoid the pain of adjustment to the environment. The second side of man is the *Abraham,* one which impels him to achieve and to add to his existence. The Adam side of man has *hygiene* needs which are satisfied through salary, working conditions, and fringe benefits. From the Abraham part of man's nature emerge needs that are *motivators.* These are the complex and crucial needs that deal with the psychological growth of individuals in the organization. Job enlargement, therapeutic actions, or self-development of personnel become the focus for activity in the growth sphere.

Field Theory

Kurt Lewin (1951) belongs in the general category of holistic theorists but his adoption of concepts and terms of physical science to describe behavior provides enought basis for separate discussion. Lewin pictured a person in a perceptual field in physical terms. The field may be considered the psychological life space of the individual with vectors or forces attracting or repelling him with respect to a goal. This topological approach to personality may be seen below when some of Lewin's basic concepts will be used to describe certain life problems and behavior encountered in attempts to solve those problems.

Cognitive Dissonance

While not a full-fledged theory of personality, Festinger's (1957) concept of cognitive dissonance has stimulated enough interest to permit brief mention of it here. Festinger postulates cognitive dissonance as being a motivating state in individuals. When two cognitions of a person are dissonant, or inconsistent with each other, the person will attempt to change one of them to conform with the other, thereby reducing the dissonance. This conceptualization is one of the few views of motivation with a cognitive rather than conative basis.

Motivation

Motivation helps answer what we have considered to be the fundamental question in the area of human behavior, the question "why" or "what is it that makes people do things." Motivation refers to something dynamic that arises on an *internal* basis; it refers to, as Berelson and Steiner (1964) put it, "all those inner striving conditions described as wishes, desires, drives, etc. . . . It is an inner state that activates or moves." Indeed, the term motivation stems from the word for movement. We are familiar with motive power or an automotive (self-moving) vehicle; these are all from the same Latin stem.

Need is a good place to begin as far as motivation is concerned, and we might sketch a simple diagram (Figure 8-1) to indicate that need is the starting point. A need is a lack or deficit of something within the system or organism (one might begin thinking at this point what these needs are). When a lack or deficit arises in the individual, it is the beginning of a chain of events. Something happens, some behavior occurs, but it is not behavior at random. The organism that feels a need does not engage in random behavior or unguided activity—it engages in activity that is directed toward a goal.

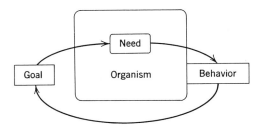

Figure 8-1. The motivational process.

Arriving at the goal satisfies the need, and the mechanism of motivation is complete. Looking at it overall, one can see that it began with the need and it ended with need satisfaction, with goal-directed behavior as a fundamental dynamic aspect of the process.

The mechanism of motivation might be looked at as a movement toward a balance; this move toward equilibrium is a *homeostatic* mechanism. This is perhaps the fundamental point to keep in mind as we discuss the behavior of the motivated organism.

Needs

Behavior which is not random but is goal directed toward a particular satisfaction of a need must now be examined a little more closely. As has been stated above, a need is a lack or a deficit within the organism. These deficits or needs are not of the same kind, and the classification of these may be made in many ways.

PRIMARY NEEDS

The human organism, without a doubt, has a need for some basic physical satisfactions, a lack of which over any long period of time may prove not only dangerous but fatal. Obviously, we need oxygen, food, and water. Clothing and shelter we do not need—closer scrutiny of what is fundamental in this instance reveals that preservation of body temperature within limits is the crucial factor and not the wearing of clothing or the maintenance of a roof over one's head. These primary needs themselves may be broken down into particular categories. Some needs are of a supply nature, providing important elements for balance, while others provide for escape from situations that threaten the integrity or stability of the organism, that is, pain, extreme cold or heat, and the like. A further basic maintenance need, sex, refers to maintenance of the species rather than preservation of the individual. In that sense, it is not as immediately basic a need as are the others. The foundations for its expression are clearly biological and innate, although, as with many other needs, the actual expression of the need shows a strong influence from acquired or learned concomitants.

SECONDARY NEEDS

A second category of needs may not be as immediate or physical, yet they emerge early in life and play a vital role. These are secondary, derived, or social needs. The social needs might be divided still further into the *affiliative* needs and the *egoistic* needs. Both have to do with people, but the affiliative needs deal with belongingness, companionship, or love of being *with* people. The egoistic needs refer to a position *over* people rather than with people. Power, status, prestige, or esteem fit under this second subclassification. Some experimenters have emphasized that a twofold classification is really too crude and that there is an intermediate class of needs between the primary and the social needs. Apparently, we have a need for stimulation, both on a physical and an emotional basis. We need physical contact, and we need the opportunity to manipulate our environment to some extent. Curiosity, for instance, can be regarded as one of the vital requisites in this third intermediate category. Even more recent experiments by Olds (1958) and others indicate that electrical stimulation of some brain centers, mainly in the hypothalamus, is a motivating mechanism. A rat with electrodes implanted in the hypothalamic area will consistently depress a lever which will provide him with slight shocks. Some investigators go to the extent of reporting that the look on the rat's face is highly pleasurable. At any rate, the rats, in many instances, maintain this particular behavior until exhausted.

MASLOW'S HIERARCHY OF NEEDS

A more sophisticated classification of needs comes in recent discussions of motivation by Maslow (1954), who has postulated an order of needs from the very basic to the highly complex. Notable in the framework is the development and refinement of the structure of needs. Not satisfied with a crude dichotomy like physical and social needs, Maslow sketches a list of basic needs which are regarded as *conative* or striving needs. Not only do these needs

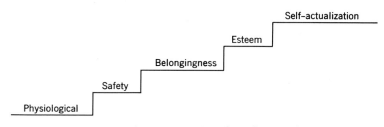

Figure 8-2.   Maslow's hierarchy of needs (Maslow, 1954).

appear in human activity, but they appear as significant in a specific ranking or hierarchy. Those which come first, says Maslow, must be satisfied before a higher need comes into play, and only when those next higher ones are satisfied are the next ones in line significant, and so on. A schematic version of this hierarchy may be sketched as in Figure 8-2, and the steps in the hierarchy may be described as follows.

Physiological Needs

The primary needs of the body are ones in which the homeostatic mechanism is ordinarily in evidence. Need to maintain the sugar, salt, calcium, or oxygen content of the blood (add many other elements to this list as well) results in some behavior which has as its purpose the filling of the lack that exists. Physiological needs dominate when all needs are unsatisfied. Other needs do not serve as a basis for motivation, and it is fruitless for one to consider any of those higher in the order. One cannot discuss with a starving Bushman the concepts of freedom or love or philosophy—these have no probity under the existing conditions.

Since these emergencies come less and less these days, particularly in western society, the important needs in a practical situation are undoubtedly those higher in the hierarchy. With the physiological needs satisfied, the next higher ones come into focus.

Safety Needs

The second step in the hierarchy consists of a set of needs which may not be fractionated as precisely as the physiological needs but are just as dominant when their turn comes. Problems of "safety-seeking" dominate the man who feels threatened. In a purer form the concern for safety is seen in the strong reactions children have to unusual stimulation, a sudden loss of support, or an illness. In a broader social setting, with adults the operation of safety needs may be seen in attempts to insure job security or broaden social security as well as in moves toward greater financial support. Safety needs manifest themselves as well in compulsive moves to order every step of daily activity; rules are adhered to religiously to avoid the unexpected.

Belongingness and Love Needs

Affiliative and affectionate needs relate to the social or gregarious nature of human relationships. These needs represent a clear-cut step up from the two below it—the plainly physical level of the physiological needs and the quasi-physical of the safety needs. Where these are not met, severe maladjustment is probable; where the hunger for companionship is assuaged, the mental health of the organism is once again on a better base.

Esteem Needs

These needs represent both the need for the self-awareness of importance to others and the recognition by others of the same. Both self-confidence and prestige are represented, but it is healthy self-confidence and a deserved respect from others, not the false or unwarranted adulation. Satisfaction of these needs leads to self-confidence and removal of inferiority or ego weakness, part of the syndrome in many neuroses.

Self-Actualization

The "desire to become more and more what one is, to become everything that one is capable of becoming" (Maslow, 1954, p. 92) is a real need. It is this impetus which makes for full utilization of one's talents or potentialities to do the best one can in serving society from the niche one has in that society. Status and role may differ, and so the external aspects of self-actualization will vary accordingly. An individual may be a physician or parent, counselor or administrator, but the drive is to be the most effective performer in the role. Needless to say, none of this is possible without the satisfaction of all the needs lower in the order. One must be physiologically and organismically as well as socially secure before he can be activated in that final thrust toward fulfillment. Despite their possession of many positive traits, it is refreshing to note that self-actualizing persons do have their faults. They are not free of guilt, they make mistakes, etc., but the healthy acceptance of these only adds and does not detract from the personality of the self-actualizer. That time plays a role is suggested by Maslow when he reports (1954, p. 200) that the sort of self-actualization he found in his older subjects was found almost never in the young.

Cognitive and Aesthetic Needs

Less described, and therefore not as well known, are the cognitive and aesthetic needs postulated by Maslow. These are not opposed to the conative or striving needs outlined above but are complementary to them. The need to know or to understand, the manipulation of the environment as the result of curiosity, or even the philosophizing that so occupies many is the expression of this set of cognitive needs. The aesthetic needs are satisfied by the getting away from ugliness and the moving toward beauty. There seems to be some scientific basis for the existence of cognitive needs (Murphy, 1947). Perhaps recent work by Harlow and McClearn (1954), in finding general needs of a manipulative and curiosity nature in animal subjects, helps to support this theory as well.

Use of the Concepts

Maslow's hierarchy has attracted much attention within academic circles and outside them, and the concepts have been applied often in practical settings. McGregor (1960) built his formulation of "Theory X" and "Theory Y" partially on this foundation; the hierarchy is used by others as well in the description of motivation in business organizations (Haynes and Massie, 1961). We may find that the model of motivation sketched by Maslow is effective in pointing out some features that motivate individuals in a business organization. One must belong to the organization, have some affiliation with the group, or some identification with the company before any needs of esteem or prestige are operative. We might go further and state that in order for individuals to do their best or to fulfill their ultimate potential, all of the needs below self-actualization must be taken care of before the organism can reach fulfillment. At the same time, incentives offered by a company to workers to satisfy physiological or safety needs (as money usually does) may be ineffective because the lower needs are satisfied. What is needed is an attempt to satisfy the higher-order needs.

Maslow's hierarchy provides researchers or practitioners neither with a system that gives complete understanding nor one that is invariate in its application, but it does provide a provocative template for the appreciation of the question of why people act as they do or "what is motivation?"

Need Nonsatisfaction

What happens when needs are not satisfied? A descriptive system of many of the aspects of the functioning of an organism (Lewin, 1951) incorpo-

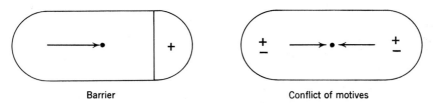

Barrier   Conflict of motives

Figure 8-3. Simple topological representation of psychological life space (adapted from Lewin, 1951).

rates the notion of a psychological life space in which a person operates. The sketch of a person operating in a life space may be useful in describing some of the aspects of problem solving that occur in life situations. Figure 8-3 depicts the psychological life space with its boundaries. The dot represents the individual, a goal represents a need and its satisfaction, while the direction of the arrow represents the thrust of the person toward the goal.

BARRIERS

The concept of the psychological life space can include a barrier which prevents the individual from reaching the goal and satisfying the need. What occurs as a result? Behavior that does occur is replete with opportunities for analysis and inferences from it for the understanding of motivation. Where a barrier exists it may be a physical, external barrier such as time, space, or lack of money; the stone wall which keeps us from our goal may be more than a figurative one. A stone wall literally keeps a motivated male undergraduate outside the exclusive girls' school which is barred at night. A lack of money may prevent the accomplishment of certain activities that would be need fulfilling. Of even greater importance are internal barriers which prevent the attainment of a goal. A lack of ability on the part of an individual who sets his heart on becoming a lawyer, a physician, or an accountant is a very real barrier indeed. Nonattainment of this kind of goal which would satisfy certain needs is productive of many serious problems.

CONFLICT OF MOTIVES

A further problem area arises on a slightly different basis (also illustrated in Figure 8-3) in the conflict-of-motives situation where, instead of a barrier interposed between the individual and the goal, there is a set of incompatible goals among which the individual must make a choice. This choice among conflicting goals is based on a conflict within the individual; different needs and their satisfaction compete for attention. The different conflict-of-motives situation may be distinguished. In one situation where there are two equally attractive goals, the conflict is called an approach-approach conflict. Where there may be two equally unattractive goals or negative goals, the individual would be caught in an avoidance-avoidance conflict. Where an individual would be both attracted and repelled by the positive and negative aspects of the goal, the conflict would be an approach-avoidance conflict. This last type of conflict-of-motives situation is undoubtedly the most common.

Reactions to Nonsatisfaction of Needs

With the focus on behavior, the next question logically becomes, "What do people do as the result of nonattainment of the goal?" What happens when needs are not satisfied can occupy volumes of description, since the variations in behavior are almost infinite. There are some patterns, however, that are more common and that can be described, albeit sketchily. Figure 8-4 contains a simple model of reactions to the nonsatisfaction of needs.

GENERAL PATTERNS

Nonattainment of a goal is frustrating. One way of handling this is to leave the "field" or withdraw. The withdrawal may be physical, as in flight

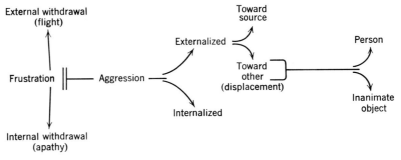

Figure 8-4.   Reactions to nonsatisfaction of needs.

from the scene, or it may be internalized and carried to the extreme lethargy seen in *apathy*.

A more common reaction to frustration is *aggression,* an act or force against someone or something. Aggression is most easily seen as a move outward. If there is a direct attack on the source of frustration in a way that can take care of the problem, this is often reasonable and healthy. It may not be "healthy," however, to punch the boss in the nose in order to remove this source of frustration. What happens all too often is that the aggression is directed to third parties or objects. This circumstance is known as *displacement.* Innocent bystanders have been known to suffer from frustrations not of their doing; when a husband growls at his wife after a traumatic day at the office, the innocent spouse should be understanding but may not be. Aggression displaced toward inanimate objects may be less taxing for humans. Kicking doors and sawing wood have long been popular. A newer and perhaps more therapeutic displacement device is the dummy resembling the boss which some few companies have introduced. The worker need only retire to a special room and punch away.

Other aspects of behavior resulting from frustration may be identified as well. Below the surface of the aggression there is hostility. Aggression differs from hostility in that aggression is an act while hostility is the deep smouldering resentment below. The continuation of the response, usually in an ineffective way, is known as *fixation.* The person persists in the response even though it may not work. He does so because it is the only way he knows to handle the problem. The accountant who gathers data according to procedures he learned in college in 1920 is in trouble when new data processing techniques are introduced.

STRESS REACTIONS

The physical reactions to stress and conflict may be viewed as an internalization of the aggression which arises in the situation. The somatic (*soma*—Greek for "body") or bodily reactions to the stress can be quite extensive or handicapping. The physical results are real, not the product of suggestion or imagination.

Psychosomatic Reactions

The emotional aspects of conflict can reach a resolution in specific somatic ways. The tension that comes with anger or resentment can be internalized as a duodenal ulcer or hypertension. The list may be longer as many researchers feel that angina pectoris, mucous colitis, asthma, hay fever, migraine, many allergies, neuritis, most industrial dermatitis, sciatica, and perhaps many others, including the "common cold," are psychosomatic ailments (Brown, 1954, p. 260). The chronic anxiety with which some men carry out their daily activities is bound to have some adverse results. The physical reactions are the effects of the physiological changes in the *autonomic nervous system*. The *sympathetic* branch of the autonomic nervous system is that which mobilizes the resources of the body to meet a threat or challenge, while the *parasympathetic* part regulates the sedentary and usual activities of the body—regular respiration, digestion, and elimination. Challenges are met by having the heart beat faster and pump more blood to the extremities, tensing the muscles, reducing the digestive activity, and speeding up the rate of breathing. These results of the sympathetic system activity utilize a great amount of energy. It is easy to see how a continuing arousal of the sympathetic system can have direct and serious somatic consequences.

The General-Adaptation Syndrome

The reaction of a human person to continuing stress is one of very real concern in practical settings. A theoretical approach toward an understanding of what happens when an organism is exposed to prolonged stress has been formulated by Selye (1950). The reaction of the organism, according to Selye, takes place in three stages: *the alarm reaction, the stage of resistance,* and the *stage of exhaustion.*

The alarm reaction is the initial alerting of the forces of the body to mobilize its efforts to meet the stress. The physical changes or symptoms of the response may be seen in various forms such as fever or fatigue. The stage of resistance is reached if the stress continues. The defense mechanisms that were mobilized may have begun to cope with the threat to the system, and the initial symptoms may have even disappeared under the adaptation by the system. If these forces overreact, however, the system shows the result of this overactivity in bodily disturbances like ulcers or hypertension. If the stress is prolonged or the forces of resistance cannot cope with it during the stage of resistance, the organism under stress reaches the final period, the stage of exhaustion. The body defenses are no longer adequate, the glandular output cannot cope with the increased pressure, and the system is in the critical terminal state.

DEFENSE MECHANISMS

Some ways of reacting to stressful situations, frustration, or anxiety are not generally complex nor do they handicap the individual to any great extent.

These mechanisms are not ordinarily, however, adequate or appropriate to the task of protecting the self concept of the individual.

Anxiety is considered by many to be the most significant product of frustration and stress. Anxiety is an unpleasant state, a disturbed feeling arising out of the inability to reach the goal. This vague, free-floating feeling cannot be tied to anything specific and, indeed, part of the problem is that the individual ordinarily is not aware of how it arises. All one knows is that one has "butterflies in the stomach," the heart is beating faster, perspiration may be profuse, and all these physiological changes are accompanied by feelings of unpleasantness. Behavior that results is a defense by the individual against the anxiety that arises. Not always is the attempt effective; if it does not succeed, it may generate a further defense by the individual in the frustration from nonsolution of the problem.

Some reactions are compromise attempts where one may "bargain one's way out" or substitute something else. *Substitution* is where one puts something else in place of an original object. A need may be met by substituting some other goal object for the original one and satisfying the need; getting to the goal to satisfy the need reduces any anxiety and "solves" the problem. *Compensation* occurs when a person may go overboard in one activity to make up for a deficiency in another area. The deficiency arouses anxiety; it is an unpleasant thing to face the fact that you "just don't have it" in one area, but to concentrate all the forces at one's disposal on a second area may bring success. *Sublimation* consists of substituting a socially desirable activity for one that is undesirable or that may not be possible at that particular time. Social service activities by women may substitute for motherhood; taking care of children is something that is a socially desirable compromise activity.

There may be *repression* of the situation and the problem in order to keep anxiety down. Repression is a mechanism that happens without our willing it. This is not deliberate process; it is an almost automatic response whereby we lose awareness of certain incidents that would arouse anxiety in us were they present in our consciousness. It thrusts into the deep recesses of the mind the particular aspects of the surroundings that would give us difficulty if we recognized them.

THE NEUROSES

More serious mechanisms, indicating a need for a stronger defense, are those patterns that are called *neuroses*. The neurotic defense mechanisms are a little more unusual; they are more handicapping and arise because of the need by the individual for a defense that would be stronger in the prevention or reduction of anxiety in the situation. Those who engage in a particular kind of behavior like hand washing every five minutes are forced to do so,

This response is a *compulsion*, as the individual is compelled to do something under penalty of increasing anxiety by not doing it. The anxiety rises to such heights that it is unbearable; even though it might be difficult to perform the act, this is a lot less painful than living with the anxiety. The bank teller who must count and recount the money at the end of the day is handicapped in more ways than just having to stay at work until ten o'clock at night. An *obsession* is an idea that constantly intrudes upon the person's thinking rather than act such as in compulsion. The two phenomena are considered as one class of neuroses.

There may be a great deal of anxiety arising in a situation where an individual is enclosed in a tight place. The person fears being in this particular situation—an irrational fear of something specific. This is known as a *phobia,* the Greek term for fear. A Greek prefix will also identify the specific phobia (as in *ailurophobia,* the fear of cats); a listing of these fears would provide an extensive collection.

A *conversion reaction* is a neurotic defense response which involves the use of a physical mechanism such as blindness or paralysis: It has no physical or organic basis but certainly prevents the individual, at least in his own mind, from performing certain activities. The purpose of the mechanism may be clear to observers but not to the individual adopting it. It represents an attempt to solve a problem in a certain way—no one can be expected to do a job when one is "paralyzed"; this relieves the burden when the person is unable to meet a crisis, as in a loss of voice, a loss of memory, or a loss of eyesight.

Some additional unusual situations may occur involving a neurotic mechanism. A totally different personality may emerge at one time or another. These *dissociative reactions* or *multiple personalities* have individuals filling a series of roles under various conditions without an awareness on the part of the main personality of the individual. Although this reaction is fairly rare, it has been recognized for over half a century and has been a very popular subject in novels and the theater.

Another neurotic defense mechanism is the use of alcohol. This continues to be one of the most pressing of our social problems. In an industrial or business setting it is a serious problem of adjustment with many concurrent implications. While some of the physiological aspects are not entirely clear, it is certain that alcohol serves as a mechanism that reduces anxiety, somewhat the way tranquilizers act. The problem does not go away, but one can feel a lot better about it after a drink or two.

While anxiety is at the base of all neurotic reactions, it sometimes is seen by itself. Where there are no symptoms other than the anxiety and its components, the neurotic mechanism is called an *anxiety reaction.* The unpleasant feeling state will be accompanied by its physiological aspects—anything from gastric upsets to rapid respiration or heartbeat. The anxiety can also lead to the adoption of mechanisms like *hypochondria,* a preoccupation with one's health, or *neurasthenia,* a general feeling of fatigue or nervousness.

Neuroses are serious enough defense mechanisms to be a handicap to the individual. The anxiety and other patterns of behavior prevent the individual from performing as he might or should in a particular position. There is, however, a recognition of reality by the neurotic. The mechanism used does not cut off the person from an awareness of real life, as in the psychoses to be discussed shortly. The neurotic may be "out in left field" but he knows a ball game is being played and he knows the score. His problem is that he always drops the ball when it comes to him. The psychotic is "outside the ball park"; the cheers of the crowd indicate to him that people are acclaiming his exploits as a national hero. This departure from reality marks the dividing line between neurotics and psychotics.

THE PSYCHOSES

This term is a label for a broad group of severe and bizarre behavior patterns. They have in common a departure from reality in the responses made by the psychotic person. Whatever the differences between the psychoses, the activity of the individual in all of the categories shows the same serious inability to respond to life situations in an appropriate or meaningful way.

The names used give little indication of basic factors in the development or onset of the disorder; the labels are little more than descriptions of behavior. In the most general breakdown of the psychoses, however, the two subclassifications give a slight indication of underlying factors. The two main groupings of the psychoses are the *organic* and the *functional* psychoses. In the former category are a few varied psychoses that arise on a physical or organic basis. There is something somatic that is responsible for the disordered activity of the person. In the functional psychoses no such clear-cut foundation for the behavior exists. No causative factors have been pinpointed as in the organic psychoses; the term functional really represents an admission of inability to fix the reasons for their emergence. What can be said is that, at this time at least, the functional group of psychoses is composed of those psychoses which are nonorganic.

The disordered behavior of the organic psychotic comes as the result of the invasion of the organism by some foreign substance, disease, or the deterioration that can accompany advanced age. Actual medical and clinical tests must be made to determine the exact organic factor because the visible behavior of some organic and functional psychotics may be similar. The patterns for the alcoholic and the senile psychoses may be so much alike as to be virtually indistinguishable.

The functional disorders provide most of the action in the mental health sphere. Not only are there more individuals affected, they are involved longer. Most of the organic psychotics are of advanced age and their affliction does not, therefore, last long. The functional psychotic may be of any age and, in one category, may even be younger than most. The number involved, the seriousness of the disability, and the lack of understanding of causation make it one of the more pressing problem areas facing society. The specific difficulties that come to the fore in any organizational setting call for the most perceptive personnel decision making.

The functional (nonorganic) psychoses may be grouped into three general categories.

1. Schizophrenia.
2. Disorders of affect.
3. Paranoia.

Each of these groupings will have some variation in behavior as part of the overall pattern, sometimes so extensive as to allow for many subclassifications.

Schizophrenia may show many forms; the latest psychiatric classification has ten categories, all labels either describing behavior or indicating the time of onset. Of these, the four most commonly found are as follows.

(a)   Hebephrenia—silly and inappropriate behavior.
(b)   Catatonia—unusual psychomotor ability or gesturing.
(c)   Paranoid type—hallucinatory behavior with delusions of persecution or grandeur.
(d)   Simple type—uncommunicative withdrawal.

Schizophrenia was known earlier as *dementia praecox,* a term that at least pointed to one of the most interesting aspects of the disorder, namely, that it does affect the young more often than other types. It is also more resistant to therapy; over half the hospital beds in mental institutions are occupied by this group—there are more of them and they stay longer.

The affective disorders have been known as the *manic-depressive* psychoses. These designations describe the dynamics of this type well. The individual may be manic, that is, hyperactive and excited, or he may be in the throes of a deep depression. Even more dramatic is the classic type of manic-depressive psychosis when the individual swings from one end of the affective scale to the other; he may be "on top of the world" at one moment and in the depths of depression soon after. Oscillation like this may occur over and over again within a relatively short period of time.

Paranoia is a disorder where the individual is beset by delusions (false beliefs) of persecution. The paranoid differs from the paranoid schizophrenic in that his delusions are organized and he ordinarily does not have hallucinations. He may be difficult to spot at first because the pattern of persecution could be believed. In a factory, the worker who indicates vehemently that others are "out to get him" often finds some sympathetic listeners. When he incorporates all stimuli into his delusional system, however, others may begin to see the disorder as it really is.

CHARACTER DISORDERS

A separate category of behavior patterns includes a variety of clinical labels with the *sociopathic personality* the most dramatic example. Sociopaths, or *psychopathic personalities,* have fascinated researchers and laymen alike in many respects. Individuals in this classification, unlike psychotics, are in touch with reality; even more, they have a keen perception of circumstances, and they use this to their advantage or the disadvantage of others. These are the confidence men who prey on the weak; they have no social concern or conscience in the usual sense and are indifferent should they violate a norm or law in their attempt to reach desired ends.

While departures from the norm are often dramatic and bizarre in the actions of sociopaths, the law generally holds them accountable for their behavior. Though their acts may be as shocking to society as those of psychotics, they do have a clear sense of reality; this is the basic test of legal responsibility. Prisons contain a high percentage of sociopaths who have been caught in swindles or worse. They have proved resistant to therapy, but this may be because of the initial classification of "criminal" rather than "ill" with the resulting few attempts at proper therapy.

Therapy

While a detailed study of the methods of therapy for disturbances of personality are beyond the scope of this book, a worker, manager, teacher, or simply an informed citizen should have some idea of the possibilities for treatment in this area. The knowledge of what can be done and where to go could be of great help in critical situations.

MEDICAL THERAPY

The treatment that medical science has been able to utilize consists of either surgical, electrical, or chemical techniques. Surgery can consist of ablation of certain tissues of the brain or the cutting of nerve fibers. Results of such surgery have been mixed and, since the technique is a radical one, the method has been used less often (Mettler, 1949). Electroshock has some positive factors that have encouraged many therapists to use it. The jolt of electricity which induces unconsciousness does seem to bring some seriously disturbed individuals back to the point where they are proper subjects for psychotherapy. They are able to adapt themselves better to the reality of the situation and often can engage in the dialogue that forms the basis of psychotherapy. Chemotherapy may consist of administering insulin or metrazol to produce a grogginess in which the barriers preventing the emergence of unpleasant material are removed. Sodium amytal is one of this class of drugs sometimes known as "truth serums." By far the most widely used and promising chemical tools in therapy, however, are the various drugs that aid in changing the emotional states of patients. Tranquilizers which soothe or energizers which stimulate the depressed do not "cure," but they do provide a climate for the more effective use of other techniques. Less violent or less pessimistic patients give an opportunity for psychotherapy where little existed before. The whole tenor of hospitals and clinics has changed as a result.

Psychedelic drugs may, in many cases, mimic the symptoms of the psychoses, particularly schizophrenia, even when they are taken by people who are not psychotic. The best known of these is *lysergic acid diethylamide,* or LSD, for short. The extent of the help or danger from the use of LSD has been a matter of controversy even within professional circles. The situation has aroused strong feelings among some who have experimented with the psychedelic drugs in the recent past and who consider them "mind expanders." Others who are concerned with the dangers are in the majority and have supported legal control of the chemicals.

PSYCHOTHERAPY

The nonmedical treatment of personality disorders is known generally as psychotherapy. While on the surface it may appear to be a simple dialogue between client and counselor or patient and doctor, the actual technique may be complex (one should say, instead, techniques because the number of approaches in psychotherapy are many and varied). The exact method used may depend on the theoretical orientation of the therapists, the nature of the problem, its severity, or what is possible in the way of therapy. Some of these may be determined from the interviews and testing procedures the clinician will use.

Directive therapies involve some positive and straightforward direction by the therapist or an alteration of the environment. Taking the patient out of a difficult situation may help somewhat but seldom is long lasting as it does little for the basic problem. In the same way, supportive help the counselor provides may calm the client but will not provide the kind of insight a less direct and more participative approach might give. Even more directive are those attempts used to extinguish or unlearn the undesirable behavior patterns and learn others that are more desirable. Hypnosis is another directive method that bears some similarity to the reeducation techniques but adds the element of the strong suggestion of the hypnotic state.

Nondirective approaches to therapy avoid the situations where the therapist tells the patient what to do or does something for him. Many therapists feel strongly that long-lasting improvements come about only when the client has the opportunity to control his own circumstances. This factor alone has been responsible for the increasing use of the nondirective approaches to psychotherapy. The best known of these techniques is *client-centered therapy,* which has been developed primarily by Carl Rogers (1951). In this approach the present emotional aspects of the individual, not the hypothesized problem, are the center of attention. The counselor mirrors the feelings of the client to make him more open to the emotional release which comes in a warm and permissive therapeutic atmosphere. The self-realization through the expression of feelings is a good basis for more substantial changes in functioning.

Psychoanalysis is a therapeutic method that follows the concepts and techniques first outlined by Freud. While it has in it elements of both directive and nondirective approaches, awareness of the basic factors in the problem is considered to be the critical requirement in therapy. This is fostered through *free association,* the talking out of anything that comes to the mind of the patient without fear of disapproval. Some *resistance* may take place which would prevent the free flow of association. *Transference,* the transfer of attitudes to the psychoanalytic situation from earlier experiences, may overcome resistance if it is positive but may hamper the analysis if it is negative and hostile. Analysis of dreams may be attempted also to further the development of insight.

Other miscellaneous techniques are often tried as therapeutic measures. *Group therapy* departs from the one-to-one relationship of client and counselor to a situation where the therapist works with several patients at a time. As a supplement to individual therapy or used alone, the group has some advantages; the social support a patient can receive from others in the group is valuable in promoting insight and problem resolution. *Psychodrama* (Moreno, 1946) is a therapeutic technique based on drama where disturbed patients act out their problems and thereby gain insight into them. For children, *play therapy* can not only give some release to the anxiety or tensions that may be present, but the technique also allows the clinician to get some better idea of the basis of the problems.

EFFECTIVENESS OF THERAPY

How well the different techniques of therapy work and how many people are helped is a difficult question to answer. No one speaks of "cures" because of the impossibility of determining just what this is. If there is recovery from a disorder for a period of time, does this satisfy the criteria for a cure? How long should this period be—one year, two, five or more years? More realistically, an individual may be judged to be able to leave the friendly environment of a hospital and return to the outside even though there is a chance that he may be reexposed to the stressful circumstances that precipitated his problem symptoms. Presumably that judgment included the view that the individual could now withstand the stress imposed by a hostile environment. If this is not the case, a relapse will send the person back to the less threatening environment.

The different approaches to therapy have been evaluated by many researchers and, while there are variations in findings, increasing numbers of patients are being released from hospitals. This indicates some increase in effectiveness although there is some other evidence that the recovery rate for untreated individuals may be as high as the recovery under treatment (Eysenck, 1952). While the comparisons may not be without controversy, it is true that spontaneous recovery does occur even with severely disturbed psychotics; that is, they can show a remission of symptoms without any psychotherapy or other treatment.

There are some clear results to report, however. Therapies or tranquilizers may not themselves produce a state in the individual that would permit discharge from a hospital, but they can provide a more favorable climate for psychotherapy. Psychotics can be calmed or "brought back to reality" and the treatment continued from that point. At the very least, tranquilizers have brought about extensive changes in the atmosphere within mental hospitals.

Organizational Problems

Problems of personal adjustment arise in many situations, of course, and the variation in kind and degree of difficulty will be great. Minor problems sometimes may be overshadowed by major disorders, but the minor ones will be met more often and, in this sense, are more important.

A word of caution is in order first. It is all too easy to memorize a few labels or the patterns of behavior described above; the danger lies in the assumption that knowledge of terms means an understanding of the dynamics involved. Much more than a labeling is needed—insight into the problem situation at least must be attempted. An opposite reaction also gives limited information. We may be overwhelmed by the amount of material to be studied or disconcerted by the apparent lack of coherence in the behavior observed.

When faced with unusual behavior, it does not do to throw up our hands and say we do not understand it. We may not but we ought to try. The "logic" of the problem-solving approach by the individual who has a particularly serious problem or who is under severe stress is not easy to determine, but an attempt to do so should be made. This may be the most important point for anyone who is involved in the work activities of others, whether he is a manager, teacher, or just an ordinary citizen. If one can try to get the view of the world of the person with the problem and attempt to recognize how this particular situation arose, there could be limited success in understanding but more will be gained through this approach than by simply memorizing a list of labels referring to adjustment and mental health. This is a suggestion not limited to any particular business and industrial situation—it extends to all activities in society.

EXTENT OF PROBLEM SITUATIONS

Two factors are of general interest as a further prologue to a discussion of specific problems faced in organizational functioning. The first finding is that most of the problems in performance in many situations come from personality difficulties. A majority of the dismissals of employees in industry (some say as high as 90 percent) come as a result of inability to adjust to the situation or to function effectively because of personality problems. This one finding alone points out the importance of an understanding of individual dynamics. There is further evidence that most of the trouble in any organizational setting comes as the result of the activities of a small number of individuals. It may well be that 80 percent of the problems in industry are caused by 20 percent of the people. It must not be assumed, however, that the incidence of neuroses and psychoses in the plant will be as high as indicated by the stated percentage of problem people. While estimates are difficult to make and vary widely, a rough guess is that one in ten in the population at large will at some time or other be admitted to a mental hospital (Morgan and King, 1966). Those affected in an industrial organization may be above or below that figure, but the supervisor should be aware that most of his time will be spent with the milder problems. With both mild and severe problems, however, the caveat remains the same—avoid "psychologizing" or simply pinning labels on events and attempt to understand the basic features of the behavior in question.

PSYCHOSOMATIC DISORDERS

We know (above) that the somatic results of emotional stress can appear in various forms, from ulcer to hypertension. Many of these, particularly duodenal ulcer, have long been the badge of the striving executive. This notion that only executives have ulcers is, however, not founded. Gibson (1960), in a study at General Motors, confirmed earlier findings that stress disorders were found at all levels of industry. The problem achieves greater importance if these stress disorders are increasing (Brown, 1954). While these are rare in rural and nonindustrialied parts of the world, they are prevalent in the United States, Britain, and Western Europe, and there is evidence of rapid increase in the newly developing nations. Even more alarming is the possibility that the age of onset is moving to younger age groups as children are more and more adversely affected by the attitudes toward performance in our society.

APATHY

The reaction to frustration where the individual will withdraw or "leave the field" can be noted often on the organizational scene. Some workers will simply depart physically for some other location. Others will stay physically but, for all intents and purposes, they are no longer there. They do their job but with a minimum of interest or effort. This apathy is hard for some managers to comprehend, yet, when analysis is made of the frustrations beforehand, the behavior patterns become more understandable. Apathy is understandable, too, as an end product of a consistent and continuing pattern of discrimination in job selection and placement.

A more serious state of apathy comes with a longer and more traumatic series of frustrations. When an individual or family has lived with a history of nonattainment of even simple goals, the results are often traumatizing. The effects of prolonged unemployment, for instance, can be devastating to the individual and his family. An early extensive description by Zawadzki and Lazarsfeld (1936) of the personal reactions to unemployment clearly shows the disintegration of individuality which accompanies apathy. What started with resentment and anxiety led to depression and finally to a state of "suspended animation."

ALCOHOLISM

The use of alcohol to the extent that it handicaps the individual continues to be one of the main problems of many societies and a source of economic loss to industry as a whole. The number of alcoholics in industry has been estimated at 3 percent of the work force (Franco, 1954), but the losses that accrue as the result of alcoholism are even greater. This reaction pattern has been discussed above in terms of the concept of a neurotic defense mechanism, and a better understanding comes with an analysis on this basis rather than focusing on handling the surface symptoms of absences, aggressive accidents, and changes in mood or personality.

ACCIDENTS

Much the same pattern prevails in accidents. People who have more than their share of accidents represent a minority of individuals, but they provide most of the problems for managers, insurance companies, and society at large. Although the correlation is far from perfect, we know that people with certain personality features have more accidents. Interestingly enough, these people who may be accident prone may be very capable individuals in other respects. They may be free from colds and have quick reactions (Dunbar, 1947). Perhaps this quick reaction time gives us an indication that there may be an element of impulsiveness in individuals who have accidents; their motor reactions may take place before their perceptual organization. This is the outcome of an interesting study along these lines by Drake (1940). The results may be summarized by the old statement "look before you leap," in that those with psychomotor reactions lagging behind perception are relatively free from accidents.

It is also fairly well established that in an extreme emotional state there is more possibility for accidents; when people are upset or disturbed, it is easier for them to have accidents.

ABSENTEEISM

Absenteeism is also a prevalent problem; while the amount of time lost on this score in industry may not seem to be as great as with accidents and alcoholism, it is significant. Absenteeism may be viewed, from the surface at least, as a withdrawal reaction. Individuals who for one reason or another find it difficult to function in a particular setting will go out of their way to avoid being in that particular setting. Tardiness is in the same category;

if a person is always late we may wonder how eager he is to be there. Often there is also a lack of awareness on the part of the chronically absent or late individual of the deeper resistance he may have to the situation he avoids.

ROLE CONFLICTS

Stress on individuals in industry may develop from their placement in the organization. The pressure from competing patterns of behavior required in the same situation puts a burden on the person in the position where his various roles may conflict. We may note further, however, that workers, foremen, and executives might have slightly different environments or there might be some different problems of adjustment at the different levels. At the executive level there might be a greater need for achievement and more of a let-down in middle age, the so-called "middle-age slump," at a time when pressures are undoubtedly multiplying. The pressures on the younger and on the older executive may not be as great as the pressures on the man in the middle part of the span; unfortunately, these pressures mount up particularly when the resistance to stress, on a psychological basis at least, decreases. The 40 year old executive may suddenly look in the mirror and wonder "what am I doing here" or "will I ever get anywhere at the rate I'm going?" Other role conflict situations may arise where an individual may find himself faced with a conflict between his notions of individual or social responsibility and the requirements of the task at hand. Moral conflicts like this have been with us for a long time and appear in all organizations.

The problems of the foreman may be little different. With work assignments, loads, materials, and methods, the first line supervisor is ordinarily responsible for coordination in the material as well as the personnel area; there are many jobs for the foreman to do, and often he may switch from one situation to the next where there are different individuals with different needs, problems, and problem-solving approaches. He may not recognize any differences between problems and is in trouble if he does not. Making it more difficult is the location of the foreman in a position midway between management and the worker where he is considered neither one nor the other. It puts him in a precarious position on top of all the problems but leaves him in the middle with tenuous ties to either side. On the one hand, he may not be considered by managers as a part of management and, on the other, is not considered one of the employees by workers under him. To the workers the foreman represents management or the company; he is the only representative of the organization with whom they regularly come in contact. For them he *is* the company even though he may have little feeling that this is so.

INDUSTRIAL CONFLICT

Most of the strife that occurs between individuals and groups may be seen as examples of aggression arising from frustration. The aggression in grievances, strikes, stoppages, and other activity may be identified easily enough and handled accordingly, but it is more difficult to recognize embezzlement or rumor mongering as the same phenomenon. Even displacement of the aggression may be seen in such diverse activities as racial prejudice and industrial sabotage.

Many of the problems in industry come to focus in the frustration and aggression stemming from the relationships between labor and management. The most notable facet may be that aggression sets off counteraggression (Stagner and Rosen, 1965). Any aggression by one side is a source of frustration to the other; the reaction is further aggression by that other side to counter the initial aggression. Escalation of a conflict comes easily under these circumstances.

Toward Positive Performance

A society, a work group, or an individual can function most effectively when conditions are such that the potentials of all can be fully developed. While the step from this obvious generalization to the execution of it in a specific situation may be difficult to make, the emphasis on that fundamental factor must be continued. The problems inherent in the fulfillment of the capabilities of individuals are not easy ones at all levels, from large aggregates to small groups, yet these remain the most important ones a society has to solve.

THE WORLD OF WORK

On the industrial scene there have been many suggestions as to the course of events to be followed in order to form a healthier framework for functioning. One such attempt appears in *Eupsychian management,* where Maslow (1965) applies his basic concepts of personality and motivation to the world of work. The kind of management advocated is that which is psychologically "good" or "healthy" and recognizes the fact that work can be psychotherapeutic in making well people grow toward self-actualization. The better a society, the more people will demand education, management, or government that will permit growth in individuals. They will resist working for an authoritarian and hierarchical management. Maslow considers eupsychian management the wave of the future because only those organizations run in this enlightened way can be competitive.

The interchange of ideas between Maslow and McGregor (1960) is obvious when one reads their works. McGregor has leaned heavily on Maslow's *hierarchy of needs* in building his *Theory X* and *Theory Y* of management, and Maslow has quoted from McGregor. The X and Y designations are used for the traditional view of management or control and the more meaningful approach, respectively. Theory X, or the traditional view, holds that people dislike work and they must be coerced into doing it. They are not self directed, have little ambition, and want only security. The elements of Theory Y, on the other hand, focus on individual self-direction and responsibility in a committment to organizational goals. Where, at present, the potentialities of individuals are only partially realized, a wider participation in organizational activity can further individual and group goals. McGregor points out in detail how management, if it wishes to remain viable, must adopt the concepts from behavioral science that are embodied in Theory Y.

A theory of effective management that may draw some of its inspiration from McGregor is one propounded by Blake and Mouton (1961). A descriptive system, called the *managerial grid,* is developed to identify styles of leadership in numerical terms. A 9,1 supervisor is one who emphasizes production over people while a 1,9 designation refers to a reversal of interests. A 9,9 supervisor is "high on both people and production" and is so because of his ability to get people to participate in constructive effort that meets their needs and those of the organization.

Similar hopes are expressed by Herzberg (1966) where, in *Work and the nature of man,* the importance of growth is stressed, much as Maslow and McGregor have done. Herzberg's motivation-hygiene theory requires that certain elements be present in a job before the job holder can find the growth that is not only possible but necessary in work. Motivators such as achievement, responsibility, advancement, interest, and possibility of development all exemplify growth principles while hygiene needs are those limited ones satisfied in salary and working conditions. Taking a view of humanity that emphasizes the growth aspects over the simple need-relating side of man is imperative, says Herzberg, if we are to realize a great society.

INDIVIDUAL DYNAMICS

Reiteration of the material in this chapter may be of greatest interest when put in normative rather than experiential terms. Hints on "how to" are often sought even though these may be of dubious value for any or all persons. No one can really tell others what to do to steady the course of their daily affairs and bring their social relationships into adjustment. What can be done, with some reservations, is to point out a few factors to which we might attend as individuals in the course of living with others. Comments such as those below serve merely as guidelines and not as absolute conditions for effective behavior. Because value judgments enter into any list of guides, the statements ought to be considered carefully.

Most researchers in the behavioral sciences will agree, however, with the importance of the concept of adjustment or equilibrium where a balanced state is approached. A "well-adjusted" individual is flexible in accepting inputs from the environment, knowing that there is no steady state in life as changes occur constantly. He understands that anxiety may arise in this and other situations but further understands the basis of motivation and does not complicate his life with defense mechanisms to meet this anxiety. Goals and objectives can be altered in these circumstances of their attainment postponed if this is required. Frustration can be met and emotions expressed in an acceptable way. Productive effort in work and social service is not hampered but, on the contrary, is emphasized. In all activities, finally, the mature and well-adjusted individual is realistic about himself through all the processes of self-understanding to which he has been exposed.

It should be emphasized again that these guidelines can be tentative only, with extensions or alterations occurring on an individual or situational basis. These are, above all, personal matters; only the individual can really handle the problem for himself.

Summary

The search for understanding of the whys of human behavior has occupied man for many centuries. Explanations have varied from the simplistic and naiive to the more sophisticated approaches of recent times. While other disciplines have contributed, the most continuous approach toward the study of the dynamics underlying behavior has been made by the personality theorists.

Personality is a broad concept which is difficult to define. There is agreement, however, that traits and mechanisms of adjustment to the environment can be fairly descriptive of personality.

Personality theorists have postulated a variety of bases for behavior. Sigmund Freud began the modern era by sketching an elaborate hypothetical structure of personality with physiologically oriented forces providing the drive. Freud's impact on the present world scene cannot be denied; even his direct disciples have departed, however, from the master's teachings. Concepts of power, anxiety, isolation, or social forces come to the fore in newer psychoanalytic approaches. A focus on traits or needs characterizes other conceptual approaches. More integrative than an organization around a specific construct are the global approaches that can be labeled "holistic."

A closer look at the specifics of behavior involves a discussion of motivation. The primary phase in motivation is in a need arising within an organism. This lack or deficit gives rise to behavior that is goal directed. Reaching the goal satisfies the need, and an uneasy equilibrium is attained. When needs are not satisfied (that is, frustrated), the reactions that take place are many and varied. It may be that an understanding of human behavior lies in the understanding of this basis for various reactions. The reaction patterns can represent attempts to solve problems; the attempts may be somewhat ordinary and routine, as in the defense mechanisms, or they may be unusual and dramatic attempts to cope with situations, as in the neuroses and psychoses.

Therapy for the aberrant personality patterns may be surgical, chemical, or electrical. More likely it will consist of a dialogue between therapist and patient. Whether long-term improvement takes place is a difficult question to answer.

The problems attendant to the emergence of a disordered personality pattern in individuals are met everywhere—in the home, in school, and in the factory. Alcoholism, absenteeism, and accidents represent a great social and economic loss to a society. Less dramatic but no less a loss is that found in individual cases of withdrawal and apathy, or the conflict within the individual, whether it is internalized in physical form or not. On a broader basis, the emergence of individual and group problems as social or industrial conflict can impress the observer but the violence may blind him to the real factors underlying the behavior.

Guides for a more positive approach toward individual mental hygiene generally or in the world of work have been promulgated for centuries. While these have many drawbacks, especially when applied without due consideration, those situations where the real needs of individuals can be met are the most productive for society and the individual in the long run.

Bibliography

Adler, A. (1927). *The practice and theory of individual psychology.* New York: Harcourt.

Allport, G. (1937). *Personality: a psychological interpretation.* New York: Holt.

Berelson, B. and Steiner, G. (1964). *Human behavior: an inventory of scientific findings.* New York: Harcourt, Brace and World.

Blake, R. and Mouton, J. (1961). *Group dynamics: key to decision making.* Houston, Texas: Gulf.

Brown, J. (1954). *The social psychology of industry.* Baltimore: Penguin.

Cattell, R. (1950). *Personality: a systematic, theoretical, and factual study.* New York: McGraw-Hill.

Combs, A. and Snygg, D. (1959). *Individual behavior: a perceptual approach to behavior* (rev. ed.). New York: Harper.

Dollard, J. and Miller, N. (1950). *Personality and psychotherapy.* New York: McGraw-Hill.

Drake, C. (1940). Accident-proneness: an hypothesis. *Character and Personality,* **8,** 335–341.

Dunbar, H. (1947). *Mind and body: psychosomatic medicine.* New York: Random House.

Erikson, E. (1951). *Childhood and society.* New York: Norton.

Eysenck, H. (1952). The effects of psychotherapy: an evaluation. *Journal of Consulting Psychology,* **16,** 319–325.

Festinger, L. (1957). *A theory of cognitive dissonance.* New York: Harper and Row.

Franco, S. (1954). Problem drinking and industry: policies and procedures. *Quarterly Journal of Studies of Alcohol,* **15,** 453–468.

Freud, S. (1953). *The standard edition of the complete psychological works.* Strachey, J. (ed.). London: Hogarth.

Fromm, E. (1941). *Escape from freedom.* New York: Holt, Rinehart and Winston.

Fromm, E. (1955). *The sane society.* New York: Rinehart.

Gibson, J. (1960). Science looks at your job: a ten-year study at General Motors. *Today's Health,* **38,** 14–15.

Hall, C. and Lindzey, G. (1957). *Theories of personality.* New York: Wiley.

Harlow, H. and McClearn, G. (1954). Object discrimination learned by monkeys on the basis of manipulation motives. *Journal of Comparative and Physiological Psychology,* **47,** 73–76.

Haynes, W. and Massie, J. (1961). *Management: analysis, concepts and cases.* Englewood Cliffs, N.J.: Prentice-Hall.

Herzberg, F. (1966). *Work and the nature of man*. Cleveland: World.

Horney, K. (1937). *Neurotic personality of our times*. New York: Norton.

Horney, K. (1945). *Our inner conflicts*. New York: Norton.

Jung, C. G. (1916). *Analytical psychology*. New York: Moffat, Yard.

Kretschmer, E. (1925). *Physique and character* (Spratt, W., transl.). New York: Harcourt.

Lewin, K. (1951). *Field theory in social science: selected theoretical papers*. Cartwright, D. (ed.). New York: Harper and Row.

McClelland, D. (1961). *The achieving society*. Princeton, N.J.: Van Nostrand.

McClelland, D., Atkinson, J., Clark, R., and Lowell, E. (1953). *The achievement motive*. New York: Appleton-Century-Crofts.

McGregor, D. (1960). *The human side of enterprise*. New York: McGraw-Hill.

Maslow, A. (1954). *Motivation and personality*. New York: Harper and Row.

Maslow, A. (1965). *Eupsychian management*. Homewood, Ill.: Dorsey.

Mettler, F., ed. (1949). *Selective partial ablation of the frontal cortex*. New York: Hoeber-Harper.

Moreno, J. (1946). *Psychodrama*. New York: Beacon House.

Morgan, C. and King, R. (1966). *Introduction to psychology* (3rd ed.). New York: McGraw-Hill.

Murphy, G. (1947). *Personality: a biosocial approach to origins and structure*. New York: Harper.

Murray, H. (1938). *Explorations in personality*. New York: Oxford University Press.

Olds, J. (1958). Self-stimulation of the brain. *Science,* **127,** 315–323.

Rogers, C. R. (1951). *Client-centered therapy: its current practice, implications, and theory*. Boston: Houghton-Mifflin.

Selye, H. (1950). *The physiology and pathology of exposure to stress*. Montreal: ACTA.

Sheldon, W. (1940). *The varieties of human physique: an introduction to constitutional psychology*. New York: Harper.

Sheldon, W. (1942). *The varieties of temperament: a psychology of constitutional differences*. New York: Harper.

Stagner, R. (1961). *Psychology of personality* (2nd ed.). New York: McGraw-Hill.

Stagner, R. and Rosen, H. (1965). *Psychology of union-management relations.* Belmont, California: Wadsworth.

Sullivan, H. (1953). *The interpersonal theory of psychiatry.* New York: Norton.

Zawadzki, B. and Lazarsfeld, P. (1936). The psychological consequences of unemployment. *Journal of Social Psychology,* **6,** 224–251.

9

Language and Communication

The importance of language and communication cannot be overemphasized in any discussion of human behavior. No other factors stress the social and the cognitive aspects of man as much as these two variables. Communication between people is not only a hallmark of social beings, it is a virtual necessity in assuring the continuing functioning of a complex group, organization, or society.

Communication is an attribute man shares with infrahumans. Various organisms can transmit some information to others—cries of pain, rage, or danger can be sent and received by many species at many phylogenetic levels. To paraphrase the popular song, even birds and bees do it (von Frisch, 1955). All this is minimal, however, compared to the tremendous variety of ideas and concepts that can be transmitted and received by the human organism by virtue of the ability to use symbols, that is, to use language. This ability is limited to man—it is species specific—and it might be argued strongly that it is this above all that separates man from all other forms of animate life.

When communication is mentioned, the first, and often only, example that comes to mind is the verbal form of communication—the written and spoken set of signs which we call our language. Communication can be non-verbal as well, however. Much information may be transmitted through inputs from the environment which are not in verbal form. Take, for example, the instance of two twelve-year-olds, one, a model young man and the other, a delinquent in the eyes of the law. As they walk along the street, they see a man in a dark blue suit approaching them, swinging a small cylinder of wood on a leather thong. His suit has brass buttons and there is a metal plaque on his chest. His cap has a thick visor. Communication is undoubtedly taking place, although the message is probably not the same for both youths.

One can find many similar examples of nonverbal communication in other settings. In industry, for instance, color codes convey as much information as do red and green lights at a street intersection. A green cross at a first aid station informs us of a safety point, while diagonal yellow and black stripes signify a danger spot. Shape coding occurs in highway signs and in industrial work layouts to communicate information more effectively to the recipient.

Even more information can come sometimes from further nonverbal aspects such as attitudes and emotions. Sometimes behavior may be influenced more by these subtle aspects than by any spoken or written version of them.

Verbal communication also includes more than spoken or written words. Other kinds of written signs are verbal; mathematics is a language system as English is—the signs vary but both relate to some pattern of ideas. We can differentiate, however, on the basis of English being a *linguistic* set of signs while mathematics is *nonlinguistic*. Often, however, we reserve the term language to a natural system (English and French, for example) and call mathematics a language or sign system.

In this discussion the term "sign" has been used rather than "symbol" as the label for the communications element that stands for something in reality. This is because most researchers in communications prefer to reserve the use of symbol for some broader cultural aspect such as the flag, the cross, Wall Street, and other representations or associations of a society.

The Process of Communication

Communication may be described schematically in a form similar to that sketched earlier for other behavioral processes. The simple model of the communication process (Figure 9-1) indicates the important steps in the systematic transmission. It begins with the cognitive material in the source in some form before it is coded for transmission through a channel. What we say to others is in a linguistic "code," our learned language. After we code the cognitive materials, we transmit them by vibrating our vocal cords or by engaging in some physical activity such as writing. Gesture language is another type of code, one the American Indians extended to a high level of sophistication.

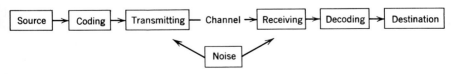

Figure 9-1. The communication process.

The message passes through a channel (air, paper, or advanced variants of the two such as electronic transmission) to a receiver. In speech transmission the process of hearing comes into play and the hearer must decode the variations in pressure which activate his auditory mechanisms. The statement «коммерческий директор» may not be one the reader can decode, however, and no real communication can take place until the linguistic code is learned. If it is a familiar one it can be decoded, and it eventually reaches the destination.

If one wishes to oversimplify the entire process of communication, it could be said that what is meant by this process is that cognitive materials move from the first step to the last. Real communication requires that the state of material in the final stage be like that put in at the beginning. Perfect correspondence is unattainable in real life, of course, but it may help to be aware of the need for efforts toward transmitting concepts from speaker to hearer which are as unchanged as possible.

Some difficulty in transmission of information comes from the presence of *noise* in the system. The term noise means more than the auditory dissonance people ordinarily think of as being noise, but it does include that condition. Noise in information technology means anything that interferes in the transmission process. While we may identify noise most readily in the channel or message phase, it can be met in any of the steps of the communication process.

Another characteristic of the process is one that can counter noise. *Redundancy* is the transmission of more information than is necessary to communicate. This additional amount may be needed to insure that the message overcomes noise and is received. It has been estimated, for instance, that the English language is over 75 percent redundant. Under appropriate circumstances, we could say as much with significantly less effort.

A final aspect of communication that plays a vital role in transmission of information is *feedback*. Here, as in other models of behavior, feedback is the information that is sent back from the outputs to serve as further inputs; in doing so, it alters or corrects the activity. Feedback enables the speaker to find out if he is "getting the message across" to his audience. Lincoln is reputed to have believed his Gettysburg address was a failure because of the silence of his audience. A company president may pick up the nodding of heads by his workers as signifying their agreement with the corporation's message. In both cases there may have been faulty feedback.

The Study of Communication

This complex process has many facets and, therefore, many are the ways in which studies may be made. Since researchers can concentrate on only a small fragment at a time, it is little wonder that a successful synthesis is not to be had.

The earliest and still most active workers in communication have concentrated on various aspects of language. These *linguists* may have different areas of interest in language related to the classification of data they have made. Some of these separable interests areas can be seen below in the discussion of language.

Other more recent approaches have attempted to sketch broad fundamental areas or to pursue the studies in depth along specifically defined lines. One fundamental area of study has given rise to the concept of *semiotics*, the general study of signs that carry information. Even more recent has been the interest in the mathematical or statistical basis of information transmission, an approach that has been labeled simply as *communication theory*.

SEMIOTICS

The study of signs or the science of elements that carry information is known as *semiotics*. This study is a broad one and is basic to all of human communication. The signals that travel from one person to another are not the basic raw material of the experience of either; these signals are the transformation of the form of the experience into a pattern or grouping of physical changes. It is important to note at this point that the changes in sound waves which we know as language represent only a part of the total store of signs. Gestures, shop signs (the three golden balls above the door), graphs and charts, along with innumerable other material arrangements also constitute signs. As was noted previously, communication and language may be nonverbal as well as verbal.

Semiotics may be broken down into three different areas: *semantics, syntactics,* and *pragmatics.* The relationship of signs to their referrents is semantics. Syntactics is concerned with the relationships of signs with each other. The matters touching on the use of signs is the concern of pragmatics. The factors of cost, speed of communication, and use of it in a behavioral setting falls in the last area. These three aspects of communication may also be described as being symbolic, systematic, and need related (Rubenstein and Haberstroh, 1960, p. 229). This means that acts of communication refer to something external and "real," relate to each other in an orderly fashion, and are important in satisfaction. It may be seen that the three points are what we know as semantics, syntactics, and pragmatics, in that order. Since we are most concerned with the more familiar set of signs known as language, a discussion of these three aspects of semiotics will be more rewarding under the heading of language.

COMMUNICATION THEORY

The origins of this approach stem from, first, telegraphy, and then from later methods of communication. Engineers have been concerned with technical problems of transmission; the capacity of the system to carry correct signals gets attention here rather than other purposes. How much information rather than what kind is the focus of inquiry.

The information content of signals is the outcome of statistical studies that may be represented in mathematical terms. Information is defined by communication theorists as a successive selection of signs from a list (Cherry 1957). Information has also often been looked at as a "modulation" in the sense that any changes that occur in the situation provide data to the acceptor of it. A radio broadcast wave is modulated by a voice; a field of snow is modulated by a hiker. Information is not synonymous with knowledge, which is the understanding of the information by the human person.

Communication theorists, in their measure of information capacity of a system, most often employ a standard measure of information called the *bit.* This is shorthand for *binary digit,* a concept already met in the earlier discussion on electronic data processing in Chapter 3. You may remember that where two alternatives are available, the bit is the amount of information possible in the single selection between those two alternatives. Alternatives like on-off, push-pull, red-green are one bit and provide two states of information.

Language

The gift of speech sets man apart from other animals and enables him to do things all out of proportion to his physical presence in the world. The power of words has been noted in many ways throughout history ("the pen is mightier than the sword"). The importance of language for the development of a social and cognitive being cannot be overstated. It is clear how valuable language is for communication with others; less clear is the vital role it plays in shaping the individual's view of the world and in categorizing or organizing a world of ideas with which he can function in his integration into a community. Language serves not only social purposes but individual cognitive ones as well.

Language is a system of arbitrary and learned signs by which human beings can communicate present conditions or remote events. The signs in a language do not necessarily bear a resemblance to the situations or events that are the subject of the communication. An animal in pain or danger may communicate to other animals through the use of cries appropriate to and taken from that situation. This is communication but not language because there is no possible substitution of other arbitrary sounds to stand for the event and transmit information about it. The transmission of information about abstractions or events not immediately present to the senses is a more complex matter that cannot be handled by a communication system tied into only the immediate circumstances.

Language has provided the behavioral scientist with problems when certain specific aspects of language have been selected for study. The difficulty of determining the content of concepts in an empirical way, for instance, has proven challenging for the researcher with a scientific bent. The propriety or even the necessity of scientific endeavor in this area has been stated for a small but increasing group of psychologists interested in the study of language. Though language behavior touches on central theoretical issues in behavioral science as well as important applications in society, in the past the area has demanded more attention while receiving less than most topics in experimental psychology (Osgood, 1953, p. 727).

LINGUISTICS

The most frequent type of study in the area of communication must still be that encompassed by the term *linguistics*. It is the study of language or, more specifically, the study of the languages and dialects that are or have been in use. The area of study is delimited by concern only with certain aspects of communication, namely, that occurring by means of speech sounds, and not by other means, in a pattern determined by the culture. Since linguistics studies the language system as a vehicle rather than focusing upon content, the emphasis is on structure more than on other aspects. How the sign system is shaped is the crucial concern of the researchers in this area.

Some of the areas of study in linguistics can be listed here very briefly. *Phonetics* is the study of vocal sound used in language systems, and the descriptions and classifications of sounds remain the chief interest of the area. *Phonemics* is the classification of sounds into those units which serve as the distinguishable auditory elements of the language. These units, representing perceptible distinctions, are called *phonemes*. *Morphology* refers to the study of form of language or the way words are constructed. Words may be broken down into elements called *morphemes*, which are the smallest units of structure that have meaning. The arrangement of phonemes into morphemes is the province of *morphology*. The arrangement of the morphemes in an order is *syntactics*.

PSYCHOLINGUISTICS

This term, combining as it does the two disciplines of psychology and linguistics, should give a hint that the integration of the two areas is what is encompassed. This is so, yet this new division of the behavioral sciences is still developing and, in its infancy, its boundaries are not as clear as those of its parents, though the overlap with them is. It can be seen that the discussion of linguistics above leaves quite a bit of language behavior untouched. Problems of learning, perception, meaning, and affect, to name a few, are areas of importance in language behavior and ones of interest to a psychologist. Some of these factors will be considered in the next section; still others can occur in various contexts throughout this book.

The Logic of Language

An analysis of language based on a semiotic viewpoint causes one to look at the sign system with the intent to study the syntactics, semantics, and pragmatics of language. Linguistics may be concerned with some aspects of the three, particularly syntactics. Most linguists, however, have limited themselves to the studies described above.

SYNTACTICS

The relation of signs to signs is known as syntactics or syntax. This study of the arrangement of signs that represent concepts is what is often known familiarly as grammar. It is more often known in a linguistic framework as the study of language structure. The study of structure may take place on the sign (word) level or on the more complex level of sign sequence or word order. Prefixes and suffixes are variations of the signs themselves which ultimately relate to the other signs and sketch the interrelationships between them. The importance of sign sequence can be seen easily in almost all useful language produced. "Man bites dog" is news because it is certainly different from "dog bites man." The signs are the same but the syntactical relationships between them are not. The set of signs must have what Kuhn (1963) calls "jointness," that is, a complete system that is operating or at least one that can operate to convey a feeling that something will happen.

SEMANTICS

The aspect of language that relates the sign to reality is one labeled semantics. This is the approach that studies meaning of words or the relationship of the sign to the concept for which it stands. The sign is really a name or label for the concept. Some concepts are shared, at least roughly, by many people (apple or chair, for instance), while a more specific or complex concept may be the exclusive possession of a single person.

The Bases of Meaning

In a primitive stage of development, an individual may perceive the sign, the label, or the word as a fixed attribute of the object to which the word refers. Children, reports Vigotsky (1939), insisted a cow was called a "cow" because it had horns. When asked whether it could be called "ink," they replied that ink was for writing and the cow gives milk. It will be seen later that some of this fixity may not be overcome even in adulthood when we focus on a name and believe that it and the object are inseparable. The clinging to outmoded and, therefore, misleading designations may be the source of difficulty. The words "machinist" or "accountant," for instance, are labels that could be replaced with other signs.

Semanticists often focus on two aspects of meaning. *Extensional* meaning is the kind of meaning that can be communicated simply by pointing to the object under discussion. The thing, "table," "chair," or "pencil," is present to our senses and may be perceived readily when the word is spoken. *Intensional* meaning is built up by using other words to define something. It is meaning derived from dictionary definitions or other verbal discussion.

Meaning may be advanced, further, by the fact that words usually appear with other words in a specific situation. The context can be very useful in promoting better communication. Words are expected to be in a proper order or sequence. Where particular words appear, as well as the kinds of words present, helps in providing a meaningful exchange of ideas.

Measurement of Meaning

The question of meaning remains one of the most difficult problems in the study of language. The difficulties stemming from communication problems can be reduced when differences in meaning disappear.

Most of the difficulty with the relating of the sign to reality comes in the individual differences encountered. A label will have different *connotative meaning* for different individuals, that is, a meaning affected by the various dynamic factors associated with personality of the individual. This is in contrast to the *denotative meaning* of a word or concept which represents a social consensus on the meaning of a word or an "accepted" definition of it.

Meaning and its measurement have fascinated researchers for a long time, primarily because of its importance in human affairs and the concomitant frustrations encountered in its measurement. Some idea of the meaning of a concept may be gained from simple methods such as analysis of responses of individuals (as in definition of words) or through word association tests ("reply with the first word that comes to mind"). Discriminating the word that does not belong in a group of words can also be a means of establishing meaning. None of these techniques has really accomplished the job and the search for other methods must continue. A substantial breakthrough in the measurement of meaning has already occurred, however, with the fairly recent work of Osgood on the Semantic Differential (Osgood et al, 1957). This method uses a set of dipolar scales with seven steps between the poles. An extensive series of polar terms may comprise the inventory. Subjects are then asked to indicate where on the seven-point scale a particular concept fits. The term business, for instance, might be placed on scale items such as the following:

BUSINESS

hard _____ : _____ : **X** : _____ : _____ : _____ : _____ : soft
fast _____ : **X** : _____ : _____ : _____ : _____ : _____ : slow

The items may continue thus to number in excess of fifty. The results not only give some indication of the connotative meaning of the term "business" for individuals but are useful also in understanding differences in meaning that may arise on a group basis. There may be, on the average, a placement of the term business by MBA students that differs from a rating by students of philosophy. Similar comparisons between cultures could promote understanding of the problems of meaning encountered on an international level as well.

PRAGMATICS

This is the area that is concerned with the relationships between signs and their users. The effects are in both directions; signs influence users, and the users are individuals whose personality dynamics affect the signs they use.

Motivation may be as important a determiner of communication as it is a factor in all other behavioral areas. Affect and emotion provide a further imprint on the process of communication as value-laden words do have an impact on our behavior in general. The emotionally charged statements may be of greater interest to a researcher on that basis rather than on the basis of their actual semantic significance. The importance of pragmatics may be most visible in the mass media and their effects. This will be discussed in a later chapter (Chapter 14) under various labels—propaganda, loaded words, and glittering generalities. One must not, however, ignore the individual dynamics, in the aggregate or on a person-to-person basis. Reactions to name calling are good illustrations of the impact of pragmatics on each of us. The inner responses to HOME, MOTHER, and COUNTRY are such as to influence our further behavior considerably, as do those reactions to COMPANY and UNION.

Development of Language

As in other aspects of human development, certain patterns in the development of language can be seen in the growing individual. While language covers more than just speech, this aspect is the one used exlusively at first, and it may continue to be more important in action than related reading and writing.

At birth, infants make a variety of sounds apparently related to the different states of the organism. In this, all babies are generally alike; there are no racial differences in the sounds made (Irwin, 1948). At two months, the infant can make all the sounds of the human voice. At this time, control over volume is achieved, then over pitch a month later and, by the fifth month, some control over sequence of sounds is attained (Osgood, 1953). Somewhere near the ninth month, the child can imitate sounds made by others, but the first word appears near the first birthday. Where the child may be able to say two words at year one, this increases slowly to between three and five words at one and half years, when combination of words takes place, until phrases and simple sentences begin to appear at age two (McCarthy, 1946). From this point on, speech develops at an accelerated rate though an exact numerical appraisal may be difficult to obtain. One classic investigation (M. E. Smith, 1926) found an increase from 272 words mastered at age two up to 2562 at age six. Other figures may result from using other criteria. M. K. Smith (1941), for instance, found "recognition" vocabularies of 23,000 words at age six with an increase to 80,000 at age seventeen.

In the development of language, girls are slightly superior to boys with respect to age of acquisition and fluency, but because of the wide overlap between groups, this interesting finding has very little practical significance. More important are the socioeconomic factors; those individuals with less opportunity to learn and practice verbal skills are less likely to do well, other things being equal. Early investigators of bilingualism, for instance, noted a handicap in English on the part of students. When socioeconomic factors are controlled, however, no such detrimental effects are noted (Kolasa, 1954).

Intelligence does play a role, however. The close correlation between intelligence and language has been the core of the standardized measures of mental ability from the Stanford-Binet to the newest tests for selection to graduate and professional programs. More recently, the links between verbal skill and test performance has been the object of some criticism arising on the broader question of whether existing tests mirror too much the narrow cultural biases of a "dominant middle class society." This may well be so, but no good culture-free measure yet exists to allow prediction of behavior in this area.

Meaning develops for the individual according to the basic principles of learning. Trial-and-error approaches may produce one vocalization that is rewarded, or a similar reinforcement may come for the completion of phrase learned by rote. Perhaps most important is the learning achieved by conditioning as F. H. Allport (1924) illustrated in his classic discussion of this type of learning. A child sees a doll held up by its mother and hears the sound "doll." It imitates the sound under these circumstances and is reinforced. Soon, the sight of the doll by itself will elicit the verbal response from the child.

Language, Culture, and Thought

Impressive evidence is easily forthcoming with repect to the close ties of language and other aspects of culture. The United States has produced, for instance, a wealth of technical terms that have eventually found their way, in one form or another, around the world. Anthropologists have long pointed out that significant conditions in a society are reflected by the language. Eskimos are said to have dozens of words relating to snow and ice as a clear indication of the importance to the individuals of those physical states (Boas, 1938).

The close interconnection between language and thought has led some researchers to a closer study of the influence of one upon the other. While the notion of thought influencing language and action is one that is accepted easily, a more intriguing reverse relationship can be postulated, namely, that language is a shaper or mediator of our thought (Whorf, 1956). This concept considers that our view of the world is determined by the constraints of the language we have learned in addition to other influences of the cultural milieu. When a language has limited possibilities for verbal categorization of time, space, color, or other perceptions, it may well be that this influences the thinking about the world. Most western languages, in contrast, have categories that promote time differentiations. The Kwakiutl Indians may be more interested in visibility than in time, since the language is structured to report "the man is coming and is visible" rather than the emphasis on the present tense in "the man is coming." The Hopi Indians use a single word for all flying objects except birds (Whorf, 1956). The fact that many primitive peoples have four or five terms for colors (the Navaho language has white, red, blue, green, and two shades of black) may lend further support for this "linguistic relativity" hypothesis.

Not enough evidence exists to accept the "world-view" concept. It may be simply that behavior important to a group is identified and named. There is no reason to believe, for instance, that the Navaho cannot perceive colors as we do even though their language has fewer color terms. In this connection Brown (1958) found that individuals can learn new discriminations when taught the words in a new language.

Language in Action

Numerous attempts have been made to encourage clearer thinking, speaking, and writing. These various efforts will, no doubt, continue as long as man remains active on this planet or elsewhere and is called on to interact with others in meaningful activity. Only a limited number of these approaches need be sketched here by way of illustration.

GENERAL SEMANTICS

The general semantics movement represents almost a crusade for clear thinking on the part of a group of linguistic logicians influenced by the writings of the late Count Alfred Korzybski and others. In *Science and sanity* (1958) the ideas Korzybski first published in 1913 give some evidence of the thinking of the general semanticists. Virtually all of our problems, say these proponents of the system, arise from the faulty basis in the Aristotelian system of logic, internalized by the individual and mirrored by his language.

Three "laws" of logic in Aristotle's system may be described.

1. The law of identity (A is A by simply stating it as being so).
2. The law of the excluded middle (everything is either A or not-A).
3. The law of noncontradiction (nothing is both A and not-A).

These bases of logic can lead to a two-valued orientation (expressed in language as "there's only one way to do this job") rather than a multivalued approach to life situations ("let's look into this further to see what the alternatives are").

More specific references to language behavior by the general semanticists focus on the relationship between the extensional ("real") and the verbal world. The word must relate to the real world as a map does to a territory. The map is not the territory nor is the word the extensional world. Troubles develop when we act as if the two were one.

More recently, Wendell Johnson (1946) has used the concepts of general semantics to explain the bases of problems in virtually every area of human behavior. Johnson refers to these problems as quandaries and likens them to "verbal cocoons in which individuals encase themselves." While he considers many pathological conditions as being related to struggles with meaning and the distortions that arise, Johnson is better known for his activities in speech pathology. It is of interest to note, for instance, that stuttering is unknown among American Indians. "The Indians had no word for stuttering" says Johnson (*ibid.*, p. 443). There is a clear recognition that Indian parents are not concerned about the verbal performance of their children in the same way that parents in our general American culture are. The lack of stress when language is being learned allows the Indian child to adopt speech habits quite effortlessly. In the general population, the growing person may respond to real or inferred pressure with a language disability, usually stuttering.

Hayakawa (1964) sets out rules for "order within and without." These guides serve to aid extensional orientation rather than the intensional thinking that leads to rigid and routine courses of action based on faulty ways of reacting to use of language. The rules note that, as a map is not the territory, so words are not things. Meanings are not in words but in use, and the meanings we derive are determined by the multitudinous contexts in which words appear. Index numbers and dates are suggested as indicators that no word has the same meaning twice ($Jones_{1967}$ is not $Jones_{1968}$). The word "is" may mislead ("business is business" is a directive, not a statement of fact). These rules attempt to remind a speaker of the need for clearer thinking and speaking through extensional orientation. This is the recognition that the word is not the event but is an abstraction that does not tell all about the event. It may even mislead us as to the salient characteristics of the situation.

CLEAR COMMUNICATION

The use of clear language so that communication can take place has been urged by many researchers in the area of language. In *The art of plain talk,* Flesch (1946) analyzed many of the problems and developed an index for ease of comprehension based on number of syllables per word, words per sentence, and personal words in sentences. The shorter the words and sentences and the more personal words in them, the easier the reading and the greater the comprehension. Flesch offers a quick formula as well as a more involved one for gauging difficulty:

$$I_d = \left(\frac{A - P}{2}\right) + W$$

A is number of affixes (prefixes) while *P* is number of personal words (we, they, etc.) per 100 words. *W* is the average number of words per sentence. A score of 13 or below means the material is very easy; standard material has an index of 29 to 36, while very difficult reading reaches a score of 52 or above.

While the measure may not always be a good one, the concept is valid and worthy of note in practical situations. Many of the guidelines for clear communication have been noted by mass communicators—newspapers, radio, or television—and put to use in "getting the message across." The problem of communication in industry is often vital and may be an area where the rules for clear communication may be of help. Most of the information in industry is in the form of oral instructions from supervisor to subordinate. The supervisor should remember to speak in a simple, straightforward style and present a limited amount of information at one time. In addition, he should be certain that all workers know promptly what they need to know so that they do not have to guess.

BASIC ENGLISH

Basic English, with a vocabulary of 850 words, was first proposed by C. K. Ogden (1934) to enable non-English speakers to learn enough English quickly to be able communicate. Ogden demonstrated that this small number of words was enough to communicate concepts and directions without any hardship. Technical terms can be added. Basic business English can serve in a wide variety of situations with the addition of 50 words to the basic list. Reading the Bible is possible with the original set of 850 words, but all passages can be handled with the addition of only 150 words. Here is an example from Genesis in a familiar version and in Basic English.

King James Version	*Basic English*
In the beginning God created the heaven and the earth. And the earth was without form, and void; and darkness was upon the face of the deep. And the Spirit of God moved upon the face of the waters.	First God made the heaven and the earth.
	And the earth was without form, and there was nothing in it; and the dark was upon the face of the deep. And the Spirit of God was moving over the face of the waters.
And God said, "Let there be light": and there was light.	And God said, "Let there be light," and there was light.

A passage in Basic English may end up being longer than the original, but it does stay within the limited number of words. It may also be at a more difficult reading level, but all the words are likely to be known to all readers.

Information Handling Systems

One of the most dramatic happenings of the present era is the "information explosion," the manyfold expansion of knowledge. Under these conditions, the use of high-speed information processing technology is not only developing into an important facet of communication, it is becoming a virtual necessity in information handling in today's world.

An information handling system will encompass activities from abstracting, indexing, and filing to retrieval operations at the output end of the system. Organizing and classifying are important functions along with the translation of material, usually from a natural language to a type of code or shorthand. Later access to the information depends on the successful execution of these earlier steps.

Translation from one natural language to another, as from Russian to English, is another type of translation for which an information system may be geared. While it does have some basic similarities with the translation to a code or index system, the translation of a natural language poses some additional problems, mainly those associated with the semantic changes arising from the context (Allen and Salkoff, 1964). Identical words have a variety of meanings depending on the words around them; a one-for-one translation produces some ambigous results.

In the following short descriptions of some of the operations encountered in information handling, the reader is urged to identify things he has been doing all along, if only in less precise fashion.

ORGANIZATION OF INFORMATION

Those who continually have problems finding something they need among their possessions may have been reminded by others of the old adage, "a place for everything and everything in its place." The need for filing of information and access to it has been a crucial aspect in the functioning of all kinds of organizations, including business ones. Where routine filing systems required only a knowledge of the alphabet, modern information handling systems require an organization based on more sophisticated methods.

Some kind of *index* must be established to fit the information processing system. The index is a categorization that makes the original material easier to find, but since the system was undoubtedly introduced to handle the increased flow of information, one may not be able to handle all the material in its original form. Not only must there be an indexing of it, but some *coding,* an indexing shorthand, must take place as well. How verbal information can be represented in a short and logical form is one of the critical problems in any system. One system that has been widely used is KWIC, or *key word in context.* Figure 9-2 is a computer printout based on the KWIC System; there, the key word is machine, and all references to the word in the original text are given. Reference systems have shown continuing growth in numbers. Some of the systems are general programs while others are tailored for particular areas, disciplines, or problems (Janda, 1967).

INFORMATION STORAGE

Where once file cabinets filled with paper copies of material were adequate for all purposes, now some other system must, of necessity, be introduced. Photo images may be miniaturized on rolls of *microfilm* or on card mountings called *microfiche.* If transformation is called for, coding must be done; after coding, the material may be transferred to a variety of media. These may be amenable to hand processing, or electronic data processing handling may be required. Punched cards, for instance, may be separated by manual systems as well as by electronic equipment; larger operations will require the capacity that only EDP equipment will provide. Paper tape or magnetic media (tape, discs, and cards) will probably see more use in the future than will the familiar punched cards.

INFORMATION RETRIEVAL

As indicated, success of the search for the required information depends heavily on the adequacy of the classification and organization of the original

294

```
                    ──→ 5258 PUNCHED CARD AND MACHINE *
                                     2195 MACHINE  –  PUNCHED CARDS /
OORDINATED DOCUMENTATION USING HAND AND MACHINE  –  2195 POSSIBILITIES OF C
               4038 METHOD – SUCH AS MACHINE – SORTING TO COMPUTERS /
                                     5134 MACHINE  APPLICATION *
                                     5135 MACHINE  COMPARIOSN *
                         5340 SOME MACHINE DESIGN PROSPECTS /
                                     5280 MACHINE DISCLOSURES *
NG THE HARVARD –    5137 LINGUISTIC AND MACHINE METHODS FOR COMPILING AND UPDATI
               5405 RAPID METHOD FOR MACHINE RETRIEVAL /
        5161 THE FEASIBILITY OF MACHINE SEARCHING OF ENGLISH TEXTS
EARCH FILES /   5350 APPENDIX D USE OF MACHINES AS AIDS IN THE PREPARATION OF S
                                     5335 MACHINES WITH LEARNING ABILITY /
```

Figure 9-2.   Representative sample of a Key-Word-in-Context (KWIC) index (Bourne, 1963).

material. A printout of references to a complete text will describe the text material adequately if the shorthand references have been arranged properly. Some retrieval systems can print out complete text material. In this case the search will be framed more extensively through the use of basic words as well as all variants and qualifying related words (Figure 9-3). Use of the system is particularly appropriate when large and exhaustive searches are called for. In the legal area, the lawyer with a problem or a state legislative committee developing statutes want to be aware of all aspects that could play a role in the determination of the problem. In business, too, with so many decisions hinging on the requirements of statute or court decisions, the value of a complete search of pertinent literature references is obvious. Retrieval of internal or external information can be of vital concern to decision making in all organizations.

Communication in Large Entities

Since communication requires more than one person, any consideration of the concept requires a discussion of many other variables involved in interpersonal relationships. These other factors have either been explicitly stated above or have been implied all along. It seems clear, then, that even more attention must be paid these factors and others when the number of people involved increases. The greater complexity of the research and applied problems of communications in larger social entities is particularly apparent when study proceeds from small groups to organizations and even larger aggregates.

Greater interest in these other aspects may be seen in discussions of communication within organizations. Considering communication in an administrative setting as a process of transmitting premises for decision making focuses on cognitive factors in the eventual making of a decision in the organization (Simon, 1957). On the other hand, the orientation toward the study of individual personality and communication in organizations attends to the problems of interaction and the possible resulting difficulties on all sides (Argyris, 1957). A study of communication in organizations also involves a consideration of factors such as size and structure of the grouping. Research in communication then becomes an inquiry into the transmission of information through many channels linking individuals situated in various levels of some type of hierarchical arrangement. Examination of the effects of different kinds of networks in communication (Leavitt, 1951) has shown that different patterns of communication were found to differ in effectiveness of performance and satisfaction of participants.

This short excursion into the area of communication in organizations

Search Statement

```
*   AUTOMATED LAW SEARCHING
*   SEARCH NO. - 6010 ON PA. STATUTES
*   REQUESTED BY - JOHN F. HORTY
*   SEARCH ANALYST - C.L. MATTERN
*   DATE - JUNE 1, 1967
*   QUESTION - RIGHTS OF PARENTS OF ABANDONED CHILDREN UP
                FOR ADOPTION
*

06/01/67  PA. STATUTES

GROUP 1      OR                      AGE
             OR                      YEARS
             WORD        65-5        OVER
             WORD        65-5        UNDER
             WORD        65-5        MORE
             WORD        65-5        LESS
             OR                      CHILD
             OR                      MINOR
             DOCUMENT                ABANDON
             DOCUMENT                ABANDONED
             DOCUMENT                ABANDONING
             DOCUMENT                ABANDONMENT
             DOCUMENT                ABANDONS
*
GROUP 2      OR                      PARENT
             OR                      PARENTS
             DOCUMENT                ADOPT
             DOCUMENT                ADOPTION
             DOCUMENT                ADOPTING       GROUP 1

                                                    GROUP 2

*   OUTPUT      PRINT%G0
*   END

*   THE NUMBER OF ASTERISKS FOLLOWING ANY DOCUMENT NUMBER
*   INDICATES THE NUMBER OF ADDITIONAL TIMES THE DOCUMENT
*   WAS RETRIEVED BY THIS SEARCH.

*   WORDS IN RIGHT MARGIN ARE WORDS THAT FORM THE SEARCH.
*   THEY NEED NOT HAVE CAUSED THE DOCUMENT TO BE RETRIEVED.

*   IF REQUESTED, PRINTING IS IN BLOCKS IN ORDER OF REQUEST.
```

Figure 9-3. Framing of a search for the retrieval of legal information and print out of the results. (below). (Horty et al., 1968).

BY THE FINDING OF ABANDONMENT IN COURT, THERE SHALL BE EMBODIED IN
THE PETITION A STATEMENT SETTING FORTH /1/ THE COURT, TERM AND
NUMBER OF SUCH PROCEEDINGS, /2/ THAT SUCH PERSON PROPOSED FOR
ADOPTION IS IN THE CUSTODY OF AN APPROVED AGENCY OR INSTITUTION
WHOSE CONSENT IS ATTACHED TO THE ADOPTION IS ATTACHED TO THE PETITION. IN
ADDITION SUCH PETITION SHALL EMBODY OR HAVE ATTACHED THERETO THE
CONSENTS IN WRITING OF THE PERSON OR PERSONS WHOSE CONSENT TO THE
PROPOSED ADOPTION IS NECESSARY AS HEREINAFTER PROVIDED. A BIRTH
CERTIFICATE OR CERTIFICATION OF REGISTRATION OF BIRTH OF THE PERSON
PROPOSED TO BE ADOPTED SHALL BE ATTACHED TO THE PETITION FOR
ADOPTION. IF NO BIRTH CERTIFICATE OR CERTIFICATION OF REGISTRATION
OF BIRTH CAN BE OBTAINED IT SHALL BE SO STATED IN THE PETITION,
WITH A REQUEST THAT THE COURT, ON THE BASIS OF THE EVIDENCE, SHALL
ESTABLISH A DATE AND PLACE OF BIRTH IN THE ADOPTION HEARING.
1925, APRIL 4, P.L. 127, SEC. 1., AS
AMENDED 1941, JUNE 5, P.L. 93, NO. 46, SEC. 1., 1941, JULY 2, P.L.
229, SEC. 1., 1947, JUNE 30, P.L. 1180, SEC. 1., 1953, AUG. 26, P.L.
1411, SEC. 1., 1959, DEC. 21, P.L. --, NO. 711, SEC. 1.
ADOPTION ACT

PA. STAT. ANN. TIT. 1 , SEC. 1.2
SEC. 1.2 ABANDONMENT
    WHEN ANY PERSON UNDER THE AGE OF EIGHTEEN YEARS HAS BEEN IN THE
CARE OF AN APPROVED INSTITUTION OR AGENCY FOR A MINIMUM PERIOD OF
THIRTY /30/ DAYS AND IT APPEARS THAT SUCH PERSON HAS BEEN
ABANDONED FOR A PERIOD OF AT LEAST SIX MONTHS, SUCH APPROVED AGENCY
OR INSTITUTION MAY PETITION THE COURT, IN THE COUNTY IN WHICH IS
LOCATED THAT OFFICE OF THE APPROVED AGENCY OR INSTITUTION HAVING THE
CUSTODY OF SUCH PERSON, FOR A FINDING OF ABANDONMENT AND ASKING FOR
CUSTODY OF SUCH PERSON.
    THE COURT WILL THEREUPON FIX A TIME FOR HEARING, WHICH SHALL BE
NOT LESS THAN TEN DAYS AFTER SUCH PRESENTATION. AT LEAST FIVE DAYS-
WRITTEN NOTICE SHALL BE GIVEN, BY REGISTERED MAIL, TO THE ALLEGED
ABANDONING PARENT OR PARENTS, AT HIS OR THEIR LAST KNOWN ADDRESS.
THE HEARING SHALL BE PRIVATE OR IN OPEN COURT, AS THE COURT SHALL
DETERMINE. AT SUCH HEARING THE COURT, BY EXAMINATION UNDER OATH OF
THE PARTIES INTERESTED IN THE PETITION, SHALL ASCERTAIN THE TRUTH OF
THE FACTS SET FORTH IN THE PETITION AND ITS EXECUTION, AND IF
SATISFIED AS TO THE TRUTH THEREOF AND THAT THE PETITION SHOULD BE
GRANTED, IT SHALL ISSUE ITS DECREE SO FINDING AND DIRECTING A
FINDING OF ABANDONMENT, /1/ DECREEING THAT CUSTODY BE GIVEN TO THE
APPROVED AGENCY OR INSTITUTION CARING FOR SAID PERSON, AND /2/
AUTHORIZING THE APPROVED AGENCY OR INSTITUTION TO GIVE CONSENT TO
THE ADOPTION OF SAID PERSON WITHOUT FURTHER CONSENT OF OR
NOTIFICATION TO THE NATURAL PARENT OR PARENTS.
    SUCH DECREE, WITH ALL THE TESTIMONY AND ALL OTHER PAPERS
PERTAINING TO THE CASE, SHALL BE RECORDED IN SUCH MANNER AS THE
COURT SHALL PRESCRIBE AND SHALL BE KEPT IN THE FILES OF THE COURT
AS A PERMANENT RECORD THEREOF, AND SHALL BE WITHHELD FROM INSPECTION
EXCEPT UPON AN ORDER OF THE COURT UPON CAUSE SHOWN, EXCEPT THAT THE
CLERK OF THE COURT MAY TRANSMIT A CERTIFIED COPY OF THE DECREE OF
ABANDONMENT, WITHOUT EXPRESS ORDER OF COURT, FOR USE IN ADOPTION
PROCEEDINGS IN A COURT OF ANOTHER DISTRICT. 1925, APRIL 4, P.L.
127, SEC. 1.2, ADDED 1953, AUG. 26, P.L. 1411, SEC. 2.
ADOPTION ACT

Annotations:

CONTINUATION OF DOCUMENT 1 FROM PRECEDING PAGE

1

DOCUMENT NUMBER

3

WORDS CONTAINED IN SEARCH STATEMENT

Right column word list:

ABANDONMENT
ADOPTION
ADOPTION
ADOPTION
ADOPTION
ADOPTION

ADOPTION

ABANDONMENT
UNDER, AGE,
YEARS
ABANDONED
ABANDONMENT
LESS
ABANDONING, PARENT,
PARENTS
UNDER
ABANDONMENT
ADOPTION
PARENT, PARENTS
ABANDONMENT, ADOPTION
ADOPTION

Figure 9-3. (Continued).

297

should serve to put the reader on notice of the nature and complexity of this aspect of communication. It should make one aware of the many other variables that come into play in this kind of setting and that, primarily on this basis, a discussion of the organizational aspects of communication departs significantly from the material already considered in this chapter. For this reason, a more comprehensive treatment is to take place in Chapters 15 and 16 as part of the consideration of small group or organizational functioning as a whole.

In the same way, a consideration of mass media and communication introduces factors that need development along with concepts other than those sketched here. Discussions of attitudes and influence processes on a large scale accompany the consideration of the broader social concepts involved in transmission of information through methods of mass communication. Material in Chapter 14 represents the research and applications from this area of human behavior.

Summary

Language and communication are significant aspects of human behavior. Language, the ability to use verbal symbols, is something that sets humans apart from infrahumans. Communication refers to the broader area of transfer of information; it includes language but also incorporates the nonverbal means of information transmission.

The communication process can be described in terms of transmitting a message, encoded at a source, through a channel to a receiver, where it is decoded for use at a destination. Feedback is present in the process as well as, most of the time, unwanted noise. Redundancy is the extra transmission of information that can overcome noise.

Communication has been studied in many ways. While linguists have studied various aspects of language, broader inquiries have concentrated on semiotics, the general study of sign systems. The study of semiotics includes syntactics, the ordering of signs, semantics or the relation of signs to reality, and pragmatics, the study of factors surrounding the use of signs. Communication theorists have focused more on the mathematical and statistical bases of information.

Language, a system of arbitrary and learned signs, can be studied from several viewpoints as well. A focus on linguistics involves the study of the structure and arrangement of sounds and written material. Psycholinguistics involves a broader look at the behavior involved in the use of language.

Of the three main aspects of language study, syntactics, pragmatics, and semantics, the last area has provided more challenges to the scientific researcher.

Semantics is the study of meaning, and its measurement is difficult to arrange. The semantic differential is one objective attempt to pin down and measure meaning.

Language develops in the individual according to a pattern. All infants are alike in terms of the sounds they are able to make from the very earliest moment. Vocal production unfolds in a set sequence until, on the average, the first word appears at age one. From that point, a geometric increase in number of words known takes place. Background factors, primarily socioeconomic, are important in the development of language ability. Sex differences in ability are slight in favor of females, but the overlap is great.

Language is a fundamental part of the culture in which it is found. The influence of culture on language is strong; some have postulated an influence the other way, namely, that the language spoken influences the way we view the world.

Some positive stands have been espoused in the matter of utilization of language. The general semantics movement has placed the blame for most human difficulties on the use of faulty logic and improper use of words. Equating the word with the real world is seen as the fundamental problem. Basic English is a different approach to the use of language—one involving the substitution of a shorter vocabulary to enable more people to learn to use English for communication in a shorter time.

Because of the great increase in information, systems to handle the information must rely on electronic processing methods. This calls for adaptation to the new techniques of already utilized concepts in abstracting, indexing, filing, searching, and retrieval. The greater speed and efficiency after programming a system helps handle information at a level that could not be reached otherwise. Communication in groups, organizations, and in mass society involves much more than mere matters of information transmission. The additional facets of the problems call for fuller development in separate treatments.

Bibliography

Allen, J. and Salkoff, M. (1964). Machine translation: the state of the art, 1964. *American Behavioral Scientist,* **7(10),** 9–12.

Allport, F. (1924). *Social psychology.* Boston: Houghton Mifflin.

Argyris, C. (1957). *Personality and organization.* New York: Harper.

Boas, F. (1938). *General anthropology.* Boston: Heath.

Bourne, C. (1963). *Methods of information handling.* New York: Wiley.

Brown, R. (1958). *Words and things.* New York: Free Press.

Cherry, C. (1957). *On human communication.* New York: Wiley.

Flesch, R. (1946). *The art of plain talk.* New York: Harper and Row.

Hayakawa, S. (1964). *Language in thought and action* (2nd ed.). New York: Harcourt, Brace and World.

Horty, J. et al. (1968). *Retrieval of legal information.* Pittsburgh, Pa.: Aspen Systems Corporation.

Irwin, O. (1948). Infant speech. *Journal of Speech and Hearing Disorders,* **13,** 31–34.

Janda, K., ed. (1967). Advances in information retrieval in the social sciences. *American Behavioral Scientist,* Part I, **10(5)** 1–32; Part II, **10(6)** 1–32.

Johnson, W. (1946). *People in quandaries.* New York: Harper.

Kolasa, B. (1954). *The relationship between bilingualism and performance on a linguistic type intelligence test.* Unpublished doctoral dissertation, University of Pittsburgh.

Korzybski, A. (1958). *Science and sanity: an introduction to non-aristotelian systems and general semantics* (4th ed.). Lakeville, Conn.: International Non-Aristotelian Publishing Co.

Kuhn, A. (1963). *The study of society: a unified approach.* Homewood, Ill.: Irwin.

Leavitt, H. (1951). Some effects of certain communication patterns on group performance. *Journal of Abnormal and Social Psychology,* **46,** 38–50.

McCarthy, D. (1946). Language development in children. In Carmichael, L. (ed.). *Manual of child psychology.* New York: Wiley, 476–581.

Ogden, C. (1934). *The system of basic English.* New York: Harcourt, Brace.

Osgood, C. (1953). *Method and theory in experimental psychology.* New York: Oxford University Press.

Osgood, C., Suci, G., and Tannenbaum, P. (1957). *The measurement of meaning.* Urbana, Ill.: The University of Illinois Press.

Rubenstein, A. and Haberstroh, C., eds. (1960). *Some theories of organization.* Homewood, Ill.: Irwin.

Simon, H. (1957). *Administrative behavior* (2nd ed.). New York: Free Press.

Smith, M. (1926). *An investigation of the development of the sentence and the extent of vocabulary in young children.* Iowa City, Iowa: University of Iowa. Studies in Child Welfare No. 5.

Smith, M. (1941). Measurement of the size of general English vocabulary through the elementary grades and high school. *Genetic Psychology Monographs,* **24(2)**, 311–345.

Vigotsky, L. (1939). Thought and speech. *Psychiatry,* **2**, 29–52.

von Frisch, K. (1955). *The dancing bees.* New York: Harcourt, Brace.

Whorf, B. (1956). *Language, thought and reality.* New York: Wiley.

10

Culture and Behavior

The widest influence on the behavior of people in societies would have to be attributed to culture. Culture has meant many things to many people and, while behavioral and social scientists do not always completely agree on the totality of a definition, they do agree on one thing, that the term covers much more than or something very different from the meaning ordinarily held by most people.

What Is Culture?

Culture does *not* mean just something "fine," aesthetic, or highly prestigeful, such as going to the opera, buying fine paintings, or engaging in similar pursuits. There should be no value judgments or ratings of particular activities. Culture is simply all that exists in the social functioning of a particular group of people. It refers to characteristics individuals in the group have in common such as language, value systems, religious beliefs, preferences, and other patterns of behavior. Culture includes the way things are done and the feelings people have about interpersonal relationships. It covers an immense number of things like concrete material objects or abstract concepts, from civil rights and justice to the automobile, and from the bow and arrow to hot dogs, baseball, jazz, and Shakespeare. Finally, culture is a learned way of living transmitted socially from one person to another down through the years, not unchanged, yet with a particular fundamental underlying pattern which is identifiable.

Dynamics of Culture

Patterns of behavior built up on a cultural basis are never static over a period of time. When groups and the individuals within them learn the behavior patterns transmitted from others and pass these on in turn, the patterns are constantly open to variation, subtle or dramatic, in all phases of the process.

CHANGE

As in so many other areas, it is inevitable that changes will take place. The change may occur slowly or rapidly but it does occur. Discovery of stone age cultures in New Guinea and other parts of the world has taken place earlier in this century. More recent views of them, particularly after the invasion of foreign troops in World War II, show the sometimes extensive changes brought about by the contact with other cultural patterns (Mead, 1956).

Generally, culture change has been brought about by contact with others. This may be the result of migration of peoples, war and conquest, trade or exploration—any opportunity for peoples to rub elbows. To a lesser extent, the changes in climate or the depletion of natural resources have been responsible in history for changes in cultural patterns. Here too, however, the immediate basis has been the increased contact with others as the result of movement prompted by ecological factors. A final and perhaps most important factor in or cause of cultural change has been innovation or technological change. The advances in technology have, since the dawn of history, provided the impetus for changes in behavior in social structure and functioning. The wheel, gunpowder, steam engine, telephone, automobile, and airplane have each brought about changes in attitudes and behavior. Even these do not stand by themselves as promoting social change; contact among peoples promotes the spread of artifacts and accentuates the changes occurring with technology by exposing more individuals and groups to the artifacts themselves.

DEVELOPMENTAL PROCESSES

Culture is effective through its pervasiveness during all phases of the development of individuals within the cultural framework. The elements of culture are learned, either from early childhood or in the course of later exposure to the patterns of behavior. The process whereby a developing person is molded by the culture is *enculturation*. When, later, there is access to other cultural patterns, as in immigration, the process of change toward the new cultural form is called *acculturation*. When the newer members are incorporated into the broad stream of functioning of the general society, it may be said that *assimilation* has taken place. Assimilation means more than mere acculturation, since it implies amalgamation or integration into the community. If merger is not complete then at least the new group finds acceptance or tolerance. Some groups may have been acculturated yet not assimilated—the patterns of behavior are similar to those of a dominant group yet the minority is not included in most activities (such as the Negro). *Accommodation* is more often met in this situation and represents incomplete progress toward a complete integration. It is a land of compromise which staves off conflict, if only for the time being.

The process of acculturation shows variation in tempo as the result of the influence of many concomitant factors. The greater the amount of contact among individuals, the faster is the acculturation of the new group. The process occurs even more rapidly when there is a broad representation by age and sex (as in entire families) and where there are few families with the same background. Since the contact is greater in that case with representatives of the main cultural groups, the speed of the change is greater. The same is true of high socioeconomic status and mobility. Greater mobility, physically and socially, as well as higher ability leads to faster acculturation (Weinstock, 1964).

CULTURE LAG

The changes that take place in a society do not come at once to all parts of the group. Even though there may be extensive interdependence in the society, the changes are introduced, transmitted, and accepted at varying rates. The period of general delay was first labeled the culture lag by Ogburn (1950), who provided many examples. One such illustration is the typewriter (Figure 10-1). When first introduced, resistance to use was great and became even

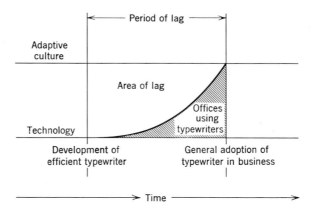

Figure 10-1. Ogburn's concept of culture lag as illustrated by the case of the typewriter (adapted from Broom and Selznick, 1963, p. 83).

greater when the question of "morality" of training young women to use it aroused extensive indignation. Similar examples could be selected from all eras of history. At present, the lag and its concomitants can be recognized in areas such as law, societal relationships, automated business procedures, or more efficient educational techniques.

Related Social Constructs

Certain aspects of broader behavior in a culture sometimes occasion confusion of terms or concepts. While they are certainly part of the picture, the roles played by factors such as race, nationality, and ethnicity are not as significant behaviorally.

RACE

Race and culture are not synonymous, nor are they even necessarily related. Race refers to the possesion of certain biological characteristics on which a classification is made, albeit a somewhat arbitrary and very often superfluous and meaningless process. Even as obvious an attribute as skin color shows such variation that a classification on this basis becomes confusing. Beyond this, individuals of different racial backgrounds often are part of a single culture, or the converse may be true—individuals with the same general biological characteristics are found in different cultures; languages, attitudes, and practices may be learned by individuals from any racial background. A similar dangerous fallacy is one based on the notion of inherent inferiority in racial differences. Margaret Mead (1958, p. 481) reports the consensus among behavioral scientists when she states:

> Extensive efforts to demonstrate the genetic superiority of one racial group of man over another have so far failed, so that the present working assumption is that, as far as their capacity to learn, maintain, transmit, and transform culture is concerned, different groups of *Homo sapiens* must be regarded as equally competent.

This does not mean that biological factors do not play a role. Factors such as general activity and emotional tone or other temperament traits which do help to make up behavior have some basis in hereditary mechanisms. These characteristics are seen in individual variation, however, and are not the source of distinction between one racial group and another.

A similar misconception is based on a frequent misuse of the term race in references to "the Irish race" or the "Jewish race." In the former case, the concept of race is confused with that of nationality; in the latter instance, the reference is really to a religious group. One has only to visit modern-day Israel to notice the great diversity of cultures admixed within a relatively small space and time where the gathering together of individuals has taken place on an ideological basis.

NATIONALITY

The term nationality itself is subject to misuse as well. The question of nationality is posed, in most situations, to identify the countries of origin of the parents or forefathers of present citizens of the country. It is inaccurate to speak of this as nationality; this is a country of origin or descent. Nationality is a purely political concept referring to allegiance to a political entity. One may be labeled simply by identifying the boundaries of the country of which one is a citizen.

ETHNICITY

An ethnic group is one which is distinguished from the general population on the basis of differences in culture. Many ethnic groups may exist within the boundaries of one particular country. Countries like Yugoslavia, for instance, have many groups demonstrating cultural variation through the differences in language, religion and, perhaps, attitudes, values, and dress as well. In the United States the term ethnic group is applied in the same way to minority groups separable on the basis of either race, religion, or national origin (or all of these), although in most cases they have fewer cultural facets that differ from the prevailing pattern of culture.

SOCIETY

A society is a large aggregate of people who have a way of life in common, a settled existence, and can be definitely located on a geographic basis. Inkeles (1964, p. 70) puts forth the test for a society as being a continued existence, in present form, of a community if suddenly all other people were to disappear. Most primitive groups and virtually all modern nation-states would thus qualify. Society refers to a group while culture indicates patterns of behavior. The two concepts often are considered together when the behavior of a social group is described. Culture can be broader than a society, however, as when we can speak of a Western culture that extends beyond ethnic and national boundaries.

Common Social Responses

Culture is so much a part of us that we take it for granted. We do the things we do so often and without realizing the reasons for doing them that they come to be looked upon as "natural." What is particularly dangerous about this situation is that all too often we come to believe that much of the activity or behavior of individuals is the result of some basic and innate predisposition or that it is the product of very substantial hereditary mechanisms. This ethnocentrism receives somewhat of a jolt when we travel to different parts of the country or the world and encounter other and different ways of accomplishing the same result. Our ethnocentricity, however, stands the test when we simply incorporate these findings into our thinking by coming to the conclusion that, because it is different, it is therefore not as good a way as the one to which we have become accustomed. The strongly ethnocentric individual may go even further and regard some different patterns of behavior as "unnatural" and, therefore, unworthy of consideration by a moral or civilized person.

This last response brings us back to the often found feeling that there must be something basic and biological about a particular behavior that we have taken for granted. The conclusion is responsible for many of our strong feelings in very simple issues to very broad and complex social problems. It may color our attitudes toward the role of women in our society as it may also determine our attitudes and patterns of behavior with respect to the civil rights of minority groups. It is quite easy to relegate women to the kitchen and to deny them entry into certain occupations solely on the basis of "women are simply not born for these things," as one gentlemanly lawyer once remarked to the author in explaining the relative absence of women at the bench and bar. In the same way, it becomes easy to explain away different patterns of behavior in minorities by simply ascribing them to inborn, innate causes.

For these and other reasons, the study of culture, with its variations and uniformities, is important for the knowledgable citizen generally and for the change-agent who wishes to proceed in a meaningful way, be he a teacher, businessman, government official at any level, or activist in any other type of institution.

Culture Patterns in
Simple Societies

Much of our information about the varieties of culture comes from the work of anthropologists. Their activities have been concentrated in the past in field studies among primitive peoples. More and more, however, the anthropologist is becoming interested in complex as well as the preliterate societies and is applying his field study techniques to the scrutiny of ongoing groups in a western or technological setting. Some historians have also joined in sketching patterns of culture by delving into historical materials. It should be emphasized, in this connection, that the study of peoples in places and times other than our own provides a fascinating and valuable picture of the diversity and the unity of human behavior patterns.

Ruth Benedict (1934) concentrated on three cultures, analyzed the integrating patterns, and compared in detail the cultural patterns of two Indian cultures of North America and a culture in New Guinea. In the United States Southwest she found the Zuni to be quiet, dignified, reserved, and restrained. Individualism was submerged by group considerations. There was very little conflict among individuals; everyone treated everyone else with kindness, consideration, and respect. Lack of competition, aggression, or even leadership was evident in this pueblo-dwelling Indian group. Moderation in all things was the hallmark of Zuni society. Benedict termed this culture an *Apollonian* culture and pointed out that it was in great contrast to the violent and aggressive cultural patterns of the Indian groups that surrounded the Zuni. These other cultures she labeled *Dionysian*. An outstanding example of Dionysian culture was that of the Kwakiutl Indians of the Pacific Northwest. Fierce competition was maintained in almost every conceivable way as they aggressively pursued their highly individualistic ways. In almost frenzied fashion they sought not only to outdistance their rivals materially but to shame them in the process. "Keeping up with the Joneses," Kwakiutl-style, meant not only amassing material wealth but giving more of it away than one's neighbor; if this could not be done, then destruction of it was called for. For the Kwakiutl there was "only one gamut of emotion, that which swings between victory and shame. It was in terms of affronts given and received that economic exchange, marriage, political life, and the pratice of religion were carried on" (p. 215).

Hostility and aggression characterize the Dobu of New Guinea. Suspicion, resentment, secrecy, and treachery, all in a highly competitive atmosphere, characterized everyday activities of Dobu males and females. The good man in Dobu culture was one who cheated and schemed, humiliated others, and usurped their place in society. Husbands and wives not only were the targets of suspicion for each other, but the family of each humiliated the opposite partner at any opportunity. "Life in Dobu fosters extreme forms of animosity and malignancy which most societies have minimized by their institutions. Dobuan institutions, on the other hand, exalt them to the highest degree. . . . All existence appears to [the Dobu man] as cut-throat struggle in which deadly antagonists are pitted against one another in a contest for each one of the goods of life" (p. 172).

In a similar set of studies, Margaret Mead (1935) set out to analyze the patterns of activity in three primitive tribes in New Guinea. She did this to determine the extent to which patterns of behavior along sex lines were due to innate biological factors on the one hand, or to learned cultural patterns on the other. Three racially similar tribes, the Arapesh, the Mundugumor, and the Tchambuli were compared. Arapesh culture emphasized gentleness and cooperation; the ideal of a mild responsive personality was characterized by Mead as being essentially feminine. The Mundugumor, on the other hand, were violent, hostile, and quarrelsome. Both men and women were expected to be competitive and aggresively sexed, and both men and women were expected to be proud and harsh without tender sentiments. The entire picture was one of extreme and exaggerated masculinity. The third group, the Tchambuli, provided by far the most interesting picture of cultural patterns for an outside observer from the Western world. Here, as opposed to the other two groups, men and women had very different and clear-cut roles; not only were the roles for each sex different, but they constituted almost a complete reversal of sex roles from those considered appropriate in Western culture and in many other societies as well. In Tchambuli society, women not only controlled the economy and did all the work but they were the dominant partners as well. Men spent their time in ceremonial huts preparing for very elaborate ceremonies, painting ceremonial masks, gossiping, and generally engaging in the Tchambuli version of the "coffee klatsch" or the women's club bridge party.

Margaret Mead perhaps is known even better for her studies of the influence of culture on the development of individuals in their particular society. She found (1928) that adolescence was not necessarily the period of storm and stress that we find it to be in Western society, particularly in the United States. She found Samoan youth to be easy-going and free of pressure, primarily because of the permissive and liberal attitudes of the large, happy family groups. That this was not a result of living in a primitive or preliterate group was amply demonstrated by Mead in a comparison of adolescent development in another society at the same technological level, the Manus of New Guinea. Here the respect for authority and the ideal of strong drive and assertiveness resembled that seen in our Western culture. Many families were not tolerant or permissive, and adolescence involved as much strain as in the United States.

Numerous other studies have demonstrated, in much the same way, the influence of culture in the shaping of behavior of individuals. The results emphasize the impact of the attitudes and values of the group in what is regarded as ideal or "normal." Behavior that might be viewed as deviant in one particular culture could be considered highly desirable in another. Then, too, our notions of what is innate or "natural" must undergo revision when we find extensive variations in matters like sex roles and patterns. Each culture has its own structure and functional pattern, and the individuals developing within that culture mirror, to a high degree, the set of values held by the group as a whole. In addition, each group is apt to regard its own ways of doing things as not just superior to other ways but even "the only way things should be done."

Culture in Larger Societies

As difficult as the study of small societies may be, research on larger, more complex modern societies is infinitely harder to undertake. Often, the student is forced to accept generalizations made about nations and their citizens that are sometimes little better than the casual stereotypes that abound. Sketching "character structures" of a national group, if such can be demonstrated to exist, may be developed on extremely tenuous ground.

RUSSIAN MODAL CHARACTER

The patterns of culture and behavior in Soviet Russia are, for example, of great interest to researchers in many areas, basic and applied. Yet the difficulty, or even impossibility, of doing research in a direct manner raises some questions about the validity of results. The Russian Research Center at Harvard, for instance, studied Russian refugees in Western Europe to obtain a picture of Soviet patterns (Bauer, Inkeles, and Kluckhohn, 1957). Nevertheless, with the limitations made clear, some interpretations can be made.

Interviews and tests were administered to a small group of well-educated urban males who had been occupationally well placed before becoming emigrés. These were compared to a control group of matching Americans to highlight any differences between the national groups.

The Russians showed a great need for interpersonal, face-to-face relationships without, however, undue concern for the opinions of others. They were more emotional and more willing to express their emotions. They had fewer defense mechanisms. Americans may be concerned about being liked, but the Russians expected to receive moral responses from the group (loyalty, sincerity, and respect). Autonomy and achievement are part of American attitudes but are not present in the Russian scheme of things.

There is some indication that variations in attitudes and values occur in the social hierarchy. Affiliation and dependency needs may be present at all levels of Soviet society, but these supportive needs are less evident at the top or elite levels.

Bauer et al. (1957, pp. 134–142) maintain, in sketching the modal Russian national character, that the central problem of the Soviet citizen is whether to grant trust to others and, especially, the regime. This great dilemma may exert some influence on the attitudes of individuals and groups in the Soviet Union toward international problems as well.

A more recent study of the Russian executive (Granick, 1960), based on a survey of professional literature plus interviews in the field, indicates that the "Red organization man" differs very little from his American counterpart in terms of desires and aspirations.

Even with similarities, differences do exist. The training of the Russian manager is that of an engineer, and he has to pick up the elements of business administration on the way. While problems of advertising or making model changes each year are nonexistent for him, the problems of procurement are overwhelming. Here, salesmanship of the first order is called for. Profit as such is also of no concern to the manager, but incentives are at the forefront. A system of bonuses, up to 100 percent of the base salary, can make the Soviet factory even more a "high pressure" situation. Risks of failure also may be greater.

AMERICAN PATTERNS

The American modal character also has been the subject for much interpretation and even argumentation. Again, the warning about stereotypes needs to be made. This has not stopped some social scientists from outlining, on the basis of their analysis, a review of the "characteristics" of American personality structure. One such (Williams, 1951, pp. 388–442) includes a listing that should occasion little surprise to observers of the American scene. Trends to personal achievement through activity and work, humanitarianism with a moral orientation, and progress toward material comfort through greater efficiency and practicality are all "major value-orientations" in the United States.

A wider audience has been gained in recent times by Riesman, through *The lonely crowd* (1950). His analysis of character patterns in modern societies, exemplified by the United States, revealed three major types.

Tradition-directed individuals are governed by an adherence to custom primarily; Riesman says few such groups exist in America today. Most numerous are the *inner-directed* individuals, who have internalized social norms and are governed by this "built in" mechanism. A more recent trend toward *other-directedness* is claimed by Riesman, especially in the upper middle class of the larger cities. Approval of and guidance from others is characteristic of the other-directed man, who has developed sophisticated methods to keep in touch with others in his world.

The three groups are not only guided differently in terms of references, they are controlled through different sets of sanctions. The tradition-directed respond to shame, but the inner-directed are moved by guilt. While the other-directed are controlled as well by guilt and shame, the main curb seems to be anxiety.

Cross-Cultural Communication

In *The silent language* (1959) E. T. Hall makes the observation that Americans have themselves been responsible for the animosity generated toward them by nationals of other countries. Despite the billions of dollars in foreign aid and the many other well-intentioned words and gestures, the response on the part of others represents a total failure of our efforts. This complete loss is laid at the doorstep of ignorance, the lack of awareness of the meaning of communications, mostly nonverbal, in cultures different from our own. The communication by behavior is the "silent language" referred to in the title.

There is a tendency to treat any departures from our ideas with disdain. Difficulties in communication can always be regarded as being caused because "those crazy foreigners have no idea of how things should be done." Hall (*ibid.,* pp. 15–16) provides some illustrations of actual breakdowns in communication. An American mission in Greece, for instance, was having difficulty in working with the Greeks. The Americans, who took pride in being outspoken and forthright, did not know that this was regarded by the Greeks as a lack of finesse. A further attempt to reach agreement on general principles and leave details to subcommittees was regarded by the Greeks as an attempt to "pull the wool over their eyes."

In the Middle East, an American agricultural expert managed to get farmers very angry by asking them what yields they expected from their fields. The basis for the anger lay in the fact that Arabs regard anyone who even attempts to predict the future as slightly insane. The farmers regarded the question as implying that they might also be slightly crazy. The Arab considers that only God knows the future and to talk about it is highly presumptuous. Arab businessmen by now may be less resistant to attempts to predict the future course of their business; it may be wise, however, for outside entrepreneurs to consider the possibility of a vestigial influence of this basic cultural aspect of the Arab world.

The silent language that communicates in a culture as powerfully as words do, says Hall, includes the language of time and space. With respect to the significance of elapsed time, cultural variations provide differences in meaning. In some foreign countries an hour's tardiness is interpreted as a five minute delay in America. An indigenous civil servant being on time in a call on an American emissary could be viewed as relinquishing freedom of action, while an hour would be insulting. Hall (*ibid.,* p. 176) reports the compromise as being tardiness of 50 minutes, a result that, needless to say, was not fully appreciated by the American. Within the United States, too, there are variations in patterns of arrival behavior. The reader may be aware of regional differences. A cocktail party from "6 to 8" in a Northeast urban area will have people arriving from 6:30 on and staying well beyond the purported ending time. In the Midwest, or some parts of it, the exact period specified will be rather firmly adhered to. When the event is a dinner, however, arrivals show much less displacement from the stated time. In all events, in different cultures the variations are a function of the type of occasion, the status of the individuals, and the way in which time is handled by the individuals involved.

"Space speaks," says Hall (*ibid.,* pp. 188–209) in describing the communication inherent in physical activity within the environment of a culture. Spatial cues abound but often the visitor from another culture is not aware of them. Pushing and shoving encountered in many parts of the world shock Americans who have grown up in a pattern that discourages touching. The Latin-American who leans close to talk is offended as the *Norteamericano* backs away uneasily.

The "language of office location" becomes known to newcomers to business enterprise in the United States. As one goes up the scale of prestige, the amount of space increases and the location tends to be more peripheral. The French manager, on the other hand, wants to remain in the center of things where he can remain in visual contact with what is going on. The French manager's office may be noisy, but that is "where the action is."

Political and Economic Patterns

The basic norms for group behavior that are fundamental in a society serve as foundations for the extensive functioning seen at all levels of simple and complex groupings of people. Cultural factors have an important role in shaping men's behavior in political and economic entities as well.

The basic norms of a group and its organizational structure may arise from even more basic changes that sometimes go unnoticed because of their simplicity. Mention has been made above about the culture changing forces of war, migration, climate, and technology. Exactly how these forces operate may, in most cases, be obscured by the complexity of the interaction of those various forces. When even simple examples are found, however, the results of these situations can be profound in their influences on the group.

FUNDAMENTAL STRUCTURING

A provocative illustration of one such change is provided by Kardiner and Linton (1939) as they report on a field study of the Tanala-Betsileo peoples on the island of Madagascar. One branch of this people was just undergoing a change from the dry method of cultivation of rice to the wet method, while the other branch apparently had made the change many generations before. An analysis of both groups indicated that a change in social structure and functioning took place concomitantly with the change in method of cultivation.

Under the dry method, villages were less important. The people were mobile because the dry method depleted the soil rapidly. When the limits of the territory were reached, however, the need to cultivate one parcel intensively was faced; the wet method of flooding the same land year after year had to be adopted. Under this change, the land became more valuable and tenancy more permanent. Tribal organization changed from one with democratic patterns to a monarchy with a rigid class and caste structure. Slaves became valuable along with other shifts in political and economic interests. Villages now had to be defended more vigorously, and a system of physical and personal protection emerged. Powers of the sovereign were extended to the point where there was no appeal from the king's judgments.

It can be argued that the unfolding of these social patterns resembles, in miniature, the development of the feudal system in the history of Western civilization. What is significant, however, is that these pervasive ramifications arose as the result of a simple change in the method of cultivation of a food.

INFLUENCES ON THE ECONOMY

The cultural determinants of business behavior have often been stated in a manner reminiscent of Adam Smiths's dictum that man acts in regard to his own self-interest. This position, even though it assumes rationality, is meaningless, however, unless one can see what alternatives are available for decision making and under what conditions the choices are made. One cultural pattern may provide the kinds of opportunities and constraints that another does not.

Discussion above of cultural patterns in primitive societies indicated a wide variety of norms and modal behaviors in all aspects of everyday life. Differences emerged from descriptions of even limited aspects such as economic behavior. Primitive societies have their aggressive "hucksters" as well as passive clients.

The same variety is possible in industrialized Western societies. The ethnocentric student of the economy might, for instance, proceed on the assumption that profit maximization is the prime determiner of the decision making of managers of industrial enterprises in the West. This assumption may not be warranted, however, when such decisions are analyzed. It is possible in Europe, for instance, that a business might be seen as furthering the continuing existence of the family under whose aegis it has been conducted. The honor and wealth of the family and business are one (Landes, 1951). Since the author focused on the France of 1951 to describe the differences with American concepts of operations, particularly in the matter of attitudes toward growth, what was true for France then probably could have been repeated for most other European countries. There is a question, however, of whether any changes have taken place since.

Broad and basic relationships between economic activity and the cultural milieu have fascinated researchers for some time. Max Weber was one of the first to sketch the idea of the close link between an economic system and a way of life influenced by a religious ideology. From a consideration of Calvinist Geneva, as one of the first cities to provide an impetus for capitalism, to parallels present in this century, Weber's concept of "the Protestant ethic" interests many observers, inside and out, of the business scene.

Weber's *The Protestant ethic and the rise of capitalism* (1958) was first published in 1904. Weber's thesis traced the basis for the economic vitality of capitalism to the asceticism and individualism so prized by Calvinism and related religious sects. The mark of heavenly predestination lay in the increasing solidity of the bourgeois merchant, who toiled long, was thrifty, and did not idle away his time nor spend his wealth frivolously. While Weber may have drawn his examples too neatly (there were, as Tawney explains in the foreword to the quoted volume, many Protestant and Catholic variations), the legacy of his incisive sketches is still with us in common references to the "Protestant ethic" with its values and attitudes reflected in business activity in today's world.

A more recent and more precise approach to this intriguing relationship has been launched by McClelland (1961). Based on an earlier theoretical formulation of the achievement motive (McClelland et al., 1953), he relates the actual economic level to the prevalence of achievement motivation. Where enough individuals display in their test results a high need for achievement (nAchievement), the level of productivity of the country in general is likely to reflect those need patterns.

McClelland acknowledges a debt to Weber in formulating his more pervasive and empirical study of achievement and economic development. An even closer link was provided by Winterbottom (1953), who was interested in parents' influence on sons' achievement motivation. She found that boys with high nAchievement scores had parents, mothers particularly, who expected self-reliance and mastery at an earlier age. This was in distinct contrast with the restrictive attitudes of mothers of those low in nAchievement. McClelland (1961, p. 47) describes the parallels with Weber's concept in the schematic form represented in Figure 10-2.

The main thrust of McClelland's thesis is that a relationship exists between the individualism expressed in Protestantism, nAchievement, and the level of economic activity. He indicates this in many ways, but the study goes beyond the positive relationships between capitalism and Protestantism to a global comparison of various cultures and even an historical review of the rise and fall of the economics of nations. In all this, the positive relationship between nAchievement and economic vitality seems to prevail. Various tools were employed: content analysis of imaginative stories told by individuals and similar analysis of children's readers were most often used. Historical studies focused on nAchievement themes in literature of all kinds, but a further intriguing analysis of ancient artistic products showed designs related to those produced by high and low achievers of contemporary times. The study of the literature of ancient Greece, Spain, and England of medieval to industrial revolution times and of the United States shows achievement motives in the writings anticipating the surge in economic activity. A lessening of such themes signals or accompanies a decline.

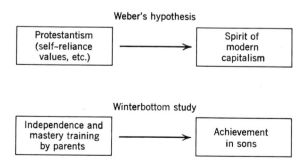

Figure 10-2. Comparison of Winterbottom's findings with Weber's concepts (McClelland, 1961, p. 47).

Summary

Culture refers to the sum of behavioral characteristics of a group of people. Limiting the term to those aspects considered prestigeful represents a value judgement that should not be made. The actual patterns of behavior of a society or group are the focus for a study of culture and its concomitants.

Cultural patterns are never static; even in simple societies, change takes place, though usually more slowly than in complex environments. Technological change, migration, wars and conquest, or climatic changes can result in new and different patterns of behavior. The adaptation of individuals and groups to such changes reveals many patterns of development. The implementation of new techniques may lag considerably behind the availability of the technology.

Race and culture are not the same. Race refers to a set of common physical characteristics. Not only is there great variation in almost any trait that may be used to establish a racial classification, but there is little of value in explaining behavior on this basis once the categories are established. Nationality is also limited in that it merely identifies the political allegiance of the individual. Ethnicity refers to a separate set of cultural characteristics within a larger group. Sometimes the term ethnic is used to identify groups within the broader American culture (Negroes, Italians, or Germans), but this separation has many misleading aspects. A society is a large aggregate of individuals who share a common pattern of behavior.

A typical response by individuals to patterns of behavior in groups previously unfamiliar to them is an ethnocentric one. "Ours is the best, or even only, way" is a representative reaction. Even stronger may be the feeling that one's way of doing things is the only "natural" way. The variety of behavior discovered all over the globe by anthropologists in the field effectively supports the concept of learned patterns in a society rather than innate biological bases for virtually all of human behavior.

Studies of culture have concentrated on the more easily studied smaller primitive groups. Attempts to describe larger complex societies also have been made with some success. Russian and American "modal character" may represent an oversimplified sketching of the characteristics of a broad national group but do provide leads for futher study.

Communication across cultures may be made more difficult by the lack of awareness of the inherent social differences in meanings in different societies. Simple concepts of time and space can convey much to those in a culture group and be misinterpreted by others outside that aggregate. The "silent language" of everyday things may not be known to strangers.

Political and economic events may be affected by the basic cultural patterns of a society. A change in conditions can affect the political structure of a group, or the norms in individual development may determine the level of economic activity. The postulated relationship between capitalism and a Calvinistic philosophy has received more specific delineation through the showing of a positive tie between independence training in childhood and mastery of an economic environment.

Bibliography

Bauer, R., Inkeles, A., and Kluckhohn, C. (1957). *How the Soviet system works.* Cambridge: Harvard University Press.

Benedict, R. (1934). *Patterns of culture.* New York: Houghton Mifflin.

Broom, L. and Selznick, P. (1963). *Sociology* (3rd ed.). New York: Harper and Row.

Granick, D. (1960). *The red executive: A study of the organization man in Russian industry.* Garden City, N.Y.: Doubleday.

Hall, E. (1959). *The silent language.* Garden City, N.Y.: Doubleday.

Inkeles, A. (1964). *What is sociology? An introduction to the discipline and profession.* Englewood Cliffs, N.J.: Prentice-Hall.

Kardiner, A. and Linton, R. (1939). *The individual and his society.* New York: Columbia University Press.

Landes, D. (1951). French business and the businessman: a social and cultural analysis. In Earle, E. (ed.). *Modern France.* Princeton, N.J.: Princeton University Press.

McClelland, D. (1961). *The achieving society.* Princeton: Van Nostrand.

McClelland, D., Atkinson, J., Clark, R., and Lowell, E. (1953). *The achievement motive.* New York: Appleton-Century-Crofts.

Mead, M. (1928). *Coming of age in Samoa.* New York: Morrow.

Mead, M. (1935). *Sex and temperament in three primitive societies.* New York: Morrow.

Mead, M. (1956). *New lives for old.* New York: Morrow.

Mead, M. (1958). Cultural determinants of behavior. In Roe, A. and Simpson, M. (eds.). *Behavior and evolution.* New York: Yale University Press, 480–503.

Ogburn, W. (1950). *Social change.* New York: Viking.

Riesman, D. (1950). *The lonely crowd.* New Haven: Yale University Press.

Weber, M. (1958). *The Protestant ethic and the spirit of capitalism* (Parsons, T., trans.). New York: Scribner.

Weinstock, S. (1964). Some factors that retard or accelerate the rate of acculturation. *Human Relations,* **17**(**4**), 321–340.

Williams, R. (1951). *American society; a sociological interpretation.* New York: Knopf.

Winterbottom, M. (1953). *The relation of childhood training in independence to achievement motivation.* Unpublished doctoral dissertation. University of Michigan. Quoted in McClelland, D. (1961). *The achieving society.* Princeton: Van Nostrand.

11

Social Structure

The way in which people in groups are brought together and the manner in which they are distinguished is a basic area of study in the social and behavioral sciences. An understanding of the fabric of a society serves as a prelude to the scrutiny of the behavior that stems from the structuring of the group.

Interaction among people is possible under various arrangements, and it can be viewed at several levels of inquiry. As a researcher proceeds with the study of structure, he may move from an initial view of the "ties that bind" to a more detailed inspection of the different building blocks of which the group is composed.

Despite proclaimers of equality and classless societies, there is no known human aggregate where all persons stand at the same level in their interrelationships with others in the group. Differentiation among people is a characteristic of human groups.

The differential standing of individuals in a society can be based on many personal and social attributes. Each grouping may show variation in the way the characteristics are evaluated, but in some way individuals are distinguished more or less on what the group has settled on as being important or contributory to the welfare of the society. People may be differentiated and evaluated differently, on the basis of age, sex, race, skills, or other individual variables. Older citizens may be looked to for guidance while men may have an easier time than women in gaining a particular employment. Negroes may be cut off altogether from the enjoyment of certain activities.

Other criteria may be added to establish strata or levels in the society. Where and how one lives, ancestry, and income are only some of the additional factors taken into consideration in a determination of social placement. The importance of each of these may vary by country or era, but the end result is the socioeconomic stratification we may know under the label of social class.

Social Organization

The patterns of social organization may be said to be the basis for further study of group functioning in any setting. The structuring of the relations between individuals and groups influences many aspects of behavior. How people interrelate can shape their attitudes, values, and virtually all other facets of personality to one extent or another.

FORMS OF ORGANIZATION

The basic forms of social organization may be stated as being (a) kinship, (b) status, (c) fealty, (d) contract, and (e) coordination. These may be found in pure form or in combination.

Kinship refers to the bond of membership in the family. Primitive societies still rely on this form, although it is not unknown in more complex societies. The family-run enterprise is still a strong entity in Europe and is not unknown in the United States.

Status is the person's place in the social system. When an individual is treated according to the position he occupies, we have relationships based on status. A king, dependent child, mother, welfare recipient, or corporation president may be recognized in terms of their position.

Fealty is the personal relationship between individuals based on trust, loyalty, or other mutual benefits. In troubled medieval times the allegiance of vassal to lord provided a basic order. The same notions of personal fealty may sometimes be seen in modern organizations where the president, for instance, may rely on the loyalty of key people subordinate to him and not to the organization.

Contract is based on the exchange of one promise for another. The social results are more far-reaching, however, than this basic legal concept might suggest. It emphasizes a free and responsible individual, one able to organize his own life as he sees fit or to "get the best bargain" on his own merits.

Coordination has been labeled in many ways. Some call it *bureaucracy,* as Weber (1946) did, while others may refer to it as an *organization society.* The interaction of individuals working together in large enterprises or activities is an outstanding feature of present-day society. It is also unlikely that this aspect will be curtailed. The organization can operate effectively only if it proceeds under impersonal rules rather than whims of individuals and under, presumably, specialists in administration and other skill areas.

LEVELS OF ORGANIZATION

Analyses of social structure can be made at various levels of societal entities depending on whether the view of the researcher is limited to small and specific units or whether he looks at the "big picture." Ultimately, all aspects must be considered.

For convenience, we may identify three levels of social organization—the interpersonal, the group, and the social order level. An inquiry at the interpersonal level pinpoints individual interactions and deals with the bonds between single persons. When interaction between a small set of individuals is of interest, the second level of analysis comes to the fore. The broadest study of group patterns of action, particularly in systems of social functioning, is a study at the social order level. At this point an entire community or society is involved.

Individual Differentiation

A society has varying expectations of the contribution each of its members can make to its functioning. Each grouping has "slots" to be filled, and each position in that social framework has certain activities that must be performed. These categories and behaviors are organized according to the society's conceptions of what is proper or effective and, in addition, values are placed on the different results.

STATUS

The positions people occupy in society are established with reference to the needs and values of that society. A status is a position that has been determined as being important in the interpersonal relationships of the group. An early developer of the concepts of status and role called status "simply a collection of rights and duties" (Linton, 1936, p. 113). Each person has a status or, more correctly, several statuses representing differences in contribution to the group. The reader may focus on the status arising on an occupational basis (teacher, cook, farmer, or shoeshine boy, for example) and overlook more fundamental ones that should be obvious. Age, sex, and social status are of consequence in most societies—our behavior is often highly dependent on whether we are dealing with a male or female, young or old.

A person has more than one status. A man with whom we place our money is a banker. He is also (we would hope) a dutiful husband, doting father, and undoubtedly much more. The status of husband and father is more latent during the day and comes to the fore when he goes home at night. When he presides at a luncheon for the United Fund, another position emerges, and when he goes to his club later, still another status appears. Individuals not only have multiple statuses but they may change, sometimes rapidly, with circumstances. The more complex a society and the more active and capable an individual, the more positions there are likely to be.

This concept of status does not carry with it an automatic value judgment. Status should be regarded only as a position and nothing more. The classifications may represent decisions of value, but an evaluation of the position should be a separate act. Some behavioral scientists may combine the concepts of position with a judgment of its value and call it status. The second aspect, however, is better handled separately as *prestige*.

Status may be described further in terms representing dynamics of the society. When positions are determined by criteria that are fixed and beyond the control of the person (sex, skin color, or ancestry), they are known as ascribed statuses. A position subject to control by the individual (occupation, residence, or religion) is an *achieved* status. The more "open" a society, the more important achieved status will be.

ROLE

Each status has a set of behavior patterns that is considered to be appropriate to it. Some variation is permitted, but the general outlines are usually crystallized. According to Linton (1936, p. 114), a role "represents the dynamic aspect of a status. . . . When he puts the rights and duties which constitute the status into effect, he is performing a role." The banker in our illustration may be aware that his demeanor and dress must reflect the solidity of the organization he represents. We would, after all, be concerned about the safety of our deposits if we observed our freindly banker playing dice in a Hawaiian sport shirt in the lobby of the bank.

As individuals have multiple statuses, so they have many roles appropriate to each. In the case of the banker, we may be less concerned about his fulfilment of the role of husband and father except insofar as it affects the state of our bank account. Multiple roles may cause problems, however, in that an individual may not recognize what is called for in a new and different status. A freshman girl new on the university campus may have serious questions about dress and behavior. A new management trainee may have some uneasy moments in a company he has joined until he learns what it is that he must do, on the job and off.

Multiple roles can cause further problems arising from the inability of the individual to make a complete shift in behavior as a change in status occurs. *Role conflict* is the condition where the changes in status and role are disruptive. A chaplain in the military may experience it. An unscrupulous businessman could be sensitive to it when he sits in church on Sunday, although he may have compartmentalized his thinking so that he feels no conflict. A shop foreman who is promoted to an executive position may have some trying moments when his blustery ways are no longer appropriate in his new position. A college girl may have learned to "play dumb" on dates under penalty of not receiving further opportunities to socialize with the opposite sex but may resent having to hide her abilities.

It should be emphasized that the term role, while it reflects its theatrical origin, does not mean that we are playacting each moment of our lives. We may or may not be completely aware of the different ways we respond to the situations in which we find ourselves. Our reactions in the different positions are learned through the process of socialization, and we behave in routine ways much more often than in consciously constructed poses.

PRESTIGE

The evaluation of status and the role that accompanies it is the basis for a ranking called prestige. The value judgments of a group can be expressed in terms representing a placement on a scale. We then speak of high status and low status. Judgments such as these are made more often in occupational terms or in ways representative of broader social placements, as in class stratification. We seldom evaluate on the basis of the status of husband or father even though society may consider these favorable.

Occupations are ranked with sufficient frequency to provide a relatively stable illustration of prestige occurring on this basis. Table 11-1 represents a survey of ratings of occupations done in June 1963 following a format in use for several decades.

While some variation in placement may take place over time, such rankings have generally been rather stable.

Social Stratification

Prestige rankings of status by the community form the basis of the broader classifications usually termed social class. Social class has been defined as "an open aggregate or stratum of people with roughly similar ranking in a particular community or society" (Berelson and Steiner, 1964, p. 459). They further note that, although many criteria are used for stratification, most of the research develops an economic basis for class. There may be some variation in the ways in which the term class is used, and some researchers avoid it altogether, preferring instead to speak of social or socioeconomic strata. There is agreement, however, on the impact of such groupings. Behavior may be influenced by

Table 11-1. Ratings of Occupations[a]

Occupation	Score
United States Supreme Court Justice	94
Physician	93
Scientist	92
College professor	90
Lawyer	89
Airline pilot	86
Banker	85
Biologist	85
Public schoolteacher	81
Farm owner and operator	74
Policeman	72
(Average)	(71)
Bookeeper	70
Plumber	65
Barber	63
Truck driver	59
Coal miner	50
Bartender	48
Shoe shiner	34

[a] Adapted from Hodge, R., Siegel, P. and Rossi, P. (1964). Data from June, 1963.

many factors, but one's social class heritage and membership play as important a role as many other factors. Since other people are influential in the socialization of individuals in a society, the impact of attitudes and values of one's membership group is seen directly in stratification.

Social strata are present in all societies even though the opportunity to have a number of strata will present itself more in complex industrial societies. There may be variations, as well, in the extent or rigidity of memberships in the groupings. India may, for instance, present a picture of a more rigid social class structure, even in this day, than is true of the United States. Class membership need not be fixed for a period of time nor is it a highly visible attribute of an individual. When social aggregates are closed with little or no movement in or out, the result is a *caste*. In American society, the Negro is a member of a caste.

In addition to differences in mobility, there may be variations in the criteria members use to place themselves and others on a social scale. History has presented examples of the extent to which social class was important but also how it was reinforced through the behavior of its members. Nobility, peasantry, clergy, and others had their prescribed costume and way of life. Not only did "clothes make the man," but speech and behavior served as identifying factors as well. It is well to point out that these variables may not be solely of historical interest in that speech patterns, for instance, may still be a distinguishing aspect of class. In Great Britain "U and non-U" speech supposedly differentiates members of classes; in the United States and other countries one's speech may also be indicative of class placement and the learning patterns that accompany it.

BASES OF STRATIFICATION

Since people inevitably classify themselves and others, it is important to determine just how this classification proceeds. The strata may be identified in one of three major ways.

(a) Objective evaluation.
(b) Subjective placement.
(c) Reputational selection.

The first approach is one where the determination is made by an objective, outside researcher who establishes the levels on the basis of certain criteria believed to be important and active in the situations with which he works. The subjective approach, on the other hand, asks the individuals to place themselves. The questioning determines the class to which the respondent himself thinks he belongs. The final approach, the reputational one, is a broader and sometimes more ambiguous attempt to get persons in the community to act as judges and assign rankings to members of that community on the basis of criteria those judges have developed. What people generally think about where individuals fit in the social scene has been the basis for much of what has been used in the past for information about stratification.

To one extent or another, the three approaches use the same general set of criteria to determine placement. The salient ones may vary with time or place, but the criteria for selection to class memberships may be identified. Max Weber (1946) indicated three criteria for stratification—political power, prestige, and economic conditions. While this was more than the one factor Karl Marx singled out (position in the production process), it represents much less than is usually considered, consciously or not, in the determination of class. Some of the criteria generally attended to are as follows.

> Occupation
> Income (amount and source)
> Education (extent and type)
> Race or ethnic status
> Religion
> Associations
> Ancestry (inherited social position)
> Manners
> Ownership of property
> Style of living
> Authority
> Power
> Public service
> Morals

One or more of the above may be used in the evaluation, and the weighting assigned to each will vary with the values imposed by the society or a dominant group within it. There is seldom a formal or objective evaluation; the classifications are made informally or casually by an amorphous aggregate of individuals.

The number of classes in a community and the percentage of the total within each category are questions for which no hard and fast answers should be given. The number of classes in American communities is mainly the result of an arbitrary decision as to how to order the data. It may be said that the number can vary from two classes (high and low, or "haves" and "have-nots") to several groupings. Two classes is too rough a dichotomy, while a large number of categories may be a more precise differentiation than really exists in the basic information. A classic study by Warner and Lunt (1941) in a New England community they called "Yankee City" established six classes on the basis of prestige rankings of citizens by the members of the community themselves. Each of the three main classes—upper, middle, and lower—were divided into two, the upper and lower (Figure 11-1). A smaller town might provide even less opportunity for fine distinctions between levels. In "Plainville" (West, 1945) the people of that Midwest small town were divided into the "prairie people" and the "hillbillies." Distinctions were made within the groups, but the overall result is a simpler arrangement than one found in a larger city.

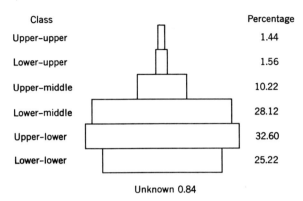

Class		Percentage
Upper–upper		1.44
Lower–upper		1.56
Upper–middle		10.22
Lower–middle		28.12
Upper–lower		32.60
Lower–lower		25.22

Unknown 0.84

Figure 11-1. Distribution of classes in "Yankee City" (Warner and Lunt, 1941).

In most situations the net result of an attempt to stratify is a loose hierarchy with vague lines of demarcation. Especially in a rapidly moving society, the merging of strata may be extensive. White collar—blue collar, for instance, used to be a convenient distinction between the middle and lower classes. Higher pay at blue collar levels with an increasingly similar pattern of consumption make distinctions harder to make.

Centers (1949) used a subjective approach to derive the class categories. He got some idea of class consciousness or the feeling of group membership in a class by asking subjects to which class they felt they belonged. The respondents placed themselves (in percentages) as follows:

Upper class	3
Middle class	43
Working class	51
Lower class	1

Centers included the category *working class* to permit a response that otherwise might not be made realistically without some emotional hedging. The two low groups can be considered as comparable to the lower class categories even though some of the respondents who would be objectively placed higher may have indicated membership in the working class category. The overall similarity to the results of an objective approach emerges from a comparison. There was a close relationship between the objective occupational rating and expressed class membership. Centers concluded that, while stratification is basically an objective arrangement deriving from economic factors, the psychological aspects are important complementary facets of the psychosocial structuring.

It has been noted above that the criteria may be weighted differently and the emphasis on factors will vary with time or place. Many stratifications emphasize the occupational membership of the breadwinner while, in Old City, a more tradition-based Southern city surveyed by Davis, Gardner, and Gardner (1941), the classes emphasized ancestry much more than other factors. A smaller town might, on the other hand, have its classes arrayed casually on the basis of area of residence ("snob hill" or "other side of the tracks"). There usually is, however, a close positive correlation between factors; that is, a professional man undoubtedly has more education and probably lives in a more exclusive section of town.

With all the criteria for class placement, it is difficult to fix on a single characteristic of class that can be identified as being present in all instances. Perhaps the most general criterion of class placement is that of attitudes. A shared set of attitudes, values, and opinions may be the one factor that is common to class members even though variation in other factors exists.

Perceptions of members with respect to requirements of class membership may be fairly uniform and clear within the strata, but the further away from one's level an individual must rate others, the less specific and precise is the sketching of criteria and membership. Davis et al. (1941) sketched the differing perspectives of the six social classes in Old City (Figure 11-2). Those looking up from far away have only a foggy notion of what it takes, while the upper classes are somewhat better oriented.

Broom and Selznick (1958, p. 179) identify the basis of the different perceptions by class as the following. "The lower classes use money as the main criterion; the middle class, use money and morality; and the upper classes, style of life and ancestry."

BEHAVIORAL CORRELATES OF CLASS

For many readers, the above material, while fascinating in itself, would be of little interest in the absence of a link between class and whatever might be encountered in life. The question is, "What difference does it make?" "At least some" is the answer, even though the exact relationships may be less clear. There are behavior patterns, large and small, associated with stratification. These may not always be shaped significantly by class membership, but the tie does exist.

Even simple demographic statistics display class differences; life expectancy increases with class membership—the higher classes live longer partly, perhaps,

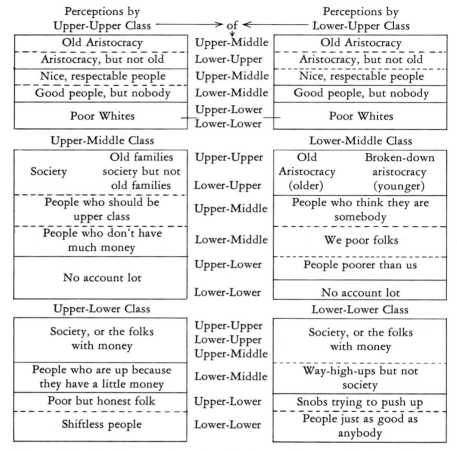

Figure 11-2. Social perspectives of social class members (Davis, A., Gardner, B. and Gardner, M., 1941).

because they are able to buy the things that help keep them healthy (Mayer and Hauser, 1953). Higher-class individuals usually belong to more organizations (and different ones—the club and lodge separating the upper from lower levels). Church membership, too, shows a relationship with class. Some Protestant churches (Episcopalian and Congregational) draw a high proportion of their members from the upper and middle classes (Schneider, 1952). More fundamentalist sects have a larger representation from lower levels, as does the Catholic Church.

More basic and more important in the long run is the effect on the growing individual of the behavior of parents and other models. This influence process is socialization. If values and attitudes vary at the different social levels, these variations will influence behavior of members who, in turn, pass on to their children the styles of life they have learned. Bronfenbrenner (1958) has summarized a long series of studies of child-rearing practices in middle and working (lower) class families. Working class parents are more likely to foster obedience in their offspring, more often through the use of physical punishment. Middle class parents are more permissive and try to induce desirable behavior through reasoning and verbal reinforcement. Guides to behavior are socially based such as, "We don't do things that way; we do it this way." Authority of lower class parents is emphasized by them while the middle class procedures are more egalitarian and permissive. With this there is more development of individual responsibility (and conscience), independence training, and achievement. Middle class families also are likely to impose more controls on aggression and sexual or other impulses. Physical aggression is particularly frowned on in middle class families, although protection from aggression is not discouraged.

Bronfenbrenner (1958) has also indicated, however, that such differences may be disappearing as a result of the increased communication of "proper practices" of child rearing to all levels. There still remains, in spite of the leveling influences of mass media, a differential in the extent of information gained. Upper and middle classes are more apt to expose themselves to such information and to assimilate it. Some information does filter down, however, to groups below.

VALUES, ATTITUDES, AND NORMS

The middle class has been known popularly for being most concerned with conformity to generally accepted standards of behavior in a society. There may be some basis in this, as evidenced by reports of fewer social problems.

Prestige is a prime motivator for middle class individuals. Since achievement is also valued highly in the middle strata, education, the most common avenue to achievement, is also valued. More children of upper and middle class families plan to go to college, and most of those do enter and finish a program. There is not the same expectation by or pressure from lower class parents. Finances may represent part of the problem, yet they do not explain away the difference entirely since the patterns of difference have persisted even recently when financial support has become less of a concern. Hyman (1953) has summarized the data by stating "that there is a reduced striving for success among the lower classes, an awareness of lack of opportunity, and a lack of valuation of education, normally the major avenue to achievement of high status."

The feelings in lower class individuals of lack of opportunity may be part of broader personality patterns. Hollingshead and Redlich (1958) noted a deep distrust of authority figures in the lowest strata. Hostility and feelings of being exploited by political officials permeated the behavior of many of those at the bottom of the social scale. Feelings like this lead easily to lack of confidence and feelings of inferiority. In the same way, individuals at the top of the social scale find it very easy to feel superior and to justify it on the basis of intrinsic abilities or exceptional achievement.

Moderation in those two sensitive areas, religion and politics, seems to be more likely in the middle and upper classes. Strong feelings in the lower strata are apt to be expressed in either radical terms in the political area or in very emotional religious activity.

Styles of life and taste in virtually all areas may vary with class placement. While stereotypes can be misleading here as in consumer patterns, social class differences can be identified with respect to factors such as taste in entertainment and use of leisure time. Even a decreasing gap between spendable income has not eliminated differences in the way money is spent. Polo and bowling belong at opposite social poles. Choices of clothing or home furnishings may show more subtle differences such as place of purchase or type of material rather than general style differences. More subtle still, yet just as important to the interested entrepreneur, is the indication by Katona and Mueller (1954) that upper and lower class individuals are more prone to purchase with less deliberation than the middle class persons who are likely to ponder over the prospective purchase to a considerable degree (see Chapter 19).

Groups

A social group is an important unit in the total structure of a society. When we speak of a group, we mean something more than just a number of persons under study. There is agreement among researchers that *interaction* of some nature must take place. Newcomb (1950, p. 492) points this out. "A group consists of two or more persons who share norms about certain things with one another and whose social roles are closely interlocking." Through interaction, the group is the point of focus for all individual activity that is affected by others. This means virtually all of human behavior.

Groups may be classified in many ways. We may concentrate on size; in this instance, we may speak of small groups, ranging from dyads (two persons) or some arbitrary and low number up to larger aggregates.

Groups may be listed as *primary* or *secondary* depending on the degree of intimacy or the directness of the relationships. Primary groups are ones with opportunities for close and frequent face-to-face contacts. Secondary groups are ones where contacts are impersonal and infrequent and where interaction is on a remote plane.

Groups may also be considered from the standpoint of whether rules for organization and behavior are clearly delineated or not. A set of rules for a structured body determines a *formal* group, while a system of interaction that operates casually and spontaneously for some of the same ends is apt to be known as the *informal* group.

A classification according to function might also be made. The purpose for which the group exists is the basis for a breakdown into religious, social, educational, economic, political, or family groups. Such classifications may be made even more precise by subdividing them in different ways.

Groups also may be considered as being either *membership* or *reference* groups. The former are those to which the individual belongs, and the latter are those in which he would like to function. The two may or may not be the same; if not, the aspirations toward the reference group may have more influence on individual behavior.

Some researchers differentiate further between *in-groups* and *out-groups*. In-groups are those with norms accepted by a dominant element within an aggregate, while the out-groups represent concepts considered to be of lesser prestige and value. What is "in" or "out" may vary from time to time or may differ with location.

Groups are of prime importance in understanding social behavior, and the study of specific kinds of groupings may be even more important to researchers of certain areas such as business. The pervasiveness and the influence of the group, particularly the small primary entities, makes a more complete discussion mandatory. Small groups will be the topic for Chapter 15.

Organizations

Associations consisting of a larger number of individuals are often known by that name but are more likely to be designated as organizations. This type of aggregate is, basically, no more than a group with characteristics that would enable one to classify it according to the systems outlined immediately above. To say that organizations are merely larger in size than small groups is not, however, the entire story. Complexity and formality accompany the characteristic of larger size and make the organization a more challenging subject for description than if it were simply a large grouping. Colleges and universities, business firms, social clubs, labor unions, and churches are all organizations, and even a casual listing such as this can give rise to many inferences about the variety and complexity of the behavior to be studied. For this reason, a more detailed view of organizations is contained in Chapter 16.

Institutions

Large aggregates with norms that govern the behavior of the members can be called *institutions*. This kind of conglomerate of individuals is sometimes held together tightly by a common bond, but most often it is the representation of a common set of values and an allegiance to one unifying concept or title. Institutions may be identified as political, economic, military, educational, or religious. The family could be considered an institution as well and is treated as such by many social researchers. It is important to note, however, that this refers to the broad concept of family—not to a single specific example which would be labeled a primary group.

The term institution does show some variation in application. As it is used here, it points directly to an aggregate governed by norms. Some researchers prefer to focus on a set of patterns of behavior that are normative in a given social setting. In this view one would speak of proportional representation, for instance, rather than a political party. The aggregate rather than the pattern is more likely to be the focus of attention, however, primarily because of the greater opportunity to arrange the data neatly.

POLITICAL INSTITUTIONS

Today the most visible structural unit for political behavior is the nation or political state. The nation is a relatively recent creation in most parts of the world, however; for much of history, the kinship group or the local community were the unifying forces. The limitation of perspective in the tribal community inhibits the functioning of a larger political entity. When, on one basis or another, a nation develops, the structural change results in a breaking down of local barriers with a concomitant integration into a uniform system that permits a more effective political structure to function. The emerging nations of the world are now following in the paths set by many Western nations as little as a century ago.

Structuring within the nation can take place along authoritarian or democratic lines. Either system, however, depends on reliable individuals to administer the activities of the state. A rational and impersonal handling of governmental duties is the hallmark of a *bureaucracy,* a virtual necessity, as Weber (1946) pointed out, for a political entity to function as a modern state.

Structuring in a democracy further takes place in the development of political parties in order for the members to play a more effective role in the political process. The relationship between basic social factors and politics is quite close. Apparently, parties in all Western countries represent three tendencies—those of the "left" have working class biases, the privileged conservatives are on the "right," and the middle classes fill the center (Bendix and Lipset, 1957). Yet political parties cannot hope to remain in the majority without attempts to phrase issues more broadly and to appeal to a wider constituency. Attempts to limit a party to a single class are bound to fail, especially in a modern industrial country. In developing or more rigidly stratified countries, parties may develop successfully along class lines or there may be regional, religious, or urban-rural bases for the structuring.

The impact of political activity in daily life is significant enough for further discussion. The dynamics of politics and more detailed data on behavior will be treated in later sections (Chapters 12 and 18).

ECONOMIC INSTITUTIONS

Without doubt the greatest impact on economic functioning has been that stemming from industrialization. The advent of industrial life brings with it more than rapid change and immediate behavioral responses. It introduces a newer and more extensive social structuring and organizational grouping. Institutions such as the business firm and the labor union owe their place in society to the changes acompanying industrialization. On the same basis, the increase in some problems of human relationships bears some scrutiny.

The rise of capitalism followed the breakdown of the feudal order. No longer bound to the lord of the manor or dependent on him, the worker was free to move wherever he might receive more for his services. Where the emphasis was on ascribed status in a fixed and structured society, the changed circumstances enhanced the opportunities for an achieved status on the basis of freedom of choice. The advent of a religious outlook based on individual responsibility further hastened the economic development (as in the Reformation, particularly creeds such as Calvinism). When science and technology contributed to the vast changes under way, the picture of industrial Western civilization approached that of the present day.

Industrialization brings with it a new and more complex system of stratification. There are more and different roles to be filled in a technological society; each new task in industry requires not only different skills but more complex ones as well. It has been noted also that more subtle changes are produced in the economy. An increase in bureaucratization takes place with a concomitant emphasis on the organization over the individual. The size of the labor force declines, and the number of individuals in service occupations increases. There is greater value placed on innovation—the "faith in technological progress" (Berelson and Steiner, 1964, p. 400). It is realistic to suggest, further, that almost all economic or even social relationships are affected by the changes brought about by industrialization.

EDUCATION

Educational institutions are important socializers in their own right, but they do not function independently of other social factors. Political and economic institutions help shape educational structure and functioning and, in turn, are influenced by the intellectual and social processes within the school systems.

The school has long been the one vehicle for the transmission of basic cultural premises as part of the educational process. The values of the school system that get transmitted are those, by and large, of the teachers and administrators. These are generally from the middle class, and they impart middle class values. One of the topics under serious consideration is whether this middle class orientation of the educational authorities puts lower class children at a disadvantage.

The relationship between social stratification and education, particularly at higher levels, has been stated often. Brim (1958) supports this in noting that, while intelligence is still a factor in the determination of who goes to college, when this is held constant there is still a difference between class levels in college attendance. After they get there, even more uniformity in attitudes and values along class lines is attained by the end of the four-year program (Jacob, 1957).

A further illustration of the interrelationships of institutions and other social variables can be seen in the link between educational level and income. Miller (1960) has shown that college graduates earn almost twice as much, on the average, as high school graduates.

Completed elementary school	$ 4,337
Completed high school	6,295
Some college	8,682
Completed college	12,269

These figures are from 1958, and there is some indication that the gaps are increasing.

To summarize in somewhat oversimplified form, stratification is reinforced as individuals from higher strata are more likely to go further in school, be available for better positions, and be able to provide more for their children who will go further in school, and so on. There is movement up from the lower strata through education, but it requires more effort and is not as likely to happen.

THE FAMILY

Conceiving of the family as an institution introduces more concepts of structure and functioning than the consideration of a family as a small and primary group. The broad social and behavioral facets of family functioning generally provide a foundation for further discussion of the dynamics of the individual family unit.

The family (or marriage, if one views this as the institution) exists, without any exception, in all known societies (Murdock, 1949); any variations in structure relate to the conception of who belongs. The family may be thought of as only the *nuclear* family consisting of husband, wife, and children, or the unit may be the larger *extended* family composed of those related by "blood." In Western society the small nuclear family is treated almost exclusively as the basic unit, while in other societies husband, wife, and children do not live off by themselves away from numerous relatives. Even within Western culture, however, there may be some subtle differences. Lower class individuals may conceive of themselves as being part of an extended family, while middle and upper classes may be more concerned with independence from relatives and greater privacy.

Other classifications may be made on the basis of number of persons in the marriage. The division may be made between:

(a) *Monogamy*—one man, one woman.

(b) *Polygamy*—more than one partner; this can be one man, two or more women (polygyny), or one woman, two or more men (polyandry).

The authority may be *patriarchal* (father dominant), *matriarchal* (mother rules), or equalitarian (equal dominance). Descent may be important in that in some societies rights accrue through a relationship in the female line (matrilineal). We may be more used to a *patrilineal* (through the father) or *bilineal* system. In Western society the importance of lineal concepts may have been stronger in past emphases, such as in *primogeniture,* the inheritance by first-born males or in the passage of property or titles through the father. Then, as now, the importance of a marriage relationship was emphasized by limiting inheritance of a child born out of wedlock to the mother's family.

In all societies most adults are married; this is especially true in agrarian, tradition-based, or simpler societies such as in India or other Asian countries. While the percentage of unmarried adults in those areas may be well under 5 percent (Davis and Blake, 1956), the comparable figure in more industrialized areas would be four to five times as high. In the United States, for instance, the unmarried represent about 20 percent of the population over age 14 (United States Department of Commerce, 1966).

Even in those societies where there is freedom of choice in selection of a marriage partner, that choice is restricted in practice by geographic limits. A large percentage of marriages are contracted by persons from the same neighborhood or within the same area. It may not be the "girl next door," but it is likely to be one not too far away.

Not only are the marriage partners more likely to be from the same geographic area, but they are also likely to be from the same stratum of the society, be of the same race and religion, and perhaps even share some physical characteristic (height or color of eyes, for example) as well (Goode, 1961, p. 428). Thus, the factors at work in mate selection further reinforce the stratification in society that is developed on the other social bases already mentioned above. A similarity in attitudes and values in mates and peers provides easy transmission of these to their children who, in turn, perpetuate these same patterns.

The family can be said to have the function of societal maintenance. Not only does it develop and maintain individuals in a pool for productive support for society, but it transmits to each person the attitudes and values of the culture as well. This socialization of individuals is the basic avenue by which there is control to bring about conformity with the needs of an ordered society. The family is used as a fundamental unit by other institutions, and changes in it are reflected by other aspects of society. Considerable evidence is present of a shift from the role of the family as a producing unit in the economy to a role as a unit of consumption (Broom and Selznick, 1963, p. 360).

The relationships between economic institutions and the family have shown some basic patterns. In simple agrarian societies children are usually an asset in that they start early to contribute to the growing of food. In a move from the soil to industrialization, children figured prominently; they often worked beside their parents as they had in the "cottage industry" of an earlier era.

Except for some part-time efforts in agriculture, children in Western society are less of an economic asset. The complex technological cast of the society calls for a longer period of dependency on adults. Education is increasingly desirable or even mandatory in order to perform effectively in industrial society. Added to earlier considerations about child welfare or fear of competition, the need for more skill has eliminated child labor in a technological environment.

The male adult has traditionally been the breadwinner in the family. A focus on this aspect, however, would distract attention from a development that has become of greater significance in business and industry in recent years. Women, including the married, have increased in number and significance in the labor force. Where, at the turn of the century, less than 5 percent of married women worked, now the figure ranges from 30 percent in the 20 to 30 age bracket to 40 percent between the ages of 35 and 65 (Broom and Selznick, 1963, p. 393).

This represents a significant change in attitude toward working married women. Previously the male breadwinner was considered a failure if his wife worked. Now, particularly at an age when children are grown or in school, married women are back in business in full force. They thus represent a significant aspect of the labor scene.

Even when not directly employed to supplement the family exchequer, the wife has a role that has increased in importance in a business setting. There may be scattered voices of concern over the demands of the business organization on the wife and family of the rising executive, but the importance of the conformity of wives to company norms remains. Whyte (1951, p. 88) lists some rules for wives of executives.

Don't talk shop gossip with the girls. . . .

Don't get too chummy with the wives of associates your husband might soon pass on the way up.

Be attractive. There is a strong correlation between executive success and the wife's appearance.

Never—repeat, never get tight at a company party (it might go down in a dossier).

These and other rules are intended to help the wife make it easy for her husband to stand the stress of work, late hours, frequent transfers, or other occupational hazards and work more effectively for the corporation.

Population and Placement

No study of social structure would be complete without a look at the major array of aggregates of people. The problem of population may, in the long run, dwarf all other concerns of professionals and citizens. The dynamic aspects of population, that is, the changes and relationships between factors over time, are the more significant ones for study. Social demography and ecology are the professional approaches to this body of data. Because most aspects of social functioning will be presented together in the next chapter (Chapter 12), only a basic identification of some structural factors will be made here.

The fundamental information about the number and types of individuals within a certain geographic or political area comes from a census. In the United States a census has been taken every ten years since 1790 to enumerate all the persons in the nation. In addition, there are other census surveys, including one for business which has been issued every five years since 1954. The decennial census also is broken down into smaller units, the *Census Tract,* for certain areas. These contain from 3000 to 6000 people for an area that is drawn to provide a homogeneous population. In 1960 there were 180 tract areas providing information on education, race, marital status, income, age, and national origin.

The results of a census give a static picture of the population, its composition, and geographic distribution. The sex ratio and age composition are the most basic bits of data. In 1960 the sex ratio in the United States was 97 (97 males to every 100 females). The number of boys born was greater than girls by 106 to 100, and the lower ratio for all ages reflects the increased mortality of males. Of added interest is the variation in the sex ratio by area. In 1960 the rural sex ratio was 104 while the urban one was 94. On a state basis, Alaska had the highest sex ratio (132) while Massachusetts had a low of 93.

Mortality and fertility can be determined readily from a sketch of the age composition of a population in any one year (Figure 11-3). A view and comparison of these population pyramids can give both a static picture and one of trends. The 1900 pyramid shows a high birth rate and a high death rate. In 1960 the death rate was lower, and the recent birth rate was still high. The pyramid also shows clearly the lower birth rate of the 1930's and the early 1940's in the reduced number of persons in the age brackets of ages 20–34.

Density of population is also of interest. England, for instance, has over 700 people per square mile, while the United States has more "elbow room" in having only about 68 persons per square mile. The implications of this in making comparisons with respect to behavior become clearer.

Furthermore, people are not likely to be found evenly distributed over the country. Industrialized nations have a higher percentage of their population in urban areas than do the countries where industry has yet to take hold.

The movement from the farms to the cities has accompanied the rise in industry for many years and, while the proportions may be leveling off, the spread of urban areas continues. This may well be the era of urban man.

The internal structure of the large city and any concomitant stratification have served as a topic for research for many years. As early as the 1920's, Park, Burgess, and McKenzie (1925) proposed the concept of concentric zones as a good way to describe the different areas of a city. These researchers sketched what looks like a target with, since they worked in Chicago, the *Loop* as the "bullseye." Outside the center, each ring could be identified as having a particular socioeconomic flavor. While this system may be helpful in trying to picture the structure of a city, in many cases some other sketch may be more accurate. Topography can make the concentric zone concepts inappropriate. Major transportation arteries can help promote an economic development along their lines, so that a city structure may look more like a many-armed star.

Grouping in the city may occur on a class or ethnic basis. People with similar identifications tend to live in the same general area. When moves further out to the suburbs take place, the choices of area are likely to be similar. Upper class and professional people are segregated into tight and exclusive

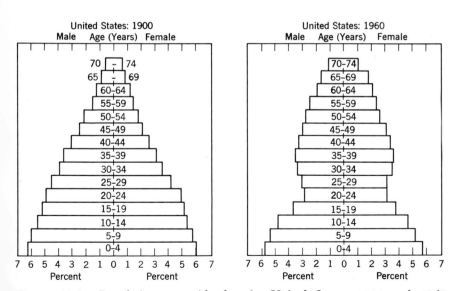

Figure 11-3. Population pyramids for the United States, 1900 and 1960 (Broom, L. and Selznick, P., 1963, p. 317).

residential areas while laborers and lower classes are, in their areas, just as homogeneous in their housing. Middle class and clerical workers show more variety in location. This resulting pattern has been called a U-shaped pattern of residence (Duncan and Duncan, 1955).

Summary

All human societies show differentiation among their members based on many factors such as age, sex, occupation, or virtually any other characteristic. In addition to treating individuals differently, a society develops strata, usually on a socioeconomic basis, that constitute a hierarchy of groups or social classes.

Individuals in a society occupy a position or status (actually there are many of these for a person) in that social grouping. Each position has a role attached to it embodying the pattern of behavior for that slot in society. The general evaluation by the larger group of the desirability of the status/role activity is prestige.

Grouping of individuals into a hierarchy called social classes occurs throughout the world. A more complex society may have more identifiable groupings; in addition there can be variation in the rigidity of these groupings. An "open" society permits more movements up and down the scale.

The bases for social stratification lie in general evaluation of individuals by others in the group. Criteria used in this evaluation show wide variation; occupation, income, education, race, religion, ethnicity, ancestry, manners, style of living, area of residence, public service, and authority or power may all be used to one extent or another. These criteria are viewed by objective researchers or by the subjects themselves in the determination of the strata. The number of classes can be determined arbitrarily. The number is not important; what is significant is that there is some consensus on the basic concepts and outlines of the system of stratification. People at each of the levels may have different views of what it takes to be a member of another stratum, but general placement is not difficult.

Within classes there may also be similar variations with respect to many variables, but the one characteristic tending to keep a social class together is that of a common set of attitudes among the members.

Some ties exist between class membership and behavior even though the exact relationships may be difficult to sketch exactly. Upper class individuals live longer and are more active in the community. Their religious and social patterns show qualitative differences from those of the lower class as well as indicate the quantitative differences. More basic is the disparity between classes in the child-rearing practices within the family. The different attitudes toward "proper" behavior at each level is the result of attitudes of individuals of that class. The pattern of behavior then further reinforces the attitude base of the individual and the group. Attitudes and values find further expression in political, religious, and economic behavior, all of which usually show class differences.

More concise groupings of individuals interacting for some purpose in common have been important in human affairs and thus have been of interest to researchers. While small groups may have been studied more intently, research has extended to larger entities. Apart from size, groups may be classified in many ways. The focus may be on the function performed by the group (family, religious, or political) or the interest may center on whether it is formally constructed or functions simply and informally. Primary groups meet face to face while secondary groups consist of individuals who interact in less direct or proximate ways. Many further conceptual references may be made in a consideration of group functioning.

An association of a larger number of individuals is known as an organization. The increase in size and complexity over small groups makes the study of organizations a challenging one. Business firms, universities, political parties, and churches represent significant organizational entities.

Institutions are large aggregates wherein the members are bound together by common norms or allegiance to a set of unifying concepts. Some behavioral scientists, however, focus instead on the patterns of normative functioning in the aggregate and label that the institution.

Political institutions emerge in a modern political state. Political parties arise on a social basis and may be related to other variables. Complexity of governmental duties and functions in a modern state requires the introduction of a corps of administrators, a bureaucracy, to maintain an effective and continuing governmental process.

In their development economic institutions can be related easily to political factors as well as to technological influences. Political and religious values emphasizing individual responsibility can be fostered in an increasingly open society. Science and technology bring with them attitudinal changes as sharp as the purely technical ones.

Educational institutions have helped to mold attitudes and behavior of those exposed to it. Not all those coming into contact with the educational "establishment" are affected in the same way, however, as those with attitudes similar to the pedagogues adapt more easily and reinforce the middle class attitudes to which they are exposed.

The family exists in all known societies, although the consideration of who belongs to it may vary. The number of male or female partners may exceed the single one of a monogamous society. Influence of the father or mother may predominate in addition to an inclusion of other relatives as part of the family group. Where choice of marriage partner exists, the selection of the mate can be remarkably similar to that which results from selection by parents. Partners are apt to come from near at hand and be similar in many variables.

Industrialization has influenced many family living patterns. A general move from the land to the factory has required the upgrading of skills. Social pressures have eliminated the child laborers once common in factories while concomitantly the role of women in industry, especially the working wives and mothers, has increased significantly.

A study of population and its placement reveals the general array of aggregates. Fundamental information comes from a census, usually organized along the lines of political divisions. Identification of variables such as age, sex, race, and education provides a profile of the population that is useful for many purposes. Density, location, birth rates, and deaths also may provide valuable patterns as the basic material is sketched.

Bibliography

Bendix, R. and Lipset, S. (1957). Political sociology: an essay and bibliography. *Current Sociology,* **6,** 79–169.

Berelson, B. and Steiner, G. (1964). *Human behavior.* New York: Harcourt, Brace and World.

Brim, O. (1958). *Sociology and the field of education.* New York: Russell Sage Foundation.

Bronfenbrenner, U. (1958). Socialization and social class through time and space. In Maccoby, E. et al. (eds.). *Readings in social psychology* (3rd ed.). New York: Holt, Rinehart and Winston.

Broom, L. and Selznick, P. (1958). *Sociology* (2nd ed.). New York: Harper and Row.

Centers, R. (1949). *The psychology of social classes.* Princeton: Princeton University Press.

Davis, A., Gardner, B., and Gardner, M. (1941). *Deep South: a social-anthropological study of caste and class.* Chicago: University of Chicago Press.

Davis, K. and Blake, J. (1956). Social structure and fertility: an analytic framework. *Economic Development and Social Change,* **4,** 211–235.

Duncan, O. and Duncan, B. (1955). Residential distribution and occupational stratification. *American Journal of Sociology,* **60,** 493–503.

Goode, W. (1961). Family disorganization. In Merton, R. and Nisbet, R. (eds.). *Contemporary social problems.* New York: Harcourt, Brace and World.

Hodge, R., Siegel, P. and Rossi, P. (1964). Occupational prestige in the United States, 1925–63. *American Journal of Sociology,* **70,** 286–302.

Hollingshead, A. and Redlich, F. (1958). *Social class and mental illness: a community study.* New York: Wiley.

Hyman, H. (1953). The value systems of different classes: a social psychological contribution to the analysis of stratification. In Bendix, R. and Lipset, S. (eds.). *Class, status and power: a reader in social stratification.* New York: Free Press.

Jacob, P. (1957). *Changing values in college: an exploratory study of the impact of college teaching.* New York: Harper and Row.

Katona, G. and Mueller, E. (1954). A study of purchase decisions. In Clark, L. (ed.). *Consumer behavior.* New York: New York University Press.

Linton, R. (1936). *The study of man.* New York: Appleton-Century-Crofts.

Mayer, A. and Hauser, P. (1953). Class differences in expectation of life at birth. In Bendix, R. and Lipset, S. (eds.). *Class, status, and power: a reader in social stratification.* Glencoe: Free Press.

Miller, H. (1960). Annual and lifetime income in relation to education: 1939–1959. *American Economic Review,* **50,** 962–986.

Murdock, G. (1949). *Social structure.* New York: Macmillan.

Newcomb, T. (1950). *Social psychology.* New York: Dryden.

Park, R., Burgess, E. and McKenzie, R., eds. (1925). *The city.* Chicago: University of Chicago Press.

Schneider, H. (1952). *Religion in 20th century America.* Cambridge: Harvard University Press.

United States Department of Commerce (1966). *Statistical abstract of the United States.* Washington: U.S. Government Printing Office.

Warner, W. and Lunt, P. (1941). *The social life of a modern community.* Yankee City Series, Vol. I. New Haven: Yale University Press.

Weber, M. (1946). *Max Weber: essays in sociology* (Gerth, H. H. and Mills, C. W., trans. and ed.). New York: Oxford University Press.

West, J. (1945). *Plainville, U.S.A.* New York: Columbia University Press.

Whyte, W. (1951). The wives of management. *Fortune,* **44,** 86 ff.

12

Social Process

In the previous chapter, the data represented static images of society in many of its ramifications. The presentation can give a misleading picture of social reality, however, since any behavior means action. The entire panorama of social behavior, therefore, cannot be seen without developing the dynamic aspects of society on the structural base built up earlier.

The individual and group forces at work in a social setting may be described in various ways. These processes involve change as a basic factor with conflict as a concomitant one. Understanding of influence and control processes adds further to the appreciation of the developments that arise from the base of social structure and its dynamics.

Development of the Social Individual

What we are in a society is due mainly to the way we have learned to respond to the influences of our social heritage and environment. It has been noted that, while there are certain biological factors of influence, the important variables are sociopsychological in nature. How the social setting is structured and how the learning in it takes place is of prime concern.

SOCIALIZATION

The process of incorporating the values of a group into the growing individual is called *socialization*. A leading sociology text (Broom and Selznick, 1963, p. 93) develops two perspectives, from the point of view of society and of the individual. From society's vantage point the individual is fitted into an organized way of life while the opportunity for the full unfolding of the person's potential emphasizes the individual aspects of socialization.

Thus the process not only deals with the transmission of attitudes, values, and beliefs, but it also serves as a means of development of individuality and awareness of self.

Socialization begins early in life. An earlier chapter (Chapter 4) has already traced the development of an individual through the life span where it was noted how other people are important in shaping the young individual. Adults, particularly parents and other family members, play a leading role in passing on their own attitudes and values as well as being the transmitters of broader cultural patterns. The impact of other people can be the result of a deliberate attempt to influence or it may follow without any conscious intent to do so. Attitudes can be transmitted very subtly as perceptive children recognize what is and is not done within the group.

Even more simple is a phenomenon arising out of the mere presence of other people. Having others in the room can make a difference in the performance of simple tasks by individuals even though there is no interaction among those present. This basic result was elaborated early in social research by Allport (1920) who labeled it *social facilitation.*

CONFORMITY TO NORMS

The rules that every society uses to point out what kind of behavior is desirable or appropriate are called *norms.* These guidelines for behavior are based on cultural values. "Cleanliness is next to godliness" reflects a norm that has recieved much support in the past, even though it may not be effective in segments of the population. Hard work and thrift may, in the same way, be less powerful guides than in previous periods.

Norms are fundamental to socialization. In this process the child incorporates the values of the society by being reinforced for following the rules. Conformity to norms is learned—rewards are in the form of social approval while punishment comes in the disapproval manifested in various ways. Ridicule can be very effective at all ages for those who do not know or follow the rules of conduct.

Aggregate Social Processes

As we have just seen, the impact of culture on the individual rests on the mediation of the cultural characteristics by others, primarily the parents. The family serves as the main channel through which the broad attitudes and values pass on to the child. The prior interactional processes of the primary group thus have their effect on single individuals, but they may be viewed in wider perspective. The changes that cultural patterns undergo and the concomitant changes in interaction among groups will be the subject of this aspect of the dynamics involved in social change.

A well-known example of an attempt to formulate a cohesive system (Parsons, 1951) emphasizes the interaction of many factors. The resultant "Theory of Action" focuses on individual actors interacting within a dynamic social setting wherein each actor develops a system of expectations.

CHANGE AS A BASIC PROCESS

An old statement, attributed by some to Benjamin Franklin, has it that "we can be certain of nothing except death and taxes." To this we can add "change" for we may be sure that no matter what else occurs, change is inevitable. We may not recognize it or otherwise be cognizant of it; we may oppose it or we may even try to accelerate it. No matter what our position may be, change makes its course in the evolution of human effort. Change may take place so slowly that it is not perceptible in one generation, or even two, or it may occur with such rapidity that we are left somewhat breathless in the wake of the waves.

Society is not a static system; it is in a dynamic state and constantly undergoing change. This is so for large systems or aggregates as well as for smaller systems or groups. And even more fundamental to society is the extension of the concept right to the ultimate unit—the individual.

On an individual basis, the most important factor may well be learning. This variable is nothing more than a change process, and the modification of behavior that takes place in learning can be considered the most basic change process of all.

Concepts of Change

Few argue the validity of the concept of change even though views of its bases vary widely. We may move from the elaborate, though less than scientific, views of Marx to the various new behavioral approaches toward an understanding of basis for change. On a broad scale, Toynbee (1948) looks for purposeful patterns in the emergence and decline of civilizations and draws upon the cyclic concepts of the Greeks and Indians with modification by the Jewish-Zoroastrian view of an unknowable divine plan.

A more molecular approach along these lines is illustrated by Mannheim

(1941) who describes the historical developments underlying change as proceeding from "trial and error" experiments of an individual to more deliberate approaches. The next phase in the process is the stage of inventing, where activities have to be thought out in advance. This concept goes beyond the production of a technological product and includes the "invention" of an elaborate organizational structure and process. The final stage historically is characterized by planning and planned thinking. This planned approach marks a long step from trial and error in that it not only recognizes individual goals but also understands what effect these will have on the broader goals in the entire pattern of relationships.

It could be said that Mannheim was not only painting a broad picture of developments in society but one that could be descriptive of events within a short period, as in community redevelopment in many specific urban situations at the present time.

In more limited and more precisely studied organizational settings, Selznick (1949) looks to forces affecting organizations from the outside and analyzes the adaptations as the consequences of these forces. Barnard (1938) concentrates more on the forces creating a push toward unity in the grouping. Selznick focuses on the aspects producing change, and Barnard on the persistence of organizational forms and the forces that keep a group in equilibrium.

Social Change

Earlier discussions of culture (Chapter 10) introduced factors associated with change. Only brief mention of some of these factors need be made here along with the additional reminder that the attitudes toward change are in themselves cultural products. In Western society, particularly in North America, practically no one remains neutral in feelings about change. There may be more positive attitudes toward finding new and "better" ways to do things, but there are also some emotional resistances to the notion.

Since the culture of a people is not unrelated to the environment, some changes in the environment may produce different patterns of behavior. Climatic conditions have not changed very drastically, however, over relatively long periods. Man's increasing ability to control aspects of the environment may provide the opportunity for witnessing more changes in behavioral patterns than has been possible in the past.

The impact of technology has been felt through the centuries. Historians have traced the growth of societies and related changes in living patterns with the introduction of agricultural innovations or the discovery of new materials. In describing progress from the Stone Age to the Bronze and then to the Iron Age, we could focus on the innovations in material without really illustrating the profound changes that accompanied those elements. A similar ordering by Mumford (1934) describes the developing industrial society in terms of certain characteristics.

Phase	Era	Material	Power
Eotechnic	1000–1750 A.D.	Wood	Wind and water
Paleotechnic	1750–Date	Iron	Coal
Neotechnic	Date	Alloy	Electricity

It may be added that atomic energy may be more a characteristic power source for the future. J. A. C. Brown (1954) has elaborated on this outline to provide a broader picture of the behavioral concomitants. In each phase, Brown says, the ideology formulated by the decision makers explained the social order or justified the social organization. Each era thought its patterns to be "right" and "natural."

Even with positive attitudes toward the introduction of new methods, there is usually a time lag between the availability of a technological innovation and the general acceptance of it. This delay, *culture lag,* has been demonstrated by the case of the typewriter (Chapter 10). Culture lag, however, extends beyond acceptance of technology. In the area of social interaction, from stratification to primary relations, the gap between old patterns and the necessary new relationships may be great. These social factors may or may not be related to technological change.

Recent events bear witness to the widespread activity involved in the links between technological and social change. For instance, mechanization of agriculture, particularly in the South, has reduced the need for human labor. Existence, though marginal, was eked out as long as some farm labor was necessary. Increased automation in the fields has sent farm hands, White and Negro, to urban areas, even to distant Northern cities. Most of the cities have been ill-prepared to accommodate the influx of large numbers of people to whom the changes mean a traumatic readjustment of behavior and attitudes. The increase in density of population served to magnify already serious problems of housing and intergroup relations.

Migration of the type just sketched and the more extensive intercontinental movements of peoples have undoubtedly demonstrated their cultural impact. Carr-Saunders (1936) estimated that over 34 million immigrants came to the United States, chiefly from Europe, during the period from 1821 to 1932; the total number coming to the Western Hemisphere has been estimated at 70 million people. This represents the largest movement of peoples in history. Even with the mass migration, however, the United States Census figures never showed more than 14 million foreign born and these always represented less than 15 percent of the total population. This will undoubtedly show a decline even more in both absolute and proportional terms. Although the cultural input to the American "melting pot" has been extensive, the newcomers have been molded even more by the receiving majority.

Change in Groups

The process of change in small groups and organizations occupies the attention of many researchers in various applied areas—industry, education, the military, and government. The critical nature of the process is recognized in the light of the need to function effectively in the midst of rapidly developing social and technological events.

The responses to change are conditioned both by individual factors and those relating to the nature and functioning of the group. Attitudes, motivation, and ability play a role within the broad area of individual personality. Group factors such as communication enter the picture as well. The interrelatedness of all these factors within specific patterns of change in social groups is a topic of importance to be treated again in later chapters (15 and 16).

Individual Factors in Change

The broad outlines sketched above have implied or even pointed to the necessity of considering psychological factors in attempts to understand the processes of change more fully. Personality variables may well be the most important ones to consider in any change procedures, since broader cultural and social factors are not likely to be under the control of a change agent.

Attitudes are very basic to the functioning of individuals. These are predispositions of tendencies to respond in one direction or another to a set of circumstances (see Chapter 13). One might have a positive attitude toward something new or be predisposed to react negatively to novel events. The position of the person may be noted on a continuum, the poles of which can be labeled in various ways. The most popular designations are *conservative* and *liberal* but these, as many others, are unsatisfactory for various reasons. First of all, the terms arouse emotional reactions that may cloud an understanding of what is really meant by them. More important is the fact that an individual will not show an unvarying response in all areas. Attitudes may be expected to show some variation. One may be "conservative" in education yet "liberal" in morals. The generality of such terms is thus open to question. With this warning provided, it is still true that we often use the quick and easy term "conservative" to label those who favor the status quo while those open to change are "liberal."

Attitudes, as will be seen, are learned in the very same way that other material is learned. The family is the prime source of attitudes, surpassing the peer group or other agencies outside the family in this respect (Newcomb and Svehla, 1937).

Motivation must be considered as an equally important factor in individual responses to change. It may seem superfluous to state that change will not be accepted unless the need for change is felt by the individuals involved. What was earlier expressed as "you can lead a horse to water but you can't make him drink" has its delineation in countless industrial and educational situations. The specific needs may not be easy to identify, however, since the simplest situations may represent a complex interaction of all types of needs and drives, conscious and unconscious (Barnett, 1953).

Factors such as age are often considered to be related to attitudes, but there are enough exceptions noted to cause some reservations on this point. It may be that youth is liberal and old age is conservative yet enough "old maids" (male and female) exist at age 20 to help us avoid the stereotype.

All of the variables that may play a role in change must be evaluated in combination. As a result of this approach, a picture emerges that may be representative of the agent of social change or of the acceptor of new developments. Sargent and Williamson (1958, p. 515) identify the most likely innovator as a deviant individual in society—"certainly nonconformist and unorthodox." These labels are neutral in themselves although the nonconforming majority often reacts to them in a negative and emotional way. This, too, is an indication of the very attitudes under discussion here.

Finally, it must be remembered that even the individual factors related to change are themselves susceptible to change. Attitudes can be altered through direct measures, or the changes may take place over time as the result of less recognizable forces. Newcomb's (1943) classic study of the liberalization of student attitudes with exposure to Bennington College norms is an old example. A well-known study from industry (Coch and French, 1948) describes the positive responses to a direct introduction of change procedures.

ACCOMMODATION

The process of adjustment that takes place when individuals accede to various compromises or develop working relationships in order to be able to function together is called accommodation. This relatively stable state is preceded by a period of conflict and differences among individuals or between the parties. A married couple reaches a point where there is a recognition of what can or cannot be done to preserve a relationship of harmonious equilibrium. Labor-management relations are characterized by accommodation processes such as arbitration, negotiation, conciliation, or compromise.

ASSIMILATION

Assimilation is the melting of individuals with previously diverse backgrounds into the general society to the point where attitudes and values are held commonly in that society. The immigrant who comes to this country finds himself faced with new patterns and styles of life. The accompanying value structures may be slowly adopted by him until his ways of thinking are those prevalent in the environment. This does not mean a complete abandonment of previous patterns of behavior or a lack of contribution to the community by the incoming individual. It is true, however, that the total fusion of thought and action patterns is closer to that of the host environment.

Many Northern communities are experiencing the problems of assimilation of migrants from the different social setting the South has fostered. Both Whites and Negroes face the difficulty of first learning the new patterns and then adopting these ways. When this process is complete, or nearly so, the fusion of social concepts and behavior is assimilation. The process may not be as complex in a limited environment such as business or industry. The fusion of workers into the general job patterns may come more easily than the assimilation into the community at large, yet even this restricted setting may provide tensions that are difficult to reduce for workers and supervisors alike.

ALIENATION

While the two processes above are ones where social forces lead to a coalescence, alienation is a tendency in the other direction. A worsening of race relations is an example of alienation as is an increasing gap between union and company in a deteriorating labor dispute. On both a group and an individual basis, the drawing apart from others or society at large is the socially debilitating process of alienation.

One of the earliest developers of the concept of alienation was Karl Marx. It was his hypothesis that the technology of an industrial and capitalist economy was responsible for the alienation of the working man from society by depriving him of the control over and responsibility for his livelihood. The isolation from ownership of property or the means of production and a growing loss of meaning lead to decline in initiative and freedom that is part of alienation. Marx later concentrated on waging the class struggle between workers and owners under the capitalist system. Perhaps this kept him from recognizing that alienation is not peculiar to a capitalist system but is recognizable in industrial societies generally. A researcher can also postulate a negative relationship between the amount of craftmanship or control of the work on the one hand and alienation on the other. The less important the person in the process (as in an assembly line), the more alienation there will be.

In a society at large, the supporters of negative or extreme solutions to social problems are apt to be those who display the highest degree of alienation. Horton and Thompson (1962) found that a mass turnout of persons of low income and education was responsible for the defeat of a school bond campaign in two New York communities. Those who felt left out of the power structure and who seldom participated in community activities were thus the alienated ones. They were also likely to be critical of education or to feel threatened by the activities of leaders of the community. Table 12-1 indicates the extent

Table 12-1. Negative Voting among Taxpayers (from Horton, J. and Thompson, W., 1962)

Attitudes of Voters	Percentage Voting No on School Bond Issue	Percentage Turning Out to Vote
University town		
Alienated	70	85
Not alienated	18	90
Company town		
Alienated	84	82
Not alienated	37	91

of negative voting of the alienated ones. The picture of alienation extends to cynicism about political events and a deep distrust or suspicion of political leaders and strangers from outside the tight little community. The negative reactions of the alienated and anxiety-prone can develop easily into behavior more destructive than merely voting down school bond issues. Civil disturbances featuring rioting and looting have been increasingly prominent features of the national scene.

INTEGRATION

The term integration, when used with respect to social organization in its broadest outlines, refers to the amount of contact existing between social groups within the society. When groups exist in harmony within a central framework and can work with each other and communicate back and forth, the essential features for integration are present. Social control and, therefore, social order are achieved because of overlapping needs and the dependency of one group on the other.

ISOLATION

The lack of integration in a society is known as isolation. Isolation of groups within a society is a matter of degree, since complete isolation is not possible if a society exists. Groups within a society may be cut off from each other because of mutual rejection. The absence of some bond between the groups causes social conflict through lack of strong social control. Broom and Selznick (1963, p. 35) illustrate isolation by sketching the history of unions. In the early years of industrialization, membership in a union was regarded as participation in a criminal conspiracy. The rejection of the concept of unionism on all sides provoked extensive conflict between adherents of the union and those who were strongly opposed to the development of representation of empoyees. With the passage of time, changing attitudes, and legislation reflecting those changes in attitudes, unions and their members became more and more integrated into the community. In some quarters the transition may be seen as incomplete, but the communication and a common outlook between all those involved is well advanced.

ANOMIE

A "normlessness" that results from an individual departure from group values is anomie. The term was coined long ago by the French sociologist Emile Durkheim, who, in his book on *Suicide* (1951) emphasized the need for sharing of values to curb egoistic drives and maintain group stability. A deviance from the consensus is anomie, a state that contributes to social conflict.

More recently, Merton (1957, pp. 131–194) has expanded Durkheim's concepts to focus on the relationship between means and ends. Anomie and deviance can arise when either the end value or the means to it (or both) are lacking. An individual, says Merton, can accept the value of pecuniary success in our culture (there is great pressure to this effect) but not have the means to achieve it. The stress may tempt him to use illegal or inappropriate means to reach the goal. The resulting deviation from values adds to isolation or alienation on any other basis.

Collective Behavior

The study of amorphous and largely unorganized social interaction is the area commonly designated as collective behavior. This is known also by the designation mass behavior. Pertinent studies deal with relatively immediate social situations such as crowds, riots, and mobs at one end of the scale to the somewhat more organized and broadly based social movements at the other end. This area also includes such social and economic phenomena as fads and fashions, cults, and crazes, as well as booms. Related phenomena are present in collective behavior and must be considered along with it. Rumor and propaganda, for instance, represent important aspects in the functioning of collectivities. A more detailed discussion on the latter factors will come in Chapter 14.

PROXIMATE INFLUENCE SITUATIONS

A glance at newspaper headlines may convince the reader that no discussion of social process can take place without the delineation of this area of behavior. A study of riots on the present-day social scene may prove interesting by itself, but the value of the study of collective behavior goes beyond this as these phenomena demonstrate again some of the basic factors in human behavior. More intriguing is the fact that these particular phenomena arise in spontaneous and highly dynamic situations that can provide information beyond what is gained in more constrained settings. This often emotional and shifting behavior seen in mass action adds to our understanding of social behavior even though much of collective activity may be more routine and less dramatic than the activity that makes the headlines.

Crowds

A loosely knit gathering of individuals in one place is commonly designated a crowd. There are, however, different kinds of assemblies that may be categorized under this heading. Some crowds may be very casual and passive or, at the opposite end of the continuum, the group may be quite emotional, expressive, or highly active. Viewed from another perspective, the mass may be an audience in a small theater, a congregation in a religious setting, a group attending a deliberative assembly, or spectators at a sports event. A wide range of emotions is possible in all of these settings.

A crowd that gets out of hand and displays aggression or other types of antisocial and destructive activity is then a mob. A mob has as its purpose a single idea, be it looting, lynching, or something similar. When more than one small group of individuals is involved in an antisocial activity, the situation can be called a riot. A riot involves widespread aggression and destruction of property, possibly by many different kinds of randomly acting crowds.

Panic

Panic is an uncoordinated and irrational response to fear. In their attempts to escape the source of the fear, people become disorganized and are unable to cope effectively with the situation. The response in panic is away from the precipitating situation and is, therefore, quite different from the pattern shown in the aggressive responses outlined above.

Rumor

Interesting by itself as an example of collective behavior, rumor is also important to note because it plays an important role in other forms of collective behavior. Rumors spring up in highly ambiguous and emotional situations, thereby helping to develop the other forms of mass behavior as well. A rumor is a "specific proposition for belief, passed along from person to person, usually by word of mouth, without reference to secure standards of evidence" (Allport and Postman, 1947, p. 34). It arises in situations of stress and is concerned with a topic of great interest to the individuals generating it or passing it along. There is not, however, much evidence on the matter, and this arouses even greater anxiety. How a rumor serves to provide meaning for an individual in an emotional state will be the subject for further discussion in Chapter 14.

BROAD INFLUENCE PROCESSES

While the study of crowds and related phenomena focuses on the influence of immediate and transitory events, behavior is shaped also by more extensive influence processes arising from longer-lasting social events. These probably have more economic and political impact in the long run than do the short and limited collective processes.

Fashion

Fashion may be described as a socially sanctioned variation in material form or activity. Changes in dress, life style, music, or art constitute areas in our culture where fashion is an important factor. Automobile manufacturers, furniture designers, and song pluggers from "Tin Pan Alley" all find their livelihood closely tied to their abilities to predict or influence the flow of fashion choices. The most dynamic and obvious variations, however, come in the area of women's apparel. Even individuals insensitive to the vagaries of style are aware of the sometimes rapidly changing fabrics and forms that develop in the area of women's high-fashion clothing. Men's fashion changes are less peceptible. While the height of women's skirts may change very drastically over short periods of time, the style changes in men's apparel have been quite conservative until very recently.

Fads

A limited and more superficial manner of dress or other behavior is called a fad. These come and go very quickly. Fads have less acceptance than fashions although they may be quite prevalent in particular areas or age groups. Goldfish swallowing of an earlier era has given away to hulahoops and telephone booth stuffing. The Davy Crockett fad of the mid 1950's has its counterpart in the cartoon character from "Peanuts" in the second half of the 1960's. Some fads get wide enough acceptance to be classified as fashions—blue jeans and bingo may be called fashions by virtue of their persistence and the sanctioning of their use by larger social groups.

Crazes

A pattern of activity that is more emotional and more intensive than a fad can be called a craze. It may sometimes be difficult to distinguish between a fad, a craze, and a fashion. Crazes, however, should have greater involvement by the individual in the patterns of behavior as well as represent greater departures from the norms in a society as a whole. Where an activity becomes the overwhelming preoccupation, as in the chain letter mania of the depression years or the witchcraft mania of the sixteenth and seventeenth centuries, the feverish activity represents much more than the mere adoption of small bits of behavior. When this emotional involvement tends to show some continuing organization, it may be said to represent a *cult*. The earlier adolescent crazes surrounding Frank Sinatra or Jimmy Dean turned into regular ongoing fan clubs, and the death of Dean was not enough to eliminate the cult completely. Fans of jazz and "rock" continue to communicate with one another in almost mystical tones. The cult of sun worshippers or other groups of individuals emotionally involved with some unifying central concepts, sometimes with religious overtones, represent further illustrations of the cult phenomena.

Booms

A more expansive and economic involvement than a craze can be called a boom. Booms usually represent responses to get-rich-quick schemes. The tulip mania in seventeenth century Holland, where the price of ordinary tulip bulbs skyrocketed to fantastic heights, is an example of a boom. The California gold rush found millions of "forty-niners" moving westward to make their fortunes. Similar minor land booms have occurred and are still occurring in various parts of the country though none recently has matched the celebrated land boom in Florida in the early 1920's.

Social Movements

Collective action on a broad scale to change the status quo and move to a better life can be designated as a social movement. These are more or less structured, large-scale organizational activities that gain a favorable reception from those disadvantaged by current events or frustrated by and insecure in the social changes taking place. Social movements are new and yet unorganized groupings that emerge as a response to a fairly widespread interest in changing the status quo, though by moderate methods rather than radical ones such as revolution. Goals may be so broad as to be somewhat unclear but are generally cast in humanitarian terms and advocated with zeal and crusading spirit by the members (Sargent and Williamson, 1958, p. 524). To be effective in its activities, the social movement must adopt certan measures of a highly practical nature. Leadership must be of the best, but it must be supplemented with a plan of action and an ideology. Watchwords, banners, and rituals add to the emotional state of the membership.

Up until the passage of the 18th Amendment shortly after World War I, the temperance movement was a powerful social and political movement. The Women's Christian Temperance Union and the Anti-Saloon League crusaded vigorously for prohibition and exercised effective control in state legislatures throughout the nation. During the depression, the Townsend Plan represented a social movement. Appealing primarily to the aged and the economically insecure, Dr. Townsend's program to aid the economy (it was highly impractical in the economic sense) brought out thousands of enthusiastic people singing "Onward Townsend Soldiers" to the tune of "Onward Christian Soldiers" at meetings and gatherings held throughout the land. At the present time, the civil rights movement may be considered as a social movement. It has not, however, been as crystallized and clear an entity as some of those seen in the past; the efforts at gaining the rights of citizenship for Negro citizens in the United States have been split somewhat. There are, however, certain factors in this overall general movement that may be strong enough to stand by themselves as an identifiable entity.

While the revival movement, as exemplified particularly by the Reverend Billy Graham, has achieved some social impact, it probably falls short of meeting the characteristics for a social movement. Moral Rearmament, on the other hand, may represent a more cohesive and continuing religious revival that has all the characteristics of a full-fledged social movement.

FACTORS IN COLLECTIVE BEHAVIOR

An understanding of collective behavior may never be attained completely, but some awareness of the social and psychological bases for the behavior may be sought. While there is much variety in collective behavior, as in other social events, certain elements can be occasionally identified.

General Characteristics

Collective behavior manifests some general aspects that may be described casually as being products of an ambiguous and changing social situation. Rapid change brings with it new and emotionally tinged values. The high degree of insecurity in the change is brought about to a large degree by the absence of any guides or social forms. People do not know what to do and, since authorities do not have any answers either, the decisions are reached on a quick and competitive basis (Broom and Selznick, 1963, p. 256). On these bases for instability in collective behavior, one can add other factors present in more specific types of collective behavior.

Emotional Contagion

Emotional contagion refers to a mood the individuals in the group or crowd have in common. A shared set of emotions can be seen in a highly excited mob or in the restrained aura of a religious service. While very dramatic events may etch themselves on our memory, it must be remembered that emotional contagion is present in quiet and routine settings as well. With a prevailing common mood, people have a tendency to act in much the same way. They get support from others in their behavior and are especially sensitive to other people's activity. The behavior further reinforces the similar behavior of others, and the process becomes a circular one. When the individuals in the group share common needs and attributes, the common behavior patterns are even more firmly ingrained. A civil rights march into a small and cohesive white neighborhood, for instance, is likely to encounter a very strong response from virtually all of the residents reacting with common emotions and behaviors.

Other mob scenes and riots illustrate the freedom from the usual restraints felt by many people who have strong ties to a norm group in this highly emotional state. Mass media can extend the size of this group as others who hear the news become emotionally involved. Of course, the further away individuals are, the weaker the contagion; those who are present in person are most involved.

The significance of emotional contagion to the individuals involved may serve as an explanation of the phenomenon. There may be a psychological unity where few other opportunities exist for social participation; there are no entrance requirements for this group—membership is as extensive as the communication of the contagion. Emotional contagion also provides for the release of impulses that would otherwise be discouraged or prohibited.

Broad Patterns

Fashion has fascinated observers for centuries. Various suggestions as to the impact of fashions on human behavior have been made in the past. There is general agreement that the reasons for fashions center on the need for some prestige or recognition and the pull of conformity in order to achieve that recognition. Sherif and Cantril (1947, p. 349) have, for instance, determined that clothes serve to "extend the self of the wearer, to enhance his ego, to display his status." Other suggestions have centered on apparel as compensation for inferiority or as a means of expression of exhibitionistic or aggressive tendencies. Comfort and convenience, while they may be a consideration, play a relatively minor role compared with some of these dynamic features. Widespread variations for reasons other than comfort indicate a relatively low importance placed on utility.

A pinpointing of the bases of fads proves to be even more frustrating for researchers. The highly transient nature of the phenomena makes it very difficult to collect any reliable information on most of the factors surrounding this dynamic and short-lived collective behavior.

Apparently fads find a rapidly changing society congenial to their development and dissemination; certainly novelty is an important determiner of success. It might be further hypothesized that fads must fit with the stream of culture, especially the interests and motivations of a broad segment of the target population, although advertising and promotion can provide much of the impetus where knowledge or interest is weak. Some of the same elements noted in fashions play a role in fads, as might be expected. Fads are most popular among teenagers at an age when they want reassurance that they are doing the "right thing." A high degree of conformity to the behavior of other individuals in the same age group does help spread the fad in a very short period of time. Status anxiety appears to be a dominant factor in the spread of fads among adolescents and sometimes even adults. The emergence of particular fads among subordinate minorities seems to be quite common as well (the relationship between long hair and social protest groups has been noted even by casual observers). Apparently this represents an additional protest against the more conventional society on the outside.

In crazes and booms the irrationality of behavior encountered is even more evident than in fads and fashions. Apart from the promotional efforts in their behalf, Frank Sinatra and Elvis Presley probably served to satisfy certain needs among adolescents. Perhaps the same basic needs for recognition and acceptance of the adolescent were met in these situations. Conformity undoubtedly contributed to the buildup in numbers of individuals belonging to the cults.

Social Mobility

Our look at the structure of society disclosed the presence of two or more layers, or strata, that emerged on a socioeconomic basis. These different levels in the social hierarchy are not static, however, since individuals within them are likely to show movement even in relatively fixed societies. Movement through the various strata may be either downward or upward; this is vertical mobility and is the situation usually thought of when the term social mobility is used. There may, however, be even more opportunity, especially in a complex society, for horizontal mobility to take place; this is the movement from one functional area to another. For instance, one might move from the area of education which is stratified in several levels to the area of business which has comparable stratifications. While social stratification is a structuring achieved on a broader basis, an individual's occupation is a significant aspect of overall social stratification and horizontal movement as well as vertical can affect socioeconomic placement.

Additional aspects of mobility are of interest to social researchers. Movement of an individual during his lifetime is referred to as career mobility. The changes that take place in a generation or two, where the focus is on the occupation of father and son, is known as generational mobility.

CAREER MOBILITY

The movement of individuals during their career has been a topic of continuing interest down through the years. It almost seems that the Horatio Alger story of a rise from rags to riches has been a central theme of American life. There is, however, little justification for this stereotype. An open society in the United States does permit movement, but many factors combine to limit the vertical occupational mobility of an individual during his career. The high educational requirements of a complex technological society, for instance, prevent many unskilled or semiskilled workers from moving much higher. Individuals in the middle part of the range may show a little more movement than those at either the bottom or the top of the occupational scale, but even these do not move very far (Lipset and Bendix, 1952, pp. 494–504). It is, and perhaps always has been, hard to move from a log cabin into the presidency.

This is not to say that there has been little mobility, particularly in an open society such as that in the United States. While vertical mobility may be somewhat more restricted than the usual stereotypes admit, horizontal mobility has been quite extensive. People do move from one occupation to another as well as between geographic areas. They do not, however, move very far from the occupation or profession for which they have prepared and had some experience. They move from one job to another at the same level.

GENERATIONAL MOBILITY

Occupational mobility from one generation to the next shows patterns that resemble career mobility patterns. There is a substantial amount of downward mobility from one generation to the next, even more upward mobility, and still more similarity between the occupational choices of different generations. That is, sons have a tendency to follow in the footsteps of their fathers (Bendix and Lipset, 1953, pp. 371–500). There may be finer variations of this basic finding in that the different levels may not show the same patterns. Miller (1955) found that almost half of the professional people he surveyed had fathers who were in business or the professions, but 20 percent of them had fathers in the lowest occupational levels. Only 30 percent of laborers and service workers had fathers at that low level but about half had fathers who were in the higher middle levels occupationally. This last figure represents a high degree of mobility downward, but one that takes place within a specific and limited set of circumstances.

On an international level Miller (1960), in a comparison of 18 countries,

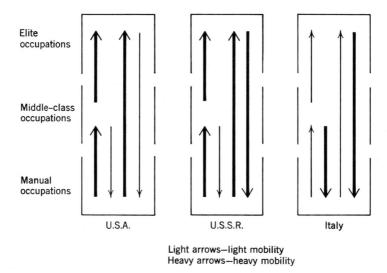

Figure 12-1.   Generational mobility in three countries (Miller, S., 1960).

found more similarity and social mobility between the United States and the U.S.S.R. than between the United States and countries like Great Britain and Italy. These comparisons are indicated in graphic form in Figure 12-1.

OTHER FACTORS IN MOBILITY

Broad social and economic factors serve as the backdrop for occupational opportunity and choice. No observer of the social scene can ignore the sometimes vast changes occurring in various countries. In the United States, for instance, many broad and basic changes have taken place nationwide since its founding. The base for the economy has shifted through the years from an agrarian to a highly industrialized one, and from a political entity of rural individuals to a conglomerate of urban clusters. The society has, for the most part, been open, with vague and rapidly shifting class lines. More important, there has always existed a general feeling of the opportunity for advancement, whether this was justified by the facts or not.

Industrial development has occasioned occupational changes down through the years. Industries requiring a large number of manual workers have declined, and those remaining (mining, for instance) are highly automated. The new technology requires individuals with a high level of education and skill. A continuing shift from blue collar occupations to white collar jobs has been noticeable in other areas as well. In earlier years waves of immigrants provided the muscle for burgeoning industry but also pushed upward those who had arrived here before them. Open spaces not only lured people westward but provided the setting for an openness in the social sense. Today the new frontier is less geographic and more occupational.

In addition, occupational mobility may be determined by the individual factors of attitudes, values, education, level of aspiration, and perception of opportunities. Many people may feel comfortable and secure in a particular setting and may never wish to move upward into newer and more challenging areas even if opportunities present themselves. Opportunities, too, are not in themselves the important determining factors; what is influential in occupational choice is the perception of opportunities by the individuals involved. An opportunity is not an opportunity unless it is perceived as such, and someone deficient in an educational way or one who lacks social awareness may be surrounded by possibilities that he cannot recognize.

The need for higher levels of education in upward mobility has been demonstrated by consistent relationships between the two factors. Of further interest in this area is the difference in the perceptions of the value of education for "getting ahead." Individuals in the upper levels more consistently place a higher value on education than do people in the lower occupational levels (Hyman, 1953). The same study delved further into attitudes of different classes with respect to opportunity in general. Professional people are more likely to believe that their own abilities and performance are the important factors in their progress while manual workers believe that political factors or "pull" are more important in the progress of an individual on the job. As a concomitant factor, aspirations of the laborers were generally quite low; few of the workers aspired to a position higher than that of first line foreman.

Most of the findings with respect to occupational and social mobility focus on the concern that probably represents the most critical feature of social functioning today. The lack of economic well-being or opportunity among a significant segment of our population in the United States has occasioned varied reactions from mild editorial concern to radical and aggressive mass action. The reduction of an economic and social disparity between those high on the scale and those dispossessed at the bottom will be cause for concern for years to come in many societies, not just our own in the United States. From the foregoing discussion, it can be concluded that the task of alleviating poverty and providing equal opportunity will be difficult tasks indeed.

Population Dynamics

Growth and decline of population and its movement from place to place are social facts of great magnitude that are, everyone agrees, of vital importance but ones that often are put aside under the pressures of more immediate fact situations. Basic social facts such as population, however, must be studied for their own sake and for the influence they exert on other factors.

The description of populations is the domain of the field of demography. The purely historical listing of data, such as that obtained from the census, is not, strictly speaking, a behavioral discipline, but some discussion of these facts must be made here and in other chapters to serve as the basis for other more pertinent information. The study of the dynamic aspects of population, that is, the discussion of birth and death rates, immigration, and mobility, is something that is representative of motivation in a general sense and, therefore, can be considered behavioral in nature. This area of study is known as social demography and, as it represents the dynamic aspects of population study, it will serve as the main focus for these broad aspects of social process to be discussed here. The basic factors in population change are births, deaths, and migration. Other factors play a concomitant role in the demographic cycle but always as influences on the three basic ones.

FERTILITY AND MORTALITY

The most significant factor in modern times in the increase of population has undoubtedly been the reduction of the death rate. Davis (1964) summarizes information from the life tables of many Western countries that points to the conclusion that the greatest drop in mortality came in the early years of the present century when the benefits of technology were beginning to be felt. This is the most significant fall in the downward trend over the past 200 years. The same author points out that the drop has been gradual down through the years and came about as the result of scientific and economic gains (housing, sanitation, and education, for example) that were generated from within the group. This contrasts with the recent and radical drops in mortality in the underdeveloped countries. In these the benefits of science and technology are provided from the outside, by the affluent and already developed nations. The mortality drop occurs, therefore, in a much earlier stage of economic and social development. Mortality rates can now be independent of economic status where earlier in the industrialized nations the two factors went hand in hand.

In the 1930's the birth rate began to drop off in Western nations so that the continuing small decline in the death rate produced a leveling-off of the population. "Experts" predicted a continuing level of population stability for the future. As another indication of how events may alter even the best of predictions, the "baby boom" of the 1940's shattered the earlier prognostications. This rise in the birth rate was accompanied by a drop in the death rate in the underdeveloped countries that exceeded any previously encountered in the industrialized countries. The result has been the "population explosion" that concerns demographers and lay persons alike for, if it continues at the present rate, the present population of almost 3 billion (3000 million) will double every 35 years.

The impact of the rise in births and drop in deaths is greatest in the underdeveloped countries. The combination produces a young population, a situation that reduces the productivity of the country by adding an additional number to feed with the same resources (most often the case). As a result, there is a tendency to put children to work earlier to compensate but it aggravates the situation because a low level of education impedes development. Thus the cycle continues.

Davis (1964), in the same report, notes some of the difficulties involved in attempts to solve the problem through control of births, presumably the only way at this time. Even if a peasant believes it in his best economic interest to limit children (and he may not since each child can, in some respects, help support him), other values and goals may be more salient. In Latin America, as in many parts of the world, the birth of children demonstrates the masculinity of the father; so much the better if they are male.

The same author hastens to add that there are some concomitant costs to be paid in the reduction of fertility. A smaller number of children and a longer lifetime for the parents means a very small proportion of a life in a household with children. If love for children is a significant factor, there is a sacrifice involved in reducing the time spent with them. Even more significant, perhaps, is the effect on the age structure. A low fertility-low death rate pattern increases the percentage of older people in the society. The problems encountered in a society top-heavy with older people would be different from those faced by a young population and might be more difficult.

The problems associated with population planning have not been attacked systematically by any society or government. The foregoing should be some evidence of the difficulties surrounding demographic decisions.

MIGRATION

Migration of peoples has been occurring since prehistoric times. Ancient and modern peoples alike have shown some geographic mobility. Even though the prehistoric Indo-European peoples moved from Asia into Europe and some of their descendants (the Greeks) moved from their city-states to colonize satellites throughout the Mediterranean world, the actual extent of wandering was fairly limited until the beginning of the nineteenth century.

Intercontinental Movement

Both in terms of numbers and distance, the migration of European peoples to North and South America represented the greatest movement of population in history. Estimates of the number of immigrants from Europe to the Western hemisphere since 1800 run as high as 70 million people (Carr-Saunders, 1936). This must be compared with the no more than 5 million people migrating in the 300 years prior to the beginning of the nineteenth century. The size of the movements is swelled even more by the number of Negroes introduced in the slave trade. Estimates of the number of Negroes moved from Africa to the Western hemisphere run as high as 20 million. Approximately 60 percent of that total were brought to the United States.

Immigration to the United States in the past 150 years has shown variation not only in numbers at particular times but also in terms of country of origin. The number of immigrants reached a peak in the first decade of this century when almost 9 million people arrived. The lowest point in 100 years was reached in the 1930's when, due at least partly to the new restrictive immigration laws, only ½ million people were admitted. The policy of restricting numbers was complimented by a restriction as to countries of origin. A quota system drastically reduced the number of people represented in the most recent migrations and favored the countries of origin most represented in the previous century.

The number of foreign born in the United States never exceeded the 14 million mark reached in 1930. The part of the total population represented by the foreign born never exceeded 14 percent. The latest figures from the census of 1960 show 9.7 million foreign born which, because of the increase of population, represents only 5.4 percent of the total population.

Migration of this nature has never failed to have a significant impact on a society and the economy of the country. The benefits to a receiving country usually far outweigh the slight disadvantages that may occur through problems of integration and assimilation. The United States, for instance, was able to develop as rapidly and as efficiently as it did in the past 100 years because of the contribution of skills of immigrants of all kinds. The human resources not only provided a labor force but also broadened the consumer base and contributed to the significant increase of the gross national product over a short period of time.

That immigration is not a matter of history only is amply demonstrated by recent mounting concern in many foreign countries over the exodus of highly trained and skilled people, primarily to the United States. Foreign countries are alarmed by the "brain drain," the loss of top level manpower to other countries. In the *Wall Street Journal,* Soderlind (1967) indicates that the number of professional workers entering the United States in 1966 represented a 60 percent increase over the same category 10 years before. While some observers may doubt the magnitude of the problem, it is clear that some small or developing countries have lost a sizable percentage of their trained manpower. There is general agreement that the United States has benefited tremendously by the additional human resources.

Internal Migration

Movement within the borders of a country can be of as much significance at times as the broad international movements they have. Mobility has always been an important aspect of the American scene. Individual initiative in an open society, being highly prized, contributed significantly to the movement of peoples to new territories, usually westward. The disappearance of the old frontier of the West has apparently not diminished the proclivities of Americans to move. Numerous summaries of mass mobility, from young company executives being moved several times in a decade to the mass migrations of southern Negroes to Northern cities, are available from the popular press and official documents (U.S. Bureau of the Census, 1966). Net migration figures for the decade from 1950 to 1960 (Table 12-2) indicate not only gains or losses in particular regions of the country but also the changing racial compositions of these broad geographic areas. Further analysis of census figures would indicate changes by state (Florida, California, Nevada, and Arizona are the biggest gainers) and also that most settled cities have showed either little gain or have declined in population while surrounding suburban areas have gained to a significant extent. To these statistics must be added the already mentioned process of urbanization, the movement of the population from rural areas into large metropolitan conglomerates.

The impact of these population changes in the political area alone is evident. At the state level particularly, representatives have been elected on an apportionment based on a population distribution typical of past decades. Election districts have slowly, if at all, been brought into line with the reality of the increasing numerical importance of urban populations. The disparity in political representation between city and countryside make a rural voter count more heavily in the results than an urban voter. Rural control of the legislature and, often, of other branches of government as well, made it easier in the past to maintain rural influences in a dominant position. The landmark case of Baker V. Carr in 1962 imposed reapportionment on state legislatures in order to meet the simple mandate of the Supreme Court—"one man one vote."

The changing racial composition of cities has brought about concomitant changes in political conditions. Increasing numbers of Negro office holders

Table 12-2.   Net Internal Migration in the United States, 1950–1960 (from The United States Bureau of the Census, 1961)

Florida	+58.3	Massachusetts	− 2.0
Nevada	+53.8	Kansas	− 2.3
Arizona	+44.0	Minnesota	− 3.2
Alaska	+32.0	Missouri	− 3.3
California	+29.7	Rhode Island	− 3.3
Delaware	+20.1	Montana	− 4.3
Maryland	+13.7	Pennsylvania	− 4.5
Colorado	+12.3	Georgia	− 6.2
New Jersey	+11.9	Wyoming	− 6.8
Connecticut	+11.7	Idaho	− 6.8
New Mexico	+ 7.7	Maine	− 7.2
Ohio	+ 5.1	North Carolina	− 8.1
Washington	+ 3.7	Tennessee	− 8.3
Michigan	+ 2.5	Nebraska	− 8.8
New Hampshire	+ 2.4	Iowa	− 8.9
Indiana	+ 1.6	Oklahoma	− 9.8
Texas	+ 1.5	Vermont	−10.0
Utah	+ 1.5	South Carolina	−10.5
Illinois	+ 1.4	Alabama	−12.0
New York	+ 1.4	Kentucky	−13.2
Oregon	+ 1.0	South Dakota	−14.4
Hawaii	+ 0.6	North Dakota	−17.0
Virginia	+ 0.4	Mississippi	−19.9
Wisconsin	− 1.6	West Virginia	−22.3
Louisiana	− 1.9	Arkansas	−22.7

are found in cities where the number of Negroes has increased, sometimes to the point of reaching a majority of the total population in the city.

A survey of the impact of Negro suffrage on politics in the South, however, indicates mixed results (Matthews and Prothro, 1966). Original high hopes for the elimination of social inequities in the South through increased power at the ballot box does not, at least at this time, seem justified. Increasing numbers of advocates of civil rights look more to federal intervention than to local elections to solve their problems. The authors believe that generally success will come at the local level if moderate approaches will be emphasized. This means the support of leaders who fall somewhere in between the "Uncle Toms" and the "Black Power" militants.

URBANIZATION

History has recorded an ever-increasing tendency for man to cluster, for one reason or another, with his fellow man in compact living areas. This is undoubtedly a trend that began well before written records documented this development. It has reached a point where we speak of the present century as being the era of urban man and are concerned with problems of pollution, transportation, and living space, especially in the sprawling megalopolis of both east and west coast. We have reached the point where in the United States over 70 percent of the population is classified as urban.

An interested observer of this clear development will ask—why the city? How does it come about and what purposes does it serve? Cities represent much more than merely a large collection of people. Many underdeveloped countries have hundreds of settlements encompassing many individuals, but few of these are cities as much as they are mere collections of farmers who till the soil. A city represents much more in the way of involvement and services for its members. It offers, first of all, a diversity of services through the specialization of its citizens in various occupations. A hierarchy develops from this specialization of tasks and a religious, political, and economic adminis-trative elite develops. The clustering serves the social needs for companionship as well as the safety needs that are threatened by hostile forces that can be kept outside the city. Perhaps just as important is the economic opportunity to exchange goods and services.

Urbanization has been a concomitant of industrialization and commercializa-tion. In Western society the city became the bastion of freedom to work and trade; indeed, a good part of the reason for the early development of European cities to their present large size was the necessity for the merchants to free themselves from the control of landholding lords who did not hesitate to impose different kinds of restraints on the activities of individuals within their territory. The Industrial Revolution simply accentuated the mass movement of peoples to the cities by requiring large numbers of workers under one roof before the latest technological improvements and inventions could be efficiently used. The move from the cottage to the factories increased or added to the number of individuals already enjoying the benefits of the city, dubious though they may have been. The close relationship between urbanization and economic development can be seen from a comparison of the economically advanced countries with those that are still in the process of industrial development. Developed countries are highly urbanized, most of them having over half of their people living in cities, while it is not unusual to find fewer than 10 percent of the people of underdeveloped countries living in urban areas (Gibbs and Davis, 1958, pp. 506–507).

Not only does the city contain a greater number of people, it also contains a much greater variety of individuals and groups than may be encountered in even widespread rural locations. The diversity of populations in the city may provide opportunities for greater social conflict, but it also has benefits that have outweighed the disadvantages. The cultural diversity of the city can stimulate creative endeavor; the impetus that comes from the necessity to debate ideas and exchange views generates a social, political, and economic output that the rural areas cannot seem to match. These dynamic factors may have an effect on the personalities of city dwellers that appear in areas such as concepts of time and space or, more important, in the greater feeling of impersonality in the interactions of a city dweller with others in the metropolis (Wirth, 1938, p. 124). One should be cautious at this point, however, about overgeneralizing with respect to such possible differences between urban and rural personality patterns. It may well be that such supposed differences are diminishing or have disappeared because of greater awareness on the part of the general population of patterns of behavior, attitudes, values, and characteristics that have been transmitted by mass media in short time through the length and breadth of the nation.

Conflict and Disintegration

The disruption that occurs on a broad front in a society has, on the basis of scale alone, serious implications for that society. The losses in any conflict or disintegration of this nature can mount in material and less tangible ways until they represent a substantial diversion of group resources. Fortunately there may be a strong social drive in individuals to take a position and try to resolve these problems. Sumner (1906) called this the "strain toward consistency."

FAMILY PATTERNS

Since the family is the first and most fundamental socializer of the individual, any discussion of social conflict and disorganization should begin with this primary unit of a society. The stability and cohesiveness of the family unit may not be the prime factor in understanding the basis for maintenance of social bonds in general, but it is an important aspect to consider.

Data from many sources (Landis, 1949; Goode, 1961) indicate that the more stable marriages are those where partners are psychologically secure and of similar socioeconomic or religious backgrounds. Divorce is, conversely, highest among those who lack these qualifications, that is, those who are in the lower socioeconomic levels and who show a great diversity in religious and other beliefs.

In the United States, the divorce rate per 1000 population seems to have stabilized at a level somewhere between 2.3 and 2.5. This is down considerably from the peak of 3.5 per 1000 reached right after World War II but is up from the level of 1.6 maintained through the 1920's and 1930's (U.S. Bureau of the Census, 1966, p. 46).

Environmental stresses on the family have their impact on its members in various ways. The strength of the relationships between members of the family and the types of bonds between them are the basic determiners of the outcome of individual actions under social and economic stress. One classic study of the unemployed man and his family (Komarovsky, 1940) focused on the effects of the "Great Depression" on family life. In viewing the impact of unemployment on the authority of the husband, the study noted that, while the status of the male breadwinner could easily suffer in unemployment, if the authority was vested in the husband as a person and if there was no deterioration in his behavior, there was little or no loss of his authority or deterioration in the family. Where authority was buttressed by coercive control, family breakdown occurred more often, particularly when the behavior of the husband deteriorated.

Similar patterns of relationships between family members may play a role in the onset and the development of some broader forms of social conflict. The status of the Negro woman in the rural South and among the lower class of the urban North, for instance, is quite strong within the family. The woman is a dominant figure in a closed matriarchal society, and she may even have more education than the male (Broom and Selznick, 1963, pp. 510–511). The system leaves little room for the influence of the male in the family or in the community; consequently, he may have such weak ties with his group that he is seldom around. These circumstances, when added to the chronic unemployment and hostility of a dominant group toward him, make fertile ground for the militant and aggressive reactions seen increasingly on the urban scene.

The relationship between family patterns and crime or delinquency is one of the more critical areas for study. Crime is antisocial behavior that is learned and the family, along with the peer group, serves as the most important training ground for attitudes and behavior. If the family lives in a setting where anti-social behavior is condoned or even encouraged, it reinforces these values within the family group; the outcome is likely to be delinquency and then crime, partly because there are so few other educational experiences.

Many researchers believe that the prime basis for delinquency lies in the breakup of the home. A more likely explanation is that delinquency results not so much from the broken home but from the unhappy home, which may or may not be disrupted by loss or uprooting of members (Nye, 1958, p. 47).

COMMUNITY CONFLICT

The complex industrial society, with its diverse and often competing elements, may be subject to disruption more than the small and well-integrated community. The onset of conflict in an industrialized urban setting is hastened by the social separation of groups into localized and limited environments. The "ghetto" can exist in a company or a city; it fosters separation by a reinforcement of attitudes and opinions through exposure to a sameness of feeling, while exposure to more identifications and many different values could reduce the chances of serious social fractionation. The localization of a compact group makes for a militant entity in mass society that can explode into a real "revolt of the masses against an administrative elite" (Coleman, 1961). This need not be a racial problem alone, and the reaction can take place in an industrial setting as well as in the community. It is as disconcerting to have nonparticipating minorities of all kinds in a factory as in a city.

A basic set of conditions seems to be the ground for the germination of civil strife and violence. A high level of tension in elements of the population that are prone to violence may exist as the result of continuing frustrations. Often this is a characteristic of rapid changes in the type of community or in the pattern of interpersonal relations. A sudden and large influx of noticeably different individuals is bound to have some effect. The presence of all of these may not produce conflict until one incident, often minor, will precipitate conflict (Williams, 1947, pp. 60–61). The violent reactions may be viewed as a protest against the conditions in which the individuals find themselves. Bowen et al. (1968) indicate that the orientation toward protest is greater among those who feel deprived, have rising expectations, or who exhibit great mobility, up or down. It may be disconcerting to some observers to realize that social conflict may increase, not decrease, as a minority group receives benefits from radical action and demands even more as its members realize what they have been missing. A disproportionate number of individuals involved in riots in urban areas recently have come from the better educated, middle class "Black

Bourgeoisie" (McCord and Howard, 1968). Brown (1954, pp. 200–201) points out the same phenomenon on the industrial scene as he describes workers wanting more after they have received something through sustained negotiations and strikes. Some observers of recent civil disorder have viewed looting in riots as an expression of the wishes of the deprived to get their "fair share" (Dynes and Quarantelli, 1968).

Discrimination and segregation are the end result of the prejudice that appears between majority and minority groups. Reactions to discrimination are like those that occur in other settings as a result of frustration. Earlier, in Chapter 8, various reactions to frustration were noted; most of those are possible in prejudice and, for simplicity's sake, they might be grouped into two categories here—withdrawal reactions and reactions of aggression. Many members of a minority group will react in the first way, that is, by withdrawing from the situation either by departing physically or through apathy and passivity. Aggression may be very pronounced in certain instances as the deprived individuals vent their hostility and resentment through direct and indirect acts of aggression toward the power structure of the dominant community.

The environmental stresses that erupt in social conflict represent a breaking down of the codes of behavior that govern the relationships between the groups and among the individuals within the groups. Some of these may be highly irrational as are the general codes of behavior in the South; a Negro, for instance, would always be addressed as "boy" or by his first name. For that matter, male and female Negroes are never addressed by the customary titles, Mr., Mrs., or Miss.

Those who are discriminated against are more likely to be involved in antisocial behavior, particularly crime and delinquency. Again, the inability to identify with a dominant group is the alienation that supports the deviation from official norms. The concomitant hostility toward the white power structure and disrespect for their property was sketched in incisive detail many years ago by Myrdal (1944) and has been observed again many times since.

Prejudice and discrimination do not, however, operate to produce uniform reactions on the part of minority group members. In some public testimony, Coles (1967) reports being amazed to find in his psychiatric practice that many children developed stable personalities under the stress of discrimination while others in more comfortable situations showed personality disorganization. As a result, he asked whether it is boredom or a sense of uselessness and futility in stress that hurts children rather than stress itself. The suggestion presents a strong challenge to society to provide meaningful opportunities for the development of the abilities of individuals with less emphasis on extraneous factors such as skin color.

In the same series, Sternlieb (1967) focused on the special alienation between owner and tenant of slum property. His survey found that the only factor ensuring good maintenance of property in the ghetto was the fact of ownership by the resident. On the basis of his findings, Sternlieb suggests consideration of an urban version of the Homestead Act. Where in the previous century settlers could acquire land under favorable financial conditions, today's ghetto dwellers need similar financial and legal assistance to get them started as home owners. With pride of ownership can come other values of a dominant society and a concomitant reduction of alienation between minority and majority.

It may be said, as a last word here, that the economic losses to society as the result of prejudice and discrimination are quite extensive. Not only is there a direct loss in human resources that could be channeled into increasing the gross national product, but there is a continuing need under discrimination to provide for the welfare and support of persons who are unable to break out of the restricted framework of the socioeconomic structure. A vicious cycle of poverty sets in and continues, often for generations, unless it is broken by strong and positive action.

The Kerner Report (National Advisory Commission on Civil Disorders, 1968) stressed the need for more housing, education, and jobs for Negroes to prevent a polarization of races in this country with its accompanying increase in violence. The recommendations are not surprising and may well be supported generally. What is disconcerting, however, is that the implementation of the recommendations could take an annual expenditure of money nearly equal to the entire national budget.

It may well be, also, that violence is a part of life and must be expected; as Ardrey (1961) has indicated, Cain, not Abel, is the father of man. This view could engender judgments of the inevitability of violence, however, when such conclusions may be dangerous. The most effective response would be to recognize that violence does exist as a natural phenomenon and to take steps to deal with it. This does not mean that it is to be repressed or denied, as now, but that it can be handled with therapeutic effects. Our educational process should allow children to become aware of thoughts of violence and help them learn to cope with them out in the open (Bettelheim, 1966). Where violence appears in racial or other social forms, it should be recognized that some of the reaction represents middle class disapproval of attacks against a vested structure of values, among them the value of nonviolence.

CRIME AND DELINQUENCY

Technically, crime is behavior that violates the criminal law. Delinquency is similar activity by a juvenile. This is behavior that deviates from official norms and is disruptive of the legal order. It is social disorganization that should come to the attention of duly constituted agents of the state and be acted on with all the machinery available to them.

Crime Data

Since specific formal procedures are called for, it might be assumed that data on crime and delinquency are precise and valid. Berelson and Steiner (1964, p. 625) quote authorities to the effect that true crime rate statistics are impossible to attain because figures are often incomplete and biased in addition to being based on definitions that vary according to political jurisdiction and time. Their warning as to the fallibility of data extends even to official statistics.

Certain factors do stand out, however, in a survey of criminal behavior. Demographic variables such as sex and age show clear-cut associations with incidence of criminal acts. Broom and Selznick (1958, 639–641) summarize the relationships with sex, age, and class position. In the United States, males are arrested ten times as often as females and imprisoned 20 times as often. This is by no means peculiar to any one country or era—the same differential has been noted over the world although the ratio may be decreasing as women achieve status equal to men. English statistics resemble those in the United States in that the crime rate is highest for those in their late teens—particularly crimes such as burglary and robbery, with car theft one of the teenage crimes of high incidence.

Lower class and certain minority groups are more often in trouble with the law. More delinquents and criminals come from broken homes and from urban areas. These statistics may be misleading in that many from upper class homes, certain geographic areas, or in professional positions may not appear in police or court records. Many kinds of informal or extralegal arrangements may be made. The embezzler may not be legally punished—he just loses his job; the son of a physician is returned to his parents for discipline rather than being handed over to the juvenile detention home. None of these results may be illegal (they may even aid in the effective administration of order), but they do emphasize the social bias often present in crime reports.

Social Dynamics in Crime

Crime and delinquency have been identified above as being deviations from the official norms of a society. The developing and continuing nonconformity to these group norms represents a disorganization of social values and relationships.

Adherence to norms is easier when a group is cohesive; that is, the bonds of relationships between individuals is strong and the values of the group are widely shared by the members. When these norms are visible, in addition, and the members of the group are also visible in their everyday behavior, conformity to and enforcement of the norms is much easier. A small and homogeneous town may have its deviants, but these undoubtedly are small in number compared to those encountered in the big city where anonymity of the individual and fewer close ties among persons is characteristic. Also, the greater variety of values among the groups encountered in large urban areas makes enforcement difficult; what may be a serious violation of norms for one group may be considered relatively minor or no cause for concern on the part of others or enforcement agencies.

Alienation of an individual or a group from the values of the society reduces the ties that may have existed and makes social conflict more likely; integration of minority groups into the cultural mainstream has resulted in a general acceptance of the values in norms of the society. This has occurred in the past with respect to the changing culture patterns among immigrant groups. Within a short time, except where there has been extreme segregation, the attitudes, values, and behavior of the incoming individuals have resembled almost completely those of the receiving groups. This is true as well with respect to conformity to the legal norms (Wood, 1947).

INDUSTRIAL CONFLICT

In the industrial world many sources of conflict can exist. Some are based on economic factors while still more stem from other individual and social bases. Conflict may also involve many different parties to the dispute. Three broad groups are involved—organizations of workers, management entities, and the government, the latter presumably being interested in furthering effective social functioning and thereby protecting the interests of the citizen. The government will generally monitor company activity and management performance in areas where government regulation of business is thought essential. Problems of antitrust, fair trade, and consumer protection are among the areas of interest to the agents of government. The union will be scrutinized for illegal activity such as secondary boycotts. Managements may compete against each other in ways that they believe will enhance their position in the industry while unions may compete for members or jobs, as in jurisdictional disputes. Internal conflict can be generated within both management and union organizations as individuals or factions fight to gain control or struggle to achieve other ends.

Union-Management Relations

The conflict that is by far the greatest topic of interest, however, is that arising between the groups representing management, on one hand, and the union, on the other. It is this conflict between union and management that occupies the center stage when industrial conflict is mentioned. While attention may focus on controversy surrounding the way in which economic returns are to be divided among the parties, as has been noted above, other factors may be even more important but not as evident on the surface of the dispute.

The union represents employees under a contract. It is upon expiration of the contract and the necessity for entering into a new one that the labor-management conflict comes into greatest focus. An inability to reach agreement before the expiration of the old contract results, usually, in the form of industrial conflict that is best known to causal observers, the strike.

While they are the best known form of industrial conflict, strikes represent merely a small part of the total discontent, controversy, or militancy present on the industrial scene. Some researchers (Stagner and Rosen, 1964, p. 101) maintain that strikes are like an iceberg; that is, they are only one-tenth of the discontent that shows above the surface; most of the controversy is hidden below. Through their high visibility, however, strikes serve as a means of calling attention to other factors. They act as an information device to people at large in the hope of gaining their sympathy and support. This is in addition to the use of the strike as one form of economic pressure on the employer.

Other forms of social conflict may be even more important in their impact on the functioning of the industrial organization. A slowdown where employees employ techniques to reduce output in order to win a point can have significant economic results. Even more drastic is industrial sabotage (the term comes from *sabot,* the French word for the wooden shoe that workers threw into the machinery to wreck it—the French version of throwing a monkey wrench into the works) which can be practiced by single workers or large groups. Management can get the message even if only one incident of this nature occurs; it is considered to be a prime cause of economic loss in industry today.

Harassment of other kinds, some of doubtful legality, are also utilized. Complaints in a continuing stream to various governmental agencies can divert the attention of management from other pressing duties, but the techniques may backfire when management files countercharges and uses legal harassments of their own. Inviting other unions to apply pressure in crucial situations is another weapon that is not unknown in industrial circles.

The Dynamics of Industrial Discord

The bases for conflict in the industrial area are no different from those in any other area of human endeavor. It must be remembered that the activity shown in many different ways during strikes and slowdowns merely represent examples of behavior that results from certain basic psychological and social factors. What has been discussed in some length in earlier chapters with respect to the dynamics of behavior of individuals and groups can be repeated here.

Industrial conflict is just another result of the activity of basic factors in human behavior. Frustration, for instance, has been discussed in some detail (Chapter 8). It is important to review the several kinds of reactions that can occur as the result of frustration, among them apathy and aggression, probably the most common. On the industrial scene, apathy can be seen in the lack of interest in the work, the company, or the union that may be manifested by the worker. There may be some of this as well in the daily activity of executives. Aggression is the response to frustration that is more likely to be seen in industrial conflict, since it represents some kind of acting-out process whereby the individual takes some physical or verbal action as the direct result of his being kept from the goal. Many acts of violence, direct and indirect, can occur in highly emotional states surrounding strikes. Direct physical aggression may take place (the employee punches the foreman) while indirect aggression can take place in a slowdown or sabotage. These injure the company and, since any such activity endangers his position, the foreman as well.

But aggression sets off counteraggression. When moves are made by one side, the other side feels threatened and moves to counter the activities of the original aggressors. This may continue to a point where original issues are lost sight of and the violence has mounted to a point where it is difficult to terminate the angry exchanges.

Conflict resolution in union-management disputes can occur in a variety of ways. A new contract and end to a strike or stoppage can come about as the result of bargaining between the parties, sometimes aided by a mediator who can only recommend but cannot force an outcome. The parties may, in a deadlock, agree to abide by the decision of an impartial third party, an arbitrator, or the arbitration may be forced on the parties in conflict by a concerned legislature. These and other factors will be met in another discussion of dynamics in business and industry (Chapter 19).

Summary

Behavior is a dynamic factor, not a static one. The basis for it lies in the learning by the individual of the requirements of a social existence; the group influences are strong and long lasting. Norms and values of the group get incorporated into the individual (socialization) in his development as the result of the learning process.

Cultural and environmental factors shape individual and group responses which then influence the broad action patterns. Change is one of the most identifiable of the features of aggregate activity. Views of change may present a general historical pattern or a more molecular view of change features in a community or group. Studies of change may focus on external factors in the developing situation or the concentration may be on the mechanisms promoting equilibrium or, on the other hand, those centripetal in nature. Cultural attitudes and values have played an important role but these, in turn, have been influenced by the technological developments of the time as well as by the concomitant factors of migration and conflict.

Change in groups must be studied first in terms of the changes occurring on an individual basis. Attitudes are fundamental in the functioning of individuals in society and are developed mainly in primary groups such as the family. Motivational and personality factors play a role—change agents are apt to be those who conform least to the constraints of the culture.

Patterns of response in social change include the compromises of accommodation or the assimilation of diversity as in a "melting pot" to provide a fairly coherent and quiescent whole. Negative reactions include alienation, the tendency toward withdrawal, and deterioration of intergroup contacts. Isolation, the lack of integration in a society, is a further possible circumstance. The lack of group norms in the individual (*anomie*) adds to further alienation.

Collective behavior, sometimes called mass behavior, includes the social and economic phenomena of fads and fashions as well as the more highly charged crazes and booms. Social movements on a broad scale and intended to change the status quo show more organization and stability. The highly emotional and more immediate influence processes may be present in the behavior of crowds; the aggressive behavior of a mob or the withdrawal as in panic may be the resulting circumstance. Each pattern often is enhanced by the presence of rumor.

The bases for collective behavior lie in the ambiguity of the guidelines for decisions in a new situation. This provides insecurity for individuals. Once responses are made in a highly changed social situation, the spread of emotional contagion provides a firm, though often illogical, basis for the action of an individual.

Further important activity in a society is seen in the movement of individuals vertically through the various socioeconomically determined levels or horizontally from one type of group to another. Studies of mobility through an individual's lifetime indicate that extensive rises in status do not occur as the traditional stereotype would indicate. More movement takes place between generations, but the similarity in occupations of fathers and sons is even greater than the differences. Industrial development provides the diversity that aids mobility. Education becomes an important contributor to movement when the requirements of a more complex technology place a premium on new or greater skills.

Demography, the study of population, provides a further basis for the discussion of social dynamics; changes in population arising from variations in the birth rate or the drop in mortality with technological development can have profound social results. Not only is there a question of numbers to support, but changes in the "age mix" which results provide other problems of administration.

Migration between countries or within them provides behavioral ramifications. Productive manpower attracted by a developing economy can help expand the material and social activity of that economy still further. Internal migration may have even more effect at present. The decline of agriculture or its mechanization has caused an exodus from the South to the North or Far West in the United States and from the farm to the cities. The political and social disruptions in the process constitute one of the country's most significant problem areas.

Urbanization is nothing new; present patterns represent a continuation of historical trends. Cities have grown because they provide diversified services to the inhabitants, but this same diversity may have undesirable consequences in the conflicts it produces. The stimulation of a city may also provide a threat for the insecure and increase alienation.

Conflict in a society has many of its roots in the primary units such as the family. Stability of a marital unit is greatest at higher socioeconomic levels and where the partners show similar backgrounds. The effects of external stress on the family depend on the attitudes and behavior with respect to the individual parents. Males with little authority or prestige in the family unit show greatest deterioration and negative responses.

The competing elements in the community provide a basis for the emergence of conflict. Frustrations in a rapidly changing set of intergroup conditions provide an emotional basis for conflict. Prejudice produces varied reactions; withdrawal or aggression and hostility may be the result, or there may be genuine growth and stability. Generally, however, the social loss in discrimination is extensive.

Criminal behavior is difficult to quantify as statistics often reflect certain biases. Young males are clearly the highest offenders, however. Lower socioeconomic status shows some relation to frequency of crime as well, though the figures may be misleading. Crime is deviant behavior by those who have not internalized the norms and values of the dominant society; either they have no norms or subscribe to the values of a deviant group. Alienation of such individuals can be reduced by incorporating them into the main cultural stream.

Industrial conflict involves various parties to the dispute—workers, management, and the political body. Each of these entities may have their own internal conflicts as well. The most visible form of industrial conflict, the strike, represents only a small part of the total discord. Restriction of output or other harassments abound. The bases for industrial conflict lie in the fundamental factors in individual and social behavior. Frustration, aggression, and counter-aggression have been well documented. Means of conflict resolution must incorporate consideration of these dynamics.

Bibliography

Allport, F. H. (1920). The influence of the group upon association and thought. *Journal of Experimental Psychology, 3,* 159–182.

Allport, G. and Postman, L. (1947). *The psychology of rumor.* New York: Holt.

Ardrey, R. (1961). *African genesis.* New York: Atheneum.

Barnard, C. (1938). *The functions of the executive.* Cambridge, Mass.: Harvard University Press.

Barnett, H. (1953). *Innovation.* New York: McGraw-Hill.

Bendix, R. and Lipset, S., eds. (1953). *Class, status and power.* Glencoe: The Free Press.

Berelson, B. and Steiner, G. (1964). *Human behavior.* New York: Harcourt, Brace and World.

Bettelheim, B. (1966). Violence: a neglected mode of behavior. *Annals of the American Academy of Political and Social Science,* **364,** 50–59.

Bowen, D., Bowen, E., Gawiser, S., and Masotti, L. (1968). Deprivation, mobility, and orientation toward protest of the urban poor. *American Behavioral Scientist,* **11(4),** 20–24.

Broom, L. and Selznick, P. (1958). *Sociology* (2nd ed.). New York: Harper and Row.

Brown, J. (1954). *The social psychology of industry.* Baltimore: Penguin.

Carr-Saunders, A. (1936). *World population.* Oxford: Clarendon Press.

Coch, L. and French, J., Jr. (1948). Overcoming resistance to change. *Human Relations,* **1,** 512–532.

Coleman, J. (1961). Community disorganization. In Merton, R. and Nisbet, R. (eds.). *Contemporary social problems.* New York: Harcourt, Brace and World.

Coles, R. (1967). Is prejudice against Negroes overrated? *Trans-action,* **4(10),** 44–45.

Davis, K. (1964). Social demography. In Berelson, B. (ed.). *The behavioral sciences today.* New York: Harper and Row.

Durkheim, E. (1951). *Le suicide* (Simpson, G., trans.). Glencoe: Free Press.

Dynes, R. and Quarantelli, E. (1968). What looting in civil disturbances really means. *Trans-action,* **5(6),** 9–14.

Gibbs, J. and Davis, K. (1958). Conventional versus metropolitan data in the international study of urbanization. *American Sociological Review,* **23**, 506–507.

Goode, W. (1961). Family disorganization. In Merton, R. and Nisbet, R. (eds.). *Contemporary social problems.* New York: Harcourt, Brace and World.

Horton, J. E. and Thompson, W. E. (1962). Powerlessness and political negativism: a study of defeated local referendums. *The American Journal of Sociology,* **67(5)**, 485–493.

Hyman, H. (1953). The value systems of different classes. In Bendix, R. and Lipset, S. (eds.). *Class, status, and power,* 426–442.

Komarovsky, M. (1940). *The unemployed man and his family.* New York: Dryden.

Landis, J. (1949). Marriages of mixed and non-mixed religious faith. *American Sociological Review,* **14**, 401–407.

Lipset, S. and Bendix, R. (1952). Social mobility and occupational career patterns. *American Journal of Sociology,* **57**, 494–504.

Mannheim, K. (1941). *Man and society in an age of reconstruction.* New York: Harcourt, Brace, and World.

Matthews, D. and Prothro, J. (1966). *Negroes and the new Southern politics.* New York: Harcourt, Brace and World.

McCord, W. and Howard, J. (1968). Negro opinions in three riot cities. *American Behavioral Scientist,* **11(4)**, 24–27.

Merton, R. (1957). *Social theory and social structure* (rev. ed.). Glencoe: The Free Press.

Miller, H. (1955). *Income of the American people.* New York: Wiley.

Miller, S. (1960). Comparative social mobility. *Current Sociology,* **9**, 56.

Mumford, L. (1934). *Technics and civilization.* New York: Harcourt, Brace.

Myrdal, G. (1944). *An American dilemma.* New York: Harper and Row.

National Advisory Commission on Civil Disorders (1968). *Report of the National Advisory Commission on Civil Disorders.* Washington: Superintendent of Documents, Government Printing Office.

Newcomb, T. (1943). *Personality and social change: attitude formation in a student community.* New York: Dryden.

Newcomb, T. and Svehla, G. (1937). Intra-family relationship in attitude. *Sociometry,* **1**, 180–205.

Nye, F. (1958). *Family relationships and delinquent behavior.* New York: Wiley.

Parsons, T. (1951). *The social system.* Glencoe, Ill.: Free Press.

Sargent, S. and Williamson, R. (1958). *Social psychology.* New York: Ronald.

Selznick, P. (1949). *T.V.A. and the grass roots.* Berkeley: University of California Press.

Sherif, M. and Cantril, H. (1947). *Psychology of ego-involvements.* New York: Wiley.

Soderlind, S. (1967). The outlook. *Wall Street Journal,* October 2, 1967, 1.

Stagner, R. and Rosen, H. (1964). *Psychology of union-management relations.* Belmont, Calif.: Wadsworth.

Sternlieb, G. (1967). The case for the tenant as owner. *Trans-action,* 4(10), 44–45.

Sumner, W. (1906). *Folkways.* Boston: Ginn.

Toynbee, A. (1948). *Civilization on trial.* New York: Oxford University Press.

U.S. Bureau of the Census (1961). *Current population reports,* series P-25, no. 227. Washington, D.C.

U.S. Bureau of the Census (1966). *Statistical Abstract of the United States, 1966,* (87th ed.). Washington, D.C.

Williams, R. (1947). *The reduction of intergroup tensions: a survey of research on problems of ethnic, racial, and religious group relations.* New York: Social Science Research Council, Bulletin 57.

Wirth, L. (1938). Urbanism as a way of life. *American Journal of Sociology,* 44(1), 1–24.

Wood, A. (1947). Minority group criminality and cultural integration. *Journal of Criminal Law and Criminology,* 37, 498–510.

13

Attitudes and Values

Predispositions to react on the basis of learned preferences are fundamental in human behavior. Ideally, individual responses in social settings can be predicted and controlled when the nature of mechanisms that trigger a reaction are known and understood. While we are still far from being able to control on an individual basis, some awareness can come from detailed data and analyses of attitudes, values, and related social concepts. Building on this awareness may provide a structure for predicting behavior and developing a salutory social climate.

Attitudes, Opinions, and Beliefs

An *attitude* is a predisposition to react, positively or negatively, to a person, place, or circumstance. It is therefore a tendency to respond and can be considered a "leaning" in one direction or another. This is what a psychologist would also term a "set." There are two main elements in an attitude, the predisposition and the direction of that predisposition.

An *opinion* is the expression of one's judgment of a particular set of facts, an evaluation of the circumstances presented to him. An opinion is a response to a specifically limited stimulus, but the response is certainly influenced by the predisposition with which the individual is operating, that is, the attitude structure. Undoubtedly attitudes are basic to opinions as well as to many other aspects of behavior. Judgments of specific circumstances are made in the light of leanings one way or the other. While attitudes are basic and influence opinions, this is not a one-way street. As an opinion is given (in line with and influenced by an attitude), the basic attitude is strengthened or reinforced, even if only slightly.

The relationship between the functioning of attitudes and opinions may be shown by the example of a person who is proeducation. When a bond issue is proposed that will pay for badly needed education facilities, he is probably in favor of it and his position reinforces his proeducation stand. Needless to say, any real decisions in complex daily activities are the result of the action of many and more complex variables along with those just illustrated. The simplified situation is, however, still a valid one.

A belief is the acceptance of a statement or a set of circumstances. When we state that we believe something, we indicate that for us, it is so. Direct contact with the events in question is not necessary, since we may accept a proposition on the basis of indirect evidence or statements from others. Beliefs are much stronger than opinions; we hold them more firmly than we do the more changeable evaluations of minor or transitory events represented by opinions. Beliefs are less affected by the pro or con positions fundamental in attitudes than are opinions, but all three aspects may influence the others. In fact, most researchers recognize that attitudes, opinions, and beliefs are so closely tied together in real life that it is difficult to separate them except on a limited conceptual basis. Much of the literature shows the high degree of overlap between them. While these concepts can be distinguished, it is common to hear someone refer to attitudes, opinions, and beliefs all in one breath.

Most psychologists have believed, however, that attitudes are more fundamental to human behavior than are the related aspects. For this reason, there has been much research on the matter of attitudes and their measurement. Attitudes will, therefore, be the focus for the discussion at this time with greater involvement in the matter of opinions to occur in a later chapter (Chapter 14). There the discussion on opinions will be related primarily to that of public opinion within the framework of mass communication.

FORMATION OF ATTITUDES

Attitudes of individuals are influenced by the culture, by the larger aggregates to which the individuals belong, and by primary groups. This does not mean that any of these act independently; all of the groups relate one to the other. Indeed, the family, as the most important primary group, has been often referred to as the mediator of the culture. The cultural attitudes are interpreted by the family to the individual. The family, the larger group to which the family belongs, and the society to which these larger groups belong all interact and are interrelated in their influence on the individual.

Group Factors

The influence of groups on the attitudes of the individual is inversely proportional to the distance of the group from the individual. Primary groups are much stronger in their influence on the members of that group; larger aggregates have less influence. The more immediate is the more powerful. Newcomb and Svehla (1937) found high correlations between parents and children with respect to attitudes in many specific areas. Overall, they found a high degree of consistency between attitudes. These investigators found a higher degree of relationship between parents and children in attitudes than they found between children and their peers. The lowest correlation was between attitudes of children and their teachers. Parents, particularly in certain phases of the child's development, may find this hard to believe, but there is a closer tie between parents and children than there is between their children and other primary or secondary groups to which children belong. Hyman (1959) reviewed studies dealing with political attitudes of parents and children. A high degree of correlation was found here as well. Hyman suggests that these learned behaviors begin very early and persist rather strongly into adulthood. This is not to say that differences between parents and children do not occur; there are changes. Goldsen et al. (1960) state that the parents who hold weak attitudes do not influence their children as much when these children are exposed to other influences under rather different circumstances than those experienced in the home. Political attitudes do show a change. The current notion that children develop attitudes through rebellion is not, however, supported by the Goldsen study. Children may differ from their parents with respect to type of music enjoyed, particular patterns of immediate social behavior, or wearing of types of clothes, but on very basic matters—social, political, and religious— the resemblance between parents and children is very great.

Other primary groups are certainly very influential; the values and norms of the primary group play a very important role in influencing attitudes, opinions, and beliefs of the members of the groups. In the area of political attitudes, Campbell, Gurin, and Miller (1954) discovered a high relationship between the voting of the respondent and his friends (Table 13-1). The close relationship between voting of parents and children has been noted in other studies. Lazarsfeld, Berelson, and Gaudet (1944) indicated that as many as 75 percent of the voters voted for candidates of the party of their parents. In Pittsburgh, straw voting held in the public school system on the general election day usually reveals results similar to the official voting generally.

It has been demonstrated, in addition, that social class and religious affiliation play a vital role. While the results may have been due in part to the influence of other factors, Berelson, Lazarsfeld, and McPhee (1954) found that persons with class placement different from their families were as much influenced by family attitudes as they were by the attitudes of the new class in which they participated. It is probably more beneficial to consider groups, when we think of influence, in terms of reference group influences rather than

Table 13-1.   Voting Behavior of Individuals
and Members of their Primary Groups
(Campbell, A., Gurin, G., and
Miller, W., 1954)

Primary Group Vote	Vote of Respondents in Percent[a]	
	Republican	Democrat
Spouses voted		
Democratic	11	88
Republican	93	7
Families voted		
Democratic	20	79
Republican	91	8
Split	41	54
Friends voted		
Democratic	17	83
Republican	84	15
Evenly split	47	50

[a] "Other" category makes percent add to 100.

membership group influences. Reference groups and membership groups may be one and the same, but where they differ the reference group undoubtedly is stronger in its influence on individual attitudes.

Personality Correlates of Attitudes

Personality differences between individuals might, on the surface, appear to be a very important concomitant of the discussion of attitudes. This area has been the subject of great interest down through the years, particularly with respect to the broader area of prejudice and social functioning. Personality dynamics underlying attitudes in this aspect of social functioning carries a great deal of weight in applications of behavioral science knowledge in many practical areas. An outstanding study by Adorno et al. (1950) sketched what the authors refer to as "the authoritarian personality." The researchers developed scales which they labeled the F (for Fascism) scale and the Ethnocentrism scale, which correlated very highly with the F scale. The ethnocentrism scale attempted to measure attitudes toward minority groups, primarily Jews and Negroes. The authors found a coherent pattern of ethnocentric attitudes including antisemitism.

The most dynamically significant part of the study consisted of a sketching of personality differences between those who scored high on the ethnocentrism scale and those who scored low on that scale. The high ethnocentric scorers demonstrated, on the whole, a rigid personality pattern. The ethnocentrics stuck to the "straight and narrow," holding conventional values, not being able to accept certain socially unacceptable impulses and, therefore, in the main, projecting these on others. Low ethnocentric scorers had more flexible organization of personality and were more affectional in personal relationships or socially constructive with respect to their value systems. They were able to accept certain ordinarily unacceptable social impulses as part of their system. The authors further traced a relationship between the personality differences and the differences in the childhood training experiences. The high ethnocentrics apparently had harsh discipline, very limited areas of approved behavior, and a family structure authoritarian in nature. Low ethnocentrics had much family love in an equalitarian family pattern with reasonable discipline by the parents. It seems clear that the dynamic mechanisms of projection and repression function as the core of attitudes, opinions, and beliefs in this area which we call prejudice. This is further reinforcement for the concept that behavior is determined more by what is inside than by what is on the outside in terms of physical reality. When McClosky (1958) studied the personality correlates of conservatism and liberalism, he found that the conservative attitudes characterized those at the lower end of the intelligence scale with less education and with less awareness of current events. He did not find a relationship between conservatism and political party preference. Campbell et al. (1960) confirmed the lack of relationship between party preference and conservatism or liberalism with respect to attitudes.

MEASUREMENT OF ATTITUDES

In a sense attitudes might be defined operationally by describing the measurement systems that psychologist use to measure attitudes. One of the most often used approaches to the measurement of attitudes has been the method of Thurstone (1929), who collected a large number of statements relating to the area in which attitudes were to be measured. Attitudes may be toward war, church, education, and so on. Statements are both favorable and unfavorable. Thurstone next had a large number of judges place statements into 11 piles denoting favorability or unfavorability; the most favorable would be placed in pile one, the least favorable or unfavorable would be placed in pile 11, with appropriate placements in between. Items on which the judges showed some agreement would be retained for use in the scale which could be administered to subjects. A scale value of a particular item was the median of the positions assigned by the judges to that particular statement. With a selection of items complete and the scale values of each item determined, the scale emerged in a form that could be adminstered to determine attitudes of individuals. Individuals would then be asked to check those statements with which they agreed. The average of the scale values of the items with which they agreed would give an indication of the person's placement along the attitude continuum. For instance, if the average were a low number this would indicate a high degree of favorableness in attitudes in this particular attitude area. If items with high scale values were checked, the person would obviously be placed at the other end of the continuum.

A method that is easier because it dispenses with the need for having judges rate the items before the scale is established is one that has been developed by Likert (1932). Likert collected a number of statements that related to the attitude area. Under each statement the respondent has a chance to check one of five boxes ranging from strongly agree at one end to strongly disagree at the other end; the five boxes are arranged: strongly agree, agree, undecided, disagree, or strongly disagree. Each box is weighted 5, 4, 3, 2, 1, in order, and the summation of the item ratings gives a final score which indicates an attitude of the individual respondent. This method is often referred to as the method of summated ratings. Before the scale receives wide use, however, an item analysis must be made to determine which items hang together. Only those which do form a cluster are used in the final form of the scale.

Probably the earliest and simplest scale of measuring attitudes was the Bogardus (1925) Social Distance Scale which is composed of a number of statements with respect to acceptance by the respondents of certain national, racial, or ethnic groups. Bogardus used a seven point scale ranging from the most favorable acceptance picture, that of acceptance to close kinship by marriage, to exclusion from the country as the other end of the scale. Other, more recent, techniques include cumulative scaling as developed by Guttman (1950). If a person gets a higher scale than another person on a set of items, we would known that on a Guttman scale his position could be easily determined for every single item. An example of a perfect Guttman scale would be where three items referring to height might be tested: No. 1, I am taller than 5 feet; No. 2, I am taller than 5 feet 6 inches; No. 4, I am taller than 6 feet. If the person says yes to No. 3, we know that he has also said yes to Nos. 2 and 1. The Bogardus Social Distance Scale mentioned above has the basic approach of the cumulative scale Guttman has proposed.

Further approaches by various individuals attempt to combine the best features of scales listed above. Edwards and Kilpatrick (1948) have attempted to synthesize the Thurstone, Likert, and Guttman approaches with a technique that they call scale discrimination. Judges are used to rate the items and those which survive the test of clarity are then presented in a scale where there are six response categories ranging from strongly agree, agree, mildly agree, mildly disagree, disagree, and strongly disagree. Another analysis, as in the Likert method, then rejects the nondiscriminating items.

CONSISTENCY IN ATTITUDES

A person's attitudes are usually consistent with each other and with other aspects of his functioning including his behavior. Circumstances arise, however, that provide some inconsistencies in perceptions or cognitions. This is a source of stress on the individual. Festinger (1957) has developed a theory of cognitive dissonance that centers on the notion of such dissonance being motivating. He states that dissonance is uncomfortable and the individual will be motivated by the resulting tension to reduce or eliminate the dissonance. This can be done either by attitude change consistent with the behavior or by perceiving the difference between the two dissonant factors as being much smaller than they really are.

A further proposition in the theory of cognitive dissonance states that greater pressure for a congruence of attitude and behavior will result in less change than will be produced by an inducement that is minimal but just enough to produce an effect. In an experiment (Festinger and Carlsmith, 1959) students who worked on a boring problem were paid either $1 or $20 to tell other students who would do the work after them that the job itself was quite interesting. In a measurement of attitudes following this, the students who received $1 showed more change in attitude toward the boring job than did those who received the $20 reward. There was obviously more dissonance in the $1 group and, therefore, more change in attitudes to reduce this dissonance. In the $20 group the subjects probably recognized that the reward was all out of proportion to the task and that anyone would do it for $20. This recognition alleviated any dissonance.

ATTITUDE CHANGE

The response of the individual to all sorts of changes in the environment surrounding him is undoubtedly related to attitudes. One leading text states that "to know how attitudes change or can be made to change is a theoretical and practical problem of great moment . . . —perhaps the most urgent psychological problem in our world today" (Krech, Crutchfield, and Ballachey, 1962, p. 215).

Any discussion of attitude change must start again with the basic factors in the formation and development of attitudes. Motivation and learning are as fundamental, of course, in this area as in others. Attitudes develop as the result of an arousal of a need and then are shaped specifically through the process of learning. Thus the most important thing to remember about attitude change is that a need to change must be present. The specific changes that occur are determined by the structuring of the learning situation.

Functional Types

Attitudes can be categorized on the basis of the purposes served. Katz (1960) has grouped attitudes into four functional types: utilitarian, ego-defensive, value-expressive, and the knowledge function. The utilitarian attitudes are adjustive ones that can be recognized most easily in change situations. Where old responses are no longer relevant in new situations, the adjustive mechanism comes to the fore. When the old activities cease to be satisfying or a higher level of aspiration is set, the way is prepared for a change in attitudes. On the other hand, the individual may "adjust" by staying as he is because he perceives this as more satisfying.

Ego-defensive attitudes protect the person from threats to the ego and the anxiety generated by them. An introduction of new business procedures or a change to electronic data processing techniques, for instance, may be perceived as a threat to one's position in the company or even as an attack on the person himself. Katz (1960) suggests that some opportunity to "blow off steam" can reduce defensiveness on the part of anxiety-prone individuals.

Value-expressive attitudes are those maintaining self-identity or leading to self-expression and determination. When old values no longer provide the basis for maintaining a good self-image, change is fostered. When the new attitudes are supported by new environmental conditions, change can occur more readily. Advertising agencies begin with a concept such as the "man of distinction" and build up the image to serve clearly as a base for identity.

Attitudes serving the knowledge function tend to promote meaningfulness in all activity. An individual strives to have completeness and clarity in what he does; ambiguity can lead to attitude change when the new patterns provide more information about the problems.

Types of Change

Attitude change may be classified roughly into congruent and incongruent change. Congruent change in attitudes involves a movement in the same direction; a mild prowar attitude may become, under change procedures, even more prowar. An incongruent attitude change involves a change toward the opposite end of the continuum (a "hawk" becomes a "dove" on a war being waged at the time). The elimination of "undesirable" prejudices is a further example of incongruent change.

All other things being equal, congruent change is produced more easily than incongruent change.

Factors in Attitude Change

Characteristics of the attitudes themselves and of the individuals holding them are factors in the strength of attitudes and their susceptibility to change. To this must be added the situational factors surrounding the individual and his attitudes.

Attitude constellations that show consistency in their composition are more stable than those exposed to the strains generated by logically related attitudes that somehow differ. McGuire (1960) found, along with a change in student attitudes toward the issues targeted by the experimenters for change, a 90 percent change toward logically related issues that were not even mentioned. This is in line with Heider's (1958) Balance Theory and its prediction that an imbalance in attitudes will provide a move toward balance. Along with this, the more central the needs served by attitudes, the stronger they will be.

Individual characteristics can be important in attitude change. Personality traits have been found to be important in the susceptibility to certain kinds of propaganda. Weiss and Fine (1955) found that respondents who showed strong aggressive impulses in projective tests were more susceptible to hostile and punitive ideas in communication. Intelligence may affect the rate of change in attitudes. While the less intelligent may be harder to reach, they may be easier to change. At least the less intelligent may be less independent and conform more to imposed conditions (Terman, 1956).

Situational factors are not only more extensive but may also play a greater role in influencing the change in attitudes. How one picks up the information— through direct contact with close friends or from an impersonal mass outlet—can make a difference in the degree of change. What he is called upon to do in that situation is also an important factor. Investigators have found repeatedly that personal influence is more effective than mass media in promoting change. A classic study of voting (Lazarsfeld, Berelson, and Gaudet, 1944) showed less influence by mass communications in the changes in voting decisions, un-doubtedly a mirroring of attitudes in the matter. In a group discussion, attitude changes are more likely to take place in the direction of prevailing attitudes. Mitnick and McGinnies (1958) found that a film on tolerance reduced a prejudice score for those highly prejudiced, but the reduction was 50 percent less when the film was followed by a group discussion that included all viewpoints (Table 13-2).

A similar social influence is found in the effect of public commitment on attitudes. Hovland et al. (1957) found that attitudes represented by public statements were more resistant to change than those stated privately. This is experimental reinforcement of the steps often insisted on by the preacher who calls for a public acknowledgment of repentance or the Chinese Communist

Table 13-2. Influence of Group Discussion on Prejudice Scores after Viewing a Protolerance Film (Mitnick, L. and McGinnies, E., 1958)

Condition	Reduction in Prejudice Score (Mean)	
	Low-Prejudice Subjects	High-Prejudice Subjects
Film alone	4.9	14.7
Film and discussion	7.5	7.6

insistence on a public confession and subsequent dedication to the official program.

Change in Organizations

The process of change in business, governmental, and education organizations is thought to be so central to the continuing existence of those entities by many observers of the administrative scene that they view the manager or executive as primarily a "change agent." This designation may not be far from an identification of the basic problem in either the instituting or the guiding of change procedures in new or established groupings. The most critical factor in such change is undoubtedly the change in attitudes and values.

There are other factors, of course. Simple structural changes in the organization or placements or people in particular locations may have consequences that either promote or hinder changes in attitudes and performance. Introduction of procedures to stimulate employee participation in organizational activities have, in the past, served to develop changes in attitudes of individuals and groups. Circumstances outside the organization, such as economic changes, also play a role in altering the values and attitudes of individuals within the organization.

It is clear, however, that the strongest bases for attitude change in groups come from the social forces acting in the aggregate of individuals. Participation of individuals in the changes taking place is of utmost importance. This may depend on the even more basic task of providing information on the changing requirements to that there is a meaning or relevance in the situation for the person (Mann, 1957).

None of these points represent absolute rules, of course, but they do serve as guidelines for the promotion of change in attitudes and, consequently, behavior.

The topic of attitude change in organizations is important enough to develop further. A more detailed discussion is due, therefore, in Chapter 16.

Stereotypes

Stereotype is a word first coined by Walter Lippmann in the 1920's to describe a rather common phenomenon consisting of an oversimplified picture of a particular group and all the individuals within that group. It is a simple "picture in our head" which tells us "all" about people who have membership in the particular group on which we are focusing. Stereotypes are evident in statements like the following: "beautiful but dumb" or "all brawn and no brains." The notion that a "highbrow" or a high forehead or a big head means superior intelligence and a low brow means quite the opposite is another common constellation of attitudes, opinions, and beliefs.

In a pioneering study of this area, Katz and Braly (1933) gave a list of adjectives to a group of university students and asked the students to select from a list traits they considered characteristic of the various ethnic groups that were presented to them. Certain traits were chosen much more often than others when there was no reason for the choice other than chance. The high degree of unanimity clearly indicates the persistence of certain ideas or notions about the characteristics of the particular national or racial groups involved. The Germans were pictured as scientifically minded and industrious, Italians were very musical, Jews were shrewd, and Negroes superstitious. In a repetition of this study by Gilbert (1951), it was noted that some changes had occurred in stereotypes even though there was some stability in that the same traits seemed to be present. This time, however, not as many individuals listed particular traits as being characteristic of the groups involved. This may mean a considerable modification of the strong stereotypes that have been held.

There is a feeling that because so many people believe some characteristics to be true of certain groups that these must be true. "Where there's smoke, there's fire" is a common contention, yet there is absolutely no relationship between the height of a person's forehead and his mental ability, nor is there a negative relationship between physical well-being and structure on the one hand and intelligence on the other. Indeed, the relationship runs slightly in the other direction. Health and mental ability are positively related. Even more dramatic are demonstrations from history of changes that take place in stereotypes or references to particular groups, changes that can hardly be explained on the basis of changes in the groups themselves, particularly when the fluctuations occur from positive views to negative ones and back to more positive views again. Schrieke (1936) analyzed the references to Chinese immigrants on the west coast from a period before the Civil War down to the turn of the century. In an earlier period, when cheap labor was much in demand, the Chinese immigrants were regarded very highly. They were considered very thrifty, able citizens, ones who would be an asset to the country. In later economically troubled times, the references in journals and newspapers changed to a more negative line. The Chinese were then regarded as unassimilable, sly, and crafty, definitely a hazard to the well-being of the country. When times got better, the stereotypes also got more favorable. This is again a confirmation of the greater importance of personality dynamics than the "reality" on the outside.

Stereotypes often invade the decision making of businessmen. Selection of workers on a basis that has little foundation in fact not only discriminates against individuals rejected, but it often deprives the firm of valuable services. Marketing managers with a limited view of what consumers are like may miss their sales targets completely. Indeed, any manager or administrator who makes decisions on the basis of biased "pictures in his head" is not likely to be an effective decision maker.

Values

Men can place a high premium on material possessions, other people, groups, interaction, offices and roles, abstract ideas or concepts—virtually anything can indicate preferential choices. These are usually tinged with an additional moral flavor. What we value is not only something "good" or "desirable"; it is "good for everyone" and, therefore, ought to be viewed in the same light by all others.

Values represent something more than just a person's acceptance of the validity of a view of facts. It is not only a belief but one with a judgment of rightness attached. Values represent what is thought to be desirable, not what may be desired. What we want may be recognized as being something we ought not to seek.

VALUES AND OTHER FACTORS

Values can be differentiated from attitudes in that the latter represent predispositions to respond. While usually there will be a close correspondence between attitudes and values that makes them difficult to distinguish, the judgments of what ought to be can represent the specific manifestation of a determining tendency below the surface of the behavior.

The close relationship to norms can be seen as easily. A norm is a rule or guide for behavior established by a consensus in the social order. The consensus represents the feelings of the group as to what is desirable or what ought to be.

Opinions, too, are related to values. The notion of what is desirable will influence the evaluation of a specific set of circumstances, but the concepts are not the same. Again, what is thought desirable will not necessarily be coextensive with the judgment, that is, the opinion.

The differences between the concepts may be delineated, in somewhat oversimplified form, as follows.

Belief—"There is no difference between Whites and Negroes."
Value—"Discrimination is wrong."
Norm—"Serve Negroes in restaurants!"
Opinion—"I think the civil rights marchers in Milwaukee are right."
Attitude—pro *x*   con
                      (*x* marks placement on a basic continuum)

It can be seen that the concepts, while not isomorphic, are all part of the same package most of the time.

Behavior may be affected by values in various ways. Actions may be influenced directly in the efforts of people to conform to a norm. In an indirect way, the behavior patterns may emerge as a by-product of the norms. There may be, for instance, no direct norm with respect to cleanliness yet middle class values incorporating the desirability of vertical mobility may indirectly develop those values.

VALUES IN AMERICAN SOCIETY

An extensive analysis of the values held by Americans has been made by many researchers, notably Williams (1952, pp. 389–442). Major value orientations have been identified by Williams as "themes" of American life. Activity and achievement, moral orientation and humanitarian mores, along with material comfort and conformity are said to characterize the main thrust of American value systems.

Continuing activity toward the achievement of "success" is, in the view of many observers, an outstanding aspect of American society. The channeling of action into productive work can be a continuation of the early needs for security on the frontier. Emphasis on activity in work leads easily to economic or occupational measures of success. Business success, with wealth as an obvious measure of it, can be viewed as a prime determiner of the strong focus on business values as central in American life. Other indices may also indicate "success," of course; these may range from prestige coming from peers in a profession to the winning of blue ribbons in a dog show.

Sympathy for the "underdog" and helpfulness may also be, to continue the analysis by Williams, a salient set of values. Along with this is a moral framework in which everything is judged in terms of right and wrong, or the Puritan ethic in its broadest application.

Material comfort values emphasize gratification of wants. There is some indication that these hedonistic forces, once started, continue to expand as luxuries become necessities in the increase of desires.

In all the dynamism of American society, the factor of conformity seems, incongruously, to dampen the vigor of the activity. In a system that values individual initiative and competition toward success, the emphasis on conformity seems out of place. An answer may be that the conformity valued is one primarily social—adherence to group goals as exemplified by the "joiner" of organizations. Promotion of technological change and the rejection of economic controls provide the field for nonconformity.

As with any complex phenonenon in society, the sketching of prevailing patterns is necessarily incomplete and, in this way, possibly misleading. Variations within the patterns are of further interest. The Lynd (1937) study of "Middletown" (Muncie, Indiana) demonstrated inconsistencies in values that were likely to put a strain on the society. Individualism was valued but joining with others was considered proper as well; education was prized but a prevailing view was that it took a "practical man" to get things done. More recent research by Mack (1956) points to further splits in values. A survey using questions based on the Bill of Rights of the United States Constitution indicated that many Americans oppose various parts of the concepts incorporated in those amendments guaranteeing fundamental individual rights.

Norms

Most groups have rules to govern the behavior of their members. These guidelines or directions as to what is accepted or prohibited are called *norms*. These can vary from very simple rules to very complex sets of prescriptions and prohibitions. In a society, the ramifications of a normative system can be extensive. Norms not only indicate to members of the group what they should or should not do, they also provide for a system of built-in rewards and punishments for the behavior. Just as norms may vary in strength or intensity of feeling and complexity, so punishment can vary in severity. Anything from mild disapproval of behavior to capital punishment can be encountered.

Norms depend on values. A belief as to what "ought to be" is fundamental to shaping of the rules for the society. If a society values property above human life, the norms will reflect this. Capital punishment finds a more fertile ground in this kind of atmosphere. A belief that one ought to give up his seat in a bus to a lady represents another value that has certain norms tied to it. In this instance, the norm represents an area to which we do not attach much importance and, therefore, a violation of this norm does not bring as severe punishment with it. Mild social disapproval is the extent of the sanction.

CATEGORIES OF NORMS

Norms governing behavior that is not considered critical in the functioning of a society are classified as *folkways*. Proper manners, style of dress, language used with other people—all those we may call etiquette—do not ordinarily arouse strong emotion. A deviation from these norms would not be severely punished; at best, mild social disapproval would result if an individual violated these rules.

Norms governing behavior of individuals in areas believed to be more important for the functioning of the society are known as *mores*. The term mores is a Latin word for authoritative and sacred customs of long standing. The name was first applied to the strong and critical norms of a society by an early sociologist, William Graham Sumner (1906), who observed that modern Western peoples had no word for the concept. While mores themselves imply stronger feelings about the behavior in question, there are variations within this classification. Some behavior may be considered by a society as sufficient threat to the continuation of that group that some formalized set of sanctions is set up. Law and law enforcement agencies thus enter the regulation of behavior. Mores do not need to be enforced by laws, however, as they maintain their influence in informal or noninstitutionalized ways. Extramarital relations in a monogamous society, for instance, would brand the guilty parties as immoral and not fit to be in the company of "decent" people in the society. This informal sanction would be powerful even if no laws governing this kind of behavior would be enacted. Additionally, however, we might look for variations in time since mores are not static. Custom may show changes representing increasing or decreasing severity of sanctions, depending on the values of the society at that particular time.

Norms that are thought to be important enough to the regulation of behavior to be organized in some formal way are laws. Laws are norms that have been institutionalized; that is, the rules are organized and enforced by the political authority of the state. Some researchers refer to these as *institutional ways*. Laws, too, show differing degrees of intensity. Those regulating the driving of automobiles are not as deeply incorporated into a society as are the sanctions surrounding murder. Traffic tickets and capital punishment are at opposite ends of a continuum, yet both represent sanctions imposed under institutional ways.

A norm that is deeply engrained in individuals in a society is called a *taboo*. The incest taboo seems to be well-nigh universal, while those prohibiting cannibalism and murder are very nearly so. While laws may have been enacted to prohibit these actions, even if there were no institutionalized norms the deterrents to action would probably be very strong. We would expect, in a taboo, that the conscience of an individual would regulate his behavior. We would also regard any departure from this behavior as an indication of a grave mental disturbance and would probably label the individual as psychopathic.

VARIATIONS IN NORMS

The great variation in intensity of norms as well as overlapping of categories sketched above should be apparent to the reader at this point. The same circumstances may be treated in an informal manner or the norms enforced in a formal and institutionalized way. This can be a source of conflict when a group in power decides that its moral viewpoints are important enough to be enacted into a statute regulating the behavior of all. Under these circumstances, what is considered immoral by a segment then becomes illegal for the entire population. A large part of the society may be governed by a set of rules foreign to them; severe stress on the society can result. The enactment of Prohibition in the United States represents one such attempt to regulate on the basis of the moral feelings of part of the total population. At the present time, restrictions such as those with respect to gambling are often bypassed because this behavior is not considered offensive to those individuals. Charitable groups often run bingo games or lotteries to raise funds for their endeavors.

Additional problems arise when institutional ways do not keep pace with changes in values and mores. Still on the books are many "blue laws" reflecting patterns of behavior of a bygone era. Most of these are seldom enforced and are regarded with humor under the prevailing social norms. Technically they can be, and sometimes are, strictly enforced, adding to the stress existing in modern-day life. Sunday closing laws for retail establishments are currently under test, and considerable discussion also exists over laws governing sex relations.

The variations, state by state, indicate wide differences in views. Some concern has been felt over the limited legal response to change or lack of a coordinated legislative or enforcement program. As a result, complete conformity to the laws is unlikely in view of the vast changes in mores over the years. More important is the fact that individual freedom and the dignity of the person are seldom advanced under arbitrary guides or regulations that do not reflect societal changes.

Prejudice

Strictly speaking, prejudice is a neutral term meaning a prejudgment of a set of circumstances but, in behavioral or social research (and, by now, in common parlance as well), the term is used to mean an attitude as the result of which an ethnic group, or a member of it, is put at a disadvantage. We immediately think of hostile attitudes toward Negroes or minority groups when prejudice is mentioned, although the negative attitudes and opinions can be, and are, just as easily expressed toward the majority or other generally more favored grouping.

Discrimination is a phenomenon often accompanying prejudice, but the two concepts differ. Prejudice is an attitude, while discrimination is the active expression of it. To feel that Negroes are no good is prejudice; to refuse to admit them to a locality is discrimination.

Conflict in community relations arises most often, and more so recently, on an ethnic basis. Since prejudice and discrimination are fundamental aspects of a broad social process, it is little wonder that researchers have been interested in this behavioral area.

CHARACTERISTICS OF PREJUDICE

The extent of prejudice toward other individuals and groups is not known exactly, but evidence from various sources indicates that it is general if not universal. Most people, whether they know it or not, have at least some bias in interpersonal relations. The hostility toward minority groups has been documented in great detail in many research reports (as well as casual observation by laymen); what is not as well recognized is that minority groups can display similar hostile attitudes toward the dominant group as well as maintaining a prejudicial hierarchy within their own group. Simpson and Yinger (1953, pp. 219–222) report that minority group members can take over the ranking basis used by the majority and even accentuate it. Negroes may differentiate on the basis of skin coloring of fellow Negroes, while whites lump them all together in one category. Jews have their own "pecking order" in prejudice within the group. Jews of German origin often look down on those coming from countries to the east of them.

Exposure to the prejudice of the "power structure" not only causes individuals to copy the system in their own groups, it can develop feelings of inferiority in those same individuals. When they adopt majority group prejudices, they do so in all respects, even those concerning themselves.

Even more productive of social conflict is the hostility built up in minority targets of prejudice to counter the initial hostility of the dominant group. Aggression develops as the active expression of hostility. Since aggression by one side breeds counteraggression, the resulting social conflict is likely to be extensive.

BASES OF PREJUDICE

There is no reason to believe that prejudice is any different from other aspects of behavior with respect to the underlying factors contributing to its development and continuation. Learning, shaped by immediate social influences, alters the personality of the individual in a way that often provides a clear-cut understanding of the forces at work in a dynamic area such as prejudice.

Personality

The relationship between the personality dynamics of an individual and the responses of prejudice and discrimination has been suggested down through the years by many researchers. Not until after World War II, however, did a deep and incisive study of these relationships take place. The now classic study (mentioned above) by Adorno and others (1950) demonstrated the specific constellation of attitudinal traits they labeled "the authoritarian personality"; they were able to identify a pattern of characteristics as the result of individual response test scales where people were asked to agree or disagree with items like the following.

1. Any good leader should be strict with people under him in order to gain their respect.
2. There are two kinds of people in the world, the weak and the strong.

It can be said that a person with authoritarian responses regards relationships between individuals in terms of force; the weak obey, the strong command, and the respondent would stand with the strong. This emphasis on power denies the basic equality of man and minimizes the importance of the ties of sympathy and love. With this personality base, it may be easy for an individual to distrust others and be prejudiced in his relationships with them, particularly if the individuals have some visible membership in a minority group.

Social Influences

There are many indications, even in the study of the authoritarian personality, that the dynamics of prejudice are much more complex than the sketch of personality patterns would imply. Patterns of prejudice have been shown to vary with the surrounding circumstances, regardless of the personality characteristics of the individuals. Sims and Patrick (1936) noted differences between Northern college students in the North and in those Southern colleges with respect to their attitudes toward Negroes. Pettigrew (1958) also noted greater prejudice in the South but found no difference between the extent of authoritarian attitudes in North and South. The higher degree of prejudice found in the South, therefore, was not a result of the larger number of authoritarian personalities. The indication is clear that surrounding circumstances play a role in prejudice at least as much as does personality. Widespread community attitudes are bound to have their impact. These may be specific norms for interaction or laws enforcing segregation. They may also be casual reactions resulting from prevailing stereotypes of minority groups held by the· dominant members of a society.

A perceived threat to one's social and economic status has been found consistently to be an element of prejudice. Feelings of being displaced from one's position by incoming minority groups feed latent feelings of aggression and prejudice against those groups. Several studies are in agreement that individuals who are downwardly mobile, that is, who find themselves slipping in the social scale, demonstrate the clearest feelings associated with prejudice (Greenblum and Pearlin, 1953; Bettelheim and Janowitz, 1950).

REDUCTION OF PREJUDICE

Elimination of prejudice is not likely to be complete, particularly in the near future. It may well be, however, that there are mechanisms that can at least alleviate the tensions that arise in intergroup relations and stem the conflict that could develop. Understanding the broad historical and social backgrounds for intergroup conflict can help somewhat; a glimpse into the needs served by prejudice can assist as well in overcoming some of the divisive factors in this form of social conflict.

Many people have placed their hopes in education on the assumption that the elimination of prejudice would occur as soon as people were exposed to the facts. As valuable as specific educational approaches toward attitude change might be, the fact remains that such attempts have not been as successful as their proponents have hoped. The reason is quite simple. Prejudice is not an intellectual matter but an emotional one, and the emotions in this area can be very strong and deep seated.

More positive and direct action has been taken in recent years to promote better relations between groups and reduce prejudice or discrimination. These have varied from changes imposed by legal fiat to an increasing of informal mingling of individuals. Despite the fact that mores are resistant to change, some direct action has been successful in changing attitudes. Stouffer et al. (1949) report on responses to integration of Negro troops into Army units in World War II. Varying degrees of integration were introduced into units of the Army. Those soldiers in units where integration was greatest reported the most favorable attitudes toward Negroes. Where integration was minimal or nonexistent, attitudes toward Negroes were highly negative. Similar findings are reported by Deutsch and Collins (1951) in their comparison of interracial and segregated housing projects (Table 13-3). Housewives in the interracial

Table 13-3. **Attitude Change after Arranged Racial Contacts (Deutsch, M. and Collins, M., 1951)**

| | Net Gain in Attitude Score (in Percent) | | | |
| | Two Integrated Housing Projects | | Two Segregated Housing Projects | |
Initial Attitude	A	B	C	D
Highly unfavorable	78	71	26	19
Moderately unfavorable	61	46	18	2
Favorable	28	13	15	−18

housing projects had more variable attitudes toward Negroes than the housewives in the segregated projects. While those who chose to live in the interracial project may have been more liberal in their attitudes to begin with, part of the positive pattern in attitudes can be traced to the increased interaction among individuals as the result of official policy decisions to integrate.

In summary, it may be stated that positive action promoting greater interaction among groups can and usually does have a beneficial effect. There is a further caution, however. Thoughtful preparations must precede action in order to provide a secure and nonthreatening environment for the relationships that are to be built up in the new social situation.

Whatever action is taken, some positive stand is necessary. The alternatives inherent in continuing segregation and discrimination are undesirable in a free society and have been recognized as such by an increasing number of individuals. While the matter had been argued persuasively before, the combination of efforts to present sociopsychological evidence of the deleterious effects of segregation came in a statement signed by 35 of the country's leading behavioral scientists. This was appended to the appellant's briefs in the landmark case of Brown vs. Board of Education of Topeka in 1954. When the Supreme Court cited the statement as a footnote, it not only pronounced segregation inherently unequal, it indicated acceptance of the validity of social and psychological factors in the determination of legal outcomes.

Job Attitudes, Satisfaction, and Morale

Morale and job satisfaction are closely tied to the basic concepts of attitudes and motivation. Indeed, some writers fail to distinguish between certain of these variables with the result that there is some variety in usage. In the light of possible discrepancies, it may be of value first to note the more common usages of the terms and to mention variations in later discussion.

An attitude is a predisposition to respond, positively or negatively, to a certain set of facts. A job attitude would be, therefore, a tendency to respond to aspects of the job. The direction and extent of attitudes on the work role or job elements themselves could be measured.

Job satisfaction is based on job attitudes but is somewhat broader in that job satisfaction relates to how the job fits into the total picture of the person's functioning. Satisfactions outside the job are *not* included except as they contribute to the person's perception of how the work role fits with his expectations, those of others, and the values that have been built up through the incorporation of cultural patterns. A machinist may be, for instance, quite positively disposed to the material aspects of his work; if he comes from a milieu where the job of machinist carries with it the imprint of a menial occupation, the impact of this on him contributes heavily to job satisfaction. The converse, job dissatisfaction, is more likely. In a family where becoming a machinist is a prized goal, the resulting picture of job satisfaction is likely to be different. Satisfaction has been considered by many to be basically a matter of needs, feelings, or expectations.

Morale is a group concept. It is the summation of the attitudes of the individuals making up the group. One may speak of high morale where the members generally have positive attitudes within the context of the group task, while a reference to a greater presence of negative attitudes indicates low morale. Viteles (1953) has added a more dynamic factor to this by defining morale as "willingness to strive for the goals of a particular group." With or without this aspect it is clear that it is incorrect to speak, as some do, of individual morale. Morale is *esprit de corps,* or the attitudes of the collective body.

Some investigators use the term morale synonymously with job satisfaction, and doing so has some empirical justification. There is evidence from morale studies that the components of both job satisfaction and morale are the same (Guba, 1958; Baehr and Renck, 1958) so that the distinction remains primarily definitional. Morale refers to a group, particularly when common goals are stressed, while job satisfaction is the individual picture of activity.

Most of the research activity has focused on job satisfaction, the area of greatest interest and importance. Since the related concepts of job attitudes and morale are either part of or so closely related to job satisfaction, a discussion of the latter factor will provide the basis for the understanding of motivated behavior on the job.

JOB SATISFACTION

The topics of job satisfaction and its determinants have occupied the interest of industrial researchers for some time, since the importance of this factor in industrial functioning has been easily recognized. Several research studies beginning with Hoppock (1935) have probed this area, with the focus not only on identifying the elements of satisfaction but, more practically, on determining the relationships with job performance or productivity. Under the aegis of the Survey Research Center at the University of Michigan, a series of studies emerged with the purpose of identifying the salient features of job satisfaction. In the pioneer study (Katz, Maccoby, and Morse, 1950), the authors surveyed the employees of a large insurance company and determined four measures of "general job satisfaction": (1) pride in work group, (2) intrinsic job satisfaction, (3) company involvement, and (4) financial and job status satisfaction. The measures were obtained from interviews and were then related to actual productivity.

A later study that has generated interest and further research on the basis of its conceptual contributions is one by Herzberg, Mausner, and Snyderman (1959). In it the authors have added the study of job content to job context, that is, what is in the job itself in addition to the social surroundings of the task. Their significant contribution to further research activity was the general finding that most of the 16 factors in job satisfaction were polar variables; this means that a factor could contribute to satisfaction but its absence would not lead to dissatisfaction. Some factors are satisfiers while others are dissatisfiers; absence of a certain factor does not lead to the opposite condition. Herzberg et al. found that five factors stood out as determinants of satisfaction—achievement, recognition for work, responsibility, advancement, and work itself. Dissatisfiers were—supervision, salary, company policy and administration, interpersonal relations, and working conditions. These dissatisfiers were named *hygiene* factors while the satisfier factors were called *motivators*.

Some questions have been raised since then as to the clarity or validity of the Herzberg two-factor concept of job satisfaction. Lindsay, Marks, and Gorlow (1967), among others, did not find hygienes and motivators to be on separate continua. They did find, however, that both motivators and hygienes were related to job satisfaction, with motivators the more important of the two concepts.

FACTORS IN JOB SATISFACTION

The element that usually comes to mind first in a discussion of factors contributing to job satisfaction is that of wages. The economist is likely to focus on this aspect of the job situation as being very important for job satisfaction, and many businessmen are doubtless in agreement that money is a crucial factor. Surveys provide mixed evidence; some have wages being placed high on a list by workers while other reports put the monetary incentives much lower, a result that appears more often. What complicates the picture is that the money may really represent other factors; money per se is seldom a factor, even when people are conscious of nothing else. Apart from the subjective evaluations going into a ranking of factors, some objective information exists that indicates that job satisfaction is positively related to income level. The higher the pay, the greater the satisfaction (Lawler and Porter, 1963).

The relationship between occupational level and job satisfaction has been of substantial interest for a long time. An early study (Hoppock, 1935) was followed by many research efforts indicating a clear positive relationship between job level and job satisfaction. In extensive and recent data, Gurin, Veroff, and Feld (1960) support this long-established finding in their national sample. Only 13 percent of unskilled workers were very satisfied, but 42 percent of professionals said they were. Since a move upward in a job means a change in the many other variables treated in this section, an assessment of the effect on job satisfaction is of value. Morse (1953) did find a positive relationship between a person's expectations of a promotion and his job satisfaction.

It has been suspected by even casual observers that the superior in the job situation plays an important role in the satisfaction of his subordinates, but the exact relationships may not have been clear. Pelz (1952) noted that the amount of influence the supervisor possesses with his superiors is directly related to the perception of the subordinates. The supervisor who can "deliver" for his men is not only an influential one but is a prime contributor to the job satisfaction of his workers. This is true as well on the academic scene. Bachman (1968) found that faculty satisfaction with college deans was highest for those deans who had greatest influence in college affairs, particularly where the influence was based on expertise rather than coercive control.

The factor of control over one's activities can play a decided role in the attitudes one brings to that task. In times of increasing specialization and standardization, one might expect some impact from these factors on job satisfaction. Walker and Guest (1952) found low satisfaction with assembly-line work over which the individual had little control, particularly in the timing of actions. In the same assembly plant, the researchers found increasing job satisfaction with an increase in the number of operations the workers were called on to perform.

It is possible to go even further and state that people may have a need to utilize their abilities to the fullest (as in Maslow's concept of self-actualization). Vroom (1962) presents empirical evidence of a relationship between job satisfaction and opportunity for self-expression in the work, while other writers use such results as a basis for related conceptualization. In *Work and the nature of man* (1966), Herzberg amplifies the concepts of hygienes and motivators. A recurring theme in this work is the strong feeling of the author that, while industry may keep people from being dissatisfied by taking care of the hygiene factors, it does very little to promote positive action and attitudes by means of the motivators. Herzberg calls the latter aspect the *Abraham* side of man as opposed to the *Adam* or animal one.

JOB SATISFACTION AND PERFORMANCE

Since the early days of studies or essays on "Human Relations," advocates of the approach (and sometimes its critics, too) have simply assumed that, since it was "good," it carried with it many positive contributions, including high performance. People basically believed that job satisfaction and morale were positively related to productivity on the job. That the actual relationships may be more complex than is first imagined is a result that has emerged from several research efforts. In their well-known study to isolate aspects of job satisfaction, Katz, Maccoby, and Morse (1950) went on to relate satisfaction to work performance.

Earlier the authors had identified 12 high producing sections and 12 low production groups to use as the basis for determining the relationship between job satisfaction and productivity. Of the four measures of job satisfaction, only the one called "pride in work group" showed a relationship between job satisfaction and productivity; that is, only this factor differentiated between high and low producing sections. The study, incidently, illustrates a problem inherent in the interpretation of many research findings, namely, the inability to pinpoint a cause and effect relationship. For instance, in this study it is difficult to decide whether the high producers are satisfied because they are high producers or are high producers because they are satisfied. It may be enough to say that the factors are related, however.

A comparison of characteristics of supervisors of high and low producing sections showed significant differences between the two groups of supervisors. The heads of high producing sections were more employee-centered than production-centered and were not given to close supervision of the employee. On the basis of the findings, it is not difficult to relate these characteristics of superiors to satisfaction of the workers even though some researchers minimize the contribution of supervisors' behavior to job satisfaction.

Direct relationship between job satisfaction and productivity are not the only aspects of interest in performance. Indirect factors can be studied as well. Morse (1953) found that job satisfaction was negatively related to variables such as absenteeism and turnover. Other evidence confirms that people are more likely to leave if the job fails to satisfy their needs one way or another (Talacchi, 1960).

In summary it may be stated that, while there may not necessarily be a relationship between job satisfaction and productivity, performance may be affected indirectly by the absenteeism or turnover which is related (negatively) to satisfaction.

Summary

Predispositions to react and related learned variables are important in human behavior. Attitudes are the basic predispositions to react in a positive or negative direction, while opinions are specific judgments influenced by attitudes. Belief is a stronger acceptance of a set of facts or events. Each of the variables influences and is influenced by the others.

Attitudes are formed very early and most immediately in the primary family group, though the broader cultural influences are present. Peers are also influential in shaping social, political, and religious attitudes but not as much as are parents. Personality and attitudes are interrelated in many respects; ethnocentric individuals are disposed to be narrow in emotions or values and less open and accepting of others and their ideas.

Attitudes are measured most often by having subjects respond to items that have been scaled earlier by the researcher. Generally, the response consists of an agreement or disagreement with the statement or a checking of the item that most closely corresponds with one's position on the question.

Attitudes show a consistency. Individuals attempt to reduce the discomfort between dissonant aspects of their perceptions by tending toward congruency in attitudes—the reduction of "cognitive dissonance."

Attitudes may change, however. Much of the kind and extent of change depends on how the attitudes are formed and the purposes they serve. Attitudes can be adaptive to situations, protective of the ego, expressive of emotions, or vehicles for meaning in activity. Change may occur in terms of intensity or direction, with the latter change being the more difficult. Generally, any changes occur in the direction of consistency—agreement with other attitudes, consonancy with personality, and similarity of response of peers. Change in groups and organizations is a more complex matter though based on individual changes.

Stereotype is an oversimplified representation of reality or, more commonly, an inaccurate portrayal of a set of facts. Pictured characteristics of individuals or groups may perpetuate myths and the prejudice stemming from them.

Values are preferred options with a moral or desirable tinge. This feeling of rightness is one which is felt to be shared by a large number. They are closely related to opinions, attitudes, beliefs, and norms. In American society the dominant themes of work and success prevail, though some inconsistencies such as the trend to conformity may be seen as complicating factors.

Norms are rules governing the behavior of members of a group. They vary in strength or importance from casual folkways to the more intense taboos. Variations in norms among segments of a society may produce some discord if what may be considered undesirable and upsetting in some subgroups is not considered so in another grouping.

Prejudice, technically a neutral term, now refers to a negative attitude that places an ethnic or social group and its individual members at a disadvantage. Such bias is extensive, since even minority group members may incorporate such attitudes in their own functioning. Hostility, aggression, and feelings of inferiority are common results of prejudice. The "authoritarian personality" shows more prejudice than do others; perceived threats in interpersonal situations intensify the response as social influences generally are important factors. Prejudice can be reduced but less by simple education than by a change in attitudes and emotions. A positive stand to remove the threats to individuals in social relations is necessary.

Attitudes toward one's work and the emotional responses from it are significant features of the present social scene. Job satisfaction is the positive response to the contributions of one's work to the general level of expectation built up through experience. Morale is a group concept although closely related to positive job attitudes and job satisfaction.

The job itself may be the source of satisfaction, or the job as it fits into the surroundings may be the provider of positive feelings. Each of these may be subdivided further. Contributing to job satisfaction are such variables as higher occupational level, higher salary (though not money alone), control over the situation, and opportunity to contribute to the fullest. Job satisfaction may not necessarily stimulate higher performance but it usually does, if only in indirect ways.

Bibliography

Adorno, T., Frenkel-Brunswik, E., Levinson, D., and Sanford, R. (1950). *The authoritarian personality.* New York: Harper.

Bachman, J. (1968). Faculty satisfaction and the dean's influence: an organizational study of twelve liberal arts colleges. *Journal of Applied Psychology,* **52(1),** 55–61.

Baehr, M. and Renck, R. (1958). The definition and measurement of employee morale. *Administrative Science Quarterly,* **3,** 157–184.

Berelson, B., Lazarsfeld, P., and McPhee, W. (1954). *Voting.* Chicago: University of Chicago Press.

Bettelheim, B. and Janowitz, M. (1950). *Dynamics of prejudice: a psychological and sociological study of veterans.* New York: Harper & Row.

Bogardus E. (1925). Measuring social distance. *Journal of Applied Sociology.* **9,** 299–308.

Campbell, A., Gurin, G., and Miller, W. (1954). *The voter decides.* Evanston, Ill.: Row, Peterson.

Campbell, A., Converse, P., Miller, W., and Stokes, D. (1960). *The American voter.* New York: Wiley.

Deutsch, M. and Collins, M. (1951). *Interracial housing: a psychological evaluation of a social experiment.* Minneapolis: University of Minnesota Press.

Edwards, A. and Kilpatrick, F. (1948). A technique for the construction of attitude scales. *Journal of Applied Psychology,* **32,** 374–384.

Festinger, L. (1957). *A theory of cognitive dissonance.* Evanston, Ill: Row, Peterson.

Festinger, L. and Carlsmith, J. (1959). Cognitive consequences of forced compliance. *Journal of Abnormal and Social Psychological,* **58,** 203–210.

Gilbert, G. (1951). Stereotype persistence and change among college students. *Journal of Abnormal and Social Psychology,* **46,** 245–254.

Goldsen, R., Rosenberg, M., Williams, R., and Suchman, E. (1960). *What college students think.* Princeton: Van Nostrand.

Gouldner, A. and Gouldner, H. (1963). *Modern sociology.* New York: Harcourt, Brace and World.

Greenblum, J. and Pearlin, L. (1953). Vertical mobility and prejudice. In Bendix, R. and Lipset, S. (eds.). *Class, status, and power.* Glencoe: Free Press.

Guba, E. (1958). Morale and satisfaction: a study in past-future time perspective. *Administrative Science Quarterly,* **3,** 195–209.

Gurin, G., Veroff, J., and Feld, S. (1960). *Americans view their mental health.* New York: Basic Books.

Guttman, L. (1950). The third component of scalable attitudes. *International Journal of Opinion and Attitude Research,* **4,** 285–287.

Heider, F. (1958). *The psychology of interpersonal relations.* New York: Wiley.

Herzberg, F. (1966). *Work and the nature of man.* Cleveland: World.

Herzberg, F., Mausner, B., and Snyderman, B. (1959). *The motivation to work.* New York: Wiley.

Hoppock, R. (1935). *Job satisfaction.* New York: Harper.

Hovland, C., Campbell, E., and Brock, T. (1957). The effects of "commitment" on opinion change following communication. In Hovland, C. et al. (eds.). *The order of presentation in persuasion.* New Haven: Yale University Press.

Hyman, H. (1959). *Political socialization: a study in the psychology of political behavior.* New York: Free Press.

Katz, D. (1960). The functional approach to the study of attitudes. *Public Opinion Quarterly,* **24,** 163–204.

Katz, D. and Braly, K. (1933). Racial stereotypes of 100 college students. *Journal of Abnormal and Social Psychology,* **28,** 280–290.

Katz, D., Maccoby, N., and Morse, N. (1950). *Productivity, supervision, and morale in an office situation.* Ann Arbor: Survey Research Center, Institute for Social Research, University of Michigan.

Krech, D., Crutchfield, R., and Ballachey, E. (1962). *Individual in society.* New York: McGraw-Hill.

Lawler, E. and Porter, L. (1963). Perceptions regarding management compensation. *Industrial Relations,* 3, 41–49.

Lazarsfeld, P., Berelson, B., and Gaudet, H. (1944). *The people's choice.* New York: Duell, Sloan and Pearce.

Likert, R. (1932). A technique for the measurement of attitudes. *Archives of Psychology,* no. 140.

Lindsay, C., Marks, E., and Gorlow, L. (1967). The Herzberg Theory: a critique and reformulation. *Journal of Applied Psychology,* 51(4), 330–339.

Lynd, R. and Lynd, H., (1937). *Middletown in transition: a study in cultural conflicts.* New York: Harcourt, Brace, and World.

Mack, R. (1956). Do we really believe in the Bill of Rights. *Social Problems,* 3, 264–269.

Mann, F. (1957). Studying and creating change: a means to understanding social organization. In Arensberg, C. et al. (eds.). *Research in industrial human relations.* New York: Harper & Row.

McClosky, H. (1958). Conservatism and personality. *American Political Science Review,* 52, 27–45.

McGuire, W. (1960). Cognitive consistency and attitude change. *Journal of Abnormal and Social Psychology,* 60, 345–353.

Mitnick, L. and McGinnies, E. (1958). Influencing ethnocentrism in small discussion groups through a film communication. *Journal of Abnormal and Social Psychology,* 56, 82–90.

Morse, N. (1953). *Satisfactions in the white collar job.* Ann Arbor: University of Michigan Press.

Newcomb, T. and Svehla, G. (1937). Intra-family relationships in attitude. *Sociometry,* 1, 180–205.

Pelz, D. (1952). Influence: a key to effective leadership in the first-line supervisor. *Personnel,* 29, 3–11.

Pettigrew, T. (1958). Personality and sociocultural factors in intergroup attitudes, a cross-national comparison. *Journal of Conflict Resolution,* 2, 29–42.

Schrieke, B. (1936). *Alien Americans: a study of race relations.* New York: Viking.

Simpson, G. and Yinger, J. (1953). *Racial and cultural minorities.* New York: Harper & Row.

Sims, V. and Patrick, J. (1936). Attitude toward the Negro of Northern and Southern college students. *Journal of Social Psychology,* **7,** 192–204.

Stouffer, S., Suchman, E., DeVinney, L., Star, S., and Williams, R. Jr. (1949). *The American soldier,* Vol. I. Princeton, N.J.: Princeton University Press.

Sumner, W. (1906). *Folkways.* New York: Ginn.

Talacchi, S. (1960). Organization size, individual attitudes and behavior. *Administrative Science Quarterly,* **5,** 398–420.

Terman, L. (1956). *Concept mastery test manual.* New York: Psychological Corporation.

Thurstone, L. (1929). Theory of attitude measurement. *Psychological Bulletin,* **36,** 222–241.

Viteles, M. (1953). *Motivation and morale in industry.* New York: Norton.

Vroom, V. (1962). Ego-involvement, job satisfaction and job performance. *Personnel Psychology,* **15,** 159–178.

Walker, C. and Guest, R. (1952). *The man on the assembly line.* Cambridge: Harvard University Press.

Weiss, W. and Fine, B. (1955). Opinion change as a function of some interpersonal attributes of the communicatees. *Journal of Abnormal and Social Psychology,* **51,** 246–253.

Williams, R. (1952). *American society.* New York: Knopf.

14

Mass Communication

That language and communication are important in human behavior has already been established (Chapter 9) on an individual basis. In the present chapter the discussion will focus on the broader and more impersonal facets of communication. While the individual variables cannot be ignored, the emphasis here will be placed more on the factors at work in the operations of mass media and opinion; most of the research in this area is centered on the effect of media on public opinion.

Mass communications originate in and are transmitted by mass media. By mass media is meant those physical or mechanical means of providing information to a large number of individuals at one time. Newapapers, radio, and television are the outstanding examples. The difference between mass and individual communications is more than simply a matter of degree. Mass communications not only reach greater numbers of people, they also operate through more effective devices at a single location to the larger number of individuals; the general grouping of individuals who are the targets of mass media presentations is known as an *audience*.

A *public,* on the other hand, is the designation for a grouping that has broader criteria for membership than an audience. Broom and Selznick (1968, p. 236) define a public as people who:

1. Regard themselves as affected by an event or activity.
2. Can in some way register that concern.
3. Are taken into account.

As a result, a public is not a formally organized group nor are the individuals assembled in one place. The number and composition of the group may change as circumstances provide different areas of concern. The areas upon which people focus can vary as well, allowing for various categories of publics. Viewers, voters, students, and stockholders all represent different types of publics. The greatest interest in publics and public opinion, however, lies in the area of political behavior. Not only is there an interest in public opinion on issues broadly affecting the nation or concerning local municipalities, there is attraction to the general political process, that is, the utilization of power moves by pressure groups in organizations or institutions of all types.

The relationship between a theoretical view of public opinion and the actuality of behavior is a lively topic. Berelson (1952) points out that the political theory of democracy sets a high standard in that it requires the electorate to be informed, realistic, principled, and considerate of the public interest. What really happens in democratic decision making is the subject of continuing behavioral studies, primarily in the field of opinion sampling. This is a central feature of the behavioral science approach to this area.

Opinions, as we have already noted, are judgments or evaluations of a specific set of circumstances. They reflect broader or more basic attitudes and values, but they arise as the result of a stimulus from a specific situation. Asking students for their evaluation of a neighborhood project undertaken by a business organization may be affected by student attitudes and values, but the specific response is tied in to that particular circumstance.

When an opinion is determined to be widely held by members of the public, we can say that a consensus exists. This wide agreement among members can be on broad national issues or on limited local and personal topics. We might say, for instance, that a consensus has developed in this country that segregation is socially undersirable and should be eliminated. There may be differences of opinion, however, as to the extent to which measures should be introduced at this time to promote integration and equal rights. This does not detract from the fact that there is a consensus on the essential validity of the civil rights movement.

Propaganda is a deliberate attempt to influence attitudes and opinions through a use of planned techniques and proper media to achieve that result. While most researchers emphasize that the term propaganda is a neutral one by itself, the word has, by now, attained a dubious reputation so that for most people it has an unpleasant connotation. Most see it as a distortion of the truth or a manipulation of the audience. To those who do not react negatively, the word propaganda simply means an attempt to influence and whether it is good or bad depends on the ends. It may well be that in practice it would be difficult to differentiate between propaganda and other techniques, such as education, for instance. This and other matters will be discussed at greater length later in the chapter.

Methodology

Gathering information in the mass communications field may be accomplished in most of the ways described earlier in Chapter 3. Some methods are more useful than others, however, and a sampling of these will serve as a reminder with respect to data-gathering methods or as an introduction to some variants that are particularly useful in communications research. Generally, survey methods are the most productive and are more widely used.

INTERVIEWS

In the area of mass communication research, as well as in other areas, the interview has been perhaps the most widely used technique of data gathering. The value of a flexible face-to-face eliciting of information can be readily appreciated. On the other hand, there is also opportunity for a variation in the use of this technique that can produce some questionable results.

The type of question and its phrasing is probably the most significant aspect of the interview. Questions may be categorized very broadly as either open or closed. An open question calls for recall of certain facts, and the response is limited only by the verbal constraints or limitations of the respondent. Because of its variety and possible length, the answer to the open-end question is more difficult to score. The closed question involves the choice of a simple response, such as *yes, no,* or *don't know.* Response may also be made to items in a list with a selection from the alternatives given. The closed question restricts responses and, while it is easy to score, the restricted answer may not give the complete information obtainable in the open question.

Both types of questions may be used in the same research study. There may be positive value in beginning with open questions to avoid a bias caused by direct and specific questioning, and then presenting some closed questions. Working from a broader range and narrowing the questions to a specific point has been called the *funnel technique.*

Phrasing is a further aspect to which close attention must be paid. Maccoby and Maccoby (1954) list several "rules of wording" that should be followed. Words with double meaning should be avoided and the questions phrased in terms of the respondent's own experience. The context should be specified and alternatives made explicit. Unfamiliar subjects should be prefaced with some explanations. The same authors add some suggestions for phrasing that could overcome emotional resistance or negative attitudes on the part of the respondents. These are designed to prevent loss of prestige or to allow the admission of what might be considered socially unacceptable responses. Questions may be phrased in euphemistic terms to help in "face-saving," although some areas require direct questioning that puts the burden on the respondent. For instance, a question such as "How large are your monthly payments?" is likely to elicit more accurate replies than a simple question, "Did you pay cash or did you buy it on the installment plan?"

The entire interview may be arranged in a specific order of questions, or there may be opportunity for varying the order and phrasing of the questions to fit the situation. The standardized interview provides consistency or reliability of results; the unstandardized interview, by being flexible, encourages answers that often represent the real situation better. Kinsey et al. (1948), for instance, found the need to vary the order of questions to establish rapport in the sensitive area in which they worked and to make sure that they used terminology that was familiar yet not too upsetting to the respondents.

Interviews may be conducted by telephone, as represented by the common surveys of audience response to radio and television programming. The often quoted ratings of programs are based on answers to telephone queries as to whether anyone is "tuned in."

QUESTIONNAIRES

Information about the effects of mass media can be gained inexpensively with large groups of people. Questionnaires may be sent through the mail or they may be administered directly to the individuals in a face-to-face situation. They are quick and easy, particularly if structured responses are called for. Open-end responses take only a little bit longer but can still provide much information inexpensively. Some response error may creep in as the result of the carelessness of the respondents, or a more subtle bias can occur if the questionnaire is structured to be answered in a specific order and the respondent is influenced by questions that should have been answered after response was made to the initial questions. Items in the questionnaire can also be skipped easily.

Comparison of the effectiveness of questionnaires as opposed to the interview has generally yielded results that were at least favorable to the questionnaire method. Stouffer et al. (1950) found that the two approaches yielded almost identical information. A later study by Kahn (1952) arrived at much the same result; in addition, the questionnaires provided a greater opportunity for frank answers because of the anonymity of the situation.

THE PANEL TECHNIQUE

Some of the information about the effect of mass media in communication comes from research studies using a panel. This technique consists of conducting a series of interviews with the same group of people over a period of time. The group of respondents is known as the "panel" (Lazarsfeld, 1948). The use of panels is particularly suited to study change over a period of time by relating data obtained at one particular point in time to information obtained later. Lazarsfeld et al. (1944) used panels extensively to observe a sample of voters in an Ohio county for six months during the presidential campaign of 1940. While the technique has been used more extensively in the area of influence of political opinion-changing programs, it is useful for determining the effects of any program intended to produce changes of opinions or behavior.

INDIRECT MEASURES

While not as widely used as direct methods, various indirect approaches have been tried where direct questioning did not seem to elicit significant or meaningful responses. Projective techniques represent the more common indirect measures of opinion. As an example Sanford (1950) used an adaptation of Rosenzweig's Picture-Frustration test (1945) based on cartoons. Respondents were to fill in the reply of a cartoon character to a statement made by another figure in the picture. The response would be called for to a statement such as, "You were telling me about something that has been bothering you. What was the problem?" Another projective measure, a word association test by Vicary (1948), has been used in market research. The subject is presented with a product and asked to respond quickly with a brand name. There are almost unlimited variations possible.

Hammond (1948) has developed an approach called the "error choice method." Subjects are asked to choose between alternatives presented to them. Several choices, none correct, vary from one extreme to another; the choice gives some indication of a basic position or frame of reference of the individual. If a question asking for the average profit of American corporations in the previous year is answered by choosing a high (and erroneous) figure, this is some indication of a basic opinion.

CONTENT ANALYSIS

Another widely used research technique in communication analysis has been the study of content. Content analysis is "a research technique for the objective, systematic, and quantitative description of the manifest content of communication" (Berelson, 1954, p. 489). While the effect of communication is the ultimate area of interest, the focus of research is on the specific syntactic and semantic dimensions of the communication. What is present is studied in a systematic and objective way to determine the impact of what is said. The technique is useful in delineating problems such as: the treatment of news stories in newspapers, the pattern of movement in the deliberations of a small group, or questions like "how can advertising be analyzed for its propaganda content?" and "what are the themes or motives in literature produced in industrialized versus underdeveloped countries?"

The most critical aspect of content analysis research studies is probably that relating to categories. In order for meaningful results to occur, these categories must be clear and appropriate to the problem studied. Berelson (1954) organizes categories into two parts—the "what is said" and "how it is said" categories. The *what* is substance and the *how* is form, although there may be overlap in practice between them. The "what is said" categories are identified as follows: subject matter; direction or orientation; standards or grounds such as morality, strength, heroism, or legality; values or goals; methods or means employed to realize ends; traits, abilities, or subjective states; actor, person, or group in a central position or as initiator of an action; authority or source for the statement; origin or place of origin of communication; and target or addressee, the group to whom the communication is directed. The "how it is said" categories are those concerned with: form or type of communication; form of statement, specifically the grammatical form; intensity or "emotionalism" and excitement values; and devices or techniques such as the propaganda "tricks" of name calling, bandwagon, and others. Ultimately, most if not all of the information derived from content analysis is used in determining the end results of communication, that is, the relationship between content and the effect of communication.

MECHANICAL TECHNIQUES

Direct measures of audience response or listening habits using mechanical or electronic devices have enjoyed varying degrees of interest. The *Audimeter* (Nielsen, 1945) is a small device that can be installed in the home to keep an accurate record of the time that both radio and television sets are in use.

The *Program Analyzer* (Peatman and Hollonquist, 1950) was first developed by Stanton and Lazarsfeld to obtain a direct record of audience preferences. Subjects in a studio view a television program and push a green button for the parts of the program liked and a red button for the parts of the program disliked. If a subject is indifferent and considers the program just average, he refrains from pushing the button. Preferences are recorded immediately on a moving tape which can later be analyzed for preference patterns.

The effect of advertising has been measured in many ways using optical or mechanical aids. Eye cameras to record eye movements while reading advertisements or tachistoscopes providing brief exposures of ads to see what is noticed have long been in use. A device known as VISTA (Visual Testing Apparatus) has been sponsored by the Advertising Research Foundation (1962) to provide even more comprehensive measures of visual efficiency of advertisements. Numerous mechanical aspects of ads may be measured in terms of four criteria of visual efficiency.

Mass Media

Public opinion owes much to the functioning of mass media. How extensive is the influence and variation among the various types of media is one central problem in a study of this area. While other individual and social factors are to be considered, a focus on the media themselves is a necessary early step in an assessment of the influence process.

PRINTED MEDIA

Newspapers and magazines have been in use longer than other mass media (excluding, of course, the popular advertising signs or public proclamations common since ancient times). The popularity of printed media has been evident and their influence generally acknowledged. Despite some agreement that the power of the press is great, there is not as much empirical data supporting this stand as might be hoped. What exists, however, indicates it can be an effective molder of public opinion.

A classic election year study by Lazarsfeld, Berelson, and Gaudet (1944) devoted much of its time to the study of the impact of newspapers on the election campaign. Newspapers were found to be significant in terms of source of information; two-thirds of the voters mentioned them as the prime source. More significant was the often recurring finding that the newspaper information is sought by a smaller number of interested people, many of whom already have made decisions. The campaign information, therefore, was reaching people who had already made up their minds and were least susceptible to the change procedures in the communication. The same authors found that while magazines may reach a smaller number of readers, there may be considerable influence occurring, especially in the reaching of specific audience through specialized magazines. *Farm Journal* was mentioned as one magazine with perhaps as much impact as those periodicals with larger national circulation.

Bauer et al. (1963) surveyed the habits of a large group of company presidents in the United States to determine how and where they got their information. Regular reading of one or more newspapers was mentioned by all. After the local paper, the *Wall Street Journal* (mentioned by one-half of the group) stood out strongly in second place. Also read were the *New York Times* and the *New York Herald Tribune*. The larger the firm, the more often readership of the "national" newspapers was mentioned.

Magazines were cited less often but three-fourths of the subjects read at least one national magazine regularly. *Time*, mentioned by one-half, led the list. General business magazines such as *Business Week* were read almost as often as the national magazines. Specific trade journals, however, had very wide circulation; these were mentioned as often as newspapers. "High-brow" magazines did not reach high readership levels—only about one-sixth said they read the *Atlantic Monthly* or the *New Yorker*. The *Reader's Digest* was checked by only 6 percent of the heads of large firms but almost four times as many from small firms did so.

Foreign printed media come to the attention of very few businessmen but travel overseas makes up for this. Only about 10 percent have never been abroad, while well over half have made more than five trips. Those who had done more traveling were more likely to take a more international view of tariffs and trade.

Oral communication between business peers and acquaintances supplements the material from mass media. In this way, business communication mirrors the "two-step" pattern of communications where opinion leaders pass on information to peers and co-workers from their (the leaders') exposure to mass media.

RADIO AND TELEVISION

Since its introduction in the 1920's, radio has been a pervasive medium. Even with the rapid growth of television after 1950, the impact of radio probably has not declined from its earlier position. It might be suggested indirectly, however, that advertisers, at least, believe the effectiveness of television on consumer decision making is superior to that of radio since considerably greater resources are placed in television channels.

The election year study by Lazarsfeld et al. (1948) of the influence on voting decisions by mass media indicated that radio was the most important source of information helping to make a choice. This was particularly true of those voters who made the switch from Republican to Democrat (it is conceded that Franklin D. Roosevelt had a magnetic radio personality). Even though only a minority changed their preferences, radio influenced either the change or a reinforcement of an existing position.

More of the interest in mass media in recent years has been in the area of television. As with many studies of communication, the focus of attention has been on the question of who listens when and where and with what effect. One of the earliest studies of television (Wiebe, 1952) attempted to assess the impact of the televised hearings on crime in the United States. Respondents indicated a high degree of interest in the televised hearings, but few indicated any positive attempts at implementing the interest through action.

In a leading study of the television viewing habits of children (Himmelweit et al., 1958) it was determined that the heaviest viewers were those children who had narrower interests or who had less opportunity or ability for achievement in other areas. Those children with lesser mental ability were those who were more likely to be avid television viewers; this was especially true in the upper grades of elementary or secondary school. Heavy viewing among those children who were intellectually able, when it was found, was the result of some insecurity or unhappiness at home or with other children. Excessive viewing of television, then, is seen as either an inability to rely on inner resources and self-generated entertainment or as a retreat from social difficulties.

The influence of television on political behavior has been studied with interest by several researchers. One study of the 1952 election campaign (Campbell, Gurin, and Miller, 1953) determined that television was considered by most respondents as being the source of most information about the campaign even though more people either read about the campaign in the newspapers or heard about it on the radio. While the authors were satisfied that television was a prime source of information, they were not certain how effective this was with regard to actual behavior. Another study (Simon and Stern, 1955) indicated that television had little influence on the vote in the 1952 campaign. They looked at earlier patterns of voting in presidential campaigns and the distribution of television sets in the 1952 election and could find no relationship between television and voting.

A review of the influence of mass media in four presidential elections (Campbell, 1968) indicates that from 1952 to 1964 television moved to a commanding position relative to other media. Not only were people "paying more attention" to political campaigns through television, but they were also "getting the most information" from it (Figure 14-1). It might be predicted that the influence of television seems likely to remain at this high level. There is some evidence that private surveys on behalf of commercial advertisers have

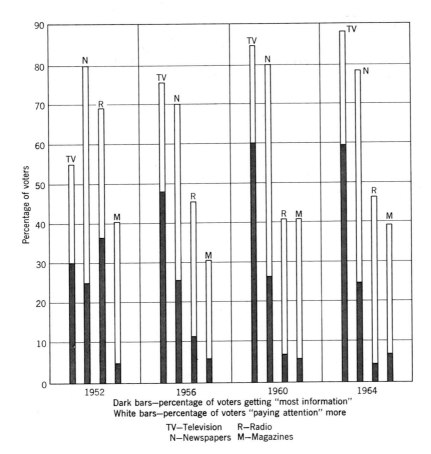

Dark bars—percentage of voters getting "most information"
White bars—percentage of voters "paying attention" more

TV—Television　　R—Radio
N—Newspapers　M—Magazines

Figure 14-1. A comparison of the effect and influence of mass media in presidential elections, 1952 to 1964. *Source.* Campbell, A. (1968). From *Psychology Today,* February, 1968.

reached similar conclusions in that a clear trend toward more extensive use of television for advertising and promotion is developing.

MOTION PICTURES

The influence of the movies on individuals in the audience has been a topic of some interest, either in popular literature or in scientific studies. One of the earliest studies of the influence of motion pictures on attitudes and opinions is that by Peterson and Thurstone (1933) with a population of school-age children. The researchers noted a sizable change in opinion which persisted over a fairly extensive period of time. On the other hand, Hovland, Lumsdaine, and Sheffield (1949), in a study during World War II, noted very few effects on opinion. There was, however, a decided change in factual knowledge as a result of exposure to specific films.

MEDIA COMPARISONS

Not enough information exists to state with certainty the extent of the differences in effectiveness of the various media. Since all mass media are in competition for the attention of a public, there is the notion that there are distinct publics for each media, that is, those who read newspapers will have their attention diverted from radio or other media. That this is not the case has been demonstrated by several researchers. Lazarsfeld et al. (1948) found, for instance, that the overlap in audiences was quite extensive; people who were exposed to a great extent to newspapers were also exposed to magazines, and vice versa, as well as being exposed highly to radio. Similar conclusions were reached by Swanson and Jones (1951), who found that television did not interfere much with the reading of newspapers or magazines although attendance at movies and listening to the radio declined slightly in favor of attention to television.

An extensive survey of this area (Klapper, 1960) presents some summary of the findings but makes the point that the great variety of conditions and circumstances provides results that are not always clear and consistent. Most supportable is the comparison that puts personal appeal higher in effectiveness than radio, which, in turn, was found to be more effective than the written word. The author hypothesized that television and films would fall somewhere between personal appeal and radio. Each of the media has its peculiar advantages. Print may be better for complex material, allowing the reader to select his own rate of exposure and leading to better assimilation. There is no doubt that television and films introduce a better sense of participation in the program or identification with a particular set of concepts.

Factors in Communication

Mass communication occurs in a complex context. In addition to the mechanical or descriptive aspects already discussed, a further delineation of concomitant factors must be made. The impact of specific patterns of presentation or an understanding of steps in the process add up, with other information about individual dynamics, to a fuller appraisal of the influence of mass communication media and techniques.

SELECTIVITY

People are more likely to pay attention to and receive communications that fit in with their preconceptions. Individuals are more predisposed to listen to messages stating things with which they have previously agreed or toward which they are partial. While there may be some exceptions, the outstanding facet of the communication process seems to be that it is a highly selective one as far as the listeners are concerned. People expose themselves to things in which they are interested; this may be correlated with age, sex, occupation, or general personality dynamics (Bauer and Bauer, 1960).

Selectivity in exposure goes further in that particular individuals not only are more interested than others in communications generally but are, concomitantly, better informed. Star and Hughes (1950) began a campaign to reach the elderly, the relatively uneducated, women, and the poor when a prior survey determined that these were the individuals most in need of enlightenment. The campaign, however, reached the better educated and younger men, the people who were already interested and informed. This has also been pointed out by Hyman and Sheatsley (1947), who labeled those perpetually uninformed individuals as the "Chronic Know-Nothings."

As the extent of exposure to communication is a selective one, so is the reception of the content of the communication. People have a tendency to perceive content as fitting in with their own position. Their own attitude and value structure causes them to misinterpret or misperceive in line with their own predisposition. Hovland et al. (1957) found that the more the communication deviates from the individual's own stand, the more the communication is perceived as propaganda. When the communication is close to the subject's own stand, the communication is perceived as even closer to the subject's stand than it really is. The effect of a communication is greatest when the recipients hold an opinion close to that presented there. Least likely to be changed are those with opinions are far removed from the message. Reinforcement of an opinion is more likely than a change (Klapper, 1960).

The identity or reputation of the communicator is another important facet in the acceptance or interpretation of the message. There is some evidence that communicators who have high prestige and are considered reliable have more influence in presenting their material than do others. This may not be the case when simple facts are presented and are to be retained over a longer period of time. Sources considered to be of low ability, however, seem to have more impact on the audience in that rejection of the contact is more likely to take place; particularly when attempts to change are made strongly, the resistance of the receivers increases greatly (Hovland, 1959).

ORDER OF PRESENTATION

After-dinner speakers, classroom lecturers, or propagandists may concern themselves with the important question of the order in which the presentation is to be made for maximum effectiveness. Cohen (1957) first aroused the fears and anxieties of students about a grading system and then presented a dispassionate, fact-oriented explanation of the system. Another group was given the facts first and then the anxiety-producing material. Those who received the facts first did not change their opinion about the grading system while those whose fears were aroused before the facts were presented were significantly more favorable to the grading group system.

McGuire (1957), in a study of the acceptability of an educational program, tried to determine whether it was better to present the desirable features of the program before the undesirable ones or vice versa. He found a greater influence on opinions when the desirable features came first. McGuire hypothesized that the undesirable features first caused the hearer to "turn off" the speaker while a pleasant series of comments caused the listener to consider the comments worthwhile and to continue listening even through the unpleasant parts.

TWO-SIDED PRESENTATION

Presenting the favored set of facts to a group without providing alternative arguments may be more effective in communicating with certain levels of the populace, particularly the less educated. In general, however, a two-sided presentation will be more effective in communicating with educated and perceptive individuals. The two-sided presentation is even more effective from the standpoint of resistance to any future counterarguments or counterpropaganda. Lumsdaine and Janis (1953) arranged a lecture to groups of students on the ability of the U.S.S.R. to develop atomic weapons (this was before Russia exploded its first bomb). Some were given a one-sided presentation while others were exposed to two sides. Some were then exposed to later counterpropaganda while the others were not. In a comparison of changes from an earlier tested position, there was no difference between the one-sided and two-sided presentations when the subjects were not exposed to counterpropaganda. With exposure to counterpropaganda, however, the magnitude of the difference between the one-sided and two-sided presentations was on the order of ten times. A two-sided presentation not only got the message across as well but served to support opinion against counterpropaganda; a one-sided presentation did not prepare the individual, and the effectiveness of the original communication was severely diminished.

OPINION LEADERS

The concept of the "opinion leader" and the "two-step flow of communication" was developed first in a study of voting behavior by Berelson, Lazarsfeld, and McPhee (1954). They postulated that information flows downward from national opinion leaders through mass media to local opinion leaders in a particular community or group. The local opinion leaders, in turn, communicate on a personal and word-of-mouth basis to rank-and-file individuals (Figure 14-2).

Opinion leaders are those individuals in a group who are trusted by others.

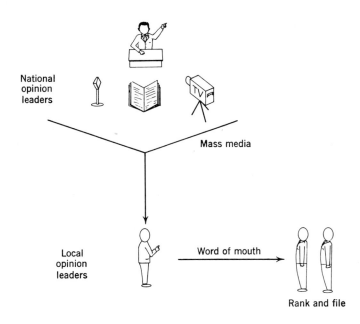

Figure 14-2. The two-step flow of communication (Berelson, Lazarsfeld, and McPhee, 1954).

These usually expose themselves to a greater amount of information and are available for the passing on of this information to others. They wield a great deal of influence in their groups. Opinion leaders, while they resemble the other members of their group, are usually a little higher in status and pay more attention to communications. They are more informed about the topics in which they are interested. Communications to opinion leaders may be effective not only with respect to them but also with the ultimate receivers, since the opinion leaders are not only respected but are familiar with the techniques of persuasion for specific individuals in their particular group.

Katz and Lazarsfeld (1955) found that opinion leaders were more exposed to mass media than were the rank and file. The influence of mass media, then, is exerted indirectly through the opinion leaders more than it is exerted directly on the individuals in the mass. There is, however, some direct influence from the mass media. Katz and Lazarsfeld found differences in the extent of this influence which direct contacts and various mass media had upon decision making. In marketing shifts or changes from one brand of household product to another, personal contacts were more important than the effects of radio advertising. Radio, in turn, was more effective than the newspaper in contributing to the marketing shift, although the newspaper was usually very effective in the small contribution it did make to the marketing shift decision. Figure 14-3 gives some indication of the effectiveness of exposure and the relative

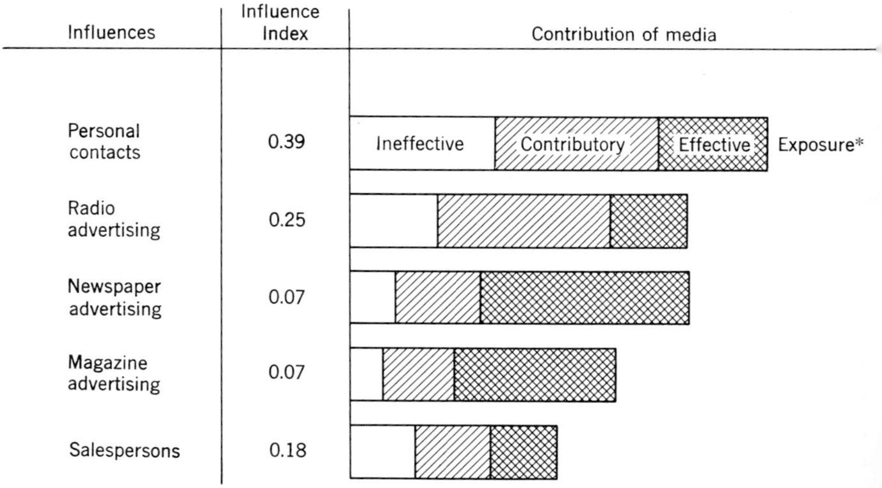

Influences	Influence Index	Contribution of media		
Personal contacts	0.39	Ineffective	Contributory	Effective Exposure*
Radio advertising	0.25			
Newspaper advertising	0.07			
Magazine advertising	0.07			
Salespersons	0.18			

Figure 14-3. Marketing shifts (changes from one product to another) under various influences (Katz, E. and Lazarsfeld, P., 1955).

effectiveness of each type of influence. For instance, personal contacts (.39) are over seven times as effective as newspaper advertising (.07). Advertising in newspapers is as effective in determining marketing shifts as advertising in magazines, but both are low in effectiveness.

These findings reinforce results found in many other comparisons of effectiveness of mass media as compared with the influence of personal contacts. Personal influence is clearly more effective in influencing behavior and decision making than are the various examples of mass media. Mass media does have some influence directly on the ultimate decision maker, and it has some influence on the opinion leaders who, in turn, influence their friends through personal contacts.

ENHANCING EFFECTIVENESS

The impact of communications can be magnified under certain conditions during the communication and after it takes place. Discussion after the message or participation in communicating leads to more effective utilization of information. Communications are retained much better if the recipient is in the position of knowing or thinking that he must do something with the information. Listening to a talk with the intent of passing this on in another speech leads to greater retention of material (Zimmerman and Bauer, 1956).

Earlier, Lewin (1953) reported on a study he did during World War II with a group of housewives. At a time when meat was in short supply because of diversions to armed forces in the field, it was considered patriotic for housewives on the home front to utilize the more readily available yet more exotic cuts of meat. Lewin had one group of housewives listen to a lecture on the need for utilization of the less desirable cuts, while another group of housewives conducted a group discussion on the same topic. It may disappoint some that a follow-up survey disclosed that only one-third of the housewives in the discussion group actually tried to use the poorer cuts of meat. This was, however, ten times the percentage of housewives who did the same as the result of listening to the lecture.

Membership in a group influences the perception of communications. Where the norms of the group are clear and the members are very active in it or are strongly attached to the group norms and values, the more their response to communications will be determined by the attitudes and values of the group. Kelley and Volkart (1952) conducted an experiment where boy scouts were given a talk criticizing the most common activities in scouting. Those scouts who were most closely identified with the organization changed their opinions least, even when they were questioned privately.

Greater exposure over a period of time, at least in political campaigns, is likely to increase the interest in the activities under discussion. Berelson et al. (1954) indicate that there is greater support for candidates as well as greater interest generally in the political campaign with greater exposure to mass media. The greater interest and exposure has the effect of increasing contacts among individuals and developing stronger ties between them. Individuals in groups have a tendency, under these circumstances, to coalesce and present the more uniform pattern of opinions. At the same time, the discrepancy between various groups in their opinions is apt to increase. During the campaign, occupational and religious groupings generally have a tendency to draw further apart. A greater disparity develops between white collar workers and union laborers in terms of their political preferences or voting intentions.

What happens when people have no strong interest in a particular matter and are caught in the middle of competing communications? In this situation they either withdraw from the field because of lack of interest or they are prime targets for influence by the majority.

Propaganda

With the rise in number and extent of mass media, propaganda has come to be a phenomenon with the potential of vast social influence and control. The anxiety over the manipulative possibilities in propaganda has undoubtedly contributed to the development of a negative image of the term. The unfavorable connotations people have when it is mentioned is, in itself, a significant fact. We are likely to label the activities of those who take a position opposing ours as propaganda and to use more favorable terms to describe our own efforts.

Strictly speaking, however, the term propaganda by itself is a neutral one. For the social researcher, propaganda means a direct effort to influence people in a particular direction; it is an attempt to change specific attitudes or values and alter the behavior of individuals in specific circumstances. Because of the opportunity to manipulate the end result much more than one might think desirable, the negative aspects have persisted. It would be better to make our value judgments with respect to the ends that propagandists strive for and then label the approach good or bad instead of attaching the negative label to the term itself. Propaganda can just as easily be used to correct misconceptions and to change undesirable behavior.

Viewed without emotion, propaganda is really indistinguishable from advertising, publicity, and even education. The lines of demarcation, if any, are difficult to draw. A press agent or public relations counsel can mount a publicity program to develop attitudes that are favorable to a product, a person, or a set of circumstances. Advertisers attempt to influence attitudes and opinions in the same way in order to achieve desired behavior on the part of the consumer. This is not to say that the activities of advertisers and public relations people are to be considered reprehensible; indeed, a strong case may be made for the proposition that much of the vitality of American society rests in the success of creating and maintaining mass markets. It would be unreasonable or even dangerous to perpetuate the extreme views sometimes pronounced by undiscerning individuals who state that nothing they see or hear in the mass media is truthful or worthwhile. It may all be propaganda but not, by virtue of that fact alone, an undesirable phenomenon.

It is just as difficult to distinguish between education and propaganda. Every educational process involves the utilization of specific approaches to alter attitudes, values, and behavior. The mere presentation of facts does not take place in a sterile setting. The teacher, the peer group, and the community in which the education takes place have their role in determining the final outcomes. Every society, in some way, has acted to implant its own specific attitudes and values. Ideally, however, education should seek to open the thinking of the individuals rather than restrict their activities along certain predetermined channels. In practice we may fall short of this, but we may still attempt to retain the concept of openness to the facts and permissiveness in the means by which individuals can proceed to make decisions for themselves.

No distinction between education and propaganda is likely to satisfy everyone; it can, however, be attempted. As one simple analogy, we may point to the picture and legend appearing on the editorial pages of newspapers belonging to a national chain. A picture of a lighthouse has beneath it the legend, "Give light and the people will find their own way." This is education. On the other hand, if we stop the rotating light and focus it along a predetermined path that everyone must follow, this is propaganda.

PROPAGANDA PRINCIPLES

The effective propagandist must consider many factors as the basis for his activity. There must be a consideration, first of all, of the characteristics of of the target group. He must consider the prevailing needs of the individuals because, without a need, no motivated behavior will exist. In this connection, frustrations and anxieties are usually the crucial factors and the propagandist must cater to these in a specific way.

There also must be a recognition of the prevailing norms in the society or group, since all effective development of techniques must take into account the prevailing social conditions. Despite the anxieties and frustrations inherent in the great depression of the 1930's, the Nazi party never achieved a foothold in this country, primarily because they naively believed that the same slogans and party trappings that were successful in Germany would achieve the same results on this side of the Atlantic. In the same way, contemporary propaganda with stilted language and an unfamiliar message fails to achieve the result expected by its framers.

The effective propagandist strives for the ego involvement of the individual or identification with the cause promoted. Unfamiliar topics or methods do not promote identification—simple ideas put forth in clear and direct fashion do the job most effectively. Since young people and those of lower status or education are more susceptible, simplicity of presentation is almost mandatory.

In addition to a simple format, repetition of the message leads to a greater impact on the target groups once attention is gained. Exaggeration, distortion, or restatement of facts in a different form are further factors contributing to the effectiveness of the propaganda.

If he cannot eliminate other competing messages, the propagandist strives to depress the effects of any countervailing communications by an adroit use of counterpropaganda techniques. In television commercials, "Brand X" always loses out to the advertiser's product.

Much of the time, the message has greater impact when the source of it is thought to be different from what it really is. A "front" group can sometimes present a message with greater impact than can an organization that is immediately recognizable as biased. The Communist Party has subsidized many student protest groups whose message either coincides with the party line or can be influenced in the direction of the dogma pronounced by the secret organization.

SPECIFIC TECHNIQUES

In furthering their objectives, propagandists are able to fall back on specific techniques or "tricks of the trade." A classic report (Lee and Lee, 1939) summarizes some of the findings by the Institute for Propaganda Analysis, an organization once very active in this area. The best known of these propaganda devices are:

1. Name calling.
2. Glittering generality.
3. Testimonial.
4. Plain folks.
5. Card stacking.

6. Transfer.
7. Band wagon.

These can be effective alone or in combination.

Name calling means giving something a "bad" label. A negative stereotype like "socialistic" has been widely used in business circles although its use has declined considerably in recent years. Many peoples of the world use the term "capitalism" in the same way. A *glittering generality* is a favorable term or "good" word used to influence people to accept the set of ideas in which it is used without looking more closely at the evidence or lack of it supporting the proposition. "Education" and "motherhood" are two examples.

Testimonial involves support from some person who is highly regarded by the public. A breakfast food company could persuade an audience of young-sters to eat a breakfast food by repeating over and over, "Morton Mandable eats Soggy Flakes" (Morton, the baseball hero, may really eat "Crunchies" for breakfast, instead). Well-known arbiters of fashion, too, have appeared in public advertisements assuring one and all that a certain activity, such as serving instant coffee at a party, is highly acceptable or even fashionable. Through the use of the method of *plain folks,* the propagandist emphasizes the solid, stable, and "down-to-earth" qualities of a person or a program. Since there are so few log cabins in these times, political candidates must search for acceptable substitutes. Pictures of the personality and members of his family mixing with other people in an informal situation indicates to the casual observer that the political personality is "one of the people."

Card stacking is the deliberate selection of facts or even outright distortion of them to put the propagandist or ihs mesage in the best posible light. The same techniques may be used to undermine opposition. *Transfer* is the use of symbols with prestige or authority in connection with a propaganda program. A political candidate who stands in front of the American flag while a stirring American march is being played has less difficulty in showing people that he too is red, white, and blue. Finally, the *band wagon* theme is—"hop on, join everybody else." The message is that everybody is doing it and one certainly would not want to be left out. While the statement "50 million Frenchmen can't be wrong" has somehow lost its appeal, many advertisements imply that 200 million Americans are united behind a certain concept or product.

LOADED WORDS

The use of "loaded words" or highly charged labels is one of the most common techniques of propagandists. A classic study of "emotional stereotypes"

(Sargent, 1939) compared the news stories in the *Chicago Tribune* with those appearing in the *New York Times*. At this time, the *Tribune* vigorously opposed the policies of the New Deal and the organization of labor unions. The terms used in its columns were deliberately selected to arouse unfavorable connotations on the part of its readers. The same events were covered in both newspapers using the following parallel terms.

New York Times	*Chicago Tribune*
Labor organizer	Labor agitator
Crop control	Farm dictatorship
Senate investigation	Government witchhunting
Regulation	Regimentation

The selective choice of words to produce the requisite emotional response was considered to be highly effective.

PROPAGANDA IN ADVERTISING

One analysis and classification of techniques in advertising (Pearlin and Rosenberg, 1952) focuses on the devices used in institutional advertising to make a favorable impression on the public for the products of a particular industry.

While each organization is in business to earn a profit, this intentional purpose has other unintentional consequences that may be stressed by the advertisers. When a company selects a strategic location for a new plant, it contributes to the prosperity of the community by paying wages to its employees. The stress of the unintentional consequences by the advertisers is called the *elaboration of latent consequences* by the authors. The industry will stress the benefits to the individual or the total society that arise from its activities. Teamwork, progress, peace and brotherhood, or the promotion of cultural values are themes running through institutional advertising.

Humanization is another device used by advertisers to provide a favorable picture of the industry. Agreeable personality and intellectual traits are used to show corporations as friendly, human, and generous—all emotionally attractive to the public.

Any possible negative aspects of opinion with respect to the industry may be met head on by an insistence on other factors. This can be done by *denial,* a rejection of ideas such as the impersonality of corporations or their exploitative or monopolistic activity. Advertising of the railroads, for instance, may refer to the owners of the railroads as being the millions of people who live right next door. If denial is too difficult to attain, then *conversion* of undesirable features to those that are more desirable can be undertaken. Big corporations, for instance, are able to develop new and more efficient ways of doing things that could not be accomplished by small concerns.

Status contagion is an attempt to achieve respectability by an association with something that has positive value. The company or industry that associates itself with "the American way of life" puts itself in a position where the positive values can be easily transferred to its activities. This is merely an extension of the basic technique of transfer.

Perhaps the most powerful device is that attempting to develop identification with the company or industry. The authors call this technique the *creation of ego involvement.* An oil company may proclaim that "your own progress and oil progress go hand in hand," or the railroads may state that "it's your railroad after all."

BRAINWASHING

Early stories of "brainwashing," particularly that instituted by the Chinese Communists, aroused widespread anxiety; although the initial emotionality has subsided somewhat in the light of more information, a residue of concern remains.

The term brainwashing is derived from the Chinese *Hsi Nao,* "cleansing the mind," a phrase describing the washing away of vestiges of the old system in China as the basic part of the reeducation or thought reform of Mao Tse-tung.

Concern was first felt by Americans for the ideological fate of prisoners of war in the Korean conflict. Schein (1956) described, on the basis of interviews, some of the methods used by the Chinese captors to influence attitudes and behavior. He concluded that any changes, at least in those repatriated, were tenuous and temporary. This was in spite of the fact that the Chinese followed the most comprehensive program to date of removing social support or information and working diligently toward a commitment to a different set of beliefs.

In a later and more fundamental analysis, Schein et al. (1961) based their conclusions on a study of cases of long-term prisoners of the mainland Chinese. As a result of their findings, the authors prefer to use the term *coercive persuasion* rather than brainwashing. The process took place in a period of general thought reform in a totalitarian society with its own peculiar history. A "passion for unanimity," common to many totalitarian systems, further influenced the attitude change processes.

The technique began with total imprisonment—solitary confinement, in most cases. Later, imprisonment with cellmates who stood as accusors aided the change process. Attempts to create feelings of guilt in the prisoner were especially effective in promoting the changes in values or identification that were supportive of later changes in behavior.

Schein et al. found nothing new or difficult to understand in the techniques. The actual results may be hard to evaluate because of the wide variation in background and experience of the subjects; successful cases were probably very few, however. Change procedures emphasized the moral aspects in political participation and encouraged ego or identity changes in the individual as well. A general model of this process can be described briefly as being one of unfreezing, changing, and then refreezing attitudes. This is a long-term procedure starting before actual change occurs and lasting some time after in the mechanisms of reinforcement.

The basic influence process can be present in institutions in other cultural settings, including our own, although the content may differ. What may be even more important for us, however, is the note that the process of persuasion may also have undesirable concomitants in that it may promote rigidity in approach to problems that call for creativity instead.

Rumor

Rumor is a phenomenon of social communication that supplements the transmission of information through the mass media. It is important as well in limited communication through interaction. While the impact may be greater in the immediate personal situations, the study of rumor is of importance on the broader scene, especially in periods of social stress or unrest.

A classic study of the psychology of rumor (Allport and Postman, 1947) outlines many of the features that are recognizable in rumors and provides some understanding of the mechanisms supporting their transmission. The authors define a rumor as "a specific (or topical) proposition for belief, passed along from person to person, usually by word of mouth, without secure standards of evidence being present." Rumors deal with temporary events in a way that implies that whatever is said is true even though there is not much information to support it. Allport and Postman assign the basic reason for the circulation of rumors as being both an explanation of ambiguous circumstances and a relieving of emotional tensions felt by people in those ambiguous situations.

A series of experiments by the authors demonstrated some of the dynamics of rumor transmission. They presented pictures of social situations to one individual of a group. The first person heard a description of the picture and then described that picture to a second person who himself did not see the picture directly. The story was repeated in much the same manner as the parlor game of "gossip" is played, the story being transmitted down the line from person to person. One picture portrayed the interior of a subway car with a roughly dressed white man holding a straight razor in his hand while saying something to a well-dressed Negro. Three men and two women, one with a baby, are seated on the bench at the side. The authors recognize the artificiality of the experiment but point out that the experimental situation should provide even more objectivity or accuracy than is present in a real life situation. We could easily assume that any findings in the experiment would be magnified in a practical setting.

An analysis of the information transmitted from subject to subject indicates the presence of three phenomena that the authors labeled (a) *leveling,* (b) *sharpening,* and (c) *assimilation.* Leveling is the phenomenon describing the shortening or simplifying of the material. As the rumor is passed on, it becomes more concise and is grasped more easily by the hearer. Fewer words or ideas are being used and reported. In sharpening there is a focusing on specific details that somehow seem to stand out. Unusual words, phrases, or ideas can be emphasized by one of the subjects and transmitted pretty much without change, even though the rest of the story shows a decay. Assimilation is a more dynamic and powerful force providing a greater opportunity for the personality of the transmitter to determine the specific content of the material. Leveling and sharpening are selective processes, but they operate in a fairly simple way. Assimilation is also a selective process, but it has the imprint of greater variety. In assimilation there is a change toward the way things "ought to be." In retelling the subway scene, the razor is moved from the hands of the white man to that of the Negro because this fits in with the popular stereotype.

This recasting of a very complex outside world to fit personal uses is a change designated by Allport and Postman as the imbedding process. This process is usually so extensive and indicative of so much distortion that rumors may generally be said to be of no truth whatsoever.

A third factor has been suggested by Chorus (1953). Where Allport and Postman say that importance and ambiguity are the two essential conditions for rumor transmission, Chorus adds *critical sense,* containing perspicacity, will-power, or decision making after reflection and consideration. This would be expressed by the formula $R \sim i \times a \times \frac{1}{c}$. The formula means that rumor is directly dependent on importance and ambiguity but inversely on the critical sense. Rumors do not occur when the factors i and a are zero and are weaker as the critical sense increases.

Caplow (1947) presents a study of rumors in a practical or field setting.

During two years of service in the Pacific Theater during World War II, the author sketched the informal person-to-person communication within groups of unconfirmed information. The number of rumors was found to be surprisingly low—less than 1 per 100 men per month. When a rumor did begin, however, it spread very quickly. "Grapevine" transmission was very rapid and effective although diffusion decreased with distance from the supposed origin of the message. Most of the rumors were transmitted along well-defined channels, each of which involved a two-way process of exchange. Despite all of the difficulties in transmission, the veracity of rumors was high and did not decline noticeably during transmission. In fact, the validity was increased during the communication process because of a tendency to select credible portions of the message. Distortion appeared on an individual personality basis rather than as a group factor.

Many industrial organizations, as well, have recognized the importance of informal channels of communication (the "grapevine"). The use of these often exceeds that of the formal information channels.

Summary

Mass media (newspapers, radio, and television) try to reach an audience and communicate information to a large number of individuals at one time. A loose aggregate of individuals with certain characteristics in common is designated as a public, and the survey of their opinions is the function of public opinion research. When the opinions of a public show some regularity, it may be said that a consensus exists. Propaganda is a deliberate attempt to influence attitudes and opinions of an audience or a public by the use of planned techniques.

Data on mass communications may be assembled using various techniques of data gathering. The interview, in its many variations, is probably the most widely used method. Results are affected significantly by the type of question used and its phrasing as well as the order in which the statements are made; further dimensions are added by mechanical aids such as the telephone. Questionnaires are paper-and-pencil variations of the interview and, while they may gather information less expensively, their set format makes them less flexible. Despite this, questionnaires have been found to be about as effective as interviews in gathering information. The panel approach simply uses interviews over and over again with the same group of people, enabling the researcher to compare responses over time and to determine changes as they occur. Indirect measures, consisting primarily of projective techniques, may provide information for analysis which the respondent has been requested to give without recognition of the purpose. The analysis of the verbal or symbolic material in the communication itself is the research technique of content analysis; the analysis focuses on what is said and how it is said. Various mechanical techniques have also been used to gather information in the area of mass communications. These devices either measure the programs being turned to and the length of time the channel is open or they go further in recording more precise preferences of audiences during the program.

The mass media themselves may be the subject of research, from the standpoint of both their characteristics and their effectiveness. Printed media, newspapers and magazines, have been in use the longest and have been effective in molding public opinion in particular ways. Written material is a source of information for those who are interested in particular issues and also serves as a reinforcement for the opinions of those who have already made up their mind. Leading newspapers and magazines have a high degree of readership, particularly among businessmen, but some of the limited magazines aimed at a specific target group may have even greater influence with the members of that particular group.

Radio has been a potent medium from its very early days and remains so despite the increasing allocation of advertising resources to television. Both radio and television can be important sources of information although a high degree of interest does not necessarily mean a later translation of this into action. Some evidence also exists that television, at least for children, is resorted to more often by those who lack the resources for intellectual or social stimulation. The influence of motion pictures in molding public opinion parallels that offered by the other related media.

Comparisons of the effectiveness of the media have indicated that those with the more direct and personal approach are more influential although the overlap between media is great. Face-to-face contacts are more important than the printed word. Some people expose themselves extensively to all media while others lack an interest in all media. People may expose themselves to mass media on the basis of interest which, further, may be correlated with age, intellectual ability, or occupational level. In addition to being selective in this exposure, people organize the information in a way that tends to fit in with their own predispositions. Reinforcement of present attitudes and opinions is more likely than change. Order of presentation of material may make a significant difference in the extent to which it influences subsequent behavior. Giving both sides of the story may not change behavior more significantly than when only one side is presented, but the two-sided presentation does resist later counterinfluences better than does a one-sided story.

One important factor in the complete flow of communications is the concept of the "two-step flow of communication" whereby the information from mass media reaches a large number as the result of being channeled first through individuals. These persons are intermediaries with prestige in their social grouping, and they serve as opinion leaders in the influence process.

The effectiveness of mass communications can be enhanced further by certain other mechanical features in the presentation. Recipients receive more information if they are alerted beforehand to the fact that they must do something with this material. Permitting discussion of the material in the recipient group leads to more effective attitude change than merely exposing the audience to a lecture. Finally, greater exposure is also likely to lead to greater interest.

Propaganda is a designation with undesirable connotations that is used to refer to direct attempts to manipulate peoples' attitudes and to have them change their behavior in a particular way. By itself, propaganda is neither good nor bad; these direct techniques could be used to influence in a desirable direction as well. The lines of demarcation between it and advertising, publicity, or even education are difficult to draw. Changes of attitudes and behavior are attempted by all of these, even though the terms education and public relations have a more positive tone. Propaganda, to be effective, must first fit into the norms of the population so that there can be involvement of individuals or identification with the cause. Various propaganda devices then can be utilized to further the emotional participation of the group toward the ends determined by the propagandist. Various verbal and other symbolic means are used to heighten the emotionality of the situation in order to influence the receiver.

A more recent variant of the influence process has been called "brainwashing," although it would be better to label it for what it is, that is, an attempt to influence or persuade under coercion. Upon analysis, brainwashing turns out to be only a more sustained and systematic use of already known influence techniques.

Rumor is the spread of ambiguous information that is passed from person to person to serve as the basis for a belief that continues to be held without much factual basis for its support. Rumors change in transmission toward simplicity or through distortion imposed by the personality dynamics of the individuals involved. Rumors can be useful in the transmission of information through organizations along informal lines. This "grapevine" can be one means of mass communication.

Bibliography

Advertising Research Foundation (1962). *The measurement and control of the visual efficiency of advertisements.* New York: Advertising Research Foundation.

Allport, G. and Postman, L. (1947). *The psychology of rumor* New York: Holt.

Bauer, R. and Bauer, A. (1960). America, mass society and mass media. *Journal of Social Issues,* 16, 3–66.

Bauer, R., Pool, I., and Dexter, L. (1963). *American buiness and public policy.* New York: Atherton.

Berelson, B. (1952). Democratic theory and public opinion. *Public Opinion Quarterly,* 16, 313–330.

Berelson, B. (1954). Content analysis. In Lindzey, G. (ed.). *Handbook of social psychology,* Vol. 1. Reading, Massachusetts: Addison-Wesley, 488–522.

Berelson, B., Lazarsfeld, P., and McPhee, W. (1954). *Voting.* Chicago: University of Chicago Press.

Broom, L. and Selznick, P. (1968). *Sociology* (4th ed.) New York: Harper & Row

Campbell, A. (1968). Civil rights and the vote for president. *Psychology Today,* 1(9), 26ff.

Campbell, A., Gurin, G., and Miller, W. (1953). Political issues and the vote: November 1952. *American Political Science Review,* 46, 359–385.

Caplow, T. (1947). Rumors in war. *Social Forces,* 25(3), 298–302.

Chorus, A. (1953). The basic law of rumor. *Journal of Abnormal and Social Psychology,* 48, 313–314.

Cohen, A. (1957). Need for cognition and order of communication as determinants of opinion change. In Hovland, C. et al. (eds.). *The order of presentation in persuasion.* New Haven: Yale University Press.

Hammond, K. (1948). Measuring attitudes by error choice, an indirect method. *Journal of Abnormal and Social Psychology,* 43, 38–48.

Himmelweit, H., Oppenheim, A., and Vince, P. (1958). Television and the child. In Berelson, B. and Janowitz, M., eds. (1966). *Public opinion and communication.* New York: Free Press, 418–445.

Hovland, C. (1959). Results from studies of attitude change. *The American Psychologist,* 14, 8–17.

Hovland, C., Harvey, O., and Sherif, M. (1957). Assimilation and contrast effects in reactions to communication and attitude change. *Journal of Abnormal and Social Psychology,* 55, 244–252.

Hovland, C., Lumsdaine, A., and Sheffield, F. (1949). *Experiments on mass communication.* Princeton: Princeton University Press.

Hyman, H. and Sheatsley, P. (1947). Some reasons why information campaigns fail. *Public Opinion Quarterly,* 11, 412–423.

Kahn, R. (1952). *The comparison of two methods of collecting data for social research: the fixed-alternative questionnaire and the open-ended interview.* Unpublished doctoral dissertation, University of Michigan. Described in Lindzey, G. (ed.). *Handbook of social psychology.* Reading, Mass.: Addison-Wesley.

Katz, E. and Lazarsfeld, P. (1955). *Personal influence: the part played by people in the flow of mass communication.* Glencoe, Ill.: Free Press.

Kelley, H. and Volkart, E. (1952). The resistance to change of group-anchored attitudes. *American Sociological Review,* 17, 453–465.

Kinsey, A., Pomeroy, W., and Martin, C. (1948). *Sexual behavior in the human male.* Philadelphia: Saunders.

Klapper, J. (1960). *The effects of mass communication.* New York: Free Press.

Lazarsfeld, P. (1948). The use of panels in social research. *The Proceedings of the American Philosophical Society,* 92, 405–410.

Lazarsfeld, P., Berelson, B., and Gaudet, H. (1944). *The people's choice.* New York: Duell, Sloan and Pearce.

Lazarsfeld, P., Berelson, B., and Gaudet, H. (1948). *The people's choice* (2nd ed.). New York: Columbia University Press.

Lee, A. and Lee, E. (1939). *The fine art of propaganda.* New York: Harcourt, Brace.

Lewin, K. (1953). Studies in group decision. In Cartwright, D. and Zander, A. (eds.). *Group dynamics: research and theory.* New York: Harper & Row.

Lumsdaine, A. and Janis, I. (1953). Resistance to "counter-propaganda" produced by one-sided and two-sided "propaganda" presentations. *Public Opinion Quarterly,* 17, 311–318.

Maccoby, E. and Maccoby, N. (1954). The interview: a tool of social science. In Lindzey, G. (ed.). *Handbook of social psychology,* Vol. 1. Reading, Mass.: Addison-Wesley, 449–487.

McGuire, W. (1957). Order of presentation as a factor in "conditioning" persuasiveness. In Hovland, C. et al. (eds.). *The order of presentation in persuasion.* New Haven: Yale University Press.

Nielsen, A. (1945). Two years of commercial operation of the Audimeter and the Nielsen Radio Index. *Journal of Marketing,* 9, 239–255.

Pearlin, L. and Rosenberg, M. (1952). Propaganda techniques in institutional advertising. *Public Opinion Quarterly,* 16, 5–26.

Peatman, J. and Hollonquist, T. (1950). Geographical sampling in testing the appeal of radio broadcasts. *Journal of Applied Psychology,* 34, 270–279.

Peterson, R. and Thurstone, L. (1933). *Motion pictures and the social attitudes of children*. New York: Macmillan.

Rosenzweig, S. (1945). The picture-association method and its application in a study of reactions to frustration. *Journal of Personality,* 14, 3–23.

Sanford, F. (1950). The use of a projective device in attitude surveying. *Public Opinion Quarterly,* 14, 697–709.

Sargent, S. (1939). Emotional stereotypes in the Chicago Tribune. *Sociometry,* 2, 69–75.

Schein, E. (1956). The Chinese indoctrination program for prisoners of war: a study of attempted brainwashing. *Psychiatry,* 19, 149–172.

Schein, E., Schneier, I., and Barker, C. (1961). *Coercive persuasion*. New York: Norton.

Simon, H. and Stern, F. (1955). The effect of television upon voting behavior in Iowa in the 1952 presidential election. *American Political Science Review,* 49, 470–477.

Star, S. and Hughes, H. (1950). Report on an educational campaign: The Cincinnati Plan for the United Nations. *American Journal of Sociology,* 55, 389–400.

Stouffer, S. et al. (1950). *Measurement and prediction. Studies in social psychology in World War II,* Vol. IV. Princeton: Princeton University Press.

Swanson, C. and Jones, R. (1951). Television owning and its correlates. *Journal of Applied Psychology,* 35, 352–357.

Vicary, J. (1948). Word association and opinion research. *Public Opinion Quarterly,* 12, 81–98.

Wiebe, G. (1952). Responses to the televised Kefauver hearings: some social psychological implications. *Public Opinion Quarterly,* 16, 179–200.

Zimmerman, C. and Bauer, R. (1956). The effect of an audience upon what is remembered. *Public Opinion Quarterly,* 20, 238–248.

15

Groups

The study of social groups is important for an understanding of behavior almost by definition, since individuals seldom, if ever, act without being influenced by others. Behavior takes place within a group, even if that group consists of no more than two people. Much of the research on social functioning in general has been done in a small group setting; it has either been concerned with the basic features of group behavior or has concentrated on the applied aspects. Studies of work teams, management conference groups, juries, or academic committees have demonstrated the ubiquitousness and the importance of the group.

While the study of groups is certainly valuable in and of itself, many researchers feel that the importance is heightened by the transfer of results to larger organizations or broader settings. Relationships in small groups are thought to be basic to all interaction in social aggregates.

This chapter will deal with the "basic unity of interacting personalities" (Burgess, 1926). This fundamental social unit is almost of necessity small so that the discussion of *group* most often refers to the *small* group. While, technically, a grouping may be of any size, the focus for research and application is in the area of small group structure and dynamics.

Definition of a Group

There are many considerations possible in determining the characteristics and qualifications for a group. Since the terms group and small group are often used interchangeably, it may be guessed that size is a consideration. The term group has come to refer to an aggregate of modest size, anywhere from two to a number (to be somewhat arbitrary about it) like 15, 20, or 25. More than just size must be considered, however, for the association of individuals to be considered a true group. There is some cohesiveness in the activity of the members. Their behavior shows a regularity which indicates that individuals recognize a guiding set of principles of interaction. They have an idea of their own position in the group with respect to others and the part each person, including themselves, plays in the group. The relationships focusing on status and role along with common values or norms are the hallmarks suggested by some theorists (Sherif and Sherif, 1956, p. 144). A little more dynamic is a related view concentrating on the psychological group as being one with an interdependent sharing of an ideology (Krech et al., 1962, p. 383). As the group works on a common task, shared attitudes develop; the members are aware that they are part of a group and perceive themselves as such.

Casual groups or aggregates of people do not qualify as a group because they ordinarily are not aware of one another or, if aware, do not interact with the other individuals in a meaningful way.

The small group is to be distinguished from a crowd or any other casual assembly of persons with no cohesive forces other than the fact that they may be viewing or listening to the same set of circumstances. A group of spectators is not a group in the sense in which we discuss interacting groups. A group need not be highly structured or structured at all. Indeed, it may be very informally arranged. Yet, if it meets the requirements set forth above, it is considered a valid example of a group.

Basis for Small Group Action

Most social researchers believe that an understanding of the fundamental functioning of individuals in a small group setting can come about best with a development of research organized around a theoretical framework. While many such conceptual organizations are possible, only a limited number need be available at this time by way of illustration.

On a molar level the question may be raised as to why people are bound to one another in groups. Answers that point to instinct or statements that imply a rational or utilitarian view are imprecise or incomplete. Gouldner and Gouldner (1963, p. 100) offer an answer in evolutionary-functional terms. They suggest that men behave in ways that provide satisfactions and that living in groups provides those satisfactions even if the result was not foreseen. This view is valid for specific small groups as well as for the general aggregation of individuals in society.

On a more precise level of analysis, Thibaut and Kelley (1959) focus on interaction, the essence of any interpersonal relationship, and its consequences for the individuals concerned. The consequences can be identified as having positive components (rewards) and negative components (costs). Rewards will vary in nature, of course; prestige, power, or material gain represent differing types of rewards. Costs will vary as well. Outcomes for the individual in any interaction can be stated as high reward and low cost or low reward and high cost, with scale values in between. Behavior in groups can be noted, then, in terms of individuals providing something of value for each other. It may be, for instance, that persons associate with others from their own social level or class because in this way they incur least cost to themselves (are more comfortable).

PSYCHOLOGICAL FUNCTIONS OF GROUPS

Groups can provide, with or without the conscious knowledge of their members, a means of fulfilling many of the needs of the individuals in them. There may be personal needs, not group needs; whether these two categories can be synchronized, however, remains one of the great assignments for any active administration of the functioning of groups.

The more significant needs met by the group can be categorized in this way.

1. Affiliative needs.
2. Egoistic needs.
3. Instrumental needs.
4. Cognitive needs.

There are, of course, other ways of categorizing the needs, and each area may encompass further variation.

Affiliative needs are provided by the group through friendships between individuals within it. The sense of belonging to a social unit or identification with it is a strong force in human affairs. The supportive nature of group ties can be felt in many settings, even in the business or industrial situations that are too often thought to be the epitome of impersonality.

Egoistic needs may be fulfilled through the development of self-esteem and status as the result of membership in the group. This can come about through opportunity for individual contributions to group functioning or as the result of some transfer to the person of the prestige of the group activities. Other egoistic needs such as security or power are met by the group as well. While these needs may be seen most easily in the area of labor-management relations, the sense of security through power over others can be met as well within white collar management circles.

Simple functional needs such as aid in daily activities, help in adjustment to work routine, or even the avoidance of boredom can be met by the group.

These are instrumental in the sense of providing a means of reaching either task-oriented or personal goals.

Cognitive needs are those that provide meanings for an individual in his own personal or task situation. The recognition of reality and the importance of a stable social environment represent a basis for motivation occurring in groupings. One's perceptions about the company regulations, job requirements, or validity of the supervisor's demands are tested by comparing them to the views of others. This consensual validation is a basic social phenomenon.

It should be noted, finally, that the need categories are not mutually exclusive. In a specific setting a number of need classes may become operative.

GROUP GOALS

To begin a task, members of a group usually determine some end results of their work. These might be called group goals. They differ from individual goals in that some *consensus* or acceptance by the individuals is needed before these can be said to exist as goals. How much acceptance is needed is a vital question; perhaps a group needs much more than minimal acceptance from its members on proposed end results in order to be effective. Highly cohesive groups will have shared values which, in turn, will promote an effective selection and acceptance of goals.

A consensus with respect to goals may develop in various ways, some of them readily apparent and others more subtle. Bennett (1955) found, for instance, that actual communications to other members may not be necessary for their acquiescence; they may simply perceive acceptance of a goal by a majority and join in that result. Participation in group discussion may promote, as it does in so many varied instances, a consensus. The workers in the Harwood Pajama Company plant (Coch and French, 1948) displayed ample evidence of the acceptance of group targets or procedures when they participated in the discussion of requirements under the new conditions of work (see below).

Types of Groups

Groups may be classified in many different ways; the basis for differentiation may be purpose or goals, duration, extent of structuring, legal organization, or setting. While classification may mislead one into thinking that this is equivalent to an understanding of their structure or function, the identification of categories that are possible can be a convenient starting point. If we remember the caveat, classification may be a starting point for a better knowledge of the nature and function of a group of interacting individuals.

FORMAL GROUPS

Groups that have been established under legal and formal authority to achieve a specific end result or to undertake delegated tasks can be called formal groups. These are structured and, in that sense, are "organized" with a definite allocation of tasks among members and a clear delineation of duties and relationships among them. Formal groups in industry, government, or education are those work units or management teams that are identified and active in the pursuit of specified goals. A work crew on an open hearth furnace and a management bargaining team preparing to enter into negotiations with union representatives in a collective bargaining session represent two clearly defined formal groups in industry. An academic department in a college or university and a field office of a governmental agency represent examples of formal groups in other settings.

INFORMAL GROUPS

Activity that is formally specified on the job probably does not occupy the entire attention or satisfy all the needs of the individuals who are operating under those guidelines. In addition to the formal patterns of interaction, individuals activate relationships along lines other than those specified. It may well be that the development of these informal groupings is a characteristic of human endeavor, since it is a widespread phenomenon and one to which attention must be directed in order to understand group behavior more fully.

Informal groups may be fostered through simple physical factors such as location, or they may arise as the result of more subtle factors such as fulfillment of specific needs of a set of individuals. Physical location in an office or a plant may give rise to the interaction among those individuals who are "held together." Physical placement may have been determined, in part at least, by the formal dictates of the job, but the development of the informal group goes beyond this base into a structuring of relationships that may not even have been anticipated by those in charge of the work force. Attitudes and values held in common or similarity in perceptions of a role in an organization in a society can give rise to the informal groupings found on all sides.

Dalton (1959) identifies three different kinds of informal groups that are found in organizations—horizontal, vertical, and random cliques. Horizontal cliques encompass members who operate at the same level or within the same area. The vertical clique is an informal group encompassing individuals from different levels within a given area or department. These members may be in superior or subordinate relationships with each other, but they interact frequently because of the opportunity for meeting goals or fulfilling needs in the informal relationships. Random groups are composed of members of various areas or departments. These are most often seen in the informal relationships that arise between individuals in different departments wherein the main basis for interaction is an opportunity to get things done outside of the regular channels. Formal structure may not be set up to provide quick repair, extra supplies, or any other sort of service that meets group or organizational goals. Some random cliques may serve to satisfy needs that arise outside the office or plant. The basis for association in the plant may arise from a continuing relationship in social organizations or religious groups on the outside.

Informal groups may arise, and usually do, from a situation in which the formal group has already been set up, but they arise out of the face-to-face situation and owe their existence only to the ongoing interaction among the individuals rather than to their having been organized by someone with the ability to control. The formal and informal groups can be one and the same when "buddies" interact to determine the production rate among themselves but are, at the same time, the duly constituted team organized by management to accomplish a certain task in the production sequence.

MEMBERSHIP AND REFERENCE GROUPS

A distinction may also be made between membership and reference groups. Membership groups are those to which the individual actually belongs, while a reference group is one with which he identifies or to which he would like to belong. One may actually be a member of a particular group yet introject the norms of another group, the group to which he "refers." The attractiveness of the reference group makes the norms of that group more attractive to the individual who aspires to it, and its norms will, therefore, become more influential in determining behavior. A discrepancy in norms and values between the two groups can be a source of conflict for the individual and for those with whom he interacts.

IN-GROUPS AND OUT-GROUPS

Another distinction of possible importance in a practical situation is that between in-groups and out-groups. The in-group represents a clustering of individuals holding prevailing values in a society or, at least, having a dominant place in social functioning. It can be a majority numerically, or it may represent the power structure with its patterns of behavior considered desirable. The out-groups are the conglomerates looked upon as subordinate or marginal in the culture; they are usually referred to as the minority groups even though they may, in certain instances, represent a numerical majority. This breakdown between in-groups and out-groups represents a source of social conflict of the kind described in earlier chapters. It is well to remember, however, that this kind of placement has shown and can continue to show considerable variation. What is "in" at one time or place can be "out" at some other juncture.

PRIMARY AND SECONDARY GROUPS

In the opinion of many behavioral scientists, the most significant distinction is that between primary and secondary groups, a distinction first developed by G. H. Cooley (1909), an early sociologist. Primary groups refer to those composed of individuals in a close, face-to-face relationship over a relatively extensive period of time. These intimate interactions take place in family, play, or neighborhood groups. Secondary groups are those where the interrelationships are more general and remote. The less frequent and less intense interactions take place within a broader setting, from the great impersonality of a large university to the functioning of a municipality or state. The secondary groups will not be discussed here, yet must be mentioned because of their influence on individuals and by way of contrast, if nothing else, with the proximate primary groups. Because most psychologists and sociologists consider the primary group to be a keystone in social relations, more extensive discussion of it will be made.

Even earlier, Tönnies (1887) developed a similar theme when he contrasted two types of associations, the *Gemeinschaft and Gesellschaft*. The former is a "communal" society where the members feel comfortable in a "natural" role in a close society into which they have usually been born. *Gesellschaft* may be translated as an association form of grouping built up on a rational and freely chosen basis in order to achieve certain practical ends. This is a salient feature of a more complex industrialized state with none of the warm and emotional support received by members from their belonging to the more simple or primitive form of grouping.

It has been noted that the critical concept in small group dynamics is that relating to primary groups. Most students of behavior consider the primary group to be a significant factor in not only the study of groups but also in the understanding of the functioning of individuals in any social setting. The closeness and warm emotional contact of small group interaction emphasizes some of the source of strong social influence for most people. Indeed, the absence of the warm ties between individuals that characterizes much of human functioning in a complex industrialized society has been suggested as the strongest source of difficulty in interpersonal relationships at the present time. In addition to being productive of social conflict under extreme conditions, it can also provide for the development of a feeling of rootlessness or loneliness— the *anomie* Durkheim first pointed out.

The primary group, by itself, is not the important factor because it merely provides a base for the activation of interpersonal ties. What is important is that stemming from it is a set of *personal relations* between individuals; it is this set of personal relations that must be analyzed in order that a better understanding of the dynamics of interpersonal relationships in groups can be gained.

Group Research Methods

Information about groups has come from studies using virtually every research technique available. The experimental method has been productive, along with survey methodology and observational techniques. More outstanding, however, are specific approaches, variations of the general classes of techniques, that have been used because they lend themselves well to the study of interaction. Sociometry and methods of observation receive mention here not only to illustrate group research but also because the results of their use provide us with a significant body of material about group activity.

SOCIOMETRY

One of the most descriptive measures of interaction in small groups is the sociometric technique developed by Moreno (1934). While the adjective *sociometric* should encompass many measurement techniques in the area of group research, the term "sociometry" has been used so frequently and almost exclusively in connection with Moreno's technique that it has acquired this specific and limited meaning. The methodology of sociometry has been discussed in a prior chapter (Chapter 3), but its use and findings from this research technique are appropriate for discussion at this time.

It should be remembered here that Moreno's sociometry provides data on choices among individuals in a small group. The results may be represented in various ways; there may be scores, indices, or other statistical descriptions. The information may also be reflected in tabular form. By far the most intriguing, however, and the most utilized are those methods where the information is presented graphically or pictorially. Graphic representations of members of groups and the relationships between them can portray the interactional picture with relative ease of communication. It is this ease of meaningful presentation as well as the relatively high reliability of the technique that has accounted for the popularity of the graphic form of presentation.

The sociometric technique has been helpful almost from the very beginning in a variety of research areas. Sociometry has been useful in portraying social dynamics in a limited setting and, by extension to other areas or through comparisons with other variables, has been useful in sketching broader social dynamics. Studies of leadership have been particularly rewarding, but measurement of social status or social adjustment have also been pursued with profit. Prejudice and other aspects of social differentiation and conflict have been topics of research using the sociometric technique as well. There is also no real limitation with respect to the kind of setting in which the study can be made; research has taken place in various types of organizations and groups—in business and industry, the military, in governmental agencies, in educational settings such as the classroom, and even in correctional institutions.

One of the first studies using the sociometric method was done by Jennings (1937) in a home for delinquent girls. She selected the girls' choice of eating companion as the basis for the description of interaction in the group, and it turned out that her results were remarkably similar to indices of leadership and performance that could be obtained on other bases.

Moreno (1934) was primarily interested in the nature of the structure of the group and the interaction among members. He was not adverse, however, to going beyond this and tracing other kinds of relationships. One of his earliest applications was in the classroom where he could identify characteristics of particular school grades and the subgroupings that arose within those grades on a sex or ethnic group basis. He also found that teachers were very poor in estimating the sociometric choices of the pupils. One of the points that Moreno has always considered significant was the use of sociometric measures to provide a basis for rearrangement of individuals in groups or to develop new groups in order to provide greater satisfactions for members or more efficient functioning of the group. In the educational setting, some of Moreno's followers have provided examples of different ways in which sociometric results may be used. Kerstetter and Sargent (1940) identified a deviant subgroup that developed delinquent patterns in the fifth grade. These individuals were separated from each other without removing group ties developed with nondelinquent class members. Zeleny (1941) developed an even more positive approach toward enhancing the functioning of pupils in the classroom. He described a method for raising the social status of individuals in the classroom setting, thereby enhancing their satisfaction in that situation.

Military applications of sociometry have been even more extensive. Again, as in most other settings, the findings can be of value in pointing out various aspects of behavior. The focus may be placed on the structure of the group and the interpersonal relationships among members of the group; this may be translated into morale terms, or the emphasis may be placed on the nature and quality of individual behavior patterns, as in leadership studies.

Williams and Leavitt (1947) attempted to relate sociometric measures to later performance in combat in World War II. Various other inventory and rating methods were used in addition to the sociometric techniques, but the sociometric measures showed a higher correlation with the criterion and predicted later performance much better than any of the other approaches. There has been some question raised as to whether these ratings of peers in the group are, in fact, popularity contests rather than accurate appraisals of ability, particularly leadership capability. In an attempt to pursue this question, Hollander and Webb (1955) determined that the sociometric ratings did measure something other than friendship. Naval aviation cadets were asked to choose three of their peers whom they would like to have lead a group on a perilous mission in which they, the rater, would be a member of the group. The investigators also asked for a list of friends and, in an attempt to delve into a relatively unresearched area in leadership studies, then attempted to gain some notion of followership. In this instance, each cadet was asked to nominate three individuals whom he would want in his unit if he himself were the leader of the group on the mission. The researchers found that there was little or no relationship between the leadership choices and those based on friendship. The cadets ordinarily ignored the ties of friendship in selection of individuals with leadership qualities. There was, on the other hand, a high degree of relationship between leadership and followership; that is, individuals who were chosen as potential leaders of the group were also chosen as individuals to be taken along as part of the group led by the rater.

The importance of various aspects of group functioning has long been recognized in business and industrial settings. The structure and functioning of work groups, along with variables dealing with the influence process, lend themselves quite readily to study through the use of sociometric techniques. Jacobs (1945) was one of the first researchers to apply sociometric techniques to industry and to describe the various uses of sociometry, from selection of supervisors to measurement of morale and performance. Browne (1951) concentrated on the executive level and related sociometric results with other intergroup or intragroup variables. The completed sociograms gave a picture of the different structures in different units of the company. Browne also found a possible correlation between frequency of interaction, responsibility and authority and sociometric choice. A study by Speroff and Kerr (1952) further illustrates the versatility of the technique of sociometry. The authors studied accident proneness in the steel mill and found it to be negatively related to sociometric choices. The more highly chosen had fewer accidents than others.

Use of sociometric choices to determine the makeup of work groups has possibilities of economic "payoff." Van Zelst (1952) studied workers in the building trades who were given the choice of determining their work partners. Small teams of carpenters and brick layers who worked with their choice of co-worker were compared with the control group where the assignments were made at random. Job satisfaction in the experimental work group increased significantly while the turnover rate decreased. Actual cost of labor and materials also declined to the extent that the benefits were estimated to be similar to that of getting one building free out of 30 built. While a self-selected group may proceed without incorporating the attitudes and values of management, the opportunity to participate and the removal of constraints on communication and interaction among members, if properly executed in a supervisory situation, can improve the performance of individuals in the group.

An interesting extension of the technique to the marketplace and the community came in the research of Menzel and Katz (1956). The researchers first derived a sociogram from interviews with almost all the physicians in a small city in New England. The resulting sociogram illustrated the usual networks and identified the isolates and the "stars," the individuals who were selected most often. Menzel and Katz then delved into pharmacy records to determine the date of adoption of a new but popular drug by the various physicians in the city. A comparison of the sociometric choices and the pattern of adoption of the drug indicated that the "stars" were not the first in adopting the drug, nor the last; whenever they did start prescribing the drug, the number of prescriptions by other physicians rose significantly. The final practical question that remained was the source of information about innovation. While many physicians mentioned that they obtained their information about the product from colleagues or the professional literature, the "stars" were more likely to be participants in a greater number of professional meetings and conventions and were also more consistent readers of the professional literature. The only source of information for the isolates, beyond the literature, was the drug company salesman.

OBSERVATIONAL TECHNIQUES

Data gathered by an observer in the situation has been one of the time-honored methods of gathering information. More recently, attempts have been made to make these observational techniques somewhat more systematic and, therefore, more valid and reliable. One of these approaches, Bales' Interaction

Process Analysis (1951), was used in Chapter 3 to illustrate one possible approach. The system identifies six problem areas that can be noted by the observer as the group functions in a task.

1. Arriving at a common definition of a situation (orientation).

2. Developing a common value system in terms of which alternative solutions are to be evaluated (evaluation).

3. Attempts of members to influence each other (control).

4. Arriving at a final decision.

5. (Dealing) with tensions which arise in the group situation (tension management).

6. (Working) at the task of maintaining an integrated group (Integration) (Heyns and Lippitt, 1954, p. 376).

Bales attempted to provide a general system whereby an observer might operate in any setting and provide a picture of the content and purpose of each act taking place in the group interaction process. Research results in a specific situation will be reported in terms of the 12 categories or six problem areas.

There are, of course, other observational techniques. Chapple (1940) for instance, has developed an approach that objectively describes interaction in noting who speaks to whom and how long it takes. He is not concerned with the content of the communication or the emotional surroundings and, therefore, no judgment by the observer need be made. Despite the limited concentration on time and order of interaction between individuals, the technique can provide much useful information. Horsfall and Arensberg (1949) extensively surveyed productivity in a shoe factory by using the Chapple technique to describe and compare work teams in their performance. Leadership, initiated activity, and social activity within teams and between teams are areas of interest that can be determined from an analysis of the results of this observational technique.

Social Influence

The influence of the group on its members can take place in many ways. Often there are well-known and accepted norms to follow, but where the standards are not very clear the actions of the individual members are affected still more by their view of the patterns of behavior exhibited by others in the group. Even definite criteria are followed, however, because of the real or implied pressures of the social group. What is of greater importance, however, is that the mere presence of other people affects the performance of a person.

In an early and well-known experiment, Sherif (1936) asked subjects in a darkened room to estimate the extent and direction of movement of a tiny pinpoint of light. (The light really did not move although people ordinarily perceived movement—a phenomenon known as the *autokinetic effect*). Individual estimates were very close together when made in a group and did not diverge significantly when the subjects were later asked to make estimates while alone. When Sherif started with subjects making estimates when no other members were present, the estimates were quite divergent. When later gathered into a group, the estimates of individuals began to converge and, while they were very close, these were not as close as the nearly identical estimates given by members of the group that started out together as a group. The earlier individual experiences clearly played a role even though the group influences were more significant.

A closer look at the influence proceses in a group setting reveals the role of already familiar social concepts such as norms in the specific context of interaction in groups.

GROUP NORMS

Norms have already been discussed (Chapter 13) as being very important in human affairs; this is no less true when we look more closely into the functioning of groups. The rules of behavior that are important for the functioning of the group become even more important when the group or the task becomes larger. Some guidelines are necessary to help the group reach a goal, although, as Thibaut and Kelley (1959) point out, the norm structure can become so complex that it interferes with the effective functioning of the group. In this situation it is likely that more attention is paid to the following of the rules to the letter than to the fulfillment of the functions those rules were intended to serve originally. Norms may be described in various ways, depending on the focus of attention. There may be a concentration on the processes at work in the social situation or on the effects of the functioning of norms. Looking at norms as sanctions emphasizes their role as a process; common behavior of group members is an immediate effect, and the support of group activity may be regarded as an only slightly more distant effect.

Real or imagined pressures to conform to the norms of the group often have been described by casual observers of the social scene. There is some general opinion that the very notion of conformity is antagonistic to individual fulfillment and, eventually, the attainment of societal well-being. Indeed it might, but such superficial pronouncements overlook the positive and sometimes necessary aspects of conformity to group norms. Cartwright and Zander (1960,

p. 159) point out that pressures for conformity can help the group accomplish its goals by providing information on "reality" to its members so that the group can maintain itself. These social pressures can provide stability and information for both individual members and the total group in the common pursuit of functional goals.

The influence of the group toward conformity can be demonstrated in many ways. An early experiment by Asch (1952) indicated that even simple tasks could be altered by group pressures. Asch had members of a small group make judgments in the presence of each other. The subjects were to match a criterion line with one of three lines presented along with it; this was a task so simple that a large number of subjects given the choices earlier made virtually no mistakes. The experimental group itself was composed of individuals who were unaware of the fact that some of the other members were instructed by the experimenter to give incorrect answers occasionally. The naive subjects, when faced with unanimous choices by the other members, often gave the same incorrect choices. This did not occur with some subjects and even those who did conform did not always do so; the number of incorrect choices, however, was quite high. Asch varied the experiment by changing the number in the group and in the majority. A majority of three was found to be as influential as any larger ones (up to 16 were tried). If one other person was present who supported the naive subject, this was enough to reduce the influence of the majority or even eliminate it entirely.

The Asch experiment called for very simple judgments—ones where there should have been little doubt as to outcome. If the group influence was strong with respect to easy judgments of lengths of lines, it should not be too surprising to find strong group influences in more common social situations where the "correct" choices are less easy to find than are the group guidelines.

Other experimenters have confirmed the basic results of Asch's study (Rosenberg, 1961). Milgram (1964) also found that naive subjects administered more pain to other subjects under the social pressure of a group (accomplices of the experimenter) than they would on their own initiative.

Some individuals finds it easier to conform than do others; the differences between the independent and the submissive undoubtedly are based in personality factors. Steiner and Johnson (1963) confirm the generally accepted guess that authoritarians are more conforming than are nonauthoritarians. The authors found an easy acceptance of the decisions of a respected group of peers. When strong needs for social approval are considered in addition to the authoritarian pattern, subjects who are highly motivated with respect to this factor are more likely to agree with expressed opinions of their peers (Stickland and Crowne, 1962).

Other variables play a role too, however. Older subjects are less likely to conform (DiVesta and Cox, 1960). The same authors found also that females and those with less intellectual ability showed more conformity. Milgram (1964) supported the latter point in finding that college graduates conformed less than those in lower educational brackets.

There is substantial evidence to support a statement that when an individual takes a stand publicly, he is more likely to be influenced by group norms than when he arrives at a conclusion in private. Raven (1959) found greater pressure to conform to the group norm when the individual either had to communicate his opinion or where possibility of rejection for nonconformity existed. Kelley and Volkart (1952) found similar results when they presented a critical speech to a group of boy scouts. Half the group was told that the results of a later questionnaire about the speech would be made public while the other half was assured that their responses would not be disclosed. Those boy scouts who were told their questionnaires would be made public tended to agree more with the speaker.

COHESIVENESS

The perceptions of the bonds between individuals are important aspects of group functioning. There is even some doubt as to whether there will be any unifying adherence to group norms without cohesiveness, the condition defined as "that group property which is inferred from the number and strength of mutual positive attitudes among the members of a group" (Lott, 1961, p. 279).

It might be expected that the influence a group will exert upon its members will be related to the cohesiveness of the group, that is, the greater the cohesiveness the greater the influence. Festinger et al. (1950) found this to be the case. The same authors described the basis for the influence as being in the attractiveness of the group for its members. Individuals may want to belong to the group for several reasons—the group may be the mediator for certain goals that are important for members, being a member of the group may have certain attractions in itself, or people may want to belong to the group simply because they like the other members.

Since norms involve criteria for behavior, they tend to reduce any anxiety about what is "right" or proper. The more homogeneous the group, the more consistent the criteria are likely to be; this, in turn, makes the group more cohesive, and so on, in a reinforcing cycle. The more the values of the group are shared, the more cohesive the group is likely to be. The "tightly knit group" means a greater sharing of values and more identification with group perspectives.

Cohesiveness of the group will be greater if changes in the membership of the group occur less or not at all (Lasswell and Kaplan, 1950). A few new members may not be resisted or may even be welcomed by the existing membership; when there is a chance of the intrusion of a large number of new participants, there is less likely to be acceptance of the new members. The newcomers, on the other hand, may come into the new situation with trepidation or feelings of inferiority (Shils, 1950). Cohesiveness may be enhanced in many different ways or through the use of many different techniques. It has been characteristic of many "in" groups that their existence has been furthered by the use of secret symbols, passwords, or any mystical arrangements that unify them and set them apart from others.

Cohesiveness of a group influences communications within it and, at the same time, communications have some effect on cohesiveness. Festinger and Thibaut (1951) found that where there was a wide range of opinion in decision-making groups, there was a tendency for communications to be directed to those members who were at the extremes of the range of opinions. There are more communications to the deviate from group norms, since these are attempts to bring him "back into the fold." The attempts are made partly because the deviate may represent a threat to the existence and stability of the group. Because of this threat, there is, in addition, hostility often expressed toward the nonconformist, the rejection being particularly strong in high-cohesiveness groups (Schachter, 1951).

Lott (1961) suggests that a more cohesive group has a higher level of communication between the members. There is also some suggestion that cohesiveness will increase if communication among members of a group increases, particularly if there are visible rewards in this procedure for the various members. This may be similar to the point that Homans (1950) has indicated, that interaction between members of a group and attractiveness were directly related. This would mean that interaction and communication would bring increased liking of other members and vice versa.

As might be expected, a cohesive group is more likely to arise in a situation calling for cooperative activity and is likely to be more effective in performance than is one where competition occurs internally. Klein (1956) has indicated that compatibility of members and similarity in characteristics of individuals lead to more effective collaboration and performance. He indicates that the badly organized group is no better than one that is composed of members in competition with one another where individuals hinder others in attainment of a goal. There is also more likelihood of communication of hostile feelings, criticism, withholding of information, and less communication in a poorly organized group. What communication does occur may be largely irrelevant or unrelated to the task.

Group discussions of problems to be faced and procedures to be followed is probably more effective in carrying out group performance than is any individual educational effort.

COMPETITION

A competitive atmosphere involving groups may play an important role in their functioning in many practical situations. It may be commonly believed, especially in industrial concerns, that competition between individuals and groups within the company is of value in stimulating higher performance. Whether this is so or not is important to determine.

Some contribution to an understanding of the effects of competition and cooperation on individual and group performance is gained through a reading of results of a basic experiment by Mintz (1951). Mintz arranged metal cones in a bottle with an opening just large enough for the cones to be withdrawn one at a time. Water was introduced into the jar from below in the experiment while the subjects were instructed to withdraw the cones without getting them wet. There were two experimental conditions; in one a reward was promised to the person who retrieved his cone without getting it wet; a fine was paid if the cone was dampened by the rising water. The second experimental variation indicated that a similar group of students succeeded in cooperating and getting their cones out within a short period of time. There were no "traffic jams" under the cooperative pattern of behavior while the reward-and-fine conditions produced blockage and nonadaptive behavior over half the time. The experimenter obtained this result with no more than the threat of a mild fear of failure or the payment of a 10 cent fine.

Another of the earlier experimental studies of competition versus cooperation was done by Deutsch (1949). His subjects performed tasks ranging from simple puzzles to more complex problems of human relations. On most tasks the cooperative groups produced at a higher level than did the competitive groups, perhaps because of greater coordination in the cooperative teams. An added feature was a friendlier spirit among the cooperators. A later attempt by Jones and Vroom (1964) to isolate key factors in a similar situation led to the conclusion that the more effective performance of cooperative groups was the result of an effective division of labor. Performance was likely to be adversely affected when members had strong preferences for a particular task. This was true in cooperative as well as competitive groups.

These results and those of other researchers give some indication of the influence of group norms and the resulting cohesiveness on the performance of the members' conformity to norms. Hammond and Goldman (1961, p. 60) phrase it in terms of "noncompetition (being) more favorable to the group process."

PARTICIPATION

In one way or another, various group studies have buttressed the view that a significant factor contributing to the effectiveness of the group is that of participation by the members in its functioning. Several research studies, particularly in industry, have indicated the importance of this factor.

The "Hawthorne studies" represent one of the most significant conceptual influences in the area of organizational behavior, particularly in an industrial setting. While the experiments focused on the influence of the group on productivity of workers, the deeper implications for a general theory of human behavior and the applications of it in an administrative framework have had great impact on organizational theorists and practitioners. These studies, begun in the 1920's in the Hawthorne plant of the Western Electric Company, have been discussed by many, including Roethlisberger and Dickson (1947) and Homans (1950).

The original interest of the experimenters in this series of studies was in the effects of environmental factors on work performance. They varied the level of illumination, for instance, and related this to measures of output, using small groups of workers selected from the general work force as subjects placed in specially prepared test facilities. During the course of the experiments, the investigators recognized that variables other than those with which they were concerned were playing a very important role in the final output. It was the recognition of the social factors contributing to performance for which these studies became justly famous. The girls who were selected for the test room experience participated in the planning of the experiment, and their views were taken into account throughout. The girls felt "it was fun" and, even though the number of observers was greater and their attention higher in the test situation than in the ordinary work environment, the girls felt no sense of anxiety because of tight control. The group developed leadership and common purpose; the work situation became a very cohesive one, where, when individuals may not have felt up to par, the other members of the group "carried" them. In short, there emerged an effectively functioning social group in a warm relationship with its supervisors. What about the original dependent variable—work output? There need not be any concern on this score by those who concentrate only on production. Output progressed to consistently higher levels without stress on the individuals and, of course, while this could not continue indefinitely, the workers were highly motivated to show increasing improvement.

This was in distinct contrast to the situation the workers said existed in their original work stations. It was also distinctly different from the situation existing in another work group that was observed without any of the preliminary discusion or participation by the workers in the new investigation. Even though there was a wage incentive system in this group, which should have provided some increase in output and wages, production figures remained remarkably constant over a period of time. Work procedures and the resulting output were influenced by the shared attitudes and values of the group; the work group set norms which maintained a ceiling on output. Those workers who exceeded the ceiling were given evidence of social disapproval, verbally or physically. Output was not exceedingly low, however, since the group norms included a floor for production, below which employees could not fall without being called a "chiseler" or something similar.

This work unit proved to be less cohesive than the original experimental one. While there was a common set of values and sentiments, the main group was characterized by a set of cliques, each with limited interests. Relationships with supervisors were less friendly and more formal than in the cohesive participating group. Workers felt more closely supervised when, in reality, there was less overall supervision in the regular work situation than in the test group. Both groups seemed to be organized; the difference arose from the fact that the test group was organized in cooperation with management for a common purpose while the second informal work group was organized in opposition to management. In both cases, however, an analysis of the informal group clearly indicated the strong influence of social factors on individual and group performance.

Another well-known study of the importance of participation in the functioning of groups was done at the Harwood Manufacturing Corporation by Coch and French (1948). While the study focused on the change process and the specific techniques possible in the overcoming of resistance to change, the techniques used and the results illustrate several aspects of group dynamics. The experiment was conducted at a time when the factory was involved in a style change that necessitated a revision of work roles and procedures. The investigators arranged to have matched groups of employees exposed to three degrees of participation in determining the new work assignments. One group had virtually no participation in the process; they were assigned tasks from the very beginning. The second group participated indirectly through a group of representatives selected from the original group. The final variation involved complete participation in the determining of programs and assignments in the changeover. After the changeover, the no-participation group showed little or no improvment in their performance. Resistance was notable among the members of the production crew, and many examples of hostility and aggression between workers and supervisors were common. The group that participated through representatives worked well with the supervisor or staff man and showed a substantial increase in performance, particularly in the second week after the change. The total participation group adapted to the change very rapidly and progressed to levels that were significantly higher than their earlier performance. The emotional tone of the group was very good; there was excellent cooperation between individuals in the group and the supervisor, and no aggression was evident.

At the end of the month, the no-participation group had made no progress and were assigned to new jobs somewhere else in the factory. When they were reassembled after a few months and permitted to participate in still another change, this group operated at the same high levels that earlier participation groups achieved, a level that, again, was significantly higher than the positions reached where they were not permited to participate. The experimenters felt that such participation leads to higher morale or better labor-management relations in addition to higher production. The entire management of the company felt that the practical results were very valuable, over and above any of the theoretical additions this study has made to concepts of group processes and intergroup relations generally.

It may be, however, that, while there is a strong motivational basis for individual participation, the strength of this factor may not be uniform for all individuals. Vroom (1959) related personality with group participation and performance. He found the highest satisfaction in the job and the best performance in those individuals who had a high need for independence. Individuals who are highly dependent and were authoritarian-oriented were affected less by the opportunity to participate and showed no relationship between felt participation and job performance. This study indicates that, while participation is related to performance and is important in group functioning, we should also look to variations in individuals in terms of the need for participation.

Broader situational and demographic variables are not, of course, without their influence on the interaction within the small group. A series of studies on an important small group in the legal area, the jury, has indicated several avenues of influence from outside the immediate group situation. Strodtbeck, James, and Hawkins (1958) determined the influence of socioeconomic status and occupation on the interaction in the mock jury. It was found that those individuals who participated more were most often chosen as foreman. Men participated in jury deliberations much more frequently than did women, and there was much more activity from those individuals in higher socioeconomic brackets.

GROUP PROBLEM SOLVING

One of the aspects of group functioning that has attracted considerable interest down through the years is that of group problem solving. The basic question has been whether the product of the intellectual functioning of a group is superior to that of a group of individuals functioning separately.

In one of the earliest studies on the question of group versus individual problem solving, Allport (1920) found a difference in favor of the group because a greater variety of ideas arose in that social setting. Lorge and Solomon (1960) replicated an earlier study by Shaw (1932) and found (as Shaw did) that, generally, groups were superior to individuals. Level of aspiration was a significant factor; no individual without aspiration was able to solve the problem, while groups were not affected as strongly. Argyle (1957) agreed in terms of superiority of the group. He isolated two factors in the process, namely, the improvement of judgment through prior judgment and the superiority achieved through a combination of individual judgments. Group problem solving increased the number of alternatives available and stimulated activity toward a typical solution to identify blind alleys that individuals might find themselves in if they pursue the task alone.

It is safe to say that most of the studies in this area report a superiority of group over individual approaches although at least one (Moore and Anderson, 1954) does not. It may be that the source of disagreement lies mainly in the conditions surrounding the task and in the individuals who are subjects. The preponderance of expert opinion, however, is in favor of superiority of the group in problem-solving performance.

There has been further interest in a specific variant of group problem solving known popularly as "brainstorming" where the focus is on unrestricted and uninhibited associative responses by members of an assembled group. The group is under instructions to be unconcerned about the logic or validity of an idea and to respond with as many as possible.

Results of experiments in this area have been somewhat controversial. Osborn (1957), among others, has noted evidence for a greater variety and creativity in group solutions under the brainstorming instructions to provide ideas without concern for their value or logic. Taylor et al. (1958) indicate that this has not been true in their experience. The latter findings may represent, however, an inability of the individuals in the group to rid themselves of limiting attitudes; other situational and relational factors also may be playing an inhibiting role.

Structural Factors

Simple physical factors affect social relationships of individuals. In a small group situation they may play an even greater role than in broad social interaction, since the more immediate psychological factors have a tendency to be highlighted in the more proximate influences of the small group.

SIZE

The number of individuals in a group can, at least at a casual initial impression, determine much of the activity of the group. It would seem logical that the greater the number of individuals interacting, the less intimate their relationships would be. The sheer volume of interactions then necessary would tend to make any concerted action much more difficult. The role of the leader would, however, be much more significant in a group of larger size.

What the "proper" number of individuals in the group may be could depend upon the circumstances in which the group operates, particularly the purpose or function. Sargent and Williamson (1958) indicate, after a survey of the field, that a fact-finding group is probably most effective when it is composed of about 14 members. An executive or action-taking group functions best at a size of approximately seven members. The validity of these figures is reinforced by information from many legislative bodies that indicates memberships in the two different types of functioning groups as hovering close to the figures given.

An experimental study (Bales and Borgatta, 1955) of the effect of size on the interaction within the group provides some empirical results. The experimenters varied group size from two up to seven and recorded observations in the 12 categories of the Bales Interaction Analysis procedure. The overall results indicate, not surprisingly, that each member is faced with the greater number of individuals with whom to interact as size increases and the amount of time available to talk to others then is reduced per capita. When specific types of interaction are considered in the increase in size, the following actions also increase: showing solidarity, releasing tension, and giving suggestion. The following activities show a decrease with size: showing agreement, asking for opinion, and showing tension. These patterns of initiated behavior probably show the increased pressure on the individuals for activities that will further the functioning of the group despite the increase in size.

Berelson and Steiner (1964) conclude that even-numbered groups show more disagreement than odd-numbered groups because of the possibility for subgroups of equal size to be pitted against each other. They further state that the "perfect" group size is five, where, if subgroups develop, a minority group of two permits participation and individual development in support of a position while a majority of three is not completely overwhelming yet strong enough to prevail.

Simmel was one of the first researchers to point out the characteristics of two-person and three-person groups and to discuss the differences between them. Three-person groups quickly break down into two subgroups, that its, two persons team up as a majority against the remaining member. This division may not be an active or aggressive one, however, since the minority of one may simply be a less interested or even apathetic member of the group. It is more stable than a two-man group in the sense of acccomplishment of purpose by the majority but unstable in that it breaks down very quickly into subgroups of two and one. The group of two is less stable because there is a great deal of tension in the evenly balanced person-to-person situation. There is, however, a recognition of the need for understanding, tolerance, and the avoidance of disagreement. The husband-wife group is a good example, and many of the characteristics of their situation can apply generally to all groups of two.

These findings have given rise to the statements of small group researchers that the dyad (two-person group) is more stable than the triad (three-person group). This may be only a newer and more precise way of stating the old maxim "two is company and three is a crowd."

PLACEMENT

Interaction between individuals and groups often is affected by their location with respect to each other. It might be expected that individuals who do not interact do not get to know each other. The converse, however, is not so readily guessed, that is, that those who do interact are more likely to be attracted to each other (Homans, 1950).

Festinger et al. (1950) compared sociometric choices with the physical distance between individuals and found a high relationship. Individuals living closest were chosen more often and, as the distances between persons increased, choices between them became less frequent. This study was conducted in a housing project where even minor distances such as a few feet were significant. Even such seemingly small factors such as placement of doorways can be significant; people whose front doors face each other directly are more likely to interact with greater frequency than when they are located in other ways.

Further evidence of the impact of physical placement on primary relationships is presented by Whyte (1956) in *The organization man.* No demographic variables such as occupation, background, religion, or education could explain the "web of friendship" that existed in the example of suburbia studied. The basis for primary social relationships turned out to be propinquity—groups at social events were composed of those who lived in the same geographic area. Whyte also noted, among other factors, the link between centrality of location and popularity. The more introverted could remain so by locating in peripheral areas.

There is much more to the patterning of groups than physical placement, of course. Similarities of interest, status, and life style are apt to be just as important as location, and perhaps even more so. The author recalls, from several years as a "participant observer" in a planned and cohesive community, that friendship groups were frequently structured along occupational lines. Just as important seemed to be the memberships of the wives in social or charitable organizations. Despite the overlapping that inevitably occurs in any complex social relationship, the common thread between individuals was most often a shared set of values and status.

Communication in Groups

Communication is a basic aspect of the interaction in groups of individuals. Whether on a person-to-person basis or on a level involving a greater number in the network, communication serves to provide information and is a prime vehicle for influencing others. Of all aspects of communication that might be of special interest in a group setting, those relating to the direction of transmission and the arrangements of networks are probably of greatest pertinence for discussion.

DIRECTION OF COMMUNICATION

Communication may proceed only one-way or the information may be transmitted back and forth; that is, two-way communication may take place. A speaker may simply lecture to an audience or a boss may not permit any questioning of his position by subordinates. In those situations, the communication is pretty much limited to one-way. Certainly, subtle cues may be transmitted by the audience back to the speaker but, for all practical purposes, the direction is unilateral. In two-way communication the channels are utilized in both directions. Statements and questions are made back and forth.

Each type of communication has its own characteristics which may determine the usefulness of procedure. Leavitt (1964, p. 143), long an active researcher in this area, has summarized the findings of experiments on direction of communication. Two-way may be slower than one-way communication, but it is more accurate. Senders in the two-way process may have more anxiety or feel under attack because receivers communicate their feelings. At the same time, the receivers feel more sure of themselves since they get a better idea of whether they are correct in their judgments. Two-way communication appears more disorderly and less efficient to an outside observer, but it works better.

The implications for a communicator in any type of organization are striking. An administrator in business or a teacher in an educational setting may feel that a one-way communication system is mandatory to preserve order and promote efficiency in the organization. While "giving orders" has been a traditional pattern of behavior in many business or school situations, there is some doubt that, apart from reducing the anxiety of "boss" or "teacher," it is an effective means of promoting organizational welfare.

COMMUNICATION NETWORKS

The structuring of communication channels between individuals in a group influences the interaction of its members and the functioning of the group as a whole. Research on communication networks was stimulated by some original work by Bavelas (1948) but was expanded upon by others, notably Leavitt (1951) and Guetzkow and Simon (1955). The experiments on the effects of communication networks, while very basic and spartan as precise experiments must be, can provide valuable information for an understanding of the functioning of communications in groups placed in various institutional settings. Small group communication networks can be structured in the patterns shown in Figure 15-1. All are patterns of communication involving individuals in groups

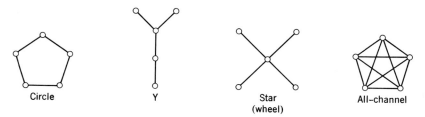

Figure 15-1. Some communication networks in groups (Leavitt, H., 1951).

of five and, while still other patterns of communication are possible (a "chain" of individuals, for example), the patterns in Figure 15-1 are sufficient for describing salient features of experiments in small group communication nets.

Those who would wish to transfer behavioral information to an applied setting would undoubtedly have greatest interest in the relationships between communication networks and performance of the group. Questions such as "which network is most efficient?" might be asked. The difficulty in answering comes in the further specification of effectiveness; speed or accuracy may be the prime consideration. In addition, the nature of the task, the order of presentation, or other conditions play a role, and there are other factors that have an additional influence on performance, if only indirectly. Motivation and morale can show some relationships with type of communication network and, as has been pointed out repeatedly, these factors can influence the performance of a group or individual.

Leavitt (1964) summarized his work and that of others in a comparison of networks operating under various conditions. The "star" network will be faster than the "circle," at least in the initial stages of organization if not throughout the entire handling of the task. The star will provide a great deal of satisfaction for the member in the central position; the others in the network are likely to be considerably less satisfied in the outcome of the task. Of possible greater importance is the difference between the star and the circle in terms of having to cope with new tasks once the networks have been organized and the earlier tasks completed. With new tasks that call for a change in approach or method of problem solving, the circle shows that it can cope much better with the changed conditions. Undoubtedly the superiority in problem solving in new situations is a result of the opportunity for greater participation by circle members in the problem-solving task. The centrality of the star network seems to be the basis for the continuing errors made in new problems.

Satisfaction in the outcome is higher in the circle networks were everyone participates in all aspects of the decision making. Morale in a group where the members are allowed to participate is much higher than in one in which few get the opportunity to play a role. Satisfaction is high, of course, for the member who occupies the central position in the star, but the peripheral members' morale is usually much lower than that of those in the circle.

With some reservations based on the fact of limited applications to "real" situations, Leavitt (1964, pp. 236–237) suggests that "good" networks are those that are equalitarian in nature, that is, where individuals have many neighbors or equal access to at least two direct channels in the group. The reader is reminded to consider these findings in connection with the earlier considerations of one-way and two-way communications.

Effective Group Activity

With increased interest in the nature and functioning of groups, there has been a growing awareness of the fact that "good groups don't just happen." It might be more accurate to say that a better understanding of the dynamics of interaction in the small group situation has led some observers to the development of more positive approaches in the early stages of group activity. The possibility that people can profit from training for group participation has been emphasized by an increasing number of supporters of varying educational approaches.

By far the most extensive program to date has been that which has developed primarily in the National Training Laboratory at Bethel, Maine. These methods have gone out with varying labels—the "T-group" method or the "laboratory method," as well as similar names for other variants of the basic method. The initial impetus for the movement arose from the work of the late Kurt Lewin and his followers in the group dynamics movement. They were soon joined by others and, with the support of the National Education Association, the National Training Laboratory first opened in 1947.

The organization has set up laboratories for various kinds of group training for effective functioning in various institutional settings. Business and industry have been widely represented, but other groups from educational, community, religious, and national organizations have joined in sending their members for the workshops.

A training program attempts to provide an opportunity for individuals to learn more about themselves and the mechanisms of interaction with others in a group situation. It provides a setting away from the work place and, hopefully, an opportunity for the "unfreezing" of attitudes that often interfere in office training programs. All of this must be done in a way that aids in the transfer of new concepts and attitudes back to the "home office."

Specific approaches in the laboratory method show variation from time to time and trainer to trainer. For this reason, no set of statements can completely portray the specific mechanics of the laboratory method, nor have many people tried to provide a comprehensive and definitive statement of procedures. Thelen (1963) has outlined his analysis of the approach and, while he has recognized that this is a single view among many, the fact that he has been active in the program and in extensions of it lends weight to the description. Thelen (*Ibid.*, pp. 131–139) states that the basic aim of the laboratory method is "to help people to learn how to behave in groups" so that the problem is solved and the individuals have a meaningful experience. Wise decisions and personal growth through learning to test for reality are central to the process; the trainer is on hand to help the group grow in this way. It is hoped that the process provides the individual with a realistic understanding of present and past experiences, eliminates anxiety, and develops images of effective processes of group functioning. The final and most important goal in the process is the transfer of all that has developed from the training sessions back to the regular setting in which the individual will continue his day-to-day interactions in real life.

In *The human side of enterprise,* McGregor (1960) outlines two broad theoretical assumptions of management. He calls the traditional view "Theory X" wherein the worker is viewed as disliking and avoiding work so that he must be closely watched and directed by those who can and will coerce through threat. "Theory Y," on the other hand, assumes that man will exercise self-direction in the effective attainment of group and individual goals, a potential that is only partially realized.

All of McGregor's discussion is important for the student of behavior, but the aspect that is pertinent to the present chapter on groups is the formulation of the theoretical assumptions in the specific context of group behavior. He has drawn on the concepts and research of the "group dynamics" movement stimulated earlier by Kurt Lewin. As a result, McGregor (*Ibid.,* pp. 235–240) distinguishes between effective and less effective groups. The "good" managerial team is one where the atmosphere is relaxed with people listening to each other without tension. People participate and try to reach agreement. When disagreements cannot be resolved, the group attempts to live with them, and criticism, while frequent, is constructive and not personal. Evaluation of group performance is constant. On the other hand, a less effective group has little idea of group task objectives. A few people dominate, and their contributions are often not to the point. Disagreements are either suppressed out of fear of conflict, or actual warfare emerges. Meetings produce tension but little of value in reaching any clear goal.

The NTL programs are seen by McGregor as producing the sensitivity and understanding that provides the characteristic atmosphere on the well-functioning group. This may well be one key to effective action of the managerial team or other organizational group.

Summary

Individual behavior is always influenced by group factors and seldom, if ever, is seen apart from group activity. The basis for social behavior may be seen in the study of groups, particularly those small and cohesive enough to be studied in more extensive fashion. Basic and applied studies of groups help to determine fundamental factors in social functioning generally and provide understanding of group activities in specific situations.

Since much of the research on groups deals with those of smaller size, the usual references met are those of small groups. This is not exclusively the case, however, as an occasional mention can be made of somewhat larger and more amorphous groupings. In a group the members interact in a relationship that is determined by their roles and guided by a shared set of values, beliefs, or a more-or-less developed ideology. They perceive themselves as a group engaged in a common task.

People tend to function in groups because of the benefits to be derived from this type of relationship. Groups may satisfy certain individual as well as social needs. Many of the activities will satisfy various concurrent needs. Group action is furthered by a common goal, that is, a consensus in the group as to the end results of group activities.

Groups may be classified in various ways. If there is a concentration on the extent of legal or formal authority in their structuring, we may differentiate between the formal group with official structure and procedures or the informal group that can be identified outside of the official structuring. The two kinds of grouping may exist side by side within a broader framework with each serving several purposes at the same time. Individuals may be identified also as to actual membership in a group recognized as part of a grouping to which they may refer or from which they may adopt a set of attitudes and values. Some clusters of individuals may represent high-prestige memberships, or the grouping may be of those who are marginal or peripheral in a society; this concept is often casually referred to as the distinction between in-group and out-group. Perhaps the most significant differentiation in the study of groups is that contrasting primary and secondary groups. The intimate, personal, and proximate relationships in the primary groupings are undoubtedly significant in their influence on individual and group behavior. Relationships in secondary groups are more general and remote and, as a result, are less likely to carry as much of an impact as do the primary relationships.

Methods of gathering data in small group research include virtually every behavioral research technique available, although certain approaches are more amenable to group research. Sociometry portrays the group choices in graphic or tabular form to provide a picture of social interaction. Sociometric results can portray the structure and extent of the grouping and can provide further insights as to its dynamics in many applied situations. Observational techniques are very old, of course, but the recent behavioral emphases have been on approaches that would provide a more systematic and comprehensive sketching of the interactions in a group. The burden is on the observer to identify and record type or content of interaction within a systematic framework previously developed.

One of the most fundamental aspects of group functioning that is of great interest to the social researcher is the capacity of the group to influence behavior in various ways. The norms of a group provide strong guidelines for individual activities; the pressure on individual members induces shared goals and common frames of reference. These enable the group to maintain itself and accomplish its goals. Various experiments have demonstrated the strength of group norms on individual behavior although variation exists as age, level of education, sex, and personality factors provide some differences in the extent to which conformity to group norms is attained. The more cohesive the group, the more the influence process will be felt. Cohesiveness is also greater with stability of membership and activities of the group.

Competition among individuals within the group appears to hinder performance of the group rather than enhance it. In problem solving, group approaches seem to be superior to those engaged in on an individual basis. Effectiveness of group functioning can be enhanced by the proper division of tasks among members of the group and by allowing each individual to participate meaningfully in the total process. Substantial results from industry indicate that participation of individuals in the total functioning of the work group provides not only a better emotional climate but enables the group to operate at higher levels of performance on the task as well. Participation may well be one of the significant factors in group performance.

Physical factors such as size of group and placement of individuals in it may have an influence on the nature of the social relationships evolving therefrom. Odd-numbered groups may show more agreement, since ties in voting may be broken. Action-taking groups may function best when less than ten in number, while fact-finding groups may exceed that, although not by too much, without harm. Interaction among individuals is often related to their physical placement with respect to each other; those who come into contact frequently are those who live or work near each other, although other personal characteristics such as age and occupation may vary the influence of physical placement.

Since communication is a basic social process, the direction and extent of communications influence the interaction among individuals in a group. Communication in one or both directions among individuals has its own advantages and disadvantages. Different types of communication networks among individuals in the group have their own peculiar characteristics. Generally those who are more active in the communication net show greater satisfaction in the results of communication activity. Centralized networks may show higher initial activity, but those nets that allow fuller participation among their members are better in coping with novel situations.

The results of research on group activity have been viewed by many as being important ultimately in the application of results to improved effectiveness of group functioning. Specific methods such as the "T-group" program have attempted to change individual attitudes in order that members can learn how to behave more effectively in groups. These and similar approaches can provide an atmosphere where individuals can work without tension and participate meaningfully in the cooperative move toward meeting the objective of the group. Individual needs are fulfilled in this way at the same time.

Bibliography

Allport, F. (1920). The influence of the group upon association and thought. *Journal of Experimental Pychology,* **3,** 159–182.

Argyle, M. (1957). Social pressure in public and private situations. *Journal of Abnormal and Social Psychology,* **54,** 172–175.

Asch, S. (1952). *Social psychology.* Englewood Cliffs, N.J.: Prentice-Hall.

Bales, R. (1951). *Interaction process analysis: a method for the study of small groups.* Cambridge, Mass.: Addison-Wesley.

Bales, R., and Borgatta, E. (1955). Size of group as a factor in the interaction profile. In Hare, A. et al. (eds.). *Small groups: studies in social interaction.* New York: Knopf, 395–413.

Bavelas, A. (1948). A mathematical model for group structures. *Applied Anthropology,* **7,** 16–30.

Bennett, E. (1955). Discussion, decision, commitment, and consensus in "group decisions." *Human Relations,* **8,** 251–274.

Berelson, B. and Steiner, G. (1964). *Human behavior.* New York: Harcourt, Brace and World.

Browne, C. (1951). Study of executive leadership in business; sociometric pattern. *Journal of Applied Psychology,* **35,** 34–37.

Burgess, E. (1926). The family a unity of interacting personalities. *Family* **7,** 3–9.

Cartwright, D. and Zander, A. eds. (1960). *Group dynamics: research and theory* (2nd ed.). New York: Harper & Row.

Chapple, E. (1940). Measuring human relations: an introduction to the study of the interaction of individuals. *Genetic Psychology Monograph,* **22,** 1–147.

Coch, L. and French, J. (1948). Overcoming resistance to change. *Human Relations,* **1,** 512–534.

Cooley, C. (1909). *Social organization.* New York: Scribner's.

Dalton, M. (1959). *Men who manage.* New York: Wiley.

Deutsch, M. (1949). An experiemental study of the effects of cooperation and competition upon group processes. *Human Relations,* **2,** 199–231.

DiVesta, F. and Cox, L. (1960). Some dispositional correlates of conformity behavior. *The Journal of Social Psychology,* **52,** 259–268.

Festinger, L. (1950). Laboratory experiments: the role of group belongingness. In Miller, J. (ed.). *Experiments in social process.* New York: McGraw-Hill, 31–46.

Festinger, L., Schachter, S., and Back, K. (1950). *Social pressures in informal groups: a study of a housing project.* New York: Harper.

Festinger, L. and Thibaut, J. (1951). Interpersonal communication in small groups. *Journal of Abnormal and Social Psychology,* **46,** 92–99.

Gouldner, A. and Gouldner, H. (1963). *Modern sociology.* New York: Harcourt, Brace and World.

Guetzkow, H. and Simon, H. (1955). The impact of certain communication nets upon organization and performance in task-oriented groups. *Management Science,* **1,** 233–250.

Hammond, L. and Goldman, M. (1961). Competition and non-competition and its relationship to individual and group productivity. *Sociometry,* **24,** 46–60.

Heyns, R. and Lippitt, R. (1954). Systematic observational techniques. In Lindzey, G. (ed.). *Handbook of Social Psychology,* Chap. 10. Reading, Mass.: Addison-Wesley.

Hollander, E. and Webb, W. (1955). Leadership, followership and friendship: an analysis of peer nominations. *Journal of Abnormal and Social Psychology,* **50,** 163–167.

Homans, G. (1950). *The human group.* New York: Harcourt, Brace and World.

Horsfall, A. and Arensberg, C. (1949). Teamwork and productivity in a shoe factory. *Human Organization,* **8,** 13–25.

Jacobs, J. (1945). The application of sociometry to industry. *Sociometry,* **8,** 181–198.

Jennings, H. (1937). Structure of leadership-development and sphere of influence. *Sociometry,* **1,** 99–143.

Jones, S. and Vroom, V. (1964). Division of labor and performance under cooperative and competitive conditions. *Journal of Abnormal and Social Psychology,* **68,** 313–320.

Kelley, H. and Volkhart, E. (1952). The resistance to change of group-anchored attitudes. *American Sociological Review,* **17,** 453–465.

Kerstetter, L. and Sargent, J. (1940). Re-assignment therapy in the classroom. *Sociometry*, **3,** 292–306.

Klein, J. (1956). *The study of groups.* London: Routledge.

Krech, D., Crutchfield, R., and Ballachey, E. (1962). *Individual in society.* New York: McGraw-Hill.

Lasswell, H. and Kaplan, A. (1950). *Power and society: a framework for political inquiry.* New Haven, Conn.: Yale University Press.

Leavitt, H. (1951). Some effects of certain communication patterns on group performance. *The Journal of Abnormal and Social Psychology*, **46,** 38–50.

Leavitt, H. (1964). *Managerial psychology.* Chicago: University of Chicago Press.

Lorge, I. and Solomon, H. (1960). Group and individual performance in problem solving related to previous exposure to problem, level of aspiration, and group size. *Behavioral Science,* **5,** 28–38.

Lott, B. (1961). Group cohesiveness: a learning phenomenon. *The Journal of Social Psychology*, **55,** 275–286.

McGregor, D. (1960). *The human side of enterprise.* New York: McGraw-Hill.

Menzel, A. and Katz, E. (1956). Social relations and innovation in the medical profession: the epidemiology of a new drug. *Public Opinion Quarterly,* **19,** 337–352.

Milgram, S. (1964). Group pressure and action against a person. *Journal of Abnormal and Social Psychology,* **69,** 137–143.

Mintz, A. (1951). Nonadaptive group behavior. *The Journal of Abnormal and Social Psychology,* **46,** 150–159.

Moore, O. and Anderson, S. (1954). Search behavior in individual and group problem solving. *American Sociological Review,* **19,** 702–714.

Moreno, J. L. (1934). *Who shall survive?* Washington: Nervous and Mental Disease Publishing Co.

Osborn, A. (1957). *Applied imagination.* New York: Scribner's.

Raven, B. (1959). Social influence on opinions and the communication of related content. *Journal of Abnormal and Social Psychology,* **58,** 119–128.

Roethlisberger, F. and Dickson, W. (1939). *Management and the worker.* Cambridge, Mass.: Harvard University Press.

Rosenberg, L. (1961). Group size, prior experience, and conformity. *Journal of Abnormal and Social Psychology,* **63,** 436–437.

Sargent, S. and Williamson, R. (1958). *Social psychology.* New York: Ronald.

Schachter, S. (1951). Deviation, rejection, and communication. *Journal of Abnormal and Social Psychology,* **46,** 190–207.

Schein, E. (1965). *Organizational psychology*. Englewood Cliffs, N.J.: Prentice-Hall.

Shaw, M. (1932). A comparison of individuals and small groups in the rational solution of complex problems. *American Journal of Psychology*, **44**, 491–504.

Sherif, M. (1936). *The psychology of social norms*. New York: Harper.

Sherif, M. and Sherif, C. (1956). *An outline of social psychology* (rev. ed.). New York: Harper.

Shils, E. (1950). Primary groups in the American army. In Merton, R. and Lazarsfeld, P. (eds.). *Continuities in social research: studies in the scope and method of "the American soldier."* New York: Free Press.

Speroff, B. and Kerr, W. (1952). Steel mill "hot strip'" accidents and interpersonal desirability values. *Journal of Clinical Psychology*, **8**, 89–91.

Steiner, I. and Johnson, H. (1963). Authoritarianism and conformity. *Sociometry*, **26**, 21–34.

Strickland, B. and Crowne, D. (1962). Conformity under conditions of simulated group pressure as a function of the need for social approval. *The Journal of Social Psychology*, **58**, 171–181.

Strodtbeck, F., James, R., and Hawkins, C. (1958). Social status in jury deliberations. In Maccoby, E., Newcomb, T., and Hartley, E. (eds.). *Readings in social psychology*, (3rd ed.). New York: Holt.

Taylor, D., Berry, P., and Block, C. (1958). Does group participation when using brainstorming facilitate or inhibit creative thinking? *Administrative Science Quarterly*, **3**, 23–47.

Thelen, H. (1963). *Dynamics of groups at work*. Chicago: University of Chicago Press.

Thibaut, J. and Kelley, H. (1959). *The social psychology of groups*. New York: Wiley.

Tönnies, F. (1st ed., 1887). *Gemeinshaft and gesellschaft* (Loomis, C., trans.) (1940). *Fundamental concepts of sociology*. New York: American Book Co.

Van Zelst, R. (1952). Validation of a sociometric regrouping procedure. *Journal of Abnormal and Social Psychology*, **47**, 299–301.

Vroom, V. (1959). Some personality determinants of the effects of participation. *Journal of Abnormal and Social Psychology*, **59**, 322–327.

Whyte, W. (1956). *The organization man*. New York: Simon & Schuster.

Williams, S. and Leavitt, H. (1947). Group opinion as a prediction of military leadership. *Journal of Consulting Psychology*, **11**, 283–291.

Zeleny, L. (1941). Status: its measurements and control in education. *Sociometry*, **4**, 193–204.

16

Organizations

This chapter continues the study of individuals as members of groups. It has been implied or expressly stated all along that study of group behavior is important because individuals spend most of their time with others and are influenced by them. What has been said of small groups may be taken as a basis for discussion of the larger groupings called organizations.

The behavior of people in formal entities larger than small groups yet smaller than great aggregates has attracted the attention of many investigators in the behavioral and social sciences, not only those from the basic disciplines such as psychology, sociology, and anthropology but also from areas that may be called the applied fields—management science, operations research, and human relations, for example. This area of group study, the area of organizations, is an area of research that has probably appealed most to those observing the functioning of individuals in business, industry, government, and in educational or religious environments as well.

There has only recently been anything approaching a systematic and unified movement toward the study of organizations and, therefore, anything even remotely resembling a theory of organization. To one extent or another, however, the interrelationships in a group such as we are viewing at this time have been the object of scrutiny and even of some theory, rudimentary and unscientific though it might have been. This area has been the object of study and thought by many philosophers and theorists of the past, some of them the very same mentioned in Chapter 2. When discussing the nature of man, these social philosophers almost of necessity had to extend their activities to a study of men in groups of all kinds. Of even more interest are those who, in the relatively recent past, have developed more rigorous theories of organization and can be called either the first of the scientific writers in the area or the progenitors of the scientific theories of organization.

The Nature of Organizations

What is an organization? The answer to this question may not be so easy to give. March and Simon (1958, p. 1) say it is easier and probably more useful to give examples of formal organizations than to define the term. They say, "The United States Steel Corporation is a formal organization; so is the Red Cross, the corner grocery store, and the New York State Highway Department." This approach is of some help but, ultimately, a verbal description of the characteristics of an organization is called for.

A definition of an organization can put the emphasis on the activities that take place (Schein, 1965, p. 8). When goal-directed activities are coordinated rationally by assignment of duties and responsibilities, this rational coordination is the organization. It should be emphasized that *activities*, not people, are the subject of coordination. Not that the human element is ignored, however, since people are involved. What is meant is that, since people belong to many organizations, their activities in the one organization under study is important. This is also a basis for the consideration of *roles* as the focus for the study of behavior in organizations. The organization may be considered as a system of roles (Katz and Kahn, 1966, p. 172). In the system each individual has a specific role to play, with each of the roles coordinated with respect to a more integrative pattern. Larger organizational roles are maintained or fulfilled through the various functions identified in motivational terms.

More specific and comprehensive descriptions of an organization may be attempted. Factors most often mentioned by theorists as characteristics of organizations are size, complexity, formality, hierarchy, and duration (Berelson and Steiner, 1964, p. 364). More than just a few people are involved, and they are operating under a set of rules defining roles. Hierarchy refers to power and authority differences between levels in an ascending scale. The organization also lasts longer than a lifetime as old members are replaced with new ones. Other features that may be added include the cooperative movement toward collective goals within a complex total field or milieu (Strother, 1963, p. 23). These last factors may be important determinants. There is little doubt that some collective action is a necessary condition, and no organizational theory can consider the organization as a closed system not receiving inputs from the outside.

Types of Organizations

By now, the reader is well aware of the fact that classification may be somewhat arbitrary and may allow, therefore, a wide variety of categories or systems. With respect to organizations, the typology that may first occur to the reader is one that is based on the specific institutional area in which the organization functions. A breakdown like this will show entries such as:

1. Business organizations (many subtypes).
2. Schools (elementary schools to universities).
3. Government agencies (municipal, state, and federal).
4. Military organizations.
5. Political party groups.
6. Hospitals.
7. Prisons and other correctional groupings.
8. Unions.

This listing is by no means complete, but it serves as a guide to the extensiveness of type-categories on this basis. All of these types have characteristics that distinguish them, but a purely descriptive approach would occupy much effort without concomitant benefits. It would tend to obscure also the undeniable fact that most features of organizations are common to all. As a result, this chapter will focus more on general factors than on specific functional types of organizations.

Another, but less common, distinction among organizations is that differentiating between formal and informal organizations. This chapter will deal with the well-structured and authoritative organizations that we call formal ones and have named "companies," "schools," "churches," and "hospitals." These should be distinguished from informal organizations such as those groupings where individuals are tied together through casual and informal bonds of friendship or through channels of communication deliberately chosen outside of those formally prescribed. While references to informal organizations may be made from time to time in discussions in this chapter, the term organization, except as otherwise specified, will refer to the formal types.

Some sociologists also recognize another type of grouping—the *social organization.* This refers to patterns of interaction on the broader social scene such as have already been described in the several immediate preceding chapters. A grouping by community or social economic level may represent some patterns of behavior and attitudes or values in common, but they seldom, if ever, involve the close coordination of activity for achievement of specifically recognized goals. This type of organization, if it can be called that, will receive little mention at this point except as the broader social phenomena influence the activities of individuals in the formal organizations.

A classification of organizations based upon authority used in the activity is a further approach. Etzioni (1961) identifies three types of organizations based on authority (Table 16-1). He distinguishes between coercive authority,

Table 16-1.   Organizations Classified by Type of Authority or Power Used (from Etzioni, A., 1961)

Predominantly *coercive* authority
    Concentration camps
    Prisons and correctional institutions
    Prisoner-of-war camps
    Custodial mental hospitals
    Coercive unions
Predominantly *utilitarian* (rational-legal authority, use of economic rewards)
    Business and industry (with a few exceptions)
    Business unions
    Farmers' organizations
    Peacetime military organizations
Predominantly *normative* authority (use of membership, status, intrinsic value rewards)
    Religious organizations
    Ideologically based political organizations or parties
    Hospitals
    Colleges and universities
    Social unions
    Voluntary and mutual benefit associations
    Professional associations

utilitarian or rational-legal approaches, and adherence to normative guides. Coercive authority uses force, the utilitarian approach uses extrinsic rewards, and normative authority is based on intrinsic value rewards. These three types may be fused in various ways to form a fourth, or mixed, type.

Blau and Scott (1962) have categorized organizations on the basis of their criterion of *cui bono,* that is, who benefits from the operations of the organizations. Four types emerged using this criterion for classification: (1) mutual-benefit associations, (2) business concerns, (3) service organizations, and (4) commonwealth organizations. There may be many borderline cases and many instances where mixed types occur as well. Mutual benefit associations primarily benefit the membership; union, fraternal associations, clubs, political parties, and professional associations are examples where the emphasis is on the benefit to members. Owners are theoretically to be the prime beneficiaries of the business concerns that have been organized to be owned and operated for profit. Service organizations exist to serve clients even though it may be considered that ultimately the public is the beneficiary of this basic function. Hospitals, schools, clinics, and social-work agencies are examples of service organizations. Commonwealth organizations exist to serve the public-at-large. Police and fire departments in a municipality as well as federal bureaus and departments (and the armed forces) are organizations where the general citizenry are served by the activities of the grouping.

Theories of Organization

At this point in time, it is possible to construct, out of the activities of many researchers in varied areas, some broad outlines of fairly consistent frameworks recognizing or explaining behavior in the larger groupings we call organizations. Some of the formulations may not have been specifically made with the intent of establishing a "theory of organizations," but the relevance of such studies to our discussion in this chapter is clear. Even at this time, however, there cannot be said to be a consistent body of theoretical material on organizations. This area is still in flux and, while interest in specific empirical research and theory construction is accelerating, it is still difficult to identify a solid body of formulation that can be called "organization theory." Nevertheless, some fairly consistent lines of development can be traced from the earliest considerations of organizational behavior in this century up to the present.

One must be aware here, as with other situation, that classification is somewhat arbitrary. "Pigeonholing" seldom portrays the complete picture of similarities and differences; overlapping in many ways is a characteristic of sets of information abstracted from a larger body of behavioral events.

CLASSICAL ORGANIZATION THEORY

A convenient way of designating a formulation that has been well established is to call it "classical." The term implies something of ancient vintage but, in the area of organizations, that means it dates from the beginning of this century. It is also important to note that, while the theory may have shown greatest vitality in the past, this does not necessarily mean that no traces of it remain. Some elements of classical organization theory are still with us, in one form or another, or their influence on some of the newer formulations may linger.

Scientific Management

The "scientific management" school, stimulated by Frederick Winslow Taylor (1907) and carried on by others through the years, focused primarily on more discrete problems of management, and thus the activities of this body of research workers developed a cohesive small body of related facts. Certainly the sketching of effective production techniques and the development of managerial approaches to implement them provide a view of the functioning of individuals in organizations that can qualify as one of the earliest theoretical formulations of organizational behavior.

Taylor's work and that of his followers established a view of individual activity in organizations based on the physical and physiological functioning of individual workers in an industrial concern. The central tenet of scientific management was outlined by Taylor's theory that there was "one best way" of doing a particular job. In a way that has been perpetuated today in many time-and-motion or "methods-engineering" studies, Taylor set out to find that best way and make certain that each individual worker followed directions to the letter. The extension of this approach from the individual to the organizational level brings with it the industrial phenomena of organization charts, job descriptions, work standards, flow charts or diagrams, and all related extensions or refinements. The careful measurement of all aspects of the job and precise programming of future activities called for a careful outlining of all duties of the manager whose responsibilities would then be matched with the authority to do the job.

Taylor may not really have ignored the human element (which plagued him because he could not control it), but the notion of individual differences played a minor role in his scheme of having the engineers specify completely and precisely how the job was to be done. It comes as no surprise that Taylor aroused a great deal of controversy, both within and outside industrial circles. When Taylor set the requirements of a handler of pig iron that he be as stupid and phlegmatic as an ox and that he "be trained by a man more intelligent than himself" (1911, p. 59), one can understand why his activities were controversial, to say the least. Yet many of his concepts, refined or unchanged, survive in the present work procedures in countless industrial organizations throughout the land.

Structural Theories of Organization

Concentration on aspects that are considered by some theorists to be underlying invariant aspects of management or administration are still current today but were developed early, primarily by Henri Fayol (1949). This body of theorists has sometimes been known as departmentalization or "administrative management theory." It has been most recently pronounced by Urwick (1943). The structural theorists view the central problem as being one where there must be an identification of the tasks necessary for achieving the general purpose of the organization and of the grouping or departmentalization to take place to fulfill those functions most effectively. Questions to be approached vary from a simple breakdown into purpose or process specialization to more generalized processes or problems of coordination. Work may also be grouped, in addition to grouping by purpose or process, with respect to time, place, or clientele.

An attempt to broaden the basis of this approach somewhat (Mooney, 1947) ends with what are called "Principles of Organization." There are five of these—perpendicular coordination, horizontal coordination, leadership, delegation, and authority. Each is considered by the author to be "basic" to all organizational activity and each is, therefore, a "Universal Principle of Management."

TRANSITIONAL ORGANIZATIONAL THEORISTS

Certain writers or groups of researchers, while active at about the same time as the classical organizational theorists, can be listed separately here primarily because of the influence they have had on present-day theorists. In many ways the individuals or groups mentioned here as transitional belong in the classical set of theorists, but their basic approaches set them apart from the physiological or structural theorists, and their activities had formed the basis for much of the significant formulation of concepts for present-day organization theory.

Bureaucracy

The concept of the bureaucratic organization and its importance in a developing society was sketched originally by Weber (1946). The reader is again reminded that the term *bureaucracy* as used by Weber does not carry the negative connotations usually attached to it at the present time by individuals who view the "bureaucrat" as an inept organizational functionary. Weber conceived bureaucracy to be a particular type of organization, one that developed in a rational way to enable a society or economy to function effectively in a situation of rapid increase in requirements. Bureaucracy is a style that Weber says is characteristic of modern officialdom in that activity is governed by rules that are carried out by people with specific qualifications. These people function in a hierarchy where authority is systematically enforced and supported by official documents. The activity is managed in a specialized and modern manner by office holders who have prepared long and well for this "vocation." Office holding is a career with tenure often guaranteed for life. New members of the organization are selected by the existing members and the organization lives on.

Weber suggested that the bureaucratic type of organization has been successful because it is technically superior to that of any other type. Official business proceeds precisely, continuously, and without ambiguity because of knowledgeable people working under known rules. This is an objective conduct of operations—a system of laws, not of men. All irrational and emotional elements are eliminated.

In their description of the formal and structural nature of organizations, Weber's formulations represent the more classical theories. His development of the concept of bureaucracy and the concomitant organizational and social dynamics, however, have stimulated much present-day research, conceptualization, and model building among the behavioral students of organizations, particularly those coming from the discipline of sociology.

The Human Relations Approach

The forceful statements and programs of Taylor and others in the *scientific management* school of thought were bound to stimulate activity that would counterbalance the sometimes extreme views held by those concentrating on the physiological and mechanical factors of organizational functioning, Surprisingly, the concepts ameliorating the scientific management positions received their greatest impetus from a study based on Taylor's work where, as further scientific verification of the impact of environmental factors did not "make sense," the investigators searched for other reasons for the organizational behavior noted. The investigators found that the workers were motivated more by the social needs in the work situation than they were influenced by economic or other incentives offered by management. The social influences of the peer group and the need for identity in social relationships influenced the worker more than any controls imposed by the company.

The original study generated an entire series of research projects that uncovered more and more the important social foundations of industrial activity. They became well known as the "Hawthorne studies" (see Chapter 15). The researchers were originally headed by Elton Mayo (1945) and the studies themselves were reported on more extensively by Roethlisberger and Dickson (1939). The emerging school of thought, if it can be called that, became the rallying point for a movement that has been labeled generally as the *human relations* movement. Labels such as *participative management* have also been used to highlight further some of the social aspects that are often important in actual organizational activity.

RECENT BEHAVIORAL VIEWS

Contemporary theories of organization that have a behavioral flavor owe something to the earlier theories discussed above. Some of the ancestry of recent conceptualization may be readily apparent; in other cases the relationship may be more remote and less visible. Even elements of scientific management (though these are less extensive) can be discerned in some of the formulations of organizational theory today.

Dysfunctional Models

The influence of Max Weber is apparent in the formulations of a group of behavioral scientists, primarily sociologists, who have focused on the concept of bureaucracy in their development of descriptive organizational models. While there are some differences between them, Merton (1957), Selznick (1949), and Gouldner (1954) concentrate on the forces that are generated in bureaucratic organizations as a result of their functioning. Interest is highest among these researchers in the dysfunctional consequences of bureaucratic organizations, that is, those forces that are unintended and with a tendency to hamper functioning or drive the elements apart.

Figure 16-1 is a sketch of a simplified model of Merton's formulation. The model concentrates on the consequences of control where, primarily, the rules function as an outcome of the concern for a consistent set of functions

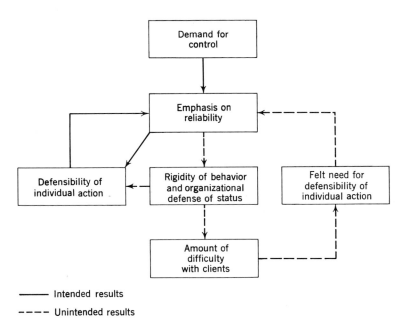

Figure 16-1. An organizational model by Merton as sketched by March, J. and Simon, H. (1958, p. 41).

and the reliability that comes with adherence to clear regulations for behavior. A similar model by Gouldner has already been used in Chapter 3 as an illustration of the organizational model.

Equilibrium Theories

A viewpoint that concentrates on the tendencies of organizations to achieve equilibrium has been developed by Barnard (1938). In many respects it is the converse of the theories that concentrate on those forces that change the organization. Barnard further concentrates on the notion of efficiency; in an efficient organization, members participate because they receive benefits or at least perceive themselves as getting certain rewards in the process. Efficiency is an individual matter relating to the satisfaction of individual motives. The effectiveness of an organization is the accomplishment of a common purpose. Both effectiveness and efficiency combine to promote cooperation. Cooperation is the most significant aspect of organizational functioning, since through it individuals are able to overcome their own biological limitations and combine to achieve ends that are not available to individuals alone.

Barnard's theoretical view of organizations was adopted by Simon (1957) and developed further in more recent work (March and Simon, 1958). In his approach, Simon places more emphasis on the cognitive aspects of functioning and stresses problem solving and rational choice. Functioning in an organization is considered to be goal oriented and, in a tendency toward equilibrium, the action in the organization is adaptive. The sequence of activities begins with the search process for alternatives, and specific or limited action programs are then developed and fixed upon in recurring paths. The critical concept in the entire process may be the fact that individuals and organizations do not optimize, that is, do not search until attaining a maximum or ideal return as the classical, rational-economic view of behavior indicated. Instead, says Simon, they *satisfice*, or strive to attain a satisfactory level. Since these concepts refer primarily to short-range problems of limited complexity, a longitudinal view of the functioning of organizations will reveal that an important aspect of functioning in organizations is the modification or change process that takes place. Problem solving remains the essential feature of the processes of innovation and change. The search for alternatives to satisfy certain requirements determines the kind of action program that will be initiated.

Need-Satisfaction Concepts

Another body of theories consists of a number stemming from or influenced by the conclusions reached in the Hawthorne studies. Several empirical studies, including those by Whyte (1955) and Zaleznik et al. (1958), conclude that social factors are much more important in job performance than are economic incentives. The central feature of the formulations is that the satisfactions gained by the workers in being part of the group are more significant than money; adherence to the norms developed in the social group could be said to take place as often as 90 percent of the time.

Other contemporary theorists who have been influenced by the Hawthorne studies are those who have given the most impetus, perhaps, to the notion of participation in organizations. Maslow's concept of *hierarchy of needs,* and of *self-actualization* as the highest of these, has already been discussed in Chapter 8. Maslow's notion that man needs to use his talents to the utmost and that industry at the present time seldom allows this has influenced much of the thinking in management circles today. McGregor developed Maslow's ideas further in his comparisons of "Theory X" and "Theory Y" (Chapter 15). The search for self-actualization, meaning in one's work, or identity of the individual in the larger grouping has stimulated other writers, both theoretical and practical in inclination, to develop similar conceptual formats. Argyris (1964) emphasizes the search by employees for meaning in their work; where this need is not met by the organizations, the employee will go to great lengths to develop it, in some instances to the detriment of the program presented by management. Herzberg (1966), too, belongs to this group when he contrasts job factors that are motivators and those that are hygienes. If the latter are lacking, the individual may be unhappy, but it takes motivators to get good work performance. Motivators are those factors that permit the feeling of accomplishment or exercise of competence in one vocational area.

Likert (1961) has developed the above concepts further and has added other empirical material to form a theory that focuses on relationships among interdependent entities in an organization. He reminds us that there are many groups overlapping in organizations and that individuals may be members of several of these groupings. The various groups may be joined by what Likert calls a *linking pin,* a term for an individual who belongs to two or more groups and can thus play a key role in communication and influence in the organization.

In an even broader approach, Schein (1965) has argued for the "complex man." He emphasizes that man is variable in his motives and, therefore, responds to different aspects of the job situation. In the light of all of the evidence, it is unwise to argue against the notion of the complexity of human behavior. It may be said, perhaps, that many of the organizational theorists mentioned here, particularly the more recent ones, also have recognized the multiplicity of variables to be considered in the assessment of individual organizational functioning but have concentrated on one accessible aspect.

A practical application of Schein's position, however, might well serve to bring this discussion of organizational theory to a conclusion. Schein says (*Ibid.,* pp. 60–61) that a concept of "complex man" has important implications for managerial strategy. He says that "the successful manager must be a good diagnostician and must value a spirit of inquiry." The good manager then must be aware of the multiplicity of motives in the men with whom he is working and must be able to recognize differences in abilities among individuals in the organization. The development of his own capacities and those of others to the fullest extent possible is indeed a challenging assignment for those who must put behavioral science knowledge to work.

Authority

It may be a safe assumption that all, or virtually all, of the variables in individual and social behavior are represented in the functioning of organizations. Factors of a general nature, such as influence processes, are even more likely to be represented. Specific types of processes within this broad general category have been of interest to students of behavior in organizations as well as to those who view broader social functioning. Within this framework there is much concern with concepts such as *control, power,* or *authority,* legitimate and otherwise.

A rationale for the existence of formal organizations is that a structuring of effort may be the most effective means of accomplishing the desired end. A study of organizations does, indeed, show that there exist various methods of exerting influence, and these techniques have often become so refined that no other entity can match them in effectiveness. This grouping is "organized" to promote reliability in effort; performance of units and individuals within the organization is specified, supervised, monitored, corrected if outside the desired range, reviewed, and altered if change is required—all to accomplish the organizational task. As most of the roles in organizational functioning vary, there is a division of labor, but all activity is interdependent with a meshing of roles being a vital ingredient.

It is apparent that to accomplish the task order, not chaos, must reign. Behavior must be specified to a high degree, and individuals or units must function according to rules. The concern for making sure that the rules are followed and that the meshing of activities takes place properly for effective action almost of necessity causes a structure to be built up. Such structuring of relationships among individuals in an organization usually ends up in pretty much the same way regardless of the nature and setting of the organization. The requirement that one person monitor the activities of others usually has as a concomitant requirement that these several others also monitor the activities of a still greater number of individuals one more step removed from the original supervisor. Thus we find the familiar organizational pyramid being built up as the result of the development of the concept of authority in the formal organization. It is because of these salient factors that, while influence and control are certainly the important aspects to be discussed in organizational functioning, specific scrutiny of the concept of authority has occupied a significant part of the attention of researchers on formal organizations.

Authority is the possession and exercise of lawful power. Leavitt (1964, p. 167) defines it as a "formal, delegable, worn-on-the-shoulders power." We are reminded that this is only one kind of power; there are others such as the kind stemming from personal traits and characteristics. Informal influences can be just as powerful as those which stem from a power delegated through legal or formal channels.

We may differentiate between the concepts in terms of their breadth or generality; influence is a broad concept embracing power, control, and authority while the most restricted of these is authority. Influence is any transaction with behavioral results. An intended influence result is control while power is a potential for influence that is backed by a force for coercion. Authority is legitimate power, that power accepted by society.

Katz and Kahn (1966, p. 220) illustrate the concepts by pointing to the example of a traffic policeman raising his hand to stop a motorist. The policeman is exercising his authority and, if the motorist heeds the signal, the officer is also exercising influence and control (if the motorist speeds up, this is also influence, but of the negative kind). A gangster brandishing a gun could also exercise influence and control the same motorist (if the driver responded to the cue). The criminal would be acting, however, without authority and the power exercised by him we call illegal or unauthorized.

A reminder is in order here that the question of authority may be quite different depending on the placement of the individual within the organization. When authority is seen by the manager or user of it, there is a tendency to view it as an instrument of control or coordination. When viewed by those who are the object of the management process, authority is seen as a means of reward or punishment (Leavitt, 1964, p. 167). This emphasizes that the psychological aspects in placement can be more important than the physical or structural factors themselves.

An even further recognition of the importance of considering authority in the light of those below who are affected by it must be made in the light of strong statements to the effect that one cannot have authority at all unless there is acceptance of it by those to whom the power or influence attempts are directed. This is the basis for the development of the "acceptance theory" of authority (Simon, 1957). Without a recognition of authority in a target group, there is no power to control, regardless of the formal or philosophical bases on which the directives are promulgated. This may be a moot point in practice, however, as in most instances the person in authority in a formal organization is perceived by others as being in a leadership position and is accepted by them as such. If not, though, tension can occur.

Conflict in Organizations

Conflict is an aspect of organizational functioning that frequently is apparent to even the casual observer and of significant interest to the student of behavioral science. One initial difficulty, however, is that the term conflict, when it is scrutinized carefully, may mean many things to many people. Conflict may be regarded as the disagreement or hostility between individuals or groups in the organization, or it may be viewed as the perception of disagreement in the individual or an inability to resolve problems arising on this basis. It could represent the result of competing demands on an individual or a group as a result of formal structuring or job definition. Rivalry and competition also can be meant.

Conflict, for March and Simon (1958, p. 112), means "a breakdown in the standard mechanisms of decision-making so that an individual or group experiences difficulty in selecting an action alternative." This definition is consistent with their concentration on problem solving as a salient feature of organizational functioning. A more conventional definition of conflict (Thompson, 1962, p. 452) views it as "that behavior by organization members which is expended in opposition to other members."

It is well to note here that these definitions do not necessarily extend to the inclusion of the physcial aggression seen in some social conflict, though they could. At the same time, these views of conflict do include intergroup competition when such activity results in an outcome that puts others at a disadvantage.

SOURCES OF CONFLICT

Since the wellsprings of conflict in an organization are many, identification of these sources can take place in varied ways. Description here, as in many other instances, depends on the level of analysis or the simple choice of vantage point from which to view events.

Some researchers prefer to focus on a unitary pattern. Gouldner and Gouldner (1963), for instance, pinpoint the greatest source of tension in organizations as being the existence of varying degrees of functional autonomy, the extent to which a segment of the whole organization is able to maintain its independence of other units in the satisfaction of its needs. Groups usually seek to maintain or enlarge their own functional autonomy; this is seen most clearly in the frequent "jockeying" for position in an organization. Workers may resent close supervision while managers complain about what they consider the increasing efforts of unions to take over their managerial perogatives. Any efforts to enhance autonomy, however, can defeat attempts toward control or coordination in an organization and can make the various moves toward equilibrium more difficult to accomplish.

A simple classification might focus on the strains arising from inputs from the outside and those resulting from internal strain or imbalance. Increasing requirements of technology, or greater control of outside administrative agencies, represent the greatest source of external pressures, although general social values may affect the organization as well.

Two kinds of internal strains are possible in an organization: (1) the competition between different functional subsystems, or horizontal strain and (2) vertical strain, the conflict between various levels in the hierarchy for power, privilege, or reward (Katz and Kahn, 1966, p. 446). Horizontal strain comes about as different departments or subgroups in an organization have different functions or concepts of directions for activity. An engineering or production facility may, for instance, have different notions about a prospective contract with a customer than does the legal department of the corporation. Furthermore, a differential in the rate of growth of different units or differences in the extent to which there may be presures for service on a department provides further occasions for stress. Competition between departments of a corporation for scarce resources is mirrored on the campus in the competition among deans of the university for increased allottments for their colleges.

Vertical strain, or hierarchical conflict, is that which separates people in various levels of the occupational ladders in organizations. Workers on the assembly line undoubtedly have sets of attitudes and values that differ considerably from those held by individuals occupying the executive suite. Katz and Kahn indicate that these vertical strains are especially important in a democratic society which emphasizes equality of opportunity.

A classification of conflict on another basis would identify three main classes of conflict in the organization: individual conflict, organizational conflict, and interorganizational conflict. Organizational conflict is of greatest interest but since some of it comes from individual problems, individual conflict cannot be ignored. The phenomena in interorganizational conflict are much the same as those arising within an organization, especially the conflict between groups.

Pursuing this line of analysis, organizational conflict may be of two types —conflict between individuals within the organizations and conflicts between groups. Conflict between individuals is likely to increase where, because of lowered environmental inputs through economic changes and the like, there is a decrease in achievement by individuals. In good times, even poor achievers in a company can "make out." When times are more difficult, there is increased hostility in the company. Intraindividual conflict is more likely to occur when uncertainty exists. Organizational policies such as frequent transfer or reduction in communication can increase the amount of uncertainty in individuals.

Intergroup conflict can be viewed in terms of differences in goals or perceptions or a need for participation (March and Simon, 1958). The greater the mutual dependence or the greater the interdependence of activity, the greater is the felt need for joint decision making. Where scheduling or allocation of scarce resources requires interdependent action, there is a pressure toward participation in relevant decisions. Unilateral actions will be met with resistance and conflict. Diverse goals of individuals and groups can be overcome by mechanics of the reward structure if, for instance, employees are remunerated to the extent that they pursue the goals of the organization. If the goals are unclear or the monetary or other rewards do not prevent individual differences in goals leading to a discrepancy between organizational and individual goals, conflict will exist. March and Simon (1958) hypothesize greater conflict in research and development organizations than in those involving, say, production where performance criteria are somewhat more clear. Further conflict can be engendered within organizations by a range of disparate perceptions or simply a lack of information because of a large number of different sources of information.

PATTERNS AND RESULTS

Reactions to conflict and its impact on organizational functioning are central issues in a discussion of conflict. Patterns of behavior characteristic of individual and group responses in the tension of conflict should be identified. Important, too, are the outcomes of the conflict situation.

In an analysis that focuses on tactics or techniques used, March and Simon (1958, p. 129) outline four major reactions to conflict in an organization: (1) problem solving; (2) persuasion; (3) bargaining; and (4) "politics." In problem solving a solution is identified that satisfies the criteria that are shared by members, while in persuasion, some aspects of goals or procedures are not shared by all and some members must be "talked into" a course of action. In bargaining, agreement is attempted without persuasion but with "gamesmanship." "Politics" is similar to bargaining except that the situation is enlarged to bring in other influential entities or allies.

A well-known study of conflict among groups (Sherif et al., 1961) provides some complementary information with respect to behavior of members of rival groups. Within each competing group, there is a tendency toward more cohesiveness, structure, demands for loyalty, and tolerance of authoritarian directives. The climate changes from an informal to a task-oriented one. Relationships between the competing groups also show increasingly striking characteristics. Each group perceives the other in an unfavorable light ("the enemy") while communication and interaction with them show a decided decrease. If interaction is forced on them, the unfavorable stereotypes are seldom changed, they are merely reinforced. Hostility between the groups continues. (These behavioral results may be quite general and may not arise in one or two types of associations. They may occur in athletic competition, labor management discord, in competition among functional departments in an industrial organization, or they may even take place at the level of relationships between nations.)

When the competition is over and, as in many competitions, there are winners and losers, the behavioral patterns emerging may also be of significance. Winning groups remain cohesive, release tension, and tend to become complacent. The positive perceptions of their own ability are enhanced as a result of the outcome. In a very friendly and happy state there is concern for the wishes and needs of members of the group; no longer is there a complete preoccupation with task requirements. Losers, if the outcome was somewhat ambiguous, have a tendency to deny the unpleasantness of the situation. There is more tension and more splintering of the group as cooperation decreases among the members. If there is a recognition of reality over time and the group accepts its loss, eventually there may be a more effective reorganization as the result of a reevaluation.

Performance in an organization in conflict will probably suffer. Where the outcome is viewed to be in terms of winners and losers, the anxiety generated in teams can be debilitating. Even individuals on a winning team may perceive that they are contributing less than they should to the outcome and be very tense in the process. What is called for, perhaps, is moderate anxiety that will motivate yet not debilitate. This is particularly so for individual effort; it is less likely that this is true for group effort.

Some types of conflict, however, may be beneficial under certain conditions. Disagreements that are aired may provide a broader range of alternatives for the group in a decision-making situation. It may result in better adaptation to changing circumstances.

Cooperative effort has generally been found to be superior to competitive activity. Deutsch (1949) early found more productivity in noncompetitive groups. Jones and Vroom (1964) have confirmed these results and suggest that the superiority in cooperative groups is a result of an effective division of labor.

REDUCTION OF CONFLICT

Conflict, it is generally agreed, often has results that impair the efficiency of an organization. Even the form that is represented by competition can have, as we have just seen, some negative impact on organizational functioning. If this is true, the reduction of conflict would seem to be one of the more pressing tasks of the administrator or manager as well as being a prime target for the behavioral researcher. Unfortunately, there is less empirical information in this area than might be desired, although there are some conceptual formulations that can be offered as guidelines.

It might be noted at this point that it is more accurate to speak of reduction or alleviation of conflict. Since conflict, like taxes, is likely to be with us for a long time, it is not realistic to think of complete elimination of strife or competition. From this standpoint, rather than speaking of prevention, we mean only certain measures that can be taken that precede, in time, the conditions wherein conflict may take place or those steps that can be taken to reduce it in extent or intensity once it has begun.

In an approach that focuses on a single and critical behavioral factor, functional autonomy, Gouldner and Gouldner (1963, pp. 411–413) offer some strategies for coping with multiple tensions arising from that factor. Functional autonomy of individuals can be reduced by selectively seeking and retaining those who are less autonomous so that there is more adherence to organizational requirements. Other strategies call for cutting off individuals from competing systems or engulfing the competitors. The corporation that takes an overwhelming interest in the private lives of its members usually does so as a means of weakening other demands on the employee. Frequent transfers to distant locations without concern for family ties and school schedules is a clear indication to all that the corporation comes first with loyalty to others a distant second. These strategies can be utilized in combination, of course, to make it easier to reduce functional autonomy among individuals. These moves also can produce the bland type of individual who has been so often labeled "the organization man."

A more positive set of guidelines for the manager who would like to reduce intergroup conflict (Schein, 1965, p. 85) emphasizes the beneficial effects of participation in group activity.

Win-lose situations should be avoided and the focus placed on the contribution of groups and individuals to the effectiveness of the total organization. Interaction, communication, and the stimulation of mutual understanding should be fostered. The main thrust of these guidelines may be the emphasis on organizational rewards based on integrated effort.

It would not be completely accurate to say that there is no room for competition. There may be times when competition among groups may be desirable in attaining a higher level of performance, particularly in industrial organizations, on short-range tasks. But it must be remembered that competition is not the crucial factor in good performance; the use of competition in ways that will be effective is the critical aspect. This is easier said than done; all too often it arouses too much anxiety in individuals and puts some at a disadvantage with respect to others. The total result is less than desirable.

Communication in Organizations

Without communication there is no meaningful activity in and, therefore, no influence on behavior in organizations. On this basis it is easy to conclude, as some organization theorists do, that "communications are central phenomena in organizations" (Guetzkow, 1965, p. 534). There is little disagreement that organizations function through communications between members; there are no inputs or outputs when there is no transmision of information. Influence, control, and cohesiveness become abstract concepts without the activating and integrating force provided by communication. Through it members are linked together in the activity of the group toward realization of group goals.

SPATIAL FEATURES

Factors such as size of the organization, distance between members, and placement in the structure are important contributors to the nature and extent of communication. It might be intuitively stated, for instance, that the greater the spread of the organizational structure, the lower the density of the communication channels. With a larger number of people involved, the possibility decreases that any two of these individuals will be in contact. Miller (1951, p. 262) summarizes this by the proposition that "the likelihood of messages passing from one person to another is inversely proportional to the distance between them." This hypothesis has been tested by researchers in many kinds of organizational settings with a great deal of regularity in results. Caplow found that the spread of rumors in the armed forces in World War II decreased with the distance from the onset of the rumor (Chapter 14), while Zipf (1946) determined that long-distance telephone calls between cities decreased in frequency with an increase in distance. In an industrial organization, Gullahorn (1952, p. 134) noted that the most important factor determining interaction rates between individuals was the distance between them.

COMMUNICATION NETWORKS

It has become clear from material in the previous chapter that purely spatial features such as distance are not, however, the final or critical determinants of communication. Other variables may play a more significant role in the process. The nature of the network may be more influential than the mere matter of distance between members of the network. A communication network based on functional variables such as specialization or on behavioral bases, formal or informal, do much more to establish the patterns and effectiveness of the communication process than does the direct feature of distance.

Nets also function along lines of prestige. As noted above, the positions of individuals in a hierarchy (their status) may have been formally determined within the official structure of the organization or they may have positions established more by external demographic or personal characteristics such as age or sex. This leads to the establishment of a hierarchy based on desirability, that is, prestige or esteem. The perception of a member's position and prestige determines the nature and extent of the interactions to a high degree and, therefore, the communication.

Authority, the power that comes from the "legally" established network of an organization, cannot be neglected. The influence of authority patterns on communication is, as might be expected, quite high. It is a mistake, however, for a superior to believe that communication exists only within those channels structured and prescribed by formal authority. Those messages originating and traveling outside the officially recognized channels may be and often are more influential in organizational behavior than those within official channels. What is more, they may be more accurate at the end of the chain as well. The "grape-vine" is well established in organizations, and the manager is well advised to stop resisting its activity or, even better, to put it to work.

While much of the information from studies of communication nets has come from analyses of laboratory groups, these experimental nets do show some of the same patterns found in practical situations; we have little difficulty recognizing the centralized committee in the "star" arrangement and the office hierarchy of the "chain" with its head and four subordinates at two levels.

Most experiments also have dealt with the problem-solving activity of the nets where a simple problem is arranged that must be solved by individuals exchanging information about that part with which they are familiar. With little imagination, the solution of this type of task resembles the more complex problems that groups of businessmen face when making a decision about production or the marketing mix.

DIRECTION OF COMMUNICATION

Communication in an organization may be horizontal, that is, side-to-side at the same level, or it may be vertical, to lower or higher levels in the hierarchy. Surrounding factors may determine the nature and extent of communication, but use of particular channels may have its social and structural consequences.

Communication upward may be part of a pattern exhibited by those who are upwardly mobile or who have such aspirations. The highly mobile subordinates are more likely to communicate with superiors than peers and to be more relevant or accurate in their communications (Cohen, 1958). Read (1962) confirmed this but found, in addition, that information, even from the mobile, is apt to be filtered in a way that will put the communicator in the best possible light. In general, then, the mobile members of the organization talk to superiors while the nonmobiles talk to each other. There is also the implication in this that initiated communication upward can bring prestige while contacts downward or horizontally do not, especially when it is to ask a favor or aid. Blau (1954) noted, in a similar view, that competent agents in a government agency had high interaction rates, not because they initiated contacts but because they received them.

Blau and Scott (1962) have indicated that individuals in an organization communicate more with each other as the pressures of work increase. Similar impact of environmental changes on communication patterns may be found in various circumstances. One of the most pertinent at this time is linked to technological requirements. Simpson (1959) indicates that mechanization reduces the need for communication between foremen and workers so that the latter keep to themselves. The relationships between foremen and their superiors are not governed by the automated processes, however, and their need for communication is not reduced. Since this communication is often thought to be one-way in the traditional industrial organization, it is valuable for the would-be manager to review the advantages of two-way communication (Chapter 15) at this point.

Decision Making in Organizations

While many of the earier concepts concerning individual decision making (Chapter 7) are applicable here, the general decision making that takes place in organizations is more complex, of course, and is affected by other variables. Not only are there more individuals involved, but the total picture of what takes place cannot be gained by simply totaling up the individual processes involved. Here, too, is an example of the whole being more than the sum of its parts. A significant part of the problem is the relating of findings in the individual approach to the group studies and vice versa when the concepts and measures are seldom similar or comparable.

METHODS OF ANALYSIS

Many analyses of the decision processes in organizations have used categories for description that have been found useful in describing individual activity. Bakke (1959, pp. 62–66) identifies 11 steps in the process of decision making in an organization (Table 16-2). These range from the initial awareness of the problem to an important aspect well beyond the solution stage, that of evaluation of the effectiveness of the solution. All too often, decision makers relax after the solution presents itself when there is little evidence as to whether the energy is worth expending then and in the future. Feedback is essential. The list represents the result of an analysis to set down categories of study and serves as a point of departure for more informative behavioral studies.

Cyert and March (1963, p. 126) have approached decision making in organizations by developing a schematic outline which they believe to be valuable

Table 16-2. Eleven Steps in the Process of Decision Making in Organizations (From Bakke, 1959)

1. Awareness of the problem
2. Exploration to get relevant information on all aspects of the problem
3. Making judgments in this exploration or structuring
4. Simplifying the problem
5. "Search and cue" to determine alternatives
6. The evaluation of alternatives
7. The decision
8. Mobilizing resources for the solution
9. Response, or the acting to carry out the objectives
10. Judgment of the solution
11. "Closure," the final evaluation to determine if the problem has been solved

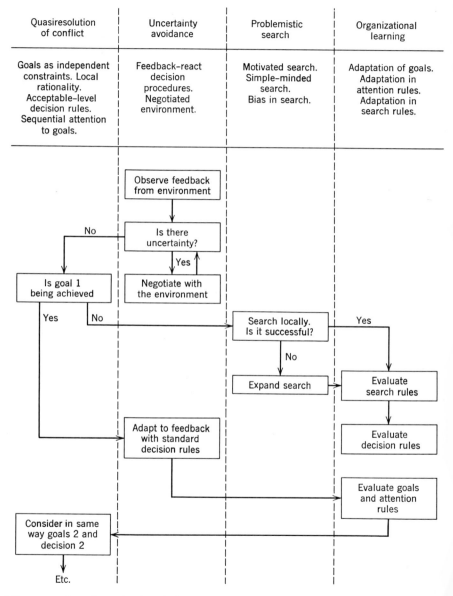

Quasiresolution of conflict	Uncertainty avoidance	Problemistic search	Organizational learning
Goals as independent constraints. Local rationality. Acceptable-level decision rules. Sequential attention to goals.	Feedback-react decision procedures. Negotiated environment.	Motivated search. Simple-minded search. Bias in search.	Adaptation of goals. Adaptation in attention rules. Adaptation in search rules.

Figure 16-2. Organizational decision process in abstract form (Cyert, R. and March, J., 1963, p. 126).

in describing the general aspects of the process (Figure 16-2). It is a more dynamic model which depicts some of the modifications that may be made as the result of varying the inputs of the system. Certainly business executives and other administrators must make decisions based on changing conditions or departures from estimates based on previous information. Dynamic processes may well be better framed in a branching diagram as Cyert and March have delineated. The various "choice points" in the ongoing process are identified. The department proceeds to gather information on objectives and goal and determines if more information is needed. If not, the goal-directed activity proceeds. If feedback from this activity indicates that the goal is not being reached, a search is made to determine the problem. When found, the problem is subjected to tests, and when better solutions are discovered, these are incorporated under a set of rules to follow to save effort in the future. The process continues in the meantime with continuing evaluation of the movement toward the goal.

Purely mathematical models of decision making in organizations imply rationality in the process, namely, that all alternatives are known and that the one that provides a maximum will be chosen. The maximization would be in terms such as "lowest cost" or "highest pay-out." Unfortunately, there are limits to rationality; all the possible alternatives are impossible to assemble for a selection to be made among them, since the number of alternatives is so great as to be unmanageable, either for an individual or for an organization.

Simon (1957) is primarily responsible for providing the concept that individuals and organizations *satisfice* rather than maximize; that is, they choose less than maximum alternatives that are the best they think they can get with the information they have available or wish to use. Those choices may not seem "rational" to others although it would be better to state instead that the actual determinants of the decision process may not have been known to the outside observer or appreciated by him.

CONTRIBUTING FACTORS

A study of other variables in the decision-making process uncovers many other influential factors. Individuals ordinarily operate under constraints imposed by the social structure of the organization. The rules (1) set limits to choice because of a need to coordinate activities, (2) determine some of the patterns of authority and communication, and (3) otherwise specify the roles of each person in the organization. When a subordinate makes a decision, he often does so on the basis of the decisions already made by superiors and, by doing so, he accepts the authority of those superiors. Since they are the originators or controllers of rewards, their opinions and activities play an important role in the actual decisions of the subordinates.

Other bases for decisions may be in biases which are built up as the result of experience or other factors. Cyert and March (1963) found, in an experiment, that graduate students playing the roles of sales and cost estimators made predictions that were larger in one direction than another. Salesmen tended to underestimate sales and cost men overestimated costs. Both were undoubtedly concerned lest the opposite result would reflect on their ability and performance.

In an experiment, Riecken (1958) found that generally the individual in the group who is most influential is the one who does the most talking. He gave the problem solution to one man in the group, unknown to the others. Where this man was the most talkative, the group accepted the solution two-thirds of the time. Where the individual with the solution was one of the least talkative, the group rejected the solution two-thirds of the time. Riecken decided that perhaps the groups confounded quantity with quality.

The social positions of the participants of the group may make a significant difference. In an experiment using Air Force personnel, Torrance (1955) noted that poor suggestions of higher status pilots were accepted more often than were the good suggestions of lower status gunners.

Group decision making also seems to involve riskier choices. Wallach, Kogan, and Bem (1962) found that where groups considered hypothetical situations in which they could make risky or conservative decisions, the tendency was toward the risky ones, especially where the groups were unanimous, rather than toward the more conservative choices they tended to make on an individual basis.

REITERATION

If one had to put the differentiating features of the decision-making process in organizations in a nutshell, the outcome might be something like the following description: choices among alternatives in organizations are made under constraints imposed by social processes as well as by the structural aspects of the situation. Limitations of size, biology, and the social *milieu* affect the decisions being made by the group or by individuals acting through and/or in the name of the group.

The extent of the problems generated on this basis would be overwhelming and intolerable for individual or group decision makers were it not for the fact that the same social bases provide patterns for better handling of those problems. The usual and, eventually, routine tasks become "programmed"; that is, a standardized response is developed to them. The nonroutine problems, then, command the time and attention of the decision makers in organizations.

Innovation and Change in Organizations

The significance of change, both on the broad environmental or cultural level and in the smaller aggregates, has already been pointed out in several places in preceding chapters. This significance may be so salient that it is well at this point to reemphasize earlier statements about the importance of change in society as a whole and in organizations in particular. A few writers have even regarded the change process as the most significant aspect of the job of a manager in that they have focused on the designation of "the manager as a change-agent" as a central concept in their formulation. It is well to remember, then, that in any ubiquitous process such as this there are forces taking place at the global and general level as well as within less extensive aggregates or elements thereof. The interdependence of these factors is, furthermore, a critical capstone for research and conceptual efforts.

The dynamics of change have already been discussed extensively in Chapter 12. Here we might make only a few additional comments pertinent to the organization and its functioning. It has been noted earlier, for instance, that technology has been the major contributor to change on the global level. Its effect on the organization has also been significant. The impact of automation has usually meant a realignment of work, structure, and norms in industrial plants (Faunce, 1958). Similar changes in organizational patterns have occurred at managerial levels. Mann and Williams (1960) noted that, in a change to electronic data processing, some formerly autonomous departments became more highly integrated into a centralized system; in the process, decision making and control moved to fewer and higher positions. The impact on other individual and interpersonal dynamics was even greater. For some persons the job enlargement was a period of growth, while for others disillusionment and failure ensued. Most important was the opportunity for management to get a better understanding of the human needs and resources of their personnel. Tolerance was an important byproduct of the policy and procedural changes. Environmental changes may represent greater or lesser demand from products or raw materials as well as changes in the structure or nature of the processes by which these materials are introduced into the economy. Changes from the supersystem are those stemming from agencies of control which may promulgate new laws or make administrative decisions that affect the functioning of the organization. Still another type of input from the environment is recognized as representing motivations and values of individuals in an organization. These are very broad and subtle influences on individual attitudes and values that may affect the perceptions and expectations of individuals in an organization. These usually go unnoticed until they reach some critical point. This may be exemplified in the increase in the demands for greater democratic participation in decision making on the part of individuals on all levels in organizations and in society.

Of the two main bases for change in organizations, external inputs and internal strains, the most significant of the two may be changed inputs from the outside. At the same time, organizations are changed by internal events. In a view that emphasizes the cognitive aspects of innovation and change, March and Simon (1958) focus on the problem-solving processes and develop a discussion of planning and control processes in innovation, the initiation of change. As a result, the model developed is one of a planning and action program through rational choice, one that is initiated to satisfy certain criteria. These criteria or requirements may be subject to change over a period of time.

Theoretical approaches to a research activity on organizations have sometimes glossed over the critical nature of the interdependence of individual and group factors in the change process as well as in other aspects of organizational functioning. Some have concentrated on individual and performance changes taking place as a result of specific inputs in a training situation; fewer have concentrated on the broader organizational changes, and still fewer have been able to incorporate the concept of interdependence in their activity.

All too often, specific individuals may be removed from the work situation and put through a training program. An evaluation may indicate success in changing undesirable behavior, but a return to the organization hierarchy places this individual back into the same system of strains and pressures which helped to contribute to his original outlook. A worker who finds that his boss has not changed at all while he was gone soon finds himself in the "same old rut" and even additional strains are imposed on him by the situation.

The foregoing statement of caution does not minimize the importance of change in individuals in an organization. Individuals are, ultimately, the organization and, furthermore, change processes may be attempted much more easily with single individuals. Even on an individual basis, however, one must be careful to recognize just exactly what is called for in the way of change. Are we interested in changing work performance, attitudes, and values, or what?

There are many ways of accomplishing or attempting changes on an individual basis in organizations. Since change involves the more fundamental process of learning, concepts developed earlier in Chapter 6 might be reviewed. Mere orientation training or the provision of traditional information may be sufficient to accomplish certain goals, while a concentration on skills training may be the more specific modification that is called for in certain situations. At the same time, certain changes may be brought about through the use of individual counseling or group therapy (Chapter 8). A technique like Sensitivity Training (Chapter 15) increasingly has become the focus of attention for industrial organizations in their attempts to alter individual behavior patterns while making certain that interactional factors are represented as well.

The now classic study of Coch and French (1948) on the effects of participation by employees in overcoming resistance to change points up the usefulness of this concept. The employees of the pajama factory who participated in determining the procedures and tasks called for in a product changeover not only adapted faster to the changes but also performed at a superior level. It is likely that participation is a factor that is basic to all activity and, when satisfied, is productive of good performance.

Probably the most important basis for real change in individuals and organizations lies in the changing of attitudes. It is likely that no real changes occur without an alteration of attitudes. In this connection some general findings from behavioral science research may provide some guidelines for promoting attitude change. A need to change must be aroused internally without arousing anxiety in the process. Group support ought to be present, and the individual should express his commitment to the new set of attitudinal choices. It is well to note individual differences in timing and extent of changes and "don't be surprised if—after trying all these ideas—attitudes still don't change (much)" (Costello and Zalkind, 1963, pp. 296–297).

Effectiveness of Functioning

No discussion of organizational functioning can be complete without devoting some attention to the question of its functioning. The primary question remains that of whether the organization is doing its job well. Unfortunately, the answer is not easy to obtain, although some cynics may respond in the affirmative simply if the organization continues in existence. In this view it would no longer function if it were not effective. Somewhat more sophisticated responses in the past have discussed questions such as "maximization of profit" or "maintenance of morale" in an industrial organization, or "providing a good service to the patient" if the organization happened to be a hospital. Determining the effectiveness of a college or university may have focused on one quantitative aspect such as number of degrees or scores on tests of achievement of its graduating seniors. One difficulty with this is that universities do more than simply teach; this reflects the fundamental fact that organizations have more than one goal and these goals may often conflict with each other.

A Measure of Viability

One attempt to resolve the complexities inherent in using multiple criteria of effectiveness is to frame a measure of functioning in terms that are more comprehensive than usual. In this connection we may draw on the work of several organizational theorists, notably Bennis (1962) and Schein (1965), to come up with a measure that focuses on adaptation to a changing environment. In this view a "healthy" organization will show characteristics such as adaptability, insightful identity, reality-testing, and coordination. Adaptability involves the ability to meet the changing demands of the environment. Reality-testing is the preliminary search stage of finding out what the real demands of the environment are and how they affect the organization. Insight by individuals and their recognition of the common demands on them and their organization involve not only perception and understanding of goals but a sharing of these by all concerned. The fourth characteristic, coordination, is the bringing together of all elements of the system in a manner that assures cohesive activity. It is the condition suggested by Argyris (1964) as "integration."

The ultimate test of the effectiveness of an organization lies in the dynamic process of adaptation to changes in the environment. Schein (1965, p. 99) has suggested the fundamental process to be exemplified by a six-stage cycle which is identified as an *adaptive-coping cycle*. The process begins with a sensing of the change and importation of information about it into relevant parts of the organization (Stages 1 and 2). Production changes are then made according to this information with a reduction of undesired concomitant changes (Stages 3 and 4). Development of new products and feedback on the success of the change complete the process (Stages 5 and 6). The cycle may be illustrated by describing the changes in a company manufacturing electronic equipment. At Stage 1 the company learns that the space program will increase the demand for its equipment. At Stage 2 this information is imported into the organization and considered seriously by those who are in a position to take some action. After management is convinced, the production processes are changed to produce more of the equipment (Stage 3); these changes must be introduced without producing other undesirable changes and must be stabilized (Stage 4). Increased marketing of products comes at Stage 5, while the final stage involves the continuing process of "checking-up" to see whether the changes in all areas have been successfully met.

Why Organizations ?

Despite the many drawbacks of the organizational structure, there are many reasons why this type of grouping continues in existence. In sketching the advantages of the organizational structure, we could almost return to the pioneering writings of Max Weber on bureaucracy by way of explanation. The opportunity to provide for a unified and coherent effort in functioning in many different areas is the outstanding reason for the effectiveness of this social form. The harnessing of directed effort toward a desired end probably is not attainable on this scale through the use of any other approach. The organizational form continues despite the disadvantages of cutting short the variability and creativity that lead to the growth and vitality of a social grouping. While continued organizational functioning is, in addition, all too often continued at significant cost to the psychological functioning of the individual member of the organization, there is little reason why an organization cannot recognize these limitations and attempt to develop a healthier and more effective existence.

To reiterate many of the points mentioned here and elsewhere, it seems clear that the effective organization will have to develop and maintain an ideology that incorporates fundamental notions of individual worth and well-being. This will be furthered by genuine commitment to group goals with activities supported by norms that have been established through participation, not dictation. Striving toward organizational goals will take place under leaders and co-workers who have been properly selected and trained to provide an atmosphere free from threat. Reality-testing, communication, and the ability to be flexible and creative will enhance the opportunity for the organization to adapt to the changing world.

Summary

The study of larger, more structured groupings has attracted the attention of social philosophers for centuries but only recently has a systematic approach to the field been started. No concise bundle of concepts yet exists, however, that may be called a theory; even definitions are diverse. A consensus has been reached that characterizes organizations as a body of individuals rationally structured in a hierarchy and pursuing a specific task.

Organizations may be classified on the basis of function, type of authority, or beneficiary of their activity.

Early theories of organizations focused on structural or mechanical views of activity. Scientific management dealt with development of a precise programming of activity. Other theorists looked for "universals" or principles of manage-ment. Somewhat more concerned with social dynamics were the formulations of Weber within the framework of the concept of bureaucracy. The human relations school arose at least partly to counteract the impersonality of scientific management.

More recent models of organizations have emphasized behavioral views. Focus may be on forces helping to maintain the organization in equilibrium or on those tending to produce dysfunctional results. Organizations viewed as need-satisfying entities have developed even more recently, some including concomitant structural-behavioral factors.

Authority has been a central feature of formal organizational views. The concept refers to the possession and exercise of lawful power. Some researchers focus on the legal basis of authority while another view concentrates on the acceptance of it by those involved.

Conflict in organizations is that behavior expended by some members in opposition to others; it represents a breakdown in choice of action alternatives. Such strains may arise within or outside of the organization. Conflict within the organization may appear as the result of competing groups at the same level or between different levels of the hierarchy. A focus on the functional aspects can bring about identification and classification of conflicts on still other bases.

Conflict may be handled in the organization through a persuasive or prob-lem-solving approach, or it may be met with political or bargaining techniques. Other behavioral concomitants of conflict may include hostility toward competing groups, tension, demands for cohesiveness, and tolerance of authoritarian direc-tives. As performance may suffer from the tension of conflict, its reduction is generally to be desired. While attempts toward removal of supports for individual autonomy may do this, a superior approach lies in the rewarding of integrated effort toward organizational goals.

Communication is of prime interest in organizations. Distance between communicators decreases the number of communications. Networks develop on the basis of prestige or other aspects of social desirability in addition to those formally established by authority. Communication increases with mo-bility of individuals in the organization as well as with an increase in work requirements.

Decision making in large groups may have some of the elements found in individual decision making, but it is more complex. Systematic models featur-ing searches for solutions may be established to attempt to put rationality in the process; the problems are so complex, however, that "satisficing" is substi-tuted for the rational maximizing attempts. Concomitant constraints may be identified in the personal and learned characteristics of individual decision makers acting alone or in concert with others. Verbal skills or social position may influence others.

Innovation and change have an impact on organizations as they have on more general structures or activities. Automation in a factory may alter organizational and individual behavioral patterns as well, although major changes are the exception rather than the rule. When major changes do take place, they are more often forced by external events. Specific efforts at change in individuals through training programs are often thwarted as the result of the resistance to change in most aspects of the host environment.

Change can take place, however, if the process is scrutinized carefully, the goals specified, and the basic concepts of learning and therapy recognized. Change of attitudes may be the single most important psychological variable to focus on in the process.

Determination of effectiveness of an organization may be a critical point but one that is often difficult to determine, since there may be various goals possible. A measure of viability of an organization may well rest on its ability to adapt to inputs in a realistic and coordinated way that, almost of necessity, includes a concern for members' needs.

Despite the pressures toward distintegration or elimination, the organization persists as a form for action because it is necessary. What is also needed is a concomitant concern for the human building blocks who help make it what it is.

Bibliography

Argyris, C. (1964). *Integrating the individual and the organization.* New York: Wiley.

Bakke, E. (1959). Concept of the social organization. In Haire, M. (ed.). *Modern organization theory.* New York: Wiley.

Barnard, C., (1938). *The functions of the executive.* Cambridge, Mass.: Harvard University Press.

Bennis, W. (1962). Toward a "truly" scientific management: the concept of organizational health. *General Systems Yearbook,* **7**, 269–282.

Berelson, B. and Steiner, G. (1964). *Human behavior.* New York: Harcourt, Brace and World.

Blau, P. (1954). Patterns of interaction among a group of officials in a government agency. *Human Relations,* **7**,(3), 337–348.

Blau, P. and Scott, W. (1962). *Formal organizations.* San Francisco: Chandler.

Coch, L. and French, J. (1948). Overcoming resistance to change. *Human Relations,* 1, 512–534.

Cohen, A. (1958). Upward communication in experimentally created hierarchies. *Human Relations,* 11, 41–53.

Costello, T. and Zalkind, S. (1963). *Psychology in administration.* Englewood Cliffs, N.J.: Prentice-Hall.

Cyert, R. and March, J. (1963). *A behavioral theory of the firm.* Englewood Cliffs, N.J.: Prentice-Hall.

Deutsch, M. (1949). An experimental study of the effects of cooperation and competition upon group processes. *Human Relations,* 2, 199–231.

Etzioni, A. (1961). *A comparative analysis of complex organizations.* Glencoe, Ill: Free Press.

Faunce, W. (1958). Automation in the automobile industry: some consequences for in-plant social structure. *American Sociological Review,* 23, 401–407.

Fayol, H. (1949). *General and industrial mangement* (Storrs, C., trans.). London: Pitman.

Gouldner, A. (1954). *Paterns of industrial bureaucracy.* Glencoe, Ill.: Free Press.

Gouldner, A. and Gouldner, H. (1963). *Modern sociology.* New York: Harcourt, Brace and World.

Guetzkow, H. (1965). Communications in organizations. In March, J. (ed.). *Handbook of organizations.* Chicago: Rand McNally, 534–573.

Gullahorn, J. (1952). Distance and friendship as factors in the gross interaction matrix. *Sociometry,* 15, 123–134.

Herzberg, F. (1966). *Work and the nature of man.* Cleveland: World.

Jones, S. and Vroom, V. (1964). Division of labor and performance under cooperative and competitive conditions. *Journal of Abnormal and Social Psychology,* 68, 313–320.

Katz, D. and Kahn, R. (1966). *The social psychology of organizations.* New York: Wiley.

Leavitt, H. (1964). *Managerial psychology.* Chicago: University of Chicago Press.

Likert, R. (1961). *New patterns of management.* New York: McGraw-Hill.

Mann, F. and Williams, L. (1960). Observations on the dynamics of a change to electronic data-processing equipment. *Adminitrative Science Quarterly,* 5, 217–256.

March, J. and Simon, H. (1958). *Organizations.* New York: Wiley.

Mayo, E. (1945). *Social problems of an industrial civilization.* Cambridge, Mass.: Harvard University Press.

Merton, R. (1957). *Social theory and social structure* (rev. ed.). New York: Free Press.

Miller, G. (1951). *Language and communication.* New York: McGraw-Hill.

Mooney, J. (1947). *The principles of organization* (rev. ed.). New York: Harper.

Pondy, L. (1966). A systems theory of organizational conflict. *Academy of Management Journal,* 9(3), 246–256.

Read, W. (1962). Upward communication in industrial hierarchies. *Human Relations,* 15, 3–15.

Riecken, H. (1958). The effect of talkativeness on ability to influence group solutions of problems. *Sociometry,* 21, 309–321.

Roethlisberger, F. and Dickson, W. (1939). *Management and the worker.* Cambridge, Mass.: Harvard University Press.

Schein, E. (1965). *Organizational psychology.* Englewood Cliffs, N.J.: Prentice-Hall.

Selznick, P. (1949). *TVA and the grass roots.* Berkeley: University of California Press.

Sherif, M., Harvey, O., White, B., Hood, W., and Sherif, C. (1961). *Intergroup conflict and cooperation: the robbers cave experiment.* Norman, Okla.: University Book Exchange.

Simon, H. (1957). *Administrative behavior* (2nd ed.). New York: Free Press.

Simpson, R. (1959). Vertical and horizontal communication in formal organizations. *Administrative Science Quarterly,* 4, 188–196.

Strother, G. (1963). Problems in the development of a social science of organization. In Leavitt, A. (ed.). *The social science of organizations.* Englewood Cliffs, N.J.: Prentice-Hall.

Taylor, F. (1907). *On the art of cutting metals.* New York: American Society of Mechanical Engineers.

Taylor, F. (1911). *The principles of scientific management.* New York: Harper.

Thompson, J. (1962). Organizational management of conflict. *Administrative Science Quarterly,* 4(4), 389–409.

Torrance, E. (1955). Some consequences of power differences on decision making in permanent and temporary three-man groups. In Hare, A., Borgatta, E., and Bales, R. (eds.). *Small groups.* New York: Knopf.

Urwick, L. (1943). *The elements of administration.* New York: Harper.

Wallach, M., Kogan, N., and Bem, D. (1962). Group influence on individual risk taking. *Journal of Abnormal and Social Psychology,* **65,** 75–86.

Weber, M. (1946). *From Max Weber: essays in sociology* (Gerth, H. and Mills, C., trans.). New York: Oxford University Press.

Whyte, W. (1955). *Money and motivation.* New York: Harper and Row.

Zaleznik, A., Christensen, C., and Roethlisberger, F. (1958). *The motivation, productivity and satisfaction of workers: a predictive study.* Boston: Harvard Graduate School of Business Administration.

Zipf, G. (1946). Some determinants of the circulation of information. *American Journal of Psychology,* **59,** 401–421.

17

Leadership

In any social aggregate some people are bound to be more active than others. There is a differentiation of roles in social groupings that gives a structure and function that, while it may not always be the same, emerges from the situation. While it may be an oversimplification to state that in groups there are people who turn out to be leaders and others who turn out to be followers, for this chapter it serves a satisfactory beginning. It is virtually impossible to discuss behavior, especially social behavior, without including something about the process and nature of leadership. There are few, if any of us who remain unaffected by the activities of leaders—assembly line workers have their foreman, college professors have their dean, Indians have their chiefs, and all of us as citizens have a president.

What is leadership? Attempts to define leadership or describe a leader have been many and varied. In the past some reviewers have focused on outstanding personal characteristics and have defined leadership around those personal traits. Others, recognizing the complexity of the social situation in which we all operate, have taken into account the many social variables that are present and interacting. Definitions of leadership depend, then, on the focus of attention. Interest in the influence process might develop the definition of a leader as one who either influences others or who causes the group to reach certain objectives. Attending to leadership as a selection process might define the phenomenon as the result of sociometric choices. A simpler representation of an accomplished fact would characterize the leader as an individual in a specified office, while a more arbitrary characterization depicts a leader as one who engages in "leadership behavior" (Gibb, 1954, pp. 800–884).

A further identification system is one that concentrates on certain descriptive functions of a leader (Sargent and Williamson, 1958, pp. 371–373). The *symbolic leader* has prestige but no power, the *administrative* leader "gets things done," while the *expert* or the theorist stands out because of his special qualifications. The *charismatic* leader has power on a supernatural or mystical-emotional basis.

Some attempt may be made, however, to focus this diversity of information toward a shorter verbal definition of leadership based on a unitary conceptual framework. The concept of *role,* for instance, is one that may be useful in a description of leadership. In this view, leadership, quite simply, is a role that is occupied by a person (Gouldner, 1950, p. 20). Defining leadership in this way identifies a leader as a member of a group where he is assigned a certain status by that group and engages in the behavior that is associated with the position he occupies.

Leadership also has been viewed basically as an influence process (Stogdill, 1950, p. 4). A leader may be defined as that person who stands out in influencing the activities of a group in setting goals and making progress toward achieving those goals. It should be recognized that we usually assign to the category of leaders those whose influence on the group is outstanding. This is important because each member of a group exerts some influence on another; leadership is more a matter of degree than anything else.

This definition distinguishes between actual leaders and the formally designated leaders who may have very little influence on the group. This is the same distinction that Kimball Young (1956) makes when he distinguishes between "leadership" and "headship." The latter category includes those who are placed in the position by virtue of authority or historical accident and who have little control over circumstances. Sometimes the activity of an individual operating under formal or legal authorities is called supervision to distinguish between it and actual leadership. Supervision is most often used in an industrial setting but it need not be limited to organizations of that type. There is also no real reason why we should call a supervisor at the higher organizational level an executive except that the latter term has by now acquired certain positive connotations that give it certain emotional motivational value. Supervision, as used here, should include the exercise of formal or legal authority at all levels in the organization; the notion still persists, however, that supervision consists of rather "low-level" activities while the executive is concerned with more exacting duties.

In this discussion leadership will refer to the wide range of influence processes that occur in group interaction. Headship or supervision are aspects of this broad social phenomena of leadership. These variants may differ from true leadership, but since those invested with formal authority often have, to some extent at least, the power to influence by virtue of their position, this is still leadership. And so it will be discussed.

General Approaches to Study

Leadership is a topic that has fascinated people down through history, sometimes to the virtual exclusion of all related areas of human behavior.

It seems that we are vitally concerned (especially in Western society) with the question of "who's who" and "who's in charge."

There are many general ways of approaching the study of leadership. From the past we can identify a basic dichotomy arising from an analysis of leaders. The most common conceptualization has been to focus on a single leader and his characteristics. In ancient Greece and Rome, Herodotus, Tacitus, and other historians concentrated on outstanding men as contributing significantly to the stream of events. More recently, Thomas Carlyle remains the chief proponent of the "great man" theory, the notion that men make the times. Others have followed in the same or similar channels; even most of those who have taken psychological approaches to this problem area have concentrated on the clinical histories of great men or, somewhat the same, basically, have tried to determine if there have been any traits that have been peculiar to leaders or that have been present in them more frequently than in others. The results of such endeavors have been disappointing, regardless of the scientific level of the approach.

The other main approach to the study of leadership starts with a framework representing the converse of the "great man" theory, namely, that the times make the man. This view has been called the "situational" or the "sociological" view of leadership and history. Under this organization of thinking, the researchers look to the group instead of concentrating on the leader, seemingly an incongruous way of approaching leadership until we realize that the situational theory (at least in its newer forms) calls for a closer look at interactions between individuals in the group (a casual way of showing the validity of this way of thinking might be to answer the question, "What does it take to be a leader?" with the not too facetious response—"followers"). Extending the situational view to encompass large aggregates would explain events in a fashion like "the temper of the times"—such factors as inflation, frustration, the personality structure common in the German family, and the search for a father image were responsible for the rise of Hitler. If not he, someone like him would have fitted into the pattern which permitted an authoritarian individual to come to the fore.

The focus here is, of course, on the interrelationships between the members of the group under study. It is conceivable that the importance of particular traits varies from one leadership situation to another. If this were so, it could be that the results of the approach concentrating on the characteristics or traits of a single individual would not explain leadership completely.

Traits

The concentration on personal traits or characteristics has occupied the attention of a significant number of researchers in the past, and the interest, in one way or another, continues to the present day. The measurement of the abilities of individuals who are classed as "leaders" and a comparison made with others represents, at least partly, a trend in study that is influenced by the "great man" approach.

PHYSICAL FACTORS

It is not surprising that physical factors such as height and weight should have been studied; the interest shown in this aspect down through the years is evidenced by the folklore and stereotypes existing in our day-to-day contacts. The main stereotype has the leader as a tall man. Gilmer (1961) tells of the three windows in the wall surrounding a construction site. The lowest was labeled "Junior Superintendent," a higher one "Assistant Superintendent," and the highest window, "General Superintendent." References in common speech such as "being head and shoulders above the crowd" contribute further to the stereotype.

In his extensive survey of leadership studies, Stogdill (1948) determined that nine found leaders taller, two found them shorter, while one other suggested that the type of leadership activity is the important feature. Similarly equivocal findings appear for weight, physique, and health.

MENTAL ABILITY

Historically, even more interest has been maintained in studies of the relationship between intelligence and leadership. Most studies agree that, in this respect, leaders are superior to nonleaders. Certainly, if the group functions in a problem-solving situation and any activity which contributes to that problem solving is seen as desirable, those who can contribute come to the fore more easily.

A study of college leaders indicated that they scored higher on the American Council on Education Psychological Examination, a well-established test of scholastic ability, than did nonleaders on the campus (Hunter and Jordan, 1939). In a study in the United States Army, Gibb (1947) found that officer candidates were clearly superior to a general army sample; 99 percent of those selected were above the general population mean. There may be upper limits, however, though these point to the situation more than to the attributes. For instance, Hollingworth (1942, p. 287) found that 30 I.Q. points was the maximum tolerable spread between the leaders and the led; otherwise the relationship either does not take hold or maintain itself.

VERBAL ABILITY

Stogdill's (1948) survey found that fluency in verbal communication was a factor to be considered in identifying characteristics of leadership. It might be intuitively stated that the ability to talk, particularly where the task is a verbal one, would be an important variable in leadership. This has since been supported in the jury studies of Strodtbeck et al. (1958) where it was noted, *inter alia,* that those who participated more in the discussions were more influential and when they spoke up at the beginning, were most often chosen as foremen.

PERSONALITY TRAITS

Leadership and self-confidence have been found to be related in most cases, though not all. Drake (1944) reported a high correlation between these factors. Richardson and Hanawalt (1944) similarly found higher scores on the Bernreuter self-confidence scale among leaders than among those who did not display leadership behavior. In a finding that is representative of the variation in results of studies in this area, Hunter and Jordan (1939) did not find a difference in their college group. They did find, however, that there was a difference between leaders and nonleaders on the Dominance Scale of that same personality measure. It seems that leaders may be more dominant in social situations, alalthough here, as with intelligence, there may be outer limits in a situation with respect to acceptability by others in the group. Too much dominance may lead to rejection. For instance, Jennings (1943) found that dominant and aggressive leaders were rejected by the group, although the result may have been partly the result of the special circumstances; the group was made up of girls in a closed community, sent there under court order.

Leaders may be more perceptive of ability and personality differences in themselves and others. In an industrial situation, Fiedler (1960) found that effective supervisors were better able to differentiate between their best and poorest workers than were the less effective supervisors. Such individuals are more psychologically distant from the other members of the group they lead.

The area of introversion-extroversion has received a great deal of attention generally. Apart from the popular and misleading approaches to this factor (the categories are not discrete and may be situationally related), there seems to be little evidence that extroversion and leadership are related. A review of studies on this factor by Mann (1959) confirms the well-known earlier review by Stogdill (1948) in stating the lack of relationship.

EVALUATION OF THE TRAIT APPROACH

While some information about traits in leadership has been gained from the many studies that have been made, there still remains a lack of substantial agreement in the results, particularly when the studies have focused on characteristics in specific situations. The most significant outcome from this approach may be the inability to generalize the findings from one situation to another.

Presentation of the findings in capsule form might be made by reiterating the results of the well-known survey by Stogdill (1948), one which is still useful though some time has elapsed since it was made. Stogdill surveyed studies of personal factors involved in leadership and found that leaders were higher in self-confidence, intellectual adaptability, and verbal facility. In age, height, weight, and dominance the picture was not as clear though there was some superiority here as well. The above, Stogdill found, represented only fair agreement between investigators; there were too many departures from the main findings.

A further complicating factor concerns the limitations placed on our thinking by a concept of a single and unitary leader. Even casual observation (though it is backed up by substantial evidence) demonstrates the fallacy of the notion, *the* leader. At least some groups function with more than one person emerging as a dominant figure, a situation that shows a good deal of fluctuation with time and place (Bales and Slater, 1955).

It seems clear that while there is no such thing as a "general leadership trait" or any trait that seems to be necessary in all situations, there may be generality or transfer of characteristics from one situation to another. As might be expected, the more alike the situations, the more the composition of leadership remained the same (Carter, Haythorn, and Howell, 1950). Even more, Katz et al. (1957) found generality across different tasks, but many of the traits in their studies were of a general kind, those which pointed to leader behavior in social situations rather than to specific personality traits.

Cartwright and Zander (1960, p. 492) express a trend to the study of *behavior* as the result of deficiencies in the trait approach. They put the focus on the interactional aspects. "Leadership is viewed as the performance of those acts which help the group achieve its preferred outcomes. Such acts may be termed *group functions*." Gibb (1954, p. 889) may have set the stage best for us in his statement that "a person does not become a leader by virtue of his possession of any one particular pattern of personality traits, but the pattern of personal characteristics of the leader must bear some relevant relationship to the present characteristics, activities, and goals of the group of which he is leader." The need to focus on the situation and the part individuals play in it emerges clearly from most studies.

Roles and Functions

One of the more precise approaches to the situational approach to leadership is that which focuses on *roles* as more descriptive of the basis of leadership. Some researchers even define leadership as "a role which an individual occupies at a given time in a given group" Gouldner (1950, p. 20). Using the concept of roles not only moves the observer away from traits and the difficulty that individual traits may not carry over from one specific situation to another, it also recognizes that even a description of a situation or the statement of a role being occupied is insufficient to encompass all the complexity of social situations that take place. A "leader" plays more than one role or his behavior serves many purposes. In addition, different individuals may emerge at different times to provide for more or less influential models or to channel the activities of others in those specific situations.

One of the most extensive classifications of leadership roles has been shaped by Benne and Sheats (1948, pp. 42–49) in which they list 27 different roles (Table 17-1). These various roles can be grouped into three general categories: (1) group task—definition and solution of problems, (2) group building and maintenance, and (3) individual roles—satisfaction of individual needs. These are all considered by the authors to be in the general description of "group required roles."

Another description of leadership patterns is that given by Krech et al. (1962, pp. 428–432) in discussing the many functions of the position (Table 17-2). They place the various descriptive classifications into two main categories—those which are primary functions and those which are merely accessory. The primary functions are those considered essential to leadership, while the accessory functions may be assumed by the leader or assigned to him by the group by virtue of his position. All the various functions can be woven into a practical situation, especially in an on-going complex and dynamic social situation. We might be able to see a little of each type to one extent or another. More complexity may emerge when the functions of a leader that are accessory in some situations may become primary in others. A religious leader, for instance, may act as exemplar or symbol, and these may be very primary in this particular setting.

A more conceptual and integrative view of roles in leadership is part of what Schutz (1961) calls his Fundamental Interpersonal Relations Orientation (FIRO) theory. In this formulation there are three fundamental interpersonal needs—*inclusion, control,* and *affection.* Inclusion is contact or interaction with people or things; control is power over social environment, while affection is social closeness. An individual functions at an optimal level when all three areas are functioning in a proper relationship. The focus is on the individual

Table 17-1.   Classification of Member Roles (from Benne, K. and Sheats, P., 1948)

A. Group Task Roles
1. Initiator-contributor
2. Information seeker
3. Opinion seeker
4. Information giver
5. Opinion giver
6. Elaborator
7. Coordinator
8. Orienter
9. Evaluator-critic
10. Energizer
11. Procedural technician
12. Recorder

B. Group Building and Maintenance Roles
1. Encourager
2. Harmonizer
3. Compromiser
4. Gatekeeper and expediter
5. Standard setter or ego ideal
6. Group-observer and commentator
7. Follower

C. Individual Roles
1. Aggressor
2. Blocker
3. Recognition seeker
4. Self-confessor
5. Playboy
6. Dominator
7. Help seeker
8. Special interest pleader

ego and its development by integrating outer reality; leadership is viewed as functioning in the same way in that the leader operates to integrate the needs of the group with reality. The function of the leader is to complete any of the process of integration that the group does not perform.

Other studies of leadership patterns of behavior have used statistical methods to determine the specific factors that are important and independent dimen-

Table 17-2. Primary and Accessory Functions of the Leader (Krech, D., Crutchfield, R., and Ballachey, E., 1962, pp. 428–432)

Eight Primary Functions of the Leader	Six Accessory Functions of the Leader
1. Executive	1. Exemplar
2. Planner	2. Symbol of the group
3. Policy maker	3. Substitute for individual responsibility
4. Expert	4. Ideologist
5. External group representative	5. Father figure
6. Controller of internal relations	6. Scapegoat
7. Purveyor of rewards and punishments	
8. Arbitrator and mediator	

sions of leadership behavior. In one such approach using the technique of factor analysis (Fleishman et al., 1955), the researchers found that a high percentage of the differences in leader behavior could be accounted for by two dimensions. "Consideration" was that behavior designed to motivate and provide satisfactions for members as harmony was being maintained in the group. "Initiating and directing" behavior coordinated goal-directed activities

Leadership behavior on the "consideration" factor stresses participation in planning an acceptance of suggestions from members and, in general, is oriented toward member satisfactions. Leadership behavior under the "initiating and directing" dimension includes definite indications by the leader of his attitudes and role in the work task and the nature and level of performance he believes is called for by the members in the work situation.

Leadership Styles

In a classic description of the climate developed by leaders, White and Lippitt (1960) describe three types of styles they believe emerged from their research studies. In several experiments they systematically varied the leadership climate in which groups of ten-year-old boys worked pursuing their hobbies. Three leadership styles were postulated and produced—the *authoritarian, democratic,* and *laissez-faire.* In the authoritarian style the leader developed all of the policy and most of the procedures. Not much went on in the group without the knowledge or personal direction of the leader himself. Under the democratic procedure, group activities were pursued after the establishment of policy through initial group discussion and decision making. Participation of members of the group was encouraged; there was, however, a need for the leader to act as a guide or controller of the discussion. The laissez-faire climate allowed opportunity for an extensive range of behavior, often at cross-purposes, in that complete freedom for individual and subsequent group activity was promoted.

This set of studies included the highly relevant question of performance of groups operating under the three types of leadership styles. The researchers noted that output of work was at high levels much earlier in the authoritarian climate than under the democratic atmosphere. The authoritarian approach presumably allowed better coordination of activities to provide the initial high level of performance. In the long run, however, the output under democratic situations closely approached the levels reached under the authoritarian style of leadership. A finer analysis of performance over the entire period revealed a most significant fact. Performance under the authoritarian approach varied considerably with the presence of the leader. When the leader was absent, performance decreased significantly while it was maintained at regular levels when he was present. Under the democratic climate, it made no difference whether the leader was present or not; performance of the group was fairly even, whether the group was on its own or not. The group operating under laissez-faire arrangements was characterized by the uncoordinated horseplay that contributed little to effective performance. Output was consistently very low in this group.

Performance of the group represented only one of the two major aspects considered in this series. The authors considered the resulting emotional responses and the feeling tone of the group to be fully as important as the quantitative measure of performance. The authoritarian climate generated a lot of hostility in the individuals comprising the group. This hostility was not directed at the leader, of course, nor was there much venting of these feelings through aggression toward fellow members. Aggression was directed primarily toward members of other groups or other outsiders. An inventory of feelings after the experiment indicated lower levels of satisfaction of performance under the authoritarian discipline. Hostility and aggression was low in the groups operating under democratic atmosphere; individuals reported feeling more satisfied throughout the democratic sessions and aggression toward others was at a minimal level. The laissez-faire group did not provide much satisfaction either, in spite of the fact that individual and group freedom in activity was almost unbounded.

It must be noted at this point, however, that the above represent general findings; there was some variation on an individual basis. Not all subjects, for instance, were content with the democratic approach nor did all function most effectively in that climate. The fact that some individuals apparently feel a need for a highly structured situation and do not do well without it is one of the significant factors to be taken into account in the evaluation of this classic study.

Other cautionary statements need to be made as well, since this set of studies has served as a focal point for countless discussions of leadership and the factors associated with it. There even may be some temptation to generalize results as far away as the international scene in order to promote ideological positions, at least partly, on the basis of studies such as this one. However valid these results may be, it must be remembered that the subjects consisted of a group of ten-year-old boys in an experimental situation. It seems likely, however, that the results can transfer to other organizational settings such as industrial work groups. For instance, a study by Baumgartel (1957) assessed the leadership style of directors of 20 research laboratories. The directors were divided almost evenly between the classic three styles of leadership. Scientists in the laboratory were then asked to discuss the leadership climate conducted by the director. The directive style (authoritarian) provided the lowest ratings of satisfaction or orientation toward research and creativity. The participatory climate (democratic) engendered greater satisfaction on the part of the scientists who seemed to enjoy the opportunity to contribute to the development of original work. In the same way, Pelz (1956) found that scientific researchers in a large government organization performed better under a democratic approach that allowed them to make their own decisions in a climate that was neither strongly directive nor completely without any guidelines.

It may be misleading, however, to suggest that an authoritarian climate necessarily leads to a condition where a superior lacks concern for the welfare of the subordinates. Blau and Scott (1962, p. 163) found that supervisors who commanded the loyalty of their subordinates were able to promote productivity even if they were authoritarian in approach. Stanton (1960) also found that an authoritarian approach need not limit concern for employees. He compared two companies, one authoritarian and the other democratic, and found that supervisors did not differ in their attitudes toward consideration of the welfare of employees.

Other ways of characterizing leadership styles exist, of course. Knickerbocker (1948, p. 39), for instance, identifies four climates: (1) force, (2) paternalism, (3) bargain, and (4) mutual means. Force is the direct use of restrictive control while paternalism is characterized primarily by loyalty of followers in a warm and cohesive setting. Bargaining involves an exchange in which certain satisfactions are gained by leaders and followers alike. Mutual means represent a fusion of individual and group goals and activities or, at least, attempts made in that direction.

Perception of Leadership

As has already been noted with frequency in earlier chapters, much of human behavior is determined not as much by what is "out there" as it is by what happens to the material when it gets inside the human processing system. The perception of the situation is usually much more important in determining behavior than is the objective reality of that situation. The attitudes and views of individuals involved in all phases of group activity are important to note; this is true as well in discussions of leadership.

If an individual serves as a leader of a group, it is quite probable that he is perceived by the members of the group as belonging to the group and sharing with other members the characteristic attitudes and values of that group. It is not likely that he would function effectively as a leader otherwise. This factor was stated very early by Brown (1936) as "membership-character" in the group. At the same time, the members probably have certain expectations, from the very mintue behavior patterns, perhaps, to the general image the leader may radiate within the group and outside it. He will probably require those skills that are judged to be critical for the task at hand and, even more, will need to excel other members of the group in this respect (Jenkins, 1947). Yet, as we have seen above from Hollingworth's study (1942), the leader cannot be too far ahead of the group, particularly in intellectual ability.

The values and norms of the group will influence that group's expectations of how the leader should behave. Blau (1955), for instance, noted that superiors in a governmental organization slipped into a directive form of leadership behavior and subordinates became submissive very readily. All this happened despite clear-cut attempts by the supervisors to develop a more equalitarian leadership climate. It was obvious that all members basically insisted that individuals follow the roles prescribed by the ideologies of the group in its functioning in the bureaucratic structure of the organization to which they belonged.

College professors, too, may have their expectations of the behavior of department heads or deans. Some campus climates may foster a directive approach by academic superiors, although it is quite likely that present trends in academe are away from a directive approach as an increasing number of academicians expect more equalitarian procedures to prevail. In this climate the dean is merely *primus inter pares*.

Many observers of the business and industrial scene have suggested that the kind of leadership expected among American businessmen is that which we have labeled autocratic or authoritarian. Individuals who are aggressive and forceful are, under this set of expectations, ones who are originally selected to come to the fore as captains of industry.

Perceptions of oneself and others are reinforced, particularly if one is well placed, by the tendency to see that an existing situation has something that is "proper" and also to believe that one possesses the traits or requirements for the position one holds. Porter (1958) found managers seeing themselves as decision makers with independence of thought and high degree of initiative, while line workers perceived of themselves in a way that reinforced a general image of followership with less independence of action. And, since the two aspects of human functioning mesh together neatly, perceptions and behavior were closely related. Bowers (1963), in noting a similarity in patterns of behavior between supervisors close together in the organizational hierarchy, indicated some reasons for the similarity. Either the lower level supervisors imitate the behavior of their superiors because this is where the payoff comes, or all supervisors have a tendency to think alike because only those who do are promoted by their superiors. There is, of course, an organizational tendency to perpetuate the organization in the way the individuals found it and to select other members of the organization that are like the existing members of the group.

Followers

It might be expected, in view of the important place of motivation in human behavior, that understanding of leadership behavior cannot be complete unless some knowledge is gained of the "why" of "leading." The same holds true of "following" as well. What needs are served in the specialized interaction involved in leadership and followership is an important aspect of motivation. A simple answer to the question of why people act as they do in the group situation can be based easily on the general model of motivation sketched earlier in Chapter 8. We might state simply that certain needs are present in individuals and that they engage in some behavior that will be goal directed. Upon reaching that goal, the needs are satisfied. In the social context this implies that some needs are satisfied for people in a leadership role, while other needs may be stronger for those who play a less active or less influential role in the group activity.

It has been stated earlier in this chapter, somewhat facetiously, that what it took to make a leader was followers. Aside from the obvious fact that leadership cannot exist without a group, a study of the characteristics of followers and the conditions under which they follow is of importance, not only to an understanding of the dynamics of their behavior, but also for the neeed to study followers in order to gain a better understanding of the leaders them-

selves. In the emphasis on leaders and their characteristics, the nature of followership has been ignored. Consequently, all too little exists in the research
literature.

One such study by Sanford (1952) surveyed a sample of individuals in
Philadelphia. After using a scale to differentiate between "authoritarian" and
"equalitarian" personalities, the researcher asked the subjects in each of the
two categories questions that would elicit their views of Franklin D. Roosevelt
(this was in 1949) and what made him a good or poor leader. The responses
were categorized into four classes—whether there was an emphasis on functioning as a democratic leader, an emphasis on material dependency (the gaining
of material benefits), a stressing of power or strength and, finally, an emphasis
on personal warmth or concern for humanity generally. In a comparison of
the two groups, equalitarians more often emphasized the function of democratic
leader and almost all of the responses focusing on personal warmth also were
given by equalitarians. The emphasis on material dependency were made by
authoritarians. It might be expected that the authoritarians would emphasize
strength of power more than the other group. Interestingly enough, however,
there was no significant difference between the two groups with respect to
their concentration on the factor of power as being important in their evaluation
of the leader. The study indicates that the response to a leader may be either
positive or negative on the part of followers, but the reasons for the reactions
can differ according to the personality characteristics of the followers. This
has important implications for leadership and its development.

Haythorn et al. (1956) used the same scale to measure the personality
dimension of authoritarianism and set up experimental groups composed of
leaders and followers on both dimensions. Ratings were made after a series
of experimental tests. As might be expected, authoritarian leaders were rated
as less oriented to others and more autocratic. Authoritarian followers were
also rated in the same way in comparison to equalitarian followers. In groups
led by equalitarians there was more opportunity for various members, authoritarian or equalitarian, to participate in the activities of the group and to exercise
some influence. In groups with equalitarian leaders, the followers were more
secure and conflict among individuals seemed to be reduced.

There may be a tendency, especially because of our casual references to
people as leaders or followers, to believe that there are consistent and real
differences in personality or other traits between the two types we have established. This is reinforced by following the trait approach toward leadership
behavior. That some caution needs to be exercised might be recognized from
the fact that conditions and circumstances differ and, therefore, differing group
requirements may call for various individuals to exercise leadership behavior
at various times. Not only is the concept of one individual (*the* leader) dominant

in all situations to be avoided, the hard and fast distinctions between leaders and followers should be carefully stated.

There may even be a high relationship between leadership and followership roles. In a study of choice behavior in leadership situations, Hollander (1961) evaluated sociometric choices of a group of naval aviation cadets. The cadets were told that they were to assume that a critical and stressful mission were facing them. They were asked to choose those fellow cadets whom they would most or least like to have as a leader of the group; then each was asked to choose those he would most or least like to have in his group if he were the leader. Finally, each cadet was asked to list his best friends. There was an extremely high relationship between the lists of leaders and followers that each cadet chose. The same people were chosen as both leaders and followers, while friendship choices were quite different. The much lower correlations with friendship indicated that, while friends were chosen at times, this was not the same as an evaluation on other bases and tends to indicate that individuals will select other members of the group, whether as leaders or followers, on attributes that are considered to be important for the task at hand. This would confirm casual observation of events like choosing up sides for games in the primary neighborhood group. Friends seem to get chosen for one's group, but the skillful players get chosen first.

Formal Structure and Behavior

The nature and extent of the organizational hierarchy play a significant role in the emergence and maintenance of leadership. By virtue of one's placement in the group and its channels of communication, opportunities to exhibit leadership behavior appear to a greater or lesser degree.

A position wherein an individual transmits all orders of a superior to those below and passes information upward to that superior represents a locus of power, whether the job description formally specifies or recognizes this or not. Whisler (1960) studied the "assistant-to" personnel in several organizations and found them particularly influential where top officers were being rotated frequently. The reliance on the subordinate in these circumstances is readily understandable. (Whisler also found that the success of the assistant was related more to how closely he resembled the boss in social, educational, ethnic, and political background than to specific job performance.) The reliance on others may be, as Miner and Culver (1955) state, a mark of the greater feeling of helplessness on the part of the executive in his meeting of complex job demands.

Communication patterns in a group may, as the result of previous success, become perpetuated so that these patterns remain one of the main determinants of the leadership function (Klein, 1956). Concomitantly, power, authority, and status are reinforced by the simple fact of positioning in the communication chain or net.

Klein (*Ibid.*) also found that *centrality* in the communication structure was important for two reasons. There is greater access to information in the central position, and this alone may provide influence and control. In addition, the occupant of the central slot is more visible and apt to be more in demand.

Further, since "nothing succeeds like success," the very fact that one has had an opportunity to practice leadership skills or at least engage in "leadership behavior" gives him a later advantage over those who have been deprived of a chance to do so. Michels (1949) notes further that the exercise of leadership activity contributes to the motivational structure of the individual. The reinforcement makes him more likely to act similarly in the future. This is, of course, consistent with all our information on learning (Chapter 6). Parsons, Bales, and Shils (1953) found that the status of leaders can carry over to a new task. Success with one task enhances the status of the person who contributes to the successful completion of that task and makes it more likely that the contributor transfers his satus to some new situation.

In management circles some of the most frequently occurring questions with respect to the organizational hierarchy and the impact on leadership has to do with the concept of span of control. Span of control refers to the number of subordinates directly responsible to the superior. Much of the activity in this limited area revolves around the fixing on a specific number in the span of control on the assumption that the time and abilities of single individuals impose certain constraints on their functioning with subordinates. Since the superior and all subordinates are not interacting constantly, this assumption may not be warranted. However this may be, the search for the "magic number" continues. Entwisle and Walton (1961) report a span of five as being the median number in their survey of two different types of organizations. They found that the presidents of small business companies and the presidents of colleges or universities had, on the average, a staff of five people reporting directly to them. They also indicate that, as the size of the organization increases, the number in the span of control is also likely to increase.

It might be sufficient to say at this point that no set figure exists with respect to the number of subordinates a manager ought to have. Much depends on the internal conditions in the organization, the type of task, the extent to which interaction is necessary for the completion of the task, the abilities or capacities of the subordinates, the communication channels, and virtually any other condition that affects the functioning of the leader and the organization.

Leadership in Change Situations

Since change is one of the more ubiquitous features of human behavior, it should occasion no surprise that change must be considered in the light of its impact on leadership. Change affects individuals and groups and, therefore, leaders as well. Changes in leadership may come about as the result of changes in group functioning induced by either internal conditions or by those arising from the external factors. Even groups that look fairly stable or appear to be in or close to equilibrium undergo change induced by both internal and external factors.

All of the forces generating conflict in groups and organizations (Chapters 15 and 16) have their implications for leaders. Attitudes of individuals toward the organization or the leader may be such that friction exists. Competition among subgroups for scarce resources or a lack of identification with group goals can upset the equilibrium far beyond the ability of the leader to reestablish it. Changes can also occur within the group as people come and go, and the membership of the organization changes.

Forces from outside the group play a role as well. Input from the environment can alter leadership behavior in many ways. Attacks or threats from the external situation can result in a change of leadership or leadership techniques to counter the external threats. Some external attacks may provide, however, an occasion for group unity rather than act as a devisive force in the group or organization. A change in technology, for instance, may force an industrial organization to reevaluate its position and go so far as to change not only its leadership but its entire structure. The challenge arising on this basis may force other companies out of business if they cannot adapt their functioning to the levels or procedures required.

The challenge implicit in change is even more pertinent for the individual in a leadership situation. Since his role usually calls for more activity than is expected of others in the group, some positive steps are required in most situations. As he is the prime influencer of group action, the effectiveness of the leader in dealing with the conditions of change assumes utmost importance.

There seems to be little doubt that personality factors more than abilities or knowledge are responsible for most of the turnover in organizations, particularly industrial ones. Success of managers, in the eyes of many corporate executives, is traceable to those same factors (Gaudet and Carli, 1957) and, more specifically, to the ability to evaluate social situations or delegate some of the responsibility in the task. The unsuccessful executives were less perceptive of their own attributes and those of others with whom they worked.

Another characteristic of successful leaders may be their avoidance of conforming behavior (Fleishman and Peters, 1962), although this may be limited to individuals higher up in the hierarchy (nonconformity at lower levels is not often tolerated). The researchers found that the executives who scored higher on a measure of conformity were rated lower by their superiors on a measure of performance in their jobs.

Effective leadership is also, according to Selznick (1957), responsible leadership. The main task of the leader is to set goals, or determine what has to be done in order to achieve what must be. "Leadership is irresponsible when it fails to set goals and therefore lets the institution drift. . . . In addition to sheer drift stemming from the failure to set institutional goals, opportunism also reflects an excessive response to outside pressures. To be sure, leaders must take account of the environment, adapting to its limitations as well as to its opportunities, but we must beware of institutional surrender made in the name of organizational survival. There is a difference between a university president who *takes account* of a state legislature or strong pressure groups and one who permits these forces to determine university policy" (*Ibid.*, pp. 143–145):

But even responsible leadership often is not enough to meet the most challenging situations an organization will face, Selznick adds. What is called for in addition to responsibility is creative leadership, a concern for constructive change in all facets of organizational functioning.

Summary

A differentiation of roles in groups leads to a study of those who are more active in group functioning than are others. Leadership may mean, however, many things to many people. Focus may be on occupancy, influence, or choice, or on leadership or specific functional behavior.

Studies of leadership often have proceeded from one of two predispositions—a concern with personal characteristics or a concentration on the situational factors. The trait approach, sometimes reflecting stereotypes about a leader, has been generally inadequate or equivocal. Mental ability or verbal skill may be important in many, but by no means all, situations. Leaders may be more perceptive and dominant in social situations, even though here, too, no invariant relationship exists. With respect to leadership, therefore, the focus apparently must be on the part individuals play in specific situations rather than on traits per se.

A consideration of leadership from the standpoint of roles puts the emphasis on behavior in a setting where relationships between individuals in an ongoing, goal-directed process are the critical factors.

Leadership styles have consequences for the behavior of group members and the performance of the entity. A climate established by the leader that permits participation by members is generally most productive of effort by the group.

Members of a group have certain expectations of their own and their leader's behavior which causes them to perceive the situation accordingly. Reinforcement of a leadership position through a specific and continuing behavior pattern is common in organizations.

Followers, too, have certain needs met by the situation. Personality patterns have something to do with how the leader is perceived and the expectations that accompany the circumstance. Sometimes the same individuals, when the choice is offered, are selected as both leaders and followers by their peers.

Leadership can depend on the physical placement of an individual in the organizational structure. A central position in the communication channel enhances the ability to control. The opportunity to engage in leadership behavior reinforces those patterns and makes it more likely that these will be used again.

The challenges of change are felt most by those in leading positions. Internal disequilibrium or external pressures command much of the manager's actions. Self-awareness, less conformity, and superior social skills may characterize the executive who can cope successfully with change. Creative leadership is a concern for constructive change.

Bibliography

Bales, R. and Slater, P. (1955). Role differentiation in small decision-making groups. In Parsons, T. et al. (eds.). *Family, socialization, and interaction process.* New York: Free Press.

Baumgartel, H. (1957). Leadership style as a variable in research administration. *Administrative Science Quarterly,* **2,** 344–360.

Benne, K. and Sheats, P. (1948). Functional roles of group members. *Journal of Social Issues,* **4(2),** 41–49.

Blau, P. (1955). *The dynamics of bureaucracy.* Chicago: University of Chicago Press.

Blau, P. and Scott, W. (1962). *Formal organizations.* San Francisco: Chandler.

Bowers, D. (1963). Self-esteem and the diffusion of leadership style. *Journal of Applied Psychology,* **47,** 135–140.

Brown, J. (1936). *Psychology and the social order.* New York: McGraw-Hill.

Carter, L., Haythorn, W., and Howell, M. (1950). A further investigation of the criteria of leadership. *Journal of Abnormal and Social Psychology,* **45,** 350–358.

Cartwright, D. and Zander, A., eds. (1960). *Group dynamics.* Evanston, Ill.: Row, Peterson.

Drake, R. (1944). A study of leadership. *Character and Personality,* **12,** 285–289.

Entwisle, D. and Walton, J. (1961). Observations on the span of control. *Administrative Science Quarterly,* **5,** 522–533.

Fiedler, F. (1960). The leader's psychological distance and group effectiveness. In Cartwright, D. and Zander, A. (eds.). *Group dynamics.* Evanston, Ill.: Row, Peterson.

Fleishman, E., Harris, E., and Burtt, H. (1955). *Leadership and supervision in industry.* Columbus, Ohio: Bureau of Educational Research, Ohio State University.

Fleishman, E. and Peters, D. (1962). Interpersonal values, leadership attitudes and managerial "success." *Personnel Psychology,* **15,** 127–143.

Gaudet, F. and Carli, A. (1957). Why executives fail. *Personnel Psychology,* **10,** 7–21.

Gibb, C. (1947). The principles and traits of leadership. *Journal of Abnormal and Social Psychology,* **42,** 267–284.

Gibb, C. (1954). Leadership. In Lindzey, G. (ed.). *Handbook of social psychology.* Reading, Mass.: Addison-Wesley, Chap. 24.

Gilmer, B. (1961). *Industrial psychology.* New York: McGraw-Hill.

Gouldner, A. (1950). *Studies in leadership.* New York: Harper.

Haythorn, W., Couch, A., Haefner, D., Langham, P., and Carter, L. (1956). The effects of varying combinations of authoritarian and equalitarian leaders and followers. *Journal of Abnormal and Social Psychology,* **53,** 210–219.

Hollander, E. (1961). Emergent leadership and social influence. In Petrullo, L. and Bass, B. (eds.). *Leadership and interpersonal behavior.* New York: Holt, Rinehart and Winston.

Hollingworth, L. (1942). *Children above 180 I.Q.* New York: World.

Hunter, E. and Jordan, A. (1939). An analysis of qualities associated with leadership among college students. *Journal of Educational Psychology,* **30,** 497–509.

Jenkins, W. (1947). A review of leadership studies with particular reference to military problems. *Psychological Bulletin,* **44,** 54–79.

Jennings, H. (1943). *Leadership and isolation.* New York: Longmans Green.

Katz, E., Blau, P., Brown, M., and Strodtbeck, F. (1957). Leadership stability and social change: an experiment with small groups. *Sociometry, 20*, 36–50.

Klein, J. (1956). *The study of groups.* London: Routledge and Kegan Paul.

Knickerbocker, I. (1948). Leadership: a conception and some implications. *The Journal of Social Issues,* 4(3), 23–40.

Krech, D., Crutchfield, R., and Ballachey, E. (1962). *Individual in society.* New York: McGraw-Hill.

Mann, R. (1959). A review of the relationships between personality and performance in small groups. *Psychological Bulletin, 56,* 241–270.

Michels, R. (1949). *Political parties.* Glencoe, Ill.: Free Press.

Miner, J. and Culver J. (1955). Some aspects of the executive personality. *Journal of Applied Psychology, 39,* 348–353.

Parsons, T., Bales, R., and Shils, E. (1953). *Working papers in theory of action.* Glencoe, Ill.: Free Press.

Pelz, D. (1956). Some social factors related to performance in a research organization. *Administrative Science Quarterly, 1,* 310–325.

Porter, L. (1958). Differential self-perceptions of management personnel and line workers. *Journal of Applied Psychology, 42,* 105–108.

Richardson, H. and Hanawalt, N. (1944). Leadership as related to the Bernreuter Personality Measures. *Journal of Applied Psychology, 28,* 308–317.

Sanford, F. (1952). Public orientation to Roosevelt. *Public Opinion Quarterly, 15,* 189–216.

Sargent, S. and Williamson, R. (1958). *Social psychology* (2nd ed.). New York: Ronald.

Schutz, W. (1961). The ego, FIRO theory and the leader as completer. In Petrullo, L. and Bass, B. (eds.). *Leadership and interpersonal behavior.* New York: Holt, Rinehart and Winston.

Selznick, P. (1957). *Leadership in administration.* Evanston, Ill: Row, Peterson.

Stanton, E. (1960). Company policies and supervisors' attitudes toward supervision. *Journal of Applied Psychology, 44,* 22–26.

Stogdill, R. (1948). Personal factors associated with leadership. *Journal of Psychology, 25,* 35–71.

Stogdill, R. (1950). Leadership membership and organization. *Psychological Bulletin, 47,* 1–14.

Strodtbeck, F., James, R., and Hawkins, C. (1958). Social status in jury deliberations. In Maccoby, E., Newcomb, T., and Hartley, E. (eds.). *Readings in social
psychology.* New York: Holt, 379–388.

Whisler, R. (1960). The "assistant-to" in four administrative settings. *Administrative Science Quarterly,* **5,** 181–216.

White, R. and Lippitt, R. (1960). Leader behavior and member reaction in three
"social climates." In Cartwright, D. and Zander, A. (eds.). *Group dynamics.*
Evanston, Ill.: Row, Peterson.

Young, K. (1956). *Social psychology* (3rd ed.). New York: Appleton-Century-
Crofts.

18

Political and
Legal Behavior

The study of man operating within political and legal systems has long occupied the interest of learned writers and teachers. From Plato and Aristotle, through Hobbes, Montesquieu, and Bentham, to the present-day writers on political behavior, the philosophy of politics and jurisprudence has been the central focus of activity; a strong trend toward the scientific study of behavior is a more recent phenomenon.

While the separation between legal science and political science has been maintained, at least in name, the two areas are part of a broader inquiry into the nature and functioning of normative systems. The fundamental social bases of political and legal behavior must be kept in mind in a discussion of this area of human activity. The study of social controls and sanctions along with the structuring of the control systems embodying certain values and leading to certain decisions represents a broad and basic approach that provides a firm foundation for behavioral research in politics and law.

Social Foundations

A small social aggregate bound together by ties of kinship is not yet a political entity. A study of the influence processes at work in such small groups easily reveals the importance of primary relations. Behavior of individuals is regulated by norms that have developed through the experience of living together over a long period of time. The norms or rules are seldom written or formalized; people simply do what has been done all along or what is considered "normal" in that setting. Sanctions exist on a casual basis and are applied on a personal one.

DEVELOPMENT OF A POLITY

While the complete process of development of the social group and the exact point at which we might say that law and a political entity come into existence may be debated, it seems clear that a growth in the complexity of a society and the increasing need for groups of individuals to coordinate their activities in a geographic area lead to the development of an entity that can be called political. This process of political development ends ultimately in the creation of a nation, the point where national boundaries are defined within which individuals depart from complete loyalty to a local community to a consciousness of being part of the larger entity. In addition to a removal of local or regional barriers to interaction and identification, the process of political integration into the larger unit is hastened by means such as a common system of education as well as identifiers of unity such as a flag, an emblem, and other symbolic representations.

The problem of when law actually comes into existence may not be too critical, but a reference here may give some indication as to some of the definitional difficulties. Max Weber (1954) has stated that law comes into existence when a coercive apparatus comes into being. This does not have to be, however, a force supported by actors of the state. It may be a psychological coercive force emanating from some other type of organization. This is, then, a more comprehensive view of law than most other students of the legal process would envision. A more characteristic view of the onset of law would tie it in with the establishment of a formal system of action by agents of a political entity. When a judicial system is set up to determine matters of controversy and a means of implementing these decisions is possible, this is when law begins.

POWER AND LEGITIMACY

One of the most pervasive and fundamental concepts inherent in political and legal behavior is that dealing with power and the variables stemming from it. Power is the ability to control, which may be exercised or built up in many ways, from its imposition through the use of naked force to its restrained action on the basis of a moral or ethical justification. The power of a political order will, however, be more stable and effective if there is some relationship between the norms and values of the culture and the channels through which the power is exercised. When the values of a society form the basis for the use of power and the power itself is justified by reference to those values, it is said that power is made legitimate. Legitimate power is called authority.

Legitimacy of a political system is one of the main factors leading to the stability of the entity. Lipset (1967, p. 442) lists three ways in which legitimacy may be achieved.

1. Tradition.
2. Rationality-legality
3. Charisma.

A political entity will have legitimacy through tradition if all members believe that the situation should be as it "always" has been. Rational-legal bases are those that have been accepted as appropriate in the system. A charismatic basis for legitimacy lies in the acceptance of a leader on faith in his outstanding ability.

Lipset says, further, that effectiveness of a political regime these days is measured primarily in economic terms. Development of the economy and a "payoff" for individual members of it is increasingly, though not entirely, a measure of effectiveness. In this connection, Lipset has constructed a simple breakdown (Figure 18-1) illustrating types of political societies with respect to their status on the two factors of legitimacy and efficiency. Box A would be illustrated by a stable country such as the United States, which is high in both legitimacy and effectiveness. A loss of effectiveness while retaining legitimacy, as in Box B, would present a crisis yet would prevent a departure from the democratic system. Box D represents those unstable nations in Latin America or the Middle East that have not developed legitimate political systems and whose effectiveness is low. Coups and other internal crises continue. Military coups do not occur in countries high in legitimacy and effectiveness, since one of the basic principles of legitimate authority is the recognition of civil authority by the military.

Legitimate power is also power that recognizes restraints on its use. The

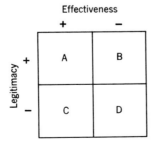

Figure 18-1. Legitimacy, effectiveness, and stability of political systems (Lipset, S., 1967, p. 446).

greatest restraint of power of a political entity lies in the elimination of its concentration. Even this, however, must be accomplished in a particular way. If power is fractionated into several small and powerful groups, either action is restricted or the small group can dominate. The most effective distribution of power comes in a balancing of interests through the participation of a large number of individuals. This system of "checks and balances" is often referred to as *pluralism*. Pluralism encourages the participation of individuals through membership in various groups and organizations, wherein they develop their political skills through interaction within the group and competition with other groups. The presentation of alternatives to the populace at large increases information generally, and the competition between these alternatives increases the chances of limiting a monopolization of power. The pluralistic society can be effective, however, only if the basic values of that society include the notion of pluralism. This concept is widely accepted in the United States and some other countries but is subjected to a severe test or is seldom considered in many other parts of the world.

Political Behavior

Discussions of politics in the past have been a blend of philosophy, art, and science—with very little of the last. Aristotle and most of his successors have maintained theoretical approaches which could not be called entirely scientific. The emphasis on the analytic and descriptive rather than on the normative is the result of the fairly recent activity of political scientists, most of whom carry the label of behavioralist or a similar designation.

Harold D. Lasswell has long emphasized the "science of politics" which requires the "systematic statement of theory and the use of empirical methods of gathering and processing data" (1936, pp. 13, 187). Most researchers who feel this way see political science as interdisciplinary in nature and incorporating concepts from the disciplines of sociology, psychology, and anthropology. Behavioralism concentrates on "rigorous research design and . . . precise methods of analysis. . . . It is concerned with the formulation and derivation of testable hypotheses, operational definitions, problems of experimental or *post-facto* design, reliability of instruments and criteria of validation, and other features of scientific procedure" (Eulau et al., 1956, p. 4).

This does not define either political science or the behavioral approach to politics, but it may give a better picture of the field than might the usual verbal forms. At any rate, the problems of definition of the area have been constant. These difficulties are met simply by Eulau (1963, p. 455) in indicating that "what makes man's behavior political is that he rules and obeys, persuades and compromises, promises and bargains, coerces and represents, fights and fears. . . ." While he recognizes that using verbs does not define politics, Eulau points out that they at least put the focus on behavior—"what man does politically and the meanings he attaches" (*Ibid.,* p. 5) are the crux of what the author calls the "behavioral persuasion."

The interest of behavioral researchers is not on the structure of government or on differentiation between doctrines; the focus is rather on the behavior of individuals and groups in a political setting. The approach is empirical though it is built on a conceptual orientation or framework. In short, the approach veers away from the purely philosophical treatment of ideology or policy as well as away from the consideration of static forms of power structures. A plain and straightforward description of the separate branches of government or the deductive results of description of judicial organizations does not qualify as a behavioral science approach.

In a classification based on well-known action systems, the areas a behaviorally oriented researcher might be interested in would be fields such as: political parties, public opinion, judicial behavior, legislative behavior, voting behavior, politics and personality, and public administration, to name only a few.

PERSONALITY AND POLITICS

The relationship between the personality of individuals and their participation in a political system has continued to be a topic of interest. In his *Psychopathology and politics,* Lasswell (1930) early developed major theses about the general relationships. Lasswell focused on power as the significant feature in the personality of politically inclined individuals. His theoretical formulation of the political type rests on a development of motivation in terms of:

"Private motives
Displaced on Public Objects
Rationalized in Terms of Public Interest."

This is a provocative conceptualization, but it needs verification through empirical research.

Other researchers since have defined the problem in terms that are more measurable and have used, therefore, a variety of personality measurements in noting relationships between test results and performance of individuals on the political scene. One of the measurement techniques that has stimulated activity in this area was developed by Adorno et al. (1950) in their assessment of what they described as the *authoritarian personality*. Their paper-and-pencil questionnaire, the F scale, measures their definition of authoritarianism. The researchers found that high scorers were fairly rigid in personality organization, more likely to adhere to conventional values or to follow rules to the letter, and were power oriented in interpersonal relationships.

Using the F scale on a national sample, Janowitz and Marvick (1953) found many relationships with political behavior. Those high on the authoritarian scale were also more strongly isolationist than those who scored low on the scale. High authoritarian subjects were also less likely to participate in political processes as indicated by their failure to vote in recent elections. It should be noted also that other factors play a role. Authoritarian attitudes were over twice as a frequent in the lower class than among the well educated upper-middle class respondents, although the authoritarianism scores were still higher for white collar workers who had low education and low incomes. The authors related the high level of authoritarian responses in this latter group to the frustrations encountered by individuals in whom social striving was very strong.

AGENTS OF A POLITY

In any political grouping, some individuals achieve or otherwise arrive at a status that allows them to exert more influence on the behavior of the group than others do. Political executives at all levels, legislators, and judicial officers are more active in the political influence processes than are ordinary citizens. With their impact on social events and the high visibility of their activity, it is no wonder that an interest in the behavioral concomitants of political leadership has been generated.

Role Perception

Analysis of the variations in roles that may be present on the political scene may be a significant part of the task of a student of political behavior. Perceptions of individual roles can be studied from the standpoint of the officials themselves or from the viewpoint of their constituents.

A study of state legislators by Eulau et al. (1959) developed three major representational types of roles based on the responses given: Trustee, Delegate, and Politico. The Trustee operates as a free agent and follows the dictates of his conscience. The Delegate acknowledges, in one way or another, that he acts under direction from his constituents. The Politico represents a midpoint on the continuum where the other two types are at the poles; this stance may represent vacillation or simultaneous overlapping. Those representatives who were oriented toward their districts were more likely to be Delegates than were the state-oriented Trustees. Politicos occupied a middle position.

Public attitudes on the same problem area were studied later (McMurray and Parsons, 1965). Subjects responded to questions pertaining to the roles of legislators and judges at local, state, and national levels. Virtually all felt that judges should be free of politics yet two-thirds also felt that they should be accountable to the people for their actions. Seven out of ten favored, rather than opposed, the Delegate type of legislator, but four out of ten also favored the role of Trustee (though more opposed the concept). The college-educated in the sample were more likely to favor the Trustee role than were those with less education. Occupational patterns were similar—the instructed Delegate role was increasingly favored by those lower on the scale.

Characteristics

Several commentators on the social scene have identified a concentration of influence through the selection of individuals on the basis of wealth and power. The main thesis of *The power elite* (Mills, 1956) is that a selection process is taking place not on participative and democratic grounds but through the concentration of power. This broad position has been challenged, also in a general way, by others who point out the social checks inherent in the pluralism they see present in American society. An empirical examination of the concepts, however, can provide a more stable basis for evaluating the validity of the various constructs.

Mann (1964) made a study of the background of men who served as executives in the federal government. The results reflect special sources for their recruitment; most were drawn from the Northeastern part of the United States and had a much higher level of education than the general population. Religious preferences indicated that Protestant members were represented in greater numbers than their presence in the general population. The largest percentage of appointments were of individuals who already were in nonelective positions in government. For almost as many, the practice of law was the primary profession, and a substantial proportion of those in government service also had law training.

United States Senators (Matthews, 1954) have shown a similar strong representation from higher socioeconomic levels. Results of this study dispel the myth of humble origins—very few Senators were born into lower class or working families, and their educational level far exceeded that of the general population. Almost 70 percent of the group had legal training, with most of these having law as a principal occupation. Religion is also a factor, since over 80 percent of the Senators were members of Protestant denominations, with the higher prestige churches overrepresented in the group.

The foregoing survey needs some qualification at this point. Even a casual review of the roster of the Senate in the 90th Congress shows the addition of Negro and Oriental representation to effect more of a balance racially. Radical changes in socioeconomic backgrounds from those pictured in the earlier study are not evident, however.

A study of the background characteristics of justices of the United States Supreme Court since the Court's foundation indicates some remarkably similar patterns (Schmidhauser, 1959). This may not be as visible as we proceed down through the various levels of the judiciary to the local county and municipal courts. Local political pressures are apt to have some impact in the increasing heterogeneity of the composition of the courts.

Of substantially more importance in the study of judicial behavior is the question of relationships between these background factors and the decision making of judges. Nagel (1962) determined, for instance, that the majority of judges in state and federal supreme courts were white Anglo-Saxon Protestants, their number being out of proportion to their proportion of the general population. In addition, judges of this background were more often found on the conservative side of split decisions in their courts than were those from other backgrounds. The author notes that, while various mechanisms in the courts can keep the influence of individual backgrounds at a minimum, the values inherent in the controversies can develop a relationship between individual backgrounds and the decisions.

These various studies indicating a positive relationship between socioeconomic status and political position do not necessarily show, however, complete support of the development of a "power elite" as envisioned by Mills (1956). The activity of the individuals surveyed suggests some degree of pluralism that is not completely representative of the tight and unified system conceived by Mills. The various studies do show, however, that a strong bias on a socioeconomic basis exists in political participation.

ECONOMIC DEVELOPMENT AND POLITICS

Relationships between the nature of the political system and the level of economic development have been studied for centuries. Aristotle may have been the first to note that the disparity between a poor mass and a wealthy elite was likely to end in either tyranny or oligarchy. This kind of dictatorship, presumably, would be less likely to occur with political participation of a larger number of individuals. The pertinence of this problem in recent times has led to surveys of the relationships between the economic levels of peoples and the political system. There is some growing body of evidence that points to the fact that developed countries, which have stable political systems allowing for participation of their members, have, as well, a greater distribution of wealth among individuals. Underdeveloped countries are characterized not only by a lower level of industrialization and urbanization, but also by a greater gulf between the "haves" and the "have nots." Coleman (1960) has noted that truly competitive political parties are more likely to be present in those countries that are more economically developed. Lerner (1958) found that the major aspects of economic development such as education, wealth, and urbanization are all interrelated and correlate highly with the level of democracy found in a political state. Lerner comes to the conclusion that democracy, a participative society, is one of the ultimate steps in the development of a modern and industrialized society. Lipset (1960) supports the relationships to democratic government outlined above. Table 18-1 summarizes these findings.

Table 18-1. Correlation of Factors in Economic Development with Democracy (Lerner, 1958)

Dependent Variable	Correlation Coefficient
Urbanization	.61
Political participation	.82
Media participation	.84
Literacy	.91

Education seems to be an important variable in the process of development with both a material and a less tangible effect. The level of education and democratic values have been found to be positively related. In many different settings, the higher the level of education the more positive are the attitudes toward tolerance of others, acceptance of social differences, and avoidance of extremest doctrines—all of the fundamentals of the democratic process (Smith, 1948; Stouffer, 1955). In Lerner's (1958) study, above, the high relationship of education to media consumption and production indicates the economic payoff accompanying the development of skills and resources; this does not occur without the development of educational vehicles.

POLITICAL PARTICIPATION

People are involved in political activity in different ways or degrees. Some are quite active in the party of their choice while others have only minimal interest. Those who are active not only participate but do so in various ways as they maintain a high degree of interest in all aspects of political activity.

Political participation is related to other personal and demographic variables. Age, sex, residence, education, and socioeconomic level all show a relationship with political activity. Lane (1959) has shown that the very old and the very young adults are not as active as the middle-aged individuals who have some status in the group, own property, or have family responsibilities. The same study identifies the greater role in politics by men; women are more apt to focus on "reform" issues or on personalities when they do show interest. Urban residents are apt to be more interested and active in politics than those in rural areas, a factor no doubt related in part to the easier access to sources of information. Greater political activity is also positively related to higher socioeconomic status. Lipset and Linz (1956) describe the relationship arising from three attributes of the situation. They believe that higher status individuals are more knowledgeable and more likely to be aware of the consquences of political activity. Higher status persons are more likely to interact with others and expose themselves more to mass media. The importance of the last point has been demonstrated many times since Hyman and Sheatsley (1947) first labeled that segment of the population which was hard to reach as the "Chronic Know-Nothings." Education, too, plays a significant role in the process, by itself or as one of the factors that are associated with socioeconomic status or residence.

Some warning with respect to overgeneralization is needed, however. Lane (1959) indicates that minority ethnic groups may be just as active as others if there is conflict in the community, if group differences are great between adjacent populations, or if the administration of justice is less than adequate or unfair. Participation is greater where minorities are permitted to participate or, even more, are encouraged by governments sensitive to these differences.

POLITICAL PREFERENCES

Selective activity on the political scene can be the result of a complex set of determiners. As with other social behavior, primary relations are important. Campbell et al. (1954, p. 99) found that two-thirds of respondents in their survey identified themselves as being in the same party as their parents, where the parents were identified as being in one party or the other. While a majority did identify with the party of their parents, there was more of a departure from parental identification with party than apparently exists in other Western countries. Such departure may occur in different ways, but one big opportunity comes with exposure to different attitudes in college. Associations of any kind are powerful influences on behavior as we have already learned in discussing attitudes and activities. Political behavior is no exception; people are more apt to vote as their friends vote.

Furthermore, the more cohesive the group and the more alike the members of that group are, the more solidly based is the preferential behavior. Berelson et al. (1954, p. 99) noted that strong Republicans were thirty times as likely when the three closest friends were Republicans than when the three closest friends were Democrats. Less than 1 percent of the strong Democrats in the sample had as three closest friends all Republicans but 38 percent of the strong Democrats had three closest friends all Democrats.

Many researchers and students of the political scene have commented on the strong homogeneity of political behavior which occurs on the basis of membership in religious, class, or ethnic groups. The notion of "bloc voting" has been with us for a long time. There are some strong relationships between voting and membership, but the complexity of the situation comes because of the large number of variables involved. Certainly the party preference of Catholics may be different from that of Protestants and Jews, but each other factor introduced changes the nature of the relationship. Socioeconomic status (or class) makes a difference as do geographical location or rural-urban conditions of residence. Some researchers believe that the religious identification is stronger than the other factors but Stouffer (1955, p. 94) states that age qualifies this considerably. Younger people seem to be more influenced by class membership than by religious affiliation. This may be further qualified by the attributes of residence and the opportunities for interaction with others holding similar positions. Strength of identification stems from greater chances for support and validation from others.

In the situations where cohesiveness is not present, the lack of homogeneity can lead to cross-pressures on the individual. These cross-pressures, especially where there is a low level of interest in political activity, cause instability of voting preferences. Lipset (1959, pp. 94–95) makes the point that political leaders recognize this factor when they make efforts to win or retain the support of party members who are more likely to switch. Multiple group affiliations and identifications with the pressures from many sides are an increasing aspect of present-day activity. This produces stress but it also provides a reduction of emotion which has been often expressed in the political arena, especially in past generations.

MASS POLITICS

Some concern has been felt in many areas about the emergence of mass activity arising on bases and working in channels outside those that have been established. That activity has been labeled mass politics. One leading researcher

(Kornhauser, 1959, p. 227) describes mass politics as that which "occurs when a large number of people engage in political activity outside of procedures and rules instituted by a society to govern political action." The stability of a political entity can be seriously affected by such mass action. Mass politics can result in either a highly volatile situation approaching anarchy or it can end in a seemingly stable and quiescent dictatorship. Kornhauser's theory of mass society allows for action by both elites and nonelites in that extensive self-governing units can be available on a private as well as public basis. In addition, however, there must be a formulation of policy by elites without continuing and hampering interference from outside pressure groups. A problem that is even more basic and one to which more attention must be paid is that mass society suffers from social alienation, the distance between an individual and society. In this view, mass society is characterized by the alienation of both elites and nonelites with a resulting rise in social discord produced by a set of dysfunctional consequences in the political arena.

Some empirical verification of these concepts has occurred. Campbell et al. (1954) found that citizens who felt that politicians were responsive to the electorate were more likely to be politically active. The level of inactivity was higher on this basis at the lower socioeconomic levels. Hastings (1956) also found that those who did not vote in political elections were more likely to be those individuals who experienced a sense of social isolation. This social distance from general society apparently makes the nonvoter apathetic in politics. A limited commitment to established institutions of society is also characteristic of this group of nonparticipants in the political process.

Law and Behavior

The role of law in the processes of interpersonal activity is one which may be stated differently by each person surveyed in various social and professional groupings. Generally, however, the most common view of law is that it is a set of rules by which people are to live in their community. The consensus reached by the average members of the community seems to regard the law as a set of regulations that are the embodiment of immutable principles—regulations clearly known to the professional practitioners of the art of advocacy. This view clearly pictures law as known and fixed, static and yielding to no effort of man to introduce a variance. With this definition of law we are concerned with finding specific answers to specific questions. "Is it legal to drive down the left side of the street?" or "May I sell my apples on this street corner?" are the kinds of questions we expect to hear under the casual view of law as a rule of behavior.

This concern with law as a logical system of rules has been the basis for traditional distinctions or classifications in the legal order. In the traditional approach a subdivision may be made on the basis of the type or broad system of law involved as when we differentiate between the Anglo-American system of common law and the civil law of continental countries. Differentiation may be made according to jurisdiction or seat of authority as in references to federal, state, or perhaps even international law. A further familiar classification may be made according to legal content as is done in the breakdown of law into contracts, torts, decedents' estates, or rules of evidence. The legal order may also be looked at from the standpoint of whether only the private interests of individuals are involved or whether the larger political entity or state may have an interest in the matter. In this case the division may be made between civil law and criminal law.

To many students of law and behavior, however, the familiar distinctions, while important and informative, have been limiting in the sense that they have not included the role of law in the influencing of broader social activity and, in turn, in being influenced by other aspects of individual behavior in a society. Narrow definitions of law that limit themselves to the outlining of rules or regulations are seldom comprehensive enough for meaningful activity. That there is much more to law than this narrow definition of rules is evident when one views the functioning of law in society today.

WHAT IS LAW?

The definition of law and a description of its bases have been topics of intellectual concern for many centuries. Controversy in this area has been fostered by the affective reactions stemming from the strong value judgments that are possible in a discussion of the nature of law.

Viewed very broadly and fundamentally, the law may be seen as a method of social control (among other types of control) or as an embodiment of certain values. It may be considered an instrument of policy or an expression of one kind of authority. It can be a means of establishing order or developing social solidarity or it may be seen as a set of social institutions, associations that serve public interests in an accepted, orderly, and enduring way. And, most fundamentally, law may be viewed as a means toward fulfilling social needs and aspirations.

A concentration on law as a set of rules has been, historically, the most frequent approach, and recourse to this concept persists today. "Positive law" refers to rules established by elements in authority. "Natural law" is susceptible to many definitions but most generally refers to a "higher law" that is more basic to human behavior than man-made law and, therefore, of greater validity in human events. Needless to say, the above two categories, along with other designations, can be considered controversial, either in their generality or their propensity to provoke emotional responses. In addition, the tendency of legal conceptualists to work within a self-contained framework of existing legal structures or concepts often has limited their consideration of social factors in human functioning.

A more recent response has been that aimed at studying how the law works. A behavioral science approach studies *law-in-action* rather than developing formal and abstract concepts. It is, moreover, a study of what "is" rather than what "ought to be." In addition, the incorporation of social and behavioral influences on activity under law can aid in the further development of concepts describing the foundations of law. Evolution under social forces, vehicles for meeting social aspirations, means of social control, providing opportunities for participation—all represent varying possibilities by way of explaining the pervasiveness of law.

As one of the early behaviorists, Max Weber was among the first to settle on an operational definition that excluded all value judgments. Weber (1954, p. 13) believed that social norms become law only when "there exists a 'coercive apparatus,' i.e., that there are one or more persons whose special task it is to hold themselves ready to apply specially provided means of coercion (legal coercion) for the purpose of norm enforcement." When a special group is set up to enforce social norms, this is where law begins. The coercion may be physical, of course, but it may also be psychological. The coercion is also not limited to agents of the political community but can extend as well to a group outside the formal state network; thus, a corporate group—church, labor, or business—may have binding influence on its members.

Others, notably Selznick (1965), have expressed belief that a definition like Weber's is too limited. Selznick states that such definitions are confined to indicators of law rather than being the means of distinguishing law from other conceptual areas. According to Selznick, "an adequate theory of law must identify the distinctive *work* done by law in society, the special *resources* of law, and the characteristic *mechanisms* law brings into play." The key concept underlying law is, for Selznick, that of authority. The obligation to act in line with norms authoritatively determined is the central factor outlining law and its study.

Some legal researchers, notably Stone (1966), have translated the concepts of an interactional social system of Parsons (1951) to a legal context. The legal system is seen, therefore, as a "structure of relations between actors"—a web of interaction. Just as important in the legal uses are the concepts of sanctions and roles. Sanctions as a central feature in the process of regulation of social order are particularly pertinent to a consideration of law. Roles and role-relationships, too, have their basic place in law; the relationships between seller and buyer, husband and wife, employer and employee, or landlord and tenant have been some of the traditional trappings of interactional processes among actors in the legal milieu.

Another prominent approach to the law has been that focusing on the process of social control. It is a means by which individuals and groups are influenced to conform to group expectations; this may occur through both formal and informal methods. Law may then be described, as Davis (1962, p. 41) and others have done, as a formal means of social control. "Law is defined as the formal means of social control that involves the use of rules that are interpreted, and are enforceable, by the courts of a political community."

Pound (1942, p. 40) has outlined three meanings of law commonly held as being the source of most of the definitional difficulty. The first concept is that of a political body ordering conduct by the application of force. A second view regards law as a body of authoritative guides to action while the third considers the legal system as a judicial process using the authoritative guides as the basis for determination. Pound states further that the idea of *social control* is the idea by which all three meanings may be unified, although two other theories of law are pointed out by him as worthy of notice.

One is the notion that law is power, the power to influence. This conceptualization is rejected on the basis that power, far from being synonymous with law, is really a force that is utilized for social control. Another theoretical view is that which regards law as an "authoritative canon of value." These canons of value are, according to those who hold strongly to this view, in the self-interest of the dominant class who then constrain others accordingly.

CONCEPTS OF CONTROL

Within the framework of the concept of law as a method of social control, the focus perhaps should be on the underlying philosophy of the system of control. Control may be seen as providing stability for the social group, or the focus may be on the opportunity for the individual to fulfill his potential and function as a total person within a group. Depending on one's attitude or value system, this might be achieved by a process that encourages certain behavior through positive means that are educational and therapeutic, on the one hand, or the behavior may be promoted by the use of directed methods to assure the behavior desired. This differentiation is a very basic one because it goes to the foundation of many of the practical problems present in society. Whether we believe in stimulating and soliciting good behavior or, on the other hand, use corporal punishment to try to prevent lapses from good behavior in a family setting has its counterpart on the social scene in the dichotomy between social sanctions for treatment or punishment.

A further way of putting the distinction might be in terms of a difference between the *laissez-faire* approach and a more paternal view of the forces of authority. In the former instance, people are considered to be more on their own and responsible for their actions. With the paternal approach, the authorities may take the position that they are acting as wise and loving parents in prescribing particular procedures that will make better students, better children and, therefore, better citizens of the state. Instead of taking a punitive approach that comes easily in assuming that individuals should be "on their own," society would seek to "help" the offender, whether he be adult or juvenile. While seemingly no one can be against education, there is a subtle danger in following through with the educational approach. Often the insistence on a particular type of "correction" really involves a punitive process rather than an educational one. Under the guise of education, we may let some of our punitive tendencies operate. It is evident that in practice what is called treatment of the individual amounts to far less and that this "treatment" may even contribute to further criminality on the part of those released from correctional institutions.

With procedures tailored to an advocacy situation, representation is possible and should be obtained so that the individual will be championed by at least an appointed advocate. If he is adjudged responsible and guilty, he is faced with a specified penalty of certain maximum duration. Critics of the less formal approaches with an educational or paternal flavor are concerned that treatment is very often worse than the ordinary punishment for the crime in terms of separation from society.

Presumably an advocate will safeguard the constitutional rights of the individual, since there could be situations arising under an educational approach that limit the rights of an individual. The dangers inherent in a situation where safeguards may be limited are seen by many observers. Social interests and, even more, the interests of the defendant may not be served by freeing an administrator, judge, or clinician from a rigorous rule of law. To do so would have the result of entrusting unlimited discretion to an individual whose personality would determine how the interests would be served. This is the main argument against widespread elimination of substantive and procedural rules in order to accomplish social objectives (Tappan, 1947, p. 22). The existence of established procedures helps to facilitate a government by rules and not of men. This concept is being extended to juveniles as well in the recent United States Supreme Court reduction of the parental role of government (In Re Gault et al., 1967).

SOCIAL AND LEGAL CHANGE

It has been said before that nothing is certain in this world except death, taxes and, in addition, change. No society, simple or complex, exists without undergoing some change. The differences from year to year or generation to generation may be minor but they do take place. In Western society, where we may be able to recognize certain specific changes taking place every day in the area of law, the relationship between the development of the social order and legal order especially needs to be scrutinized.

Social change is basic to other change, including that in law. Legal form and function are affected by the more extensive patterns of behavioral variation in time and place. Increased mobility and wider participation in social events has increased pressure on governmental services and decreased the hitherto existing behavioral controls grounded in close ties with kin and community (Selznick, 1965). These changes themselves have promoted a more interdependent set of relations with broader social interests taking precedence over private ones.

The modern corporation has grown in size and influence to a point where it represents mass society. Regulation of its activity in many sectors of social functioning, including a concern for the rights of its members, has made the distinction between private and public law a tenuous one (Selznick 1965). All of these aspects are, in one way or another, subjects for discussion of legal activity apart from change itself.

Social change overall and legal change more specifically occur together, though the development is not always synchronic; at times, laws lag behind public opinion and, at times, general sentiment may not keep up with enactments of the legislature. These variants of culture lag can be productive of considerable unrest on the social scene as enforcement becomes a difficult matter when either lag exists. At the present time, civil rights legislation in the South is resisted by the individuals and groups who have learned to live with different norms. William Graham Sumner may not have been completely accurate when he said that folkways and mores can nullify law because law has a very potent normative effect *qua* law, but the statement readily emphasizes at least the immediate reaction to the dissonance caused by the culture lag between law and custom.

On the other hand, law may be a potent force in itself for promoting social change. Social change through legal agencies may come through legislative bodies, the judiciary, or through quasi-judicial groups such as administrative agencies or boards. Legislation is perhaps the easiest and quickest means of effecting social change through utilization of the legal order. Despite disclaimers, courts can and do effect changes in the social order through changes in interpretation of statutes, though the process is necessarily slow. A change is even more gradual in countries following the common law methods in judicial decision making than it is in the civil law countries. The common law, with its strong basis in previous decisions, does not make any radical change from past performance on the basis of single cases or a short series of cases. In its dedication to analogy on the basis of general principles, the civil law provides a method that can introduce change more readily and may be better than common law in attacking new problems on a broad front where the piecemeal, empirical, and limited fact basis of the common law limits it to very restricted situations. In addition to situations where lag is found, there are some synchronous situations where dissonance exists because of a lack of understanding of the problems or procedures that are involved. Virtually all of the activity of a lawyer or law enforcement agency may be viewed as maneuverings, sometimes even with malice, because the layman may have no clear-cut perception of the purposes served.

Further difficulties arise when the attitudes and values toward particular institutions are not consonant with each other. To take the juvenile court as an example, the body of lawyers would likely look upon the functioning of the juvenile court as primarily a matter involving law. Other professional groups may well take the stand that the social and psychological factors involved are much more important than the legal ones. This lack of agreement may arise in policy matters, or it may come about with respect to very specific personnel and procedural questions.

The fundamental nature of contracts illustrates the emphasis placed on individual activity in a laissez-faire society. It represents a particular policy determination in the regulation of transaction between human beings. The inadequacy of the concept of contract is shown in daily happenings in the practical world. Today relationships between individuals turn out to be often in the nature of status relationships rather than contractual relationships. Even in business, seemingly an area constrained by contractual decisions, variances from strict functioning according to legal prescriptions is common. Macauley (1963, p. 55) notes that "businessmen often fail to plan exchange relationships completely, and seldom use legal sanctions to adjust these relationships or to settle disputes." That other considerations may be present may be seen from the rather common occurrence whereby department stores seldom stand on their contractural rights in their relationships with the customer and will adjust the outcome of a transaction for public relations purposes.

Concern also is being felt in many quarters at the increasing activity of administrative agencies in government. On the one hand, there is some feeling that legislative duties may be delegated improperly, in part at least, to the agencies. Adjudication, too, is increasingly moving to quasi-judicial bodies within both public government and private agencies. Many claims of right are now being settled by organs of an executive agency of government with infrequent appeals of verdicts to the established system of courts. Courts are also reluctant to interfere in most of the mechanisms of private government. Any controversy must first be taken through all available channels until remedies within the organization are exhausted. Even before this, various agreements between individuals and groups call for the use of laymen acting in a judicial capacity. Examples of impartial arbitration, in the industrial area particularly, are the rule rather than the exception.

It may well be that in other civil matters the entire complexion of legal practice and, therefore, the legal profession itself will change. The deluge of accident and personal injury cases before the courts accounts for most of the backlog of cases; in some jurisdictions this backlog runs to three years and more. Whether this and other factors will lead to an entirely different procedure in this area of the legal order is one of the prime topics of discussion. A radically different approach worries some practitioners, yet we already have had some departures from the traditional adversary-in-court system in the area of injury at work. Workmen's compensation laws superimposed an almost completely new system on the centuries-old pattern without, apparently, any serious difficulty.

Other recent developments touching the law have components arousing the anxieties of many people. The development of mathematical models to understand legal behavior or the use of electronic data processing equipment in legal problems are perceived by some as threatening (perhaps at the prospect of being eliminated by a computer program or an "electronic brain"). It is already certain that, wherever electronic aids have been introduced, they have lightened the routine of the worker, laborer, or professional. A complete search of statutes can be accomplished in a fraction of the time it takes with traditional systems and the lawyer, for one, is freed for much more meaningful activity.

All of the above changes and problems point to what may be the final and fundamental issue, namely, the need for a review of the traditional concepts which have developed in this broad area of legal and social activity. One hundred years ago, Sir Henry Maine, in his famous work *Ancient law,* outlined a pattern of development in the law which he identified as a movement from status to contract. In it, relationships between people in primitive societies are pictured as being determined by their placement in the society. As societies developed in complexity, the emphasis from a reliance on status changed to a concern with relationships developed on a contractual basis. In a status condition an individual receives what is given him under the social rules of his group; in a contract situation he receives what he bargains for. It may well be that in many respects we now are reversing the direction of the development and are moving from contract back to status.

Welfare benefits or similar forms of governmental services may hardly be thought of as being contracted for by the parties receiving them. Instead, it is their particular position (poverty, motherhood, neglected child) that is the determining factor in their participation. An example of the approach is the suggestion that decisions as to procedure and the protection of individual rights should be based on the question of whether there will be an effect on social position, safety, comfort, or rectitude rather than whether the case fits into the traditional categories of "civil" or "criminal." The distinction between different forms of property (as in distinguishing between real and personal property) does not seem to be as important now as it has been in the past. What may be more important is that we increasingly are experiencing the impact of "new forms of property" in the form of government benefits and services. Even private employers have been taking into account the new demands on them by the workers whereby employment begins to be governed by social obligations rather than legal ones.

It should be added, finally, that such views of change do not mean a total abandonment of all that has been useful in the past. What has stood the test of time may have some basis in rationality and validity. To say, however, that these are the best possible approaches and that we should maintain them as they exist today does not seem realistic. The conditions of a society are not static; the moves toward balance keep taking place. Under these dynamic conditions, change occurs as it always has. With a better awareness of the foundations of behavior, a more effective adaptation can take place.

LEGAL POLICY MAKING

Perhaps the most fundamental of the newer conceptual approaches to law is the attempt to determine the real variables which underlie behavior in a legal and social order. This also demonstrates the basic approach of behavioral scientists who study the activity of individuals as it really is. When researchers are interested in uncovering bases of decision making and policy making, they concern themselves with aspects that are of importance yet ones that may be taken for granted and glossed over. When real-life decisions are made, as when laws are enacted, these may assume certain relationships between the rule and the behavior that the rule is intended to influence. Intuitively we may say that a particular regulation will prevent a specific type of behavior which is considered as undesirable by a social body. Often, however, we find that in many cases the regulation enacted proves to be ineffective. We might ask the obvious question, "Does punishment actually deter?" On the basis of limited personal experience, it may be evident that punishment does influence in some way but the question really should be, "What sort of punishment deters, how often, who is deterred and who is not, and why not?"

The contribution of the behavioral sciences seems to be appropriate for providing the empirical base for action which is intended to meet certain objectives (indeed, the original objectives may be defined by the same processes). Reform of the legal order, both substantive and procedural, may be founded on the investigations within a behavioral or social framework, when that framework incorporates not only the purely legal concepts but those concepts affecting actual social functioning as well. This has been, in the past, one of the distinguishing characteristics of the school of Sociological Jurisprudence, especially as exemplified by Pound's theory of social interests in his overall concern with the social foundations of law. The "legal realists," primarily Jerome Frank and Karl Llewellyn also emphasized the basis of law in social norms.

More direct use of "legal engineering," much as Pound and others have proposed, comes to the fore in recent attempts to outline a basis for legal policy from empirical data. By far the most ambitious have been attempts to develop a "science of legal policy" (Podgorecki, 1962).

Something similar can be done by setting up an experimental situation to gather data on basic policy questions. There is some information in a few areas regarding the effectiveness of sanctions. One study of the compliance with income tax laws (Schwartz and Skolnick, 1963) tested different kinds of sanctions to determine which seemed to be most effective. Another sociological study on rent control violations (Ball, 1960) showed that the degree of violation of the regulations was not related as much to severity of the sanctions as it was determined by the feelings of fairness or unfairness in those who were faced with the procedures of control.

Just as basic and important are those studies which provide information for policy in other social areas. Evidence for either policy making or more limited judicial decision making may be obtained by survey or experimental studies attacking problems involving fundamental issues in law such as "the standard of the reasonable man" or "the sense of the community as the standard of judgment." Researchers can go beyond intuition or speculation and gather data as to the opinions and attitudes of a large segment of the community. Scientific evidence provides a better base for legislation or judicial decisions than do opinions of a single individual or a group with cultural bias. Presumably the awareness by the Supreme Court of the finding of social deprivation in the segregation of Negro children helped that court decide in the landmark case of *Brown v. Board of Education of Topeka* (1954) that separate facilities for members of two races were in and of themselves unequal.

JUDICIAL DECISION MAKING

Analysis of court decisions and the individual judge's role in the process is not a new activity. More recently, however, the focus of attention is increasingly on approaches with a quantitative basis. The techniques have reached the point where various psychological and mathematical models are being used to describe and to predict judicial behavior. In this the researchers have been aided by electronic programming techniques and machinery. Many of the re-researchers refer to this field as jurimetrics, a term used to refer to part or all of the study of judicial decision making (Schubert, 1960; Baade, 1963).

The development of research procedures utilizing an electronic computer, either in the formulation of day-to-day activity or in the prediction of judicial behavior, has aroused some anxiety in legal quarters. There are those interested in legal processes who find the models overly simplistic (which, indeed, they are), but the advantages accruing to the administration of legal processes are those that have been discovered to be valuable in other functional areas of our society. Stone (1964), for instance, points out the savings to the lawyer in time spent in a long bibilographic search. Even more, the prediction of outcomes at the initial and appellate level may save a great deal of needless time spent in litigation and appeal. What Stone is concerned about, however, is that the approach will solidify the course of judicial decision making so that the usual impetus to change in law mirroring changes in society will not come as easily when future decisions are overly constrained by predictions from past decisions. This seems a more valid concern than those expressed in opposition on the basis of novelty of psychological and mathematical predictive models.

LAW IN MASS SOCIETY

An aspect of the legal order that is the object of even more concern is the area of administration of justice in a complex and changing society. With a rise in numbers and the increased mobility of the population, the opportunities for social friction and discontent with the legal order mount. Even ordinarily simple administrative problems in the distribution of justice become overpowering through sheer numbers alone. The preservation of the ideals of individual rights becomes difficult when law officials must operate with procedures tailored for one-tenth of the case load that actually exists. The situation becomes a fertile ground for what might be described as "bargain-basement justice." Not only is justice apt to be more casually applied, but the element of bargaining also enters in where, in return for a guilty plea, the prosecuting officials are often willing to recommend a shorter sentence or probation. The decision hinges more on the effectiveness of defense counsel in "getting a deal made" than on the appropriateness of correctional methods or placement in therapeutic settings.

More subtle, and perhaps more important, is the related matter of the differential in enforcement that develops along socioeconomic lines. Police blotters are more likely to contain the names of those who live at the bottom of the social ladder. The basis for this does not lie completely in the fact that we expect more crime as the result of unfavorable economic conditions. Still more significant is the differential in law enforcement imposed by different attitudes and values of officials. Often what promotes prosecution is that activity which most violates the sensitivities of the prosecutor. What at one stratum of the social order is regarded as inoffensive may be looked upon by others, because of their different set of values and attitudes, as a very obnoxious or even immoral act. An official with middle class values may find those influencing legal outcomes.

It is important to remember at this point, however, that our legal system, along with others generally, is an adversary system. Each side relies on representation by counsel, each of whom is charged with the responsibility of working diligently toward an outcome favorable to his client. Various notions of what constitutes a victory, however, exist in the minds of all litigants or those, as in society at large, who have an interest in the outcome. What may be correctional in the opinion of some may not coincide with ideas of others, so that decisions as to the validity of "justice" may not be made easily.

Since representation is crucial, a point that has long been of concern has been the lack of representation of indigent defendants. Various recent Supreme Court decisions have stimulated action by states and municipalities toward the establishment of means of assuring some representation for defendants, particularly in serious criminal matters.

Recent events have indicated also that there is room for even greater activity in the legal representation of groups of people, who may be tenants, consumers, or just plain citizens of a community. The traditional one-to-one relationship between lawyer and client will be subject to change as a result of the problems raised in "mass society." Group legal services have the potential for providing legal services for those who need them most (Schwartz, 1965).

PRIVATE GOVERNMENT

One of the most visible aspects of mass society is the immense number of organizations and groups, many of them of tremendous size, each with a power to control, to one extent or another, the activities of many individuals. These normative systems represent a special kind of "law" with an influence that may be equal to or greater than the influences in the legal order of the polity. The examples of business or industrial organizations immediately come to mind even though there are numerous other areas to consider in this context—education, religion, mass communications media, and various social and beneficial organizations. Certainly the extent of economic power alone gives industrial organizations an impact on the social scene which the other types of organizations seldom possess. There are some who believe that this authority far transcends the ordinary bounds of economic activity and represents a type of control comparable to that exercised by early governmental bodies. The influence on individuals in or out of the organizations may be all out of proportion to the numbers involved. According to at least one observer, the concentration of power in a few individuals in a few corporations would make "the medieval feudal system look like a Sunday school party" (Berle, 1964, p. 102). With over two-thirds of the productive assets owned by not more than 500 corporations and the decision making in each of those organizations resting in a few persons, the sheer economic power exceeds any seen in world history. The conclusion Berle comes to on the basis of this realization of the power of a private entity is that a corporation or other body should be subject to the same types of restraints that are applicable to governmental bodies under the Constitution. Due process of law, individual rights, or judicial review might be envisioned as concepts that are directly applicable.

The occupational position of an individual may well be the most significant aspect of his ego functioning and self-perception. When questioned as to who he is, a man more often will reply in terms of his job—"lawyer," or "carpenter," for example. Often one of the first things others will wish to know is what a man does or what his occupation is. The importance of the job reference and its continuance seems clear. The need to maintain it is such that dismissal from employment is often referred to as "industrial capital punishment," and such action is seldom entered into without considerable thought. Indeed, the emotional (and economic) aspects of job loss are undoubtedly the reasons for the success of unionization and the power through collective action that results.

The labor union, as an institution, can be just as restrictive. There may be barriers to entry into the group in the first place and, consequently, no opportunity to work at that trade. A union member who may not completely agree with a particular union policy may find himself cut off from the opportunity to earn a living, a matter that often affects his future more than a sentence or punishment by a civil or criminal court.

Other institutions may be just as powerful even though their direct economic power is slight. Educational bodies have come into the limelight more and more in recent times with respect to the personal functioning of individuals connected with them. The growing importance of an education in our society makes separation from it as serious a matter as dismissal from a job.

Riots and "free-speech movements" on college campuses underscore the shortcomings inherent in approaches institutions may have utilized in the past; the concept that the university stands *in loco parentis* for the student and, therefore, may use methods parental in nature and form is being challenged in many organizations simultaneously. Questions of due process and notice are being raised with respect to even ordinary academic procedures, much less the unusual ones which arise when campus activities spill over the boundaries of the academic.

The fundamental question here concerns the approach that should be taken. Is academic dismissal, for instance, to be dealt with in terms similar to those imposed in a criminal court or should more flexible procedures be followed, thus mirroring a familial concept of control? Recent events indicate a trend away from informal and sometimes arbitrary decision making by academic administrators. Increasingly successful challenges in court by aggrieved students have either forced or suggested formal (and effort-consuming) procedures on the campus. The concern for individual rights has finally reached into the academic structure, though the implementation of a formal approach does bring with it some possible losses.

Not only do such problems affect the student members of the group but faculty as well. Historically, staff members have been even more concerned with academic freedom and due process even though these concepts have not been crystallized as they have in courts of law. Earlier general principles have not provided adequate procedural guidelines, and the American Association of University Professors, for one, has set up a special committee to aid in the task of establishing clear conceptual bases of action (AAUP, 1965).

LAW IN AN INDUSTRIAL SOCIETY

Industry today functions under constraints imposed by social groups or other aggregates. Political regulation of enterprise has been exercised in one way or another along with unwritten rules of behavior as well. Certainly the formal and legal regulations have been of greatest visibility even though the influence of the informal rules and sanctions persists; the forces of custom, mores, and folkways have power to influence behavior in complex industrialized societies as much as they do in preliterate and simple ones.

Historical Foundations

The basis for much of present-day legal influence on business in the United States lies in the Anglo-American tradition of common law, although other systems have affected it. Common law differs from the civil law tradition of the continental countries in that more emphasis is placed, in common law, on prior judicial decisions and the prevailing patterns of the community. This is often expressed in the term *stare decisis,* let the decision stand. Civil law jurists are apt to rely more on logical analogies and legal scholars in interpreting the codified laws of their jurisdiction.

Many civil law countries have special codes covering business which are administered by separate courts. No distinctions between businessmen and others now exist in the Anglo-American system of jurisprudence, but there was a separate "law merchant" in English law until two hundred years ago. The law merchant developed in medieval times when the vigorous expansion of trade on land found merchants still constrained by the already crumbling feudal concepts of regulation of activity. The "custom of merchants" decided many controversies among tradesmen, regardless of their political fealty, in the same manner that maritime law, developing from customary behavior, decided among seafaring litigants. Early industrial enterprise was concentrated in small units— single individuals with one or two helpers or single families. The craft guilds of medieval times imposed their own private law upon the bodies of workers and, for these groups or others indirectly concerned, the regulation was effective. The extent and influence of the guilds, even in the middle ages, may have been overdrawn, however. Tawney (1947) states that only a small minority of medieval workers were ever members of a craft guild. Nine-tenths of the population were peasants on the land, and even in the cities a high proportion must have been casual workers never organized into the friendly societies of craftsmen. Nevertheless, certain other legal concepts were powerful. Strong prohibitions against the charging of interest existed in church law as well as the law of the state. Notions of a "fair price" that may have been propounded by Acquinas and others crept into medieval regulation of the marketplace by the sovereign lord.

The industrial revolution brought with it a change in attitudes along with the development of wealth and power. Fortunes were tied less and less to the land; legal and social actions were geared increasingly to the development of climates favorable for industrial investment. Medieval constraints on interest and fair price gave way to a laissez-faire approach allowing for little, if any, regulation of activity. These values were undoubtedly reinforced by the post-Reformation attitudes favoring individual enterprise and responsibility.

Inevitably, some reaction had to take place. A concern with unlimited power and its undesirable social concomitants may have been present in the minds of some all along, yet the effective responses to unbridled economic activity have been so recent as to place them within the present era. This pattern will emerge, therefore, in the immediately following description of contemporary events.

Contemporary Regulation

The interest of society, as mirrored by agencies of government, in industrial enterprise is manifest in virtually every area of activity. From the creation of the business entity to its external relationships in society, the organization is the object of scrutiny by officials of government.

Creation. Government regulation begins with the very establishment of the business entity. Corporations, particularly, must fulfill certain requirements to become a legal "person" and do business. Fiscal actions are also scrutinized carefully from the start, with issuance of stock monitored by the Securities and Exchange Commission. Further, other regulatory agencies may be empowered to oversee the actions of specific types of business enterprises.

Antitrust Regulation. Reactions in the area of legal regulation in present-day industrial and commercial behavior may be shown against the broad historical backdrop of generalized attitudes with respect to economic functioning. Certainly political and social objectives have had an influence on attitudes toward competition. On the one hand, competition has been viewed as being the hallmark of the free enterprise system; on the other, it has been approached with reservations stemming from ideas of equality of opportunity, avoidance of concentrated economic power, and reliance on "fair play." This abundance of ambivalence has generated legal and other social controls on economic behavior, ostensibly to maintain the balance thought desirable. There may be some question, however, as to the actual end result of governmental or social activity of this nature, not only with respect to the broad socioeconomic functioning but also in the many concomitant conditions. At any rate, the writing of legislation in this area has been variable, showing changes in intent as social conditions have changed. Since it did not arise as a coordinated or coherent effort, antitrust legislation not only mirrors the variation in values over time, it makes a complex and perplexing area of study as well.

The most significant activity with respect to business enterprises undoubtedly has been in the area of preservation of competition among business organizations. While concern over economic power was felt early in this nation's history, not until the latter part of the nineteenth century did any significant regulatory activity take place. The rise of huge combinations or trusts after the Civil War resulted in a combination or concentration of power that could not be ignored by Congress, and the Sherman Act of 1890 became the first of a series of statutes in the antitrust area. The act established the illegality of any combination in restraint of trade and proscribed any individual or group activity that monopolized trade or commerce.

The Sherman Act was a significant landmark in the history of government regulation and provided some checks on excessive activity but, since some vagueness inherent in its general terms limited prosecution under the act, need was felt for further legislation. In 1914 the Clayton Act and the Federal Trade Commission Act were passed to plug some of the loopholes. The Clayton Act proscribed more specific activities in restraint of trade, such as price discrimination, while the Federal Trade Commission Act established the Federal Trade Commission, an independent agency that was empowered to enforce the Clayton Act and maintain competition in other ways.

As time went on, newer business practices called for additional definitions. In 1936 the Robinson-Patman Act refined the prohibitions against price discrimination and added criminal penalties to the Clayton Act; yet, reflecting the tenor of economic events, there were some other aspects to the act that could be interpreted as protecting established economic structures and reducing competition.

Later development of the economy after World War II disclosed bases of power that may not have been evident earlier. A more general approach to limiting concentration was evident in the latest antitrust statute. The Celler-Kefauver Act of 1950 was intended as a means of limiting those mergers of assets of corporations that tended toward monopoly in "any line of commerce in any section of the country."

It should be noted here that there have been, at various times, deviations from the main thrust of antitrust. The National Recovery Act of 1933 provided some exemptions from antitrust laws that were intended to promote economic recovery during the Depression. Other attempts in those troubled times promoted "fair-trade" in order to maintain retail sales prices agreed to between manufacturers and retailers. Numerous other exemptions in specific occupational categories exist, beginning with the Capper-Volstead Act of 1922, permitting farmers to asociate in the processing and marketing of agricultural products.

Patents and copyrights also represent, in a sense, the other side of the coin of antitrust. Here the government expressly confers limited monopoly upon the developer of an invention or the creator of the literary or artistic product. Trademarks, the specific identifiers of a product, service, or company, are similarly protected. If, however, patents and trademarks are employed in restraint of trade the constitutional protection will be withdrawn.

Marketing and the Consumer. Activities of industrial enterprises are regulated in still other ways in the marketplace. In a general effort to eliminate unfair competition with other business entities, federal statutes, particularly an amendment to the Federal Trade Commission Act of 1938, have reinforced the common law prohibitions against misrepresentation of merchandise, disparaging the competitor or interfering with his business activities, or engaging in other unfair and deceptive practices.

More in the way of consumer protection is contained in other legislation. The Food and Drug Act of 1906 was the beginning of a series of statutes in the consumer interests. Since it concerned only the misbranding of foods and drugs, the many gaps were indifferently filled down through the years. While some legislation designed to control misleading practices in various industries has been passed in the interim, there has been nothing to match the flood of legislation protecting the consumer that emerged from the 90th Congress, particularly in 1967. Auto and highway safety, meat inspection, and air pollution probably represent the greatest activity in the consumer interest in these areas.

The course of this legislation clearly shows the increasing interest in government agencies with respect to the protection of the consumer from any practice likely to put him at a disadvantage. The trend might be described as a move away from the laissez-faire notions of *caveat emptor,* or let the buyer beware, to the point where the maxim might be more accurately stated as *caveat vendor.* The same tendency is recognizable in court decisions indicating that liability for injury from use of manufactured products or services is being extended, all to the further benefit of the consumer.

Personnel relationships. The conditions under which individuals work and their activity vis-à-vis others and the corporate entity are still other areas in which extensive government interest exists. Hours of work, compensation, working surroundings, and selection are some of the more pertinent areas of regulation. Job disputes and collective efforts of workers to resolve these add a complicating dimension to the fundamental interactional problems.

Concern over working conditions mounted considerably after the various exposés of the circumstances surrounding labor at the turn of the century. Eventually, the prohibitions against child labor found a place in the Fair Labor Standards Act of 1938. The same act established what it considered a living wage (40 cents per hour then) and determined further that the limit for a work week was 40 hours and any excess was to be reimbursed at one and one-half times the regular rate. Many workers were left out of the act, either under its provisions or because they were in intrastate industry. Discrimination in employment has been prohibited by a variety of state and local Fair Employment Practices Acts.

The most significant break with legal history, however, has come in the rights and duties arising from risk and accidents in the work situation. Under traditional concepts of tort liability, negligence has to be shown before recovery can be had. In a hazardous occupation, furthermore, as long as the employer took all reasonable steps and pointed out the risk, it could be said that the employee assumed the risk and could not recover. With the increasing complexity of industrial work, the risks of accidents often mounted. With little possibility of recovery, the injured worker could not support himself, much less pay the expenses. In the early years of this century, most states enacted Workmens' Compensation Acts that substituted a payment plan for injuries at work based on an insurance program. The move away from the finding of fault to an evaluation of disability and an award of money on that basis marks a significant departure from common law concepts.

The right of workers to join together in collective action has developed over the years in ways similar to the manner of emergence of the legislation described above. Unionism was considered an illegal conspiracy under common law until the case of Commonwealth v. Hunt in Massachusetts in 1842. As long as the means and ends were lawful, united action was legal. Union growth was slow, however; the first union of any consequence, the Knights of Labor, was started in 1878 but soon disappeared, leaving the American Federation of Labor in its place in 1886. The AFL developed slowly along trade or craft lines but was virtually alone until the Depression years. Changing industrial practices called for an organization along industry lines, and the Congress of Industrial Organizations (CIO) was formed. When the membership of the two reached the same level, a merger took place.

In the period of labor union growth, attitudes toward unionism were frequently negative. An answer to the workers' most potent weapon, the strike, was a court injunction to restrain workers from their activities. Attitudes (or those of agents of government) swung to a prolabor position along with more generalized economic value changes in the early Depression years. One of the first acts liberating labor expressly outlawed the injunction (Norris-LaGuardia Anti-Injunction Act of 1932). The Wagner Act of 1935 went further in establishing labor unions as a potent force by introducing collective bargaining. Subsequent growth of unions was not checked seriously during or after World War II, but the scales swung a bit the other way as the Taft-Hartley Act in 1947 imposed more controls on unions. The Landrum-Griffin Act in 1959 maintained the balance and added further areas for government regulation.

Summary

The study of behavior in political and legal areas rests on inquiry into the fundamental nature of normative and control systems of a society. While it is not always clear when a social group becomes a political or legal entity, clearly, as complexity of social functioning increases, the need for an organized system of sanctions and enforcing agents grows. The power to control in the society becomes an important factor; when it is exercised legitimately, it is called authority. Legitimacy and the economic effectiveness of a political entity are important factors in its stability. Legitimate power is also one that recognizes restraints on its use, often through pluralism, the distribution of power among subgroups.

Political discussions have only recently focused in part on the systematic collection and analysis of primary behavioral data. This empirical approach concentrates on individual and social behavior rather than on description of structures or philosophical views.

The relationship of personality to politics, since power underlies the process, has fascinated observers of political behavior for some time. Recent approaches have focused on measurable constructs such as the authoritarian personality and its functioning in a political framework. Further analyses of characteristics of political achievers have isolated some concomitants of successful striving in the public arena. Officials may perceive their roles in ways that vary from a free-agent leading the way to a trustee subservient to the will of the constituency. As to educational and social background, political officials in all branches of government are more likely to be products of favored environments.

Economically developed countries are more likely to have a higher degree of participation in political activity. Stability of the political process is related as well to the concomitants of economic development—education and urbanization. Participation does vary, however, with age, sex, and socioeconomic status. Those of middle age with status, property, and a higher educational level take a greater interest in political issues. Minority groups may increase their participation however, when circumstances are favorable for it.

Political preferences are based strongly on primary group influences. Although departures do occur, people are apt to vote as their family and friends vote. Aggregate statistics may be misleading; the concept of "bloc" voting does not take into account the many variables, other than the one scrutinized, that may be important. The cross-pressures from membership in diverse groupings are significantly strong.

Mass political action outside the institutional procedures and bodies has been called "mass politics." Such activity often results from alienation and may produce discord and other dysfunctional consequences.

The view of law as a fixed set of rules has produced conceptualization and action that, while valuable in certain ways, has limited consideration of dynamic social foundations for legal behavior. Such concern has stimulated a move from defining law in terms of given regulations to a recognition of the legal system as a means of providing social control or satisfactions. This behavioral approach focuses on law-in-action rather than on formal or abstract concepts. It brings in all activities surrounding the interaction of individuals in a broadly defined legal framework.

When the concept of law as a form of social control is at the core of research and action, the results may have greater meaning for a society. There are, however, some implications in this approach that must also be faced. The basic philosophy of control, ranging from directive to laissez-faire, colors the actual activity of social agents.

Change in the legal order must also be faced. Social change and legal change may lag behind each other, and the resulting gaps produce social discord. Social relations may be altered by legislation, but the force of folkways and mores persists. In these and other matters, the perceptions by the general populace of the actions of legal agents may be negative ones. Disruption of communication between interest groups may occur. In addition, changes may take place whereby legal formulations are no longer followed in real situations. Adaptations to changed circumstances result in new and different agencies or activities. Present and future conditions may call for an accelerated alteration of concepts and techniques of legal functioning.

Behavioral science can play an active role in serving as the basis for determination of policy. Empirical research ought to be able to provide information that would serve as the basis for legislative activity. Judicial decision making, properly researched, can provide a significant basis for the reinforcement of more effective conflict resolution.

Mass society, through rise in numbers and expectations, provides a severe test for the application of justice. Techniques useful in times long past are no longer adequate, while attitudes toward behavior may no longer coincide with the letter of the law or its enforcement.

Organizational functioning may represent a "private government" and "private law" that can rival or surpass the public bodies and statutes in importance in present social activity. Business firms, colleges and universities, or labor unions may have greater impact on the course of an individual's life than any agency in the public sector.

The development of an industrial society is marked by certain concomitant progressions in the form and functioning of the legal system. The growing importance of trade and commerce to a society leads to a consideration by and inclusion into a legal framework of those concepts that are viewed to be beneficial to economic and social growth. Earlier ethical or behavioral concepts to the contrary are transformed. Only when the disparities are manifest is there a counterreaction in order to bring about a semblance of equilibrium.

The development of business and industry in the United States has been accompanied by the political and legal responses sketched immediately above. Regulation of corporate activity from the very inception of the business entity is a feature of the present environment. Concern over the control of economic life by a small number has stimulated antitrust regulation, even though these manifest a mixed set of values and attitudes toward bigness in business. Economic fluctuations and other social conditions have had their influence on the area as well.

Concern for the consumer appeared somewhat later but has shown great strength more recently. Protection of the individual in his dealing with those operating from a more substantial base is the hallmark of present governmental activity. Similar orientation toward the individual in his work relationships with business entities provided the basis for organization of collective action in order to approach parity with the more secure company.

Bibliography

Adorno, T., Frenkel-Brunswik, E., Levinson, D., and Sanford, R. (1950). *The authoritarian personality*. New York: Harper.

American Association of University Professors. Report of the Special Committee on Procedures for the Disposition of Complaints Under the Principles of Academic Freedom and Tenure, *A.A.U.P. Bulletin,* **51(2)**, May 1965, 210–224.

Baade, H. (1963). Jurimetrics. *Law and Contemporary Problems,* **28**, 1–270.

Ball, H. (1960). Social structure and rent-control violations. *American Journal of Sociology,* **65**, 598–604.

Berelson, B., Lazarsfeld, P., and McPhee, W. (1954). *Voting.* Chicago: University of Chicago Press.

Berle, A. (1964). Economic power and the free society. In Hacker, A. (ed.). *The corporation take-over.* New York: Harper and Row, 101–102.

Brown v. Board of Education of Topeka (1954) (347 U.S. 483).

Campbell, A., Gurin, G., and Miller, W. (1954). *The voter decides.* New York: Harper and Row.

Coleman, J. (1960). The political systems of developing areas. In Almond, G. and Coleman, J. (eds.). *The politics of the developing areas.* Princeton: Princeton University Press.

Davis, F. (1962). Law as a type of social control. In Davis, F., Foster, H., Jr., Jeffrey, C., and Davis, E. *Society and the law.* New York: Free Press.

Eulau, H. (1963). *The behavioral persuasion in politics.* New York: Random House.

Eulau, H., Eldersveld, S., and Janowitz, M. (1956). *Political behavior.* Glencoe, Ill.: Free Press.

Eulau, H., Wahlke, J., Buchanan, W., and Ferguson, L. (1959). The role of the representative: some empirical observations on the theory of Edmond Burke. *American Political Science Review,* **53,** 742–756.

In Re Gault et al. (1967) (387 U.S. 1).

Hall, J. (1963). *Comparative law and social theory.* Baton Rouge, La.: Louisiana State University Press.

Hastings, P. (1956). The voter and the non-voter. *American Journal of Sociology,* **62,** 302–307.

Hyman, H. and Sheatsley, P. (1947). Some reasons why information campaigns fail. *Public Opinion Quarterly,* **11,** 413–423.

Janowitz, M., and Marvick, D. (1953). Authoritarianism and political behavior. *Public Opinion Quarterly,* **17,** 185–201.

Key, V. (1961). *Public opinion and American democracy.* New York: Knopf.

Kornhauser, W. (1959). *The politics of mass society.* Glencoe, Ill.: Free Press.

Kornhauser, W. (1965). *Political society.* Englewood Cliffs, N.J.: Prentice-Hall.

Lane, R. (1959). *Political life: why people get involved in politics.* Glencoe, Ill.: Free Press.

Lasswell, H. (1930). *Psychopathology and politics.* Chicago: University of Chicago Press.

Lasswell, H. (1936). *Politics: who gets what, when, and how.* New York: McGraw-Hill.

Lerner, D. (1958). *The passing of traditional society.* Glencoe, Ill.: The Free Press.

Lipset, S. (1959). Political sociology. In Merton, R. et al. (eds.). *Sociology today: problems and prospects.* New York: Basic Books.

Lipset, S. (1960). *Political man: the social bases of politics.* New York: Doubleday.

Lipset, S. (1967). Political sociology. In Smelser, N. (ed.). *Sociology: an introduction.* New York: Wiley, 438–499.

Lipset, S. and Linz, J. (1956). *The social bases of political diversity in western democracies* (unpubl.). Quoted in Berelson, B. and Steiner, G. (1964). *Human behavior.* New York: Harcourt, Brace, and World.

Macauley, S. (1963). Non-contractual relations in business: a preliminary study. *American Sociological Review,* **28,** 55–67.

Mann, D. (1964). The selection of Federal political executives. *The American Political Scientist,* **58,** 81–99.

March, J. (1955). An introduction to the theory and measurement of influence. *American Political Science Review,* **49,** 431–451.

Matthews, D. (1954). United States Senators and the class structure. *Public Opinion Quarterly,* **18,** 5–22.

McMurray, C. and Parsons, M. (1965). Public attitudes toward the representational roles of legislators and judges. *Midwest Journal of Political Science,* **9(2),** 167–185.

Mills, C. (1956). *The power elite.* New York: Oxford University Press.

Nagel, S. (1962). Testing relations between judicial characteristics and judicial decision-making. *Western Political Quarterly,* **15,** 425–437.

Parsons, T. (1951). *The social system.* Glencoe, Ill.: Free Press.

Podgorecki, A. (1962). Law and social engineering, *Human Organization,* **21,** 177–181.

Pound, R. (1942). *Social control through law.* New Haven: Yale University Press.

Schmidhauser, J. (1959). The justice of the Supreme Court: a collective portrait. *Midwest Journal of political Science,* **1,** 2–49.

Schubert, G. (1960). *Quantitative analysis of judicial behavior.* Glencoe, Ill.: Free Press.

Schwartz, M. (1965). Foreword: group legal services in perspective. *U.C.L.A. Law Review,* **12,** 279–280.

Schwartz, R. and Skolnick J., (1963). Televised communication and income tax compliance. In Arons, L. and Way, M. (eds.). *Television and Human Behavior.* New York: Appleton-Century-Crofts, 155–165.

Selznick, P. (1965). Sociology of law. Forthcoming article prepared for the *International Encyclopedia of the Social Sciences.*

Smith, G. (1948). Liberalism and level of information. *Journal of Educational Psychology,* **39,** 65–82.

Stone, J. (1964). Man and machine in the search for justice. *Stanford Law Review,* **16,** 515–560.

Stone, J. (1966). *Law and the social sciences.* Minneapolis: University of Minnesota Press.

Stouffer, S. (1955). *Communism, conformity, and civil liberties.* New York: Doubleday.

Tappan, P. (1947). *Delinquent girls in court.* New York: Columbia University Press.

Tawney, R. (1947). *Religion and the rise of capitalism.* New York: Harcourt, Brace.

Weber, M. (1954). *Law in economy and society.* Rheinstein, M. (ed.). Cambridge, Mass.: Harvard University Press.

19

Economic Behavior

The importance of economic factors in social functioning has been undisputed even though the specific bases for this functioning and the myriad roles played by individuals or impersonal forces may not always be agreed on. Exchanging of goods and services, though not always on a monetary basis, has long been a significant aspect of human behavior. Most often the focus may be on material things represented in monetary terms, but we could make the mistake of focusing too much on goods and forgetting about services. If we do this, we gloss over contributions to society that are becoming increasingly important. An advanced society cannot ignore the services of professionals and nonprofessionals—medical aid, personal services, industrial consulting, and (not the least) educational services. In none of these is there a "product" except in the most extended sense.

The Economy

In a general way, economics can be regarded as a study of the structures and processes of production and allocation of limited goods or services. While this definition may stimulate divergent refinements, those differences are not likely to be as great as if the term behavior is added. When behavior is mentioned, economists are likely to think of the area of economic principles and analysis of economic events along a broad spectrum representing activity implied in factors such as production, national income, demand, and prices. Other behaviorally oriented researchers may focus on more specific molecular data gathered directly from individual and group behavior. This latter orientation will be the primary basis for discussion in this chapter with some broader analysis serving as a background.

Economic activities have traditionally been placed into three categories—production, distribution, and consumption. The factors in production have been viewed as land, labor, capital, and organization. Closer inspection of these factors, either on an historical or an analytic base will indicate that the relationships between them have been the source of much ideological or even mundane discord. The Marxian notion that it was exploitation of labor to withhold part of output as profits represents only a small part of the wide range of values. In distribution the focus is on money as a medium of exchange; this is a true market situation as opposed to the more primitive mechanisms of gift or barter. An industrial system would be impossible without the use of money as a medium of exchange. Mechanisms as seemingly diverse as advertising agencies and banks are mechanisms supportive of the distribution in a monetary market. Consumption is the "end of the pipeline" of economic activity. While the individual consumer or the household represents the most immediate example of the consumer, it must be remembered that various business, governmental, and private organizations are also significant consuming entities.

HISTORICAL FOUNDATIONS

While one could reach far back into history in discussing the antecedent conditions for present-day events, it is not necessary in reality to go any further back than the late Middle Ages to recognize the first real stirrings of widespread commerce, industrialization, and the rise of capitalism. The Medieval era, with its social structuring and relationships patterned by the principles of feudalism, represented a clearly ordered society. Numerous and savage petty wars, religious persecutions, and raging plagues marred the scene, but generally people lived out their lives in a regularity that was recognized and followed by most individuals without complaint. It was an era summarized by McGuire (1963, pp. 14–18) as one of stability, security, universalism, and religion.

Attitudes and values with respect to trade and industry were somewhat equivocal. The universal church did not exactly discourage commerce, but it did not encourage it either. It was a period where a saintly father of the church, Thomas Acquinas, ranked commerce last among the professions in terms of its contribution to the welfare of society. Charging interest was usury, a grievous sin. Work was considered less as intrinsically good than as expiation for one's sins.

Many different events in the late Middle Ages and early Reformation times occurred together to provide the more immediate foundations of capitalism. Increasing trade and commerce was a result of greater mobility and, in turn, encouraged wider movement of people, not just merchants. The loosening of Feudal ties proceeded apace when it became clear that all parties in the relationship were hampered by it. The increase in urbanization provided the basis for an impetus in manufacturing and trade. Cities grew as people flocked to them, either in anticipation of the enjoyment of greater freedom within their walls or because tilling small tracts no longer provided the revenue for the lord that the grazing of livestock would provide. In the England of Henry VIII much of the disruption with which Thomas More concerned himself came at a time when large landowners were turning out small leaseholders so that the land could be used for sheep grazing. The early stirrings of science and technology went hand in hand with the same vigorous and inquiring spirit that drove seafarers to all parts of the world. Part of this restlessness and quest for change and the challenging of the status quo manifested itself, often in violent terms, in an overturning of established religion and the development of a new creed.

The attitudes and values of a system of beliefs that put the focus on individual responsibility and the virtues of hard work and thrift were characteristic of the more puritan types of denominations developing under the Protestant Reformation. The relationship between the emergence of Protestantism and the strengthening of capitalism is undoubtedly no mere coincidence. These ties have been remarked upon extensively by many, notably Max Weber (1948) and Tawney (1947). It could be argued whether one thrust preceded the other, but the important thing is that these value systems coincided and provided support for the development of each other.

During this period, the advances of science and technology provided further impetus for industrialization. The advent of the Industrial Revolution is somewhat arbitrarily placed at the middle of the eighteenth century, presumably because it was at this point in time that so many important inventions were made. The steam engine provided unprecedented power for the complicated and profitable machines that spun or wove. While all this required the increasing concentration of workers under one roof and living in cramped quarters near the factory, the truth is that the beginnings of a massed work force and the expenditure of large sums to start an enterprise were becoming commonplace centuries before.

Significant industrial expansion came, of course, with the development of steam power based on coal as the fuel and iron as the material. This was the age of coal and iron which Mumford (1934) described as the Paleotechnic era, an age superseding the eotechnic age of wood, wind, and water. But even before this widely acknowledged beginning of the Industrial Revolution, the foundations of capitalism were being laid. Brown (1954) describes the sizes of early enterprises and the capital required to launch them. As early as 1371, a weaving mill at Amiens had 120 workers while, not long after, a certain Jack of Newbury built one with 200 looms and 600 workers. Blast furnaces and copper mills required several thousand pounds of capital to start up production in the late sixteenth century while at the time of Charles I a London brewery required capital of 10,000 pounds (present-day exchange rates do not begin to reflect the importance of an investment of this magnitude).

The middle of the eighteenth century can be used, however, as a starting point for discussions of the philosophical foundations of economics and business. Adam Smith, in his massive work *An inquiry into the nature and causes of the wealth of nations* in 1766, set forth his notions of what constituted the basis for the functioning of a business system. Smith postulated a natural system in economic affairs whereby each individual was motivated to serve his own interests and to pursue his own advantage in the marketplace. This pursuit of self-interest was not without control, however. Smith believed that the "invisible hand" of the market, stemming from competition between the parties, would regulate and control the activities of individuals in the public interest. With respect to labor, Smith felt that increasing specialization of work would lead to greater productivity. Increased productivity would not only result in larger output but greater profit which, in turn, would permit fair wages. The overriding principle is that of laissez-faire, where supply and demand would regulate and adjust the relationships if government would not interfere.

Further support for the laissez-faire approach to business and the economy came with the adaptation by Herbert Spencer of the elements of Darwin's theory of evolution. Spencer argued that the process of selection was a "natural" one and only the fittest of the species would survive. Any tampering with this process, he argued, was an interference with one of the basic laws of society. It was a theoretical stance that fitted in neatly with the attitudes and values of many of the captains of industry of this period in the United States during the few decades following the Civil War which were marked by an almost unbridled growth in the economic and political power of industrial enterprises. "Social Darwinism" was the justification for any method used by the businessman to get to the top. Unbounded reliance on this philosophy generated the concerned counterreactions which led eventually to the type of government regulation of enterprise described in the previous chapter.

The most significant set of concepts to be introduced from that time to the present (important enough to be called the "new" economics) was the evolutionary set of propositions propounded by John Maynard Keynes (1936) in his *The general theory of employment, interest, and money,* where he pieced together some already enunciated concepts into a novel framework. Coming as it did during the Great Depression, the main thrust of his work dealt with proposals to alleviate economic distress and unemployment. One of the main aspects on which he focused was the consideration of wages as not merely costs of production but as a representation of the purchasing power of individuals. This, he believed, was one of the important bases for the demand for goods and services, a condition upon which an economically healthy business and industry depended. The emphasis on purchasing power requires direct governmental activity in support of public works while deficit spending is not necesarily to be avoided. Despite a certain lack of enthusiasm for the "new" economics in many business circles, the concepts have been adopted, at least in part, by many businessmen without their recognition of the fact.

INDUSTRIALIZATION

In ancient times economic units were small, self-contained, family or extended-family organizations. The commerce of classical times flourished throughout the then-known world, but those engaged in trade operated most often within a geographical area of limited scope. These enterprises were limited by the individual or small group efforts of the artisan, his family, and any slaves bound to the effort.

The scope of activity or the nature of economic roles did not change much in medieval and feudal times. Occupational roles were sketched simply and continued to be based on social custom. One was a farmer or a blacksmith or a tailor and remained so for the extent of his life. Not only did one have a clear sense of occupation, this was passed on to the rest of the family; children followed in their father's footsteps. In addition to the fixing of economic behavior through custom and tradition, feudalism reinforced the social relationships through the maintenance of a fixed set of rights and duties of lord and laborer.

The breakdown of feudal society brought with it an increased freedom of the individual to move both geographically and socially. Instead of being tied personally to the lord under rigid customary rules, the individual could and did bargain for his labor or the products of his activities. The opportunity to engage in employment in other parts of the world and to sell one's labor is a prerequisite for the development of an industrial society, and other factors in industrialization depend on this condition. While this increased mobility, occupationally and socially, provided the basis for industrial development, it should be noted that other conditions resulted from this that may have proved disadvantageous to some. In the feudal system there was at least a clear recognition of one's place, a certainty of role, and a security that comes with that knowledge. A temporal lord and a spiritual church into whose care an individual is entrusted may alleviate much of the ordinary anxiety generated in everyday events. Close ties with family and neighbors reinforce this pattern. The need to depend on one's own abilities can be challenging and productive of effort in the long run; it can also produce a pattern of anomie, alienation, or anxiety in those cast adrift in a changing and competitive world.

This set of circumstances provided the basis for outlines of the relationship between the rise of capitalism and the development of a set of values which Weber (1948) called the "Protestant Ethic." In this set of values individualism occupies a prominent position. One is responsible to his Creator for his activities here on earth, and an indication of one's standing in the next world is his attainment, primarily economic, in this world. The emphasis is placed on hard work that comes from initiative, self discipline, and competition with others. Weber and others have indicated that these values enabled an entrepreneurial class to develop and, when the other conditions for an industrial society emerged, the foundations for capitalism and an industrialized society took place.

Some further conditions are necessary for the full emergence of an industrialized economy. Certain scientific or technological conditions or changes must take place along with the development of entrepreneurs and mobile laborers as sketched above. Technological advancements to permit the more effective use of labor to convert materials into finished products, the necessity for the management of the laborers in one location, the need for capital investment of great magnitude to provide these conditions, and the need to broaden concepts of marketing and distribution of the products in freer trade are all interrelated factors in the emergence of an industrial society.

The departure from the feudal system may be seen in many specific ways. An industrial organization depends increasingly on specialization of effort. The broad industrial categories of the Middle Ages became no longer applicable; one craftsman could not be responsible for the entire production effort as before nor was industrial efforts furthered by the limitation of occupation to hereditary lines, that is, on the basis of ascribed status. Concentrating on achieved status rather than placement on the basis of birth fits in better with the concepts of capitalism and the requirements of an industrialized economy.

The rise of industrialism was not without its broad social ramifications. In addition to its role in the decline of primary relations in the family or the peer group, industrialism was the primary force in the creation of other social institutions. Chief among these are the large industrial enterprise, the corporation, and the often countervailing collective efforts of workers, the labor union.

The Firm

The requirements of large-scale industrial activity are of such magnitude that organization of effort must be accomplished. The organization may adopt the legal form of a corporation, although this is not necessary. What is required is that some differentiation of function in specialization of effort be made along with a continuity of work force under managerial activity.

BASIC FACTORS

In the early days of industrialization most companies were family enterprises, begun by a single individual and often continued by his direct and collateral heirs. This type of family management is often called patrimonial. It is easy to see that the family-managed enterprise represents the first stage in the transition of a business organization from the earlier reliance on the family as a primary social and work group (Harbison and Myers, 1959).

Some family managed companies still exist though their ranks are dwindling. More characteristic of present-day affairs are the industrial organizations that are managed by professional and, presumably, impersonal managers. This type of management has been labeled by Max Weber and others as bureaucratic management. Bureaucratic management came into being of necessity as the complexity implicit in change or the greater financial requirements of the industry necessitated a greater participation by individuals beyond the limited family. In the process of moving from the family type of management to a bureaucracy, the organization undoubtedly moved from the close, personal, and probably warm relationship between the family head and others to a more impersonal functioning of the professional under a stable and clear-cut system of rules and procedures. "Sound management principles" and "efficient methods" are represented as being characteristics of the bureaucratic style in the administration of an industrial organization.

SOCIOTECHNICAL SYSTEMS

The impact of industrialization on primary and secondary relationships continues. Changing technology leaves its imprint, as we have seen, on structure and function. Influence is present in the other direction, however, as people influence the operations of the technology. This two-way interrelationship is important and has caused some researchers to concentrate on it. The situation has been described briefly as a "socio-technical system" (Emery and Trist, 1962, pp. 18–25).

Consideration of an industrial work situation within the framework of a sociotechnical system involves scrutiny of the specific technology used, the way in which the work patterns are organized, the formal structuring of inter-personal relationships, and the informal patterns that emerge in the work group.

Automation represents the ultimate triumph of technology if one considers the popular stereotype of a factory without workers. Despite the traumatic picture of computers organizing and running a system without human intervention, the complexity of industrial activity today often requires a greater number of human beings, albeit different ones, than under nonautomated techniques. Some processes cannot be adapted to a complete turnover to automated methods because of the diversification of activity, while still other tasks require more than routine solutions. There is no one clear situation called automation; the variety and nature of the various uses of automatic techniques defy any simple description (Bright, 1958). The technological changes involved in automation can be described somewhat by superimposing them on some traditional descriptions of differences in technological activity. Broad designation of activity in industry has been made most frequently on a threefold basis. First, in craft technology, the craftsman is a skilled worker with individualized output under conditions where the individual maintains his own pace. Second, on an assembly-line, the worker is one who performs the limited and usually less-skilled task under conditions established by others. A worker who has to assemble a small part on a product moving past him on a conveyor belt has little or no control over the pace of work. Third, in continuous-process technology, operations take place in a complex system of reservoirs and pipelines. The individual is far removed from the actual process except for controls of the networks of raw materials and product. In the petrochemical industry, for instance, the flow of materials proceeds without any direct influence by human hand. The skilled worker does play a significant role, however, in that he controls or monitors the activity taking place.

It should be remembered that these three traditional types of industrial technology represent convenient categories. In reality, work situations in any significant industrial setting represent complex combinations of types of activity. When we add the many variations that are possible in automating an industrial work situation, we find the type of technology extremely mixed.

The impact of technology on individual and group functioning in the work situation can be a significant problem area. Introduction of automated techniques does not differ, in its impact, from other change processes that occur. New requirements in terms of skills and work patterns often generate anxiety in those facing change. Often, too, the changes represent only the beginning points in a series of continuing changes. Generally, the new technology requires workers who are more flexible, adaptable, and more highly skilled. Indeed, one of our society's most significant problems may be the fact that there are fewer and fewer opportunities for utilizing the unskilled. Those employees who remain probably experience the greater responsibilities and, because any interruption in work performance is expensive, the need for coordination among units of the organization and interaction with other workers is heightened. These same factors, however, provide some concomitant features that may not be as welcome. The simplification of work activity that comes with automation also removes much of the direct contact with work and the freedom of movement or control over that activity (Champion, 1967). The loss of meaning or purposefulness in one's work is the feeling of alienation (Chapter 12), one of the salient aspects of the impact of technology remarked upon much earlier by Karl Marx. This feeling of lack of responsibility or meaning in the job probably is present more often in assembly-line operations than it is in the craft or continuous-process work situations. The limited task on the assembly line and the restricted opportunity for participating in meaningful social and occupational relationships undoubtedly provide a basis for a detachment from the larger group. It should be remembered, however, that there is danger in overemphasizing this factor as well. The relative number of employees in a pure assembly-line position is small—probably no more than 5 percent of the work force is thus engaged. This small percentage may receive much more attention in critical commentaries of American industry than its proportion warrants.

THEORIES OF THE FIRM

Traditional economic theories of the firm have generally emphasized action of an aggregate unit using rational elements for decision making to achieve a goal. The unit is a coordinate one often called the entrepreneur acting under the stimulus of an incentive. The incentive is represented in monetary terms and may reflect economic results such as costs, price, or, more generally, profit. Rational behavior of the firm means selecting from among alternatives those which will provide the most incentive. This is the assumption that the firm will maximize, that is, achieve the most by making a rational choice. Not quite so evident in the traditional economic theory of the firm is the assumption that the environment is such that the firm can make decisions on price and quantity in the market without being concerned about competition from other firms or about the impact on the market of its own actions. It also assumes that there are no dysfunctional consequences of the activity of the firm, since the entrepreneur is viewed as if it were a single organism. In short, the strengths of the traditional economic view of the firm are also a weakness. A unitary model in quantitative terms can be manipulated and certain results measured, but the number of interacting variables in a real situation that are not considered in the economic theory make for a complexity that leaves many behavioral researchers dissatisfied with concepts of the economic model.

Views of the firm that take into consideration a larger number of variables on a molecular or aggregate basis as well may be more difficult to put to use but may be more representative of actual situations in the long run. The frame of reference that is often labeled as behavioral views the behavior of individual actors in the unit being analyzed in a complex environmental structure and process. Assessment of personality, interest, and abilities of individuals as they interact in situations involving intertwining individual and group goals provide some basis for behavioral concepts of the firm.

Significant approaches with a behavioral emphasis have been topics for discussion in earlier chapters, particularly Chapter 16. A short reiteration at this point will help to set the general material into the specific economic perspective of the firm. Much of the present-day discussion of organizational functioning can trace its ancestry to Max Weber's early writings on bureaucracy. The more recent discussion of dynamics by Merton (1957) and that by Selznick (1949) focus on the dysfunctional consequences of the striving of the aggregate of individuals toward a goal. In these, more attention is paid to the forces tending to fractionate the firm, since these are considered more important in the total end result, than to the integrative activities of the firm. A somewhat different organizational approach is exemplified by Barnard's (1938) concepts of cooperation among elements of the unit in order to assure the survival of the entity. This view concentrates more on the forces having to maintain an equilibrium toward a continuing functioning of the firm. Barnard identifies three factors that are required in proper combination for a firm to survive— common purpose, willingness to serve, and communications. Despite a possible disparity in individual motivations, these three factors represent the shared willingness of all members to perpetuate the organization. Simon (1957) has extended Barnard's notions while continuing to emphasize the complexity of patterns of interaction in the organization. By far the most interesting contribution by Simon, especially with reference to an economic organization, lies in his rejection of the importance of rationality in decision making by members. Individuals in organizations, says Simon, do not maximize but curtail their search and choose among alternatives when the satisfactory and less than optimum situation presents itself. Organizations, says Simon, "satisfice" rather than maximize. This may well be a more realistic representation of the actual situation faced by decision makers in business. Rationality in traditional economic theory is represented by situations where a decision maker is aware of the probability of each result and the payoff that accompanies it. The concept also implies that the payoffs are ordered and, therefore, are amenable to comparison for the final selection to take place. It might be guessed intuitively that decision making is never carried to these lengths, even if the possibilities were theoretically available. Moreover, there is some good empirical evidence that satisficing does take place and that it is possible to predict the actual decision making of executives. Clarkson (1963) developed a model that stimulated trust investment behavior. With it, he was able to predict securities that would be chosen by investment trust officers when he assumed that alternatives would be considered in a certain sequence until an acceptable level goal was reached.

The concept of roles within organizational functioning has been used in few behavioral analyses of functioning of firms. The notion of role has been attended to by others in the past but has not been fully developed in the industrial or business context. Gross et al. (1958) have used role theory, for instance, as the basis for describing the complex functioning of an educational organization. Katz and Kahn (1966) have developed some of the ramifications of roles and functioning in an industrial organization but this delineation is a mere part of a broader approach they follow. They have sketched a more comprehensive formulation which they have called open-system theory. The theory conceives of energic input leading to an output and its absorption by the larger environment. The significant central part of the process points to motives and behavior of the individual carriers of the input.

In another extensive effort, Cyert and March have developed several models describing the behavior of a "large, multi-product firm operating under uncertainty in an imperfect market" (1963, p. 115). Behavior of the firm is viewed primarily from the standpoint of the decision-making processes of the organization. Several variables are considered under the categories of organizational goals, expectations, and choice. Even more closely related to the business decision making itself is the set of four relational concepts developed by them: quasi-resolution of conflict, uncertainty avoidance, problemistic search, and organizational learning. The relationship between the factors can be described generally in the flow chart appearing in Figure 19-1. The quasi-resolution of conflict comes about from a recognition of goals as independent constraints. Conflict is resolved by adhering to decision rules while solving one problem at a time. Resolution is furthered by assigning primary responsibility for decisions along lines of specialization; that is, a production department would be primarily responsible for production goals and procedures. Uncertainty is avoided by organizations in the short run by reacting to immediate feedback; long-range reactions are handled by atempts to "negotiate the environment." These are approaches whereby certainty is reduced through common adherence to conventional practices of the industry or following cutsomary procedures internally and in the market. This does not mean, as the authors point out, collusion between the companies; it is simply a general pattern of behavior to which the competitors conform. The search is the third fundamental aspect

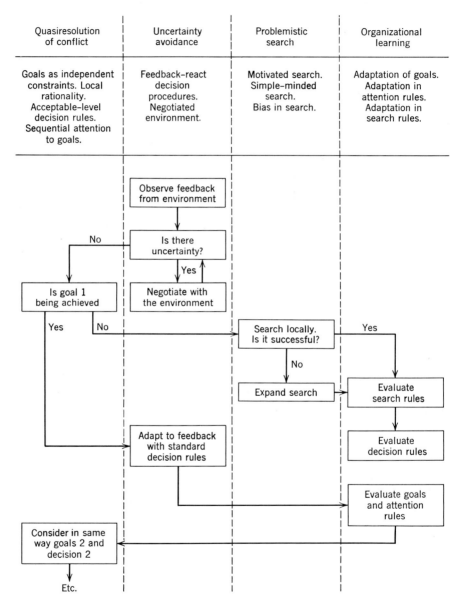

Quasiresolution of conflict	Uncertainty avoidance	Problemistic search	Organizational learning
Goals as independent constraints. Local rationality. Acceptable–level decision rules. Sequential attention to goals.	Feedback–react decision procedures. Negotiated environment.	Motivated search. Simple–minded search. Bias in search.	Adaptation of goals. Adaptation in attention rules. Adaptation in search rules.

Figure 19-1. Organizational decision process in abstract form (Cyert, R. and March, J., 1963, p. 126).

of the concept of choice for decision making. In addition to being problem directed, the authors asume that it is also motivated, simple minded, and biased. The three factors simply mean that search is stimulated by a problem, is based on simple concepts of relationships, and reflects special experiences or training within the organization. The final relational concept of organizational learning refers directly to the adaptive behavior of organizations as the result of experiences over time. Adaptation can occur with respect to goals and aspiration levels as well as in attention or search under rules. Changes in all areas are the result of experience that represents the learning behavior on the part of the organization.

Behavioral concepts of the firm are, of course, more extensive and diverse than this short reminder may indicate. At the same time, virtually all share characteristics that put the focus on behavior of individuals and groups in a complex set of interactions. The concentration on psychological and social factors present in the behavior of actors within a large aggregate engaged in a move toward a complex goal represents the behavioralists' answer to a somewhat less extensive model such as economic theory of a firm. Perhaps Barnard (1938, p. 65) has expressed it as concisely as possible when he defined his system as "a complex of physical, biological, personal, and social components which are in specific systematic relationships."

THE WORK FORCE

An outstanding characteristic of a developing economy is the continuing increase over time in the number and proportion of individuals occupied in nonagricultural occupations. In underdeveloped countries, the percentage of inhabitants engaged in agricultural pursuits represents a high majority of the population. This has been true in the history of any preindustrialized nation. In the United States, for instance, more than three-fourths of the population was engaged in agriculture at the founding of the nation. As industrialization proceeds in this setting, the advantages of science and technology accrue to the farmer who is then able to produce more per unit of work. This and developing opportunities in the nonagricultural spheres of manufacturing and services swell the number of nonfarm workers and help to increase the number of urban dwellers. A significant part of this change has taken place even in recent times in the United States. From 1950 to 1966 the number of persons employed in agriculture was cut in half, from 8 million in 1950 to 4 million in 1966. The 1966 figure means that about 5.8 percent of the total work force was employed in agriculture (United States Bureau of the Census, 1967).

The United States labor force is composed of those individuals who are gainfully employed or who are able to work and are seeking it. It also includes members of the armed forces. The labor force does not include anyone under 14 years of age, students, institutionalized persons, the retired, housewives, or those who are unemployable. A significant feature of labor force statistics down through the years has been the increase in the percentage of women in the total work force. At the turn of the century, less than 20 percent of the work force were females, but by 1966 the total number had increased to almost 26 million, a figure representing 37.3 percent of the labor force (United States Bureau of the Census, 1967, p. 229). An additional feature of the work force is the higher age of entry into the labor force. With more individuals extending their education, often well beyond high school, entry into gainful employment is postponed.

The labor force may be described further by determining the number of individuals employed within the broad industrial categories. Industries may be considered as:

1. Primary—agriculture, fishing, and forestry.
2. Secondary—manufacturing, construction, and mining.
3. Tertiary—trade, finance, transport, and all services.

Table 19-1 confirms the continuation of trends in the United States toward a substantial drop in the primary industries. At the same time, it indicates

Table 19-1. Industrial Distribution of Workers in 1900 and 1960 (United States Bureau of the Census, 1965)

Major Industrial Category	Percentages	
	1900	1960
Primary industries	38	9.7
Secondary industries	30.6	33.7
Tertiary industries	31.4	56.6

a maintenance of secondary industries at relatively the same level and a significant increase in the tertiary or service industries (United States Bureau of the Census, 1965).

Another look at the labor force that is often meaningful is one where the categories are on an occupational scale. Figure 19-2 gives percentages of employed persons by major occupational groups to indicate their distribution,

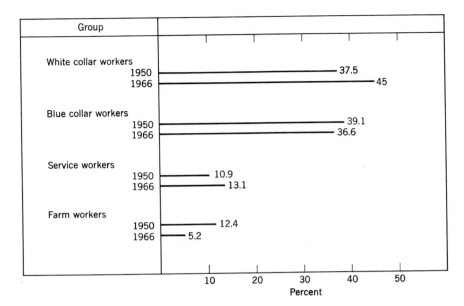

Figure 19-2. Employed persons by major occupational groups, 1950 and 1966 (U.S. Bureau of the Census, 1967, p. 230).

and some idea of trends can be gained by a comparison of recent statistics with similar figures obtained earlier. Striking differences have occurred in as short a period as 16 years; changes since the turn of the present century are even more striking. The changes along occupational lines have mirrored those changes described above that have taken place in terms of industries. The decline in agricultural employment is clearly sketched. At the same time, it is clear that the rise in the service area comes primarily in the professional, semi-professional, and clerical occupations. Personal service occupations characterized by semi-skilled or unskilled activities do not show a commensurate increase.

SELECTION

Industrial firms recruit and select for posts in organizations somewhat along the lines suggested by Max Weber in his earlier writings on bureaucracy. White collar workers and, more particularly, executives increasingly are selected from a pool of individuals with higher education. While those without college training are not necessarily barred from executive positions, for all practical purposes this is the case as the rise of individuals in manual or blue collar occupations seldom reaches outside those areas. The college degree is looked on by virtually everyone as the "club card" for significant managerial posts. A survey by Warner and Abegglen (1955) emphasizes the higher level of education of business leaders in the United States over a period of time (Figure 19-3), a finding that reflects the values of this segment of society.

Recruitment by industrial and, increasingly, governmental and educational organizations takes place primarily on the college campus. Selection techniques begin with the interview in the placement office of the college or university and may continue with the use of the psychological measures outlined in Chapters 3 and 4. The process of selection relies on these objective or other techniques but is not influenced entirely by the results. Indeed, other factors may be seen to emerge when the entire process is more closely scrutinized. While the principles of rationality in hard decision making are subscribed to by the selectors, it becomes evident that other social factors play a role in the determina-

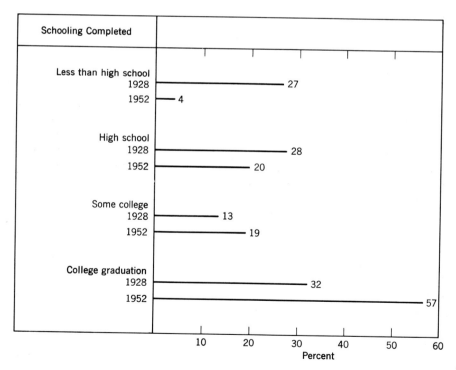

Figure 19-3. Education of business leaders in 1928 and 1952 (Warner, W. and Abegglen, J., 1955, p. 108).

tion. An extensive description of the organization and functioning of a bank by Argyris (1960) not only described the milieu of the organization but vividly illustrated the differences in personal and social functioning of individuals located in various areas of the bank. Individuals of the "right type" were hired; these happened to be primarily persons with characteristics possessed by those who were already functioning in the organization. This tendency of a business organization to perpetuate itself in the same fashion over a long period of time is a feature that has been considered by many as characteristic of organizations generally.

Manual or "blue collar" workers enter the company most often through the selection processes employed by the personnel office. The tests used, if any, are usually those measuring the specific abilities that are called for in the task (Chapter 3). In certain situations, however, there are restrictions imposed that serve to preselect the individuals making application. Craft unions, for instance, may have apprenticeship programs through which they control the selection of members. Some have been criticized in recent years for maintaining a policy of discrimination on racial grounds.

PROFESSIONALISM

Many of the members of industrial organizations identify themselves as professional persons and, whether others regard them as such or not, the label and the identification it represents can shape the attitudes and values of the members of the group and affect their functioning in the organization. While there may be some who do not agree, professionalism is usually defined in terms of four attributes. Professional persons function under a code of ethics that is internalized and/or enforced by an association of peers. Professional functioning is in areas requiring high levels of systematic knowledge with work orientation and rewards, to a great degree, in the community interest rather than centering exclusively in limited or monetary individual self-interest. While all four attributes are looked upon as being necessary to the professional state, the extent to which each or all of the factors is present will vary; professionalism is, then, a matter of degree. Medicine and law have long been considered professional areas. Many other occupational groups have attempted, for one social and psychological reason or another, to achieve similar status. Organizations with qualifying examinations for entry seem to be springing up at present in all possible occupational areas. Conceivably, even door-to-door encyclopedia salesmen will begin to believe that theirs is professional activity and will organize on this basis.

The implications for business are many. There has been extensive discussion as to whether business generally was a professional area or whether particular occupations within it could qualify for the term. At any rate, many staff members represent occupations or disciplines that have qualified. The presence of medical examiners, legal counsel, or scientists in the research and development laboratories is a strong representation from acknowledged professions. That factor in itself may have important ramifications. Individuals who consider themselves autonomous in their decision making as a result of an identification with a professional area may find it difficult to respond positively to orders promulgated by individuals in an organization who have been accustomed to giving them.

There is the further consideration of service to community or the society at large. This is, at least technically, one of the important considerations of the professional group. Business, on the other hand, may well be described as achieving its greatest force in being individualistic more than welfare oriented. However, individuals as diverse as Durkheim, Tawney, and Mr. Justice Brandeis have advocated the development of professionalism in business not only to develop the ethical foundations of business activity but to build on it to further the community interest in the functioning society (Barber, 1965, p. 16).

Labor Relations

The rise of labor organizations paralleled the industrialization of the community. Different kinds of union groupings have developed historically, most of which can still be seen at the present time. The type of union movement that tries to further the immediate material welfare of its members through collective bargaining has been known as "pragmatic" unionism. This approach represents the abandonment of a broad ideological and political struggle in favor of immediate objectives that can be achieved within the framework of collective bargaining. Earlier attempts in the United States to organize labor in a broad, all-encompassing ideological movement took place in the latter half of the nineteenth century with the formation of the Knights of Labor, whose influence extended almost to the present century. A more radical labor organization, the Industrial Workers of the World (IWW), attempted to achieve the same basic ends by organizing militant action to transform society.

It is safe to say that, while ideological and militant influences remain in the union movement, the emphasis is overwhelmingly retained in pragmatic approaches. The attempt to use unionism as a broad and basic political lever, however, may still play a role in the political affairs of underdeveloped countries (Galenson, 1959, pp. 8–15).

POWER AND CONFLICT

While a description of structure and procedures of union-management relationships is of interest, a focus on more dynamic processes such as conflict or power are more illustrative of behavioral science approaches. The concepts of conflict and power that have been discussed previously in a general context are applicable here although some researchers have proceeded to incorporate these concepts into the specific industrial setting. Dubin (1960) has developed a model relating the two factors of power and conflict in union-management relations. The model is based on "fundamental issues," defined by the author as those not part of the collective bargaining process. When fundamental issues are of concern, the disparity in power between the union and the company determines the extent of the conflict. Conflict is greatest when the power is evenly balanced and is lowest when the disparity in power is greatest. The amount of conflict is, therefore, inversely proportional to the disparity in power between the parties.

CONFLICT RESOLUTION

Strikes, slowdowns, and work stoppages represent militant means of settling disputes. Much of the time, however, parties to the industrial disagreements prefer to have these settled through less disruptive approaches. Bargaining is the basic process whereby both sides try to establish the new relationships under which they will operate for a future period, that is, to establish the contract. Each side tries to communicate to the other the circumstances of work and remuneration that it considers to be proper.

There are other approaches that can be used to help in the termination of disagreements. In mediation an outside party, generally a staff member of a state or federal agency, may be invited or may offer his services to the parties when it may be clear that the serious differences have difficulty in being resolved. The mediator cannot make decisions binding on the parties; he is present only to suggest alternatives or, more importantly, to point out the differing perceptions of the parties or break down the communications barrier between them.

Arbitration involves calling in an outside umpire to determine the dispute with finality. Arbitration can be imposed by government regulation or, more commonly, it comes as a result of an agreement between the parties to select an impartial outsider. In 1962 a compulsory arbitration law was passed by Congress to settle the conflict between the operating employees and the management of American railroads, the first enactment of a compulsory statute in the area of arbitration. When the parties themselves agree that the dispute should go to private arbitration, they agree as to the impartial third party, usually selected from a panel offered by an independent organization such as the American Arbitration Association; the arbitrator's decision is final and binding. While parties who fail to agree on a new contract in the bargaining sessions may agree to take the matter to arbitration, it is more often encountered in the determination of disputes that arise under the provisions of the contract. The contract may provide, for instance, that the grievances under the provisions of the contract, if unresolved between the union and management, end up in final arbitration. Here the arbitrator decides whether the worker is indeed justified by his grievance that the company has violated a provision of the contract in his individual situation.

BARGAINING DYNAMICS

Both labor and management are required by law to enter into collective bargaining in good faith and to keep at it for a reasonable length of time. Needless to say, the interpretation of the terminology leaves a wide area for disagreement. Apart from this, even more disagreement may stem from the basic provisions of the contract itself. Both sides will approach the negotiations with certain fears, attitudes, and expectations. The union may be concerned about arbitrary actions of management which would put in jeopardy the job security of its members. Management, on the other hand, will feel concern over the erosion of their prerogatives through the union's attempts to determine the condition of work.

Both sides probably enter into the bargaining session with some preconceptions as to tactical limits and alternatives of action. Figure 19-4 gives a graphic account of the expectations and limits that each side perceives in the process. Somewhere between the ideal situation conceived by both sides there is a bargaining zone between the positions on the continuum that both sides can tolerate.

Any process such as bargaining is helpful for establishing a common set of percepts and attitudes for the parties involved. Individuals bring to the bargaining session variations in perceptions, attitudes, and values in the experiences that have been built up over a period of time on the job. The same facts may not be seen in the same way by individuals on both sides of the bargaining table. What is perceived as an unsafe situation by the worker may not be viewed similarly by the manager or his staff man in charge of the safety program. The opportunity to talk as the bargaining session progresses is the kind of communication process that is educational for the individuals

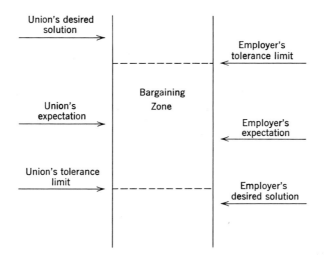

Figure 19-4. Desires, expectations, and tolerance limits determining bargaining zone (Stagner, R. and Rosen, H., 1965, p. 96).

involved; both sides begin to see, hopefully, the situation as others see it. Communication is hindered by the fact that workers and managers seldom "speak the same language." Executives are, more and more, being selected directly from the ranks of recent college graduates and have had little or no experience on the production line. While words do have a different meaning often for both groups, the matter goes much further than this. Workers and managers are selected or select themselves from different groups with different backgrounds and experiences. The resulting patterns of attitudes and values make communication between different occupational and social groups even more difficult because they not only speak but perceive things differently and are motivated in dissimilar ways (Haire, 1955).

In an attempt to provide a comprehensive behavioral model of collective bargaining, Walton and McKersie (1965) recognize the necessity for integrating concepts from various disciplines in the behavioral sciences to provide a theoretical framework stressing conflict resolution in a setting that is socially purposeful. Bargaining is looked upon as a rule-making, goal-directed process with four systems of activity identified as subprocesses. Distributive bargaining resolves conflicts of interest while integrative bargaining functions to find complementary interests of the parties. Attitudinal structuring focuses on influencing attitudes and, finally, intraorganizational bargaining attempts to achieve consensus within each group.

ORGANIZATIONAL DYNAMICS

The contribution to social conflict that the structure of management and the union provides must be taken into consideration. To this must be added the meshing of personality dynamics of the individuals involved in both groupings. In both union and management, perhaps the type of individual who emerges to make a more significant contribution to overall activity than others do is one who has a high level of general activity and who is alert and vocal. With continuing frustration these individuals may become even more aggressive than the average members to the point where their beleigerence actively feeds the industrial conflict under way. Some individuals in the process of negotiations can get so emotionally involved and have such deep-grained hostility toward the other side that they can run great risks of destroying the very thing for which they battle (Selekman, 1947).

The organizational structure and its functioning have an impact on the conduct of the activities of both the union and the company. The company is not a monolithic and autocratic organization. Executives proceed in varied ways to win the confidence and following of others in the organization or to reach other goals. The overall impact is one that resembles the pluralism of the larger society. Neither is the union always the democratic organization that it purports to be. With widespread apathy among union members, a few vocal and aggressive individuals may play a role all out of proportion to their number. In labor as well as company organizations, there are a multiplicity of motivations and various and changing constituencies that must be satisfied.

One of the more significant findings in the area of workers' attitudes is that indicating the prevalence of dual allegiance to company and union (Purcell, 1960). It was found that a majority of workers held favorable attitudes toward both the company and their union rather than a strong attachment to either and might respond in similar ways to both. This factor often is not noted, a result that is to the detriment of all parties.

Periodically, some concern has been voiced over the future of the union movement. Recent percentage decreases in the number of blue collar workers that are traditionally attracted to union membership has caused some observers of the industrial scene (Bell, 1954) to predict that unions will decrease in importance in the future as growing numbers of white collar workers take their place in the industrial scene. White collar and professional people generally have been cool to unions, considering membership in them as "unprofessional." Increasing militancy of some professional unions, especially those events culminating in widespread teachers' strikes in 1967 and 1968, indicates that some white collar attitudes are changing. Garbarino (1968) predicts, from experience in California, that professionals in education in the future will cease to take their goals and status aspirations from an "ideal academic" professional model (intellectual autonomy in a "community of scholars" and joint decision making in curriculum, for example) and will take their tactics from the professional union model with its pragmatic approach utilizing the technique of collective bargaining and group pressures.

BEHAVIORAL CONCOMITANTS

While the focus of attention in a bargaining situation may be on the material outcomes that are generally considered to be the topics under negotiation, there are many concomitant factors that may be just as important in the long run. Selekman (1947) was one of the first to recognize that the negotiating process served to reduce intergroup tensions as a by-product of the main task of resolving the conflict situation. He was also aware of the use of bargaining techniques by an immature administrator, not to conclude the bargain but to keep the union "in its place" through continuing the conflict. On other hand, more positive and therapeutic results of the "warfare" may be the working through of an individual's feelings so that he can behave more appropriately in the situation (Blake and Mouton, 1961). Bargaining tactics may reward and punish, provide learning situations, be cathartic, or provide virtually any other behavioral base.

Consumer Behavior

In any society, the bases of economic activity lie fundamentally with the individuals who, through their acceptance of the goods and services provided for them by the producers, determine the levels of economic functioning. Consumer behavior is often described as being the end result of an influence process with the flow of influence from producer to consumer frequently referred to as the marketing mix. Three aspects of the marketing mix are crucial and may be extracted for study. These are:

1. *The goods and services mix.* Producers must provide the kinds of materials the consumers want.
2. *The distribution mix.* Somehow the goods or services must reach the consumers.
3. *The communications mix.* Unless the consumers know what producers have to offer, it is unlikely that any movement of goods or services will occur.

The goods and services mix deals with the product or brand choices and the basis for them. While the reasons for the specific choices are fundamental, researchers would be interested also in brand preferences, purchase frequency and continuity (loyalty), variations resulting from price or other attributes and changes over time. Distribution aspects are primarily descriptive and deal with such factors as location and number of outlets, placement of products, assortment, prices, and method of selling. The factors in communication relate to information transmission and any promotional activity. Sources of information and their influence on consumer decision making are significant factors in behavioral studies of the economy.

Determination of specific behavior or limited relationships between factors in the mix may be of great interest to those whose job depends on knowing the answers to some marketing questions. Where to put the "Crunchies" cereal in the supermarket and how many children will buy it if it is advertised on television are specific questions of great import to certain researchers. They receive little mention here, however, in favor of more general organization of concepts and data.

CONSUMER DECISIONS

Behavior in the market is little different from that encountered in other life situations. The myriad individual and social factors in motivated activity that have been seen up to now are usually present, and virtually all may come to focus in the specific behavior identified as consumer decision making. Individual personality dynamics, the patterning of primary group attitudes and values, broader social processes, and the specific mechanisms of mass media—all these and more provide the basis for market decisions.

It is important to recognize at the outset that all behavior in the market is not necessarily the result of deliberate decision making. In *The powerful consumer,* Katona (1960) differentiates between habitual behavior and genuine decision making. Habits are those actions which are engaged in so repetitively that their regularity is firmly established. They are operative somewhat automatically and are not really influenced by attitudes or feelings. Genuine decision making is problem-solving behavior; it requires deliberation with respect to alternatives and a choosing among them. It is rare, is subject to group influence, and occurs under strong motivational circumstances. It is called for in new circumstances and where the results are substantial. Of the two kinds of choice behavior, those engaged in from habit are very much in the majority.

The kinds of conditions or economic circumstances that lead to genuine decisions have been outlined by Katona (*Ibid.*, pp. 289–290). These include major and rare expenditures such as buying a house or car (but even a new dress may be an important event) as well as first purchases. Unsatisfactory past experience or awareness of discrepancy between one's behavior and that of a group to which one belongs will make a prospective purchaser pause as will strong stimuli (threat of war, inflation, or powerful advertising). Finally, certain personality characteristics and education also will be associated with genuine decision making. The main alternative to this type of problem-solving behavior is not impulsive or whimsical choice, it is habitual behavior. The learned patterns are important to understand, of course, since much of market behavior is on this basis. What is necessary at this point is to distinguish between them.

ATTITUDINAL BASES

Attitudes, motivation, perception, and values are no less important in the economic area than in other areas of human behavior. Some idea of how the consumer (and the businessman) views the general state of affairs or specific features of the economy may prove to be amenable to study and the results of value to interested parties. Katona (1960) and others at the Survey Research Center have extensively sampled attitudes and expectations of various groups, particularly consumers. In relating the replies to actual economic events, the researchers are able to describe the changes in the market as a function of attitudes as well as objective levels of monetary ability. They would, for instance, survey expectations of consumers with questions phrased, "Do you think that in the country as a whole during the next twelve months we will have good times financially, or bad times, or what?" (*Ibid.,* p. 16). The level of sales during the period is demonstrated to be a function of both the willingness and the ability to buy. Attitudes of optimism or pessimism are directly related to level of sales (Figure 19-5).

Many other possibilities for study remain. Motives in buying automobiles, life insurance, and appliances point directly to underlying bases for the behavior of the consumer. Katona (*Ibid.*), for instance, studied the motivations of purchasers of life insurance. This survey of the awareness of purposes served by insurance noted that those purchasers who were aware of more reasons for insurance were also more heavily insured. Those who believed that insurance was good protection for the family in the case of the loss of the breadwinner bought significantly less than those who looked upon insurance as a means of savings, helping with education, or serving as a "nest egg" for retirement.

In a similar study of automobile purchases (*Ibid.,* p. 81), the answers to the question "Do you people expect to buy a car during the next twelve

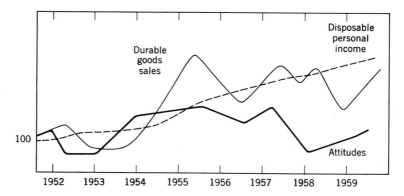

Figure 19-5. Sales of durable goods as related to consumer attitudes and income (Katona, 1960, p. 52).

months or so?" by a representative sample of urban families were compared to the actual buying behavior of those families in the ensuing year. Of those who either planned to buy or said they might buy a car, 35 percent bought within the first 6 months and 28 percent more bought within the next half year, for a total of 63 percent within a year. Those who said they did not expect to buy demonstrated far less purchasing. Only 6 percent bought within 6 months and 11 percent bought within the next 6 months, for a total of 17 percent within the year.

Katona cautions the reader that while the above may represent the not-too-surprising approach of the car salesman when he spends his time with those families whom he knows are planning to buy a car, there are other factors that make prediction of purchase on an individual basis difficult. Only 20 out of 100 of those queried said they planned to buy a car. If 60 percent did buy, then 12 cars were sold. If 16 percent of the 80 percent who said they did not plan to buy actually did buy, then 13 cars were purchased by this group. We can be sure of knowing where only half the cars will be sold if we limit ourselves to the survey.

PERSONALITY AND MOTIVATIONAL FACTORS

Studies of the individual bases of consumer behavior must, of necessity, go beyond the tracing of relationships between demographic variables and consumer preferences or the study of social influences on market behavior. Determination of personality characteristics of consumers or the needs met by the purchase of products provides some difficulties for the researcher, but the rewards are commensurate. This area may well be the crux of consumer behavior, if only, as Martineau (1957) puts it, that the buyer's personality is expressed in brand choices or product identifications.

The study of the motivational and personality factors in consumer behavior is often labeled *motivation research*. This term may have stimulated more emotional reaction than virtually any other term used in the area of consumer behavior. Perhaps this is partly the result of some of the questionable activity that purports to be in this category. Some of the reaction points to the importance of the approach generally. The concept is a fundamental and an important one, certainly, because it attempts to answer the very basic question of "why." Trying to uncover the reasons for consumer behavior are much more likely to be of significance in a theoretical or practical sense than a mere count of items stocked or sold in a supermarket, although that, too, is informative to a degree.

The attempts to determine the motivation of consumers have utilized virtually every data-gathering technique described in Chapter 3. Wide use is made of interviewing, with many of its practitioners labeling their technique *depth interviewing*. The approach may show wide variation in execution, but its users see themselves as spending more time in the process of delving more deeply into the behavioral foundations by exploring symbolic meanings or emotional context. Projective techniques of various kinds are also used, particularly those that are amenable to group administration, such as the Rosenzweig Picture-Frustration Test where the respondent fills in the statements he thinks cartoon characters would make. The Thematic Apperception Test and the Rorschach are less widely used because of limitations of time and trained personnel. More characteristic of activity in this area is the use of personality questionnaires. These paper-and-pencil techniques, through the ease of administration and scoring, are very widely used. These very same factors, however, produce problems, since the simple format lulls many into believing that their interpretation is also easy.

Useful techniques may be simple, however, as a now classic study in this area reveals (Haire, 1950). The researcher presented a group of housewives with two hypothetical shopping lists. Each housewife was asked to try to visualize the person who would be going to the supermarket with one list. The lists were identical except that one included instant coffee while the other contained regular ground coffee. The investigator was working under the hypothesis that the resistance among housewives to instant coffee soon after its introduction on the market came as a result of certain perceptions. Respondents describing the carrier of the instant coffee list described her as lazy and a spendthrift, while the housewife with the second list containing regular coffee received few such labels. From these results it is easy to conclude that a stereotype was the main block to the acceptance of instant coffee.

An illustrative use of personality measures was made by personnel of a large advertising agency (Koponen, 1960). The study used the *Edwards Personal Preference Schedule,* which measures the strength of needs in 15 areas. Needs such as affiliation, dominance, and achievement are surveyed by the scale. The scores on each of the 15 needs were related to frequency of purchase of several common items from cars to cosmetics. For instance, cigarette smokers were compared with nonsmokers. Smokers, especially heavy smokers, were higher on the heterosexuality, aggression, and achievement scale. Nonsmokers were higher on the order and deference scale. Nonsmokers were more compliant, therefore, and in need of an ordered regularity of existence.

The same personality measure was used earlier to determine if there was a difference between Ford and Chevrolet buyers (Evans, 1959). Evans found none but the study itself stimulated lively discussion and further research. Later, Westfall (1962) used a similar measure, the *Thurstone Temperament Schedule,* and found that convertible owners were more active, impulsive, and sociable than were the owners of standard or compact cars.

Many observers of motivation research recognize that the end results of the use of the technique need careful handling. Despite the opportunities for development of hypotheses or the emergence of stimulating concepts, many of the findings are difficult to validate. They are often done with small and sometimes unrepresentative groups. They require careful interpretation by highly trained individuals. While these limitations may restrict the confidence we are able to place in the outcomes, the studies represent a source of stimulating concepts in consumer behavior.

PRIMARY GROUP INFLUENCE

The impact of membership in social groupings on individual decision making has been a phenomenon of recurring interest in discussions of behavior. We might expect that the activity of individuals in the marketplace is no different, and our surmise is confirmed by numerous studies. Face-to-face relationships provide the most influential bases for consumer choice.

Katz and Lazarsfeld (1955) found that in almost all product areas the verbal and visual interaction on a personal basis was most effective in determining consumer behavior. The primary relationships were not ordinarily the initial or greatest source of information (newspapers and magazines were, prior to television), but the mass media lacked the impact of the direct contacts with friends or family. Rogers and Beal (1958) determined that commercial sources of information were effective in the earlier stages of decision making, while personal sources became more effective in later stages. In the adoption of a new drug, physicians were found to have salesmen and advertising as important information sources (especially if they were "isolates" with little or no contact with others), but sociometric patterns and adoption relationships indicated that prescriptions were made as the result of primary influences (Menzel and Katz, 1956). Bauer (1961) confirmed this in finding that personal contacts counted with new or risky drugs although the reputation of the company was taken into account. Salesmen (another kind of personal contact) were influential in the selection of ordinary or well-tested drugs.

STRUCTURAL FACTORS

Choice of brand, product, or place to shop represents a more specific problem for the researcher, but there are some general patterns that may be of wider interest. Initial choices are of concern to market researchers but, given a preference, the marketer probably would be even more interested in knowing whether such choices would be sustained over time. Loyalty to brand or super-market means more in the long run.

Tate (1961) indicates that people have a tendency to shop in relatively few stores; many shop in only one. This is especially true in lower socioeconomic levels. The consistency in pulling power is just as marked in the matter of brand. Loyalty to a brand is not a trivial matter or based on differences even though it may seem so to outside observers. Some purchasers will be loyal even when the only difference between two products is the brand itself. Kuehn (1962) noted that brand loyalty was a function of frequency of purchase; those who bought more often were more likely to stick to the same brand. The choice behavior was conceived to be primarily learned. There is a caveat from the author, however. The brand loyalty was not developed so strongly as to cause complete acceptance of the brand or rejection of others.

ADVERTISING

Since advertising is one form of communication, many of the basic factors have been discussed in Chapters 9 and 14. Advertising may also be viewed as an attempt to influence where the desired outcome by the advertiser may be something directly measurable, such as the purchase of a product, or something less tangible, as in the development of a favorable image for the company or the product.

Research

One of the first concerns in arranging an advertising program is whether the target population is likely to attend to and perceive the message. Choice of media, placement within it, and the organization of material are topics for decision making. Audience or leadership surveys are attempts to determine the auditory and/or visual impact of the advertising message. Advertising in newspapers or magazines will be checked through readership surveys with attention being paid to factors such as size of the advertisement and its position, the effect of color or illustrations, and the impact of frequency or repetition of the ad. Time placement of advertisements and their length in radio and television programming is a similar area of concentration for advertisers. The more specific responses of members of the audience of both radio and television programs have been measured in objective fashion as have preferences for various types of programs (Chapter 14). Telephone surveys establish the extent of the listening audience of any particular program; preferably the contact is made during the course of the program on the air with a mechanical device such as the audimeter (Nielsen, 1945).

Results

Readership studies have been made with great frequency, since this represents an area of immediate interest to advertisers when they spend their money. A great majority of these are reported for in-house consumption and are, therefore, in limited circulation. One study (Rudolph, 1936) remains a valuable one because of its scope and proper execution. The researcher found no difference in effectivenes between right- and left-hand placement in magazines. He did find an increase in readership with increase in size of the ad but not a proportional one. Two-color ads received only 1 percent more readers than black and white ads, but four-color ads raised the readership by 50 percent. Advertisements with pictures of women in them were more often read by women while those picturing men were read more by men. Evidently, each group felt the ads were meant for them when their sex was represented.

One of the more frequent questions asked in advertising is that dealing with the effect of frequency or repetition. It might be expected that, if one insertion of an ad is effective, then two will be even better, if not quite twice as good. In a summary of evidence along this line, Simon (1965a) concludes that there are no economies of scale in advertising. Expenditures should be dispersed, therefore, rather than concentrated.

Image

The associations evoked by a product or the feeling tones connected with it are often referred to as "image." The image may be that of an entire corporation, or it may extend to a product line generally or to a particular brand of product. The image is in the nature of a stereotype, a simple "shorthand" representation of reality. It may even be developed beyond an individual corporation to encompass an entire industry, such as the steel or the railroad industry. The corporation might try to develop a positive "personality" by stressing activities in the general welfare; "better things for better living through chemistry" represents one such corporate attempt. More specific emphases have been seen in the use of tattoos in advertising to project an image of masculinity connected with a specific brand of cigaretes. In the same way, tea has been described as robust and hearty to overcome earlier associations with little old ladies in tea rooms.

Subliminal Perception

While stimuli below the threshold of individual perception have been used in the psychological laboratories for years, widespread interest in "subliminal advertising" reached a peak in the late 1950's. Great concern was felt for the consuming public who presumably would be influenced as a result to purchase products without their willing it. Controlled experimental studies (Byrne, 1959; Champion and Turner, 1959) have indicated a lack of effect in use of subliminal cues. Attention to it has since waned, and the phenomenon remains one of historical interest only.

MODELS

General or more specific models of marketing decision making or consumer behavior have been developed in recent years. Cyert and March's (1963) model deals with price and output in a retail department store and relates more, therefore, to a marketing management problem. Kuehn (1962) has developed a model of consumer choice and brand shifting that is based on probabilistic models believed to be equivalent to those describing some learning models. The model is, furthermore, related to those proposed by others, notably Frank (1962).

The decisions surrounding allocation of resources for advertising may be aided by attending to models of the process. A relatively simple approach by Simon (1965b) is his model for advertising appropriations using only cost of capital, rate of sales decay, and an estimate of the functional relationship between advertising and sales.

It should be noted that none of the models provides a complete picture of the complexities in consumer behavior. What is important is that they represent an increasingly fruitful approach to the analysis of situations, and their role in assessing marketing and other functional problems will show a commensurate increase.

Summary

The production, distribution, and consumption of limited goods and services long has been an important part of social functioning. This economic activity began to gather even more momentum in the restlessness following the Middle Ages. The decline of Feudalism with resulting mobility and urbanization brought with it increasing commercial contacts; the process aided or was helped by concomitant changes in attitudes and values. Industrial activity was already of consequence at the acknowleged beginning of the Industrial Revolution in the mid-eighteenth century, although the advent of coal and steam-powered technology certainly accelerated the development significantly. At this time, concern for the intellectual bases of economic endeavor began to manifest itself as well. The ideas of natural and basic laws of the market flourished in this early period and the laissez-faire philosophy was reinforced by borrowings from Darwinian thinking. The move to an economy influenced by deliberate acts of planners represents a very recent countervailing philosophy.

Socially, industrialization has meant the disintegration of familial production entities and generational succession in occupations. Fixed primary ties were severed as social and religious conditions called for increasing individuality. Greater achievement may have resulted but at the accompanying cost of individual alienation from the rest of a competitive society. Even less interest in individuality came with the need to focus on technology and mass its productive units under one roof.

The increase in industrial complexity carried with it the necessity for more orderly management of the enterprise. The corporation has arisen, in part at least, because the small and often warm familial-like body could no longer provide the leadership needed. The complexity of relations between man and machine in an organization has been referred to with validity as a "sociotechnical system." The way work is organized provides greater or fewer satisfactions to the operator—those with greater control over the activity have more positive attitudes.

Economic theories of the firm focus on the decision making of units under the stimulus of an incentive. Traditional models have been based on the concept of a simple and rational attempt to determine optimal levels of activity. The complexity of the process, interwoven as it is with individual and social forces, has been recognized so that further attempts have included these relevant factors. This behavioral emphasis has provided views of interaction in organizations and the forces leading to equilibrium or dynamic development. In decision making the search process has been identified as one leading to a solution that is not the perfect one but is satisfactory in terms of the effort involved. Conflict and uncertainty are avoided, an the organization learns in the process.

A developing economy changes the mix of the work force from one that is primarily agricultural to one that is urban and industrial. At the well-developed stage, as is shown clearly in recent American experience, the service functions expand greatly while the basic manufacturing functions maintain a relatively static position. The trend is further reflected in the rise in professional and clerical occupations.

Recruitment for managerial posts in organizations is taking place increasingly from a college-trained population. Objective measures for selection are used, but other social factors play a role. Organizations have a way of perpetuating themselves with new members in the image of the old. At lower levels, the procedures of the unions often regulate the characteristics of the workers. When the members of the organizations identify themselves as professionals, they indicate some acceptance of the positive values in the pursuit of knowledge with more than self-interested service under an ethical code. Whether business is or is not a profession is being debated at present, but the opportunities for larger service are undoubtedly being recognized.

Associations of employees have grown with development of industry. Labor unions at times have adopted the guise of broad ideological movements or have been content to concentrate on immediate and limited conditions of work. Such pragmatism is characteristic of American labor today. In attempting to achieve its ends, labor's posture vis-à-vis the company emphasizes the power and conflict that underlie the relationships existing between the two. Conflict resolution may be through militant means such as strikes, but the bargaining process can avoid this. In any case, a mediator may help bring the parties together. Arbitration, the resort to an impartial third party, may also produce a set of conditions for continued activity under a contract or solve problems arising from it later. The dynamic course of the bargaining process itself is based on many of the behavioral concepts already covered in earlier chapters. Fears, attitudes, and perceptions influence posture and strategy. The entire course of agreement may be viewed as a rule-making, goal-directed process. While active individuals may sometimes force greater cleavages between the parties, there is generally a recognition of the basic commonality of interests. The bargaining process may also have some therapeutic value as well.

The consumer represents the ultimate basis for the economic viability of an endeavor. Consumer decisions are based, of course, on behavioral variables that do not differ from those encountered in other areas of activity. Some bases for market behavior are cognitive while some are affective in nature. All are based on learning. Attitudes and motives, while they may not always be identifiable, are important bases for behavior. Expectations or levels of awareness of purposes can be related to specific purchase behavior, and a campaign can then be tailored to fit.

Personality factors have been of great interest to researchers, particularly those who are partial to motivation research, a technique at least technically involving deeper probes into underlying factors in motivation. These and surface techniques have produced a few intriguing relationships between personality and product preferences. Not to be overlooked is the ubiquitous influence of the primary group. As in other areas, the impact of face-to-face relationships is powerful. Environmental factors or those related to the product itself play an additional role in determining choice behavior.

Advertising research concentrates on the extent to which the communication process is achieved and whether any desired behavior results. Readership or audience surveys may obtain data on one or both of those points. Advertisements may attempt to induce action in the form of purchase or there may be a desire to build and maintain a favorable image for a long-term relationship. Subliminal perception has aroused interest, but it does not seem to be of any direct utility in advertising.

Models of the marketing and advertising process have been of increasing interest. Decision making of either consumer or marketer often can be viewed more clearly when the choice points in the process are illustrated graphically.

Bibliography

Argyris, C. (1960). Excerpts from "Organization of a bank." In Rubenstein, A. and Haberstroh, C. (eds.). *Some theories of organization.* Homewood, Ill.: Irwin 210–228.

Barber, B. (1965). Some problems in the sociology of professions. In Lynn, K. (ed.). *The profession in America.* Boston: Houghton-Mifflin, 15–34.

Barnard, C. (1938). *The functions of the executive.* Cambridge: Harvard University Press.

Bauer, R. (1961). Risk handling in drug adoption: the role of company preference. *Public Opinion Quarterly,* **25(4),** 546–559.

Bell, D. (1954). Industrial conflict and public opinion. In Kornhauser, A., Dubin, R., and Ross, A. (eds.). *Industrial conflict.* New York: McGraw-Hill, 240–256.

Blake, R. and Mouton, J. (1961). Reactions to intergroup competition under win-lose conditions. *Management Science,* **7,** 420–435.

Bright, J. (1958). Does automation raise skill requirements? *Harvard Business Review,* **36,** 85–98.

Brown, J. (1954). *The social psychology of industry.* Baltimore: Penguin.

Byrne, D. (1959). The effect of a subliminal food stimulus on verbal responses. *Journal of Applied Psychology,* **43,** 249–252.

Champion, D. (1967). Some impacts of office automation upon status, role change, and depersonalization. *Sociological Quarterly,* **8(1),** 71–84.

Champion, J. and Turner, W. (1959). An experimental investigation of subliminal perception. *Journal of Applied Psychology,* **43,** 382–384.

Clarkson, G. (1963). A model of trust investment behavior. In Cyert, R. and March, J. *A behavioral theory of the firm.* Englewood Cliffs, N.J.: Prentice-Hall, 253–267.

Cyert, R. and March, J. (1963). *A behavioral theory of the firm.* Englewood Cliffs, N.J.: Prentice-Hall.

Dubin, R. (1960). A theory of conflict and power in union-management relations. *Industrial and Labor Relations Review,* **13,** 501–518.

Emery, F. and Trist, E. (1962). Socio-technical systems. In Walker, C. (ed.). *Modern technology and civilization.* New York: McGraw-Hill, 418–425.

Evans, F. (1959). Psychological and objective factors in the prediction of brand choice: Ford vs. Chevrolet. *Journal of Business,* **32,** 340–369.

Frank, R. (1962). Brand choice as a probability process. *Journal of Business,* **35(1),** 43–56.

Galenson, W., ed. (1959). *Labor and economic development.* New York: Wiley.

Garbarino, J. (1968). Professional negotiations in education. *Industrial Relations,* **7(2),** 93–106.

Gross, N., Mason, W., and McEachern, A. (1958). *Explorations in role analysis: studies of the school superintendency role.* New York: Wiley.

Haire, M. (1950). Projective techniques in market research. *Journal of Marketing,* **14,** 649–656.

Haire, M. (1955). Role perceptions in labor-management relations: an experimental approach. *Industrial and Labor Relations Review, 8*, 204–216.

Harbison, F. and Myers, C. (1959). *Management in the industrial world.* New York: McGraw-Hill.

Katona, G. (1960). *The powerful consumer.* New York: McGraw-Hill.

Katz, D. and Kahn, R. (1966). *The social psychology of organizations.* New York: Wiley.

Katz, E. and Lazarsfeld, P. (1955). *Personal influence.* Glencoe, Ill.: Free Press.

Keynes, J. (1936). *The general theory of unemployment, interest and money.* London: Macmillan.

Koponen, A. (1960). Personality characteristics of purchasers. *Journal of Advertising Research,* 1(1), 6–11.

Kuehn, A. (1962). Consumer brand choice—a learning process? In Frank, R., Kuehn, A., and Massy, W. (eds.). *Quantitative techniques in marketing analysis.* Homewood, Ill.: Irwin, 390–403.

Martineau, P. (1957). *Motivation in advertising.* New York: McGraw-Hill.

McGuire, J. (1963). *Business and society.* New York: McGraw-Hill.

Menzel, H. and Katz, E. (1956). Social relations and innovation in the medical profession: the epidemiology of a new drug. *Public Opinion Quarterly,* 19(4), 337–352.

Merton, R. (1957). *Social theory and social structure* (rev. ed.). Glencoe: The Free Press.

Moore, W. (1967). Economic and professional institutions. In Smelser, N. (ed.). *Sociology: an introduction.* New York: Wiley, 273–328.

Mumford, L. (1934). *Technics and civilization.* New York: Harcourt, Brace.

Nielson, A. (1945). Two years of commercial operation of the Audimeter and the Nielson Radio Index. *Journal of Marketing,* 9, 239–255.

Purcell, T. (1960). *Blue collar man: patterns of dual allegiance in industry.* Cambridge, Mass.: Harvard University Press.

Rogers, E. and Beal, G. (1958). The importance of personal influence in the adoption of technological changes. *Social Forces,* 36, 329–335.

Rudolph, H. (1936). *Four million inquiries from magazine advertising.* New York: Columbia University Press.

Selekman, B. (1947). *Labor relations and human relations.* New York: McGraw-Hill.

Selznick, P. (1949). *TVA and the grass roots.* Berkeley: University of California Press.

Simon, H. (1957). *Administrative behavior* (2nd ed.). New York: Free Press.

Simon, J. (1965a). Are there economies of scale in advertising? *Journal of Advertising Research,* **5(2),** 15–20.

Simon, J. (1965b). A simple model for setting advertising appropriations. *Journal of Marketing Research,* **2,** 285–292.

Stagner, R. and Rosen, H. (1965). *Psychology of union-management relations.* Belmont, Calif.: Wadsworth.

Tate, R. (1961). The supermarket battle for store loyalty. *Journal of Marketing,* **25(6),** 8–13.

Tawney, R. (1947). *Religion and the rise of capitalism.* New York: Harcourt, Brace.

United States Bureau of the Census (1965). *Historical statistics of the United States, Colonial times to 1957.* Washington, D.C.

United States Bureau of the Census (1967). *Statistical Abstract of the United States* (88th ed.). Washington, D.C.

Walton, R. and McKersie, R. (1965). *A behavioral theory of labor negotiations.* New York: McGraw-Hill.

Warner, W. and Abegglen, J. (1955). *Occupational mobility in American business and industry, 1928–1952.* Minneapolis: University of Minnesota Press.

Weber, M. (1948). *The Protestant ethic and the spirit of capitalism* (Parsons, T., trans.). New York: Scribner's.

Westfall, R. (1962). Psychological factors in predicting product choice. *Journal of Marketing,* **26(2),** 34–40.

20

The Individual,
the Organization,
and Society

One of the more significant phenomena in present-day events may well be the ability of the designations in the title of this chapter to provoke discussions, sometimes very heated ones. Singly or in combination the terms have become "buzz words," popular words with power to influence.

This basic confrontation of possibly competing concepts is not really new, however. In one way or another, the problems of individual rights and responsibilities vis-à-vis an aggregate have been topics of great concern for a long time, at least since the days of Socrates. The longevity of discussions centering on these concepts and the heat they can generate point clearly to the central place they occupy in the set of values held by many. Karl Marx was concerned with the inability of individuals to free themselves of the restraints of a class structure; more recently, Fromm (1941) has had similar fears though he has postulated different bases for the behavior. Whyte (1956), Packard (1962), and similar observers of the contemporary social scene present still other causes for concern.

Much of what has been said should be scrutinized carefully however. The content of pronouncements without an immediate empirical base can betray the influence of tradition or limited experience rather than indicate the presence of objectively based behavioral data. What results can be a mixture of stereotypes and illusions instead of factual material.

The major disparities between percepts and realities on the American social scene at present are seen by Skolnick (1965, p. 4) as being centered in the lag between past idealizations and already developed circumstances. While we profess social equality, we are really stratified. Local autonomy with primary group controls, long viewed as an essence of American functioning, has given way to the depersonalizing effects of a remote centralized government. Finally, we consider ourselves a nation of individual capitalists but the power is held by large organizations of all types where decisions are made by a few people. While there may be variations in the extent to which these conditions exist or how the perception of them takes place, it is certain that much of the difficulty in a dialogue on social issues arises on this basis. Sometimes we may be talking about an America that does not exist or may never have existed.

One additional concomitant of behavioral studies that makes its first clear appearance here needs to be mentioned. Discussions of the interrelationships of individuals and groups in society often lead to a consideration of the ethical foundations of behavior. Individual and group activity has been treated throughout this book in the empirical and analytical framework that behavioral scientists adopt as a necessary part of their approach to the study of human endeavor. The focus has been on what actually is, rather than on what "ought" to be. Many ethical implications have been present, however, at every stage of the discussions of human behavior even though these have been treated only in some indirect fashion. This is representative of the long-standing feeling among behavioral scientists that normative considerations ought not to play a role in a scientific endeavor. More recently, however, there have been some behavioral scientists who have argued for their greater involvement in public policy making, an activity that would imply at least some decision making on a prior ethical or normative basis. Seaborg (1962) has indicated that scientists recently seem to be more aware of the values present in relating themselves and their work to broader social objectives. Ericksen (1963) views the increased activity of behavioral scientists in pursuing the ethical and normative questions of policy making as a sign of increased professional responsibility. Business, too, may not be far behind.

The normative questions of behavior in business settings have generated extensive discussion of business ethics and the broader impact on the community of corporate functioning.

Most of the members of organizations would undoubtedly agree that there is more to their activity than pursuit of the main goal for which their organization exists. The importance of subsidiary goals and values may be of more concern to business organizations than to others, although social and educational organizations feel some of the same stresses. Businessmen are generally in agreement that, while the pursuit of profit is the main goal of enterprise, there is the subsidiary goal of "being a good citizen of the community." A survey by Baumhart (1961) indicates that virtually all of them believe that social and moral considerations play a role, or should, in corporate activities. To disregard the requirements of a society is viewed as unethical. Virtually 100 percent agreed that sound ethics and good business were virtually identical, at least in the long run. Closer observation of these results may show, however, that at least some may have meant that if profit is gained this is, in and of itself, ethical.

Individualism and Freedom

The concept of an individual free from the constraints of a restrictive social or political structure has been a significant part of a set of values that many casual observers have long felt to be part of the American character. The stereotype paints the picture of American society as placing a high premium on the importance of individual functioning; attainment in the economic sphere or in other areas on a basis of one's own abilities without any help or hindrance from the group seems to be a central tenet of this ideology.

This stereotype covering the pattern of attitudes and values has probably been present since the early years of this country. De Toqueville (1956) noted it and discussed it extensively in describing the spirit of the frontier. One hundred years ago de Toqueville may have been concerned about the separation of an individual from a group with the detrimental effects to the person and society that could result, but it has been obvious down through the years that the concept has been voiced as an ideal.

In the years of economic expansion after the Civil War, the emphasis on individualism began to be seen in the glorification of material attainment. The Horatio Alger story and the idealizing of the self-made man were prevalent in the folklore of the era of rapid industrial expansion. Even those, like Andrew Carnegie, who felt some concern about the role of their wealth in society at large, conceived of their mission in paternalistic terms when they considered themselves as trustees for those less able than they. Yet, in all of this, there was the beginning stirring of the same concern that de Toqueville felt earlier about the normlessness in the separation of the individual from a society. Just as strong have been the feelings for the maintenance of autonomy in individuals or the freedom from undue restraints.

The cause of individual freedom has undoubtedly enlisted more support through recent centuries than has any other ideal. With the development of the behavioral sciences in more recent times, the insights into personal and group dynamics provided by conceptualization and research have added further facets for understanding.

In a psychoanalytic approach to the problems of freedom and the individual, Fromm (1941) outlined the dynamics of the psychological forces within the social structure. While he wrote during World War II and was influenced by it, there is little reason to believe the treatment of authoritarianism and freedom would differ much today. Fromm was concerned about the emergence of man as an individual in present society. In this process man has two alternatives; he can either become one with the world in love and productive effort or he can seek a kind of security that destroys his freedom and integrity of self. The "escape from freedom" causes the individual to adopt the personality patterns given him by others. Man would become free to act if he knew what he wanted, but he does not know. The insecurity in the isolation from society provides no meaning for him, and he tries to escape this by adopting a self that is not really his. As a general guide toward positive action, Fromm indicates that the future for democracy lies in developing an initiative for freedom in man, not only in private matters but, even more, in the fundamental activity of work. This society is seen as being required to master the social problems; to do it requires concerted effort without the centralizing forces that limit freedom. Fromm was astute enough to see this as the critical problem in execution of social effort.

Complementary views of freedom and the individual round out the picture. Frankl (1959), whose main focus is on man in a search for meaning in his life, has posed the concept of responsibility as being the criterion of freedom. Man is not able to be really free, says Frankl, unless he has responsibility to something outside himself. This also may be the main theme of Herzberg (1966) who notes that healthy individuals look for challenges and responsibility in their activities, particularly at work.

The same basic concerns may be expressed in other ways. Some commentators on the current scene may focus on related psychodynamic variables such as the cognitive or perceptual ones. It is illustrative of the strong concern, perhaps, that symposia on "control of the mind" have received support from unlikely sources and have generated wider interest than usual (Farber and Wilson, 1963). In the second volume of the series, Rollo May (1963) describes freedom as originating from the self acting as a totality—the *centered self*. It is, however, a freedom involving social responsibility and, therefore, having limits. The "beatnik" is not really free, for freedom is not license. Freedom also means the capacity to cope with anxiety or the ability to live with it and accept it in a constructive way. We do not have, nor can we have, freedom from anxiety—to run away from it means to surrender our freedom. What we do need to eliminate is neurotic anxiety, the kind that blocks constructive effort as it debilitates the individual. Anxiety is a necessary and a dynamic aspect of freedom; as May quotes Kierkegaard, "Anxiety is the dizziness of freedom."

In the same vein, Crutchfield (1963) reinforces the conceptualization outlined above by presenting some empirical evidence of conformity-proneness (or "flight from freedom"). Such individuals are vulnerable to anxiety and have an inability to cope with stress. They have feelings of inferiority and inadequacy because their activity lacks openness and freedom of expression of emotion. Finally, there is a deficiency in the individual's cognitive processes in that he is less aware of what is really happening around him. These characteristics were visible from experimentation as well as observable in natural settings.

The area where many of the considerations of the principles of individual rights seem to be coming to a focus is in the right to privacy. We may not have progressed from a situation where the company or other type of organization takes the paternalistic view that the individuals in the organization are to be governed by thoughts of what the company or its managers feel is good for them. The present concerns of the company for its employees may range from seemingly innocuous matters of place of residence or style of living to questions of inducing employees to participate in certain civic or political activities.

Even greater concern might be felt for the positions of employees or applicants with respect to their individual rights to privacy and freedom from invasion by mechanical or psychological means. Psychological exams, particularly personality tests, have been atacked as invasions of privacy as have the polygraph, or "lie detector" tests. The use of electronic audio or visual surveillance techniques of employees, even in their private activities, also have aroused a great deal of resentment.

The line of demarcation between what is the company's business and what is the individual's may be a line that is hard to draw. Garrett (1966) suggests that the difficult area of privacy may be handled best by resorting to a process of collective bargaining whereby a contract is entered into between employer and employees which specifically states the procedures that may be used. As a result of this dialogue, both sides agree voluntarily on the conditions rather than enter into a situation where unilateral activity takes place.

On the broader social scene, the concern for the preservation of individual privacy in behavioral research has led to the enunciation of guidelines for those engaged in such activity (Panel on Privacy and Behavioral Research, 1967). Acceptance of responsibility by researchers and administrators, the obtaining of consent, the maintenance of confidentiality, and an emphasis on the ethical aspects of research represent the salient features of the recommendations.

The Individual and the Organization

Discussions of individual freedom and autonomy are being framed increasingly around the relationships between individuals operating within larger social structures. This strong concern in present-day society for the fate of the individual faced with big government, mass organizations, and organized activity in all spheres of life is not a new one, however. As has been pointed out above, earlier social philosophers have commented on some of the functional difficulties in interaction. Within the last half century, however, concern for the individual in the organizational setting has shown an increase, undoubtedly the result of the significant growth in size, number, and importance of the organizational form of activity. Where Montesquieu could expound generally on the political mechanisms to promote freedom and Marx would look to a withering away of classes to do the same, today's crusaders are apt to focus more on the organization, notably in the business area.

One of the better known dissertations on the social impact of organizational activity is by Whyte (1956) in *The organization man,* where he develops his description of the individual in corporate society in a way that puts the focus on the deficiencies of the system with respect to its providing a basis for personal growth or actualization. Lest anyone believe that this is a phenomenon peculiar to business alone, Whyte (*Ibid.*, p. 3) hastens to add:

> The corporation man is the most conspicuous example, but he is only one, for the collectivization so visible in the corporation has affected almost every field of work. Blood brother to the business trainee off to join DuPont is the seminary student who will end up in the church hierarchy, the doctor headed for the corporate clinic, the physics Ph.D. in a government laboratory, the intellectual on a foundation-sponsored team project, the engineering graduate in the huge drafting room at Lockheed, the young apprentice in a Wall Street law factory. They are all, as they so often put it, in the same boat.

Whyte says these people do not just work for the organization, they *belong* to it. In it, men and women work as a team and give up much of their individuality as they do so.

A later popular look at the same area by Packard (1962) outlines, perhaps without intending to do so, the same psychosocial costs of the large aggregate. More of the same comes from Anthony Jay (1967) who vividly portrays the dynamic interrelationships between the individual and the business organization using analogies from history. Not only are Machiavelli's guides adapted to corporate politics; in addition, Jay describes present structures and functioning of corporate life in terms of historical characters and events. Individuals in corporations may not be kings, barons, or popes, but the comparisons may provide a stimulus for further analysis of the organizational activity.

There is little reason to delve more deeply into these specific delineations of organizational activity. Some comments made are, furthermore, often without direct empirical support. What is of greatest importance, however, is the fact that these are a small part of what is being said and written about the problems of the individual in the organization. This alone is a significant indicator for future research and action.

Critical commentary is easy and popular (and it sells books). The resolution of the problems does not come quite as effortlessly, although some proposals for alleviation of difficulties have been advanced. The programs have had to be concerned with the difficult paradox involved in ambivalent feelings toward individualism and organizations. On the one hand, while the idealization of the individual has a long history in America, the dangers that de Toqueville saw one hundred years ago are still present in the unchecked satisfaction of individual needs. On the other hand, the economic and administrative realities of present-day functioning have made some kind of organized effort a necessity. The dilemma is an old one. To paraphrase a saying just as old, our problem is "how to have our good cake and eat it, too, without indigestion."

Admittedly some kind of organized effort is called for. The idea of a collective, or at least a description in those terms, certainly has been foreign to the American social scene, however. The emphasis on this kind of social unity exemplified by the authoritarians of both right and left has been rejected in American society with great consistency. The question has remained, however, of the proper circumstances for the maintenance of equilibrium or a viable society. One proposal by *Fortune* (1951, p. 176) outlines a solution in this dilemma by purporting to identify a trend.

> The concept that appears to be emerging, as the answer of the modern individual to this challenge, is the concept of the *team*. It is an old concept but it is being put to new uses. As a member of a team an individual can find full opportunity for self-expression and still retain a dynamic relationship to other individuals.

This series of articles then goes on to illustrate that the stature of an individual will increase rather than the growth of government, and the individual will find a "higher expression of himself" through involvement in the community at all levels. This seems like a happy thought, and yet it is evident that it may be no real solution taking us out of the paradoxical situation. Can there be true incorporation of the individual in a group without his willing it? If others impose their ideas of what is best in group activity for the individual, is this really the growth factor for a person? Argyris (1964) paints the basic problem as being the requirement of the individual to experience dependence and submissiveness as the result of a "grand strategy" in the organization of effort to achieve certain objectives. In attempting to eliminate the dilemma, Ward (1964, pp. 75–76) points out that considering the individual versus society is a vital question. In demonstrating the necessity for some means of resolution, he states that there is no choice between organization and something else; the choice lies between organizations that serve our needs and those that do not. If we believe that society exists to serve the individual than we must proceed with imagination to develop organizations so that they serve this ideal. There is recognition of the fact that reaching an optimal or ideal objective is unlikely. Argyris (1964) agrees that one should be realistic and expect that it would be possible only to "satisfice" rather than maximize an integration of the individual and the organization; but we can try.

Social Responsibility

The suggestion that a business organization has some obligation to the society in which it operates is bound to engender controversy whenever the point is raised. On the one hand, there are those who consider that the corporation, because of its size and power, should be even more concerned with its responsibility to society. If individuals are called on to maintain some social consciousness and act responsibly in the community, even more should that legal but fictitious person, the corporation, do so. Even if single individuals are called upon to participate in United Fund drives, contribute to other charities, or serve in community endeavors, the corporation can do so as an entity beyond encouraging its members to action.

The drive to "sell" industry to the American people and to burnish the general image of business enterprise has sometimes been conducted with a patently emotional appeal. The type of approach may have varied along with the affective level of the communications, but the overall message pointed to the same general goal. There may be, however, a change in a progress from the relatively unvarying attitudes of businessmen in the past. Cheit (1964) detects a decided change from the "Free Enterprise sales campaign" containing phrases like "security" and the "free enterprise system" to the point where there is much less effort to revive the capitalism of pre-New Deal days and more concern with listening to the problems that face Americans and American businessmen today. In short, social responsibility is the topic of more discussion than ever before with respect to the proper role of business in society.

The move to greater awareness of the requirements in today's society is accelerating despite occasional vociferous pleas to return to the basic values of the past. The warnings of danger may even be echoed in academic circles (Levitt, 1958; Friedman, 1962) and by others who take a dim view of any action of a corporation other than that of making money for their stockholders. Those who look askance at this role of business organizations most often maintain that such pursuits are not within the proper sphere of activity of the corporation. Its role, the say, is to maintain a healthy economic existence with benefits to the community accruing directly from this position. Levitt (1958) is one of the major exponents of the notion that business should stick to "business." He indicates that its business is making money, not welfare. If welfare does not come automatically under this system, it becomes the government's job. Instead of all major groups trying to intrude on our private lives, they should "fight each other" so that none dominates our society. This approach leaves little room, if any, for a corporate role not arising on a competitive and economic basis.

Another position, and one that has more validity, is the stand that maintains that the corporation's managers may not dispense the funds of the organization in a manner extraneous to the enterprise; this view states that the money is not theirs to give, it belongs to the stockholders. The officers of the company merely manage the money and, as such, they are operating under a trust for the benefit of the stockholders. It may be strongly argued, however, that the legal basis for corporate gift giving remains the same as it has always been. Katz (1960) indicates that the justification lies within the well-established managerial duties to develop customer or community good will. The extensive distribution of scholarships or direct grants to colleges and universities and the support of community projects or artistic activities such as a symphony orchestra and opera is an indication of the extent to which companies have expanded their activities in a community-oriented framework. It might also be argued that urban renewal projects instituted on a private basis by corporations such as Alcoa and the Penn-Central represent some civic consciousness in overlooking the economic risks involved beyond those justified by the levels of profit expected from the investment.

The crucial point in this discussion may be that the concept of cost should not be considered too narrowly. McGuire (1965, p. 27) indicates that when costs are taken to encompass more than economic variables it may be that socially conscious corporations do not have higher unit costs. Employees may accept lower wages in favor of better relations. Customers may pay more for a product based on their feeling that it was made by a company with integrity. Social responsibility may thus fit within a traditional economic framework. This may be the best answer to those who challenge these actions of the corporation, either as a matter of principle or on the basis of the economic impact on the status of a stockholder.

Other expressions of concern stem from different considerations. Some commentators view the tremendous power of the corporation and consider that the interest in the social responsibility of business is really an attempt by anxious businessmen to legitimize the awkward state of a business that has outstripped the controls that would keep it functioning in the public interest. Earlier (Chapter 18) the warnings of Berle (1964, pp. 101–102) concerned the need to introduce legal constraints on those private entities which have become so large and powerful that they constitute a private government with as much power as public government.

While this view of the social responsibility of business which regards it as a dangerous rationalization is shared by many, different conclusions have been reached. Cheit (1964), for one, sees the "Gospel of Social Responsibility" as a response to the changing environment and is only concerned with whether the appropriate responses can come fast enough. There is no question in his mind of legitimacy because the stockholders and the public generally accept and approve of the managers' actions (even if they are not owners, the managers act like it). Power is so diffused that control is seldom a problem; where it does become a point at issue, the problem is really one of a clear-cut delineation of the duties of business under the doctrine of social responsibility. These guidelines are the responsibility of government.

Whatever else happens, however, social responsibility of business is likely to remain an important concern of society. It seems clear that the area of most social concern for business in the future is likely to be that combination of factors in poverty and civic participation that already occupies much of the thinking and activity of businessmen as well as other citizens of the community. In the beginning stages of the present "war on poverty," Galbraith (1958, p. 331) urged an "investment in individuals" to enable them to meet the requirements of their environment or escape it. Others have taken up the challenge, even in the more prosaic economic circles. Hazard (1968) has issued a call for business to organize an effort to apply its leadership and skills to aid in the struggle—to "put up" or "shut up" as the government fumbles in the interim.

Challenges of the Future

Some unknown cynic has indicated that he would choose to predict happenings far off into the future as the safest course, since no one would remember several years hence what his prediction was and could never check on the validity of it. With the confidence inspired by this attitude, one can look at immediate and past events and cast an eye toward the future. Perhaps it is not too far out of line to make some further comments to add to the implied predictions made earlier at various points.

To begin with, it seems quite possible that organizations of all types will function under conditions indicating a better awareness of the individual and group dynamics that are present in their own particular setting. Business organizations are attempting already, whether for reasons of social responsibility or not, to do something about some of the social inequities that surround their very headquarters in large urban areas. With a greater understanding of the dynamic qualities of human behavior, they will, perhaps, be ready to cope with initially strange social phenomena because they have coped successfully with more inanimate financial and economic mechanisms. Knowledge accumulating to their benefit from conceptualization and research in behavioral science will play a significant part of an expanded role for business in our society. Riesman (1950, pp. 372–373) has predicted something similar using familiar marketing terms. He indicates that people will learn to "buy the larger package" of a neighborhood or way of life much as they buy a package of groceries now. In a way, this sounds vaguely reminiscent of the earlier equating of business and the "American way of life." The dangers inherent in this view of the role of corporate entities is stated in forthright terms by Berle (1960, pp. 96–97) who warns that public consensus must determine a value system and corporations will fail if they attempt to do so. While he sees some dysfunctional consequences, Berle (*ibid.*, p. 98) ends with the heartening prediction that "we shall, in 1985, prove George Orwell wrong."

Paralleling a strong behavioral thrust will be the continuing impact on behavior from the technological changes that surely will continue to take place. The power of computers is not limited to the assembly and analysis of data; electronic aids will have their impact upon the individual and the organization in changing the relationships between people working together. In another look toward 1985 within the context of technological development, Simon (1960) sees some aspects of organizational functioning surprisingly remaining much the same as they appear today. Few "workmen" in the traditional sense will remain, with a larger number in maintenance or long-range planning. Personal service occupations will increase significantly. Management will be automated at varying speeds—well-structured problem solving will be automated completely (possible now) while programming of supervision will proceed most slowly. "Middle management" is likely to disappear while those relegated to top levels of the organization will be spending more of their time in thinking with a long-range perspective. All in all, the human beings in society will remain in the same general array of occupations as at present. As a final reassuring note, Simon foresees that, while we will possess the technical means to manage corporations by machine, the technical requirements will not be all that important as long as we recognize how to use the products. Simon notes that the driver of the 1910 automobile had to know more about the machine than his counterpart in 1960. This should be reassuring to many readers.

A final statement on the complex social processes involved in pressing domestic and international demands on our society defies delineation within the limiting constraints of this book. Suffice it to say that the results of increased conceptualization and research in the behavioral and physical thrusts of technology will be available and, hopefully, will be put to good use. For what ultimate purpose? Perhaps, as Galbraith (1958, p. 351) has stated, a very practical one.

> A society has one higher task than to consider its goals, to reflect upon its pursuit of happiness and harmony and its success in expelling pain, tension, sorrow, and the ubiquitous curse of ignorance. It must also, so far as this may be possible, insure its own survival.

This remains the ultimate challenge confronting society and the individual.

Summary

Concepts covering the relationships of individuals and the social entities to which they belong have been topics of great interest for a long time. Most of the discussions have been lively and, all too often, based on inaccurate perceptions of the actual bases for individual and social behavior.

Ethical concepts have edged into recent considerations by behavioral scientists because many are beginning to recognize the need for some ultimate use of scientific data in a way that has normative bases. This is increasingly true of applications of data to business.

Individualism represents a significant part of the American stereotype, and the values inherent in the drive toward individual attainment may still be strong today. Concern for individual freedom may be voiced today, but the basis for this concern may vary. Some analysts fear that individuals too often adopt an artificial self as the result of pressures by peers while other researchers may concentrate on meaning and responsibility as prime motivating forces. Anxiety, too, may be a basic drive in everyday living; it can be constructive in providing an impetus to action. For some individuals, those prone to conformity, anxiety can be stressful and debilitating.

The right to privacy is an area where many of the concerns for individual freedom are coming into focus. Freedom from invasion by psychological or mechanical means is considered to be crucial to individual dignity in any organizational or primary setting.

The role of the individual in a modern business corporation (and many other kinds of organizations) has attracted additional researchers and commentators. Critical outpourings are easy; the difficulty lies in using the beneficial (or even necessary) aspects of the organization to achieve a goal without stultifying single individuals in the process. We have no choice as to whether organizations stay; what can be done, however, is to make sure that these are able to serve the needs of those involved in them.

Social responsibility of business organizations also has been a central topic in discussions of the role of business in society. Views emphasizing that the duty of business is to make money undoubtedly are exceeded by those recognizing the broader impact business can and does make on the larger social scene. Justification for this activity lies within the nature, purpose, and goals of corporate action.

The excessive use of corporate power has also been a point of concern when the matter of responsibility is raised. Increasing diffusion of the basis for control in addition to the awareness of responsibility makes this aspect less troublesome.

Programs designed to improve the image of business have changed complexion through the years. Most recently, the concern for social values has been expressed in the declaration of war on poverty and other social problems.

Challenges of the future for individuals, organizations, and society seem to center on the problem of maintaining the individuality of each member of the social unit at the same time the improvements in organization and community functioning are taking place. The survival of a healthy society is our most significant task.

Bibliography

Argyris, C. (1964). *Integrating the individual and the organization.* New York: Wiley.

Baumhart, R. (1961). How ethical are businessmen? *Harvard Business Review,* **3(4),** 7 ff.

Berle, A. (1960). The corporation in a democratic society. In Anshen, M. and Bach, G. (eds.). *Management and corporations, 1985.* New York: McGraw-Hill.

Berle, A. (1964). Economic power and the free society. In Hacker, A. (ed.). *The corporation take-over.* New York: Harper and Row.

Cheit, E. (1964). The new place of business: why managers cultivate social responsibility. In Cheit, E. (ed.). *The business establishment.* New York: Wiley, 152–192.

Crutchfield, R. (1963). Independent thought in a conformist world. In Farber, S. and Wilson, R. (eds.). *Conflict and creativity.* New York: McGraw-Hill, 208–228.

Ericksen, S. (1963). Legislation and the academic tradition in psychology. *American Psychologist,* **18,** 101–104.

Farber, S. and Wilson, R. (eds.) (1963). *Conflict and creativity.* New York: McGraw-Hill.

Fortune (Davenport, R., ed.,) (1951). U.S.A.: the permanent revolution. *Fortune,* **43(1)**.

Frankl, V. (1959). *From death camp to existentialism.* Boston: Beacon.

Friedman, M. (1962). *Capitalism and freedom.* Chicago: University of Chicago Press.

Fromm, E. (1941). *Escape from freedom.* New York: Holt.

Galbraith, J. (1958). *The affluent society.* New York: Houghton-Mifflin.

Garrett, T. (1966). *Business ethics.* New York: Appleton-Century-Crofts.

Hazard, L. (1968). Business must put up. *Harvard Business Review,* **46(1)**, 2 ff.

Herzberg, F. (1966). *Work and the nature of man.* Cleveland: World.

Jay, A. (1967). *Management and Machiavelli.* New York: Holt, Rinehart and Winston.

Katz, W. (1960). Responsibility and the modern corporation. *Journal of Law and Economy,* **3**, 75–85.

Levitt, T. (1958). The dangers of social responsibility. *Harvard Business Review,* **36(5)**, 41–50.

McGuire, J. (1965). The social responsibilities of the corporation. In Flippo, E. (ed.). *Evolving concepts in management: proceedings of the 24th annual meeting.* University Park, Pa.: Academy of Management.

May, R. (1963). The psychological bases of freedom. In Farber, S. and Wilson, R. (eds.). *Conflict and creativity.* New York: McGraw-Hill. 199–207.

Packard, V. (1962). *The pyramid climbers.* New York: McGraw-Hill.

Panel on Privacy and Behavioral Research (1967). Preliminary summary of the report of the panel. *Science,* **155**, 535–538.

Riesman, D. (1950). *The lonely crowd.* New Haven: Yale University Press.

Seaborg, G. (1962). Scientific society, the beginnings. *Science,* **136**, 505–509.

Simon, H. (1960). The corporation: will it be managed by machines? In Anshen, M. and Bach, G. (eds.). *Management and corporations, 1985.* New York: McGraw-Hill.

Skolnick, J. (1965). The sociology of law in America: overview and trends. *Law and society* (a supplement to the summer issue of *Social Problems*).

Toqueville, A. de (1956). *Democracy in America.* Heffner, R. (ed.). New York: Mentor.

Ward, J. (1964). The ideal of individualism and the reality of organization. In Cheit, E. (ed.). *The business establishment.* New York: Wiley, 37–76.

Whyte, W., Jr. (1956). *The organization man.* New York: Simon and Schuster.

Credits

296 Figure from publication of J. Horty and Aspen Systems Corporation (1968) and reproduced with permission.

297 Figure reproduced by permission of J. Horty and Aspen Systems Corporation.

304 From *Sociology* 3rd Edition by Leonard Broom and Philip Selznick; adaptation, figure III:3, use of the Typewriter (Harper, 1963).

309 Quotation from Benedict (1934), *Patterns of culture,* by permission of Houghton-Mifflin, Inc. and Routledge Kegan Paul.

316 Figure reproduced from McClelland (1961) *The achieving society* with the permission of Van Nostrand.

325 Extracted from Hodge, Siegel, and Rossi (1964), *American Journal of Sociology,* courtesy of R. Hodge and the University of Chicago Press.

328 Figure from Warner and Lunt (1941), *The social life of a modern community.* Reproduced through permission of Yale University Press.

330 Figure reproduced from Davis, Gardner, and Gardner (1941) *Deep South.* By permission of the University of Chicago Press.

341 From *Sociology,* 3rd Edition by Leonard Broom and Philip Selznick. Figure IX:2 Population Pyramid, United States: 1900 and 1960 (Harper, 1963).

350 Terminology extracted from Mumford (1934). *Technics and civilization* © Harcourt, Brace and World.

354 Table extracted from Horton and Thompson (1962), *The American Journal of Sociology,* courtesy of J. E. Horton and the University of Chicago Press.

370 Table from the United States Bureau of the Census (1961), *Current Population Reports.*

389 Table extracted from Campbell, Gurin, and Miller (1954), *the voter decides,* by permission of Row, Peterson.

405 From Deutsch & Collins (1951) *Interracial housing,* courtesy of the University of Minnesota Press.

416 Brief exerpt from page 236 in *Sociology* 4th edition, by Leonard Broom and Philip Selznick (Harper, 1968).

425 Figure from Campbell (1968) in *Psychology Today.* Reproduced through courtesy of CRM Associates, Corona Del Mar, California.

430 Figure from Katz and Lazarsfeld (1955), *Personal influence,* courtesy of the Free Press.

434 Propaganda devices from Lee and Lee (1939) *The fine art of propaganda.* Used courtesy of Clyde Miller and Alfred McClung Lee.

470 From H. J. Leavitt, "Some effects of certain communication patterns on group performance," *Journal of Abnormal and Social Psychology,* 46, 1951, 38–50. Copyright 1951 by the American Psychological Association, and reproduced by permission.

483 Table based upon Etzioni (1961) *A comparative analysis of complex organizations* © 1961 by the Free Press.

488 Figure reproduced from March and Simon (1958), *Organizations,* courtesy of John Wiley and Sons, Inc.

501 Tab e from Bakke (1959) in Haire (ed). *Modern organization theory,* courtesy of John Wiley and Sons, Inc.

502 From Richard M. Cyert and James G. March, *A Behavioral Theory of the Firm.* © 1963, Prentice Hall, Inc., Englewood Cliffs, N.J.

522 Table extracted from Benne and Sheats (1948), *Journal of social issues.* Used through the courtesy of Kenneth Benne and the Society for the Study of Social Issues.

523 From *Individual in society* by D. Krech, R. S. Crutchfield and E. L. Ballachey © 1962 by McGraw-Hill. Used with permission of McGraw-Hill Book Company.

539 Figure from Lipset, S. (1967) in Smelser (ed.), *Sociology,* courtesy of John Wiley and Sons, Inc.

584 From Richard M. Cyert and James G. March *A Behavioral Theory of the Firm* © 1963, Prentice Hall, Inc., Englewood Cliffs, N.J.

586 Material from the United States Bureau of the Census (1965) *Historical statistics of the United States.*

587 Material from the United States Bureau of the Census (1967), *Statistical Abstract of the United States.*

588 Material reproduced from Warner and Abegglen (1955), *Occupational mobility in American business and industry, 1928-1952,* courtesy of the University of Minnesota Press.

593 From *Psychology of Union-Management Relations* by Ross Stagner and Hjalmar Rosen. © 1965 by Wadsworth Publishing Company, Inc. Belmont California. Reproduced by permission of the publisher.

598 From *The powerful consumer* by George Katona. © 1960 by McGraw-Hill. Used with permission of the McGraw-Hill Book Company.

615 Quotation from Whyte (1956). *The organization man* © 1956 by Simon and Schuster, Inc. and used with permission.

616 Extract from *Fortune* (1951). © 1951 by and quoted with the permission of *Time,* Inc.

621 Quotation from Galbraith (1958), *The affluent society,* with the permission of Houghton-Mifflin, Inc. and John Kenneth Galbraith.

Author Index

629

Subject Index

Industrial Workers of the World, 590
Industrial work force, 585–587
Infancy, 111
Inferiority complex, 244
Informal group, 333, 450–451
Information, cognitive model of, 231–232
  handling systems, 292
  organization of, 293
  processing index, 293
  receiving, 153–161
  retrieval, 100, 293–297
  storage, 293
  theory, 20
In-group, 333, 451–452
Initiating, by leader, 523
Injunction, 566
In loco parentis, 561
Inner-directed, 311–312
Innovation, by individuals, 352
  in organizations, 505–507
Input, in a behavior system, 153–161
  biological basis of, 124–125
  computer devices, 98–99
  in organizational change, 506
Insight, 222
Insightful learning, 179
Instinct, 51
Institutional ways, 401
Institutions, 334–339
Instrumental learning, 177–178
Instrumental needs, 448–449
Integration, as a social process, 354–355
  organizational, 508
  racial, 405
Intelligence, and attitudes, 394
  creativity and, 233–234
  distribution of, 114
Intelligence Quotient, 70, 113–114, 233, 518
Intensional meaning, 285
Intensity, in audition, 157
  in perception, 216
Interaction in groups, 332, 468–469
Intercontinental migration, 368–369
Interests, 135
Internal migration, 369–371
Internal strains, in organizations, 506
Internship, 194
Interorganizational conflict, 494–495
Interpersonal level of organization, 322

Interval scale, 74
Interview, 62–63, 418–419
Intrinsic programming, 202–203
Introversion in leaders, 519
Invention, 233, 349
Inventive level, 233
Investment in individuals, 619
I.Q., 70, 113–114, 233, 518
Iris of eye, 156
Isolates, 456, 601
Isolation, 355
Italy, 364

Jack of Newbury, 575
James, 11, 42
Jews, 26–27, 305, 403
Job attitudes, 406–407
Job content, 407–408
Job context, 407–408
Job enlargement, 505
Job satisfaction, 406, 407–410
Jointness, 284
Judges, 543, 544, 558
Judgment, 211, 220–221
Judicial decision making, 558
Jung, 45, 46, 244
Jurisprudence, 16–17
Jury, 465, 466, 519
Jus civile, 30
Jus naturale, 30
Juvenile Court, 554
Juveniles, 552

Katona, 49–50
Kerner Report, 376
Key-word-in-context, 293
Kinesthetic sense, 160
Kinship, 321
Knights of Labor, 566, 590
Knowledge function of attitudes, 393
Knowledge of results, 184–185
Köhler, 7
Kwakiutl Indians, 289, 308
KWIC, 293

Labor, government regulation of, 565–566
Labor-management communication, 592–593
Labor relations, 270, 378–380, 590–595
Laboratory method, 472–473

Time magazine, 423
Timocracy, 28
Tonal islands, 125
Townsend plan, 359
Tract, census, 340
Tradition, legitimacy by, 539
Tradition-directed, 311
Training, apprentice, 193
  group method, 194, 196–197, 472–473
  managerial, 194
  objectives in, 193
  on-the-job, 193
  programs, 192–198
  school, 194–195
  sensitivity, 196–197
  simulation, 195
  simulators, 200
  supervisory, 194
  system, 195–196
  transfer of, 186–187
  vestibular, 195
Traits, 114, 517–520
Trait theories of personality, 245–246
Tranquilizers, 264, 266
Transaction, 8
Transfer, 435
Transference, 265
Transfer of training, 186–187
Translation, 292
Tree diagram, 92–93, 224
Triad, 468
Trial-and-error learning, 179
Trustee role, 542–543
Truth serum, 264
Tschambuli, 309
Two-sided presentation, 428–429
Two-step pattern of communication, 423, 429–431
Typewriter, 304
Tyranny, 28

U hypothesis, 168
Ulcers, 268
Uncertainty, 227–228, 583, 584
Unconditioned response, 177
Unconscious, collective, 244
Unemployment, 373
Union-management conflict, 378–379
Unions, 355, 482, 483, 560–561, 566, 590–595

United States, Army integration, 405
  Senators, 543–544
  Supreme Court, 552, 557–558, 559
United States Steel Corporation, 481
Universal principles of management, 486
Unmarried, 338
Unsuccessful executives, 531–532
Upper class, 327–329
Urbanization, 371–372, 574–575
U-shaped pattern, 342
U speech, 326
Utilitarian attitudes, 393
Utilitarian organizations, 483
Utility, 37–38, 228–229
Utopia, 51

Validity, test, 70, 119
Value, law as, 551
Value-expressive attitudes, 393
Values, 397–399, 611
Variance, analysis of, 90
Veblen, 43
Verbal ability, 287–288, 519
Vertical clique, 450
Vertical communication, 500
Vertical strain, 494
Vestibular sense, 160
Vestibular training, 195
Vigilance research, 162
Violence, 374, 376
Viscerotonia, 246
Vision, 124, 155–157
VISTA (Visual Testing Apparatus), 422
Vocabulary development, 287–288
Voting, 388, 394, 547

Wagner Act, 566
Wall Street Journal, 423
War on poverty, 619
Watson, 13
Watt, 36
Wealth of Nations, 36–37, 40
Weber, 14, 19, 43–44, 315, 486–487, 509, 579, 582, 587
Welfare benefits, 556
Western Electric Company, 463
White collar workers, 594–595
Whole learning, 186
Wives, corporation norms for, 339
Women's Christian Temperance Union, 359